Balzac's
Comédie Humaine

by
HERBERT J. HUNT

UNIVERSITY OF LONDON
THE ATHLONE PRESS

First published in 1959 *by*
THE ATHLONE PRESS
UNIVERSITY OF LONDON
at 2 *Gower Street, London* WC1
Distributed by Constable & Co Ltd
12 *Orange Street, London* WC2

Canada
Oxford University Press
Toronto

U.S.A.
Oxford University Press Inc
New York

Reprinted with corrections, 1964

First printed in Great Britain by
Western Printing Services Ltd, Bristol
Reprinted by offset-lithography by
William Clowes and Sons Ltd, London and Beccles

PREFACE

THE AIM OF THIS BOOK, which was preceded in 1957 by an
account of Balzac's life,[1] is to give a descriptive history of the
'Comédie Humaine'; to watch Balzac's purpose unfolding from
1829 to 1848, and to put the individual works into their general
chronological context and their relationship with one another—
in so far as that is possible for one person at a time when so much
research on the novels remains to be done and when good critical
editions are still comparatively few.

The trail has already been blazed. By M. Maurice Bardèche
in his excellent *Balzac romancier*,[2] a searching and subtle inquiry
into the development of Balzac's inspiration and technique which,
however, does not go, and in view of its particular nature scarcely
needs to go, beyond *Le père Goriot*. By a group of American
scholars, in *The Evolution of Balzac's 'Comédie Humaine'*, edited
by Messrs E. Preston Dargan and Bernard Weinberg,[3] a work of
great utility, but which, alas, is only selective. By M. Léon
Émery,[4] in a study which, though penetrating, is analytical and
reflective rather than historically informative. And, in a more
positive way, by Joachim Merlant, in a compendium of *Morceaux
choisis* in which extracts from the important novels are linked
together by introductory notes and comments.[5] That a complete
and detailed history of the 'Comédie Humaine' has not yet been
published is due partly to prudence in face of so strenuous
an undertaking, partly to the fascinating variety of particular

[1] *Honoré de Balzac: a Biography* (Athlone Press, 1957); hereinafter referred to
as *Biography*.
[2] Listed in Bibliography as Bardèche (1). The same system of reference is
used throughout this book.
[3] See, in Bibliography, under Dargan and Weinberg and, more especially,
under Dedinsky.
[4] See, in Bibliography, under Émery.   [5] See Merlant (1).

vii

research subjects which the study of Balzac offers, and partly to the need which readers of Balzac in successive generations have continuously felt, and to which critics have continuously responded, for general assessments of the meaning and value of Balzac's work.

This present enterprise, though perhaps too ambitious in one sense, is a modest one since its primary object is not such a general assessment. It does not claim to give anything like a definitive judgment on Balzac. Criticism of great authors is so often carried on in the clouds, and assessment of values so often starts from the assumption that the reader is already familiar with the works treated, or expects him to take for granted the critic's own knowledge as well as the competence of his judgment. In the case of a novelist who wrote so much and whose works are so closely interrelated, is there not something to be said for an attempt to set forth the basic facts as a foundation on which sound judgment may repose?

Not that criticism and appreciation are here eschewed. They take the form of a running commentary rather than a comprehensive verdict. A number of valuable general studies have been written in which criticism, being more free of factual impedimenta, can soar unfettered over this vast domain and offer a panoramic view; they are of course included in the Bibliography. Mention may however be made here of one remarkable work of recent years: M. Félicien Marceau's *Balzac et son monde*, which is copiously informative—far more than the present study can hope to be—about Balzac's characters, and which also brings the insight of an experienced novelist to their examination. But it is not a historical study. That is legitimate enough in the case of an author who makes no claim to special erudition in this field. But to consider Balzac's characters without paying any attention to their development in Balzac's mind and the moments at which they came to life in his novels[1] is to deprive oneself of important information for the understanding of them.

Of course the historical approach has its difficulties and raises some knotty problems. The order in which Balzac's writings are considered in this book may sometimes seem exceptionable.

[1] See below (93–7), on *le retour des personnages*.

Nothing could have given a more chaotic impression, or been more misleading, than the automatic device of treating each work as it appeared. Balzac had so many irons in the fire at once. He was continually revising or rewriting previous works and taking up anew projects long since conceived—many of them during his formative period—or begun and interrupted. Within a limited range of time, it was generally a mere matter of luck for one work, or one group of works, to be published before another.[1] On the other hand, to have treated the works, as Marcel Barrière did, according to their exact place in the logical scheme (or schemes) which Balzac devised for them, would have been to give up all pretence of a historical conspectus. So my grouping together, in more or less homogeneous chapters (e.g. Chapters IV, IX, X, XIV), of contemporaneous or roughly contemporaneous works has its primary justification in the fact that, during successive phases of his creative career, Balzac's attention was in the main directed to certain subjects or *milieux*. Sometimes logic, conforming to an approximate historical sequence, has enabled me to group works (e.g. Chapters IV, VII, VIII, etc.) in accordance with Balzac's own theoretic categories. But at all times the reader should keep in mind the fact of relative simultaneity (for instance Chapters II, III, IV show a simultaneity of advance in different directions during the period 1830-5), and give due attention to those sections of chapters (III, i; VI, ii; IX, i; X, i; XI, i; XIII, i) which recall the actual historical succession in the order of publication. And allowance should always be made for an apparently adventitious or capricious element in the flow of Balzac's inspiration.

Lengthy as this book is, and scrupulous as I have tried to make it, I would not presume to suggest that it exhausts the subject, or that I have infallibly given emphasis to the right things, or hit upon the right proportions in the constitution of its parts. No two people perhaps would assign exactly the same importance to this or that novel or *nouvelle*. Other investigators embarking on a similar task would no doubt find room for other things; for there are plenty of other things to say, and many other aspects of Balzac which would merit bringing into the limelight. Yet, as Henry

[1] No better illustration of this could be given than M. Pommier's masterly but intricate study of *La Torpille*. See Pommier (8).

PREFACE

James wrote, 'it would verily take Balzac to detail Balzac'; and I would willingly urge this truth as an excuse for all those short-comings which have persisted in spite of assistance and advice I have received and which I here take pleasure in acknowledging. My very warm thanks are again due to Mr H. O. Stutchbury and Miss Mary Pemberton for indispensable help generously be-stowed. And again to Mr Stutchbury for the unfailing interest he has taken at all stages in the composition of this study, for his indulgent comments and suggestions, as well as for the shrewd and sometimes trenchant criticisms he has made in his anxiety that justice should be done to a writer who only too often, in this country and in our own times, has been the object of ill-founded disparagement. I am grateful to my revered friend, the Abbé Philippe Bertault, both for sympathy and information on points of detail; to M. Jean Pommier for the kindness he has shown me at Chantilly; to MM. Jean Ducourneau and Roger Pierrot for other points of information; and not least to the Secretary of the Athlone Press for many apt criticisms and valuable suggestions.

H.J.H.

CONTENTS

Part I: 1829–35

Part II: 1835–41

CONTENTS

CONTENTS

Part III: 1841–8

CONTENTS

ABBREVIATIONS

Works frequently referred to in the footnotes, and periodicals listed in the General Bibliography (below, pp. 466–81), are abbreviated as follows:

Biography   *Honoré de Balzac: a Biography*. By H. J. Hunt. Athlone Press, London, 1957.

Conard   *Œuvres complètes de H. de B.* Edited by M. Bouteron and H. Longnon. 40 vols. 8°. Conard, Paris, 1912–40.

Conard O.D.   The three vols. of *Œuvres diverses* in the above edition.

Éd. Déf.   *Œuvres complètes de H. de B.* 24 vols. 8°, Calmann-Lévy, Paris, 1869–76 (the erstwhile 'Édition définitive').

E   *Lettres à l'Étrangère*. Edited by Spoelberch de Lovenjoul and M. Bouteron. 4 vols. 8°. Calmann-Lévy, Paris, 1899–1950.

L.F.   *Lettres à sa famille, 1809–50*. Edited by W. S. Hastings. Albin Michel, Paris, 1950. (First published in 1934, Princeton University Press.)

Z.C.   *Honoré de Balzac. Correspondance avec Zulma Carraud*. Edited by M. Bouteron, Gallimard, Paris. Edition of 1951.

FS   *French Studies*. Basil Blackwell, Oxford.

MF   *Mercure de France* (the periodical, not the edition).

RHLF   *Revue d'histoire littéraire de la France*.

RLC   *Revue de littérature comparée*.

RSH   *Revue des sciences humaines*.

In general, references in footnotes cite only the name of the author quoted. When a number follows the name [e.g. Bertault (2), Bouteron (8), Lovenjoul (4)], it refers to the particular book or article listed opposite that number under the author's name in the General Bibliography.

PART I

1829–35

I

BALZAC IN 1829

i. 'Tout cela sera rangé, classé, étiqueté . . .'

A VIVID, DYNAMIC LITTLE MAN, this descendant of Langue-
doc peasants, this native of Tours transplanted to Paris; already
rotund, with a mane of coarse black hair, usually unkempt; large
head, wide brow, strong nose, mobile and sensual mouth, bright,
compelling eyes. Bouncing, vain, self-assertive, not at all chastened by the considerable debt he had contracted from 1826 to
1828 as publisher, printer and type manufacturer, in fact quite
willing to swell it as the years went by. Genial, loquacious, happy
to dominate, to monopolize a conversation when the opportunity
occurred. Expansive, least refined when trying to appear so, but
fascinating even by the strain of vulgarity in him, so indicative it
was of robust vitality. On the whole a self-taught man, notwith-
standing his six years as a boarder at the Collège de Vendôme, his
year at the Lycée of Tours, his two years in Paris as an aspirant
for the *baccalauréat*, his three years there as law student and
lawyer's clerk. Probably he had drawn more spiritual sustenance
from the subjects he moiled at on his own, however second-hand
his approach to some of them may have been: the 'philosophie' of
the Encyclopaedists and the Ideologues, the introspective psychology and the aesthetics of the Eclectics, the physiology of
Bichat and Broussais, the psycho-physiology of Cabanis, the
'physiognomy' of Lavater, the phrenology of Gall, the 'magnetism' of Mesmer, Deleuze, and Koreff, the near-illuminism or
illuminism of Charles Bonnet, Saint-Martin, then of Swedenborg
and Ballanche. His predilection for philosophy is revealed in the
scribblings of his late teens: *Notes sur la philosophie et la religion*,
Notes sur l'immortalité de l'âme.

We can credit him with prodigious readings, now haphazard,

now systematic. During his boyhood and after, he had an enormous appetite for fairy-tales and oriental fiction like the *Thousand and One Nights*. For educational background there were the seventeenth-century French classics, Molière above all, and the great writers of the eighteenth century from Montesquieu and Voltaire to Diderot, Rousseau and Beaumarchais; also Laclos, Rétif de la Bretonne, Bernardin de Saint-Pierre and André Chénier. He had a special and growing taste for Rabelais—chiefly, at first, a Rabelais transmitted through Sterne. He had a general acquaintance with certain world classics: Dante, Shakespeare, Milton, Cervantes; with the more recent Germans, Klopstock, Schiller, Goethe; the fascination of Hoffmann did not come perhaps until 1829, when Loève-Weimars translated the *Fantastic Tales*. His scientific or pseudo-scientific and theosophic readings produced in him a quaint blend of materialism and mysticism. It would be hard to say, during his formative years, which of two opposing outlooks, scepticism and effusive religiosity, was fighting the winning battle in his speculative mind.[1] By tradition and upbringing he was a middle-class liberal, instinctively prizing the achievements of the Revolution and venerating Napoleon as a superman, for his infancy and boyhood had been bathed in the effulgence of the Imperial conquests. The thoughts which the uneasy and uncertain regime of the restored Bourbons inspired in him he kept mostly in reserve for his writings of maturity, for it needed the Revolution of July and the more supple constitutionalism of Louis-Philippe to give him a clear view of the direction in which France was moving. With all his Gallic commonsense and positivism he was intermittently but impetuously responsive to the influence of pre-Romantics and Romantics: after Rousseau and Saint-Pierre, Chateaubriand, Mme de Staël and then Byron, Moore, Nodier, and to some extent Lamartine. Moreover, for one who in later years was to make a great show of Anglophobia, he was an insatiable and strangely unselective student of English literature—in translation. He read, at first or second hand, Hobbes, Locke, Otway, Pope, Swift, Addison, Steele; the novelists Defoe, Fielding, Richardson, Sterne, Goldsmith; Macpherson (the *Ballads of Ossian*) and the then popular poet Crabbe. He steeped

[1] See Bertault (2), Parts I and II, and Bertault (3).

himself in the novelists of terror, Horace Walpole, Anne Radcliffe, 'Monk' Lewis, Mary Shelley; from 1819 onwards he was a devotee of Maturin, and *Melmoth the Wanderer* was almost as a bedside book to him. He was at one with his contemporaries in yielding to the charm of Scott. To Byron as the apostle of Satanic rebelliousness he added Godwin, author of *Caleb Williams*. Soon he was to be fascinated by Fenimore Cooper and the 'Leatherstocking' series.

There is little doubt that he embarked on a large part of these and other readings in order to develop his own talent as a novelist. That is the case with Scott, the reviver of times past; with the authors of *romans noirs* and melodramas—France too had many cultivators of this genre, foremost among them being Ducray-Duminil and Pixérécourt; with the authors, or rather the authoresses, of sentimental novels, from Mme de Krüdener to Mme de Staël, not forgetting the Irishwoman Maria Edgeworth; with the adepts in the *roman gai*—such best-sellers as Pigault-Lebrun, Paul de Kock and Victor Ducange, who swam against the current of sentimentality and terror and poured out hilarious stories of middle-class and low-class life, burlesques which in their way were no less extravagant than the genres they set out to ridicule.

For the Balzac of 1829 already had some ten years of literary effort behind him. He had failed in an initial attempt at tragic drama and turned—provisionally at first, it seems—to prose fiction. The six novels which in 1836–7 he authorized Hippolyte Souverain to publish under the title *Œuvres de jeunesse*[1] (he had originally produced them under the pseudonyms of Horace de Saint-Aubin and Lord R'Hoone) form only a small part of his *juvenilia*. He had begun with a strange mystery story, *Falthurne, Manuscrit de l'abbé Savonati* (1819–20?), and a predominantly Rousseauistic novel, *Sténie ou Les Erreurs philosophiques* (1820–1821?). Neither of them was finished, nor did they get into print until the twentieth century. Another fragmentary sketch, also entitled *Falthurne*,[2] was perhaps written in 1823–4, and was to

---

[1] To them may be added two novels, *L'Excommunié* and *Dom Gigadas*, which he had sketched out, and which he left to his two amanuenses, de Belloy and de Gramont, to finish off.

[2] For the dating of these abortive works, see Guyon (1), 720, 723, 736–7, and Castex (1) (Étude préliminaire, x–xi).

develop later into his Swedenborgian novel, *Séraphita*. In the meantime he had gone into collaboration with the literary adventurer Le Poitevin de l'Égreville and others of that ilk. Between 1821 and 1825 he helped to flood the market with mediocre novels whose purpose was to regale the average reader with medleys of Scott, Maturin and Pigault-Lebrun. They were presented to the public under anagrammatic signatures.

In how many of these works did Balzac have a hand, and what was the extent of his collaboration? It is generally agreed that he was chiefly responsible for *L'Héritière de Birague* (1821), which is at once an imitation and a parody of Scott and the types of novel enumerated above, and *Jean-Louis ou la Fille trouvée* (1822), inspired mainly by Pigault-Lebrun. But there were many more, and to hold the literary divining-rod over such pot-boilers is a very hazardous kind of activity. It is safer to gauge his early talent by recourse to those works which are indisputably his own: *Sténie* and the two *Falthurnes*; *Clotilde de Lusignan* (1822—*L'Israëlite* of 1836), a weak imitation of *Ivanhoe*; *Le Centenaire* (1822—*Le Sorcier* of 1836), which springs directly from *Melmoth the Wanderer*; *Le Vicaire des Ardennes* (1822), a sentimental novel which hovers over the theme of incest and degenerates into melodrama; *La dernière Fée ou La nouvelle Lampe merveilleuse* (1823), which starts like a fairy-tale and ends up as a story of amorous disillusionment; the sequel to *Le Vicaire des Ardennes*, *Annette et le criminel* (1824—*Argow le Pirate* in 1836), which continues the history of a far-off precursor of Vautrin, the murderous gangster who, so unlike Vautrin in this respect, is redeemed by the love of a pious girl; and *Wann-Chlore* (1824—*Jane la Pâle* in 1836), in which, treating the theme of a man torn between two wives, Balzac makes his most determined effort since *Sténie* to avoid blood-and-thunder and achieve something like a psychological novel.

This survey practically covers the first phase of Balzac's arduous but financially unprofitable apprenticeship. In our century much interest has been focused on this phase and the subsequent phases in his early development as a writer. The axiom of all researchers—it has some foundation—has been that the author of the 'Comédie Humaine' is latent, and already perceptible in the author of these works. André Le Breton set an early example in this kind of research.[1] That *comparatiste* of genius, Fernand Baldensperger, opened many vistas in which the works of Balzac's maturity stand out against the background of his early readings and writings.[2] The inquiry of L. J. Arrigon[3] is biographical rather than analytical. P. Barrière[4] made the first systematic analysis, though a brief one, of Balzacian features to be found in the *juvenilia*. A. Prioult[5] has delved indefatigably into sources and influences. He detects Balzac's handiwork in a surprising number of novels, and finds themes and character-types of the 'Comédie Humaine' in all of them. Yet, strangely enough, he is not far from denying Balzac any inventive power, and regards the *juvenilia* as a repository in which he stored up innumerable gleanings for eventual use. He carries his thesis too far, but it does serve to confirm the aphorism of Baldensperger: 'Balzac peut beaucoup donner parce qu'il a beaucoup reçu: et s'il a "absorbé" de toutes parts, ce fut pour restituer immensément.' M. Bardèche[6] has given, in a closely woven texture, a valuable study of Balzac's developing technique and conceptions from the earliest days to *Le père Goriot* of 1834–5. With enviable ingenuity he makes everything fall into place, and characterizes the period 1820–5 as the one in which Balzac, by dint of an imitation which is half ironic and parodistic, mastered the tricks of his trade. 'J'ai écrit sept romans comme simple étude: un pour apprendre le dialogue, un pour apprendre la description, un pour grouper les personnages, un pour la composition.'[7] As M. Bardèche sees it, Balzac had progressed as far as he could in the technique of novel-writing by 1825. He had yet to learn to be himself in his presentation and interpretation of human personality and also to relate his characters and themes, which he now possessed in abundance, to a social setting.

A new phase began as Balzac, from about 1824, came under the influence of another literary jobber, Horace-Napoléon Raisson who, while exploiting his talent and energy no less extensively than Le Poitevin de l'Égreville had done, diverted his attention

---

[1] See Bibliography, op. cit., ch. ii.   [2] Baldensperger (2).
[3] Arrigon (1).   [4] P. Barrière (1).   [5] Prioult (1).   [6] Bardèche (1).
[7] A remark of Balzac reported by Champfleury, quoted by Bardèche (1), 114.

to an increasingly popular type of literary composition—admittedly second- or third-rate—which in the eighteen-twenties was observing and humorously describing the normal life of the age. Leaving the pretentious and the extraordinary—outlaws, devil's emissaries, lurking villains, persecuted heroines and their heaven-sent 'protectors'—Balzac turned to the common foibles of humanity, already at least glanced at in *Le Vicaire des Ardennes* and its sequel. The product of this new collaboration was a number of 'Codes' and 'Arts', jesting manuals which gave ironical advice on dress, manners and comportment in society. These exercises trained Balzac to concentrate his attention on the life he saw around him in the Paris with which the years had made him so familiar, and to seek originality by utilizing the first-hand material he had amassed since his lawyer's-clerk days as he mixed with his literary and journalistic associates; material shortly to be swollen by his experiences as an unsuccessful businessman from 1826 to 1828. From these experiences in fact were to spring some of his most personal creations in the 'Comédie Humaine'—Raphaël de Valentin,[1] Lucien de Rubempré,[2] César Birotteau,[3] and David Séchard.[4] He also learned to observe individuals and types in the light of the theory of Lavater—to deduce character and temperament, not only from physiognomy, but also from dress, gait, personal peculiarities and mannerisms. And so came the habit of including comic 'physiologies' in the 'Codes' and 'Arts' he helped to multiply.

Here again the extent of Balzac's production is uncertain,[5] but the value of this new orientation can be seen in two authentic works: the first draft of *La Physiologie du mariage* (begun about 1824 and printed by Balzac himself in 1826 or 1827) and *Le Code des gens honnêtes* (1825). The published *Physiologie du mariage* of 1829 will soon come under our scrutiny. *Le Code des gens*

[1] *La Peau de chagrin.*
[2] *Illusions perdues.*
[3] *Histoire de la grandeur et de la décadence de César Birotteau.*
[4] *Illusions perdues*, Parts I and III.
[5] M. Bardèche himself, though more circumspect than M. Prioult, has not completely avoided the dangers which beset this kind of research. *Le Dictionnaire des Enseignes*, printed but certainly not written by Balzac (see B. Guyon (1), 745), is pressed into service and given a place in the novelist's development. But there is no doubt that Balzac learned something from it.

honnêtes, in its broad outlines perhaps derived from the sermon delivered by a perspicacious Abbé in *Annette et le criminel*, is significant because it shows Balzac taking cognizance of the multifarious rogueries of his day, realizing the immense power which money was already wielding in the eighteen-twenties and was to wield ever more triumphantly as the century wore on, and cataloguing the many tricks by which greedy people could appropriate it without incurring the penalties of the law. Here is a foundation for his studies of human rapacity in the 'Comédie Humaine'! Such an exercise involved a closer inspection of individuals, classes and avocations than he had ever consciously made before, and pointed to the aim which he later summed up in the phrase *faire concurrence à l'état civil*: the civil registers were to be no more complete and precise than his own records of quality, status and occupation.

A third phase in Balzac's development is the lull in creative effort—though not in assimilation and absorption—necessitated by his bid for fortune in the printing and publishing trades. As soon as he was cured of that ambition, he returned to his real vocation, from which in future nothing was to divert him, not even the desire to become a politician which took possession of him between 1830 and 1833. The period of imitation and accumulation had sufficed to give him more than a glimmering of what he wanted to do. He was becoming aware that the novel offered him a means of saying all that he had to say. Throughout the years, and notably in *Sténie*, the two *Falthurnes* and *Le Centenaire*, he had been constructing a metaphysic which he was to develop and incorporate in the 'Comédie Humaine': a singular metaphysic, one part science, one part illuminism, one part Hoffmannesque fantasy. The craving for passionate experience, which with the desire to achieve fame was a permanent trait in him, was finding at least temporary assuagement in his relations with Mme de Berny, 'La Dilecta'. A few years later, in *Le Lys dans la vallée*, it furnished the essential clue to the character of Félix de Vandenesse, another of his semi-autobiographical creations. Through 'La Dilecta' he obtained, with some initiation in the more spiritual aspect of love, more direct insight into feminine psychology; and this further whetted his curiosity about women, especially in the higher ranks

9

of society. Her loving devotion, and soon his increasingly intimate liaison with the Duchesse d'Abrantès, gave him better equipment than all his book-learning for studying the psychology of passion; through Laure d'Abrantès, moreover, his circle of aristocratic acquaintances was in due course to expand considerably. From now on, and throughout his life, it is easy, if not inevitable, to correlate such study with his amorous attachments: after Mme de Berny (though her image persists to the end), Mme de Castries, Mme Guidoboni-Visconti and, from 1833 increasingly, the vicissitudes of his wooing of Mme Hanska. But for the present it suffices to note that the first, like the second *Physiologie du mariage*, in spite of its mocking tone, reveals a deep interest in the problems of love and marriage, and even in that respect leaves far behind such works as *La dernière Fée*, the two *Argow* novels and *Wann-Chlore*. Hitherto he had found it difficult not to adulterate his studies of passion with *roman noir* absurdities. He was never entirely to cure himself of this defect, nor of the urge to imagine his lovers as dispossessed princes and sultanas imported from oriental fiction, endowed with all glamour and prestige and pre-destined—but for the even more imperious claims of depressing nineteenth-century reality—to bliss and glory.[1] His unique discovery was that the novel of sentiment and passion could support, and indeed must be supported by a background of actuality; and that not only primary, but also secondary characters furnished with an 'état civil' could achieve three-dimensional verisimilitude. He was always to remain under the spell of the romantic, the fantastic and the 'metapsychic', so much so that he saw commonplace existence transformed and transmuted by them. But he saw commonplace existence in its turn justifying and even creating them. Hence proceeded not only his idea of the 'Comédie Humaine' as 'Les Mille et une Nuits de l'Occident' but also his perception of a fourth dimension in human experience.

Coincidentally—or conversely—the sociologist in him was beginning to pierce through and give sense and purpose to the would-be philosopher. His head was buzzing with subjects and personages. It is not extravagant to suppose that by 1829 the substance of the 'Comédie Humaine' was present in his mind, and

[1] See Baldensperger (2), ch. i.

that it only needed bringing out and organizing. The will to organize had been taking hold of him for some time, and he was now ruminating on the way to do it. What matters above all is that, even then, he was not minded to produce a string of disconnected fictions.

In this context the example set by Scott assumes paramount importance. Nor is it sufficient to say with André Le Breton:[1] 'Scott lui a appris à préparer fortement le drame, à le situer dans un décor déterminé, à le peupler de types expressifs: et il est le décorateur, il est le costumier chez qui Balzac est allé en apprentissage.' The Waverley novels also gave him an inkling of what miracles the novel could perform in bringing past ages to life. Even in 1820 or 1821 he was hoping to do for France what Scott had done for his own country, but to do it more systematically by making the novel a medium for the interpretation of recorded historical fact. 'Il ne suffit pas d'être un homme, il faut être un système, disait-il.'[2] He had contemplated, and was still contemplating a series of fictions which should link century to century. The periods he most favoured were those of civil strife and change: those marked by the dissensions between Armagnacs and Burgundians, between the Valois monarchs and the Guises; and naturally the period of the Revolution itself. This idea still possessed him in 1828 when he emerged from his business ventures. *Le Gars*, soon to develop into *Le dernier Chouan*—the first novel which was to find a place in the 'Comédie Humaine'—was in part an attempt at realizing it. In a sense *Le Gars* was a false start; but the application of his historical sense to so recent a period as the Royalist rebellions in western France, coupled with the interest in his own times which his collaboration with Raisson had awakened in him, brought him to the very threshold of his ultimate purpose. He was in fact about to embark on a most audacious undertaking: that of presenting and evaluating, in an interwoven sequence of novels and short stories, the life and civilization of his own country during a period which in the main was not to exceed the span of his own vital experience; a presentation which indeed was founded on and compounded of that experience. Although bursting with energy, and conscious of the tremendous power

[1] Op. cit., 90.   [2] Reported by Félix Davin, Lovenjoul (1), 50.

which lay within him, he did not become immediately aware of the scope and magnitude of the task he was approaching. Our endeavour will be to watch his purpose gradually becoming clear and working itself out.

The French proverb—*à force de forger on devient forgeron*—might almost have been invented for Balzac: not only the Balzac of 1819–29, but also the Balzac who, in the literary sense, only begins to exist in his own right in 1829. We must not underestimate the importance of the period of gestation, of what might well be called pre-natal growth. But the palpable and visible 'Comédie Humaine' offers a wide enough field for investigation. We see him then, in the region of 1829, girding up his loins for the fray. With what special aptitudes—innate no doubt but also sharpened and polished by long and painful practice—was he endowed?

One was an unparalleled talent for story-telling. Vivid tribute has been paid to this by General and Mme de Pommereul, who were his hosts at Fougères in the autumn of 1828.

En arrivant, il avait déclaré qu'il voulait payer sa pension: mais comme il n'avait pas d'argent, il ajouta qu'il payerait en histoires: chaque soir donc, lorsqu'on était réuni, Balzac racontait son histoire: 'Tout ce monde, disait-il, vit, aime, souffre, s'agite dans ma tête, mais si Dieu me prête vie, tout cela sera rangé, classé, étiqueté dans des livres, et de fameux livres . . . vous verrez, madame!'

. . . Il avait une façon de raconter extrêmement saisissante, qui vous faisait croire que 'c'était arrivé' . . . Il débutait souvent ainsi: 'Général, vous avez dû connaître, à Lille, la famille de X . . . pas les X . . . de Roubaix, non . . . ceux qui sont alliés aux Z . . . de Béthune? . . . Eh bien, il s'est passé dans cette famille-là un drame digne du boulevard du Crime . . .' Et il partait, tenant ses auditeurs sous le charme de sa parole et de son imagination. Quand il avait fini, on se secouait pour rentrer dans la réalité. 'Est-ce vrai, Balzac?' lui demandait son hôte.

Balzac le regardait un instant de son œil où rayonnaient toutes les finesses, puis avec cet éclat de rire qui faisait trembler les vitres et qui lui était habituel:

'Pas un mot de vrai! s'écriait-il, du Balzac tout pur! . . .'[1]

Few readers of the 'Comédie Humaine', whether for other reasons well or ill disposed to Balzac, will deny the force of the spell Balzac can cast. Charles Rabou also acknowledged it when in 1832 he

[1] Robert du Pontavice de Heussey, quoted by Étienne Aubrée, 98.

upbraided him for loading his stories with metaphysics and exhorted him to be a 'conteur comme la nature vous a fait et non embêteur comme elle a fait Victor Cousin'.[1] At greater length, and with vivacious humour, a contemporary of Balzac, the critic Philarète Chasles, paid him a similar tribute in an article of 1838.[2]

Another obvious quality in Balzac was the gift for minute observation, enhanced and extended by an uncanny faculty for sympathetic divination, and converted by a phenomenally retentive memory into the most valuable of assets. Each and every novel of Balzac gives ample evidence of this. It aroused surprise and admiration even in himself. In a story of 1836—*Facino Cane* —he describes the detective work which, during his years in the attic of the Rue Lesdiguières, he carried out on people he walked behind in the streets, and tells how the scraps of conversation he overheard enabled him to get inside their skin and appreciate every detail of their daily lives and worries. 'Quitter ses habitudes, devenir un autre que soi par l'exercice des facultés morales, et jouer ce jeu à volonté, telle était ma distraction.'[3]

His reflexion on this activity shows that he was not inclined to explain it merely in terms of acute physical perceptivity or training in the art of observation. Again in 1828, he had sketched out a preliminary *Avertissement* for *Le Gars*, which he was then intending to attribute to an imaginary author named Victor Morillon. In some respects Morillon is a replica of himself, and the *Avertissement* served him later as a nucleus for his more or less autobiographical *Louis Lambert*. In it he enlarges on the faculty which Morillon, a young and inexperienced peasant, possessed, and which extensive reading had developed but not created, for describing, with minute and circumstantial detail, sensations and sentiments he had never felt, narrating scenes and events he had never witnessed, and making subtle moral observations about people he had never met. For the benefit of an interested schoolmaster, Morillon

. . . décrivait les plaisirs d'une immense fortune avec une étonnante vivacité de couleur; lui parla des ivresses ressenties au sein des bals où il avait admiré la nudité des femmes, leurs toilettes, leur fleurs, leurs

---

[1] From a letter quoted by A. Levin, 234, n. 113.
[2] Ibid., 150–1.   [3] Conard XVI, 372–3.

diamants, leurs danses et leur regards enivrés, lui peignit le luxe des appartements qu'il habita, leurs ameublements, la richesse des porcelaines, la beauté des tableaux, les dessins de la soie et des tapis, entra dans le détail des voitures somptueuses, des chevaux arabes qu'il avait possédés, des modes suivies par les fashionables et du choix des étoffes, des cannes et des bijoux dont il avait usé, sans avoir rien vu de tout cela par sa prunelle extérieure et visible . . .[1]

This is also *du Balzac tout pur*. How often, when reading the 'Comédie Humaine', shall we remain puzzled as to whether Balzac, in such and such a rhapsody, is recounting his opalescent day-dreams or drawing upon his later and broadened experience! Are we to ascribe this faculty, which he so super-eminently possessed, to an exceptionally vivid imagination building on a store of facts observed or vicariously experienced, or perhaps to an abnormal capacity for self-deception or hallucination? Balzac himself was not content to leave it at that. He regarded it as the manifestation of an occult power, latent in all men, highly developed in himself. He called it (after Scott) 'second sight' or 'vision interne' and, as we shall see, linked it up with the philosophy he had formed about the relationship between mind and matter, the 'vital fluid' and the potentialities of thought, emotion and will. Whatever judgment we may pass on that philosophy when we come to study it, we shall find it difficult to deny that Balzac the scrutinizing observer is supported and transformed by the *voyant*[2] whose intuitive apprehension of reality transcends mere experience and enables him, to use his own expression, to 'invent truth'.

Yet other qualities were needed if he was to justify his claim to 'carry a whole society in his head' and consign to the written word its divisions and categories, its drifts and tendencies, its light and shade, its greatness and weakness. He needed—and he possessed—a sublime confidence in his own genius, in his ability to express his view of life, a sure conviction that it was worth expressing—this conviction was certainly strengthened in him, in 1829 and 1830, by the perfervid preachings of the Saint-

[1] Abraham (2), 84. Now available in the Garnier edition of *Les Chouans*, 415.

[2] Philarète Chasles was the first to apply this term to Balzac (*Journal des Débats*, 24 Aug. 1850). Baudelaire called him a 'visionnaire passionné' (*Œuvres complètes*, Pléiade, ii, 473). Cf. Béguin, ch. ii.

Simonian socialists on the theme of the 'artist's' sacred mission—
and lastly, but superlatively, the indomitable will to express it to
the full, despite debts, distractions, discouragements and advancing sickness; and, we may add, despite the obstinate urge to
bring each of his works, however swiftly conceived or drafted, to
all possible perfection by means of an incredible number of corrections and revisions. That these qualities combined to furnish
the necessary driving-force will become evident as we see him
tirelessly cutting out and shaping the multiple pieces which were
sooner or later to fall into place as parts of his ever-evolving
design.

ii. *Le dernier Chouan*

Le Gars, whose title was changed to *Le dernier Chouan ou La
Bretagne en 1800* on the advice of Mme de Pommereul, had been
conceived in 1827, if not before, as a companion-work to another
projected novel, *Le Capitaine des Boutefeux*, which was to have
been about the civil wars of the fifteenth century. It was composed in what was to be Balzac's usual manner—expansion of an
original draft with innumerable corrections and additions on
proofs—between September 1828 and March 1829. It was sponsored by his friend Hyacinthe de Latouche, writer, critic and
journalist, and published in March 1829 by Urbain Canel. Some
significant facts about it have already been noted It reveals a
dominant and permanent trait in his outlook, the tendency to
look at life through the eyes of a historian. Indeed the already-
mentioned *Avertissement* expresses his views on how history and
historical novels should be written. It also shows what great importance he now attributed to setting and atmosphere, for he
spent several weeks at Fougères, collecting facts and local traditions, and absorbing local colour. Furthermore it was the first
novel which he signed with his own name, which means that
Honoré Balzac, or, a little later, Honoré *de* Balzac, was henceforth
asserting himself as a reputable author.

The subject of *Le dernier Chouan* is the guerrilla warfare between Revolutionaries and Royalists, 'Blues' and 'Whites', which
had flared up in 1799 on the confines of Normandy and Britanny,
in succession to the regular civil war which had raged in La

Vendée from 1793 to 1796. The hero of the novel is the fictitious Alphonse de Montauran, nicknamed 'le Gars', whose followers were known as 'Chouans' because they imitated the hooting of the owl as a form of signal. In 1833–4 Balzac carefully revised the work and published a second edition of it under the title *Les Chouans ou La Bretagne en 1799*. Today, thanks to the recently published Garnier edition, any reader can compare the two versions. There are important differences. By 1834 Balzac's political outlook had evolved. He had abandoned the almost conventional liberalism of his formative period in favour of legitimist principles.[1] In opposing 'Blues' and 'Whites' therefore, he was kinder in 1834 to the latter than he had been in 1829, though he was still not too kind. Moreover his views on women and love had become more sophisticated, in accordance with a deepening experience which his growing intimacy with Mme Hanska was perceptibly enriching. The heroine of the second edition is indeed more mature, more psychologically complex. But both versions of the novel offer the most passionate and, in the everyday sense of the term, the most 'romantic' love story that Balzac had written or was ever to write. It has been likened for this reason to Shakespeare's *Romeo and Juliet*.

Balzac's Juliet is Marie de Verneuil, who has the misfortune to be illegitimate, though of good family, and to have had her reputation undeservedly besmirched even before the collapse of the Old Regime. Caught up in the Revolutionary whirlpool, she had been by her own account 'married' to Danton on the eve of his fall, and then became involved with Fouché and his secret police. She has now come to the Royalist west, in company with Fouché's right-hand man, the foppish and wily Corentin, with orders to seduce and betray the leader of the Chouans and the promise of 300,000 francs as a reward.

Balzac's Romeo, the Marquis Alphonse de Montauran, is a noble and intrepid youth whose disinterested loyalty is in sharp contrast with the calculated adherence which most of his fellow aristocrats give to the Bourbon cause. But he is less strongly fortified against the lure of passion. He and Marie de Verneuil are brought together by a set of plausible chances, at the Hôtel des

[1] See *Biography*, 45 ff.

Trois Maures in Alençon. He is in disguise, for there is a price on his head; she is escorted by Corentin and a company of 'Blues' with Commandant Hulot in charge. Montauran quickly comes under suspicion. Marie, divining his identity, and already taken with him, uses her special authority to save him from arrest. They continue their journey together towards Fougères, chaperoned by the woman who is masquerading as Montauran's mother, but who is in fact an adventuress, hardened in atrocity, and jealously in love with Montauran. She calls herself Mme du Gua Saint-Cyr. She and Corentin are the villains of this sombre drama.

The book owes its originality and fascination to the fact that from the instant when this pair, Marie and Montauran, feel curiosity quickening into admiration, and admiration into love, their relationship becomes a duel to the death. In the heart of each rages a conflict between self-esteem and self-surrender. The psychology of Marie de Verneuil is, by Balzac's intention if not in all the details of execution, mysteriously subtle. She has to contend, within herself, with a certain guilt-consciousness due to her sense of having lost caste, her association with the Revolutionaries, and her reluctant collaboration with Corentin, whose energies and intelligence are bent to one purpose, the destruction of Montauran and the conquest of Marie, both for his own enjoyment and for the furtherance of his ambitions. Marie has lent herself to Fouché's plan, partly for gain, and partly because she is the product of her age—one of those Amazons whom periods of turmoil throw up, who are in love with adventure and danger, but still eminently feminine, as Balzac is anxious to prove. Which means that their appetite for life is so intense that the risk of sudden and violent death is freely accepted. Even while she plans the seduction and betrayal of Montauran, she is ready, nay, eager, to give up all thought of her project if her proposed victim can bring her to the total self-abandonment to which her soul aspires. She has as maid and confidante, Francine, a Breton peasant, whose faithful attachment to the grimmest of Montauran's lieutenants, Marche-à-Terre, exerts an important influence on the action of the story. To her she confesses (in the 1829 version): 'Veux-tu savoir ce que je cherche ici?—Un homme . . .'

Montauran's situation is similarly ambiguous. Pride of race, and suspicion of one whom for a time he believes to be nothing but a *fille d'Opéra* well schooled in her meretricious arts, make him turn suddenly against her. Only a few hours after their first encounter and their first cautious exchanges of sentiment, he condones an act of black treachery towards her and the 'Blues' whose safety he has guaranteed. Her budding passion is apparently changed to violent hatred. The urge to vengeance for so unpardonable an affront, as well as reluctance to believe in his real guilt and the burning desire to clear herself of the slander that Mme du Gua and the irresponsible Comte de Bauvan (in the 1829 version he is the Marquis de Marigny) have put upon her, sets her plotting for a new encounter with him. She forces Bauvan to introduce her to an assembly of Royalist rebels who have gathered at the village of Saint-James for a ball. Passion flames up anew between her and Montauran, and she reveals her past to him. But her misgivings as to his complete sincerity are acute enough for her to demand of him, before surrendering herself, proof of his readiness to renounce everything for her, even his service to the Royalist cause. She obtains it in the end, but only by a concatenation of events, not too clearly narrated, which leads them to the consummation of their desires: a wedding which gives them one night of love and brings them death in the morning.

Such is the theme of an enthralling tale whose interest is supported, though not created, by the historical motive that impelled Balzac to write it. *Le dernier Chouan* is a novel in the Scott manner, and with some of the Scott mannerisms. But Balzac departs from Scott in at least one important respect. The work as a historical novel is coloured by a theory that Balzac many times expressed in later years, namely, that Scott falsified psychology and history by his puritanical conception of woman and by the neutral, passive rôle he assigned to her in the preparation of historical events.

La femme porte le désordre dans la société par la passion: la passion a des accidents infinis. Peignez donc les passions; vous aurez les ressources dont s'est privé ce grand génie pour être lu dans toutes les familles de la prude Angleterre.

18

This is the counsel of the sage d'Arthez to the would-be historical novelist, Lucien de Rubempré, in *Un grand Homme de province à Paris*.[1] And Balzac was to repeat this conviction in the Foreword (1842) of his 'Comédie Humaine': 'la passion est toute l'humanité. Sans elle la religion, l'histoire, le roman, l'art seraient inutiles.'

Les Chouans illustrates this thesis, since it shows a civil war being nipped in the bud by a military leader's surrender to a Delilah; for Marie is a Delilah, however passionately virtuous she may be in Balzac's intention. It is also a notable effort on Balzac's part to approach the history of his own times and resuscitate recent events without bringing real figures into the foreground. Moreover its success in this sphere lies in the description of background and the creation of atmosphere. Here again Balzac continues Scott, and even perhaps excels his master. The region round Fougères with its wild countryside is admirably evoked as a perfect terrain for guerrilla warfare, ambushes, surprise attacks, sudden withdrawals and a confusion of manœuvres due to the absence on one side of uniformed troops. The ideological elements are even more important: a superstitious peasantry, easily duped by the hope of plunder and celestial reward, its appetite for slaughter and pillage whetted by the priests whose function should be to restrain them; uncouth but picturesque subalterns like Marche-à-Terre, Pille-Miche and Galope-Chopine, whose cunning savagery recalls, and is in fact likened to that displayed by the Mohicans of Fenimore Cooper; unwilling conscripts drafted into the Republican train-bands, looking for the opportunity to desert or join forces with their rebel brethren. And on the other side the Revolutionary troops with their rugged, valiant, honest commander, Hulot, for whom war means the exchange of musket-shot and bayonet-thrust, and not the wily plottings of government commissaries who use women as decoys; of one mind with him are the jovial, swearing, fearless soldiers, Merle, Gérard and Beau-pied, who believe in the Revolution, who idolize the First Consul, who fight and die like the Imperial *grognards* they are in course of becoming.

And here the perspicacity of Balzac, who was treating a well-

[1] *Illusions perdues*, Part II, 1839, Conard XII, 72–3.

pondered subject, helps in some measure to attenuate the implication of the love-plot itself, the suggestion that sexual passion, like Cleopatra's nose or the Duchess of Marlborough's glass of water, is all-powerful to deflect the course of history. In *Le dernier Chouan* at any rate, Royalism as represented by the Pretender and his satellites at Coblenz, as well as by those who are risking their heads in civil war, is a losing cause. The greedy nobles who cluster round Montauran in the sinister castle of La Vivetière, the scene of the treacherous massacre of the 'Blues', or who parade their elegance and cupidity at the ball at Saint-James, are out for what they can get. As Marie de Verneuil, although half-disposed to change sides under the impulse of passion, turns her gaze at La Vivetière from the Chouan nobles to the Republican officers whom her caprice has brought into mortal danger, her admiration goes perforce to the latter.

'Oh! là est la nation, la liberté!' se dit-elle. Elle jeta un regard sur les royalistes.
'Et là est un homme, un roi, des privilèges!'

Such confrontation and opposition is the essential historical theme in *Le dernier Chouan*. But it is still, in a large measure, ancillary to the love theme. Everything contributes to the sublimity and tragedy of the central tale: the ebb and flow of the struggle between 'Blues' and 'Whites', the strokes and counterstrokes, the confused skirmishes, the menacing ubiquity of the Chouans with their sinister hootings, their sordid plundering of the dead and their merciless execution of the suspect Galope-Chopine, the grim slaughterings in the darkness at La Vivetière and the final closing in of the Republican forces on the fog-surrounded cottage at Fougères in which Marie and Le Gars are finishing their 'journée sans lendemain'. The very opaqueness of the plot has the same effect. For there is some obscurity in the motivation of the two main characters, or at least in the sequence of impulses which determine Marie's oscillations between 'Blues' and 'Whites'. This sense of mystery is enhanced by the blurred outline of the events which lead up to the tragedy: Montauran's foolhardy actions, the steps taken by Barbette, Galope-Chopine's widow, to avenge her husband by betraying Montauran; Corentin's tortuous and equivocal bargain with Marie; the interferences of the malevolent Mme du Gua Saint-Cyr; the violence of Marie's fluctuations, and the strange mental or moral paralysis which prevents her from trying to save her husband before the arrival of dawn has destroyed their last chance of escape.

There is still in this story enough of the *roman noir* tempestuousness, incoherence and melodrama for M. Bardèche to judge it as being the last of the youthful works rather than the first work of the 'Comédie Humaine'. Nevertheless, in spite of traces of naivety and lack of skill in relating mental reactions and dialogues to subsequent action, it is certain that for the freshness and vigour and passion that inspire it, this 'Scene of Military Life' will remain a strong favourite with readers of the 'Comédie Humaine'.

iii. *La Physiologie du mariage*

The distinction between what is usually called '*La physiologie du mariage* pré-originale' and the completed work published in December 1829 is far greater than that which separates *Le dernier Chouan* from *Les Chouans*. M. Bardèche, in his edition of the 'pré-originale' (1940), has compared the two in order to show Balzac's progress, between 1824 and 1829, towards the master conception of the 'Comédie Humaine'. In the 'Préoriginale' Balzac was merely exploiting a vein of literature which 'Codes' and 'Arts' and 'Physiologies' were making popular. The *Physiologie* of 1826 'est un manuel du geôlier, et, d'abord, elle veut l'être'.[1] Beginning with a crude statistical computation of the inroads made into conjugal solidarity by the 'Minotaure'—the ubiquitous philandering bachelor seeking whom he may devour —Balzac intended, as its provisional title of 1828 shows (*Code marital ou l'art de rendre sa femme fidèle*), while tracing the progress of satiety and disillusionment in the minds and hearts of married couples, to catalogue the signs and symptoms of approaching infidelity, to instruct any husband in the numberless ruses and artifices whereby his wife may elude his vigilance, and to show him how to anticipate and thwart them. Here was an opportunity for witty comment and innuendo, for cynical jovialities, for

[1] Bardèche (2), introd., 51. Cf. Le Yaounanc (1), 525–32.

21

exercises in the style of Rabelais, for facetious subtleties in the manner of Sterne, for rapid character-sketches and pithy anecdotes which Balzac seized on and developed to the full in the expanded and final version, with its mock geometrical array of 'axioms' and 'theorems', imitated from Spinoza via Condillac,[1] its multiplication of 'Méditations' and its store of aphorisms, dialogues and apologues, a device borrowed from Brillat-Savarin's *Physiologie du goût*, which Balzac had read and assimilated since 1825.

But he did not remain content merely to gloat over feminine guile. Personal observation, reading and the conversation of his friends had by 1829 enriched his stock of incidents and stories and extended his knowledge of women and of married life. While his taste for manifestations of male stupidity and female subtlety was not diminished, he was ready to take a more serious view of marriage and its problems. 'Tout en raillant, l'auteur a essayé de populariser quelques idées consolantes.'[2] In the 1829 *Physiologie* his sympathy, even his tenderness for 'le petit sexe' is in evidence. He considers, without adopting it, the view of Diderot that all the mishaps of conjugal life, and indeed all forms of feminine activity, are attributable in the last resort to the sexual urge. He is well aware of 'l'égoïsme, l'insouciance et la nullité des maris', and the expanded work is full of reminders, both frivolous and grave, that estrangement between the partners is most frequently due to offences against the woman's self-respect and sense of modesty, her 'pudeur'. In a word, he no longer bases his entire work on the assumption that lasting love and happiness are impossible in marriage.

L'amour est l'accord du besoin et du sentiment, le bonheur en mariage résulte d'une parfaite entente des âmes entre les époux. Il suit de là que, pour être heureux un homme est obligé de s'astreindre à certaines règles d'honneur et de délicatesse. Après avoir usé du bénéfice de la loi sociale qui consacre le besoin, il doit obéir aux lois secrètes qui font éclore les sentiments. S'il met son bonheur à être aimé, il faut qu'il aime sincèrement: rien ne résiste à une passion véritable.[3]

[1] Spinoza: *Tractatus de Intellectus Emendatione*, translated by Condillac: *Traité des Systèmes*, ch. ix.

[2] Introd. to *Physiologie du mariage*, Conard XXXII, 12.

[3] Conard XXXII, 69.

The superficial intention of the book is to study, in its three successive parts, the progress of married life from that unfortunate invention, the English honeymoon, to the initial misunderstandings ('Considérations générales'); from the first symptoms of disintegration to the plots and counterplots that herald infidelity ('Des moyens de défense à l'intérieur et à l'extérieur'); and from open warfare to the final accommodation when estrangement is philosophically accepted ('Guerre civile'). But the first part abounds in reflexions on the causes of adultery and the attitude of the Code Civil towards it, and culminates in an Epilogue in which the author puts himself forward as a serious social reformer. After embarking, with a professorial dogmatism characteristic of Romantic historians, upon a history of conjugal relations in East and West, from antiquity to modern times, he takes his stand on the Letters of Mirabeau and a misinterpretation of Rousseau's *Nouvelle Héloïse*, and advocates a reversal of the commonly received idea that virginal chastity is more important than wifely fidelity. He proposes that public opinion should recognize and approve experimental, pre-marital unions, and also asserts the right of the unmarried girl to learn how to choose before making her choice; but he insists on rigorous fidelity once that choice is made. In a word, freedom before marriage, and bondage afterwards. Reducing this to terms of commonsense one may legitimately see in it merely a criticism of arranged and conventional marriages, and a conviction that careful selection, and not infatuation based on inexperience, opens the best avenue to happy wedded life. Since Balzac deliberately restricts himself in *La Physiologie du mariage* to the consideration of marriage among the well-to-do, the economic aspect, and even the material interests involved in the marriage contract, are left out of account: a surprising fact in view of the importance that economics are to assume in the 'Comédie Humaine'. Indeed the precautions which Balzac advises a potential cuckold to take would be beyond the means of the average man.

But to overstress this serious note in *La Physiologie du mariage* would be to give a false impression of the work. It is predominantly light-hearted, and only its gaiety prevents it from being merely ribald or salacious. It is an assemblage of cynical witticisms, sometimes obvious, sometimes pungent or subtle; often suggestive, but never definitely coarse. At times it even attains to a sort of humorous lyricism, as in the apostrophe to migraine, that never-failing resource of a wife forced to the defensive.

O migraine, protectrice des amours, impôt conjugal, bouclier sur lequel viennent expirer tous les désirs maritaux! O puissante migraine! Est-il bien possible que les amants ne t'aient pas encore célébrée, divinisée, personnifiée! O prestigieuse migraine! O fallacieuse migraine, béni soit le cerveau qui le premier te conçut! Honte au médecin qui te trouverait un préservatif! Oui, tu es le seul mal que les femmes bénissent, sans doute par reconnaissance des biens que tu leur dispenses, ô fallacieuse migraine, ô prestigieuse migraine!

And yet, by its vivid presentation of matrimonial scenes, by its diagnosis of matrimonial situations, by its crystallization of matrimonial crises in rapid evocations which are sometimes miniature *nouvelles*, it gives a foretaste of many 'Scenes of Private Life'. So also, by its serio-comic analyses of female psychology, by its divination of feminine frustrations, by its plea for a better understanding of feminine aspirations, it points the way to a series of fictions whose appeal to the female heart was to become wellnigh irresistible.

This could not have come about if Balzac had continued to laugh at women, no matter how tender his chuckle or guffaw. In 1830 he took up with zest an activity in which he had occasionally indulged during previous years, that of free-lance journalism; in articles written for *Le Voleur*, *La Mode*, *La Caricature* and *Le Charivari*, he was for some time to carry on, in the spirit of the 'Codes' and 'Arts', with his mocking sketches of prevalent characters and types. Also a new genre, affiliated to the eighteenth-century 'Proverb' made famous by Carmontelle, was coming into fashion, that of semi-dramatic sketches whose aim was still dominantly satirical or comic. In 1827 Auguste Romieu, a wag and scatterbrain of the period, published his *Proverbes romantiques*. In 1828, in collaboration with Vanderbuch and Loève-Weimars, he published *Scènes contemporaines*. Both works were printed at the press of Balzac and Barbier, and attributed to the pen of 'feue Mme la Vicomtesse de Chamilly'.[1] In 1830 the

[1] Hanotaux and Vicaire, 147–8.

caricaturist Henry Monnier gave to the world his first collection of lithographed drawings combined with humorous letterpress: *Scènes populaires*. Almost simultaneous with the work of Monnier, who claims to have known Balzac since 1825, was Balzac's collection of *Scènes de la vie privée*. One of these Scenes, *La Paix du ménage*, recalls Carmontelle and strangely anticipates Musset's 'proverb' *Un Caprice*, of 1837. But what separates Balzac's Scenes from their immediate predecessors is that they have become a serious medium for the portrayal of real and normal life, especially that conjugal life at which Balzac had only recently been laughing. The term 'scene' may at first glance appear to be something of a misnomer. The destiny of these Scenes is to begin as *nouvelles*—we may distinguish the *nouvelle* from the *conte* as being more concerned with situation and state of mind than with narrated fact—and to develop into novels. But gesture and dialogue have their place in them, and the later and longer 'scenes', those which have in fact developed into full-length novels, will still be conceived by Balzac as a series of dramatic episodes linked by preparatory description and narration. The man who had failed at tragedy and melodrama, and who in the course of the next twenty years was often to renew his assault on the footlights, still thought of his world as a stage, and his episodes, peripeteias and conclusions as essentially dramatic material. The habit of dramatizing everyday life was often to involve him in misrepresentations of reality, but it was to add to the fascination he exercises on his readers as a galvanizer of the commonplace.

II

FICTION AND THOUGHT

i. First and second *Scènes de la vie privée* (1830–2);
Le Curé de Tours (1832); *Le colonel Chabert* (1832)

AFTER *Le dernier Chouan* Balzac did not publish another novel
until August 1831, when *La Peau de chagrin* appeared. In the
meantime he produced about a score of 'contes' and 'nouvelles',
some of which he was composing in the autumn of 1829, and
many of which appeared in periodicals before they were gathered
into volumes. A glance at them shows that he was striking out in
two directions: through the stories connected with domestic life
and intimate sentiment to the 'Études de Mœurs', and through
tales of mystery and horror to the 'Études Philosophiques'. He
was conscious of having at once three functions to discharge: those
of moralist, observer and thinker.

It was ostensibly a moral purpose which led him to group together the six stories composing the first two volumes of the
Scènes de la vie privée.[1] He was perhaps desirous of atoning for the
apparent levity of *La Physiologie du mariage* by giving almost
avuncular advice on courtship and marriage to inexperienced
girls. Three of the tales are variations on the theme of the spoilt
child, and show how snobbery (*Le Bal de Sceaux*), romantic
sentimentality (*Gloire et malheur*, now *La Maison du chat qui
pelote*), and wilfulness (*La Vendetta*) may either prevent a happy
marriage or lead to a disastrous one. In the other three he turns
his attention to the pitfalls of married life. *La Paix du ménage*
depicts a young wife recapturing an errant husband's affections
under the expert guidance of an older woman. *La Femme vertueuse* (now *Une double Famille*) appears to have been written in
a mood of fierce anticlericalism, and shows how a wife's puri-

[1] Mame-Delaunay, Apr. 1830.

26

tanical coldness may drive a husband into another woman's arms. The title of *Les Dangers de l'inconduite* (now *Gobseck*) speaks for itself; it is a tale of adultery culminating in the break-up of a family.

Extremes meet in this first collection of tales. The relative insipidity of *La Paix du ménage* and *Le Bal de Sceaux* is offset by the lurid drama of *La Vendetta, La Femme vertueuse* and *Les Dangers de l'inconduite*. Their value lies, not in the moral they point, but in the glimpses they afford of life in Imperial and Restoration times (Napoleon himself figures in *La Vendetta*), and more so still in the opposition of characters and the clash of wills which give a piquant flavour even to the most edifying of them. Like Mérimée, Balzac makes good capital of the Corsican blood-feud theme in *La Vendetta*, even though many years elapsed before he put the final touch to the Corsican father's ferocity by making him rejoice at the sudden death of the hated son-in-law who has brought the news that his daughter has died of starvation: 'Il nous épargne un coup de feu . . .' *La Femme vertueuse*, although open to criticism for the duality of its structure, gives a penetrating study of a priest-ridden *dévote* and portrays with great poignancy the cynical misanthropy of a husband whom both marriage and illicit love have grievously disappointed. *Les Dangers de l'inconduite* reached only an intermediate stage of composition in 1830. It had begun (in *La Mode*) as a 'physiologie': *L'Usurier*. As a scene of private life its main theme is the conflict between the Comtesse de Restaud and her ill-used husband who, even on his death-bed, has to fight hard to preserve the family heritage from falling into her hands. The moneylender Gobseck, one of the most memorable figures in the future 'Comédie Humaine', did not achieve his full stature until the story was reconstructed in 1835; but he already stands out as an inexorable creditor whose gloating enjoyment of the power which money can bring is tempered by a certain harsh kindliness—he is austerely benevolent to the narrator of the story, a struggling solicitor who has never tried to get the better of him in a bargain, and he sides with Restaud against the Comtesse and her lover.

Gloire et malheur is undoubtedly the best of these tales. It is a perfect Balzacian novel in embryo. It eschews the lurid, gives that true picture of the middle-class home which Balzac had

promised in his preface, and does so with such restraint and such
attention to background detail that it started critics in the habit
of emphasizing the affinity between Balzac and the Dutch school
of realist painters. It furnishes a structural pattern which he was
often, though not invariably, to follow in the future: an initial
incident, conversation or situation, a 'close-up' of the protagonists, with an account of their antecedents and environment, then
a series of scenes or dialogues which culminate in a decisive act,
from which in turn derive new scenes of mounting intensity until
a climax is reached and a conclusion precipitated.

It is a story of misalliance. Augustine, the pretty and ingenuous
daughter of a stolid cloth-merchant, loves and marries a brilliant
young painter, Henri (in later versions Théodore) de Sommervieux. Her 'gloire' consists in being lifted into a station of life for
which she is not fitted; her 'malheur' consists in being unable to
adjust herself to it. A similar antithesis was later to inspire
L'Histoire de la grandeur et de la décadence de César Birotteau.
The definitive title, *La Maison du chat qui pelote*, is inspired by
the picturesque sign, a relic of earlier times, which hangs over
M. Guillaume's shop, and is more indicative than the 1830 title
of Balzac's main purpose, which was to reveal the physical and
moral background from which the heroine, for her own misfortune, emerges: the world of the *petits commerçants* wrapped up
in their daily business of buying and selling, and totally incapable
of understanding the meaning of art and the Bohemian temperament of the artist. 'Est-ce donc bien amusant,' asks M. Guillaume,
when confronted with the painting Sommervieux has made of
the shop and its curious sign, 'de voir en peinture ce qu'on rencontre tous les jours dans notre rue?' His chief assistant, the worthy
Joseph Lebas, replies with the only argument he and his like are
capable of urging in favour of art: 'Cela pourra nous faire vendre
quelques aunes de drap de plus.' Mme Guillaume's attitude is
even more trenchant: 'Comment, mon enfant,' she says to her
daughter, 'ton mari s'enferme avec des femmes nues, et tu as la
simplicité de croire qu'il les dessine?'

The Guillaumes and their household, though targets for satire,
win enough of Balzac's sympathy to be real and coherent figures.
They set the standard for his future depiction of the mercantile

middle class, generally honest creatures, but comic because they are ignorant of their limitations. Augustine, who is sensitive enough to realize hers, is pathetic, and her progress towards disillusionment and heartbreak is patiently unfolded. The crisis is reached when, in her innocent simplicity, she appeals to the better feelings of her worldly and contemptuously pitying rival, the Duchesse de Carigliano. This device of confronting the wolf with the lamb, to the inevitable discomfiture of the lamb, is one which Balzac was most frequently to use—and here the case of César Birotteau again leaps to the mind—as a means of bringing his action to a pitch of dramatic intensity. More than any other device, it established his reputation for ironic pessimism. The Duchesse also is aptly hit off in her hard wisdom, as she tries to convey to Augustine that only cunning and histrionic ability, and not passionate attachment, can bring refractory husbands to heel.

Gloire et malheur is a masterpiece in miniature: three social *milieux* set in opposition; the idiosyncrasies of the 'bourgeois', the unstable, temperamental artist and the fashionable *mondaine* economically and dispassionately evoked; a young woman's sentimental experiences subtly and sympathetically analysed; and all this in the space of some seventy octavo pages. Balzac's readers in 1830 were more impressed by his scrutiny of the female heart than we can be today after a century of similar exploration, but he stood forth as a pioneer in an age when Stendhal was misunderstood and neglected. 'C'est M. de Balzac qui a inventé les femmes', wrote Jules Janin maliciously in 1833. In 1830, indeed, Balzac was already meditating a whole series of 'Études de Femmes'. Even in March of that year he had printed one story bearing the title *Étude de Femme*, which examines the mixed emotions of a society prude on receiving a love-letter intended for another woman, and gives valid proof of his insight into feminine psychology. But this exquisitely sarcastic sketch could not be included at that moment among the Scenes of Private Life because it offered no message to the unsophisticated.[1]

Balzac's deceptively naïve sense of responsibility to the young continued for some time to influence his conception, and still predominates in the third and fourth volumes of Private Life Scenes,

[1] It was made to rank as a philosophical story in 1833.

which were added in May 1832. It accounts for *La Bourse*, which, in contrast to *Gloire et malheur*, relates the happy union, after a misunderstanding, of another young painter (Hippolyte Schinner) with a girl who is poor but nobly born. It provides him with an avowable motive for writing *Le Message*, preceded in the 1832 collection by *Le Conseil*, which defends the morality of contemporary literature, and followed by the gruesome story of a husband's vengeance (*La grande Bretèche*). *Le Message* is also, in principle, a warning against adultery, despite the sympathy with which it describes the grief of a wife suddenly bereft of her young lover. This same concern for edification is moreover the ostensible reason for writing, in the course of 1831 and 1832, a group of six 'tableaux' which he completed and put together in 1834 under the title *Même Histoire*, and which only acquired their definitive title, *La Femme de trente ans*, in 1842.

As a composite novel relating phases in the life of a 'mal mariée' this work is incoherent, and also, at moments, takes us back to the melodramatic absurdities of *Annette et le Criminel*. As a group of semi-independent 'scenes' it is more digestible, and the earlier episodes have considerable value as a study of aristocratic society during the period of Napoleon's decline and fall, and the years immediately succeeding. The 'Dernière Revue de Napoléon' with which the first part begins ('Premières Fautes', originally entitled 'Le Rendez-vous') had first appeared in *La Caricature* in November 1830, and gained instant popularity for the vivid glimpse it afforded of the Man of Destiny. But as far as both morality and psychology are concerned the work shows divergent tendencies. Certain episodes support the lesson of *Scènes de la vie privée*. An impetuous love-match leads to rapid estrangement between a dull husband and a quickly dissatisfied wife; then to a romantic and improbable triangle situation from which the third party, the chivalrous young Englishman, Lord Arthur Grenville, reaps nothing but a painful death; and then to a guilty liaison whose consequences, some of them atrocious, extend to the second generation and beget, in the hearts of the children concerned, hatred, rebelliousness and cynicism. Once more it is a question of 'les dangers de l'inconduite'.

Nevertheless, by the time these episodes were brought together to comprise the fourth volume of the *Scènes de la vie privée*, Balzac's sympathy for the unsatisfied woman, and his instinctive approval of individual passion at odds with social law and convention, had played havoc with his edifying intentions of 1830. 'Cette histoire', he wrote with particular reference to what is now the third chapter of the work, 'explique les dangers et le mécanisme de l'amour plus qu'il ne le peint.' He was obviously more absorbed in the study of its mechanism than he was perturbed by its dangers. The tribulations and temptations of Julie d'Aiglemont (until 1842 she went by different names in the various episodes) and the stages by which she reaches unfaithfulness to her nonentity of a husband, are inspected with minute and sympathetic attentiveness, even though Balzac makes the eventually successful seducer, Charles de Vandenesse, grumble over the patient and elaborate manœuvres necessary before a woman of society in France, so unlike her Italian sister in this respect, can be conquered. By such sophistication he no doubt went some way towards meriting Sainte-Beuve's dry characterization of him as 'le romancier qui savait le mieux la corruption de son temps, et il était homme à y ajouter'.[1]

Moreover, in this same episode (*A trente ans*) Balzac makes his first notable plea on behalf of the Woman of Thirty, declares her superiority over the insipid *ingénue* in depth and intensity of passion, and delights his women readers by prolonging the period of sentimental and passionate experience beyond the conventional age-limit. The caustic Sainte-Beuve again has his word to say on this topic:

M. de Balzac a plus que personne son cortège de femmes, celles de trente ans en masse et d'au-delà, dont il a si bien saisi le faible et flatté l'infirmité secrète, toutes ces organisations nerveuses qu'il a eu l'art de magnétiser.[2]

Le Message, of contemporaneous inspiration, carries this thesis a stage further, and brings even the woman of forty[3] back into circulation: here speaks the lover of Mme de Berny and Mme d'Abrantès. The appendage to it, *La grande Bretèche*, and another

---

[1] *Causeries du Lundi*, xi, 483.   [2] Ibid., ii, 64.
[3] '. . . l'âge où les passions des femmes acquièrent leur dernier degré d'intensité', he had written in *Le Vicaire des Ardennes*.

short story, *Adieu*, which had first appeared in *La Mode* (May–June 1830) but which was included in the 1832 Scenes of Private Life under the not-too-appropriate title of *Le Devoir d'une femme*, have a different kind of interest. They are specially good illustrations of his talent, which we have seen recognized by Mme de Pommereul and Charles Rabou, for telling ingenious and exciting tales. He most frequently exercised it during the years 1830–3, and contributed several such tales, in the guise of conversational improvisations, to *Contes bruns*, a miscellany of short stories published in 1832;[1] but as a rule he grouped them in the category of philosophical tales. *Adieu* itself was to take its place among these in 1835. It is a fine example of the rapidity with which Balzac can devise a setting, key his reader up to tense expectation, keep him agog until he has reached the heart of the matter, and then take his narrative to a climax of poignancy. A Napoleonic officer who has returned from imprisonment in Siberia goes for a day's hunting, happens upon a neglected manor which houses a demented young woman, recognizes her as the mistress from whom he had been parted in tragic circumstances at the passage of the Beresina in 1812, makes patient efforts to bring her back to sanity and recognition of his identity, and succeeds at last in doing so by artificially reconstructing the scene which had driven her out of her wits—but only to have her collapse and die in his arms. The two outstanding features of this story are Balzac's account of the Beresina episodes and his description of the pathetic animality to which Julie (later rechristened Stéphanie) de Vandières has been reduced by witnessing them.

La grande Bretèche is even more cunningly complex. Its subject is the classical one of the immurement of a lover in the presence of the guilty wife. The narrator—from 1837 onwards he is identified with Horace Bianchon, one of the medical celebrities of the 'Comédie Humaine'—tells how he has visited a deserted house at Vendôme and become curious to account for the air of desolation that surrounds it. The *frisson* Balzac communicates to his reader in evoking this chilly ruin shows how instinctively, around

---

[1] His contributions were *Une Conversation entre onze heures et minuit* and *Le Grand d'Espagne*. See below, 314, n. 1 and 315. His collaborators were Charles Rabou and Philarète Chasles.

the nucleus of a striking fiction, he wrapped all that was needed in the way of atmosphere. Then also the development of the story reveals the sureness of his technique. Into contact with the musing visitor, anxious to ferret out the facts, come three persons in turn: a fussy little notary with his mannerisms and his legal jargon, a jovial and garrulous innkeeper's widow, and her servant whose confidence can only be won by amorous advances. Thanks to them he gets to the core of the mystery. The narration thus proceeds by well-devised stages, while at the same time the touch of Balzac's wand is able to convert three secondary figures, simply and economically, into real people to each of whom physiognomy, gesture and turn of speech give marked individuality.

Two other works belonging to the 1832 period are of more obvious importance as a landmark in Balzac's progress as a social historian. One is *Le Curé de Tours*, entitled *Les Célibataires* in the third volume of Private Life scenes. The other is *La Transaction*, which had appeared independently in *L'Artiste* in February and March of 1832 and which, in its later expanded form, is now known as *Le colonel Chabert*.

These two fairly long 'nouvelles' bring Balzac almost into the heart of his domain as an observer of manners. In them the romantic sentimentalist is temporarily eclipsed and the apology for passion gives place to a close scrutiny of social groups in their more prosaic or more material preoccupations. *Le Curé de Tours* relates the conflict of petty interests within the precincts of a cathedral close—'une tempête dans un verre d'eau'. It is a dramatization of the commonplace: a mild, inept, comfort-loving priest-vicar, 'dont la bonté allait jusqu'à la bêtise', is driven from the snug quarters in which he is ensconced by the combined efforts of an intriguing colleague and a resentful old maid. *La Transaction* is built on less ordinary data, but pierces through to the core of social life. Its hero is a Napoleonic veteran who, after being reported killed on the battlefield of Eylau, returns to Paris many years later to establish his identity and reclaim his wife and fortune. The wife has married again and achieved a brilliant but precarious social position which his reappearance threatens to destroy; she is the incarnation of ignoble selfishness, and seeks only to thrust him back into the anonymity and squalor from which his solicitor, the upright and benevolent Derville, has rescued him. Although victory is within his grasp, indignation and contempt for his wife's baseness prompt him to give up the struggle, and he prefers to end his days as a pauper in an asylum. In *Le Curé de Tours* a tone of restrained irony is discernible under the matter-of-fact narration. It dilutes our sympathy for the feeble Abbé Birotteau; it gives pungency to the rapid sketch of the frustrated spinster, Mlle Gamard; it brings out sharply the contrast between the benevolent intentions of Birotteau's supporters and their pusillanimity when they find that the sanctimonious Troubert is pulling strings to endanger their interests. In *La Transaction* the dominant note, especially in the enlarged version of 1835, is one of sardonic bitterness, intensified by a feeling of pity for the victims and outcasts of society.

In these two stories then, with a new-found consistency and potency, Balzac begins more conspicuously to exploit one of his most remarkable veins: the exposure of social triviality, egoism and cruelty. Moreover it is clear that he is advancing beyond the single category of Scenes of Private Life. In 1833 *Le Curé de Tours* was to constitute one of the first *Scènes de la vie de province*, not merely because the action is staged in a provincial city, but also because it was to be part of his plan to reveal the seething passions, born of petty interests, which live under the apparently untroubled surface of provincial life. *La Transaction* remained unclassified until 1835, but with its evocation of Parisian backgrounds, particularly that of a solicitor's office, it points the way to a third series, the *Scènes de la vie parisienne*.[1] It is however true that these were already implicit in many of the *Scènes de la vie privée*.

ii. Philosophical Tales (1830–3)

As a student of nineteenth-century France Balzac had necessarily to take the recent past as his field of investigation, but only in *Étude de femme* had he set the action so late as 1829. *Le Bal de Sceaux* had served to reflect the outlook of the returned aristocracy during the early Restoration period. Life during the Empire

[1] Balzac's final intention was to put it into the Private Life category.

was at least the point of departure for situation and action in the other stories, and it is not surprising that some of the Scenes of Private Life are bathed in the atmosphere of the Napoleonic legend. At the same time, in 1830 and 1831, Balzac was also sending to the periodicals stories which he conceived as having philosophical rather than directly social import, or at any rate as implying criticism of the principles on which social life is based rather than description of the course it takes.

Many of these are also set against a Revolutionary or Imperial background, and in accordance with the taste of the time and the trend of contemporary fiction, the episodes they relate are startling or tragic, although their real interest is intended to lie in the reflections they incite on strange facets of human experience. A work of early 1830 in whose composition Balzac collaborated, the alleged *Mémoires*[1] of Henri Sanson, official headsman of Paris during the Revolutionary years, stands apart from these stories, but in common with them it encourages the prevalent taste for the morbid and the atrocious. Yet even here, in those parts which can be more surely assigned to Balzac, the sensational serves to give a jolt to thought. In the first chapter, for instance, a chance confrontation of Sanson with Napoleon at the height of his glory elicits from the former the admission that, if the occasion arose, he would execute the latter with the same devotion to duty as he had executed Louis XVI. And perhaps with less reluctance: for from the theme of Sanson's remorse for having to behead an innocent king, Balzac drew the story which provides the Introduction to the *Mémoires*, which he republished in 1843 as *Une Messe en 1793*, and which now has its place in the 'Comédie Humaine' as the moving *Épisode sous la Terreur*.

Among the *Contes* themselves, *Les deux Rêves* (May 1830), afterwards to form part of the composite novel *Sur Catherine de Médicis*, takes a curiously opposite standpoint to that of the *Mémoires*, which have their place in the literature inspired round about this time by the movement for the abolition of capital

---

[1] The parts of this work attributed to Balzac were included in the Definitive Edition of the 'Comédie Humaine' as *Les Souvenirs d'un Paria*. In the Conard edition (*O.D.* I) M. Bouteron discusses this attribution and prints in an appendix the other chapters of the *Mémoires*.

punishment.[1] Through the fiction of two hallucinations experienced in 1786 by the future terrorists Robespierre and Marat, *Les deux Rêves* justifies on political and social grounds the holocaust of 1793–5. However, incidents of the military campaigns furnish Balzac with more material than the Revolution itself: one reason for his taste for them is that they enable him to convey through fiction his admiration for the forthright, passionate temperament of the Spanish and Italian peoples. *El Verdugo* (January 1830) tells of a whole family of Spanish nobles condemned to death in 1809 for guerrilla warfare; the eldest son is granted his life on condition that he carries out the sentence upon the rest of them, and he does so at their earnest persuasion. *Adieu*, though we have seen that it was temporarily misplaced in 1832, can be legitimately included among these stories; its 'philosophical' interest lies in the study of a young woman's dementia. *Une Passion dans le désert* takes the reader to Egypt in 1793, and describes the strange infatuation of a female panther for a soldier cut off from his comrades in the Sahara. It is a disconcerting story in which some critics have discerned the study of a monstrous sexual aberration; but its real intention seems to have been a humorous one—a comparison between the felinity of women and the femininity of panthers.[2] Two tales of 1831 can be added to this list: *Le Réquisitionnaire*, a study of telepathic sympathy between mother and son, and *L'Auberge rouge*, which superimposes, on the story of an officer facing the firing-squad for a murder that he had committed in imagination but not in fact, the discussion of a moral problem. Except for spasms of neuralgic torture brought on by remorse of conscience, the real criminal has escaped scot-free and become a millionaire; should the man who

[1] In the pseudo-memoirs the plea for the removal of the death penalty is coupled with one in favour of the rehabilitation of the hangman, a figure of universal horror and reprobation; it curiously anticipates that made by Vigny in 1836 on behalf of that other 'pariah', the serving soldier. It is not easy to surmise how much of this comes from Balzac's pen, and how much from that of his collaborator, Lhéritier de l'Ain. It seems likely that those responsible for the *Édition Définitive* were ready to attribute too much of the *Mémoires* to Balzac on the later testimony of Lhéritier. But see Goulard.

[2] It had first appeared in *La Revue de Paris*, 24 Dec. 1830, and Philarète Chasles asserted that this story made Balzac's reputation (*Journal des Débats*, 16 Aug. 1838). For Balzac's views on affinities between men and animals, see Baldensperger (2), 94–5.

loves his daughter, but who knows the facts, marry the girl and so acquire a fortune which is tainted with blood?

A type of story somewhat different from the above, but destined also to swell the list of philosophical tales, shows Balzac more patently vying as a dealer in the fantastic and the preternatural with such contemporaries as Charles Nodier, Jules Janin and the recently translated Hoffmann. As a rule, for the subject and setting of these tales, he dips further back into the past. *Sarrasine* (November 1830) conjures up eighteenth-century Rome and treats the theme of indeterminate sexuality in a castrated male. *Le Chef d'œuvre inconnu* (July–August 1831), whose scene is set in early seventeenth-century Paris, is one of Balzac's best short stories, and one of the most penetrating inquiries a writer of fiction has ever made, in so limited a space, into the central problem of æsthetics. It shows a fanatical old painter, Frenhofer, driven to delirium and suicide in his attempt to reach beyond the consecrated technique of line and colour, beyond form itself, and so achieve on canvas the perfect illusion of life—or rather, perhaps, his own incommunicable vision of life. Much of this is no doubt inspired by the ideas and practice of Eugène Delacroix; but at moments it reads like a brilliant anticipation of trends in modern painting from Monet to Picasso.

In *L'Élixir de longue vie* (October 1830) Balzac enriches the Don Juan legend with a horrific story of filial impiety, and enlarges with much cynicism on the parricidal tendencies of children anxious to succeed to their parents' property. *Les Proscrits* (May 1831) draws a contrast between two exiled poets living in fourteenth-century Paris, the rugged but embittered Dante and the mystical Godefroid de Gand. Both poets are in quest of the transcendent, and the real object of the story is to put a summary of the illuminist creed, to which Balzac was turning with increasing fervour, into the mouth of Sigier, the famous Sorbonne doctor who, in actual fact, had died some twenty-five years before the action of the story begins. Like *L'Enfant maudit* (January 1931), a story not completed until 1836 which narrates the birth, life and premature death of a hypersensitive child in the early seventeenth century, *Les Proscrits* gives a foretaste of Balzac the metaphysician. Finally there is the charming legend of *Jésus-Christ en*

Flandre (September 1831), which transfers to the neighbourhood of the Flemish coast and to an indeterminate period of the Middle Ages the Gospel story of Christ walking on the waters, and shows Him saving a handful of simple-hearted folk from drowning. To it was to be added, in 1845, a separate story also written in 1830–1 and entitled *L'Église*.[1] Here Balzac uses a fantastic vision as a means, first of denouncing the Church for the crimes it has committed through the ages, and then of acclaiming it as the creator of science and civilization. This acclamation was confirmed in 1845 by the addition of a concluding paragraph:

'Croire, me dis-je, c'est vivre! Je viens de voir passer le convoi d'une monarchie,[2] il faut défendre l'ÉGLISE!'

One month after publishing *La Peau de chagrin* in August 1831, Balzac assembled nearly all these tales, together with the *nouvelle* entitled *Étude de Femme* (March 1830) and a boisterous, satirical fantasia, *La Comédie du diable*,[3] in a somewhat disparate three-volume collection entitled *Romans et contes philosophiques*. In December the *Revue de Paris* printed his *Maître Cornélius*, a story owing much to Scott's *Quentin Durward* for its structure and the view it gives of Louis XI and his minions; but comparable with the completed *Gobseck* for its study of a miser, in this case a somnambulist, so obsessed with the fear of losing his hoard of treasures that he steals and hides it in his sleep. This, with *Madame Firmiani* (February 1832), whose subject is the restitution of dishonestly acquired property which a young heir makes in order to win the hand of a virtuous and charming woman, and the first version of the semi-autobiographical *Louis Lambert*, went into the 1832 volume of *Nouveaux Contes philosophiques* which also found room for *L'Auberge rouge*. But Balzac's standing as a moralist-philosopher depends rather on the three full-length novels he produced between 1831 and 1835: *La Peau de chagrin* (1831), *L'Histoire intellectuelle de Louis Lambert* (1831–5) and

[1] See Pommier (1).

[2] This is probably an allusion to the death in 1842 of the Duke of Orleans, in whom had been placed the hopes of the Orleanist dynasty.

[3] It had first appeared in *La Mode* (13 Nov. 1830) and *La Caricature* (18 Nov. 1830). It stages a 'Convention des Morts' in Hell, presided over by the Devil. See Conard, *O.D.* II. It is not a work of great originality, and was never incorporated into the 'Comédie Humaine'.

Séraphita (1834–5). The clusters of stories just characterized, varied and picturesque as they are, may legitimately be regarded as mere satellites of these novels, which are worthy of more detailed attention.

iii. *La Peau de chagrin* (1831)

La Peau de chagrin is a paradoxical achievement: it is a fantastic novel, as fantastic as any of the *Thousand-and-one Nights* so often quoted in connection with it, and yet it is a novel about contemporary society. There is no time-lag between the period when Balzac was writing it (late 1830 to July 1831) and the period at which the action reaches its climax. He calls in the supernatural to give colour and relief to the theory about life which the tale unfolds; the action is contemporaneous because that theory is intimately concerned with the relationship between the individual and society at what was for Balzac a critical moment in human history.

La Peau de chagrin is a work of great power and exuberance, offered to French readers at a time when these two qualities were more appreciated, and more often displayed, than economy and restraint. Had Balzac's literary production stopped short at this point, *La Peau de chagrin* would still rank as one of the great literary monuments of the early eighteen-thirties, displaying as it does both the virtues and the faults of the age. Viewed as a whole, it is a work of complex and sinuous design. Hence the adoption for its epigraph of the serpentine squiggle which, in *Tristram Shandy*, Corporal Trim had traced in the air as a symbol of celibate independence: 'drame qui serpente, ondule, tournoie', as Balzac himself stated of his work in one of the many puffs which he wrote, or caused to be written, about it.[1] Even the order in which the three parts of this 'drama' are narrated is significant for the philosophy it reveals.

In the first part, now entitled 'Le Talisman', on an October evening of 1830,[2] after losing his last gold coin at the gaming-table, a young man on the point of suicide steps into an old

[1] A review in *La Caricature*, 11 Aug. 1831, by 'Alexandre de B.'
[2] Unaccountably the texts after 1833 give 1829, although the July Revolution has taken place.

curiosity shop and loses himself for a while in contemplation of the welter of disparate objects it contains—relics of all ages and civilizations. A strange, wizened centenarian, the owner of the shop, offers him a mysterious parchment, a fragment of shagreen, on which King Solomon had cast a spell. Its possessor has only to express a wish, and it will be granted; but with every wish the skin will shrink, and with it his span of life.

Incredulous but reckless from despair, Raphaël de Valentin tests the virtue of the skin by calling for an immediate orgy. As he leaves the shop he falls in with a trio of friends, one of whom, a poet, 'Émile' (later developed into Émile Blondet, one of the most ubiquitous journalists of the 'Comédie Humaine') is concerned with the launching of a supposedly anti-ministerial newspaper sponsored by the government, and proposes to make Raphaël its editor-in-chief. The latter is led off to a dinner offered by the banker[1] who is financing the venture to a crowd of writers, artists, scientists and courtesans. At the end of it Raphaël is still sober enough to pour his life-story into the more or less sympathetic ears of Émile. This furnishes the substance of the second part of the novel: 'La Femme sans Cœur.'

It is the first of many pictures from Balzac's pen, inspired by his own experience, of youthful poverty, struggling for recognition and success in a Paris which is indifferent to everything save wealth and pretentiousness. Raphaël has spent three years living in a garret on a franc a day, at work on a philosophical treatise which is to make his reputation. A young elegant, Rastignac, who believes that the secret of social success lies in idleness and dissipation, persuades Raphaël to try an easier alternative: that of climbing upwards by the conquest of a rich and beautiful woman, Fœdora, semi-Russian in origin, 'espèce de problème féminin'. But Fœdora is the 'femme sans cœur' battening upon the adoration of men and determined to give nothing in return; and all the while Raphaël has ignored the disinterested love of Pauline Gaudin, his landlady's daughter. Reduced to fury and desperation,

---

[1] He is the 'ancien fournisseur' of *L'Auberge rouge* (see above, 36) which Balzac wrote at the same time as *La Peau de chagrin*, when staying at La Bouleaunière, Mme de Berny's house near Nemours. This character, Mauricey in the short story, was renamed Taillefer later. See below, 97.

and still tutored by Rastignac in the art of making ends meet, first by the prostitution of his name and pen, then by gambling and living on credit, Raphaël has decided to end his life in debauchery. At this point in his confession to Émile he remembers the wild-ass's skin so recently acquired, and decides to test it again by demanding an income of 200,000 francs. The orgy is over. The next morning, as the merrymakers emerge from their stupor, the news comes that he has inherited a princely fortune. Raphaël discovers that the skin has already shrunk, and becomes panic-stricken.

The third part, 'L'Agonie', shows the Marquis Raphaël de Valentin attempting to eke out his frail and dwindling existence by the avoidance of all emotion and volition. His needs are automatically supplied by the old family servant whose business it is to spare him the necessity of uttering the fatal words 'I wish', even as a formula of conventional benevolence. Chance throws him again into the company of Pauline Gaudin. 'Je veux être aimé de Pauline,' he cries, and the skin does not shrink. Not knowing that this particular wish is gratuitous since she has loved him for years, he believes the spell is broken, and abandons himself to the bliss of perfect union with her—until he finds that the skin is now the size of a lady's pocket-handkerchief. Panic returns. He suffers the inane loquacity of a zoologist, a mathematician and a mechanic in the vain effort to have the skin stretched by artificial means. He consults a group of medical specialists in the hope of getting a diagnosis and finding a cure for the disease—is it mental or physical?—that is draining away his life. He goes to Aix-les-Bains to arrest its progress. There the hostility of fellow-patients involves him in a duel and forces him to further expenditure of his vital span by willing his opponent's death. He buries himself in a peasant's cottage in a remote corner of Auvergne and tries to attain a state of vegetative calm in intimate communion with nature: the curiosity and tactless solicitude of his hosts drive him back to Paris. But the uncomprehending Pauline rejoins him there and he dies in a paroxysm of erotic frenzy.

Some critics have regretted Balzac's use of a magic talisman as a gauge for measuring the wasting life of a nineteenth-century Frenchman in tall hat and gaitered trousers. Had he not enough 'realism' at his command to dispense with the supernatural in depicting the anguish of a man who at every turn comes up against the inexorability of doom and the hard indifference of a selfish world? But Balzac was not a mere 'realist': *La Peau de chagrin* is as much a poem as it is a novel. The wild-ass's skin symbolizes the choice which, according to him, every mortal makes between two ways of life. The inevitability of this choice is the dominant theme of the book, worked out through the opposition of characters, the interweaving of analogous episodes and the approximate symmetry of the parts.

'Je vais vous révéler en peu de mots,' [says the satanical dealer in antiques to his impecunious customer] 'un grand mystère de la vie humaine. L'homme s'épuise par deux actes instinctivement accomplis qui tarissent les sources de son existence. Deux verbes expriment toutes les formes que prennent ces deux causes de mort, VOULOIR et POUVOIR. Entre ces deux termes de l'action humaine, il est une autre formule dont s'emparent les sages, et je lui dois le bonheur de ma longévité. *Vouloir* nous brûle, et *pouvoir* nous détruit, mais SAVOIR laisse notre faible organisation dans un perpétuel état de calme.'

This is the early expression of a conviction which haunted Balzac, which he often repeated, and which provided him with a ruling principle for the conception of his most striking novels. The critic Philarète Chasles enlarged on it in a preface he wrote[1] for the 1831 edition of the *Romans et contes philosophiques*. It can be summed up in the term *l'usure par la pensée*, the destructive function of thought. To reinforce this truth Chasles called in the testimony of Rousseau in a distorted aphorism which Balzac himself had already misquoted: *l'homme qui pense est un animal dépravé*. Intelligence and the habit of analysis are in a sense a deviation from nature, a derivative of civilization; they lead to a disastrous exacerbation of the instincts and desires, to a lust for experience, pleasure, passion, wealth and power which wears out the human organism.

'Pensée' for Balzac is a generic term. In *Les Martyrs ignorés*, a fragmentary work written in 1836 which found no permanent place in the 'Comédie Humaine',[2] he defines it thus:

[1] Reproduced in Lovenjoul (1), 171–7 and A. Levin, 130–7.

[2] Conard, *O.D.* iii, 116–42. It is a philosophical discussion between half a dozen eccentrics, one of them (Raphaël) evidently Balzac himself. It is often

Les passions, les vices, les occupations extrêmes, les douleurs, les plaisirs sont des torrents de pensée. Réunissez sur un point donné quelques idées violentes, un homme est tué par elles comme s'il recevait un coup de poignard.

So, according to Félix Davin (another friend of Balzac writing at the end of 1834 at the latter's own prompting), the majority of Balzac's stories, but especially the *Contes philosophiques*, illustrate this universal principle: *the blade wears out the scabbard.*

Ainsi, dans l'*Adieu*, l'idée du bonheur, exaltée à son plus haut degré social, foudroie l'épouse. . . . Dans *Le Réquisitionnaire* c'est une mère tuée par la violence du sentiment maternel. . . . Dans *El Verdugo*, c'est l'idée de dynastie mettant une hache dans la main d'un fils . . . dans l'*Élixir de longue vie* l'idée hérédité devient meurtrière à son tour. Dans *Maître Cornelius* c'est l'idée avarice tuant l'avare dans la personne du vieil argentier. *Le Chef-d'œuvre inconnu* nous montre l'art tuant l'œuvre. . . . Un être débile tué par la terreur est le résultat de l'histoire intitulée *L'Enfant Maudit* . . . *Jésus-Christ en Flandre* est la démonstration de la puissance de la foi, considérée aussi comme une idée.[1]

Vouloir, as conceived by the antique-dealer, is a projection of thought towards a given aim, a tension which has *pouvoir* for its objective. Already in *La Peau de chagrin* we find the adumbration of another ruling idea, that will is a material substance, a 'masse fluide' which, when concentrated, wielded and directed, can become an irresistible force. But *La Peau de chagrin* is the work of a moralist rather than that of a metaphysician, and so leaves this notion undeveloped. Here Balzac is almost wholly preoccupied with the slow or rapid expenditure of vital energy. In short, as he was to state explicitly later on, each individual is endowed with a certain quantity of energy; it is for him to squander or to husband it according to the dictates of his temperament.

The antique-dealer has chosen to husband his vital energy, and has achieved remarkable longevity by withdrawing his life from the body and nursing it within the brain. So thought is cheated of

taken to be a record of conversations which Balzac had at the Café Voltaire, in 1825 or 1827. Two of the interlocutors have been identified: one with the Prussian 'magnetiser', Dr Koreff, the other with the Polish mathematician, Hoëné Wronski. See Baldensperger (2), 101–18 and 237–59.

[1] Lovenjoul (1), 204–6.

its destructive properties and becomes for him what we might call *pensée-contemplation*. He vicariously enjoys all the varieties of experience, thanks to the wide range of his knowledge and the multitude of curios he has gathered around him. When Raphaël renounced his studious asceticism, he had chosen the spendthrift course: 'Je veux vivre avec excès!' he had cried as he grasped the skin. In her frigid egoism, Fœdora stands beside the antique-dealer, with this difference that her aim is to excite passion while feeling none: 'Je n'appartiendrai à personne.' Among the crowd of courtesans recruited for the banker's orgy, Aquilina,[1] 'l'âme du vice', and Euphrasie, 'le vice sans âme', have by diverse routes reached an egoism as hard as that of Fœdora, but they stand with Raphaël as the champions of a brief and hectic life. Then, by an ironic reversal, the figures in this weird minuet cross over. The antique-dealer, through a vengeful wish uttered by Raphaël, becomes a belated *viveur*, while Raphaël hoards with frantic parsimony what little life remains to him; and even, in the hope of attaining the insensibility of plants and inert things, anticipates the aspiration of Flaubert's Saint Anthony: 'être la matière'. This pattern of antithesis and alternation persists to the end, when the well-meaning Jonathas seeks to divert his master by preparing a replica of the banker's feast. Raphaël recoils from the last temptation to self-expenditure, only to yield to it anew in the arms of Pauline.

This theme applies not only to the individual, but also to collective humanity.[2] *La Peau de chagrin* represents Balzac's first major attempt to diagnose the moral sickness of his century, aggravated though not caused by the advent of the Orleanist regime: the disintegration of society through individualism. The guests at the orgy tear the world to pieces in a riot of cynical utterances whose very incoherence bears witness as much to the anarchy of the times as to the drunken elation of the speakers. Yet the indictment is of all society as such, and not merely that of

[1] Her name is borrowed from Otway's *Venice preserved*, a work which Balzac greatly admired.

[2] Philarète Chasles was discerning enough to bring this fact into relief, not only in the preface he wrote for the *Romans et contes philosophiques*, which was partly inspired by Balzac, but also in his previous article on *La Peau de chagrin* (*Le Messager des Chambres*, 6 Aug. 1831). See A. Levin, 127–9.

1830. Balzac's intention is made clear in the *bravura* passages which give exceptional brilliance to the work, all bearing in one way or another on the instability or corruption of society: the whimsical sketch of a Parisian gambling-den with which the book begins; the description of the old curiosity shop and its jumble of exhibits, a phantasmagoria worthy of a place in Hugo's *Légende des Siècles*; the banqueting scene with its glut of foods and wines, its rising tide of drunkenness and lasciviousness, and its aftermath of livid crapulence; also the interview with the pedantic scientists whose classifications are a cloak for ignorance and the doctors whose addiction to fads and formulas anticipates that of the physicians satirized by G. B. Shaw. But the recurrent motive is the heartless and murderous treatment which society metes out to the individuals it rejects. Fœdora with her posturing beauty, her calculated charm and her self-refusing coquetry is human society personified, as a belated addition to the Epilogue admits. And society's attitude to those it has vanquished and condemned is summed up in the maxim: 'mort aux faibles'!

. . . si quelque volatile est endolori parmi ceux de la basse-cour, les autres le poursuivent à coups de bec, le plument et l'assassinent.

It is true that Balzac's considered judgment will make him, in the long run, approve of society as an instrument of discipline and a means of individual betterment, but he never forgets that the clash of social interests develops man's propensity for evil. This strain of pessimism, so fertile a source of inspiration throughout the 'Comédie Humaine', already permeates *La Peau de chagrin*. But the work has many other points of interest.

It is the first novel in which the money motive is well to the fore: money which is not only the prize in a relentless conflict between opposing interests and ideas, but also a trivial, daily necessity, the lack of which may cause sharp embarrassment or even torture to self-esteem. It was this aspect of *La Peau de chagrin* which caused Gautier to write his famous sentence:

. . . dans *La Peau de chagrin* il [Balzac] eut le courage de représenter un amant inquiet non seulement de savoir s'il a touché le cœur de celle qu'il aime, mais encore s'il aura assez de monnaie pour payer le fiacre dans lequel il la reconduit.

45

Furthermore, the novel, before *Louis Lambert* and *Le Lys dans la vallée*, has its autobiographical significance. There is a good deal of Balzac himself in Raphaël de Valentin: his adolescent ambition, his almost arrogant persuasion of inherent genius, and the strange blend of idealism and opportunism in the reflections on love and the function of woman with which 'La Femme sans cœur' is filled. Even while watching Fœdora and Pauline take shape, the reader finds himself speculating as to what experiences of real women—others besides Laure de Berny, Mme d'Abrantès and Olympe Pélissier[1]—have been flung into the melting-pot of imaginative creation. He marvels at the candour with which Balzac reveals certain traits which we know that he himself possessed.

Si d'abord, animé d'une volonté ferme et du désir de me faire aimer, je pris un peu d'ascendant sur elle [Fœdora], bientôt ma passion grandit, je ne fus plus maître de moi, je tombai dans le vrai, je me perdis et devins éperdument amoureux.

If such self-knowledge is garnered from the past, how aptly also it applies to the future, to the real lover of Mme de Castries and Mme Hanska, and to how many other fictitious lovers in the 'Comédie Humaine' who advance from calculation to infatuation![2] How much of *La Duchesse de Langeais*, to quote a particular case, is already implicit in *La Peau de chagrin*, many months before he even knew of her who is credited with having furnished the model for the self-centred coquette! And yet, enticing as such speculations may be, it is prudent to recognize that Raphaël de Valentin is not the Balzac we know, but one of the potential Balzacs that coexisted with the adolescent of the Rue Lesdiguières. Another Balzac that might have been is the figure of Louis Lambert in the novel bearing that title. If Raphaël de Valentin had been less passionate in his pursuit of life and love, and more delicate in his physical and spiritual make-up; if he had persisted in his effort to understand the nature of things, he

[1] See *Biography*, 43.
[2] In Feb. 1834 Mme Carraud (Z.C., 173) criticized him for making this habit of calculation persist even in the heart of a man who has reached complete infatuation. There can however be no doubt that this combination was a facet of Balzac's own experience.

might have become that Louis Lambert whom a different form of self-expenditure, the straining after transcendental truth, brought also to an early grave.

iv. Science, Metaphysics and Religion: *Louis Lambert* (1832–5); *Séraphita* (1834–5)

Louis Lambert appears to have started as the expansion of a few lines in *Le Curé de Tours* referring to the devoted attentiveness of one Pauline de Villenoix to her demented lover. While he was writing the *Notice biographique sur Louis Lambert* during the summer and autumn of 1832, Balzac's ambitions for this novel developed considerably. He took up threads from his own past works, notably the biography of one of his other selves, 'Victor Morillon', incorporated in the 'Avertissement' he had written in 1828 for *Le Gars*. *Louis Lambert* tended to become a history of Balzac's own mental development. He was particularly interested in that intuitive faculty to which reference has already been made, that capacity for divination which was enabling him to conceive characters and evoke physical and social backgrounds with a minuteness and accuracy of perception for which the limited range of his experience could with difficulty account. He often speculated on this power.[1] It was in the original preface of *La Peau de chagrin* that he defined it as 'une sorte de seconde vue', which allows such poets or writers as are 'réellement philosophes' to divine truth in all possible situations:

. . . ou, mieux encore, je ne sais quelle puissance qui les transporte là où ils doivent, où ils veulent être. Ils inventent le vrai, par analogie, ou voient l'effet à décrire, soit que l'objet vienne à eux, soit qu'ils aillent eux-mêmes vers l'objet.

Since he was so conscious of enjoying this gift, it is not surprising that he wished to understand it and relate it to the scheme of things. And so *Louis Lambert*, ostensibly the biography of a fellow-scholar at the College of Vendôme, took shape as an incursion into the realm of metaphysics which became bolder and reached even farther as the *Notice biographique* of 1832 expanded

[1] As for example in *Théorie de la Démarche* of Aug.–Sept. 1833 (Conard, *O.D.* II, 625).

47

into the *Histoire intellectuelle de Louis Lambert* of 1833, and then into the almost definitive *Louis Lambert* of 1835.

The hero of the novel is presented as an exceptionally studious lad, a voracious reader superlatively endowed with those occult faculties whose source and origin Balzac is trying to investigate, including a prodigious memory and vivid imaginative power. To call Lambert an introvert would be to misapply modern terminology. He is one who from childhood was left free to cultivate the 'inner life'. Not that he was indifferent to the external world —he lived in close contact with nature—but the attention he gave to this was as it were an extension of his inner contemplation and speculation. At the age of fourteen, through the intervention of Mme de Staël, who one day surprised him immersed in Swedenborg's *Heaven and Earth*, he found himself flung into the uncongenial life of the College of Vendôme and the unwelcome companionship of the healthy, uncomprehending animals that schoolboys normally are. There he spent four years, which were sweetened only by the love and understanding of the young Balzac. The two became bosom friends.

The account that Balzac gives of life at Vendôme throws welcome light on his schooldays: it is the best part of the novel *qua* novel. But narration and description are only incidental to his purpose, which is to show how, thanks to the spiritual sanctuary in which Balzac and Lambert are able to take refuge by the very fact of being misfits at school, they come to the threshold of psychological and metaphysical discoveries. Both of them are interested in the nature of thought and its mode of generation, and this brings them straight up against the ontological problem in metaphysics. As a precocious disciple of Swedenborg, Lambert is inclined to believe in the coexistence of two 'natures' or substances, spirit and matter. As a votary of science, Balzac inclines to materialism. Lambert is of course only an objectification of one aspect of Balzac's personality and thought, and this means that the real Balzac is searching for a reconciliation of opposites and reaching foward to a monist explanation of reality. On the occasion of the two friends' visit to the neighbouring castle of Rochambeau, Lambert is confronted with a new experience of 'second sight'—he has the hallucination (a schizophrenic one,

according to modern theory) of having seen Rochambeau the previous night in a dream, though he knows he has never before
visited it in the flesh. Meditation on the possibility of the mind
possessing the power to transcend the laws of time and space
inspires him to draft a *Traité de la volonté* analogous to the
Théorie de la volonté which Raphaël de Valentin had composed
during his period of studious asceticism. His form-master confiscates and destroys this draft, but Balzac gives a summary of it
—one much expanded in the 1833 version of the novel. Speculation still goes on as to whether Balzac himself had composed such
a treatise when a schoolboy.

Instead of postulating two natures in man, the spiritual and
the physical, the *Traité de la volonté* (and also the fragmentary
Pensées which conclude the work, again much expanded after
1832) adopts a physiological explanation of the phenomena of
Will and Thought, and, building mainly upon the theories and
practice of Mesmer, equates them with a 'substance éthérée', a
'fluid' akin to electric current, heat-waves and light-waves, discharged from the brain. To state curtly and crudely what Balzac
himself expounds at greater length, and with tumultuous eloquence, Thought expresses itself in ideas which are an internal
activity of man, Will in concrete acts which impinge upon the
outer world. Because thinking involves willing, Balzac gives
priority to Will over Thought. But both are in the first resort
inner activities; volitions and ideas are part of the inner man, the
'être actionnel': when translated into objective acts they are part
of the 'être réactionnel', the outer man.

The 'être réactionnel' is subject to the physical laws governing
the outside world. The 'être actionnel' has no such limitations.
'L'Être actionnel peut s'isoler complètement de l'être réactionnel,
en briser l'*enveloppe*, faire tomber les murailles devant sa toute-
puissante vue.' Those mysterious fluids, Will and Thought, are
'forces vives', physical realities, though not at present discernible
or measurable as such. So are the sentiments and passions which
go to swell the irresistible current of Will which, when the 'être
actionnel' projects them into the outside world, can achieve miraculous or terrible effects. As for ideas in their entrancing variety
and multiplicity, Balzac-Lambert looks upon their production as

E   49

being the essential function of man. We need not dwell on the lyricism with which he expatiates on this theme. The upshot is that from the enumeration of these 'laws' which constitute the 'formula of our intelligence' he deduces the existence of those occult faculties, the power to reconstruct the past or foresee the future, or to witness events taking place at vast distances, of which he cites numerous examples.

'Second sight' is a natural gift accorded to those in whom the 'être actionnel' predominates over the 'être réactionnel'. In the *Pensées* at the end of the book, the distinction is amplified and clarified. There are, in ascending degrees of intelligence and spirituality, three types of human being, the *instinctif*, the *abstractif* and the *spécialiste*. The first type merely acts, being purely 'réactionnel'. The second one thinks, being half-way between the 'réactionnel' and the 'actionnel'. The third type ('spécialité, *species*, vue, spéculer, voir tout, et d'un seul coup') is completely 'actionnel'. He acts, sees and feels 'par son intérieur'. His particular faculty is intuition, he is approaching the peak of human destiny: 'il aspire à Dieu qu'il pressent ou contemple'. Lambert's nature is exceptional because in him the 'être actionnel' already predominates, and because he is on the way to reaching the stage of 'spécialité'. This spells disaster from the practical and mundane point of view because, despite the robustness of constitution which Balzac attributes to him, he is becoming increasingly ill-adjusted to the world around him, and the 'être réactionnel' is likely to collapse under the strain.

This is what happens eventually. In the meantime we may observe that Lambert, alias Balzac, has succeeded provisionally in reaching the desired monist position. There is one principle, one substance, subtle, impalpable, but material. After Locke and Voltaire, Balzac sees no impiety in supposing that God conferred on matter the faculty of thought. His intention seems to have been, especially in the intermediate stages of composition, to show Lambert temporarily receding from the Swedenborg thesis that the material world is symbolic of or 'correspondent' to the world of spirit, that the purpose of man is through a succession of lives to achieve a completely spiritual existence, and pinning his hopes of further enlightenment on science and a positive method curiously defined. And so, on his removal from college, after a sojourn with his uncle at Blois, he proceeds to Paris, comes into contact, like Raphaël de Valentin, with social egoism, and plunges into scientific and philosophic studies. But after three years he is disillusioned, as he explains in a letter to his uncle which was not added to the novel until the third edition of December 1835.[1] The scientists of his day are too self-centred, and scientific studies too subdivided and centrifugal. Reverting frankly to mysticism and to Swedenborg envisaged as the latest and greatest contributor to philosophical and religious truth, he returns to Blois to meditate on Swedenborg's theosophy and to draw from inner illumination the knowledge he seeks of the meaning and purpose of life. There he falls deeply in love with a rich young Jewess, Pauline de Villenoix. The drafts of a series of letters he writes to her show that the habit of analysis and introspection have already profoundly disturbed his mental equilibrium. The intensity of his passion, with all its sensual implications, completes this disorganization, and, on the eve of his wedding, pushes him over the brink of sanity. The devoted Pauline tends him for the remaining three years of his life, during which he remains, except for rare intervals, in a sort of cataleptic trance. Pauline refuses to consider him insane, and explains his condition as being one of uninterrupted contemplation, of inner lucidity. In fact the suggestion is that he has reached a plane of 'angelic existence'; and, in an afterthought added to the text in 1842, Balzac suggests that the true reason for his collapse had been the realization that the physical pleasures of marriage would be an obstacle to 'la perfection de son sens intérieur et à son vol à travers les mondes spirituels'.

So on the surface it would seem that, from curiosity about certain obscure powers of the mind, Balzac passed to the elaboration of a philosophy which he wished to build on a substratum of scientific (or pseudo-scientific) notions, and that the insufficiency of scientific knowledge at this period—he never appears to have abandoned the hope that one day science would find the key to complete knowledge—brought him to a system in which science and illuminism, uncomfortable bedfellows, were amalgamated.

[1] *Le Livre mystique*, published by Werdet.

In actual fact, to suppose such a single chronological sequence would be to sacrifice the complexity of truth to the desire for clarity, for the turmoil of notions confusedly expressed in *Louis Lambert* had been whirling about in Balzac's head since 1819 at least. Nevertheless an advance towards mysticism is plainly perceptible in Balzac's thought from 1831 to 1835. Baffled by the inability of logical reasoning to solve the enigma of God and Creation and the relationship of man to both, he had recourse to, and adapted to his own requirements, the esoteric pronouncements of those eccentric minds who, from Jacob Boehme in the sixteenth to Saint-Martin in the beginning of the nineteenth century, while claiming fidelity to a 'revelation' handed on from primitive times, drew from their own intuition the 'light' with which they sought to illumine their fellow-beings. Swedenborg, whom Balzac had only read at second hand, was the special prophet under whose ægis he elected to pursue his further investigations and give his gospel to the world. Already, in 1831, in *Les Proscrits*, he had put Swedenborg's doctrine, as he conceived or amended it, into the mouth of Sigier. From early 1834 to late 1835, while still expanding *Louis Lambert*, he was at work on *Séraphita*[1]—'une œuvre dévorante pour ceux qui croient', he claimed, in a letter to Mme Hanska.[2] It was written partly for her edification, but his desire to draw her from the strait path of Catholicism and prove that love not hallowed by the Church could yet lead to spiritual heights, does not suffice totally to explain the effort and enthusiasm he brought to the task.

As a novel *Séraphita* reaches the limits of fantasy and perhaps of absurdity. Such action as there is, placed in a Norwegian setting, centres round a person who, passing from love of Self to love of the World, and thence to love of Heaven, through Hope, Charity, Faith and Prayer, has climbed rung by rung the mystic Ladder of Existence and is ready to be received into the company of the angelic hosts. For, according to Swedenborg, 'Dieu n'a pas créé d'Anges spécialement, il n'en existe point qui n'ait été homme sur la terre. La terre est ainsi la pépinière du ciel.' This strange creature is androgynous, and appears to the Promethean

[1] Conceived, he says, after seeing the sculpture by Théophile Bra of the Virgin and Child being worshipped by the angels. *E* I, 88; 17 Nov. 1833.
[2] *E* I, 242; 30 Mar. 1835.

wanderer Wilfrid as a beautiful and desirable woman, Séraphita; whereas for the ingenuous and docile Minna, daughter of Becker, the local pastor, 'Séraphita' is 'Séraphitus', the incarnation of manly wisdom and strength. Both of these young mortals are in love with Séraphita-Séraphitus, but she has passed beyond earthly love, and her role is to reveal to the human couple 'le chemin pour aller au ciel'. Becker himself has a double and curiously inconsistent part to play: to instruct Wilfrid about the life, personality and doctrine of Swedenborg and yet, as a mind imprisoned in ratiocination and scepticism, to stand as a foil to Séraphita.

She possesses miraculous powers; like Flaubert's Saint Anthony she is tempted by the forces of evil manifested in fantastic forms; in a purely didactic chapter of this very didactic novel (*Les Nuées du Sanctuaire*) she demolishes human science and substitutes for the rationalist idea of creation *ex nihilo* the illuminist idea of a universe emanating from God through the virtue of His Word and evolving according to the principles established by that Word; in the course of a further chapter she expounds a theory of Prayer which, as the Abbé Bertault has shown, owes more to Saint-Martin than to Swedenborg; and finally she proceeds through death to apotheosis in the ethereal regions.

Such is the 'myth' of Séraphita, invented by Balzac in order to formulate a system of which a trained philosopher has written: 'Il y a là une telle accumulation d'absurdités que la philosophie ne saurait mordre là-dessus.'[1] It may be a matter for astonishment that a man so close to earthly reality should have set up as a seer and hoped that contemporaries would accept as a revelation his turgid arguments and apocalyptic rhapsodies. Yet this was undoubtedly Balzac's hope in writing the three novels (*Les Proscrits, Louis Lambert, Séraphita*) and publishing them together as *Le Livre mystique* towards the end of 1835. But the early nineteenth century was the age of spurious revelations, and Balzac belonged to his age. Nor is his attempt to work out a philosophical and religious creed devoid of interest. Two noteworthy books, the sensitive and charitable treatise of the Abbé Bertault and Dr Evans' penetrating and ingenious thesis on *Louis Lambert*,[2] bear witness

---

[1] Quoted by Bertault (2), 218, n. 3.

[2] Evans (2). See also Curtius, Bardèche (4), Estrada, and Eigeldinger, who

to a protracted effort of documentation and cerebration on Balzac's part. As a rule, until very recent times, the resultant system has been a matter for derision rather than discussion, and the vast majority of Balzac's readers have been interested in the novelist and not the philosopher and would-be illuminate.

The fact remains that the activities of all three are intimately intermingled throughout the length and breadth of the 'Comédie Humaine'. In the latter half of the nineteenth century it was customary to discern in Balzac only the 'realist' whose aim was: *faire concurrence à l'état civil*—or the 'naturalist' who observed humanity with the eyes of a scientist and, in Taine's words, gave posterity 'le plus grand magasin de documents que nous ayons sur la nature humaine'.[1] If he was recognized as a philosopher at all, it was as a pre-positivist or positivist philosopher, whose guiding principle was that of determinism, who saw the whole pattern of events, human or otherwise, as a complicated network of causes and effects, and whose essential achievement was to show the close and reciprocal relationship between character and environment, in accordance with a conviction which indeed he many times stated: 'la vie extérieure est une sorte de système organisé, qui représente un homme aussi exactement que les couleurs du colimaçon se produisent sur sa coquille'.[2]

That this is an important, perhaps a preponderant aspect of Balzac's work, is beyond question. Viewed from a certain angle, the monistic theory which he was at such pains to work out appears as sheer materialism. Moreover, he seems unable, and indeed unwilling, to escape from the 'irrefragable verity' of universal causation. Hence his persuasion of the scientific soundness of the theories of Lavater and Gall, and the wholesale enthusiasm and frequent absurdity (a matter for parody by contemporary journalists such as Albéric Second) with which, early and late, in posing his characters, he suited the material envelope to the inner disposition, and rendered moral traits in terms of physical and facial conformation, clothes, gestures, grimaces, manner of speech,

relates Balzac's æsthetic doctrine to his metaphysics and allows it high value as a contribution to modern theories of poetry, painting and music.

[1] Biré (preface, viii–x) reacted strongly against this point of view.

[2] *Traité de la vie élégante*, Oct. 1830; Conard *O.D.* II, 170.

habits of life and types of domicile. 'La vie habituelle fait l'âme, et l'âme fait la physionomie', as he said in *Le Curé de Tours*. It needed but a short step, one he was already taking in the early eighteen-thirties, to pass from individual to collective determination and envisage social groups as products of race, environment, upbringing, ways of life and thought, and avocation. And this he did always at the solicitation of science and in deference to it. Even his belief in the supplementation of observation by intuition was expressed in terms of the admiration he felt for Cuvier, the founder of palæontology, who was capable of deducing the structure of antediluvian animals from the meagre data of fossil bones. We have seen that Balzac carried his *scientisme* so far as to postulate a material origin for intellectual activity; and just as Cuvier's rival, Geoffroy Saint-Hilaire, was asserting a biological principle of 'unity of composition' and reaching out towards Darwinism, so Balzac affirms the development of all species and varieties, vegetable, animal and human, out of his primordial 'substance éthérée'.

His philosophical novels, even if they had no other value, would serve to correct such a one-sided view. It is possible that a systematic study of Balzac's manner of treating the relationship between character and environment would show, whatever his theory may be, that his instinct is more frequently to reveal the imprint of the former on the latter than the reverse, or to see in the latter a prolongation or crystallization of the former.[1] A penetrating critic of Balzac, M. Ramon Fernandez, has argued that he first conceived his characters and types in the abstract, then worked back from this initial conception to an appropriate physiognomy and environment, and finally, by a sort of poetic artifice, claimed to deduce the former from the latter.[2] So that the determinist pretension may, in effect, be no more than a creative technique. Yet it would be a poor compliment to Balzac to suppose that his characters are no more than conceptual abstractions; another critic, Mr. Samuel Rogers, is nearer the truth when he points out that there is much in them that is unpredictable, that they are, in

---

[1] See G. Poulet. M. Poulet's subtle though difficult chapter on Balzac's apprehension of space and time lifts his thought well above the materialist plane.　　　　　　　　　　　　　　　　[2] Fernandez, 148 ff.

fact, endowed by their creator with an independent and developing life for which neither the habit of preconception nor the addiction to a determinist philosophy could wholly account.[1] However this may be, it is as true to say that Balzac spiritualizes matter as it is to say that he materializes spirit. From his monism and scientism emerges a theory of life according to which the triumph of spirituality is the goal and purpose of existence, and this theory permeates the 'Comédie Humaine'. Ideas are living realities, enjoying an independent existence. Marat, in *Les deux Rêves*, says of a patient on whom he was about to operate:

Ses idées étaient des êtres qui naissaient, grandissaient, mouraient; ils étaient malades, gais, bien portants, tristes, et avaient tous enfin des physionomies particulières; ils se combattaient ou se caressaient. Quelques idées s'élançaient au dehors et allaient vivre dans le monde intellectuel.

Human activities, conflicts, crimes and disasters are explained in terms of the projection of Will. Raphaël de Valentin told Fœdora:

que, dans le monde moral, rien ne résistait à cette puissance quand un homme s'habituait à la concentrer, à en manier la somme, à diriger constamment sur les âmes la projection de cette masse fluide; que cet homme pouvait à son gré tout modifier relativement à l'humanité, mêmes les lois absolues de la nature.

The 'Comédie Humaine' was to offer innumerable demonstrations of this power. Over the preoccupation with material things and the petty realities of psychological and social determinism presides this visionary, this theosophical doctrine to which the conception of the outstanding figures of the 'Comédie Humaine' is due.

At this juncture we come back to the 'Savoir, Vouloir, Pouvoir' of the antique-dealer in *La Peau de chagrin*. The idea that '*Vouloir* nous brûle, et *pouvoir* nous détruit' receives enormous expansion in the stories Balzac wrote after 1831. The many monomaniacs in the 'Comédie Humaine' are those whose feelings and passions have been gathered into one channel, whose will has

[1] Rogers, iii ff. For an earlier discussion of Balzac's determinism see Baldensperger (2), ch. xii.

become concentrated on one sole aim: the acquisition of gold, as with Félix Grandet, the pursuit of alchemy, as with Balthazar Claës, the enjoyment of power, as with Gobseck. They have become the victims of an *idée fixe*; and so also, by the extension of its range of activity, have their families. Nor does *Savoir* always leave 'notre faible organisation dans un perpétuel état de calme', as the antique-dealer fondly believed. The life of the mind has its dangers, as *Louis Lambert* and *La Recherche de l'absolu* show. At one time Balzac was projecting a novel, *Ecce Homo*, which was to prove the converse of the theorem: in opposition to Louis Lambert, 'ce centenaire de 25 ans', a cretin was to be shown living for a hundred years, by virtue of his complete mental inertia. But it is not necessary to consider extreme cases in order to see the destructive power of ideas in operation. A curious feature in the 'Comédie Humaine' is the frequency with which simple, innocent and unselfish people become victims of a violent emotion, and are killed off by their creator with a promptitude which leaves him little hope of providing plausible medical grounds for their demise. Mme Jules Demarets, in *Ferragus*, is a case in point; likewise Mme de Mortsauf, in *Le Lys dans la vallée*.[1] This 'law' which Balzac erected into a universal principle is half a truism, and half fantastic. One may object that it does not always make for good psychology—Balzac's capacity for compelling us to believe in his monomaniacs is a mystery hard to explain—but it certainly does not make for prosaic 'realism', even though all this, according to him, is part and parcel of the natural scheme of things.

But furthermore, in Balzac's philosophy, on to the natural scheme of things is grafted a supernatural one. How interesting, how amazing to watch is the conflict fought out in his mind, throughout his whole life, between an irresistible inclination to believe in the occult, in thaumaturgy, mesmerism, somnambulism, cheiromancy, cartomancy, and a persistent desire to explain it away scientifically! He is more or less satisfied with the explanations he invents, but he allows the occult and the mysterious at least as important a place in his re-created world as he allows to normal and everyday facts. In the long run, had his mind not

---

[1] Conard XXVI, 283. He even criticizes the habit of attributing such deaths to known physical maladies.

been equally solicited by the promptings of positive good sense, he would in all probability have given priority to the occult: a recent critic, M. Vouga, has roundly scolded him for not having done so! The ideas of the angelic spirit, Séraphita, are also disseminated in the 'Comédie Humaine'. *Savoir, vouloir, pouvoir* which, on the human plane, are such dangerous activities, in her conception are the very condition of advancement on the spiritual plane. Besides the monomaniacs, besides the suffering and struggling rank and file, we find in the 'Comédie Humaine' many figures who, to a lesser or greater degree, have some of Séraphita's angelic qualities—those whom Balzac wished to hold up to admiration as virtuous or beneficent souls. There are minor figures who love, serve and sacrifice themselves to individuals—they are generally women. There are major figures who, like Dr Benassis, devote themselves to the general welfare of their fellow-creatures. These bring wisdom and purposefulness to their task of aiding Providence, and it is not fanciful to surmise that they are offered as examples of the right use of Séraphita's *savoir, vouloir, pouvoir*. Balzac's exploration of the attractions of platonic as opposed to carnal love, as in *Le Lys dans la vallée*, is traceable to the same source. And even so late as 1841 a quaint theory of the autonomous existence of ideas, already illustrated in an unfinished work of 1834, *Aventures administratives d'une idée heureuse*, is strongly demonstrated in the novel *Ursule Mirouët*; here again, as in *Louis Lambert*, mysticism rubs shoulders with realism.

Usually, however, the two elements are more imperceptibly blended. The progress made by Balzac in the art of novel-writing from 1831 to 1835, and the production by the latter date of a number of undoubted masterpieces, can be explained only by the more perfect fusion in him of the realist and the philosopher, the conscious observer and the intuitive 'spécialiste'.

III

'SOCIAL STUDIES'

i. Expanding Projects

'Un génie est une place forte, qu'il faut investir de tous les côtés. Thèbes a sept portes. Un vrai grand homme, un homme complet, est *un* . . . mais en cet *un*, combien d'êtres! Son unité d'art n'a rien à voir avec l'unité pauvre, réduite, compartimentée, qui suffit peut-être à ses commentateurs.'[1]

IF THE STUDY of an artist's unity is difficult, that of the gradual unfolding of his unity in diversity, *sub specie temporis*, is even more so. Balzac's activity might be compared to the continuous emission, from a radioactive centre, of particles varying in direction and penetrative force; or, to borrow a metaphor from organic life, a vigorous young tree putting forth its branches towards every point of the compass, crossing and intertwining its shoots and boughs, but stretching out in a total effort to obtain a maximum of air and light, in spite of the obstacles and impediments which its own superabundant vitality creates. There is no conspicuous effort to canalize the creative flow, no rationally controlled advance towards a single goal, but simultaneous or closely consecutive surrender to divergent inspirations. Simultaneous was the impulse to write 'Scenes of Private Life' and 'Philosophic Tales', though on the whole it may be said that from May 1832 Balzac marked time with the former, while the urge to establish a philosophic basis for the many fictions which were seething in his brain carried him along to the *Séraphita* of 1835. By that year the reflective and prophetic vein had been sufficiently exploited for one major category of the future, the 'Études Philosophiques', to have attained full existence; and in fact the publication of them by Werdet as a series began in January 1835. Meanwhile, in the

[1] Romain Rolland, *Goethe et Beethoven*, ed. du Sablier (1945), 137–8.

Scènes de la vie privée, and also, with less immediacy, in the philosophic stories, the greatest of the categories, the 'Études de Mœurs' was implicit. From 1832, in fact, two new waves of expansion are discernible. By the end of 1833 the *Scènes de la vie de province*, and by the spring of 1834 the *Scènes de la vie parisienne* have acquired full status. At the same time *Le Médecin de campagne* opens the way to the *Scènes de la vie de campagne*.

Other categories too were in Balzac's mind, and before approaching the works involved above it will be useful to watch him groping his way along during those critical years towards his definitive project. His 1830 plan for a series of 'Études de femmes' has already been mentioned. Although this title would be appropriate to a large number of his shorter and to some of his longer works, he dropped the idea by 1833, probably because he was tending to study women less and less *in vacuo* and more and more in relation to a social milieu. In 1830 too he was intending to write a series of 'Études analytiques' which was to include a *Pathologie de la vie sociale* and a *Monographie de la vertu*. Only fragments of these ever saw the light. His acquaintance with the Napoleonic veteran, Périolas, a friend of the Carrauds, fired him with the ambition to write a novel about the Wagram campaign —*La Bataille*—and so initiate a category of *Scènes de la vie militaire*. He conceived the idea in 1830, was obsessed by it in 1832, and, through pressure of other commitments, virtually abandoned it in 1833. The short story *Adieu*, with its description of the retreat from Moscow, gives a vivid idea of what Balzac might have achieved had he carried out his purpose. To 1830 again belongs his initial promise of a series of *Scènes de la vie politique*, of which *Les deux Rêves*[1] had been a sample, and of which a satirical *Histoire de la succession du marquis de Carabas*, a pendant to *La Peau de chagrin*, was to be the mainstay.[2] By the end of 1832, whilst at work on *Le Médecin de Campagne*, he was proposing a series of *Scènes de village*.

[1] In *La Mode*, 8 May 1830.

[2] He wrote in Aug. 1831 '. . . [elle] formulera *la vie des nations*, les phases de leurs gouvernements et, sous une forme meilleure, démontrera évidemment que les politiques tournent dans le même cercle et sont évidemment stationnaires, que le repos est dans le gouvernement *fort* et hiérarchique' (letter to Montalembert, 'Formes et Reflets' edition, xvi, 78).

In the midst of these glimmers and hesitations, he was so aware of moving towards a total plan that he could write to Baron Gérard, before 1831 was out, 'le système général de mon œuvre commence à se démasquer'. In January 1833 he was voicing his ambitions to 'L'Étrangère':

. . . représenter l'ensemble de la littérature par l'ensemble de mes œuvres . . . construire un monument, durable plus par la masse et par l'amas des matériaux que par la beauté de l'édifice.

In the course of that year he was drafting schemes for the organization of this 'ensemble', and in October he signed with Mme Béchet the contract for twelve volumes of 'Études de mœurs au dix-neuvième siècle'. By now he had ruled out such provisional categories as *Scènes de salon*, *Scènes de la vie du monde*,[1] and had fixed definitely on Private, Provincial and Parisian Life as the nucleus of the 'Études de mœurs'. Publication began with two volumes of provincial scenes in December 1833, and continued with two volumes of Parisian scenes in March 1834, and two more in May and November 1835. The four volumes of Private Life scenes (September 1834, May and November 1835) offered nothing new except *La Recherche de l'absolu* (September 1834) and *La Fleur-des-pois* (*Le Contrat de mariage*, November 1835). The Provincial Life series was not completed in this edition until February 1837. In 1833 Balzac had still a little way to go before his threefold plan of 'Études' was clarified and established, but what matters for the moment is the history of the progress he made, by means of individual novels, between 1832 and the end of 1834, when his achievement up to date was crowned by the publication of *Le Père Goriot* in *La Revue de Paris*.

ii. Between Private and Provincial Life: *La Grenadière*
and *La Femme abandonnée* (1832); *Eugénie Grandet*
(1833); *La Recherche de l'absolu* (1834)

Balzac's inquiries into the sentimental life of mature women continued in 1832 with *La Grenadière* and *La Femme abandonnée*. Both are studies of society women who have sought love outside

[1] *Pensées, sujets, fragmens* (Crépet), 99.

marriage and found it bitter-sweet. In *La Femme abandonnée* the Vicomtesse de Beauséant (*née* Claire de Bourgogne) retires to a country estate in Normandy to escape from the malice or unwelcome sympathy of Parisian society. The naïve adoration of a young neighbour, Gaston de Nueil, attracted to her in the first place by the sensation her love-affair with a Portuguese noble, Ajuda-Pinto, has caused, brings her eventually into his arms, after much heart-searching and reluctance to incur new scandal or run another risk. The new liaison lasts nearly ten years, after which Gaston, like his predecessor, abandons her for the more respectable bond of marriage. Mme de Beauséant has feared this second catastrophe, and takes the initiative when she sees it approaching. But Balzac's contention appears to be that a woman of her attractions and experience cannot be loved and then dropped with impunity; she has given Gaston delights, and variety in delights, that no frigid wife can offer, and the loss of her drives him to suicide. It is not fanciful to see in this conclusion, as indeed in the whole work, a tribute to 'La Dilecta'. By mutual agreement, Balzac had ceased to be her lover, and while he was writing the story at Angoulême in July 1832 he was hoping to play the part of Gaston de Nueil with Mme de Castries. The latter's attitude to him is no doubt reflected in Mme de Beauséant's reluctance (at first) to incur social opprobrum by committing a second 'faute'; it is likely therefore that he was already seeing cause for regretting the 'union parfaite de deux êtres' that he had experienced with Mme de Berny.

Although the data of the story are basically acceptable, *La Femme abandonnée*, like many of Balzac's probings into feminine sentiment, is likely to set up resistances, at any rate in the mind of an English reader, less dazzled than the French usually are with the religion of love and the correlation of the physical and the metaphysical in that religion. A questionable feature is the mixture of brusqueness and special pleading in the manner of Gaston's wooing. Probably this is an embellishment of Balzac's own overtures to Mme de Berny, and perhaps also to Henriette de Castries; but one would suppose that its success with any society lady would be no greater than that of Balzac with his target for 1832. Perhaps the real basis for criticism is that the artificial sublimity of the language, which apparently Balzac and his contemporaries accepted as normal, seems incompatible with the situations and motives, real as they are at bottom. This convention of lofty diction, as a means for concealing average human emotions and calculations, is hard to swallow in the twentieth century. Probably *La Grenadière* seems lachrymose and cloying for the same reason. Lady Brandon also is a woman who has sinned and suffered. She takes her two children, born of adultery, with her to the house near Tours which Balzac and Mme de Berny had found so attractive in the summer of 1830. There, stricken with one of those diseases attendant, according to Balzac, upon intense emotional upheavals, she awaits death and lavishes affection on her sons, especially the heroic but priggish Louis Gaston: here Balzac shows little talent for depicting children. The further episode added in 1834 to *La Femme de trente ans* (*Souffrances inconnues*, now chapter II) is written in a similar vein. We are shown Julie d'Aiglemont giving vent to the broodings of self-pity, in the interval between losing her platonic admirer, Lord Grenville, and yielding to the attractions of a more worldly lover, Charles de Vandenesse.

By their nature these *nouvelles* are studies of women more or less abstracted from their social background. Only in *La Femme abandonnée* does Balzac take the trouble to characterize a local society, that of the Bayeux gentry whose unintelligent conversation and adherence to narrow etiquette give the Parisian Gaston de Nueil a strong motive for seeking the more enlightened company of Mme de Beauséant. It is true that he likes to place episodes of his stories—the first part of *La Femme de trente ans* for example—in Tours or Touraine: could the idea of provincial scenes have been born of the predilection he felt for the valley of the Loire? In any case *La Grenadière* and *La Femme abandonée*, both ultimately to be classified as scenes of private life, went into the first edition of provincial scenes. But the true archetype of these was *Les Célibataires* (*Le Curé de Tours*), and in August 1833 Balzac informed Mme Hanska that 'à la fin du mois . . . il y aura une *Scène de la vie de province* dans le genre des *Célibataires*'. This was *Eugénie Grandet*. An amusing short story, *L'illustre Gaudissart*, was written only a few weeks later. These two works,[1] with *Le Curé de Tours*, constitute the first authentic provincial scenes, for they alone make any pretence of evoking life in the provincial towns and villages. In *L'illustre Gaudissart*, Balzac creates an immortal figure, that of the Parisian commercial traveller—jovial, glib, self-confident, irrepressible, ready to sell everything, even subscriptions to unsaleable socialist newspapers —but only in order to show that he is no match for the inhabitants of Vouvray in deceptiveness and guile. This is a light squib, let off with Rabelaisian verve; but *Eugénie Grandet* is a serious study of manners and local types in the town of Saumur.

Si tout arrive à Paris, tout passe en province: là, ni relief, ni saillie; mais là, des drames dans le silence; là, des mystères habilement dissimulés; là, des dénouements dans un seul mot; là, d'énormes valeurs prêtées par le calcul et l'analyse aux actions les plus indifférentes. On y vit en public.

So runs a sentence in the Preface to the work, and Balzac insists on the delicacy of touch with which such scenes must be painted:

. . . pour sonder une nature creuse en apparence, mais que l'examen trouve pleine et riche sous une écorce unie, ne faut-il pas une multitude de préparations, des soins inouïs, et, pour de tels portraits, les finesses de la miniature antique?

This is precisely what he has done in unfolding his 'drame dans le silence', a purely domestic conflict between a miser and his daughter.

Félix Grandet, cooper, landowner and mayor of Saumur, is Balzac's first notable illustration of the psychology expounded in his philosophical novels: the relentless application of the will towards a given end, in this case the acquisition and conservation of gold. The much-argued question of Grandet's prototype in real life and the exact localization of his house in Saumur is of little importance. What matters is that he stands out as the most complete expression of avarice in human shape to be found in literature. Allowing for the difference of form and scope between comedy and the novel, Balzac has here attained a classicism akin

[1] First published in Dec. 1833, in vols. I and II of the *Scènes de la vie de province* (Béchet edition of 'Études de mœurs').

to that of Molière. Félix Grandet has in common with Harpagon
the fact that everything in him—physiognomy, gesture, thought,
tricks of speech, grimaces, reflexes and actions—reveals and
expresses the master-passion.

Financièrement parlant, M. Grandet tenait du tigre et du boa; il
savait se coucher, se blottir, envisager longtemps sa proie, sauter dessus:
puis il ouvrait la gueule de sa bourse, y engloutissait une charge d'écus,
et se couchait tranquillement, comme le serpent qui digère, impassible,
froid, méthodique.

'Il semblait économiser tout, même le mouvement.' He has his
hair cut once a year. In his house he adheres to a systematic parsimony in the use of fire, candles, bread, sugar, etc. If ever he
gives his wife money, he borrows it again. He is generous only
with rotten fruit which farmers feed to their pigs: 'Régale-toi,
Nanon.' His every utterance is a concise revelation of his passion.
To his servant's objection against making crow-soup on the
grounds that crows eat corpses, he retorts: 'Est-ce que nous ne
vivons pas de morts?' His usurer's creed is expressed thus:
'Vraiment, les écus vivent et grouillent comme les hommes. Ça
va, ça vient, ça sue, ça produit.' When his wife lies dying, he
thus adjures the doctor: 'Si l'on peut sauver ma femme, sauvez-la,
quand même il faudrait dépenser pour ça mille ou deux mille
francs!'—in later editions Balzac reduces this to 'cent ou deux
cent francs', so urgently does he feel the need to press the man's
avarice to the point of caricature. On his death-bed Grandet gloats
over his hoard of gold coins: 'Ça me réchauffe.' He snatches
covetously at the enamelled crucifix held to his dying lips, and his
last recommendation to his daughter and heiress is this: 'Aie bien
soin de tout: tu me rendras compte de ça là-bas.' The 'là-bas' is
grimly ambiguous.

The difference from Molière is that Grandet's avarice is no
matter for laughter, nor is his vice suspended in a vacuum.
Grandet's financial operations have their repercussions throughout Saumur, and the reactions of its inhabitants to them are
recorded: he is a triumphant amasser of wealth who inspires fear,
envy and respect in a community of similarly acquisitive beings.
But more important is the effect of his miserliness on life in the
dark cheerless house which reflects Grandet's mania in its most

intimate details. The tyranny of this passion produces a sort of paralytic torpor in wife, daughter and servant. Yet the essence of the story is to show how that tyranny comes to be challenged and eventually defeated through an unexpected event: the arrival from Paris of the handsome nephew, Charles Grandet, a few hours before his father's bankruptcy and suicide. For Grandet this is an occasion to show his mettle in cheating his dead brother's creditors. For Eugénie, it means an awakening to life and individuality. The submission of Mme Grandet is absolute. Eugénie's pity and love for Charles (who turns out to be worthless, as we should expect) change her into a critic of her father and an unhesitating rebel. In the view of Mr Frank O'Connor, Charles 'becomes her monomania'.[1] The 'silent drama' reaches its climax after Charles' departure for the Indies, with Eugénie's treasure of gold coins in his trunk. Grandet had given them to his daughter, but only on condition of safe-keeping. His discovery of her generosity starts a civil war, with Eugénie imprisoned in her bedroom and condemned to a diet of bread and water. Mme Grandet wilts and dies. Grandet capitulates when he realizes that now, if she wishes, Eugénie can claim her mother's inheritance. He cajoles her into renunciation of this. Then he too dies, and Balzac finds his first opportunity to stage the scene of a monomaniac's last paroxysms.

Although the figure of 'le père Grandet' dominates the work, it does not throw Eugénie into the shade. She is Balzac's first study of a middle-class girl since Augustine Guillaume, but more effective because the study is less rapid and because the development of Eugénie's character is more consistently related to a single background. She begins as one of Félix Grandet's living chattels. She is also a pawn in the game of financial chess played out between two affluent and influential families of Saumur, the Cruchots and the Grassins. As the prospective heiress of a millionaire (Balzac was criticized for his overstatement of Grandet's wealth), she is a prize to be fought over; and every move in this subtle and heartless game is made in the name of 'le seul dieu moderne auquel on ait foi, l'Argent en toute sa puissance'. But through the power of virginal love she loses the passivity and

[1] O'Connor, 93.

spinelessness which Balzac was inclined to associate with maidenly virtue. As the struggle becomes more intense it becomes more and more clear that she is her father's daughter. When she learns that Charles has betrayed her, she accepts the situation, but controls it; her marriage to the Cruchot candidate (a Pyrrhic victory for him) is motivated by her resolve to organize her future life for the exercise of charity and beneficence. In her personal habits, as a mature woman, her father's traits reappear in her.

Like many of Balzac's works, *Eugénie Grandet* began as a *nouvelle*, and only in course of composition acquired the dimensions of a novel—chiefly because the time-factor was becoming more important for one who was discarding static for dynamic psychology, and combining the latter with the depiction of manners. The work is universally popular as one of his most characteristic masterpieces. Its structure is impeccable. It affords an excellent example of the art of preparation by whose means carefully proportioned items of description and incident are coordinated until the essential action is unleashed. Also it well illustrates the art of winding up a story, for the conclusion achieves that happy blend of subjectivity and objectivity, of sympathy and sardonic detachment which shows Balzac at his best. All Balzac is present in this novel: the hard-pressed debtor whom bitter experience is persuading of the all-importance of money and the struggle for it; the disciple of Gall and Cuvier determined to discover, or to invent, the intimate harmony between the physical and the spiritual world; the psychologist who has found, in the theory of wills in action and wills in conflict, a potent recipe for classical 'typisation'; the keen-eyed observer of humble people who has made a memorable creation of the rugged but valiant and kindly household-drudge, Nanon; the sentimentalist who still accords superiority of value, though not worldly victory, to self-effacing love and dutifulness; and even, though discreet and subordinate, the illuminist searching for a 'créature transitoire entre l'homme et l'ange', and finding the makings of one in Eugénie herself. This quest can and does sometimes lead to insipidity in his heroines, but Eugénie is almost free of it, since heredity and environment are called in to adjust the balance. Her greatest moment is when, in a gathering of 'Cruchotins' and

'Grassinistes', her choice lights on the President Cruchot de Bonfons as the man she is to marry on her own terms: her 'Restez, Monsieur le Président' has been compared for its significance to the sinister command of Racine's Roxane to her reluctant and ill-fated suitor, Bajazet: 'Sortez'. Eugénie is as much the master of her Saumur satellites as her father had been.

The theme of opposition between father and daughter, already tentatively treated in some of the Private Life scenes, is again strongly developed in a novel written between June and September 1834: *La Recherche de l'absolu*. This work, though it is a further study of monomania, stands on a higher spiritual plane than *Eugénie Grandet*. One may well find that Félix Grandet is too exclusively a personification of avarice, dead to all values except money, with an intelligence that is inoperative outside that domain. Balthazar Claës has for fifteen years been a good husband and father, maintaining the traditions and courtesies of his position as the head of an old aristocratic family of French Flanders. Only a chance encounter in 1809 with a Polish visionary—modelled possibly on the mathematician-seer Hoëné Wronski whose acquaintance Balzac made, or perhaps renewed, in August 1834—sets him on his quest for the 'Absolute': the attempt by chemical processes, with the paraphernalia of retorts, furnaces and pneumatic machines, to reduce all the elements to one and discover 'le principe constituant de l'électricité', the unknown force modifying the 'unique substance' and determining its myriad differentiations in material creation. From that moment 'il n'était ni mari, ni père, ni citoyen, il fut chimiste'. He squanders his own fortune, that of his wife, and a large part of his children's heritage, on the purchase of chemical equipment and material in the obstinate pursuit of his vain experiments. This goes on for twenty years—the time-element thus receives a fuller expansion in this novel—but with interruptions, for Claës has his periods of contrition and sanity during which his normal virtues reassert themselves and his laboratory remains deserted. But each repentance is followed by a relapse, and Balzac, with his usual extravagance in the manipulation of figures, makes him run through seven million francs during the course of those twenty years.

Another analogy between *La Recherche de l'absolu* and *Eugénie*

Grandet is the choice of a provincial setting. His motives for choosing Douai, which he never seems to have visited, are uncertain, but the choice is probably best explained by his earlier intention (1832–3) of making the sixteenth-century ceramist, Bernard Palissy, the hero of his story, under the title *Les Souffrances de l'inventeur*, later adopted for a quite different work. It is well known that Palissy, in dire poverty, broke up his furniture and the floor-planks of his house to feed his furnaces; and when Balzac decided to replace Palissy by a nineteenth-century chemist, the choice of Douai enabled him to make an ingenious application of that datum by providing the 'maison Claës' with a rich collection of Flemish furniture, plate and pictures which Claës was to dissipate, not indeed by direct combustion, but by sale and mortgage. Moreover the blend of civilizations and traditions in Flanders,[1] the fusion of Flemish sobriety and stolidity with the splendour and passion of Spain, gave him the basis for an effective contrast between Balthazar's instinctive habits of economy and the recklessness with which he flung his wealth into the melting-pot. Thus the 'Rue de Paris' at Douai became as appropriate a centre for the Claës drama as the 'Grand'Rue de Saumur' had been for the Grandet conflict. So there is here a similar effort, less thorough as some readers may feel, to link character and action to environment. None the less, possibly because Balzac could not personally vouch for the truth of the Douai background as he could for that of Saumur, he never seems to have been tempted to place *La Recherche de l'absolu* in the Provincial Life category. It first appeared as a Private Life scene,[2] and finally (1845) was classed as an 'Étude Philosophique'.

As a scene of Private Life it has evident importance. The family struggle of *Eugénie Grandet* is here repeated with greater intensity, and yet it is more protracted. Unlike Mme Grandet, Mme Claës possesses culture and intelligence; but because a physical deformity has given her a sense of inferiority to her husband, she has not the stamina to call a halt to his depredations. Marguerite Claës, though a model of filial virtue and piety, has 'un caractère

[1] A friend of Balzac, S. H. Berthoud, was publishing between 1831 and 1834 a series of short stories entitled *Chroniques et traditions surnaturelles de la Flandre*.

[2] Sept. 1834, t. 3, Béchet. But *Les Amours d'une laide* (Crépet, 106: first title for *Recherche*?) was listed 1833 as provincial scene (Guyon, *MF*, July, 1958).

de fer', and the steps she takes, after her mother's death, to save the remnant of the family fortune enable the author to indulge in typical monetary calculations. The story has its psychological weaknesses. Though Balzac's analysis of Mme Claës' relations with her husband is wellnigh perfect, and the study of Claës himself one of his greatest achievements, there is a postulate of basic perfection in Marguerite, and in her lover Emmanuel de Solis, which is more romantic than real. So also is the account he gives of their progress as sweethearts from timid appreciation through observant respect to silent tenderness—a sequence of emotions which twentieth-century youth is likely to find unenterprising and unconvincing.

Perhaps the early nineteenth-century taste for glozing over the physical and instinctively egoistic elements which are present even in virtuous love (as *La Femme abandonnée* shows, it is less in evidence when 'fashionable' love is concerned) is what most separates Balzac from novelists and novel-readers of today; the more so because Balzac finds Marguerite's delicate spirituality not incompatible with a business-like readiness to hand over her sister Félicie in matrimony to the mercenary notary, Pierquin ('il t'aimera comme la plus jolie des propriétés, tu feras partie de ses affaires'). This calculating person comes nearer to the Balzacian norm and is much more akin to the Cruchot or des Grassins type; but he is allowed enough basic integrity to give him a part in the reconstruction of the Claës fortunes. There is, moreover, a conspicuous fairy-tale element in Balzac's use of the financial ingenuity of the two lovers, the generosity of relatives, the benevolence of public officials and convenient marriages, to provide a comparatively happy ending whereby the dilapidations of Balthazar are wiped out and the 'maison Claës' completely refurbished. A wave of the Balzacian wand, and all is set right.

Yet the artist's hand does not falter in giving the final touches to the central character. It is true that *La Recherche de l'absolu*, considered as a philosophical study, has some disconcerting features. Balthazar is a man of genius; his quest for the Unique Substance is at bottom the quest of Balzac himself; and the condemnation of Balthazar's folly is attenuated by sympathy for the goal he has set himself. His wife, his daughter and her lover are half-inclined to believe this goal to be accessible. And so is Balzac. Balthazar's results are not altogether nugatory. His absurd apparatus, functioning spontaneously during his five years' absence, mysteriously produces a synthetic diamond; and later, as the septuagenarian lies dying, a last conviction of the possibility of success—*Eureka!*—stirs him from his paralysis. In spite of this, Balzac's overruling commonsense—perhaps the secret of Balzac's fascination lies in the intermingling in his work of the chimerical and the real—saved him from becoming the dupe of his own creation. The persistence of Balthazar's delusion to the end is presented in the main as a mere trait of human psychology, the incorrigibility of a man whom a fixed idea can never abandon. The final and stable impression that Balthazar Claës leaves on the reader is not that of one who dies on the threshold of a great discovery, but of one who rides his chimæra to the gates of death, as Félix Grandet had done, as 'le père Goriot' and many others were to do. The ultimate validity of *La Recherche de l'absolu* considered as a philosophical study resides less in its alchemistic extravagances or in its fanciful anticipations of twentieth-century nuclear physics than in its renewed presentation of the underlying thesis of *La Peau de chagrin*. But this thesis has taken on human shape; it has given poetry and power to a psychological conception.

iii. *Le Médecin de campagne* (1833)

This work, begun in September 1832 and completed in the summer of 1833, is closely connected with Balzac's abortive political career and his sentimental relations with Henriette de Castries. The Revolution of July 1830, and the weak, vacillating conduct of public affairs in the period immediately following it, had quickly cured him of the traditional liberalism of his class, which had already shown signs of modification during his formative years. By 1832 he had thrown in his lot with the more intelligent legitimists like the Duc de Fitz-James, Berryer and Laurentie, though the programme which he elaborated was perhaps too intelligent, and certainly too disrespectful of such intransigent doctrines as that of 'divine right', for the collaboration to be completely harmonious. It was Balzac's independence of mind, rather than the smart he suffered at Mme de Castries' refusal to be his mistress, that brought his partnership with the legitimists to an end in the course of 1833. *Le Médecin de campagne* was not likely to heal the breach.

Balzac's private affairs are reflected in this novel, but only incidentally, and we need not dwell on the idea which came to him of working into the fiction his grievance against Mme de Castries by means of what is now well-known as the 'Confession inédite'.[1] *La Duchesse de Langeais* offered him a better opportunity for this. What matters is that *Le Médecin de campagne* is the first novel in which he gave a frank exposition of his political philosophy and proclaimed Monarchy and Church to be the twin bulwarks of society. He called for a firm hierarchy and strong authoritarian government: king, hereditary peerage, an executive and a legislature of competent experts, with an elected body merely to vote supplies and register laws. The criticism of the electoral principle which, with his usual unconcern for the maxim of 'art for art's sake', he works into the novel has much cogency if one is content to remain in the realm of the abstract. He subscribes to none of the contemporary illusions about the fitness of the working classes for a share in government: the proletariat must be kept in perpetual tutelage. But he offers two safeguards. One is that the social and political hierarchy shall be flexible enough for real talent to find its place. The other—his whole system depends ultimately on this—is that the Church shall provide those moral and religious sanctions which alone can correct the natural egoism of men and women of all ranks. His mouthpiece is the hero of the story, Dr Benassis who, while making no pretension to statesmanlike capacities, has all the qualities needed for carrying out the more immediate purpose for which the novel was written: to show how the acquisitive instinct of the French peasant can be harnessed and utilized for the public good. So *Le Médecin de campagne* is at once a piece of political propaganda, an apology for Catholicism as a socializing force and a personal way of life, and a treatise of rural economy. It marks the point in Balzac's career when he realized that he could achieve greater conquests, gain more prestige as a European

[1] See *Biography*, 51–6; also Guyon (1), Part III, iv; and Guyon (3).

DR BENASSIS

figure, and so more effectively emulate Napoleon, by his writings than by political activity. 'Ce qu'il n'a pu achever par l'épée, je l'accomplirai par la plume.' But it is also the story of an individual who finds his way through suffering to altruism. And it is the first sample of a 'Scene of Country Life'.

This attack upon the liberal theory of constitutional monarchy and representative institutions was to be often repeated in the course of the 'Comédie Humaine', and calls for no further comment here.

As an apologia for Catholicism *Le Médecin de campagne* has this much in common with Chateaubriand's *Génie du Christianisme*—it illustrates, in a poetic style that recalls the elegiac effusions of the pseudo-Ossian, the power of rites and ceremonies, in this case solemn funereal observances, to bind families and societies together. As a treatise of rural economy it reposes on the principle enunciated and applied by its hero, Dr Benassis: *Il ne faut que du bon sens pour améliorer le sort d'une commune.* As a study of individual psychology (reference here is of course made to Benassis' definitive 'Confession' and not to the far more personal 'Confession inédite') it is of unequal value. It is the by now familiar story of a young man who goes to Paris, yields initially to the temptations which that city offers, seduces a girl and abandons her, and is brought by her death, then by the death of their son, but most of all by contact with a rigorously Catholic family and the unfulfilled hope of marriage with the uncompromisingly virtuous daughter of that family, to a sense of reprobation which determines his conversion and his subsequent career of self-abnegation. Of the virtuous daughter, whose part in the story is short, one thing only need be said. Granted that 'Évelina' was conceived as a tribute to Mme Hanska, it is still surprising that Balzac, who hated puritanism above all else, could have brought himself to invent such a paragon of maidenly rectitude, even under the spur of edifying motives and the hope that the book might win him the 'Prix Montyon', awarded annually to the literary work which the selecting jury deemed most beneficial and conducive to virtue. For the rest, Benassis' regeneration and transformation are reasonable postulates: Balzac's account of his hero's spiritual development is a close and subtle one, although

73

it is embellished with the flowery rhetoric so dear to his age.

What is the value of *Le Médecin de campagne* as a picture of peasant life? The considerable amount of space allotted to propaganda and argument, which have much historical interest but little entertainment value, might well have ruined it as a novel or a study of manners. But the artist in Balzac was not asleep as he composed the story. This is proved by the way in which he first establishes Benassis as a somewhat enigmatic personality and postpones the 'Confession' which explains the enigma until nearly the end of the book. A Napoleonic veteran, the commandant Genestas, arrives at a village in the region above Grenoble, and for a day or two is escorted round the canton by Benassis who, as he makes his doctor's rounds, tells him how, by a constant appeal to self-interest and the prestige of results achieved one by one, he has won universal respect and approval and turned the whole countryside into a hive of agriculture and industry. This fiction of the conducted tour is the means whereby Balzac brings his readers into contact with normal and generally convincing people. Much use is made in this work of the Napoleonic legend. The countryside of Dauphiné is resonant with memories of 'le petit Tondu', and the book is punctuated with anecdotes told about him by Genestas and two other veterans, Gondrin and Goguelat. The long political discussion that takes place, in the third chapter of the definitive edition, round Benassis' supper-table, is immediately followed by what is usually regarded as the *pièce de résistance* of this work, that part which had previously been printed in *L'Europe littéraire* as 'L'Histoire de l'Empereur racontée dans une grange par un vieux soldat.'

It can be argued that these many illustrations of the aura of superstition that surrounded 'le Napoléon du peuple', agreeably as they may gild the pill of didacticism, do not necessarily make for a faithful picture of peasant life. But that picture rings true in most of its details. Not only is Balzac at great pains to get his geographical setting correct—he had explored the neighbourhood of La Grande-Chartreuse with Henriette de Castries—and to contrast the poetry of Alpine background with the reality of human habitations and occupations: he takes his readers, as Benassis takes Genestas, from hovel to cottage and from cottage to farmhouse, and each visit reveals a different aspect of peasant life or a different type of peasant character. The sentimental note is occasionally too insistent, as in the study of 'La Fosseuse', a wayward and temperamental soul whom the capricious patronage of a local châtelaine has unsettled and whom Benassis befriends. But Balzac can say with Benassis: 'Je n'ai point fait des idylles sur mes gens, je les ai acceptés pour ce qu'ils sont, de pauvres paysans, ni entièrement bons ni entièrement méchants.'

There is, for instance, a shrewd sketch of the seed-merchant Taboureau, whose usurious activities in the buying and selling of grain are reluctantly tolerated by Benassis because on the whole they serve the interests of the canton; but who, when involved in a dispute with a dishonest dealer, wins from Benassis a favourable opinion on his case by pretending that he is himself the offending party. 'Eh bien,' says Benassis . . . 'croyez-vous qu'à Paris cet homme-là ne serait pas bientôt millionnaire?' Balzac's contention, to be reiterated in later 'Scenes of country life', is that an able and partial administrator can make cupidity and even sharp practice profitable to the community; as mayor of the commune he has succeeded in eliciting social virtue from amorality and egoism. Nor does Balzac forget that, even on the most solemn occasions, the acquisitive instinct is never entirely stilled—witness the significant comment terminating his highly emotional account of the widow's lament at the funeral which Benassis and Genestas climb into the mountains to attend.

She cuts off her hair and lays it in her dead husband's lap as a guarantee that she will not marry again. 'Beaucoup de parents attendaient sa résolution.' Did they await this as the conclusion to a moving ceremony or as an assurance that their part in the family heritage would not fall into alien hands? We may be sure that the latter thought was not far from Balzac's mind as he added this laconic phrase.

Le Médecin de campagne is not one of his greatest novels. But it is far from being a failure as a novel. Nor is its hero an impossible ideal. At least three real persons have been proposed as models for this paragon of country doctors.[1]

[1] For a discussion of their respective claims, see Guyon (3), 68 ff. and 97 ff.

75

IV

THE 'INFERNO' OF PARIS

i. *Les Marana* (1832–3); *L'Histoire des Treize* (1833–5)

FROM THE SPRING of 1833 until the spring of 1835 Balzac was intermittently at work on *L'Histoire des Treize*, comprising *Ferragus, chef des Dévorants, Ne touchez pas la hache* (*La Duchesse de Langeais*), and *La Fille aux yeux d'or*. They formed a nucleus for three volumes of *Scènes de la vie parisienne* published as part of the 'Études de mœurs' in March 1834 (volumes II and III), and May 1835 (volume IV). Such scenes, like those of Provincial Life, evolved almost spontaneously from the Scenes of Private Life, though they were enriched by the themes emanating from the philosophical romances. The point is worth noting that even Balzac's most exotic characters tend to be sucked into the Parisian maëlstrom: the Corsicans of *La Vendetta*, for example. A story anterior to *L'Histoire des Treize*—*Les Marana*—published in the *Revue de Paris* in December 1832 and January 1833, illustrates the same fact. It has something of the flavour of *Le Réquisitionnaire* in that it records a telepathic sympathy existing between a mother and her daughter. The mother, La Marana, the last of a long line of Italian courtesans, senses the danger to which her daughter Juana, far away in Tarragona, is exposed by the advances of a would-be seducer, and hastens to her rescue— but too late. It is also a story of vicarious expiation, that perennial theme of the illuminists: the mother wishes her daughter to live purely and thereby atone for the sins of her forebears. Juana does so as the wife of a stupid, coarse-fibred Frenchman, Pierre-François Diard, whose sole claim to her gratitude is that he takes her over from her seducer. That is why Balzac added to his original conception the account of her life with Diard in Paris. For the sake of the children she tries to further him in his career as a Civil Servant. But he fails and takes to speculation and gambling.

. . . il pratiqua le vol décent auquel se sont adonnés tant d'hommes habilement masqués, ou cachés dans les coulisses du théâtre politique: vol qui, fait dans la rue, à la lueur d'un réverbère, enverrait au bagne le malheureux, mais que sanctionne l'or des moulures ou des candélabres.

He ends up as a murderer, after which Juana shoots him and passes it off as suicide, to save her children from disgrace. By its didactic content, as well as by the luridness of its beginning and conclusion, *Les Marana* is qualified to rank among the 'Études philosophiques', to which indeed it was eventually relegated. But by its insistence on the recurrent theme of 'le vol décent', which according to Balzac is a staple industry in Paris, it deserves the place originally allotted to it among the Paris scenes.

The more so because Balzac was not yet ready—did he ever become so?—to eschew the sensational in writing his Scenes of Parisian Life. His obsession with the wickedness rampant in the French capital expresses itself in startling ways, and for its anarchic ruthlessness he compares life in Paris, as he had compared that of the 'Chouans' in Brittany, with life in the prairie as described by Fenimore Cooper. He sees Paris as the hunting-ground of three sorts of criminals: the footpad and cut-throat, the financial shark and embezzler, the unprincipled adventurer of high society. In *L'Histoire des Treize* as a whole, and, more particularly, in *Ferragus*, he brings the first and third varieties together. That mysterious ex-convict, Gratien Bourignard, alias Ferragus, chief of the 'Compagnonnage de l'Ordre des Dévorants', or Devoirants (it is not easy to see why Balzac connects him with the Compagnonnages, those respectable craftsmen's fraternities which dated back to the Middle Ages), is a link between the footpad and the gentleman criminal, since he is a prominent and powerful member of the 'Association of Thirteen', which Balzac invents as an aristocratic secret society.

Il y eut donc dans Paris treize frères qui s'appartenaient et se méconnaissaient tous dans le monde; mais qui se trouvaient réunis, le soir, comme des conspirateurs, ne se cachant aucune pensée, usant tour à tour d'une fortune semblable à celle du Vieux de la Montagne; ayant les pieds dans tous les salons, les mains dans tous les coffres-forts, les coudes dans la rue, leurs têtes sur tous les oreillers, et, sans scrupules, faisant tout servir à leur fantaisie. Aucun chef ne les commanda, personne ne put s'arroger le pouvoir; seulement la passion la plus vive, la circonstance la plus exigeante passait la première. Ce furent treize rois inconnus, mais réellement rois, et plus que rois, des juges et des bourreaux. . . .[1]

Thus, in the Preface to *Les Treize*, Balzac promises to steep his readers in the blood-curdling and the horrible. The childishness of this is manifest. It is as if he were harking back to the *roman noir* and, beyond that, to the cloak and dagger romance. No doubt he was gauging the taste of his time, which had been fed on singular events, truths stranger than fiction, of the Imperial and early Restoration years.[2] His contemporaries loved this sort of thing as well as sentimental effusions about ladies and lovers in boudoirs, just as today we have a marked weakness for thrillers and crime-stories. Balzac was even to have the satisfaction of learning that *Ferragus* enthralled the Duchesse de Berry, who at that time was atoning in captivity for her romantic attempt, in male guise, to raise the banner of Bourbon counter-revolution in France. He also no doubt needed, if that were possible, to work the *Argow le pirate* obsession out of his system. And so, in *Ferragus*, we see a young philanderer, Auguste de Maulincour, brought to a lingering and atrocious death because he has interfered with the domestic bliss of Mme Jules Desmarets, suspected of being Ferragus' mistress, but in actual fact his daughter. Her clandestine visits to her father, divulged by Maulincour, arouse the torment of suspicion in the heart of her husband, and bring her to an untimely end. Maulincour's execution is Ferragus' concern, but the hand of the Thirteen is visible in many incidents of the story.

So also, in *Ne touchez pas la hache*, when General de Montriveau decides to prevent Antoinette de Langeais, who has played with his passion and destroyed his belief in love, from

---

[1] Balzac never mentioned more than five of the Thirteen by name: Ferragus, Henri de Marsay, Armand de Montriveau, the Marquis de Ronquerolles and Maxime de Trailles.

[2] See Castex (4), introd., 29–31.

breaking other men's hearts—by branding her on the forehead with a red-hot cross—the Thirteen are there to serve him if he adheres to his purpose, which he does not; and also when she has repented of her frivolity, failed through impatience to regain contact with him, and buried herself in a Majorcan convent as Sœur Thérèse, the Thirteen undertake to snatch her from her sanctuary and restore her to Montriveau. That they only succeed in abducting her corpse is not due to any lack of daring, skill and determination.

In *La Fille aux yeux d'or*, their activities are less important, largely because the interest there is concentrated upon one of their members as a representative Parisian. For this reason this *nouvelle* demands separate consideration. Are the other two worth serious attention in spite of their melodramatic substructure?

The first point that may be made in their favour is that *Ferragus* and *Ne touchez pas la hache*, though the mystery-story element is conspicuous in them, are both to a large extent 'études de femmes'. The dilemma in which Clémence Desmarets finds herself bears some mark of truth: loyalty to a father she cannot openly acknowledge battles against confident trust in a husband with whom she is ideally happy. Desmarets in his turn is divided between a well-founded faith in his wife's virtue and suspicion of her dubious relationship with Ferragus. Doubt and jealousy drive him to ruse and espionage. Enlightenment and reconciliation come too late to save their happiness: how could she be sure henceforth that Jules' knowledge of her origin would not poison his love for her? Stripped of its incidental improbabilities, *Ferragus* treats in its way the subject of *La Princesse de Clèves*, and has in fact been compared with that acknowledged masterpiece. It has other interesting or significant features. It provides more than one 'léger croquis de la vie parisienne'. It uses two incidents—Clémence's burial at Père-Lachaise, and Jules' efforts, ineffective until the Thirteen intervene, to obtain permission for his wife's remains to be cremated—as an occasion for denouncing the red tape of officialdom and the callous 'administrationalisme' of the cemetery authorities. Furthermore the violence of paternal passion in Ferragus himself anticipates that of 'le père Goriot':

Te perdre, ma fille . . . te perdre par la curiosité d'un misérable
Parisien! Je brûlerais Paris! Ah! tu sais ce que c'est qu'un amant, mais
tu ne sais pas ce qu'est un père.

It is the one trait which gives the hint of truth to this bogy of
Balzac's invention, this unaccountable bandit the touch of whose
fingers[1] can induce a mortal disease in the man who has wronged
his daughter.

Ne touchez pas la hache survives by virtue of the full-length
portrait it gives of a society coquette, Antoinette, Duchesse de
Langeais, a portrait sandwiched between the account of Armand
de Montriveau's discovery of her (as the organ-playing Sœur
Thérèse) in the convent at Majorca, and his attempt to abduct her
with the aid of the Thirteen. This central part is preceded by that
scathing criticism of the aristocracy of the Faubourg Saint-
Germain which was a tactical feature of Balzac's political campaign of 1831–3: the condemnation of a social caste unable to
modernize its ideas and attitude. A similar denunciation occurs
later in the novel when four representatives of the old nobility
meet to form a kind of family council and reveal the ineptitude
of their normal conversation, their deep concern for the preservation of their family estates and public reputation, and their
underlying indifference to moral and religious values.

' Renoncez à votre salut en deux minutes,' [they say to the now reckless Antoinette] 's'il vous plaît de vous damner, d'accord! Mais
réfléchissez bien quand il s'agit de renoncer à vos rentes.'

Balzac's motive for this detailed inspection of a social milieu
was not merely political. Antoinette de Langeais is a representative
of her caste; her character and conduct are in large measure explained by reference to it; she is in fact the first of Balzac's great
ladies to become a living social type. As such she is 'la femme sans
cœur' already symbolically outlined as Fœdora in *La Peau de
chagrin*; but, thanks to his unsuccessful wooing of the Marquise
de Castries, he was now able to pass from the symbolic to the real.[2]

---

[1] Steeped in a solution of arsenic? See Garnier edition, introd., 31.

[2] See *Biography*, 56 and 76. There is a tendency to exaggerate the part
played by the supposedly coquettish Mme de Castries in the genesis of this
novel. See Thouvenin (2).

Antoinette de Langeais is as close a study as he ever made of the psychological and sentimental make-up of a high-born trifler with men's affections. Only the Princesse de Cadignan, in later years, is worthy of comparison with her. As is his wont, he mingles much sympathy with much disapproval in unfolding her motives and methods for enslaving the austere, high-minded Montriveau, to whom she is willing to assign first place among her crowd of admirers, and to accord such privileges and familiarities as will heighten his passion, while she withholds her ultimate favours. Her marriage to the Duc de Langeais has been a purely conventional one. By worldly standards this should make conjugal infidelity seem more excusable, but Balzac hints at the persistence of genuine scruples of chastity which, with more frivolous considerations, will enable her to keep her dalliance on the safe side of a subtle and provocative coquetry.

Elle savait être à son gré affable, méprisante ou impertinente, ou confiante. Elle semblait bonne et l'était. Dans sa situation, rien ne l'obligeait à descendre à la méchanceté. Par moments, elle se montrait tour à tour sans défiance et rusée, tendre à émouvoir, puis dure et sèche à briser le cœur.

On the other hand Montriveau, the soldier and explorer whose life has been spent in action, knows nothing of women, and up to a point is as wax in her hands. His resolve on meeting her— 'J'aurai pour maîtresse madame de Langeais'—is pitifully ineffectual in face of the ruse and guile of 'cette machine à larmes, à manières, à évanouissements, à phrases fondantes'. When hard-pressed, she harps upon the themes of wifely duty, reputation and the sanctions of religion. But she has after all been too self-assured in daring to 'finger the headman's axe'. Her error is to suppose that a man of heroic stamp, fiercely passionate and possessive, will remain indefinitely content with a spiritual relationship, after the foretastes she has allowed him of less ethereal satisfactions. The advice of one of his friends precipitates the crisis. Montriveau tries to force her defences, and the steely, insolent rebuff he receives drives him to the preparation of his strangely brutal act of 'justice'. The interview between them, while the branding-iron is being heated for her forehead, transforms Antoinette. Her coquetry and coldness give place to ardent submissiveness; she is ready to throw reputation and fortune to the winds and become the slave of the man whose unique qualities she now appreciates, but who henceforth is on his guard against further dupery. Up to this point Balzac has shown considerable penetration and subtlety: is this peripeteia acceptable?

'Les duchesses sont dures, mon cher Armand, et ces natures de femmes ne s'amollissent que sous les coups.' So de Ronquerolles has affirmed, thus voicing the old and vulgar theory that resistant women are more amenable to cruelty than to kindness.[1] Here the theory gains piquancy from the fact that it is applied to the most exquisitely artificial product of an artificial society. In such circumstances it would seem to be acceptable only on the *credo quia absurdum* principle; but in spite of the melodramatic colouring Balzac gives to Antoinette's 'conversion', in spite of the probability that a wish-fulfilment relative to Henriette de Castries determined this peripeteia, it carries conviction. The change in Antoinette is not posited as a sudden revulsion of feeling. It has been prepared by a week's uncertainty during which Montriveau's cold rage and cryptic threats have thrown her into a state of uneasiness and vague fear. When she is brought in bonds to Montriveau's flat, while she listens to his strictures and sees herself through his eyes, fear of his intentions and shame at her own mortification disappear. She even offers her brow to the hot iron, for it will mark her as his possession for ever. Paradoxical as this may seem, her surrender to this man who now disbelieves and scorns her is so extravagant as to command credence. She glories in the thought of becoming a target for scandal, of being transformed into the uncomplicated 'bourgeoise', the 'grisette' he had wanted to find in her. This brusque abandonment of race tradition and personal fastidiousness is clearly intended by Balzac to show that, underneath the fashionable trifler, there is a generous-hearted woman who needed a violent shock to bring her to self-knowledge. The only challengeable note is the return to sentimental religiosity in the letter she sends to Montriveau before disappearing from sight, and the promise she gives him of spiritual protection under 'the wings of divine love'. There is always some-

[1] One of the *Contes drolatiques—Dezesperance d'amour* (Second 'Dizain', published July 1833)—is based on the same theory.

thing insipid about a religious vocation born of disappointed passion. But such easy transition from sexual love to the love of God was yet another convention of the age.

There is a certain disparateness in the ingredients that go to the making of *La Fille aux yeux d'or*, the more apparent because it is a work of slender dimensions. The introductory pages give an astonishing example of Balzac's genius for description, but they might serve better as a preface to the *Scènes de la vie parisienne* in their entirety than as a prelude to a very strange story. He looks at Paris through the eyes of a Dante and evokes the five 'circles' of the modern Inferno. They are the five social groups— the proletariat, the lower and upper middle classes, the world of artists and the fashionable world. His object is to describe the perpetual agitation of their lives, ruled as they are by the 'loi d'airain', the quest of gold and pleasure; struggling, climbing, amassing, spending; each class having its particular forms of relaxation or debauch; each dissatisfied, exhausted, hideous, desiccated, diseased; and, at the social summit, shallowness, frivolity, boredom, satiety. There could be no more brilliant disquisition on the theme: *propter vitam vivendi perdere causas*, a vain self-expenditure manifested at every rung of the social ladder. This schedule of callings and occupations offers a general programme for the study of human types: a programme which the 'Comédie Humaine' was to carry through in detail.

Descending from these Dantesque heights, Balzac then singles out a special type of Parisian, and this constitutes the second element in the *nouvelle*. Those who now claim his attention stand in contrast to the vast majority of the Parisian population, listless, weary and wizened: they are the young elegants who flaunt their beauty, charm, wit and sartorial splendour on the fashionable parade-ground of the Tuileries Gardens. From them in turn he singles out Henri de Marsay as the personification of the 'flibustiers en gants jaunes, et en carrosses ayant des gens, des armoiries', whom he has transplanted from Byron's *Corsair* and similar works into the heart of Parisian society as examples of those who refuse to bend themselves to the yoke of laborious endeavour or to plod along in patient mediocrity; who prefer to win their way to supremacy by exploiting their personal

for Rastignac in *Le père Goriot*. As an 'immoraliste' rising triumphant over society, using it but flouting its laws and conventions,
he prepares the way, in conjunction with Ferragus, for Vautrin
in the same story. For the Béchet edition of the *Scènes de la vie
parisienne*, the group of stories was now complete. To *Les
Marana* and *L'Histoire des Treize* were added the *Étude de
Femme* (entitled *Profil de marquise*) and the *Sarrasine* of 1830,
Le colonel Chabert (rechristened *La Comtesse à deux maris*), and
Madame Firmiani, which was extracted from the philosophical
series but eventually, in 1842, found its place among the Scenes
of Private Life. Also, to furnish the missing volume I in November 1835, Balzac temporarily robbed the Private Life compartment of *La Femme vertueuse*, *Les dangers de l'inconduite* (rechristened *Papa Gobseck*) and *La Bourse*. Like so many of his stories,
they are at home in any category according to the angle from
which they are viewed.

ii. *Le père Goriot*—'histoire parisienne' (1834–5)—
and the Reappearing Characters

All Balzac's previous efforts appear to converge on this novel, and
all of his favourite themes to be caught up in it. It is, most
conspicuously, his third great study of a monomania,[1] though here
the emphasis is shifted. The ex-manufacturer of vermicelli, Jean-
Joachim Goriot, is not, like Félix Grandet and Balthazar Claës, an
egocentric whose mania inflicts unmerited suffering on his family.
He himself is the victim of the idolatrous love he bears his two
daughters, a passion natural enough in its origins, since it is the
transference to them of a 'religious adoration' formerly lavished
on his now defunct wife, but one which in course of time has become exclusive, uncritical, monstrous. It has expressed itself
originally in the expensive education he has provided for them,
in the marriages he has arranged for each of them according to
her taste: Anastasie to the Comte de Restaud, on account of her
'aristocratic leanings', Delphine to the Alsatian banker, Nucingen,
in order to satisfy her craving for wealth and display. Its growth
in monstrosity is measured by the way in which, after having

[1] Gobseck had not yet attained his full dimensions. See below, 97–8.

made over to them the bulk of his wealth for their dowries, he strips himself by degrees of all he has left in order to gratify their whims or extricate them from embarrassment. Knowing our Balzac by now, we should expect him to translate this denudation into terms of money and status: Goriot's gradual ascent from well-furnished first to drab third floor in the boarding-house he occupies, the deterioration in dress and appearance, and the rising hostility and scorn which this degeneration inspires in his landlady and her other lodgers. It is more dramatically illustrated in a scene in which Goriot is discovered twisting up his plate before selling it for the precious metal it contains. When he has mortgaged even his meagre annuity and cannot bleed himself any further for his rapacious daughters, his distraught mind leaps to impossible schemes—he will sell himself, he, a septuagenarian, as a substitute conscript or, decrepit as he is, rush to Odessa to corner wheat supplies and resume his manufacture of Italian paste.

The reward which this plebeian King Lear reaps is that he has a Regan and a Goneril, but no Cordelia. Anastasie and Delphine are ashamed of their father. He is excluded from their lives and homes, and reduced to the humiliation of loitering in streets and parks to watch their comings and goings, overjoyed to catch a glimpse of them as they pass by. His squalid garret is only lit up by their presence when they want to extract more money from him. Viewed sympathetically, as Balzac of course does view it, this infatuation has all the intensity of religious devotion. In fact Goriot's willing self-martyrdom for his strumpets of daughters is such that Balzac does not shrink from referring to him as 'ce Christ de la paternité'. Goriot himself says:

'Quand j'ai été père, j'ai compris Dieu. Il est tout entier partout, puisque la création est sortie de lui. Monsieur, je suis ainsi avec mes filles. Seulement j'aime mieux mes filles que Dieu n'aime le monde, parce que le monde n'est pas si beau que Dieu, et que mes filles sont plus belles que moi.'

Viewed from the ethical angle, the passion of this man, who shows himself ready to equip Delphine's lover with a luxurious *garçon-nière*, so that he may be allowed to bask in the reflected warmth of their illicit joys, would be profoundly immoral were it not so patently pathological:

J'aime les chevaux qui les traînent, et je voudrais être le petit chien qu'elles ont sur leurs genoux. Je vis de leurs plaisirs.

At dinner in the flat he has furnished for Eugène de Rastignac, he embarrasses the lovers by his ecstatic fawnings:

Il se couchait aux pieds de sa fille pour les baiser, il la regardait longtemps dans les yeux; il frottait sa tête contre sa robe; enfin il faisait des folies comme en aurait fait l'amant le plus jeune et le plus tendre.

Indeed this canine devotion is so extreme in its manifestations that it has something of the flavour of an unnatural vice. The penalty he pays for it is atrocious. 'Il aimait jusqu'au mal qu'elles lui faisaient'; but when the rapacity and mutual hatred of the two sisters have brought him to his death-bed he is at last forced to acknowledge what in fact he realized all along, despite the fanaticism which has driven him to find excuses for them and blame their husbands or lovers for the callousness they have shown: namely, that they have not an atom of real affection for him. His delirious ravings, when he lies yearning for a last glimpse of them, mark the climax of the book: moments of clear-sightedness when he admits their worthlessness and his own guilt in corrupting them; invocation of the law to protect the rights of fathers and compel his daughters to visit him—'Envoyez-les chercher par la gendarmerie, de force!'; denunciation of marriage which robs a father of his children. Reproaches and entreaties, maledictions and endearments pour from him tumultuously; yet this drawn-out agony ends with his delusion reinstated.

As an example of one of 'ces horribles supplices infligés dans l'intérieur des familles . . . aux âmes douces par les âmes dures',[1] *Le père Goriot* is pre-eminently a 'Scene of Private Life'; but it is so perfectly merged into the Parisian setting that one can only approve of Balzac's earlier decision to include it in the Parisian life category, even though he rescinded that decision in 1845. Goriot is scarcely conceivable save as a denizen of Paris. His martyrdom only attains its morbid grandeur in relation to the two social *milieux* which are set over against each other as two opposite poles throughout the story. One is the 'Pension Vauquer',

[1] *Les Martyrs ignorés*, Conard, *O.D.* III, 141.

whose fly-blown mediocrity, like that of the quarter in which it is situated, is so tellingly conveyed in the opening pages of the novel that it has become the very type of the middle-class boarding-house, with its dilapidated and greasy furnishings, its stale smells, its odious landlady—'sa personne explique la pension, comme la pension implique sa personne'—and its motley and vulgar crowd of lodgers and daily boarders. The other is the superb Faubourg Saint-Germain residence of Mme de Beauséant, the heroine of *La Femme abandonnée*. Thanks to his self-denudation Goriot lives as the most penurious and the most despised of Mme Vauquer's paying-guests. Through his daughters he is indirectly linked to Mme de Beauséant's salon, for Anastasie, by virtue of her marriage, has access to it, while Delphine would sell her soul—and bleed her father white—to be admitted there. Moreover, between these two *milieux* oscillates the person on whom the action of the story is pivoted—the impecunious young Gascon noble, Eugène de Rastignac. Financed by self-denying parents to study law and win his spurs by hard work, he decides to take the short cut to prosperity by exploiting his social privileges—his kinship with the influential Mme de Beauséant—and by using women as stepping-stones to fortune. 'Le démon du luxe le mordit au cœur.' A snub from Anastasie de Restaud throws him into the arms of her sister, Delphine de Nucingen, so that, later, he is able to rise to wealth as an associate in the Alsatian banker's shady speculations.

And so another theme is interwoven with the King Lear one: that of a decent and honourable young man corrupted by ambition, and learning to dispense with scruples. Although the process of corruption is only in its beginnings in *Le père Goriot*, and although Rastignac remains a sympathetic figure throughout by virtue of his kindness to the old man, the steps in his moral downfall are clearly designated. He exploits the generosity of his mother and sisters, at home in the Angoûmois, for money to start his campaign for the conquest of society. He seizes his chance to catch Delphine on the rebound when she is cast off by a former lover. As is frequent with Balzac's heroes, his first advances to her are prompted by cold calculation—'Le mors est mis à ma bête, sautons dessus et gouvernons-la.' Then the 'passion de commande' becomes a genuine one, though it can be little more than sensual. His wooing of Delphine is closely associated with the sympathy and protection he accords to Goriot; but the further he advances in her favour and the more intimately he becomes involved in the threefold drama enacted between father and daughters, the more certain does he grow of the arrant selfishness of both women. In Delphine's case the crucial moment occurs when he finds himself obliged to confront her with the choice of attending Mme de Beauséant's ball, on which her heart is set, or of consoling her father in his last moments. She attends the ball. Yet he never has the courage to break with her. He overcomes the nausea he feels, and after escorting Goriot to his pauper's grave, continues his liaison with her. He has fully realized that Paris is a wicked city and that conscience and kindliness must be stifled in the effort to conquer it. But conquer it he will: '*À nous deux maintenant!*' This challenge, which he utters as he gazes down on it from the cemetery of Père-Lachaise, has become famous. In bringing Rastignac to such a decision Balzac fulfils the promise implied in the introduction to *La Fille aux yeux d'or*. While de Marsay remains for the present the symbolical representative of 'le flibustier en gants jaunes', Rastignac is, so to speak, the working model of the type. Over against him stands the gay but hard-working medical student, Horace Bianchon, who takes his meals at the Pension Vauquer; a close friend of Rastignac, and like him sympathetic and charitable to Goriot; but holding himself aloof from any compromise with the forces of evil.

—As-tu lu Rousseau? Rastignac asks him at one juncture.

—Oui.

—Te souviens-tu de ce passage où il demande à son lecteur ce qu'il ferait au cas où il pourrait s'enrichir en tuant par sa seule volonté un vieux mandarin, sans bouger de Paris? . . . s'il était prouvé que la chose est possible et qu'il te suffit d'un signe de tête, le ferais-tu?[1]

Bianchon needs little reflection before he gives his emphatic reply: 'Eh bien! non.'

One might well imagine that, with the Goriot and the Rastignac themes thus intertwined, the author of *Le père Goriot* had material enough to keep his readers interested. But, in these early

[1] In *Annette et le criminel*, the Abbé Montivers had propounded a similar case.

years and even later, he was scarcely able to conceive of an 'histoire parisienne', however close its correspondence to life as he saw it, without setting it against a melodramatically sinister background. Ferragus and the Thirteen here give way to a new invention, that of the arch-criminal Jacques Collin, alias Trompe-la-Mort, who lives in the Pension Vauquer as the coarse and jovial Vautrin. Balzac had several models to pose for him as he fashioned Vautrin, among them Vidocq, the ex-convict turned policeman who was chief of the French *brigade de sûreté* from 1811 to 1827 and again from 1831 to 1832, and whose *Mémoires* of 1828–9, unscrupulously 'revised' by Émile Morice and Lhéritier de l'Ain, had given the world a highly coloured account of his violent and varied career. It was apparently through meeting Vidocq, in company with Sanson, son of the executioner of Louis XVI, at a dinner given by the philanthropist Benjamin Appert in April 1834[1] that Balzac got the idea of developing *Le père Goriot*, originally intended as a simple *nouvelle*, and making of it the complex work it had become by the autumn of that year. Vautrin is a diabolic, but not unsympathetic figure, destined to play a prominent part in later stories. Sent to the galleys for a forgery for which, though innocent, he shouldered the responsibility, he had escaped and made himself the leader and financier of the Parisian criminal world. He has declared organized war upon society. Homosexually inclined, he becomes interested in Eugène de Rastignac, divines the struggle going on inside him between innate rectitude and the urge to succeed at all cost, and offers to smooth out his path by marrying him to another lodger at the Pension Vauquer, the pale and passive Victorine Taillefer, after arranging the death by duel of her brother, who stands between her and the inheritance of an immense fortune.

Eugène rejects the bargain with righteous horror, even though Vautrin, before he is ferreted out and arrested by the Paris police, carries out the plan for assassination with brutal efficiency. His unmasking through the agency of two other lodgers at the pension, its sudden invasion by armed policemen, and Vautrin's

---

[1] See Bouteron (3), Vernière, and Savant (1) and (2). According to M. Savant, Balzac had known Vidocq since 1822, and obtained from him many ideas and episodes for his novels. See also Gozlan (2).

cool self-mastery when it is a question of avoiding being killed 'while resisting arrest', go to make a well-told chapter eminently fitted for a *roman policier*. But Vautrin has found his way into *Le père Goriot* not merely as a means for adding still stronger seasoning to an already pungent story. He inherits something of the symbolic role of the characters in *La Peau de chagrin*, whilst yet appearing as a very real and vivid scoundrel, with his brick-red hair, concealed by a powdered wig, his dyed whiskers, his robust physique, resonant voice, piercing eyes and penetrating intelligence. He is to Rastignac what Mephistopheles is to Faust, and serves not only as a tempter, but also as a mentor who gives Rastignac an objective view of the alternative ways of life between which he is hesitating: laborious mediocrity and callous opportun-ism. Or, more exactly, he foresees the choice Rastignac will make of the second of these two ways, and puts a further alternative to him: the choice between candid and hypocritical unscrupulous-ness. His contempt for society is based on the contrast, already emphasized in *Le Code des gens honnêtes* and *Les Marana*, be-tween that sort of criminality which openly flouts the laws and ends up on the scaffold, and the respectable roguery which wins wealth, fame and consideration. Vautrin echoes Balzac's own fulminations against Paris, a mud-pit of which he says 'ceux qui s'y crottent en voiture sont d'honnêtes gens, ceux qui s'y crottent à pied sont des fripons'. Alternatively, with Fenimore Cooper in mind, he sees Paris as

une forêt du Nouveau-Monde, où s'agitent vingt espèces de peuplades sauvages . . . qui vivent du produit que donnent les différentes chasses sociales; vous êtes [he is talking to Rastignac] un chasseur de millions. Pour les prendre, vous usez de pièges, de pipeaux, d'appeaux. Celui qui revient avec sa gibecière bien garnie est salué, fêté, reçu dans la bonne société.

This then is the choice which the cynic of the Pension Vauquer proposes to the aspirant to honours and fortune:

Savez-vous comment on fait son chemin ici? Par l'éclat du génie ou par l'adresse de la corruption. Il faut entrer dans cette masse d'hommes comme un boulet de canon, ou s'y glisser comme une peste. L'hon-nêteté ne sert à rien.

It is a view of things which impresses Eugène so much the more because he has already listened to similar sentiments expressed by the bruised and disillusioned Claire de Beauséant:

Le monde est infâme et méchant. . . . Plus froidement vous calculerez, plus avant vous irez. Frappez sans pitié, vous serez craint. N'acceptez les hommes et les femmes que comme des chevaux de poste que vous laisserez crever à chaque relais, vous arriverez ainsi au faîte de vos désirs.

'Vous arriverez.' In spite of his youthful compunction, that is Rastignac's one aim. He is appalled at Vautrin's outspokenness, though in the end he learns that Vautrin is right. But he still wishes to make his way by means which soothe and drug the conscience. The challenge he flings to the city of Paris from Père-Lachaise leads to no great heroic gesture, but merely to a cosy dinner with Delphine de Nucingen. M. Félicien Marceau puts the matter bluntly: Rastignac makes his way as a 'gigolo'.[1]

Le père Goriot is universally acclaimed as one of Balzac's greatest novels, for the complexity of its structure, the realism with which it lays bare certain permanent features in social manners and conduct, and the vividness and truth of its characterization, a truth which must be admitted if, while allowing for the fact that Goriot and Vautrin transcend the bounds of normal human verisimilitude, one reflects on the wide range of representative personalities the book offers—from the superior ladies of the Faubourg Saint-Germain to the simple-hearted slavey of the Pension Vauquer; from insolent dandies like Maxime de Trailles to the imbecile little rentier and informer Poiret; from the voracious and squabbling Goriot sisters to the shrill and treacherous Mlle Michonneau. But a memorable innovation in *Le père Goriot* gives it a special importance in the history of Balzac's work. It is the first novel in which he consciously and systematically applies a device which constitutes one of the most original features of the 'Comédie Humaine'—the use of recurrent characters.

According to Laure Surville, this idea—*relier tous ses personnages pour en former une société complète*[2]—came one day to

[1] Marceau, 47.　　　　[2] *Œuvres complètes, Éd. Déf.*, XXI, xxvii.

Balzac with all the effulgence of a revelation. 'Saluez-moi, nous dit-il joyeusement [as he burst into his sister's flat], car je suis tout bonnement en train de devenir un génie.' The date of this inspiration is uncertain. 'Vers 1833', says Laure, 'lors de la publication de son *Médecin de campagne*'.[1] Although the idea must have been simmering for a considerable period, he did not begin to apply it deliberately till the autumn of 1834, when writing *Le père Goriot*. In the preface to the first edition in book form (March 1835), he attributed the device to scruples arising from criticism made of his earlier works. Their morality had been so much called in question that he would permit himself only one new 'mauvaise femme' in *Le père Goriot*—Delphine de Nucingen, and keep to the ration of erring women, Mme de Beauséant, Lady Brandon, the Comtesse de Restaud and the Duchesse de Langeais, already offered to the public. The statement is undoubtedly ironic, for his obvious aim was to give a stronger flavour to his 'Études de Mœurs' by establishing as it were a pool of characters, families and *milieux*, so that he might move from one to another in different novels, throwing the limelight on each one in turn while leaving the others in the shade. The more easily might the impression be created of a closely knit society in which, as in real life, the reader would continually be coming upon people he had met before, whose family connections and personal history he would know in part, and whose every appearance would increase the store of knowledge he already possessed about them.

This he proceeded to do in *Le père Goriot* and subsequent works. Not content with this, in his new editions of former works he made continual changes, replacing anonymous or named persons with more familiar ones, and so bringing into circulation a world of fictitious people in whom readers tend to become so interested that they have blessed the enterprise of Cerfberr and Christophe (1887) and Fernand Lotte (1952) in compiling their respective 'Repertory' and 'Dictionary' of Balzacian characters.[2] Thanks to these compilations a reader of any novel of Balzac may

[1] She may have been thinking of the second edition of 1834.

[2] In 1839 Balzac himself, reporting that his publisher Souverain had jestingly proposed such a 'Repertory', gave a sample of what this might be by summarizing the life history of Eugène de Rastignac (pref. to *Une Fille d'Ève*, *Éd. Déf.*, XXII, 523).

obtain full information about the antecedents and future career of any character appearing in it.

This ingenious device has of course not escaped criticism. He applied it in the main to his Parisian Scenes, and the constant reappearance of the same figures and the same families, such as the aristocratic Grandlieus, Granvilles and Sérisys, the society queens like the Duchesse de Maufrigneuse, the Marquise d'Espard, Mme Firmiani, the middle-class Popinots, Birotteaus, Crottats, and Camusots, and the same usurers, bankers, courtesans, etc., has given rise to the not very convincing objection that we have here a singularly small world to represent the teeming population of Paris. But certainly the system has some weak points. The retrospective substitution of names demanded greater care and attention than Balzac was able or willing to spare. The merging of two originally independent characters sometimes created difficult psychological problems. For instance, it was only in the course of composing *Le père Goriot* that he decided to equate his newly invented careerist, who thus makes his first appearance in the Paris of 1819, and whom he originally intended to call Eugène de Massiac, with the blasé opportunist of *La Peau de chagrin*, the Rastignac whom we have seen giving advice to Raphaël de Valentin in the late eighteen-twenties.[1] Also Balzac involved himself in sometimes inextricable chronological difficulties, as anyone will realize who attempts to work out a satisfactory time-sequence in *Gobseck*, *César Birotteau* and *La Femme de trente ans*,[2] a work to which the principle of recurrent personages was not consistently applied until 1842. And furthermore, to read the life-story of such and such a character, for example Andoche Finot, Émile Blondet and the poet Canalis, in Cerfberr and Christophe or Lotte, can be irritating to one who knows by what sudden impulses, by what hesitant and fitful steps, by what shifts of amalgamation and modification Balzac brought them into his repertory. A more fascinating study is that of the appearance and development of the recurrent characters in Balzac's own conception, but that involves the task of collating manuscripts, proofs and successive editions of the works.[3]

[1] See Pommier (3).   [2] See the amusing article, Lotte (2).
[3] A useful beginning was made in 1934 by A. Canfield. Some information is to be found in the *Avertissement* and *Notes* of Lotte's *Dictionnaire*.

On the other hand the device has inestimable value in tying the different works together. Each one, although perfectly complete in itself, explains and enriches the other, just as each new appearance of a character reveals a fact at which a previous appearance had only hinted, and takes the reader backwards or forwards to the beginning, the middle or the end of his career. For with the 'Comédie Humaine', unlike the 'roman-fleuves' of our own century, there can be no steady, no simultaneous march forward in time of all the characters. On the contrary, as Balzac was to observe in the Preface to *Une Fille d'Ève* (1839):

. . . il en est ainsi dans le monde social. Vous rencontrez au milieu d'un salon un homme que vous avez perdu de vue depuis dix ans; il est premier ministre et capitaliste; vous l'avez connu sans redingote . . . puis vous allez dans un coin de salon, et là quelque délicieux conteur de société vous fait, en une demi-heure, l'histoire pittoresque des dix ou vingt ans que vous ignoriez. . . . Il n'y a rien qui soit d'un seul bloc dans ce monde; tout y est mosaïque.

Such a method puts each novel, and each character, in perspective; and behind the mass of separate novels, one glimpses a sort of hinterland,[1] in which people are moving, developing and changing as they do in real life.

No better example than *Le père Goriot* can be cited of this enrichment of one novel by episodes and reminiscences absorbed into it from previous ones, or of the illusion of depth and fullness it derives therefrom. In the first flush of enthusiasm for his new-found device, Balzac incorporated into this novel lengthy enumerations of the social celebrities he had created one by one in the course of four years. To this somewhat mechanical expedient he was often to resort in later novels. But far more ingenious and salutary is the way in which, by the reappearance of certain personages, other fictions are assumed into the novel. Claire de Beauséant, whom *La Femme abandonnée* had shown as a recluse in Normandy, nursing her wounds before finding a new lover, is moved backward into 1819 at a moment when her first lover, the Marquis d'Ajuda-Pinto, is mustering up courage to take a wife and desert her: she serves as Rastignac's kindly and noble-hearted cicerone in the brilliant society of which she is a leader. The

[1] See Bardèche (1), 359.

Duchesse de Langeais, at the climax of her misunderstanding with Montriveau (Balzac's chronology is weak here), plays her part as a malicious, then a sympathetic friend of Claire, and also is called on to give Rastignac such sketchy knowledge of Goriot's past as polite society possesses. Henri de Marsay, the elegant philanderer from *La Fille aux yeux d'or*, the events of which were situated in 1815, lurks in the background as the sated lover of Delphine de Nucingen whom Rastignac replaces. Mme de Restaud, the unfaithful wife who, in *Les Dangers de l'inconduite*, has pawned the family jewels for the sake of her lover, now expressly named as the profligate Maxime de Trailles, is transformed into Anastasie, Goriot's elder daughter. De Restaud's discovery of her transactions with Gobseck, his intervention, and the implacable firmness with which he forces her to sign away her fortune in favour of her eldest son, together with the refusal of Delphine's husband, the Baron de Nucingen, to relax his grip on his wife's marriage portion, determine the final paroxysm and death-throes of Goriot—while at the same time offering some slight attenuation of the daughters' guilt in failing to appear at his death-bed. And so *Le père Goriot* achieves additional significance by virtue of its relationship with the previous stories. And to them can be added several others. In the early versions of *Le père Goriot* Lady Brandon, from *La Grenadière*, made a momentary appearance, and was not to be excluded from it until 1843. Likewise *L'Auberge rouge* soon became permanently linked with it, since the banker Taillefer, father of the pathetic Victorine, was given in 1836 the role of the murderer, formerly named Mauricey, in that story. Moreover Balzac had only to give Taillefer's name to the Amphitryon of the Bacchanalian orgy in *La Peau de chagrin* for a second link to be forged between that novel and *Le père Goriot*. The *Étude de Femme* of 1830 was also to be brought into its orbit in its later editions, the careless lover who sends a love-letter to the wrong woman being identified with Rastignac, while the rightful recipient of the letter naturally becomes Delphine de Nucingen.

Le père Goriot met with resounding success which filled Balzac with jubilation. As a kind of postscript he rewrote *Les Dangers de l'inconduite*, now virtually a satellite story, and published it as *Papa Gobseck* in November 1835. The lawyer whom Gobseck has befriended, and who is a witness of the Restaud conflict, is identified with the Derville of *Le colonel Chabert*. The usurer himself is magnified into a figure worthy to stand beside Grandet, Claës and Goriot as the incarnation of a devouring passion which in its turn reaches its culmination in the delirium of a death-bed. For this, and no less for the fact that Balzac has now achieved an equilibrium by the perfect blending of his social and philoso-phical themes, in such wise that the latter, though present, do not obtrude, we may well endorse the judgment of M. Lalande in his study of *Gobseck*: 'En 1835, le génie de Balzac arrive à sa maturité.'

This does not of course mean that he was to remain for ever on the same pinnacle of achievement. He was still capable of min-gling the good with the bad, and remained so to the end. The work he produced in 1835, after *Le père Goriot*, shows an interesting diversity of talent and inspiration. It is the year when, in sharp contrast to his normal activities, he was intermittently occupied with the third instalment of his *Contes drolatiques*, to which it is high time we gave some attention. It is the year, as we have seen, when the mystical *Louis Lambert* and *Séraphita* reached com-pletion. It is the year when the exceedingly sentimental *Lys dans la vallée* was being hammered into shape.[1] It is the year of *Le Contrat de mariage*, that ruthless piece of sardonic realism, com-parable to, as it is wellnigh synchronous with, *Papa Gobseck*.[2] A mixed bag in very truth; but the consideration of these three last-mentioned works in conjunction with one another may well serve to illustrate Balzac's astonishing and sometimes disconcerting versatility.

[1] It began to appear in *La Revue de Paris*, 22 Nov. and 27 Dec. 1835. Then Balzac discovered that the editor, François Buloz, had sold it (in uncorrected proof) to *La Gazette Étrangère de Saint-Pétersbourg*, which had printed instal-ments of it in Oct., Nov., and Dec. He withdrew the work from the *Revue de Paris*. After the ensuing lawsuit with Buloz, which Balzac won, the complete novel was published by Werdet in two volumes in June 1836. See *Biography*, 83–5.

[2] It was published, in Nov. 1835, in the second volume of the *Scènes de la vie privée*, in Mme Béchet's 'Études de Mœurs'. *Le Lys* was evidently intended in 1835 for the *Scènes de la Vie de campagne* (see Lovenjoul (1), 49), but became a Provincial Scene in 1844. Balzac's last intention was to make it a Scene of Country Life.

V

MISCELLANY

i. The *Contes Drolatiques* (1830–7)

BALZAC WAS EVER a devotee of François Rabelais.[1] It was as if he had inherited a host of treasures from the sage of Chinon, in whose physiognomy 'Socrates and Aristophanes, once foes, but made friends in him, blended their images.'[2] Balzac had the same zest for life, broad humour, and gusty laughter, the same delight in tale-telling and word-spinning, the same love of Touraine, in which delectable province beat the very heart of ancient France with its robust sanity and its tradition of epicurean jollity. The *Contes drolatiques*, which stand apart from Balzac's main work, are above all else the expression of this local patriotism and this Rabelaisian cult, though they draw inspiration from many other sources too: Boccaccio, Poggio, the author of *Cent Nouvelles nouvelles*, Marguerite of Navarre, Noël du Fail, and Béroalde de Verville.

It was in the course of 1830 that he had had the idea of reviving the *contes grivois* which in their various ways these authors, whether blunt, loquacious or sententious, had exploited, and then of couching them in Rabelaisian diction and style—for his own amusement and relaxation, in reaction to the sentimental mysticism which was gaining possession of him at times, and, characteristically, in response to a fashion of the day when he saw that even such third-rate writers as Paul Lacroix were acquiring some popularity as resuscitators of the medieval. But he also undertook this curious task because he feared that his countrymen, thanks to the pervading gloom of German and English Romanticism, were in danger of losing their instinctive joyousness, their taste for the

---

[1] See Lecuyer. Also Massant (1) and (2).
[2] *Contes drolatiques*, 2me Dizain, *Le Prosne du Ioyeulx Curé de Meudon*.

earthy and the racy. The true point of departure for the *Contes drolatiques* may well be found in the *Complaintes satiriques sur les mœurs du temps présent*, printed in 'La Mode' in February 1830.

... il y a cent mille fois plus de talent dans un conte à rire que dans toutes les méditations, les odes et les trilogies cadavéreuses avec lesquelles on prétend régaler nos esprits. ... Les hommes qui s'intéressent à la patrie et à la figure qu'elle fait au dehors, devraient se réunir et soutenir le petit nombre de ceux qui essayent de restaurer l'école du rire, de réchauffer la gaieté française, de ceux qui ont le courage de plaider pour cette vivacité gauloise qui n'a empêché ni les *Pensées* de Pascal, ni *l'Esprit des lois*, ni l'*Émile*, ni la Révolution d'apparaître.[1]

So the impulse to take part in or to lead such a revival came simultaneously with his desire to carve a name for himself as the historian of the manners and sentiments of his own age. He aimed to produce a hundred 'droll tales', divided into groups of ten—'dixains' or 'dizains'. One such tale, *L'Archevêque*, which was written in modern French, appeared on the 4th November 1830 in *La Caricature*. It introduces 'la belle Impéria', a Roman courtesan whom he transplanted from the end to the beginning of the fifteenth century, and for whom was reserved a prominent place in this miniature 'comédie humaine'. In fact her adventures at the Council of Constance were the subject of the first 'droll story' to be printed,[2] and since this represents his first published experiment in sham Middle French, it is reasonable to suppose that the idea of linguistic transposition occurred to him during the last months of 1830 or the early ones of 1831. The first Dizain was brought out by Gosselin in April 1832, the second in July 1833. A large part of the Third Dizain, already in print, was destroyed in December 1835 by a fire which gutted the store-house in the Rue du Pot-de-Fer where it was awaiting completion, so that Balzac had to rewrite it from the proofs. It therefore fell to Werdet's lot to publish it two years later. Fragments of a Fourth and Fifth Dizain have since been edited by M. Bouteron,[3] to-

[1] Conard, *O.D.* I, 347–8.
[2] 'La belle Impéria', *Revue de Paris*, 7 June, 1831. See Massant (3).
[3] *Cahiers balzaciens*, No. 4 (1925), and Conard XXXVII.

gether with a note in which Balzac explained his further intentions, and a Prologue to the 'Quint Dizain'. In default of the 'septante iolis contes' announced, his reputation as a continuator of the late medieval and Renaissance humorists must rest on the three finished volumes.

One inescapable fact about these stories is that they are frankly and jovially licentious. Faithful to his purpose of crying up the lusty vitality of the French race, and more especially that of the lords and ladies, priests, monks, nuns, provosts, judges, craftsmen and peasants of Touraine, he takes as an axiom, and indeed as a highly commendable trait in human nature, the lubricity of all and sundry. From queen to cow-girl, from châtelaine to laundress, from High Constable to needy vagrant, young and old alike are avid for erotic enjoyment. From this principle springs the plot of most of the stories: the uninitiate seeking experience, the initiate renewing it at all times and seasons; violations, seductions, clandestine debauchery, trickery, retaliation for trickery, horse-play and humiliations, and all the varieties of knavery which salacious ingenuity can devise in the pursuit of fleshly satisfaction. Balzac's late Middle Ages abound in courtesans and trollops, lascivious wives and enterprising gallants. There is gleeful narration of other kinds of events, but the theme of universal concupiscence is played on to the point of monotony.

No fastidious person is likely to enjoy these stories, but it is not sufficient to dismiss them as mere experiments in pornography, or to relegate them to the tap-room or harness-room as untimely revivals of a crude and prurient taste in humour which cultured society should have outgrown. The *Contes drolatiques* have their redeeming features, as a glance at some of the subjects treated will show.

It must be admitted that some of them are boisterous and cruel in their comicality, like *Les trois Clercs de Sainct-Nicholas*, *L'Héritier du Dyable* and *Les Joyeulsetez du roy Loys le unziesme*. They relate the coarse pranks of scholars and the means they adopt for defrauding an innkeeper of his just due; the rivalry of three cousins for the heritage of a moribund canon and the grim victory achieved by the reputed simpleton among them; the sadistic mystifications practised by Louis XI and his mistress at the expense of his cronies. Many more are just bawdy or dirty, like *La Pucelle de Thilhouze* and the disgusting *Bons Propos des relligieuses de Poissy*. Some, however ribald may be their theme, are told with a light and amusing touch, like *L'Apostrophe* and *Le Dangier d'estre trop coquebin*: the former with its conclusion of a guilty wife's agonized cry at the sight of her husband's sword suspended above her lover—'Arrête, malheureux, tu vas tuer le père de tes enfants'; the latter with its pretty sketch of a naïve young couple's uncertainties as they stand on the threshold of married life. Others achieve a delicately sentimental or pathetic tone. Among these may be counted *Le Péché vesniel*, which Balzac himself acclaimed as 'un diamant de naïveté'—the naïvety being that of a frustrated bride who draws means of consolation from a quaint casuistry never yet consigned to the manuals of moral theology. Another of them is *Le Frère d'armes*, in which a young nobleman's resistance to temptation reaches heroic heights, and enables the author, incongruously perhaps, to touch on the theme of platonic love, as well as providing him with a subject which he some time later treated anew—and less successfully— in *La Fausse Maîtresse* of the 'Comédie Humaine'. There is also the charming *Perseuerance d'amour*, undoubtedly the purest of these stories, for it tells how a rich and virtuous goldsmith (naturally a Tourangeau) willingly stoops to serfdom in order to marry the girl he loves. *Le belle Impéria mariée* carries the history of a once proud and impudent courtesan to the point where real love overtakes and transforms her, so that she pays with her life for the bliss of lawful union, marred only by her failure to bear her husband the children he desires.

There is a bitter-sweet tang to such tales, and some of them strike the tragic note. In *La faulse Courtizanne* Balzac's inspiration soars high above its normal level, and he paints the portrait of an irreproachable, high-minded lady who dies of grief because the purity of her conjugal relations has been sullied through the contrivance of a libertine prince. It is a striking variation on the theme of the Rape of Lucrece. *Dezesperance d'amour* is virtually a transposition of the Duchesse de Langeais situation into a much more appropriate setting—the Château of Amboise in the later fifteenth century. *Berthe la repentie*, one of the longest stories, develops a humorous conceit which is very much in keeping with the general spirit of the *Contes drolatiques*—it tells of an incredibly unsophisticated wife duped into adultery; but gay absurdity gives place to sombre drama, and Berthe's repentance consists in returning good for the evil her murderous husband has done. *Le Succube* is the longest story of all, and by far the most original. It conjures up a vision of thirteenth-century Tours and relates the strange case of a Saracen girl whose charms are so irresistible and so fatal to her lovers that she is condemned by an ecclesiastical court and burnt at the stake as being, not a woman, but a lascivious demon.

The point about even the most uninhibited of these stories is that the manner of their telling usually goes far to atone for the distastefulness of the subject-matter. Perhaps Balzac's chief reason for adopting the Rabelaisian idiom was that indecencies and crudities seem less shocking when expressed in the exuberant and forthright language of an age which revelled in them. But a stronger motive still was undoubtedly his discovery that comic effects could be heightened and narration could be made more spicy and vivid by recourse to the verbal acrobatics for which Rabelais is famous.

There are notable artificialities in Balzac's 'drolatic' diction which bespeak an imperfect understanding of the older language. His use of quaint spellings and parasitic letters is not always in accordance with the etymological principles, genuine or false, which determined the orthography of Middle French; and he frequently misconjugates verbs like *ardre*, *ouïr*, *chaloir*, etc. His distortion of *laire* ('to let') into a first-conjugation verb *lairrer*, and *haïr* into a non-existent *haïter* are tiresome defects. And many of his word-creations have a modern ring. But the mimetic faculty was strong in him, and, at his best, and especially in his 'Prologues', he does in large measure recapture the flavour of the Gargantua-Pantagruel cycle, with its copious vocabulary, its multiplication of synonyms and derivatives, its accumulation of epithets and its endless strings of paraphrases. Though Balzac's enumerative passages are often lame and short-winded in comparison with those of his master, his medium is well suited for playful and even lyrical narration; it lends itself to vivacious dialogue, rapid alternations of ribaldry and tenderness, dramatic reversals of situation, ironic and epigrammatic comments, and the pointing of morals whose object is to amuse but certainly not to edify. Underneath the quips and witticisms we can discern a fine appreciation of human foibles which is the more effective because it is free from the pretentious philosophizing which on occasion may mar his serious writings.

. . . Rarement se choleroyt, à moins qu'on ne maugreast Dieu devant lui, ce qu'il ne toleroyt poinct, parce qu'il l'avoyt maugréé pour les aultres en sa folle jeunesse.[1]

. . . Enfin, ne pressoyt les Juifs qu'à tems et lorsqu'ils estoyent enflez d'usure et de deniers; il les laissoyt amasser leur buttin comme mousches à miel, disant qu'ils estoyent les meilleurs collecteurs d'impôts.[2]

. . . le bon chier homme s'estoyt enamouré d'elle avecque une passion de vieillard, laquelle augmente en proportions géométrales, au rebours des passions de jeunes gens; pource que les vieux ayment avec leur foyblesse qui va croissant; et les jeunes avecque leurs forces qui s'en vont diminuant.[3]

. . . En ceci l'homme se distingue de la beste, vu que aulcun animal ne ha perdue l'esperit par dezespoir d'amour; ce qui prouve d'abundant que les bestes n'ont point d'asme.[4]

. . . Treuvez en toute la chrestienté iusticiarde, ung prevost moins malfaisant? Non, tous les prevosts pendent trop ou trop peu, tandis que cettui-la pendoit iuste ce qu'il falloyt pour estre dict prevost.[5]

. . . Ce dict abbez estoyt ung pernicieulx compere qui soubs le frocq couloyt aux dames forces contes ioyeulx auxquels elles ne refroignoient qu'aprest les avoir entendeus, vu que pour iuger, besoin est de ouir les choses.[6]

Tribute has sometimes been paid to Balzac for the truth and accuracy with which he portrays French life and manners in the fifteenth and sixteenth centuries. In view of the peculiar orientation of his interests, such eulogy is probably excessive, though the

[1] Conard XXXVI, 31. [2] Ibid., 32.

[3] Ibid., 173. Cf. the same idea expressed in more serious mood: '. . . on n'a de véritables passions que dans l'âge mûr, parce que la passion n'est belle et furieuse que quand il s'y mêle de l'impuissance et qu'on se trouve alors à chaque plaisir comme un joueur à son dernier enjeu'. (*Le Lys dans la vallée*, Conard XXVI, 271.) Balzac never tired of repeating this 'axiom'. Cf. *Théâtre*, t. II (Conard) 25, 485.

[4] Conard XXXVII, 17. [5] Ibid., 40–1. [6] Ibid., 54.

glimpses his tales afford of court, castle, cloister and other kinds of domicile have much of the charm of illustrations in illuminated manuscripts and early printed books. The procession of types as we pass from story to story puts one vaguely in mind of the *Canterbury Tales,* and as a rule the characters are sketched out with vigour and concision, or developed with subtlety and penetration. However lewd may be his churchmen (he intends no anti-clerical malice thereby), his courtiers, burghers, students and pilgrims, they are not cold abstractions. His strumpets are spontaneous in their guile and mischievousness. His jealous husbands and gulled philanderers are not the limp puppets one finds in *Cent Nouvelles nouvelles.* From his skill in setting characters in opposition proceed energy and even violence of action. It matters little that the plots of *Le Péché vesniel, Berthe la repentie* and *La belle Impéria mariée* are lacking in basic verisimilitude: Blanche de la Roche-Courbon, Berthe de Basternay and the rehabilitated wanton from Rome spring to life, capture interest and sympathy under Balzac's pen. As for *Le Succube,* it is a masterpiece of its kind.

His device for the telling of this story is the supposed transcription of documents recording the unfortunate Zulma's trial. First of all a string of picturesquely varied witnesses stand forward one by one. By the venom of their hatred and fear, or by the warmth of their sympathy, they raise a great query in the reader's mind: is this entrancing but dangerous creature really a succubus,[1] or a victim of gossip and prejudice? The interrogatory to which she is next subjected does nothing to clear up the mystery, and— though this statement may seem outrageous considering the scabrousness of the theme—her situation is not without a poignancy akin to that of Joan of Arc confronting her judges. Zulma's demoniac status seems to become established when the Grand Pénitencier in charge of the investigation avows that he too has succumbed to her infernal enchantments. But this confession *in extremis* savours more of hallucination than truth, and the reader might well put it down to the ravings of pent-up eroticism, were it not followed by the revelation of his scribe who, many years after, tells how the Grand Pénitencier had been tortured into

[1] A 'female demon having sexual intercourse with sleeping men'.

making his spurious avowal through the malevolence of his would-be successor. The scribe's account of events seems to point clearly to Zulma's innocence regarding the sin of witchcraft. So much more appalling then is the brutality of her final torment. Balzac's cunning in plunging his readers into the dark labyrinth of medieval superstition, rendered more tortuous still by the criss-cross of individual lust, envy and intrigue, is a great artistic achievement.

And indeed Balzac demanded consideration for his *Contes drolatiques*, not only as a form of diversion and an effort to renovate the frank and innocent merriment of past ages, but also as a work of art which, so he extravagantly asserted in August 1833,[1] would constitute his chief claim to survival and glory. They were addressed, he also averred, to an élite of connoisseurs; and no doubt the special edition of them published by Dutacq in 1855, with the famous illustrations by Gustave Doré, would have particularly pleased him. When accused of servile imitation, he defended himself[2] first on the grounds that his stories were 'cut from the diurnal, nocturnal and faultlessly woven cloth that the human race weaves every minute, hour, week, month and year'; and secondly 'because the majesty of art is at stake'. It is true that the plea of art can be urged to cover a multitude of obscenities, and from 1832 onwards there have been plenty of critics, French and English, who have refused to admit the plea and cried scandal on the work. Ruskin is conspicuous among them. But 'connoisseurs' have not been lacking, even among the female sex. Mme Hanska was not too queasy to stomach them, and Zulma Carraud, who had provided Balzac with a relatively innocuous episode which he absorbed into *Les bons Propos des relligieuses de Poissy*, was enchanted above all with *Le Péché vesniel*. 'Il y a un vernis de chasteté dans cette révélation des mystères de l'amour,' she wrote to him, 'que vous devez sans doute à quelqu'inspiration du bon ange.'

This 'glaze of chastity' would often be sought in vain in the *Contes drolatiques*. In February 1831 Dr Véron, director of the *Revue de Paris*, to which *La belle Impéria* was offered, had written the charming phrase: 'Si c'est possible, soyez chaste, ne fût-ce

[1] *E* I, 33 and 60.   [2] 2nd Dizain, *Prologue*.

que pour montrer toute la variété de votre talent.' As the tales
succeeded one another, Balzac's interest in the more spiritual
aspects of love became more marked. He consciously yielded to
this tendency in the Third Dizain. In *Le Lys dans la vallée*, one
of the major productions of 1835–6, it was to triumph almost
completely.

ii. *Le Lys dans la vallée*

The rival claims of spiritual and fleshly love were a frequent
theme in Romantic literature. That love could be purged of its
grosser elements, lifted into the region of the infinite, and so
acquire the sanctity of a religious experience, was what Rousseau
had attempted to prove in *La nouvelle Héloïse*. George Sand, who
knew enough about love in its physical aspects to yearn for something higher, published in 1833 her novel, *Lélia*, in which the
two types of love were personified in the aspiring idealist, Lélia
herself, and her half-sister, Pulchérie, the voluptuous courtesan.
A like antithesis runs through the novel which, in all probability,
moved Balzac to write *Le Lys dans la vallée*: Sainte-Beuve's
Volupté, of July 1834. According to Sainte-Beuve himself, Balzac
was eager for vengeance after the critic's disparagement of *La
Recherche de l'absolu* in November of that year. 'Je referai
Volupté.' But a more compelling motive was Balzac's belief that
Sainte-Beuve had fumbled with the subject, and that he himself
was better equipped for the task.

Volupté is a long-winded, slow-moving fiction which Sainte-
Beuve wrote in one of his most sanctimonious moods, notwith-
standing the fact that it was inspired by his far from chaste
relationship with the wife of one of his best friends, Victor Hugo.
'Un livre puritain', says Balzac. It is the account given by a
middle-aged priest, Amaury, of the circumstances which had
brought him, during his youth, to repentance and conversion.
After flitting hesitantly round a marriageable girl, he had fallen
in love with a woman who was both a loyal wife and a devoted
mother. In so far as Sainte-Beuve's real intentions can be seized—
so subtly reticent is his language that one cannot be altogether
sure—Mme de Couaën was never even tempted to grant Amaury

more than friendship, although she gave him her confidence and made full use of his services at a time when her husband was under suspicion of dabbling in plots against the First Consul. The impossibility or unlikelihood of ever making further progress with her drove Amaury to seek consolation in mercenary loves, and also to make advances—with what success it is again difficult to say precisely—to a more sophisticated and rather shallow Parisian, Mme R . . .

'J'avais voulu près d'elle,' [writes Amaury] 'me soustraire à la plus pure des passions et aux plus impurs désirs, assembler en une liaison choisie assez d'âme et de sens, assez de vice et de délicatesse . . .'

So he experienced the two extremes of love, and tried to steer a middle course as well. From the sentimental and moral complexities of this situation Amaury found escape in a religious vocation.

In writing *La nouvelle Héloïse*, Rousseau's purpose had been to explore the possibility of an amorous couple finding happiness in spiritual communings, with a magnanimous husband looking on and approving. In this pilgrimage on which Saint-Preux and Julie de Wolmar embark, the latter takes the initiative and maps out the route. In *Volupté* we have no such clear-cut case of two people climbing hand in hand the uphill path to love untrammelled by desire. Amaury's desires are patent enough, and the value of the novel lies in the minuteness of his self-analysis. Mme de Couaën, to quote Balzac again, 'n'est pas assez femme'. It is true that she experiences jealousy, and regards the premature death of her son as a punishment visited upon her 'pour avoir désiré quelque chose hors du cercle tracé, hors de la famille'. Farther than this the unctuous Sainte-Beuve, garbed in his borrowed surplice and stole, does not take his heroine. He does not let us into the secret of her innermost thoughts and reactions as he does for Amaury. We learn far more of M. de Couaën, of his 'grand caractère' and his anti-Napoleonic fanaticism. Mme R . . .'s personality also stands out in relief, despite the ambiguity of her liaison with Amaury. Incidentally, what little tangible action there is in the story is provided by the Georges–Pichegru–Moreau conspiracy in which Amaury is half-heartedly involved.

In consequence Balzac had good reason, while borrowing superficial data from *Volupté*, for harking back to Rousseau and taking
his cue from the genuinely triangular situation envisaged in *La
nouvelle Héloïse*. The most notable change that he made was to
discard the noble and sympathetic husband in favour of one whose
defects might easily be expected to throw wife and lover into each
other's arms. But his debt to Rousseau is no less paramount, and
leaps to the eye even in the many pages of idyllic rhapsody in
which the delights of domestic rusticity are described; and for
this, behind *La nouvelle Héloïse*, one senses *The Vicar of Wake-
field*. Balzac's object, in *Le Lys*, is to portray a woman in love
with another than her husband, sorely tempted but remaining
'complètement vertueuse'; to celebrate in her 'la perfection
terrestre, comme *Séraphita* sera la perfection céleste'; to make her
virtue appear 'sublime et point ennuyeuse'; and to convey all this
in the language and style of the great preacher Massillon.[1] What
qualifications had he for such a task? He belonged to an age whose
tendency was indeed to rhapsodize over sexual love, but to glorify
it by attempting to spiritualize what Balzac calls 'la poésie des
sens' rather than by repressing the sensual urge. No one has
better illustrated that tendency than Victor Hugo, who worked
his way, between 1830 and 1858, to the astounding thesis that
physical possession is in itself a religious act:

> . . . on ne peut, à l'heure où les sens sont en feu,
> Étreindre la beauté sans croire embrasser Dieu![2]

Echoes of this fantastic mysticism, which the Abbé Bertault has
finely analysed and gravely condemned,[3] are frequently to be
found in the works and correspondence of Balzac. Mortification of
the flesh was no cardinal virtue in his eyes. The establishment of a
mother-and-son relationship with Mme de Berny had been the
terminus ad quem and not the point of departure of his dealings
with her. His wrath with Mme de Castries had been due to the
fact that he could not find contentment in the 'menus suffraiges'

---

[1] *E* I, 277, 278. Cf. ibid., 337, where he writes thus of *Le Lys*: 'autre
Séraphita, qui, celle-là, est orthodoxe'.
[2] *Le Sacre de la femme* in *La Légende des siècles*, Première Série.
[3] Bertault (2), 178–83.

with which Antoinette de Langeais tempered the austerities of platonic love for Armand de Montriveau, and Anne de Maillé, in *Le Frère d'armes,* for Le Sieur de Lavallière. Not even the love between Louis Lambert and Pauline de Villenoix had been uninterruptedly platonic; while the sexless or double-sexed Séraphita is a special case.

We may well therefore expect Balzac, as he dons his sacerdotal raiment after the example of Sainte-Beuve, to show some creases in his surplice and to wear his stole a little awry.

The figures forming the triangle in *Le Lys dans la vallée* are M. de Mortsauf,[1] a returned émigré of fifty-five, soured by exile, crotchety, hypochondriacal; his wife Blanche-Henriette, tormented by his querulousness and by the anxiety she feels over the ill-health of their two children, burdened also by the responsibilities which her husband's incapacity to manage their estates puts upon her shoulders; and the twenty-year-old Félix de Vandenesse. It is he who narrates the story in order to appease the curiosity of a woman with whom he has become entangled in later life, the Comtesse Natalie de Manerville. Up to a point, he can be identified with Balzac himself, except for the distinction of his birth. He is the neglected child and yearning adolescent that Balzac, in his self-pitying moments, made himself out to have been. Like Balzac, he is a native of Tours, and the phases of his education are in close parallel to those of Balzac. Vexed by the solicitations of puberty, he by chance attends a ball at Tours in 1814, and finds himself sitting in a quiet corner of the ballroom near to the yet unknown Mme de Mortsauf. He is so moved by the contemplation of her bare shoulders—'de pudiques épaules qui avaient une âme', as he absurdly puts it—that he flings himself on them and covers them with kisses. In spite of the rebuff he naturally receives, this uncouth gesture alters the course of his life. The quest for his unknown divinity quickly leads him to her in her château of Clochegourde.[2] There he is pardoned for his impetuous assault and soon welcomed into the bosom of her family, making friends with Mortsauf by his readiness to lend an ear to his eternal com-

---

[1] The strange origin of the House of Mortsauf is related in *Contes drolatiques, Les Joyeulsetez du roy Loys le unziesme.*

[2] A mansion of composite invention which Balzac situates near Saché.

plaints, and winning the affection of the two children, Jacques and Madeleine.

Henriette de Mortsauf has in common with Félix the memory of an unhappy childhood, which explains the title of the original first chapter: *Les deux Enfances*. It recounts the establishment of a sentimental *modus vivendi* between them, and the second one, *Les premières Amours*, the growth of a mutual tenderness which Félix hopes to turn into passionate love. Henriette's role is to school him in the ways of uncomplaining devotion and to keep him satisfied with immaterial rewards—a communion of confidential sympathy, a sharing of thoughts, aspirations and reveries from which Mortsauf is excluded by his very self-centredness. More tangible guerdons are few and infrequent; hand-pressings, hand-kisses, the privilege of gathering bouquets for her to convey his yearning through the language of flowers; the gift of her fallen hairs, and, on one occasion, the lifting of her forehead for him to kiss. It is against his will that Félix allows himself to remain 'dans les abusives croyances de l'amour platonique', but he has to remain satisfied with the 'langueurs enchanteresses', the 'moments de suavité divine', and the 'contentements qui suivent de tacites immolations'. In the course of time he comes to accept the situation with a sort of ecstatic reverence: 'elle devint ce qu'était la Béatrix du poète florentin, la Laure sans tache du poète vénitien, la mère des pensées, la cause des résolutions qui sauvent, le soutien de l'avenir, la lumière qui brille dans l'obscurité comme le lys dans les feuillages sombres'.

The irritating part about all this is that the *reader* finds it difficult to accept the situation. Even as seen through Félix's eyes, Henriette gives us the impression of a woman who subsists on his adoration and exploits it to her own advantage. She is grateful to him for his kindness to her children, and more so still because he humours her husband and shields both them and herself from his outbreaks of petulance. As Félix is nine years younger than she, and as he was both physically and morally immature when he came under her influence, she adopts the motherly attitude and professes to treat him as Jacques' elder brother. Balzac's debt to *La nouvelle Héloïse* has been emphasized. His debt to the *Confessions* is also manifest. Despite the fact that, in the 1836 preface

111

to *Le Lys*, he reprimanded Rousseau for his indiscreet revelations about his 'maman', Mme de Warens, there is something of Mme de Warens in Henriette. Félix lends himself to this nonsense. This false maternity is ridiculous enough. More so still is the translation of this equivocal relationship into terms of a different kinship. Deprived of her own mother's affection, Henriette had drawn much comfort in her childhood from the sympathy of an aunt. And so the bond between her and Félix expresses itself in a phrase which recurs like a refrain throughout the book: *Aimez-moi comme m'aimait ma tante.* Rarely had Balzac's sense of humour so completely deserted him. In *Les premières Amours* Félix's role is chiefly that of sick-nurse to the intolerable Mortsauf, whose hypochondria has made him seriously ill; and their joint effort to save the man who is the sole obstacle to their happiness as lovers forges a new link of attachment between them. But all the time the drift of discourse in this 'religieuse mariée pleine de résignation sainte' is the affirmation: 'Je ne puis être la source de vos plaisirs.'

Though the upshot will of course show that the motive for Henriette's apparent exploitation of Félix is unimpeachable, somehow or other Balzac has not succeeded in making all this ring true. But at any rate Henriette is concerned for the young man's future, and does not see fit to tie him for ever to her apron-strings. So she sends him away to make his career in Paris, in the diplomatic world renewed by the return of Louis XVIII, that amused cynic who takes this faithful royalist as his confidant and assigns him missions which establish his reputation as a statesman in embryo. It is at this juncture that another objectionable feature in Henriette's make-up comes into prominence—a pedantry which Balzac lends her out of his own stock, but which sits ungracefully on the shoulders of a recluse with no experience of the world. To make up for her deficiencies in social experience, Balzac again pulls his 'second sight' out of the bag, and this gift conferred on her enables her to write Félix a letter of more than 5,000 words, containing full instructions about his conduct in society, the principles which must govern his behaviour in public, and his relations with women. A female Polonius! Armed with this miniature Bible in whose literal inspiration he almost implicitly believes, but more practically supported by the influential people she has interested in his welfare, he sallies forth to the conquest of a position worthy of his talent. Henriette sees in him a high-minded genius. The reader, alas! thinks of him mainly as a prig and a booby.

In Parisian society the platonizing 'Mademoiselle de Vande-nesse', as Louis XVIII calls Félix, is something of a nine days' wonder. Then he is brought into contact with that proud, im-petuous, possessive Amazonian, that shameless siren, the English-woman, Lady Arabella Dudley, wife of a tired debauchee, step-mother of Henri de Marsay. Her instincts as a man-eater are aroused by the tale of Félix's enduring fidelity to his far-off paragon of virtue, and Félix yields, after some resistance, to the calculatedly passionate advances of this native of Lancashire, 'pays où les femmes meurent d'amour'. She plays the part of 'demon' to Henriette de Mortsauf's 'angel', that of the 'maîtresse du corps' opposed to the 'épouse de l'âme'. Sainte-Beuve's Mme R . . . is left well in the shade, for Arabella sates Félix with the carnal blisses he has never yet enjoyed. Then when Henriette ceases to write him letters after being informed of his fall from grace, he returns in trepidation to Clochegourde, and there meets with a chilling reception. Arabella has insisted on following him and taking up her quarters at La Grenadière.

In this third part of the story—Les deux Femmes—Balzac begins to come into his own again. The confrontation of the two women reawakens his sense of drama. Henriette's reactions to what Félix smugly calls 'la plus excusable des fautes' are, for a time, those of a real woman, outraged at the triumph of a rival. Arabella's reactions are no less positive—'On se donne, ou l'on se refuse; mais se refuser et moraliser, il y a double peine.' Henriette summons up courage to efface herself and offer her blessing to the unholy union of Félix with the Englishwoman. But she is mor-tally hurt. Ostensibly she dies of a stomach cancer, but the real cause is her grief and listlessness, or rather, as her doctor asserts, 'l'inertie d'un organe dont le jeu est aussi nécessaire à la vie que celui du cœur'. Félix returns once more to Clochegourde to see her die, to be confronted once more with Mortsauf's crass incom-prehension, and to incur the stubborn hatred of Madeleine, who holds him responsible for her mother's death. Henriette dies in the odour of sanctity, assured by the Abbé de Dominis of ascending to the regions of light. But, before resigning herself to a Christian death, this repressed daughter of Eve goes through paroxysms of doubt and regret. The revolt of nature wrings from her the momentary admission: 'Tout a été mensonge dans ma vie.' In the original edition this last-minute rebellion was expressed in almost blasphemous terms; but Mme de Berny convinced Balzac that he had painted in too glaring colours this 'combat de l'esprit contre la matière' in the heart of a dying Catholic. He toned the passage down. Before her death Henriette has found time and lucidity enough (like Julie de Wolmar in *La nouvelle Héloïse*) to write a last letter to Félix and confess that his 'terribles baisers' at the ball at Tours had disturbed her to the depths of her being; that she had loved and desired him all along; and that only his timidity had saved her. 'Ah! si dans ces moments où je redoublais de froideur vous m'eussiez prise dans vos bras, je serais morte de bonheur.'

'Nowhere else', says M. Allem, in the Preface to his edition of *Le Lys*,[1] 'has Balzac put more of himself into one of his characters' —namely Félix de Vandenesse. One may add that in regard to no other work have commentators on Balzac shown more assiduity in identifying the characters as real persons. Henriette de Mortsauf is Mme de Berny (for this at least there is supporting testimony from Balzac himself).[2] Or she is Sarah Guidoboni-Visconti, whose acquaintance he had recently made. Likewise Sarah is the model for Lady Dudley, as also is Lady Ellenborough. And Natalie de Manerville, for whom Félix is writing this account of his life, is Mme Hanska, whom Balzac was thus assuring of the innocence of his relations with 'la Dilecta'. And M. de Mortsauf is M. de Berny or M. Hanski[3] or the valetudinarian husband of Zulma Carraud. If certain characters of the 'Comédie Humaine' were indeed so easily recognizable as real persons, it is a wonder Balzac ever kept a friend.

[1] Garnier. For other discussions see Serval (4), Le Yaouanc (1), Hunt (7) and (8).

[2] *E* I, 344.

[3] Like M. de Mortsauf, he has his 'blue devils': cf. *E* I, 146 (3 Apr. 1834) and *Le Lys*, Conard, XXVI, 229.

We may brush such speculations aside, for what matters is that, during the greater part of the novel, both Henriette and Félix appear as insupportable creatures. Henriette is insufferably patient, angelic, monopolizing and moralizing by turns. Félix is an incredible compound of smug idealism, respectful ardour and (as regards Lady Dudley) ungrateful self-righteousness. And behind him looms Balzac of whom he is only too clearly the spokesman; the Balzac, who, in his zeal to recapture the suave style of Massillon, has indulged beyond normal limits his propensity for baroque rhapsody, forced metaphor and turgid platitude.

Significantly enough, the characters whom he obviously wished to make the least attractive are precisely those who have most life and reality in them. M. de Mortsauf is fairly convincing. So is his daughter Madeleine at the end of the story. In a frenzy of Anglophobia Balzac pounces upon Lady Dudley as the very incarnation of English materialism, steely-heartedness and flaunting immodesty set off by puritanical conventionalism. Yet, in spite of himself as it were, he has made her a vivid and amusing creature, who commands our sympathy in everything except the favour she squanders on Félix. And Natalie de Manerville, the hitherto passive recipient of Félix's confidence, shows wit, vigour and discernment in her reply to his plea for her compassionate love. No doubt *Le Contrat de mariage* establishes her as a cruel and rapacious woman, but is not her mockery of Félix well justified? She laughs at him for expecting her to combine in her person the contrasting perfections of Arabella and Henriette, but lashes him for his weak disloyalty to the women who, after all, had lavished affection on him and furthered his worldly career. 'Quand on est aimé ainsi, que peut-on demander de plus?' It is difficult not to share her disdain and endorse her condemnation.

Such are the reactions which, unfortunately, the reading of this novel tends to provoke. One is inclined to feel that Balzac, in the very year succeeding the publication of *Le père Goriot*, has belied the promise of 1834–5. And yet not a few critics have gone into raptures over this 'drame d'amour'. This much at least must be said for *Le Lys dans la vallée*: the final episodes of the 'drama', the dying Henriette's revulsions, her desperate attempt to grasp at the now unattainable sweets of love, her last letter, and Natalie de Manerville's piquant verdict on Félix's temperament and conduct, do a great deal to revive our respect for Balzac as a psychologist. It is necessary for the reader to remind himself that, as the fiction has it, it is not Balzac himself, but Félix de Vandenesse who is narrating and commenting throughout the whole work. Certainly it is only too easy to equate the two, largely because both the observations of Félix and those he attributes to Henriette are so often and so strongly redolent of Balzac in his most portentous and his most sentimental moods. If however we could assume that Balzac was entirely detached from his creation, we should conclude that he had indeed intended to show up Félix as the inept 'Chevalier de la Triste-Figure' that Natalie de Manerville sees in him, that he intended also to reveal the unconscious egoism which is perceptible behind Henriette's highmindedness and maternal solicitude. We should suppose that Balzac actually meant her position to appear as essentially false and the sentiments in which she takes refuge intolerably prim. We should suspect that Arabella's charm, vitality and impetuous passion were real and genuine, and that Félix's prudish denigration of her was prompted by the sourness of disillusion; and even perhaps that Félix had exaggerated M. de Mortsauf's egoism and hypochondria.

Regrettably, this impression of Balzac rising triumphant over the edifying intentions expounded in the *Lettres à l'Etrangère* and elsewhere, recapturing his objectivity and letting his instinct for psychological truth take control, does not begin to prevail until the last section—*Les deux Femmes*—is well under way. But from that point onwards it becomes more and more insistent. Even though the original violence of Henriette's revolt was attenuated in deference to Mme de Berny, the final episodes bring the light of real truth to a situation which has too long been seen through the eyes of Félix alone. Natalie's letter above all puts the events of *Le Lys* in their true perspective. We may therefore conclude with a more favourable judgment: if for a time Balzac has seemed to be the dupe of his own effusions about platonic love and angelical purity, his commonsense wins through in the end. In view of this, it is perhaps a pity that he had followed the lead of Sainte-Beuve and elected to entrust the narrative to the man we must call, for want of a more fitting term, the 'hero' of the story, who has simultaneously to discharge two functions, that of invented character and author's spokesman. According to a remark he made to Mme Hanska in January 1837,[1] Balzac realized that 'le caractère de Félix est sacrifié dans cette œuvre'. He announced his resolve to remedy the defect. This of course he could do only by bringing him into a new 'scene', which he did two years later in *Une Fille d'Ève*. In the meantime, his appearance as a background figure, in *Le Contrat de mariage*, put him in an even less agreeable light.

iii. *Le Contrat de mariage* (1835)

This novel is an offshoot of *L'Histoire des Treize*. It is linked up with *La Fille aux yeux d'or* through the persons of Henri de Marsay and Paul de Manerville; but also with *Le Lys dans la vallée* through the persons of Félix de Vandenesse and Natalie de Manerville.

Paul de Manerville is one of the society 'elegants' defined in *La Fille aux yeux d'or*. But his appearance there was brief, and he now becomes the subject of a complete study. He is an exception to the general type. He is simple and honest. He has been brought up in the arts and graces of his class, and has enough of the charm and the *savoir-faire* of the Parisian to cut a prominent figure, and to earn the nickname of *la fleur des pois*[2] in the society of his native Bordeaux, to which he returns after spending some years in Paris and other European capitals. He is physically courageous, but lacking in moral strength. The desire to marry marks him out as an easy prey for scheming women.

They are to hand in the shape of two Spaniards who have settled in Bordeaux, Mme Évangélista and her daughter Natalie, who have noble connections, but much of the Creole in their temperament. Paul is the most brilliant match that Bordeaux can offer. He is easily ensnared, the more so because he believes Natalie to be as rich as he is. But there are obstacles to a happy union. Since her husband's death in 1813 Mme Évangélista has controlled her

[1] *E* I, 376-7.
[2] 'The pick of the bunch.' Hence the original title of the work, *La Fleur-des-Pois*.

daughter's inheritance and squandered a great deal of it. She has brought up her daughter in habits of ostentatious luxury. Worse still, though of course Paul does not suspect it, she is one of the most virulent harpies of the 'Comédie Humaine', and is in a fair way to modelling her daughter on her own example. 'Comparé à Madame Évangélista,' comments Henri de Marsay, 'le papa Gobseck est une flanelle, un velours, une potion calmante, une meringue à la vanille, un oncle à dénouement.'[1]

The capture of Paul de Manerville, which is necessary if the two women are to be able to leave Bordeaux and enjoy more exhilarating social life in Paris, depends on Mme Évangélista's success in distracting Paul's attention from the hole she has made in her daughter's fortune. But this is a matter for the family lawyer, Mathias, who negotiates the marriage contract with Mme Évangélista's representative, Solonet. The former stands for the old-fashioned type of notary, grotesque in appearance and habits, but loyal, punctilious, incorruptible and wide-awake; the latter for the Restoration type—a dandy, but wily, shifty, unprincipled and self-interested. The duel between the two constitutes the central 'scene' which Balzac has admirably prepared and staged. It is a subtle and exciting battle—Balzac uses military metaphors to describe it—with Mme Évangélista anxiously watching over the moves and counter-moves in an action closely concerted between her and Solonet, with the amorous Paul becoming more and more distressed at Mathias' determination to keep the affair on a strictly business footing, and Natalie waiting, when defeat is threatened, to bring up the reserves in the shape of starry-eyed, uncalculating innocence. Balzac had refreshed his legal knowledge in order to present a solid case of clashing interests. Mathias is naturally concerned for the intregrity of the Manerville fortunes and the future of the children who may be born of the marriage. He fights with his back to the wall, thanks to his client's ineptitude; but he turns the tables on his opponents by proposing a scheme of entailment which will put the Manerville estates out of reach for the predatory females he perceives the Évangélistas to be. His victory brings Mme Évangélista to a pitch

[1] i.e. a benevolent uncle who arrives in the last act of a comedy to smooth out financial difficulties.

of dissimulated fury which makes her resolve on the ruin of her son-in-law, whom infatuation and her stratagems have reduced to moronic unwariness.

Subsidiary to the central scene are the manœuvres Mme Évangélista executes between the settlement of the contract and the wedding ceremony, by means of which she succeeds in undoing a good deal of Mathias' skilful work and extracting a fair nest-egg for herself and daughter from the remnant of their fortune, destined by the contract to be merged with the Manerville assets. Subsidiary also, but amusing and perfectly relevant in the light it throws on normal human nature, is Balzac's reproduction of the gossip, born of curiosity and malice, in which the matchmaking mothers of Bordeaux indulge during those weeks when the much-discussed marriage appears to be hanging fire. All this adds more fuel to Mme Évangélista's resentment, and increases the store of tribulations which she is preparing for the hapless Paul. Wearing the mask of fond motherhood, she arranges to take into her own hands the management of Paul's estates while the young couple disport themselves in the capital.

In the space of five years she has reduced Manerville to penury. One of Balzac's best achievements in this work is the heart-to-heart conversation he stages between Mme Évangélista and Natalie on the eve of the wedding: a mother advising a daughter, who is not as yet hopelessly selfish and corrupt, how, by exploiting her husband's passion while being careful not to share it, by measuring or withholding the concessions she makes to it, she may acquire complete domination over him. The instinct for domination (as Balzac had shown earlier on, in one of those ingenious physiognomical developments in which his novels abound)[1] was manifested in every detail of the young Natalie's person, and she establishes absolute rule on the first night of their marriage. Its effect is to make Paul a slave to her every whim, and eager to allow her any luxury, however costly, she craves for; and

[1] An amusing example is to be found in *Le Lys*, where even Mme de Mortsauf's manner of articulation is made out to be significant. 'Sa façon de dire les terminaisons en *i* faisait croire à quelque chant d'oiseau; le *ch* prononcé par elle était comme une caresse, et la manière dont elle attaquait les *t* accusait le despotisme du cœur.' Balzac took delight in Mme Hanska's Slavonic mispronunciations of French.

thus she is free to complete the dissipation of Paul's resources while her mother draws from the Lanstrac estates the wherewithal for them to live at their ease once Paul is disposed of. When the five years have ended, Paul sails off to India in the hope of making a new fortune. On the eve of departure he is still besottedly infatuated, and still persuaded that Natalie and her mother love him 'autant qu'un homme peut l'être en ce bas monde'.

Balzac winds up his story with the relentless cruelty of a great artist. When Paul's ship is already on its course, Paul reads two letters which had been brought to him at the moment of embarking. One is from Natalie, nauseatingly affectionate and replete with protestations of gratitude, admiration and eternal fidelity. The other is from Henri de Marsay who, with a merciless frankness prompted by the desire to wean Paul from his stupidity and make a man of him, opens his eyes to the true character and conduct of the Évangélista couple, and confirms a suspicion that had already been dawning in Paul's mind, namely that his supposedly blameless wife had for long been the mistress of Félix de Vandenesse.

It would be superfluous to insist on the power and acuity of perception which Balzac displays throughout *Le Contrat de mariage*, on the astringency of its conclusion, on the 'Que leur ai-je fait?' by which Paul de Manerville gives a final demonstration of his guilelessness and anticipates the 'C'est la faute de la fatalité' of Charles Bovary, his middle-class counterpart in Flaubert's great novel. It is food for reflection that *Le Lys dans la vallée* and *Le Contrat de mariage* are almost simultaneous productions. Balzac with an axe to grind is very different from the Balzac who lets his insight dictate his work. In so far as the two stories touch on one another tangentially, we are made aware of two curiously divergent angles of approach: Félix de Vandenesse who here is a pious prig, and there the cuckoo in a conjugal nest; a Natalie who here is a sensible but shrewd-tongued woman, and there the slyest of unfaithful wives. But the juxtaposition of the two novels does allow a fleeting vision of that hinterland of reality to which reference has already been made,[1] and which results from the continuous availability, as it were, of the recurrent

[1] Above, 96.

characters. The reader finds himself asking questions to which there can be no answer. How long has the Félix-Natalie affair been going on?[1] How did it manage to drag out until 1827 (the year of Paul de Manerville's ruin and emigration) in view of the exasperation which Félix's melancholy, born of the Mortsauf affair, aroused in Natalie? Was Félix writing his life-story for her just about the time of Paul's departure for Calcutta? In this case Natalie's breach with Félix is clearly imminent, if not complete. Was the child she was expecting—so says her letter to Paul—the fruit of her adultery with Félix? Or was her pregnancy a fiction? —it would be an audacious one, since Paul himself has misgivings when he reads the news. And what became of the unfortunate Paul after *La Belle Émilie* had carried him on to India?

In the length and breadth of the 'Comédie Humaine' such questions no doubt arise because of Balzac's negligence in establishing a clear chronology for his characters' careers and his forgetfulness when fitting new details into their lives as one novel succeeded another. But this objection can hardly apply to the almost simultaneous *Lys* and *Contrat de mariage*. So one must pay tribute to Balzac's ability to confirm the illusion of reality by deliberately leaving these uncertainties, and thereby inveigling his readers into trying to remove them.

The case of Henri de Marsay is more straightforward. What we learn of him in *Le Contrat de mariage* is a useful supplement and corrective to the information we obtain in *La Fille aux yeux d'or*. There the sinister side of the man is emphasized. He possesses 'un immense pouvoir inconnu . . . le pouvoir autocratique du despote oriental . . . Henri pouvait ce qu'il voulait dans l'intérêt de ses plaisirs et de sa vanité . . . de Marsay condamnait froidement à mort l'homme ou la femme qui l'avait offensé sérieusement.' In fact he appears to draw this power from diabolic sources.[2] In *Le Contrat de mariage* there is nothing so redolent of the wicked magicians from *A Thousand and One Nights*; without altogether losing his Byronic superiority, de Marsay is reduced to the

[1] De Marsay says it was beginning at the time when he was going on a tour in the East with Montriveau, de Ronquerolles, etc. M. Lotte surmises that this tour was invented to camouflage the expedition to Majorca to kidnap Antoinette de Langeais. This would make it 1823, one year after Natalie's wedding.

[2] *La Fille aux yeux d'or*, Conard XIII, 377–8.

common human measure through his contact with and his exploitation of the ugliness and meanness of the age. His character and outlook are fully revealed in the advice he gives at the beginning to Paul de Manerville on marriage—'Tu n'as pas le poignet assez fort pour gouverner un ménage'—and in his letter to Paul at the end. He is sarcastic, ironic, outspoken, completely sceptical about love and the virtue of women. He is gay, adventurous, fearless, though no more scrupulous than in *La Fille aux yeux d'or*. His ability to plumb the depths of human egoism and stupidity, and to rise superior to the hypocritical slogans of political parties, is bringing him to the threshold of his career as a statesman in the Talleyrand tradition. He has decided to augment his resources by taking to wife the ugly niece of a London brewer, and the caricature he draws of his wife-to-be gives the measure of his cynicism. But he is a staunch friend, opens his purse widely to Paul in his need, and does his best to dissuade him from leaving France by offering to take him under his wing as a budding politician; yet without disguising his calculation that the ingenuous Paul will be serviceable to him only as a 'stooge'. 'La politique est impossible sans un homme d'honneur avec qui l'on puisse tout dire et tout faire.' Henri de Marsay is a person who grows more interesting as he flits to and fro across the pages of the 'Comédie Humaine'.

PART II

1835-41

VI

CLASSIFICATION[1]

i. The Total Scheme

IN THE LATE AUTUMN of 1834 Balzac had made a grandilo-quent affirmation in a letter to Mme Hanska.[2]

Nous avons atteint à l'*ère de l'intelligence*. Les rois matériels, la force brutale s'en vont. Il y a des mondes intellectuels et il peut s'y recontrer des Pizarre, des Cortès, des Colomb. Il y aura des souverains dans le royaume universel de la pensée.

The sovereignty of art and letters was the basic creed of Romanticism, and Balzac was ready to claim a lofty rank among his brilliant contemporaries. In the same letter he outlined the threefold plan of the 'Social Studies', for which he had not yet found a more arresting title.

Les 'Études de Mœurs' représenteront tous les effets sociaux sans que ni une situation de la vie, ni une physionomie, ni un caractère d'homme ou de femme, ni une manière de vivre, ni une profession, ni une zone sociale, ni un pays français, ni quoi que ce soit de l'enfance, de la vieillesse, de l'age mûr, de la politique, de la justice, de la guerre, ait été oublié.

Cela posé, l'histoire du cœur humain tracée fil à fil, l'histoire sociale faite dans toutes ses parties, voilà la base. Ce ne seront pas des faits imaginaires; ce sera ce qui se passe partout.

Alors, la seconde assise est les *Études philosophiques*, car après les *effets* viendront les *causes*. Je vous aurai peint dans les *Études de Mœurs* les sentiments et leur jeu, la vie et son allure. Dans les *Études philoso-phiques*, je dirai *pourquoi les sentiments, sur quoi la vie*; quelle est la partie, quelles sont les conditions au delà desquelles ni la société, ni

---

[1] 'Le génie n'est complet que quand il joint à la faculté de créer la puissance de coordonner ses créations.' F. Davin in *Introduction to 'Études de Mœurs*, quoting Balzac himself.

[2] *E* I, 200–6 (26 Oct. 1834).

l'homme n'existent; et après l'avoir parcourue (la société), pour la décrire, je la parcourerai [*sic*] pour la juger. Aussi, dans les *Études de Mœurs* sont les *individualités* typisées; dans les *Études philosophiques* sont les *types* individualisés. Ainsi partout j'aurai donné la vie: du type, en l'individualisant, à l'individu en le typisant. J'aurai donné de la pensée au fragment; j'aurai donné à la pensée la vie de l'individu.

Puis, après les *effets* et la *causes*, viendront les *Études analytiques*, dont fait partie la *Physiologie du mariage*, car après les *effets* et les *causes* doivent se rechercher les *principes*. Les *mœurs* sont le spectacle, les *causes* sont les *coulisses et les machines*. Les *principes*, c'est l'auteur. . . .

The same letter computes the eventual dimensions of his work —twenty-four volumes for the 'Études de Mœurs', fifteen for the 'Études philosophiques', and nine for the 'Études analytiques'. Although Balzac's immediate object was to assure Mme Hanska that, with such a task on his hands, he would have no time for philandering with other women, one is struck with the sublime self-confidence and the invincible conviction of genius that the letter conveys. So comprehensive a scheme is evidently beyond the compass of any one man. 'Ce ne seront pas des faits imaginaires': this assertion may provoke a smile when one considers Balzac's exuberance of mind. There can rarely be a clear distinction between the 'individualités typisées' of the 'Études de Mœurs' and the 'types individualisés' of the 'Études philosophiques', except in such obvious cases as the Duchesse de Langeais and Eugène de Rastignac on the one hand and Fœdora and Raphaël de Valentin on the other.[1] The function assigned to the 'Études analytiques' is left in obscurity, and was to remain so. But such theoretic objections give way to admiration for the progress Balzac had already made towards the fulfilment of his programme, and to curiosity about the stages by which he intended to carry out the rest of it in the years which were left to him.

However much the intention behind the 'Études analytiques' may be left in the shade, the meaning and purport of the other two categories were, almost immediately, to be well illustrated and advertised, in two analyses written by a friend and admirer

[1] Félix Davin (see below) will base the distinction on the opposition between Grandet, 'un avare qui semble être l'avarice tout entière', and Maître Cornélius, 'l'avarice aux prises avec elle-même . . . personnage allégorique'.

of Balzac, Félix Davin, who was thoroughly primed for this task by the novelist himself. One of them was written as an introduction to the first volume of *Scènes de la vie privée* in Mme Béchet's edition of the 'Études de Mœurs', the other as an introduction to Werdet's edition of the 'Études philosophiques'. It so happened that the publication of the former work was delayed; in consequence the second of these introductions appeared first, in January 1835, and the first, adapted to suit the change of order, followed it in May 1835.[1]

Davin's Introductions are, in the main, eulogies tempered with mild but often pertinent criticism. They enlarge on Balzac's boldness in undertaking to outdistance Scott by writing the social history of his own age. They acclaim him as a renovator of the novel in substituting everyday types of people and passions, and meticulously studied reality, in place of the false and the grandiose. They marvel at the range of his vision and the acuteness of his intuition in evoking so many *milieux* and creating so many grades and shades of character; at the vividness of his sense of drama, the richness and variety of his backgrounds and the beauty of his landscapes; at his ability to divine the thoughts and motives, to steep himself in the life of all ranks and classes; at the universality of his knowledge, which enables him to move at ease in the realms of philosophy and the sciences. At the same time Davin admits certain flaws: 'une description un peu longue, une analyse un peu minutieuse, une réflexion refroidissante, un coloris trop vermillonné, des préparations trop coquettes, quelques répétitions de mots, quelque périodes verbeuses . . .'[2] But what he most insists on is the spirit of synthesis and the architectural sense which bind the different and still sometimes fragmentary parts together. In fact he gives in most respects a fuller and more systematic account of Balzac's ambitions and intentions than anything Balzac himself had written, or was later to write. The analysis of the 'Études philosophiques' does little more than elaborate and exemplify the basic doctrine—'la lame use le fourreau'—expounded in 1831 by Philarète Chasles.[3] But Davin knits the six divisions of the 'Études de Mœurs' into a closely reasoned coherent scheme,

---

[1] They are reproduced in Lovenjoul (1), 46–64 and 194–207.
[2] Lovenjoul (1), 200.   [3] See above, 42-3.

which must claim our attention because, for this part at least of his *exposé*, he was virtually writing at Balzac's dictation.

The principle linking the series of Scenes together is at once ingenious and ingenuous. Balzac's object in brief is to watch the individual in contact and conflict with society as he or she passes through the successive stages of life. Thus the Scenes of Private Life are to study pure and unsophisticated youth in its progress from puberty to maturity. It is the period of unreflecting emotion, confident sincerity and imperious desires, when young people fall into error and misfortune through ignorance of a world which is ruled by convention and calculation. The Scenes of Provincial Life are to show the transition from the generous impulsiveness of the twenty-year-old to the hard-headed self-interest of the man or woman of thirty. This decade is one of incipient disillusionment, of family and social friction; the power of money asserts itself and the quest for material well-being chills, then kills idealism, and puts reason in the place of feeling. The first of these two stages could not be situated in any particular type of *milieu*; but the provincial setting, 'le plus harmonieux, le plus riche en demi-teintes', with its petty rivalries and parochial jealousies, gives a perfect background for the second stage. The Scenes of Parisian Life are to portray the development of man from maturity to the verge of 'decrepitude', the climactic period of life. That Balzac should have chosen Paris as an appropriate setting for this phase is consistent with the view which he had already put forward. Paris is not only the centre of intellectual, artistic, social, commercial and political activity, but also a hot-bed of vice, iniquity, luxury, greed, hypocrisy and cynicism: it is that point in the universe where individualism is rampant and the exploitation of fools by knaves is the rule of life.

After the Parisian scenes, according to the logic of this classification, the portrayal of individual life falls temporarily into abeyance. With the Scenes of Political Life Balzac will pass from the clash of individual to the clash of collective interests. In studying 'l'effroyable mouvement de la machine sociale' he will stage grandiose and tragic conflicts between characters who symbolize contending principles—the monarchy and the people, the past and the present; conflicts in which sentiment has no place and the moral scruples which, however imperfectly, temper individual savagery are no longer effective. The Scenes of Military Life proceed from those of Political Life and are to show a nation organized for war under predestined leaders; life in camp and on the battlefield; the clash between France and Europe illustrated in the civil wars of La Vendée and Brittany; the whole nation in her triumphs and defeats. And then, 'après les étourdissants tableaux de cette série, viendront les peintures pleines de calme de *la Vie de campagne*', whose purpose will be to show men and women retiring from the struggle for life, seeking repose from the turmoil of political and military activity. Here the clash of interests will still be operative, but softened down. The Country Scenes will depict the evening of life. In the peaceful regularity of rustic settings, religion, true philanthropy—Balzac was for ever declaiming against the false variety, the emotional humanitarianism of his day—unassuming virtue and pious resignation will find their sphere of action. 'Partout les cheveux blancs de la vieillesse expérimentée s'y mêlent aux blondes touffes de l'enfance.' Here, through Davin, Balzac seems to promise pictures of country life which would relieve the pessimism and temper the cynicism of his darkest as of his lightest tales.

ii. Hesitations and Revisions

The reader of Davin's Introductions is bound to discern the *a posteriori* element in this scheme of development. The four ages of man—the age of illusions, the age of disillusionment, the age of bitter conflict, the age of appeasement, reconciliation and resignation—are those which Balzac happened more or less fortuitously to have studied in his earliest 'scenes'. His thought as a moralist had taken this direction from 1830 onwards. That is how things had worked out as he passed from Private to Provincial and then to Parisian life, from *Le Bal de Sceaux*, for instance, to *Eugénie Grandet*, and then to such stories as *Le colonel Chabert*, *Ferragus* and *Le père Goriot*; from presumptuous adolescence to saddened maturity, and then to that onset of 'decrepitude' which is in evidence in the characters of those whose names give titles to the three last-mentioned 'Parisian' studies. Davin, or rather

Balzac concealed behind Davin, was forced to improvise when it came to the as yet practically non-existent studies of Political Life. For the Military Studies he could only build on the analogy of *Les Chouans*, or expatiate on the intentions so often expressed with regard to the abortive *La Bataille*. *Le Médecin de campagne* was the obvious and sole model for the study of old age in a rustic setting which was to be the theme of the Country Life scenes.

The stages Balzac indicates in the painful business of growing up are in the main a matter of common experience; and in future years he was to keep them sufficiently in mind for them to provide a leitmotif throughout the 'Comédie Humaine'. But their attachment to particular or successive types of locality is a palpable artificiality. The unlocalized Private Life cadre could stand up to logical inspection if it were not so obviously a universal category. The Provincial cadre justifies itself partly by the frequent recurrence of those 'tempêtes dans un verre d'eau' which, as in *Le Curé de Tours*, ruffle the apparently placid surface of provincial society; still more by the attention given to regions, *milieux* and localized types of persons. But many stories tend to fall in an indeterminate area lying between Private and Provincial life. The age criterion is frequently inapplicable. To take novels we have already analysed, *Le Lys dans la vallée* could well be a Private Life scene, since its hero is a youth on the threshold of manhood and love, and since it treats of the intimacies of family relationships. It could also be a Provincial scene, since the action of the story takes place between Félix de Vandenesse's twentieth and thirtieth year of age. It could also be a Country Life scene, since a fair proportion of it is devoted to the description of rural occupations. It is as such that Balzac evidently conceived of it at the time of Davin's Introductions, before it had begun to take shape on paper. Yet it scarcely has as its topic 'le repos après le mouvement . . . les cicatrices après les blessures' . . . 'les cheveux blancs de la vieillesse expérimentée' mingling with 'les blondes touffes de l'enfance'. That is perhaps why Balzac removed it to the Provincial category in 1844; but in the end he reverted to his original intention. *Le Contrat de mariage* could be attached to Provincial Life for two reasons: Paul de Manerville is twenty-seven when his troubles begin, and Bordeaux is the scene of his initial tribulations; but it remained as a scene of Private Life.

The attribution of Parisian scenes is logically more clear, even though Balzac vacillated over the question whether *Le père Goriot* should be allocated to Parisian or Private Life. As time went on, this third category acquired more and more stability, for the simple reason that Paris became the favoured setting in which Balzac chose to pursue his study of professions and avocations—the merchant in *César Birotteau*, the Civil Servant in *Les Employés*, the banker in *La maison Nucingen*, the journalist in the second part of *Illusions perdues*, and the artist in *Pierre Grassou* and elsewhere. He never reached the point of devising a special sub-category for such stories, although *La Fille aux yeux d'or*, in its introductory part, had implied the promise of attention to the different walks of Parisian life. But he did sometimes think in terms of other sub-categories. The 1832 title of *Le Curé de Tours* —'Les Célibataires'—gave him a clue first of all for the Provincial scene of *Pierrette* (1840) and then for that of *La Rabouilleuse* (1841–3). The 'bachelor' series belongs logically enough to the Provincial compartment, since the celibates concerned are usually the centre of a 'tempête dans un verre d'eau'. Other divisions however cut spasmodically across the Provincial series. Two Provincial studies, *La Vieille Fille* (1836) and *Le Cabinet des antiques* (1836–9), were bracketed together in 1844 as 'Les Rivalités', one aspect of their subjects being the struggle between individuals and social classes in the town of Alençon. In 1843 *La Muse du département* was to suggest a subordinate series 'Les Parisiens en province', and later still *Le Cabinet des antiques* seemed likely to provide the nucleus for a counter-series 'Les Provinciaux à Paris'. These were ideas Balzac never found time to develop. *Pierrette* also suggested a promising series of 'Poor Relations'; but when the two authentic 'Parents pauvres' scenes—*La cousine Bette* and *Le cousin Pons*—materialized in 1846–7, they were unmistakably Parisian in setting, tone and atmosphere.

These few considerations reveal some of the weak points in Balzac's scheme, a brilliant improvisation prompted by certain aspects of his extant works but undoubtedly also inspired by the desire to deal with every facet of French life. The categories devised in 1834 proved useful as a means of provisional grouping; but Balzac was not so pedantically systematic as to let them tie his hands in the future. This determination to preserve his creative freedom became apparent almost before the ink from Davin's pen was dry. Naturally enough, the period immediately succeeding the revelation of Balzac's ultimate purpose was applied primarily to the task of completing the 1833 contract with Mme Béchet for the twelve volumes of the 'Études de Mœurs' and the 1834 contract with Werdet for the thirty volumes of 'Études philosophiques', which pressure of other commitments eventually reduced to twenty. Werdet had to take over the completion of the 'Études de Mœurs' by publishing the third and fourth volumes of Provincial Life scenes in February 1837. By that time Werdet himself had ceased to be Balzac's 'sole publisher'. It is true that the third group of five volumes of 'Études philosophiques' was published with his name on the title-page in July 1837; nevertheless the real publishers were Delloye and Lecou. The last group of five volumes was not published until 1840, when it appeared over Souverain's name with the title *Livre des Douleurs*.

Stories already published provided the greater part of both series, and it looks as if Balzac's first concern was to meet his contracts. For this purpose he had no scruples about moving his stories from one category to another, or about providing temporary homes for hitherto uncollected stories in categories for which they were not pre-eminently or permanently suited. Since the four Béchet 'Private Life' volumes were complete by November 1835 he gave no further attention to the compartment for several years. In 1834 and 1835 he had had virtually to create the Parisian cadre, with *L'Histoire des Treize* as a nucleus, in order to satisfy Mme Béchet's demands; *Le père Goriot* was not to achieve classification as a Parisian life study until 1843, and then it was only a temporary one. Of the rest *Sarrasine*, which had started life as a 'conte philosophique', alone entered the Parisian cadre to remain there for good and all. *Les Marana* only remained in it until 1846, when it became a Philosophical Study. *Étude de Femme* (for the present redubbed *Profil de marquise*) and *Madame Firmiani*, which had both been philosophical tales in 1831 and 1832 respectively, became Parisian Life studies in June

1835, and were shifted to Private Life in 1842. Even *Le colonel Chabert* (temporarily *La Comtesse à deux maris*), so patently Parisian, was finally destined for 'Private Life' in Balzac's posthumous notes. Three other stories, originally scenes of Private Life, now became Parisian in November 1835, but were restored to their original compartment in 1842: they were *La Bourse*, *Une double Famille* (still entitled *La Femme vertueuse* in spite of Davin's objection to the title as cynical) and *Le papa Gobseck*, which did not obtain its shortened title of *Gobseck* until 1842.[1]

For the completion in February 1837 of Mme Béchet's provincial stories mentioned above, Balzac put together three tales of 1832 under the title *La grande Bretèche*[2] *ou Les trois Vengeances* and wrote *La vieille Fille* and the first part of *Illusions perdues*. But during the same period he was much more occupied with the task of swelling out the 'Études philosophiques'. To this series he added two short stories in 1835: *Un Drame au bord de la mer*, which one may regard as a by-product of the *Louis Lambert* inspiration, since his 'spécialiste' hero and the latter's fiancée, Pauline de Villenoix, figure in it, and *Melmoth réconcilié*. They were of such a nature as to remain definitively in this series. So also were two of the stories first printed in Balzac's *Chronique de Paris*: the second part of *L'Enfant maudit* and *Le Secret des Ruggieri*, which was later to form the second part of the philosophical study *Sur Catherine de Médicis*. Such was not the case with the other contributions to the same short-lived periodical: *Facino Cane*, which was lodged among the 'Études philosophiques' in 1837 but passed to the Parisian category in 1844; *L'Interdiction* and *La Messe de l'athée*, both of which, temporarily philosophical (the former in 1836, the latter in 1837), became 'Parisian' for some years, and were finally designated by Balzac as Scenes of Private Life. Even *César Birotteau* was thought of in 1834 as a philosophical study, although by 1837 Balzac was preparing it for publication as an 'Histoire Parisienne', which it so evidently was.

Obviously then the criteria given in the Davin Introductions were uncertain, and expediency was at least as important a ruling

[1] Many of these intermediate changes were apparently decided in 1840. See article by M. André Chancerel.

[2] See above 31–3.

principle as reasoned classification. As we watch Balzac advancing to the conquest of his imperfectly charted domain, we are aware of continued improvisation: a multitude of projects adapted to momentary purposes, incompletely executed and abandoned for new ones whose fate it often was to be superseded in their turn. Wave followed wave of heterogenous creative activity. Balzac's *daemon* drove him onwards with fiery energy, and of few authors could it be more aptly said that 'the spirit bloweth whither it listeth'. Behind Davin's Introductions of 1834–5 we can sense Balzac reaching out in all directions, carrying in his head some works which were never to come to fruition and others whose growth was slow and painful, like *Illusions perdues*, conceived in 1833, promised and discussed in Davin's Introductions and else-where, but only passing beyond the embryonic stage so late as 1837, 1839 and 1843.

Are we then to ignore the categories as being of little effect? That they furnish no satisfactory basis for a study of the 'Comédie Humaine' in the abstract is unintentionally demonstrated by the submissively systematic, though usefully informative compilation which Marcel Barrière produced in 1890. They lend themselves only reluctantly to the purpose of this present study, which is to survey the 'Comédie Humaine' in its historical development. The task becomes increasingly difficult. Balzac had so much on his hands at once that it is often impossible to say to which member of a group of stories chronological priority should be assigned. None the less, it is possible to discern lines of development in the clusters of subjects on which he was working at successive moments in his career, just as it is possible to detect the emergence of groups of characters who spring to life during a given period and are forthwith distributed among the novels of that period. An attempt will be made here to examine Balzac's productivity from about 1835 with those ends in view, but without losing sight of the categories of the 'Études sociales' as a framework which may indeed have been forced to bend to his needs, but which he never dreamed of discarding.

VII

PHILOSOPHICAL POT-POURRI,
1835–43

i. Further fantasies: *Un drame au bord de la mer* (1835);
Melmoth réconcilié (1835); *Facino Cane* (1836)

THE FIRST TWO STORIES are of 1835, the third of 1836. The
seaside drama recaptures the horror of 1830 tales like *El Verdugo*.
Balzac's art is applied to the task of conjuring up the forbidding
figure of an old Breton fisherman who is atoning in dreadful soli-
tude for a murder dictated by his own integrity: he has executed
his own son as an incorrigible criminal. To quote Félix Davin, 'Là
aussi l'idée a porté ses ravages, la paternité, à son tour, est
devenue tueuse.' Pierre Cambremer's history is narrated to Louis
Lambert, who is enjoying a period of convalescence between two
bouts of mental derangement; and this circumstance throws welcome light on the companionship between Louis Lambert and his
fiancée Pauline, so much left in the shade in *Louis Lambert*. An
incidental feature of the story is the expression it gives to Balzac's
sympathy for extreme poverty, that of a lobster-fisher who cannot
afford to fish from a boat, and sells his hard-won lobsters for
15 sous.

Melmoth réconcilié bears witness to Balzac's abiding admiration
for Maturin's famous thriller. Its off-hand, and somewhat mocking use of the supernatural, as well as the apparent inconsequence
of its conclusion, recalls *L'Élixir de longue vie*. Though short, it is
of a composite nature. It begins with a 'physiologie', that of the
bank cashier, in this case the ex-soldier, Castanier, envisaged as a
human machine destined to subordination and routine; and this
gives Balzac an opportunity to repeat his denunciation of the
financier as a law-abiding 'corsair', and to offer his reader a rapid

glance at the Paris Bourse and the high-priests of speculation. It also establishes links with *Le père Goriot* in the person of Nucingen, and with *La Peau de chagrin* in the person of the courtesan Aquilina.

The philosophical core of the story lies in the repentance of Sir John Melmoth, a dour and sinister Irishman of puritanical bearing who has grown weary of the supernatural powers, which include that of reading other people's minds and foreseeing the future, conferred on him by his pact with the Devil. Satan alone can persist eternally in the love of evil; to know everything within the human range of knowledge creates a thirst for the Unknowable. Terrifyingly ubiquitous—Balzac enjoyed sketching him as he had done with Argow the Pirate, and was still to do with the irrepressible Vautrin—Melmoth tracks down Castanier, driven to desperation by the demands of an expensive mistress, forces him to take over the pact, and dies in the odour of sanctity. The satisfaction Castanier derives from his new-found power and wealth is short-lived, and gives place to the fear of Hell. So this new wild-ass's skin, the pact with Satan, passes swiftly from hand to hand, and its virtue is squandered in a few days' debauch by its final possessor. By this time satire and humour have got the better of serious intention in Balzac's mind, and the story ends, incoherently, with mockery of German pedantry. Indeed, in a note appended to the edition of 1835,[1] he confesses that his intention had been to make fun of Parisian acquisitiveness—the original Melmoth could find no one to relieve him of his bargain with the Devil, whereas in Paris he would have found would-be substitutes tumbling over one another in their haste to succeed him. The description of solemn religious rites (the requiem for Melmoth's soul) does little to mitigate the frivolity of this impetuous improvisation.

Facino Cane[2] ranks high among Balzac's short stories because it begins with reminiscences of the Rue Lesdiguières period and contains his reflexions on his powers of observation and the gift of sympathetic divination accorded to him.[3] Moreover, though of slender proportions, it is one of his most successful blends of

---

[1] See *Éd. Déf.*, XXII, 417-18.
[2] *Chronique de Paris*, 17 Mar. 1836.   [3] See above, 13.

realism and fantasy. The opening scene is a working-class wedding-dance in a cheap wine-shop. The band consists of three blind men, one of whom, the clarinettist, is singled out as an extraordinary person. After the dance comes the unfolding of a picturesque story which in one respect anticipates Dumas' *Monte Cristo*: that of the clarinettist as an erstwhile Italian prince imprisoned at Venice for his escapades; his discovery of the Doges' treasure in a cellar through which he digs out his passage to freedom; his escape with part of the treasure; his squandering of it until blindness and a woman's infidelity reduce him to beggary; and his desire to take the narrator of the story back to Venice with him to recover the rest of the gold and precious stones.

This little masterpiece gives something of the eerie impression of *Les sept Vieillards* in Baudelaire's *Fleurs du mal*. Also it is Balzac's most concise study of an obsession akin to those of Félix Grandet, Maître Cornélius or Gobseck. 'J'ai pour l'or', says Facino Cane, 'une monomanie dont la satisfaction est si nécessaire à ma vie que, dans toutes les situations où je me suis trouvé, je n'ai jamais été sans or sur moi; je manie constamment de l'or. Je sens l'or. Quoique aveugle, je m'arrête devant les boutiques des joailliers.' Perhaps Facino Cane's hallucination is one of the forms in which dreams of enrichment came to Balzac himself, or at any rate a symbol of the motive which lay behind his financial struggles and his perpetual calculations of affluence awaiting him round the corner.

ii. Personalities and Plots: *La Messe de l'athée*;[1] *L'Interdiction*[2]

These two works, the short story and the long *nouvelle*, are on the borderline between philosophical and Parisian studies. The theme of the former is the gratitude of a free-thinking doctor, Desplein (modelled on the famous surgeon Dupuytren), which impels him to have masses said for the soul of a Paris water-carrier, the Auvergnat Bourgeat, who had befriended him as a needy student during the early years of the Restoration.

[1] *Chronique de Paris*, 3 Jan. 1836.
[2] Ibid., Jan.–Feb. 1836.

La Messe de l'athée is not only an effective story. It is admirable for the touching portrayal of the water-carrier, a man who, though eking out a precarious existence, is the incarnation of simple, pious selflessness. It gives a full-length portrait of the hard, avaricious, unsociable, apparently misanthropic, but fundamentally benevolent Desplein, a new addition to the reappearing characters of the 'Comédie Humaine'. It also gives fresh information about Horace Bianchon, who is deemed to be telling the story in 1851, and who has developed, since his student days at the Pension Vauquer, into a busy doctor, the medical consultant of society hostesses; in spite of that a man of integrity and candour, charitable to the poor, sociable and faithful in his friendships; in fact one of the upright members of Balzac's vast company.[1] He is however one of those who, throughout the novels, like Henri de Marsay, have to be content with brief appearances and the addition of incidental touches to enrich the impression we have of their character. The part he plays in *L'Interdiction* is scarcely less ancillary; but he still stands as a foil to the unprincipled climber Rastignac, as a man with a sense of real values, disgusted with and hostile to the elegant and haughty women whom Rastignac uses for his own advancement. Like Bianchon, the latter has stepped straight out of the pages of *Le père Goriot*, but here Balzac appears to have had a special motive for bringing him back. The Rastignac of *La Peau de chagrin*, *Étude de Femme* (the hero of this story was not identified with him until the edition of 1835), and *Le père Goriot* are not perfectly fused.[2] The Rastignac of *L'Interdiction* seems to bridge the gap between the still naïve and good-hearted protector of Goriot and the 'condottiere de l'intelligence'[3] of *La Peau de chagrin*.

But *L'Interdiction* (*The Commission of Lunacy*) has greater importance. It is one of the best of Balzac's fictions. Its subject is a battle between an examining magistrate, Jean-Jules Popinot—shabby, ugly, unambitious, generous but wide-awake—and Balzac's most hard-faced and hard-hearted *femme du monde*, the

---

[1] For the identification of his prototype see Borel; according to this article Bianchon's model was a protégé of Dupuytren, one Mardochée Marx. But see also below, 344, n. 1.

[2] See Pommier (3).

[3] This expression occurs in *L'Interdiction*.

Marquise d'Espard, over her attempt to get the management of her husband's estate handed over to her on the ground that he is out of his mind. This entails a succession of typical and excellent Balzacian 'scenes': a conversation between Bianchon and Rastignac, in the course of which the latter, enlisted in Mme d'Espard's cause, tries to persuade Bianchon to use his influence with Popinot, who is his uncle; a glimpse of Popinot in his dirty old house in the Rue du Fouarre, first of all dispensing alms to the poor of his quarter, then reading with sarcastic comment the case put forward by Mme d'Espard's solicitor[1] in support of her petition of lunacy; Popinot's interrogation of the Marquise, during which she and her sinister brother-in-law are unable to disguise the flimsiness of her case; his interrogation of the Marquis d'Espard, from which it becomes clear that the latter is no lunatic but a man of unusual honesty determined to make restitution for a theft committed by his ancestors; and a curt scene in the Palais de Justice where Popinot learns that the Marquise has pulled strings in order to take the case out of his hands, knowing full well in whose favour he would make his report. So corruption and intrigue combine to prevent the triumph of justice. Readers of the 'Comédie Humaine' were not to learn until much later—in *Splendeurs et misères des courtisanes*—that private influence again intervened, in the person of Lucien de Rubempré, to defeat injustice. For the moment, at the end of the story, the Marquise's victory seems probable. Lucien's intervention was no doubt an afterthought.

Judge Popinot stands out, with Benassis, Mathias and Derville, as one of Balzac's rare good men who are not imbeciles, but a match for the rogues of either sex in which 'La Comédie Humaine' abounds. Like Victor Hugo, Balzac is often inclined to combine the grotesque and the sublime in the characterization of the good; but he confines the grotesque element in Popinot to personal appearance, habits of dress and negligence in mode of living. There is nothing sickly or priggish about this upright judge, just as there is nothing, in this story, of the fairy-tale with a happy ending. Popinot is pitted against people whose worldliness and

[1] In 1836 one Plumet, later replaced by Desroches, who was first born to the 'Comédie Humaine' in *La maison Nucingen*, composed 1837–8.

wickedness put his competence to the test. In this work Balzac
continues his study of fashionable women. To the Duchesse de
Carigliano, the Duchesse de Langeais, Mme de Beauséant, Mme
Firmiani, Mme d'Aiglemont, and others, he adds, by portraying
Mme d'Espard, the complete type of 'la femme à la mode'. After
the retirement of the Duchesse de Langeais, the Vicomtesse de
Beauséant and Mme Firmiani as reigning queens of society, their
sceptre passed, we are told, to Mme d'Aiglemont,[1] from whom it
was subsequently snatched (the events of *L'Interdiction* belong to
1828) by Mme d'Espard. She is mercilessly characterized by
Bianchon, who has learned as a doctor to read below the surface
of a woman's make-up and the 'singeries' of her behaviour in
public, in order to warn Rastignac that he would be rash to stake
his future on the reception of the Marquise's favours.

Ta femme à la mode ne sent rien, sa fureur de plaisir a sa cause dans
son envie de réchauffer sa nature froide, elle veut des émotions et des
jouissances . . . comme elle a plus de tête que de cœur, elle sacrifie à
son triomphe les passions vraies et les amis, comme un général envoie
au feu ses plus dévoués lieutenants pour gagner une bataille. La femme
à la mode n'est plus une femme; elle n'est ni mère, ni épouse, ni
amante; elle est un sexe dans le cerveau, médicalement parlant; aussi
ta marquise a-t-elle tous les symptômes de la monstruosité: elle a le bec
de l'oiseau de proie, l'œil clair et froid, la parole douce, elle est polie
comme l'acier d'une mécanique, elle émeut tout, moins le cœur.

As wife, Mme d'Espard has deserted the Marquis as soon as the
generous purpose of restitution dictated to him a reduction in his
standard of living. As mother, she has ceded to him the custody
of their two sons—the more willingly because the presence of
stalwart children is inconvenient to a woman who wishes to
remain on the right side of twenty-six. Her greed and luxurious-
ness are brought out the more strongly by the penury to which her
husband—eccentric only in so far as he is absorbed in the task of
privately printing and publishing an *Histoire pittoresque de la
Chine*—has condemned himself. In introducing the Marquis
d'Espard to his readers Balzac has made his first notable effort to

[1] Replaced in later editions of *L'Interdiction* by the Duchesse de Maufrigneuse, whose actual entry into the Balzacian world dates only from *Le Cabinet
des antiques* (1838).

paint an authentic representative of the real aristocracy of France, faithful to the traditions and responsibilities of his race.

Considéré comme un débris de ce grand corps nommé la féodalité, M. d'Espard méritait une admiration respectueuse. S'il se croyait par le sang au-dessus des autres hommes, il croyait également à toutes les obligations de la noblesse; il possédait les vertus et la force qu'elle exige.

Also he was bringing up his children to a true sense of the dignity of their rank and the qualities it demands. These two boys make only a brief appearance in *L'Interdiction*, but it is a graceful one; and it is interesting to see Balzac piercing through the façade of aristocratic life, which he had had many opportunities to observe since 1830, to a creditable reality which the showy brilliance of the more emancipated nobility served to conceal. That there was an element of pitying contempt in his attitude to the more solid and virtuous gentry becomes more evident when one reads a work which he was already beginning in 1836, *Le Cabinet des antiques*. But this disdain was a legacy of his dealings with the legitimist party in 1832–3, and was born of impatience with the rigidity and immobility of their attitude and mental processes.

Works like *L'Interdiction*, in which Balzac's social snobbery and native sentimentality remain dormant, show that he was able to achieve genuine realism in his portrayal of 'high-life' as well as in his presentation of the ways and outlook of the middle classes. But not even the populace is neglected in *L'Interdiction*. Popinot has a clientele of down-and-outs who collect in his ground-floor consulting-room to await their turn with the shrewd old judge who will assess their characters, weigh their merits and award them the succour he deems appropriate. These types of paupers Balzac himself recommends to the attention of a modern Rembrandt after having sketched the silhouette of half a dozen with his own pen. As in *Un Drame au bord de la mer*, his sympathy is evident, but he cherishes no illusions about the submissiveness of these mendicants. 'La résignation de ces âmes, aux prises avec tous les besoins de la vie, était une spéculation fondée sur la bienfaisance.' They constitute as it were the spiritual *milieu* in which Judge Popinot lives, and they provide better furniture for Balzac's novel than the streets and houses whose minute description has by now become an instinctive part of his technique.

iii. Musicalities: *Gambara*[1] and *Massimilla Doni*[2]

These two works are a by-product of the Italian journeys and also the fruits of an enthusiasm for music which seems to have overtaken Balzac in the middle eighteen-thirties. The characters in *Gambara*, dedicated to his 'secretary', de Belloy, to whom he pays tribute for having suggested the subject, are nearly all Italian, though the action is situated in Paris. The setting of *Massimilla Doni* is entirely in Venice. It sings the praises of the Venetian aristocracy and their way of life, and disparages French manners and culture about the same time as Stendhal was doing the like in the 'Avertissement' written for *La Chartreuse de Parme*. It extols the Opera-House of Venice as a social and artistic centre. In both stories music is the dominant theme, although in *Gambara* Balzac appears to take sides with the Germanophiles in the current controversy over the respective merits of Italian and German music. In *Massimilla Doni* the situation is reversed, and Rossini is lauded to the skies.

In what respect are they 'philosophical studies'? Balzac's Preface of 1839[3] links them and *Le Chef d'œuvre inconnu* to *La Peau de chagrin*, as providing further illustrations of 'le désordre que la pensée arrivée à tout son développement produit dans l'âme de l'artiste'. Gambara is an eccentric musician who has settled in Paris after much roving, and within the domain of his art is pursuing a chimæra similar to that of Frenhofer. In his view music has its roots in physics and mathematics, and is therefore a science as well as an art. As a composer—he has also invented a fantastic instrument, the *panharmonicon*—he is trying to go behind and beyond the established rules and principles of euphony and build his *magnum opus* on a purely intellectual theory of the relation between sound, thought and emotion. The result, when he tries out his composition on an audience, however sympathetic, is a series of excruciating cacophonies which earn him his repute as a

[1] *Revue et Gazette musicale de Paris*, July–August 1837.

[2] Begun 1837, completed and published 1839 (by Souverain, together with *Une Fille d'Ève*). Republished with *Gambara, Les Proscrits* and *Séraphita*, in *Le Livre des douleurs*, Souverain, 1840. On both works, see Regard (1).

[3] *Éd. Déf.* XXII, 528—originally a letter of 29 May 1837, addressed to the editor of the *Revue et Gazette Musicale*.

madman. An inference we might draw from this is that Balzac-Gambara was looking forward into the future and anticipating modern schools of music, just as Balzac-Frenhofer had perhaps foreseen some modern schools of painting. It would probably be an unwarranted inference. In so far as Balzac was serious in writing this curious *nouvelle*, he was trying to link up his newly acquired notions about music with the fantastic physics already outlined in *Louis Lambert*.[1] But how serious was he? Jacques Barzun has suggested that the detailed programme for the opera *Mahomet*, which Gambara is made to unfold with such enthusiasm, was concocted as a hoax by Berlioz and Balzac together.[2] The theory that Balzac may have been writing with his tongue in his cheek is supported by the fact that, when Gambara is drunk, he is sufficiently alive to sensation and emotion, as being the essential elements of music, to produce ravishing melodies and harmonies, and to share the popular enthusiasm for Meyerbeer's *Robert le Diable*. And Gambara has a comic counterpart in the restaurant-keeper, Giardini, who entertains a similar delusion about his own culinary art; when sober he conceives and concocts dishes that no one can eat; when intoxicated his cooking is normal and palatable. Yet Balzac was always too easily excited by the ingenuity of his own word-spinnings not to have accorded some basic sympathy to Gambara's crazy dreams.

Massimilla Doni is a case-book of curious aberrations. There are two melomaniacs in it. The one, Capraja, finds the most exquisite joys in the 'roulades' of tenors and sopranos. The other, the Sicilian Duke Cataneo, an aged debauchee and complaisant husband of Massimilla, finds a quasi-erotic or quasi-epileptic voluptuousness in the 'accord parfait' achieved by the marriage of two voices or that of one voice with the strains of the violin. Another pathological case is that of the patriot Vendramini, whose sorrow on behalf of an enslaved and decadent Venice drives him to the pipe-dreams of opium. But the main theme of the story is the strange love of Prince Emilio Memmi for Massimilla Cataneo. It is so absolute that Massimilla's beauty and purity, and even the

[1] Gambara, he says in the Preface quoted above, is 'the Louis Lambert of music'.
[2] Barzun, t. I, 262.

knowledge that his love is returned, induce impotence in him in spite of his violent desires, which he can satisfy only in the arms of the *prima donna* La Tinti, whom he not only does not love, but treats with contumely. La Tinti in turn is loved by the operatic tenor, Genovese, whose passion is so intense that when he is singing with her and trying to put his whole soul into his voice, he succeeds only in emitting raucous noises which resemble the bellowing of a stag or the braying of a donkey. From his particular frustration Memmi is rescued by the stratagem of a French doctor, whom today we should no doubt call a psychiatrist: the simple substitution of Massimilla for La Tinti under the cover of darkness. No such subterfuge is needed to restore Genovese to sanity and vocal normality.

This story of strange inhibitions borders on the comic, and imposes a strain on average credulity. The beautiful, graceful and cultured Massimilla is an attractive figure, but her credibility reposes on the belief, which Balzac shared with Stendhal, that a passionate Italian will shrink before no crime or, as in this case, no self-abasement for the sake of the man she loves. So Massimilla plays the courtesan to save the desperate Memmi from suicide, and La Tinti, herself madly in love with Memmi, consents to the substitution and consoles Genovese instead. It is not surprising that George Moore admired this story, even though it arrives at the prosaic conclusion of Massimilla's pregnancy. For in *Massimilla Doni*, as in many of Balzac's most romantic stories, we are in the end brought down with a bump to earthy reality. *Gambara* also is suffused throughout with a human interest: the devotion of Marianna Gambara to her ineffectual husband, her flight with Andrea Marcosini when she realizes that his mania is incurable, and her return after Andrea has grown tired of her to take up again her role as blind-man's dog to this penurious, wayward genius.

An aspect of these two stories which remains to be considered is their value as an incursion into the realms of musical criticism.[1] Balzac's taste in music and his comprehension of music scarcely rise above the elementary. Early in 1835 one of his female cor-

[1] For Balzac's knowledge of music see Bertault (1) and Maurice-Amour (1) and (2).

respondents complained that, at the Paris Opera, he paid more attention to the audience than to the performers. Yet he knew many musicians—Rossini, Berlioz, Liszt and Chopin—and went often to concerts at the Conservatoire. For *Gambara* he studied J. Fr. Fétis' *La Musique mise à la portée de tout le monde* (1830), and round about 1836 and 1837 received regular instruction in the meaning and technique of music from that eccentric composer and musical factotum, Jacques Strunz, who was later to provide him with a model for Schmucke in *Une Fille d'Ève* and *Le cousin Pons.* Strunz schooled him for *Gambara,* and Balzac postponed the completion of *Massimilla Doni* until he had deepened his knowledge of music; the work was dedicated to Strunz. This curiosity about the technicalities of music bore fruit in the *morceaux de bravoure* with which both stories are sprinkled; descriptions of operas like Gambara's *Mahomet* and Meyerbeer's *Robert le Diable,* and, above all, in *Massimilla Doni,* Rossini's *Moses.* Massimilla herself is entrusted with the musicographer's task in this latter case.

Balzac's performance is not convincing. His attempts at technical description are pitiable; he writes of keys and modulations and cadences, of *stretti, ottetti* and *quintetti* with the naïvety of a school-boy. From a study of these efforts—to which we may add the description of Sœur Thérèse's organ-playing in *La Duchesse de Langeais,* of Beethoven's C minor Symphony in *César Birotteau,* and the fiction in *Modeste Mignon* of the heroine composing a ballad tune without knowing a note of music—the fact clearly emerges that Balzac's comprehension of music is entirely dependent on his familiarity with Opera. As painting had been for Diderot, music for Balzac is ancillary to literature. The art of the musician consists in supporting a story or evoking the feelings appropriate to such and such an emotional or dramatic situation. Musical criticism consists in giving free rein to the purely individual reveries which the hearing of music by a layman evokes. As Massimilla says, '. . . chacun de nous interprète la musique au gré de sa douleur ou de sa joie, de ses espérances ou de son désespoir'.

And yet Balzac makes his Massimilla adumbrate the theory of synæsthesia: 'Quand je vous ai parlé des sombres couleurs, du froid des notes employées dans l'introduction de *Mosé*, n'étais-je pas autant dans le vrai que vos critiques en nous parlant de la couleur de tel ou tel écrivain? . . .' This theory, epitomized by Baudelaire in his famous line *Les parfums, les couleurs, et les sons se répondent*, was certainly 'in the air' long before Baudelaire and the Symbolists took it over. It probably came to Balzac from Swedenborg, as a sentence in *Séraphita* suggests—'La lumière enfantait la mélodie, la mélodie enfantait la lumière, les couleurs étaient lumière et mélodie'—but it was a current article of the Illuminist creed, and he may have discussed it with his musician friends, Rossini, Berlioz or Strunz. Also, in connection with the tribulations of Genovese, we find him voicing a more general æsthetic principle, applicable to any and every art. Genovese's trouble is that he is striving to express, through his art as a singer, the white heat of his emotion. The French doctor puts his finger on the spot:

Quand un artiste a le malheur d'être plein de la passion qu'il veut exprimer, il ne saurait la peindre, car il est la chose même au lieu d'en être l'image. L'art procède du cerveau et non du cœur. Quand votre sujet vous domine, vous en êtes l'esclave et non le maître.

iv. Philosophy of History: *L'Enfant maudit* and *Sur Catherine de Médicis*

We now approach two works whose component parts were written at wide intervals of time. A first instalment of *L'Enfant maudit* had appeared in January 1831; it was finished in 1836,[1] at a time when Balzac was also occupied with *Le Secret des Ruggieri*.[2] *L'Enfant maudit* is not a historical novel, but it does owe its creation in part to Balzac's interest in the Wars of Religion and their aftermath. The Comte d'Hérouville, father of the boy whom he believes to be the fruit of his wife's adultery and whose birth, upbringing and premature death the novel relates, is a product of those anarchic times: Spartan, brutal, tyrannical and vengeful. The opening scene, the grim castle in which Jeanne d'Hérouville waits in terror for the doctor whom her suspicious husband selects for her confinement, is reminiscent of Scott, but is also a good

[1] *Chronique de Paris*, 9 Oct. 1836.   [2] Ibid., Dec. 1836–Jan. 1837.

sample of the authentic Balzacian style in sombre description and the narration of dramatic events; it has a flavour reminding the reader of the Hugo who was to write *Éviradnus* and the Gautier who was to describe the castle of Segonzac in *Le capitaine Fracasse*.

But once the jealous Count has for a time stepped out of the picture and Balzac has turned his attention exclusively to mother and child, and more so still in the instalment of 1836 (*La Perle brisée*), where he relates the idyllic love between the frail and unworldly Étienne d'Hérouville and the equally fragile Gabrielle de Beauvaloir, the novel takes on a good deal of the lyricism and sentimentality of *Le Lys dans la vallée*. The novel as a whole appears to be a response to several urges inside Balzac. The 'amoureuse maternité' of Jeanne d'Hérouville is probably the expression of Balzac's yearning after a maternal devotion he himself was conscious of having lacked. The tragedy of Étienne and Gabrielle is patently devised as an illustration of the theory of angelic souls adumbrated in *Louis Lambert* and *Séraphita*: exquisite but delicate beings who are exiles in this world and cannot stand up to the rough-and-tumble of life. At the end of the story the young lovers are puffed out by the blast of d'Hérouville's wrath at seeing himself thwarted over the conventional marriage he has arranged for his son. In addition the glances which Balzac throws from time to time at astrology and the occult sciences renew in part the atmosphere of *Les Proscrits* and anticipate that of *Le Secret des Ruggieri*.

The odd fact about Balzac's second great attempt at historical resuscitation, *Sur Catherine de Médicis*,[1] is that it was written backwards. Part III—*Les deux Rêves*[2]—belongs to 1830. Part II—*Le Secret* (later *La Confidence*) *des Ruggieri*[3]—belongs to the period 1836–7. Part III—*Le Martyr calviniste*—appeared as *Les Lecamus* in *Le Siècle* in March–April 1841, but it had been announced under various titles at various times since 1837, and existed at least in fragmentary form several years before 1841.

[1] On the whole work, and especially the second part of it, see Crain (2), an excellent study. It is a great pity that Dr. Crain's critical edition of *Le Secret des Ruggieri* has had to remain in manuscript.

[2] See above, 35–6.

[3] *Chronique de Paris*, Dec. 1836–Jan. 1837.

Then in 1842-3 the whole was published by Souverain as *Catherine de Médicis expliquée*, with a long Preface which, in the 'Comédie Humaine' edition of 1846, was modified and served as Introduction to the at last definitive work bearing its definitive title. Naturally readers of the 'Comédie Humaine' read the work in its logical order, but here it will not be without interest to examine the parts in the historical order of their composition.

Like *Les Chouans*, *Sur Catherine de Médicis*, for which Balzac had been gathering material since about 1825, stems from Scott, but from a Scott corrected and enriched by Balzac's own philosophy of history, two elements in which may here be relevantly emphasized. The first is his conviction of the importance of human passions, and of women, in history. The second is his idea of the continuous action of thought in moulding the actions of France from age to age. This was the motive behind his abortive plan of October 1836 for introducing into the 'Études philosophiques' '. . . autant de scènes historiques qu'il y a de siècles depuis l'invasion des Francs jusqu'en 1800, pour montrer le ravage des hautes idées dans la politique, ce qui a fait l'esprit des siècles, l'antagonisme, et cela dans les proportions du Secret des Ruggieri.'[1] Balzac never had time to apply this general principle to the centuries preceding the Renaissance, but in regard to the modern era it found particular expression in two ideas which became tantamount to an obsession in his historical thought.

The first one had been tersely formulated, in June 1834, in *Les Aventures administratives d'une idée heureuse*.

. . . les idées de Luther ont engendré Calvin, qui engendra Bayle, qui engendra Voltaire, qui engendra l'opposition constitutionnelle, enfin l'esprit de discussion et d'examen.[2]

In brief, minimizing the importance of the Humanist movement, Balzac blames the Reformation for undermining the spirit of hierarchy and discipline in France, for encouraging rationalism and the philosophic movement and thus preparing the Revolution of 1789, the fall of the monarchy and the triumph of the parliamentary system. This is an excessive simplification of history, but

[1] *Pensées, Sujets, Fragmens*, Crépet, 138. Quoted by Crain (2), 290.
[2] Conard, *O.D.* II, 662.

it has some justification, for modern political thought can be traced back to Huguenot criticism of absolute monarchy during the Wars of Religion. The second of Balzac's *idées fixes* is a corollary of the first. It is that Catherine de Medici, a much misunderstood woman, was the only politician in sixteenth-century France who really understood the issues at stake. Her policy alone could have saved the monarchy. Only the destruction of the Huguenot party in its infancy and the eradication of Calvinism could have restored stability and good government. The only thing wrong about the St. Bartholomew massacre, engineered by Catherine, was that it was hastily improvised and imperfectly executed. Throughout her effective political career (1559 onwards) Catherine's policy, apparently tortuous and necessarily opportunist, was at bottom consistent—and salutary. She should therefore be exonerated for the crimes which she committed, or with which she is credited, in pursuit of that policy.

This apologia is the underlying theme for the whole of *Sur Catherine de Médicis*. It is the burden of *Les deux Rêves*, whose chief concern had been to give a convenient setting (an aristocratic salon in 1786) to an invented episode of the terrorist Robespierre's early career: the dream he relates of an interview with Catherine, who defends herself by the argument that a timely blood-letting can prevent rivers of gore from flowing. What this amounts to is the monstrous doctrine, to which Balzac obstinately adhered, that calculated massacre can stem the tide of thought. Had Catherine's holocaust been more thorough, the Reign of Terror would never have happened.

Le Secret des Ruggieri gives a close view of Catherine and her son Charles IX in their mutual antagonism during 1573. Here, by Balzac's own showing, Catherine is a wicked and odious woman, ruled by the lust for domination and the superstition of astrology; using her sons and her satellites as expendable instruments; corrupting the youthful Charles and encouraging him in voluptuous excesses in order to diminish his will to rule—the favour she shows to his mistress, Marie Touchet, is part of this design. None the less, Balzac's sympathy goes out to her, for when great issues are pending, considerations of private morality are beside the point. But his sympathy goes also to the harassed

Charles, worn-out at twenty-four, alternating between spurts of febrile energy (his nocturnal excursion over the roof-tops of Paris is one of these) and moods of bitter lassitude, able to rely only on the affection and fidelity of Marie Touchet.

As a historical resuscitation[1] the work has many points of interest. In conformity with the Romantic habit, Balzac emphasizes the sixteenth-century addiction to alchemy, astrology and the use of poisons from Italy. Again in accordance with the method and style of Scott, he gives vivid glimpses of the Renaissance Louvre and its purlieus, of court-life under the Valois, with its intriguers and time-servers grouped about the person of the Queen-Mother. There are admirable scenes and dialogues between Charles and Catherine, Charles and Marie Touchet, and the two Gondis who are the tools of Catherine. But the climax of the story is reached when two fascinating figures, the alchemist Lorenzo Ruggieri (probably an invented personage) and his brother Cosimo, purveyor of horoscopes and predictions, both of whom are in league with Catherine and therefore suspect to Charles, are called upon to allay Charles' suspicions in the interview which follows their arrest at his orders. Lorenzo throws dust in Charles' eyes by means of a long lecture on the ultimate aim of alchemy: the prolongation of human life as a goal for which man should strive once he has rid himself of the delusion that he possesses an immortal soul. This lecture brings us back to the occultist fancies of *Les Proscrits*, *Louis Lambert* and *Séraphita*. Balzac treats it as a piece of pompous loquacity and charlatanry, and although it certainly carries the thesis of atheistic materialism a long way, in view of Balzac's addiction to bizarre philosophies we may slightly suspect the sincerity of his implied condemnation. In any case, when Lorenzo arrives at the theme 'L'Europe en est aujourd'hui à la Religion, demain elle attaquera la Royauté', there can be no doubt that his voice is the voice of Balzac.

Oui, Sire . . . si le peuple triomphe, il fera sa Saint-Barthélemi! Quand la religion et la royauté seront abattues, le peuple en viendra aux grands, après les grands il s'en prendra aux riches. Enfin, quand

---

[1] Balzac made liberal use of Dreux de Radier's *Mémoires historiques, critiques, et anecdotes des reines et régentes de France*, first published in 1764. See Crain (2), 351 ff.

l'Europe ne sera plus qu'un troupeau d'hommes sans consistance, parce qu'elle sera sans chefs, elle sera dévorée par de grossiers conquérants.[1]

Les Lecamus, or *Le Martyr calviniste*, is the longest and most fully developed of the three instalments. It narrates events leading up to the Tumult of Amboise (17th March 1560), the death of Francis II (5th December 1560) and the Colloquy of Passy (late 1561).

Balzac's attempts to 'explain' Catherine de Medici, from Part III to Part II, and from Part II to Part I, with which we are here concerned, improve as he moves backwards across the sixteenth century. He now gives a complete and subtle picture of Catherine as the spurned and humiliated widow of Henry II, with the Cardinal of Lorraine and his brother the Duc de Guise dominating the boy-king Francis through his wife Mary Stuart. Against the Guises, who are making a bid for the crown, are ranged the Bourbon princes, Louis de Condé, the feeble Antoine, King of Navarre, and the Catholic but fiery enemy of the Guises, the Constable Anne de Montmorency. Catherine's sole resource is to play them off against one another. The fiction element resides in the invention of Christophe, son of the Parisian furrier Lecamus, who has become a Calvinist, and is commissioned by Calvin's agents, Chaudieu and La Renaudie, acting in conjunction with the Prince de Condé, to take a treaty project between Catherine and the Calvinists to Catherine at Blois, under pretext of supplying the royal ladies with furs. His real purpose is detected by Mary Stuart, and Catherine has to abandon him to interrogation by torture, which he suffers bravely without betraying her or Condé. The Huguenot plot to seize the person of the King at Amboise is thwarted by the Guises, and Catherine's position becomes entirely precarious until the illness and death of Francis II enable her to turn the tables on the Guises and secure the regency during the minority of Charles IX through the collaboration of Montmorency and the Bourbons.

In *Le Martyr calviniste*, guide-book descriptions of the Castle of Blois are a little overdone, and the desire to bring in personalities of the time—Brantôme, Du Bellay, De Baïf, etc.—is a little too obvious. But once the story gets under way the interest

[1] The quotation is from the final version of the story (Conrad XX, 334).

becomes absorbing: moves and counter-moves between Catherine and the Guises; lovers' meetings between Francis II and Mary Stuart; the arrest of Christophe Lecamus and the gruesome details of his torture; the execution of the rebel nobles captured after their abortive attack on Amboise; the uneasy manœuvres of Catherine who has to feign approval of the Guises' vindictiveness; the lofty heroism of Condé, who also stands in danger of execution; the efforts of the elder Lecamus to save his son; and the duel between Catherine and the Guises around the death-bed of Francis II. It is in this latter scene that the struggle becomes most intense. Catherine's triumph depends on the death of Francis, just as later, in 1573, it will depend on that of her second son, Charles. Francis' life can be saved if the surgeon, Ambroise Paré, is allowed to perform a trepanning operation on him: Catherine succeeds in preventing it. Morally speaking, her action is tantamount to the murder of her son.

The rest of the picture—Catherine playing for time in order to make sure of her victory—was only developed in the Souverain edition of 1842–3. It enables Balzac to switch the interest from Blois to Geneva and show Jean Calvin in conference with his lieutenants, Théodore de Bèze and Chaudieu. All Balzac's anti-Protestant rancour is pressed into service in the portrait he draws of the arrogant, self-centred Man of God, a violent, choleric politician whose aim is to bring France to anarchy and found his theocratic tyranny on the ruins of the monarchy. He even finds significance in Calvin being a Picard, like his forerunner, Peter the Hermit, and his successor, Maximilien Robespierre. In fact the gist of his thesis is that Calvin was the Robespierre of the sixteenth century. 'Sur un théâtre plus vaste que Genève, Calvin eût fait couler plus de sang que n'en a fait couler le sanguinaire apôtre de l'Égalité politique assimilée à l'Égalité catholique.' His attack on this austere bigot is vigorous and stimulating, though it detracts from the dignity of what might otherwise have been a first-rate historical novel. Purity of religious zeal is the last virtue that Balzac will allow either to Calvin, or to the elegant and foppish Théodore de Bèze, or to the French nobles and burghers whose support of Calvin is founded solely on political opportunism or on material interests. Not even the hero of the story, Christophe 'the

Martyr', is allowed to preserve his incorruptibility; in the end we see him profiting by Catherine's gratitude for his refusal to betray her in the torture-chamber, renouncing his heresy, marrying his well-dowered fiancée, and settling down as a Councillor in the Parlement of Paris.

Finally, Balzac put the last touch to this, his latest and most trenchant 'philosophical study' by adding the Preface or Introduction to the composite work published in 1842–3, and then re-published in 1846. This Introduction comprises about fifty pages of political argument and historical narration. The latter consists mainly of a sketch of the rise of the Medici dynasty and a biography of Catherine up to the death of her husband, Henri II, so that the reader can take up the thread in the beginning of *Le Martyr calviniste* and follow her fortunes still further in *La Confidence des Ruggieri*. The former reiterates the idea which inspired the whole work, and culminates in the assertion that from the principle of free judgment ('libre arbitre') proceeds that of freedom of conscience, and from that political freedom. Man in society has no right to any of these freedoms; as a subject he needs only guarantees against the sovereign which give rise, not to liberty in the abstract, but to 'des libertés définies et caractéri-sées'. Moreover, what Pascal calls a 'pensée de derrière la tête' runs through the whole Introduction and the whole work. It is expressed in a passage[1] which Balzac cut out from the Introduction of 1846. 'Le pouvoir ne doit jamais être astreint aux règles qui constituent la morale privée.' The Ten Commandments have no relevance to the government of states. France's loss of ascendancy in Europe since the fall of Napoleon, and particularly during the crisis of the Eastern Question,[2] is due to its rulers' adoption of middle-class morality as a principle of political conduct. Perhaps the passage was dropped in 1846 as too blatant a profession of Machiavellian principles. It is however more likely that by then the heat of political feeling had died down in Balzac. It is clear from *L'Envers de l'histoire contemporaine* (1842–8) that he was becoming more Christianly inclined, and thinking less of

[1] Given in Lovenjoul (1), 187–8.
[2] One page of the extant Introduction (Conard XXX, 12) reads as if it had been written in the neighbourhood of 1840.

political expediency and more of private virtue and self-abnegation as a corrective to the impersonal, merciless rigour of the
political, administrative and judicial machine. The addition he
made in 1845 to *Jésus-Christ en Flandre*[1] was perhaps prompted
by this thought.

So, by these four stages of composition, *Sur Catherine de
Médicis* arrived at its final form. As a work of art it suffers from
the intrusion of Balzac's opinions and prejudices. If he had had
the inclination or the leisure to pare it down and prune away the
excrescences, the first and second episodes at least might stand as
a fascinating and picturesque historical novel, and deserve the
praise that André Bellesort gave it when he called it 'une de nos
plus fortes études de nos Guerres de Religion'. Whatever opinion
may be held of its value, it is the last of Balzac's completed
Philosophical Studies.[2]

[1] See above, 58.
[2] For the very complicated history of the publication of these Studies and
Balzac's uncompleted projects, see Lovenjoul (6).

VIII

PROVINCIAL STUDIES, 1836–40
EPITAPH FOR THE OLD NOBILITY

i. The Alençon stories

BALZAC PLACED the main action of these two novels in the little lace-manufacturing town of Alençon, on the borders of Maine and Normandy. He had first visited it in 1825, or perhaps in 1823, but improved his acquaintance with it in 1828 during his stay with the Pommereuls at Fougères. He had made it one of the key-towns in the guerrilla warfare between 'Blues' and 'Whites' described in *Les Chouans*.

Le Cabinet des antiques appears to have been conceived before *La vieille Fille*.[1] On the 2nd November 1833[2] he told Mme Hanska that he had 'invented it laboriously' and produced seventeen consecutive sheets. In August 1834[3] he wrote of this work, which he had discussed with the Hanskis at Geneva at the turn of the year, as if it were shortly to be published in *La Revue de Paris*. It is clearly a by-product of his political meditations as an independent legitimist. But none of it came to light until the 6th March 1836, when three quarto pages of it appeared in his own *Chronique de Paris*. They correspond only roughly to the first seventeen pages of the final version of the novel as printed in the Conard edition.[4] After that Balzac diverted his attention to *La vieille Fille*, which appeared serially in *La Presse* in the autumn of 1836, and then found its way into the Béchet-Werdet

---

[1] A manuscript fragment of 1832 bearing the title 'La vieille Fille' has nothing to do with the novel of 1836. Originally Balzac also used the same title for what eventually became *Le Curé de Tours*. An embryonic fragment of the definitive *Vieille Fille*, entitled *La Fleur des Pois* (not to be confused with *Le Contrat de mariage* which, in Nov. 1835, bore that title), belongs to the beginning of 1835. See Castex (5), Introd. and 'Premières Ébauches' (233 ff.).

[2] *E* I, 72. [3] *E* I, 177. [4] Conard XI, 1–18.

'Études de Mœurs', whose last two belated volumes of Provincial Scenes were printed over Werdet's name in February 1837.[1] The continuation of *Le Cabinet des antiques*, entitled *Les Rivalités en province*, did not appear until the autumn of 1838—in *Le Constitutionnel*. In 1839 Souverain published the complete novel in two volumes, with *Gambara* as a make-weight. It was now much expanded, and was given a preface whose purpose was to link it up with the forthcoming second part of *Illusions perdues* as a preliminary illustration of the magnetic pull which nineteenth-century Paris exerted on ambitious natives of the provinces. The expansion occurred mainly in the latter part of the novel,[2] and its obvious motive was to work into the text a number of aspiring junior magistrates whom Balzac had recently invented and were now acquiring status as 'reappearing characters'.[3] Finally, in 1844, *La vieille Fille* and *Le Cabinet des antiques* were published together in the Provincial Scenes of the 'Comédie Humaine'.[4] They were offered as Parts I and II of a series entitled 'Les Rivalités'.[5]

Thus the two works not only overlap in the order of their composition and publication: they constitute a novel-cycle. The *Chronique de Paris* portion of *Le Cabinet des antiques* had brought forth a character, Boutron-Boisset (later du Croisier), who, under the name of du Bousquier, is given a prominent role in *La vieille Fille*, which therefore may be regarded as being almost implicit in the first instalment of *Le Cabinet des antiques*.[6] But the events

[1] These volumes were in reality sponsored by Delloye and Lecou. *La vieille Fille* was included in vol. iii (i.e. vol. vii of the complete 'Études de Mœurs').

[2] Comprised in Conard XI, 120–60. For the few pages which this expanded version replaced, see Lovenjoul (1), 94 ff. See also Maxam and Bartlett. But their comparison of texts does not go farther back than the 1839 edition, which is a pity, since the 'pre-originals' of 1836 and 1838 throw interesting light on the evolution of the story.

[3] Maître Camusot, the younger Michu, etc. The new version also provided the journalist Blondet with an Alençon background and a reputed father in the person of Judge Blondet, President of the local Tribunal.

[4] Furne, Dubochet and Hetzel. See below, 268–9.

[5] Balzac revised his intention after 1844, so that, in the *Éd. Déf.*, *Le Cabinet des antiques* is presented as the first work in a series 'Les Provinciaux à Paris' which was never continued.

[6] It should however be noted that this instalment contains no allusion to the essential subject of *La vieille Fille*—du Bousquier's courtship of a middle-class spinster.

of *La vieille Fille* go back to 1816, while those of *Le Cabinet des antiques* cover the period 1822–4; so that when the latter story was taken up again in *Le Constitutionnel*, it was plainly shown to form a sequel to *La vieille Fille*. Yet even today the closeness of the bond between them remains uncertain. This is because the introductory part of *Le Cabinet des antiques*, while claiming that the story is a true one, asserts that the names of the families involved are disguised; and also because Balzac, perhaps in order to keep up this pretence of discretion, did not proceed with the identification of leading characters in both novels until after their joint publication in 1844. It was never carried out completely. And all mention of Alençon itself is carefully avoided throughout *Le Cabinet des antiques*.

As the collective title of *Les Rivalités* implies, these novels have for their general theme the conflict of interests and claims between the dominant elements in Restoration society: on the one hand the old nobility, nursing its inviolability as a caste and reluctant to admit that the upheaval of Revolution and Empire had been anything but a temporary disturbance of social values; on the other hand a moneyed middle class, conscious of its newly acquired importance, eager to push forward the industrialization of France and the development of the new capitalism which in due course was to effect such profound changes in the national economy. In between these two social groupings, definable in terms of their political leanings as 'Ultras' and 'Liberals', stood an indeterminate and heterogeneous one: upstarts of pre-Revolutionary and Revolutionary times whose aspiration to patrician status was a matter of scorn for the aristocracy of birth; war profiteers who had made and sometimes lost fortunes as Army contractors or speculators in military supplies; and what Balzac calls 'la petite noblesse à poste fixe'. These latter were magisterial, fiscal and administrative officials who were often the Vicars of Bray of the period, many of them having retained their functions through changes of regime and owning no fanatical allegiance to the restored monarchy whose interests and policy they were expected to further. From the ranks of this intermediate group emerged those would-be leaders who, having membership of the Chambre des Députés, the peerage and high office as their objective, while professing to be champions of Throne and Altar, challenged the political and social pretensions and worked for the discredit and ruin of the aristocratic caste, threw in their lot, secretly or openly, with the liberals, favoured the new economic tendencies by encouraging industrial enterprise, and prepared the way for the 'constitutional' monarchy whose cause they were in fact to espouse in 1830.

ii. *La vieille Fille* (1836)

That at any rate is how Balzac interpreted the social conflict of the Restoration period. In setting the action of *La vieille Fille* and *Le Cabinet des antiques* against such a background, he was giving deeper significance to the *Scènes de la vie de province*, and to some extent making them serve as prolegomena to his projected *Scènes de la vie politique*. This purpose is more intently pursued in *Le Cabinet des antiques*, but it is important even in *La vieille Fille*. In this story of the wooing of a rich middle-aged spinster, two of the three rival suitors are socially representative —the Chevalier de Valois[1] stands for the old aristocracy, du Bousquier for the pushing, liberal upstart. But the title of the novel gives the clue to its dominant interest. Balzac had already touched on the theme of the frustrated spinster in *Le Curé de Tours*. Yet Mlle Gamard in that work had merely been the type of acid female whose sense of frustration expresses itself in religious devotion and personal rancour; she is but a feeble anticipation of Balzac's most venomous spinster, 'la cousine Bette'. Rose-Marie-Victoire Cormon is in a very different category. She is not only innocuous, but honest, benevolent and kindly; hence we may be sure from the start that she will prove to be not a scourge but a victim. The picture of her which Balzac builds up shows that, in the main, he composed *La vieille Fille* in a satirical, if not a Rabelaisian frame of mind. He certainly has a large amount of sympathy for Rose Cormon, but in dealing with her he comes within a measurable distance of caricature.

---

[1] At Fougères, in 1828, Balzac met a Chevalier de Valois (still alive in 1836) who is supposed to have furnished a model for the fictitious character. See Pontavice de Heussey, Aubrée and Castex (5). The similarity between the two is not striking.

She is 'pure comme un ange, saine comme un enfant, et pleine de bonne volonté, car la nature l'avait destinée à tous les plaisirs, à tous les bonheurs, à toutes les fatigues de la maternité'. In fact, her whole being cries out for marriage and motherhood, although the fear of being married for her considerable wealth has prolonged her spinsterhood into the forties. Balzac displays much verve in depicting her generous proportions and the rubicund robustness which, in her youth, had passed for beauty, but which advancing years have turned into 'excessive amplitude'. He emphasizes her stupidity, her piety—'il est extrêmement difficile de décider si les personnes stupides deviennent naturellement dévotes, ou si la dévotion a pour effet de rendre stupides les filles d'esprit' —her ignorance of normal feminine strategy in the battle of the sexes, her naïvety about even the elementary 'facts of life'. In short, with a joviality which is almost derisive, he stamps this middle-aged Agnès as a woman doomed in spite of herself to die 'a virgin and a martyr'. The manner in which he shows her moving towards this lamentable end marks *La vieille Fille* as a truly original exercise in sardonic narration. In fact, the tone of it is such that a reader may easily see in Rose Cormon a figure of fun, rather than the well-deserving but unfortunate dupe of her own inexperience. This is because one way which Balzac has of showing tenderness or pity for his characters may be deceptive. Sometimes he gives rein to sentimental effusion; but sometimes, as here, he allows a lambent wit or even cruel-seeming irony to guide his pen. Some of his contemporaries were aware of this element in his technique, and were disheartened by what a biographer of Henry Monnier has called an 'irony whose underlying bitterness disenchants without consoling'.[1]

Since Rose is financially speaking a prize worth winning, the rivalry she provokes between the Chevalier de Valois and du Bousquier is a purely mercenary one. The Chevalier is a somewhat fly-blown survival of the Old Régime; a middle-aged fop with a tradition of *galanterie* and libertinism behind him; one who keeps up a desperate pretence of ease and elegance but depends for a meagre livelihood on the free meals he gets at the houses of the well-to-do and his winnings at their whist-tables; amiable,

[1] Melcher, 174 and n. 7.

popular with the laundress over whose premises he lodges as well as with her assistants, on whom he is now no longer able to lavish anything but cheap trifles and paternal benevolence; tactfully attentive to Rose Cormon and hoping to win her by the address he shows in saving her from the ridicule to which her artlessness in conversation exposes her. There is no such old-world urbanity about the disgruntled and scheming du Bousquier, the erstwhile 'fournisseur des armées de la République', whose rise to affluence has been checked by the unexpected triumph of Napoleon, who is smarting from the snubs inflicted on him by the genuine aristocracy and is counting on marriage with Rose Cormon for the wherewithal to jockey himself into power and place; a stout and muscular man of fifty-six who looks like a Hercules but is virtually impotent through youthful excesses. As the sort of husband Rose requires he is even a poorer proposition than the Chevalier de Valois.

A third suitor exists in the shape of a young man of twenty-three: Athanase Granson, whom Balzac conceives as a budding genius, full of ambition and promise—presumably as a prospective administrator or politician—but devoid of self-assurance and too diffident to declare himself. Unlike the others, he is wholeheartedly in love with Rose. It is true that in the beginning this 'passion vraie' had been tainted with self-interest; but, by some strange process which costs Balzac several embarrassed pages to explain, it has reached such a pitch of intensity that Rose's plenteous proportions have become an additional attraction for him. 'Les jeunes imaginations, continuellement avides et courageuses, aiment à s'étendre sur ces belles nappes vives. C'était la perdrix dodue, alléchant le couteau du gourmet.'

Of these three, Athanase is the only aspirant capable of satisfying Rose's urgent needs. The tragi-comedy of her frustration depends upon a chain of events whose coincidental nature Balzac does not hesitate to emphasize. 'Le hasard est le plus grand de tous les artistes.' The laundry-maid Suzanne, later self-styled 'Mme du Val-Noble', in order to raise money to set up as a courtesan in Paris, tries the blackmail of fictitious pregnancy on Valois. Ungullible but amused, he refers her to du Bousquier, whose close-fisted response to an insinuation which he none the less finds flattering, decides her to ruin his reputation in Alençon by spreading the rumour that he has seduced and abandoned her. As a presumptive proof of du Bousquier's virility, this slander betters instead of destroying his chances with Rose. Another fortuitous event, the arrival at Alençon of the Vicomte de Troisville, which puts Rose into a fever of matrimonial expectation, and her mortification on discovering that this object of her flustered attentions is already married, brings her to the point of making an immediate choice between her suitors. A further contingency, the fact that, while the Chevalier wastes time at his dressing-table, du Bousquier forestalls him with his proposal, settles the issue. She accepts du Bousquier. The disappointed Chevalier goes to pieces and sinks into decrepitude, while Rose is chained for life to a man who cannot give her the children she longs for—'moi, j'achèterais un enfant par cent années d'enfer'—who makes a submissive and even servile tool of her, and uses her wealth to put himself at the head of the Liberal faction in Alençon. Many years later, at the age of sixty, she is still lamenting over the prospect of carrying her virginity to the grave.

This coincidental element in the plot is an interesting development in Balzac's technique. It is prompted by the belief that the contingent and the unforeseen form an important part of the texture of real life. And Balzac supports this contention by insisting on another fact: the unpredictability of human reactions. In this respect too he escapes from the narrow and ineluctable determinism in which critics like Taine have sought to imprison him.

Il est absurde de vouloir ramener les sentiments à des formules identiques; en se produisant chez chaque homme, ils se combinent avec les éléments qui lui sont propres, et prennent sa physionomie.

Although he urges this as a justification for an ancillary episode in the story, it stands as a statement of principle which may often serve to rationalize apparently inexplicable reactions of his later characters. But justification is still lacking for what appears to be a real weakness in the plot and motivation of *La vieille Fille*: the tragic outcome of Athanase's passion for a woman who is twenty years older than he, and one at whom Balzac has mocked to some extent. Rose's marriage with du Bousquier so disheartens Athanase that he drowns himself in the Sarthe. His moral collapse and suicide are difficult to swallow. They can only be excused on the ground that once more, in *La vieille Fille* as in *Le Lys dans la vallée*, *La Duchesse de Langeais* and *La Peau de chagrin*, Balzac is romanticizing his own adolescent Wertherism, and here propounding the idea of a youthful Balzac who might have died of a sense of unfulfilment.[1]

Nor is the part given to 'Suzanne du Val-Noble' in the later stages of the novel altogether acceptable. Her natural role is that of a sprightly and malicious intriguer; but a brief encounter with Athanase on the eve of her departure from Alençon had kindled love in her heart, so that, after achieving a whirlwind success in Paris, she returns at the end of the story with the intention of aiding Athanase's career by the 'angelical ruse' of an anonymous gift of money. *Je l'aimais*, she avows to Mme Granson, when she discovers that she has arrived too late. As many a later novel was to show, Balzac's sympathy for the courtesan in love is one of his amiable weaknesses. About Suzanne's potentialities as a successful harlot he has left us in no doubt. In fact his estimate of her is as hyperbolic as his appraisal of the baleful Abbé Troubert's Hilde-brandine potentialities in *Le Curé de Tours*: in other ages, he avers, 'elle eût été la rivale des Rhodope, des Impéria, des Ninon'. But to her, as to Coralie in *Un grand Homme de province à Paris*, and to Esther van Gobseck in *Splendeurs et misères des courtisanes*, he allows a heart of gold. The paradox is unconvincing. We are left then with the impression that *La vieille Fille* is, on the whole, a study well worth a place in the 'Comédie Humaine', but that it is not a flawless specimen of Balzac's art. Perhaps he worked in the sentimental features to offset the spirit of *gauloiserie* which gives it its special flavour, as an antidote to the disrespect with which, forgetful of his more edifying intentions, he treats spiritual values throughout the work; a disrespect which prompted his conception of Rose's uncle, the Abbé de Sponde, as the very model of a nar-

[1] For a development of this idea, in particular with reference to Balzac's early passion for Mme de Berny, who, it may be remembered, had died only a few months before *La vieille Fille* appeared in *La Presse*, see Abraham (2), 39–45. Étienne Arago tells that, *circa* 1824, Balzac had thought of drowning himself in the Seine—Arrigon (1), 184–5.

row-minded, comfort-loving priest, who is totally unable to understand what is going on in his niece's mind or give her effectual guidance in her fumbling bid for happiness.

iii. *Le Cabinet des antiques* (1836–9)

The Abbé de Sponde has one positive feature in his psychological make-up. He holds in Pharisaical abhorrence such of his clerical brethren as, in his view, had betrayed the Church by accepting the 'Civil Constitution' of 1791. He is thus the expression, in ecclesiastical terms, of that spirit of political and social immobility whose survival in the Restoration period it was the object of *Le Cabinet des antiques* to study. In this second novel, du Bousquier, renamed du Croisier, pursues his vendetta against the *noblesse de sang* into whose ranks he had vainly sought, in Imperial times, to gain admission by marriage. His attack is directed against the very citadel of aristocratic self-complacency, the salon of the Marquis d'Esgrignon, jestingly nicknamed the 'Cabinet des antiques',[1] because its frequenters live solely on the glories of the past and feed their racial pride on the delusion that they spring directly from the loins of the Frankish conquerors of Gaul. The Marquis d'Esgrignon is the embodiment of this *morgue aristocratique*. Although the Revolution had robbed him of most of his estates and revenues, he had refused to emigrate or adapt his ceremonious style of living to his straitened circumstances; when the monarchy was restored he refused also to become a mendicant or hanger-on at the Court of Louis XVIII. He is supported in his stiff-necked but high-minded allegiance to a lost cause by his half-sister, Armande-Claire, the lady whom du Croisier had hoped to marry, and his former intendant, the notary Chesnel, a lawyer of the same loyal breed as Mathias in *Le Contrat de mariage*, who in his idolatrous subservience to his haughty and condescending master does not hesitate to sacrifice his own resources to the needs of the d'Esgrignon family. All three centre their hopes in the Marquis' son, Victurnien, a weak young egoist

---

[1] A collection of medals, coins, cameos, etc., begun by Francis I, completed by Louis XIV, and now housed in the Bibliothèque Nationale as the 'Cabinet du Roi'.

whose insolent frolics at Alençon have inspired du Croisier to mark him down as the victim through whom he can strike at the d'Esgrignons, humiliate the local aristocracy, and secure the triumph of the 'noblesse à poste fixe' whose representative and agent he has made himself.

After Victurnien has sowed his wild oats at Alençon, Chesnel finds the money for him to go to Paris where, relying on his name and rank, he hopes through royal favour to begin a brilliant career in diplomacy or the army. He soon finds that this is an idle dream, but falls in with the fast set of Parisian elegants, headed by the Chevalier de Valois' Parisian counterpart the Vidame de Pamiers, Henri de Marsay and the journalist Blondet; he launches out as a dandy. His downfall is assured when he attracts the attention of a high-society siren, Diane, Duchesse de Maufrigneuse, later Princesse de Cadignan, who is henceforth to occupy a prominent position among the noble Circes of the 'Comédie Humaine'.

She is in truth well worthy of a place beside the Duchesse de Carigliano, the Marquise d'Aiglement, the Marquise d'Espard and the Duchesse de Langeais. She far outclasses the latter in the technique of seduction, the more so because, unlike the Duchesse de Langeais, she does not linger indefinitely on the chilly heights of platonic inaccessibility. De Marsay, her original guide in eclectic profligacy, looks on amusedly while she sets to work on Victurnien. 'Mon cher,' he observes to Rastignac, 'il sera *uist*! sifflé comme un polichinelle[1] par un cocher de fiacre.' For Victurnien's capture she adopts the role of the immaculate angel, 'semi-catholique et semi-ossianique', and Balzac rises to the height of his powers in the three or four pages he allots to the description of her wiles and graces.

Toutes les femmes se demandaient comment la jeune étourdie était devenue, en une seule toilette, la séraphique beauté voilée qui semblait, suivant une expression à la mode, avoir une âme blanche comme la dernière tombée de neige sur la plus haute des Alpes; comment elle avait si promptement résolue le problème jésuitique de si bien montrer une gorge plus blanche que son âme en la cachant sous la gaze; comment elle pouvait être si immatérielle en coulant son regard de côté d'une façon si assassine. Elle avait l'air de promettre mille voluptés par

[1] A glass of brandy.

ce coup d'œil presque lascif quand, par un soupir ascétique plein d'espérances pour une meilleure vie, sa bouche paraissait dire qu'elle n'en réaliserait aucune. Des jeunes gens naïfs . . . se demandaient si, même dans les dernières intimités, on tutoyait cette espèce de Dame Blanche, vapeur sidérale tombée de la Voie Lactée.

The tale of Victurnien's relationship with her, which includes a trip to Italy, is one of astronomically mounting debts. Du Croisier watches him from afar, encourages him to draw bills of exchange in his name, and then abruptly withdraws his credit; so that at last, in despair, Victurnien utters a forged bill for 200,000 francs. Du Croisier pounces on his victim and has him arrested when he returns panic-stricken to Alençon. The rest of the story is concerned with the efforts of Chesnel and Armande d'Esgrignon to save him from the consequences of his crime. They are aided by Diane, who comes to Alençon in male attire, with royal authorization to get the proceedings against her lover quashed, and armed with a phial of poison he is to take if these efforts prove futile.[1] In this way the story resolves itself into a strange mixture of romantic masquerade and legalistic wire-pulling.

Victurnien's extrication from the risk of trial before the Assize Court and condemnation to the galleys throws interesting light, both on the public morality of the times, and on Balzac's attitude towards an aristocracy which he simultaneously derides, in conformity with his adopted principle *castigat ridendo mores*,[2] and almost passionately defends, in conformity with his political creed. It suits the purpose of du Croisier and his satellites to stand out, hypocritically of course, for the principle of the equality of all in the eyes of the law. The view of Louis XVIII, his ministers and magistrates, is that the arraignment of a young noble for forgery is contrary to public policy. The problem is solved in a surprising way: a sleight-of-hand trick whereby the embezzled sum is paid back to the sympathetic royalist, Mme du Croisier, who is suborned into thwarting her husband—it is the only revenge that the erstwhile Rose Cormon ever wreaks against the man who had

---

[1] In *Le Constitutionnel* (7 Oct. 1838) it is the austere Chesnel who offers to hang Victurnien if things go badly.

[2] See his *dédicace* to *Illusions perdues*.

hoodwinked her into marrying him—by antedating the receipt for it by five days. The task that remains is for Chesnel and Diane to persuade the magistrates to cancel the charge and release Victurnien, whom Diane now contemptuously discards as a lover. The magistrates' motives are fully explained in the forty-odd pages by whose means Balzac expanded the novel for the 1839 edition. Paris is a Mecca for ambitious lawyers like Maître Camusot, as it has been for impecunious youths like Rastignac and Victurnien; the prospect of being appointed to higher posts in the capital prompts them to build up such proof of Victurnien's innocence that the examining judge (Blondet senior) dismisses the case in all good faith. So du Croisier is foiled in his immediate purpose. Yet his victory is only postponed. The Marquis d'Esgrignon, ignorant of his son's delinquency, is allowed to live on in his fool's paradise until his death in 1830. But the financial ruin of the d'Esgrignon family is so complete that, once his father is in his grave, Victurnien is obliged to make the misalliance on which du Croisier has set his heart by marrying the latter's grand-niece. This catastrophe for all intents and purposes marks the fall of the House of Esgrignon.

Le Cabinet des antiques is, I believe, a better-conceived novel than *La vieille Fille*. It has no disparate mixture of sentiment and satire, and the element of caricature is more restrained. Even in the younger Blondet's vivacious picture[1] of the 'Cabinet des antiques', with its ancient dowagers and wizened seigneurs, there is a measure of reverence as well as mockery, and the effect is more convincing. The novel is not without defects. For instance, it carries the zeal for material description too far. Such description is indeed indispensable for the 'Cabinet des antiques' itself, and it is superbly done. But it is redundant when it comes to depicting the houses and furniture of certain secondary characters—magistrates like Camusot, du Ronceret, Michu, and perhaps even that horticultural maniac, the elder Blondet. This excess is no doubt due to Balzac's anxiety, when adding such figures to his list of reappearing characters, to give them full physiognomy and background. The romantic element—Diane de Maufrigneuse romp-

[1] In the *Chronique de Paris* instalment Blondet is not introduced. The author tells the whole of the story.

ing about the country in the guise of a young 'tigre'—is harmless enough. And though the dénouement of the story—Victurnien's rescue from the clutches of the law—seems more ingenious than plausible, Balzac's contemporaries would have had no difficulty in accepting the idea of Diane de Maufrigneuse carrying the Procureur du Roi in her pocket, of a *raison d'état* prevailing over the demands of ordinary justice.

In fact the main purpose of the novel—to show up the pathetic sublimity of a disappearing caste, out of tune with the times—is triumphantly achieved. The Marquis d'Esgrignon, Armande d'Esgrignon and Chesnel are excellent museum pieces, the more so because they stand in sharp opposition to those of their class who accommodate themselves to the new age: the cynics and profligates of Parisian high society. To his 'Antiques' Balzac metes out compassion as well as condemnation. His distaste for the liberals, industrialists and careerists who supplant them is as strong as ever. His comments on the death of Chesnel, worn out in the vain struggle to save his patrons from disgrace and ruin, amount to an epitaph on the class which he had already criticized in the second chapter of *La Duchesse de Langeais* and which it had been his political ambition to rehabilitate. In *Le Cabinet des antiques* he is at once a social historian, a social critic and an observant psychologist.

iv. Angoulême. *Illusions perdues* I (*Les deux Poètes*, 1837)

It was to be expected that Angoulême would arouse Balzac's interest as the centre for a provincial study. Since the Carrauds had moved to the gunpowder factory, a few miles from Angoulême, in August 1831, Balzac had paid them three visits there: in December 1831, from July to August 1832, and from April to May 1833. It was on the third of these visits that he gathered certain data for a novel. In particular he met a local blue-stocking, Mme de Saint-Surin, who no doubt provided him with a first model for his heroine, Mme de Bargeton, upon whose literary and social activities the story was to pivot.[1] He roamed about Angoulême in the company of a hero-worshipping school-boy, Albéric

[1] See Fouquerre.

Second, who when he launched out a year or two later as a journalist in Paris, forgot his hero-worship to the extent of writing mocking criticisms of Balzac. He decided to transfer his own experiences as an unsuccessful printer to a young man whose surname he discovered on the spot and to credit him also with projects for the manufacture of a cheaper kind of paper with which he himself was concerned round about 1833.

A place was allotted to *Illusions perdues* in the list of 'Scenes' which early in 1834 inspired Félix Davin's Introduction to the 'Études de Mœurs'. But he did not set to work on it until the summer of 1836; it was on the 26th June of that year that he wrote his oft-quoted letter to Zulma Carraud asking her for topographical details about Angoulême[1]—two years after the Carrauds had retired from the gunpowder factory and taken up residence at Frapesle, near Issoudun, and one year after Zulma had besought Balzac to befriend a young protégé of hers, Auguste Chevalet, who was starving in Paris as a result of his efforts to establish himself there as a writer. 'Ce jeune homme est toute notre époque', had been Balzac's comment.[2] 'Quand on ne peut rien faire, on se fait homme de plume, homme de talent.' And from this general truth, enriched by the memory of his own vicissitudes, he derived the major theme of the novel-cycle into which *Illusions perdues* was to be expanded. The first novel in the series, whose original title was *Illusions perdues: Les deux Amis*, was for the most part written towards the end of 1836 and the beginning of 1837. It was published in February 1837 in the fourth volume of the *Scènes de la vie de province*, completing the Béchet-Werdet 'Études de Mœurs', with a preface which made it clear that he already had the second part, *Un grand Homme de province à Paris*, in his head, and intended that it should be an exposure of the scandals of Parisian journalism. But on the 27th December 1836[3] he had told Mme Hanska that he would be too busy to carry on with it for three years. And yet his darting inspiration, stimulated (as always) by the demands of editors and publishers, enabled him to look far beyond this project and write *La Torpille*, thus laying the foundations of *Splendeurs et misères des courtisanes*, which was destined as a sequel to the whole of the *Illusions perdues*

[1] Z.C. 224.   [2] Z.C. 206, Aug. 1835.   [3] E I, 373.

series. He published *La Torpille* in September 1838, and then turned again to *Un grand Homme*. In the early part of 1839 he was proceeding with it resolutely, and in June, after two extracts from it had appeared in *L'Estafette*, it was published by Souverain. By now he also had the third part in mind. There are occasional references to this in his correspondence from 1840 to 1842. It appeared at last in 1843, at first serially, and then as volume VIII of the 'Comédie Humaine'. There was some hesitation over titles. In 1843 Part I acquired its final title: *Les deux Poètes*. But it was only in the Édition Définitive that Part III, *David Séchard*, or *Ève et David*, settled down as *Les Souffrances de l'inventeur*.

What was Balzac's motive for the general title: *Illusions perdues*? As far as Part I is concerned the motive is implicit in the nucleus of the story. Mme Marie-Louise-Anaïs de Bargeton, whose ambition is to make her salon the cultural centre of Angoulême, 'discovers' a talented (and handsome) young poet, Lucien Chardon, son of a plebeian father, a chemist, and of a patrician mother, Charlotte de Rubempré. She tries to set him on the way to fame by admitting him to her salon, fails through the indifference or hostility of the local big-wigs, and decides to take him to Paris to make his name there. The protective relationship develops into an amorous one, with more ardour on Lucien's side, although (or because) in 1821, the year in which the action takes place, Louise is thirty-six, and Lucien only twenty. The attachment remains innocent, but raises a scandal and occasions a duel in which her elderly husband, in all other respects a nonentity, shows unexpected vigour and dignity, and seriously wounds his wife's traducer.[1] Once installed in Paris, living and moving in the polite circles to which her cousinship with the Marquise d'Espard gives her access, Mme de Bargeton takes stock of her lover; so does he of her. The scales fall from their eyes. Lucien sees her as she is before her commerce with Mme d'Espard has transformed her into one who can pass muster as a Parisian: 'une femme grande,

---

[1] The case of M. de Bargeton is one of those which S. Rogers (op. cit., see above, 55) urges in order to prove the independent vitality of Balzac's characters, even his so-called 'types'. Dinah de La Baudraye, in *La Muse du département*, is another.

sèche, couperosée, fanée, plus que rousse, anguleuse,[1] guindée, précieuse, prétentieuse, provinciale dans ses paroles, mal arrangée surtout'. She sees her 'grand homme de province' as he is, even after he has exchanged his provincial rig-out for one he believes to be more in keeping with Parisian standards of elegance: an awkward, inexperienced, unsophisticated young man, whose lack of *savoir vivre* and conversational adroitness are brought into painful relief by the disdainful presence of the dandies—de Marsay, Félix de Vandenesse, Montriveau and Eugène de Rastignac. In comparison with the amiable, fashionable, witty, gentleman-poet who was later to go by the name of Canalis, this jay in peacock's feathers, this chemist's son who, on Mme de Bargeton's own prompting, has illegally taken to himself his mother's patronymic and styled himself Lucien de Rubempré, cuts a sorry figure as a poetaster with a very slender literary baggage—a few sonnets and an unfinished historical novel. This mutual disillusion is simultaneous, but Mme de Bargeton, spurred on by Mme d'Espard, acts first and discards Lucien. He is left to fend for himself, 'car il était seul dans Paris, sans amis, sans protecteurs'.

It was at this point that, in the edition of 1837, the first part of *Illusions perdues* ended, and, in 1839, *Un grand Homme de province à Paris* began. In 1843 and subsequent editions Part I ends with the exit of the lovers from Angoulême. Thus the original Part I had a noticeable artistic symmetry. Lucien's first individual disillusion, the one he has experienced in Mme de Bargeton's salon in his native city, where the snobbish assembly of Philistines was bored by his declamation of André Chénier's poems, preferred the whist-tables to the hearing of his own verses, and brought him to contumely as the son of a professional midwife and the sister of a laundry-worker, is matched by the scene in Mme d'Espard's box in the Paris Opera. But Balzac's plans for further disillusionments—that of Lucien when he attempts to conquer Paris by the versatility of his pen, and that of his mother, sister and brother-in-law when they see his initial egoism developing into corruption, disloyalty and dishonesty—determined him to redivide the parts. Moreover, the idea of presenting *Illusions perdues* as a link

---

[1] When his infatuation for her has given place to resentment and hostility, he nicknames her 'l'os de seiche'—'the cuttle-bone'.

between Provincial and Parisian scenes made it desirable that
Part I should finish at Angoulême, and that Part III, when at last
it came, should terminate the action of the novel in the place
where it had begun.

Also, as a Provincial Scene, *Les deux Poètes*, whose composition
from the chronological point of view is sandwiched between *La
vieille Fille* and *Le Cabinet des antiques*, continues the socio-
graphical studies of the period 1836–40. Balzac renews in a different setting his scrutiny of aristocratic exclusiveness. But this time
he is not concerned with rivalry between two virtually contiguous upper classes—a provincial 'Faubourg Saint-Germain' and
'une seconde société',[1] but with the attempt made by a young man
of talent—of genius in Balzac's hyperbolic language—to penetrate
the closed ranks of a local élite composed of supercilious gentry and
higher officialdom. The division of Angoulême into two areas—
the upper and older city, the residential quarter of the élite, and
the lower and modern suburb of L'Houmeau, the centre of trade
and industry—offered him a convenient symbol of social cleavage,
since the semi-plebeian Lucien, his mother and sister, live in
obscure poverty in L'Houmeau. But this opposition of background
is not logically perfect, for Lucien's bosom friend, benefactor and
future brother-in-law, the young printer David Séchard, has his
premises and domicile in the older part of the city. In any case,
Lucien's conquest of a place in the genteel circles of Angoulême
is intimately connected with the Séchard printing-press. He is
David's foreman, and the printing-house to some extent provides
him with a springboard for his venture.

From this it results that the fictional interest in *Les deux
Poètes* is threefold: it involves the history of the Séchard press
itself, that of the young aspirant to greatness, Lucien, and that of
Mme de Bargeton, the queen of Angoulême society. David's
father, the former pressman Jérôme-Nicolas Séchard, who had
plodded along for years with his cheaply bought, ill-equipped and
antiquated press, is one of Balzac's striking plebeian creations: a
miser who takes his place beside Grandet and Gobseck, who like
Grandet combines two occupations—he is a vine-grower as well
as a printer—but whose originality lies in the fact that his

[1] See *Le Cabinet des antiques*, Conard XI, 9.

avarice is ancillary to bibulousness. Séchard senior is one of the
few drunkards of the 'Comédie Humaine'. He naturally gives
Balzac full opportunity to display his descriptive powers. He is
drawn with a truly Dickensian picturesqueness and humour, with
the usual attentiveness to the minutiae of his physical appearance
and dress.

> Ce costume où l'ouvrier se retrouvait encore dans le bourgeois con-
> venait si bien à ses vices et à ses habitudes, il exprimait si bien sa vie,
> que ce bonhomme semblait avoir été créé tout habillé: vous ne l'auriez
> pas plus imaginé sans ses vêtements qu'un oignon sans sa pelure.

His retirement—for the purpose of more assiduously cultivating
the vine and the bottle—is the occasion for the merciless bargain
which he drives with his intelligent and sensitive son over the
transference of the business and its equipment: an eagerly
grasped opportunity for Balzac to live over again the days of his
own printing-press, for much of the substance of this aspect of
the novel is furnished from Balzac's own projects and reverses of
1826–8. There is no doubt something of the younger Balzac in
David Séchard. He is another genius, in his way a poet like his
friend Lucien; that is to say, he is a young man of ardent
imagination whose tastes and proclivities urge him, not indeed
to the penning of sonnets, but to the invention of improved processes in printing and paper-making. His bent is scientific, and for
Balzac too science was a form of poetry. But his modest, tender
and melancholy nature, his incapacity to exploit his own talents
or stand on his rights, make him the easy victim, first of his own
rapacious father, then of his adroit and cunning rivals, the
Cointet brothers. This does not prevent him from placing his precarious resources at the disposal of the Chardon family, for he
adores Ève Chardon, and shares her and her mother's idolatry for
the handsome, effeminate, self-centred and ambitious Lucien.

Lucien Chardon, better known as Lucien de Rubempré, is the
central figure of the story, as he is also to be in the second and
third parts of *Illusions perdues* as well as in *Splendeurs et misères
des courtisanes*. In a different milieu, and with a different personality, his case is not dissimilar to that of Victurnien d'Esgrignon, for he too is a young man spoilt by infatuated relatives who

sacrifice all their interests to his. His access, as a promising poet, to the high society of Angoulême is in the first place due to a miscalculation on the part of Baron Sixte du Châtelet, an ex-Imperial beau and elegant, in some respects a variation on the du Bousquier-du Croisier type, a Director of Tax-Collection aping the grand gentleman and paying assiduous court to the dissatisfied, yearning, over-cultured Louise de Bargeton. In the latter we have Balzac's first sketch of the would-be *femme de lettres*, a type to whom he later gave considerable attention. At the time when the publication of *Illusions perdues* was in progress it was an accepted view (voiced in particular by the publisher Didier[1]) that her adventure with Lucien Chardon was based on that of George Sand with Jules Sandeau. But there is much more of Jules Sandeau in Lucien than there is of George Sand—if indeed there is anything at all of her—in Mme de Bargeton.

We have seen that a living model for Louise was not lacking in Angoulême itself: Mme de Saint-Surin. Nor was there a dearth of other possible models in an age when scores of women, talented or not, were, to Balzac's continued displeasure, emulating Mme de Staël, the Duchesse de Duras and others. Even Caroline Marbouty, the heroine of Balzac's Italian escapade of 1836, has been cited in this connection. But Mme de Bargeton has no single prototype either as a woman (there is in her a touch of the maternal affection of 'La Dilecta', and she has auburn hair like Mme de Castries) or as a feminine Mæcenas. Balzac's lengthy and perspicacious analysis of this provincial Egeria is noteworthy. So too is his description of her vain attempts to awaken æsthetic feeling in the minds and hearts of her social satellites. No less so are his portraits of these satellites, gathered in her salon to hear, and to damn with faint praise, the embarrassed Lucien's recitations. Among them are the foppish Stanislas de Chandour, the man whose later indiscretion exposes him to the painful chastisement of M. de Bargeton's pistol; Astolphe de Saintot, the reputed 'puits de science' in matters agricultural, who covers up his extensive ignorance by means of well-conned tags from Cicero; the musical bore Adrien de Bartas, and the amateur draughtsman Alexandre de Brebian with their apparently interchangeable wives; the local

[1] See Regard (2).

Nimrod Jacques de Senonches, who, despite his Othello-like jealousy, takes no umbrage at the intimate understanding that exists
between his wife and his factotum Francis du Hautoy; and all the
shallow, simpering and spiteful women who appear as worthy
consorts to these empty-headed notables. Add to these the well-
meaning Bishop and his Archdeacon, the local Prefect and the
anonymous general, together with various small fry, and the scene
is perfectly set for the ludicrous poetic soirée whose description,
with that of Lucien's subsequent discomfiture at the Opera
after his migration to Paris, is one of the high-lights of the
story.

These two scenes placed opposite each other reveal another of
Balzac's concerns in this novel: to contrast the boorishness of the
provincial élite with the snobbish brilliance of the Parisian 'smart
set', while illustrating the effeteness of both. As regards the
Angoulême élite, he gives quarter to only two families of real
gentility whom he keeps tactfully in the background—the
Pimentels and the parents and sisters of the careerist Eugène de
Rastignac, who is cutting a fine figure in the capital. But the
Séchard printing-house is in the meantime not neglected as a
focus of interest. While Lucien is writhing under the insults put
upon him and his family in the Bargeton salon, the devoted David
is screwing up courage to propose marriage to Ève—a delightful
scene in which the young woman's blend of modesty, affectionate
playfulness and tender anxiety make her one of the most charm-
ingly virginal heroines of the 'Comédie Humaine'. His wooing is
successful.[1] The rest of the action at Angoulême deals with the
preparations for the wedding and the deprivations to which the
young couple submit, willingly yet with misgivings, for the sake
of Lucien's problematical advancement, and then in order to
facilitate his precipitate departure with Louise to Paris, after the
Bargeton-Chandour duel.

The part played by du Châtelet in bringing about this duel, as
well as his pursuit of the lovers to Paris so as to turn defeat into

[1] In his corrections made *circa* 1845 on the Furne edition of the 'Comédie
Humaine', Balzac here transfers from the third part of *Illusions perdues* a long
dissertation by David on the problem of paper-manufacture in nineteenth-
century France. This transference adds an incongruous note of pedantry to the
love-idyll. See Garnier edition, 115, 578 and notes.

victory and procure Lucien's disgrace with Louise by more subtle means, gives the finishing touch to that symmetry of opposition which, as we have seen, characterizes the structure of the original story. But the task assigned to the Séchard couple (and Lucien's mother) is clearly perceptible. They stand out as an immovable centre of simple virtue and self-abnegation; as a standard by which the progressive deterioration of the 'grand homme de province' may be measured. Their further tribulations, due in large measure to Lucien's future turpitudes, but due also to the uncombative David's incapacity for hard-headed business, were to remain in the background of Balzac's consciousness for many years, while he turned his thoughts to the new, and even more poignant disillusionment which awaited Lucien in Paris.

None the less it would be a mistake to judge *Les deux Poètes* as the simple tale of a rake's progress opposed to the exemplary life of modest paragons. Balzac blends censure and criticism of Lucien with much heartfelt compassion. He feels for him in his social disappointments, for we may be sure that in the early eighteen-thirties at least, he had suffered many a similar snub at the hands of society exquisites. He sympathizes with him also as the type of struggling man of letters against whom Paris directs its hypocritical and destructive malevolence. In this respect his development of Lucien as a brilliant, unprincipled genius was destined to entail a denunciation of the social order which inflamed, thwarted and then damned the aspiration of youth in his day. But over and above all this is the private and particular affection in which the author holds his weak-kneed and shiftless creation. In spite of all, Balzac seems to be half in love with the girlish Adonis whom in after-days the homosexual Vautrin was to adopt and protect. But Balzac's tenderness for nearly all the creatures he invented, however reprehensible they may seem, is a constant and characteristic feature of his novels.

v. Provins. *Pierrette* (1840)

We shall see that *Pierrette*, although separated by a year or so from the Provincial Scenes under consideration, fits in naturally enough with them. Balzac first announced it as a forthcoming 'nouvelle' in July 1839,[1] and mentioned it again in the following November.[2] As being appropriate reading for the young, he already intended to dedicate it to Anna Hanska, now aged fourteen. The composition of it caused him much trouble. 'Cela a été fait treize fois', he wrote in December.[3] It appeared serially in *Le Siècle* in January 1840. Then there was further delay in its publication as a book. Three pirated editions of it, copied from *Le Siècle*, appeared in Brussels. At last Souverain published it in December 1840, together with *Pierre Grassou*.

When in 1843 it was incorporated in the 'Comédie Humaine', it formed the first novel in a group entitled 'Les Célibataires'. This was a title he had first used in 1832 for *Le Curé de Tours*. The preface to the 1840 edition of *Pierrette* contains a humorous disquisition on celibates and a list of bachelors he had already created—the Chevalier de Valois, the Chevalier d'Espard, Henri de Marsay and others. Pretending to be sensitive about reproaches made to him for putting so many dangerous and unprincipled bachelors in his works, he points out that he has already killed off de Marsay,[4] married off Eugène de Rastignac,[5] and that he is also about to marry off the 'monstre' Maxime de Trailles.[6] As for the incurable celibates, he is going to prick them off for his museum as rare and curious insects. After *Pierrette* and *Le Curé de Tours*, *Le bonhomme Rouget* (*La Rabouilleuse*) was to be the third in the series.

In some minor respects *Pierrette* presupposes *César Birotteau* and *La maison Nucingen*, which did in fact precede it in order of composition and publication. Yet it is affiliated to the *Vieille Fille* group, not only by its treatment of the theme of celibacy, but also by its sociological content. The 'Célibataires' in question in *Pierrette* are primarily two haberdashers, brother and sister, Jérôme-Denis and Sylvie Rogron, natives of Provins who, after making a sufficient fortune in Paris, have retired to their native town to enjoy the comfortable existence now possible. In giving

[1] *E* I, 517–18.   [2] *E* I, 522.
[3] *E* I, 523.   [4] In *Une Fille d'Ève.*
[5] Rastignac's betrothal to Augusta de Nucingen is mentioned in *Une Fille d'Ève.*
[6] In that work already announced under various titles, but never finished: *Le Député d'Arcis.*

his attention to Provins, Balzac gazes on lower social strata than those he had been concerned with at Alençon and Angoulême, though the theme of social rivalry is still the dominant one. This time the élite in this petty provincial town on the borders of Champagne is a set of ex-shopkeeping families (who likewise have made their money in Paris, as silk-merchants or haberdashers) allied in marriage to and clustered round the local Président du Tribunal and his wife, M. and Mme Tiphaine. The latter, the daughter of a defaulting Paris lawyer whom readers of Balzac had already met with in *César Birotteau*, is 'la reine de la ville'. This Tiphaine group is a closed society to which all the leading professional men of the locality belong: the doctor, the notary, the public attorney, the district tax-collector, etc. Except for having the local newspaper in their hands, they are quite without literary pretensions; but they have their own standard of living, their superiority of taste, their social occasions with boston or whist as their favourite distraction. Representing the official class at Provins in the middle years of the Restoration period (1824–8), they are royalist and *bien pensant*, although as the conclusion shows, like the functionary class at Alençon, they are ready to trim their sails to the wind and go over to the Orleanist dynasty in 1830. Over against them is set a liberal clique, headed by the 'Satanic' barrister, Vinet—'figure vipérine à tête plate, à bouche fendue, ses yeux éclatants à travers des lunettes'—and the stout, bewhiskered, unconventional but perspicacious Napoleonic veteran, Colonel Gouraud. In their wake are sorrier personalities not socially accepted by the Tiphaines—another notary, another doctor, an innkeeper, some farmers, etc. Their aim is, by the same methods as those of the reigning coterie—well-calculated marriage alliances, mutual support, the foundation and control of another local journal—to outrival and eclipse the Tiphaine faction and hoist themselves into desirable posts. The local curé, the Abbé Habert, and his sister Céleste, a rapidly but excellently sketched 'school-marm' on the look-out for a husband, stand in an embarrassed and ambiguous position between the two groups.

Into this environment step the Rogron pair. They are among the most odious people that Balzac had yet delineated. He goes backwards in time and shows them running their haberdashery in Paris, the mind of each 'entièrement absorbé par l'entente de leur commerce, par le Doit et Avoir', wheedling their customers, cantankerous with their employees, having no time or inclination for the softer aspects of life. Denis Rogron is almost a cretin in all matters not connected with the details of his trade; Sylvie is domineering and shrewd; both of them are scraping, grasping, pitiless in their acquisitiveness: 'deux natures . . . excessivement filandreuses et sèches, endurcies par le travail, par les privations, par le souvenir de leurs douleurs pendant un long et rude apprentissage'—an apprenticeship foisted upon them by an unnatural father who had thought that kicks were a better viaticum than coins. 'Pour eux, la vertu, l'honneur, la loyauté, tous les sentiments humains consistaient à payer régulièrement ses billets.' In mitigation of their lack of the milk of human kindness, and probably also in recollection of his own experience, Balzac had already pointed out that, as babies, they had been put out to nurse.

Balzac heaps page on page in evoking their shrivelled souls in a chapter which might well have been entitled: 'Physiologie du mercier.' Their one human sentiment is the nostalgia for their native town, and their dream of the embellishments they are going to make in their dead father's house once they return to it. And Balzac dwells on the untutored enthusiasm with which they reshape and redecorate it with disparate adornments in a desperate attempt to outshine their neighbours, the long-established denizens of Provins. Adopting a device which might have been admirable had it been less pedantically executed, Balzac diverges a little from his habit of direct description, and puts into the mouth of the scornful Mme Tiphaine a minute account of their rooms and furniture, the better to bring out the vulgarity and bad taste which have directed the alterations. All their expenditure and ostentation, all their crude efforts to get on terms of reciprocal hospitality with the Tiphaine set, fall flat. Tiring of the monotony born of this ostracism, they lend a ready ear to the blandishments of Vinet and Gouraud, who count on enticing them into their camp and exploiting their ignorance and their wealth.

It is thanks to the rebuffs they have received that the heroine of the story, Pierrette Lorrain, comes into the picture. She is a 'poor relation' of the Rogrons, a Breton orphan whose grandparents are no longer able to keep her and ask their kinsfolk to give her a home. The Rogrons had at first ignored the request, but have now changed their minds in the vain hope that such an act of charity will bring them credit with the Tiphaines. The treatment which this frail and sensitive child, only twelve years old when the action begins, receives from her unloving and unlovable cousins, during three years of nagging cruelty, lifts the story to the plane of tragedy. Sylvie Rogron's growing harshness towards Pierrette, who is soon depressed to the rank and duties of a slavey, is not only the expression of her hard and despotic nature; it is intensified by jealousy. First of all she resents the kindness shown to Pierrette by the Provins families so contemptuous towards herself. Then Pierrette becomes unwittingly the centre of a complicated intrigue, the bone of contention in an obscure conflict of interests in which the Rogrons, Vinet, Gouraud and the Haberts are concerned. Vinet plans to marry Denis Rogron to the impecunious but comely and aristocratic cousin of his wife, Bathilde de Chargebœuf, while Céleste Habert stands by as a not very formidable competitor. Sylvie, in spite of her physical and moral repulsiveness (she has added a totally selfish religious devotion to the list of her unattractive qualities), is through her wealth matrimonially acceptable to Gouraud: 'il était colonel de cavalerie, il avait donné ses preuves de courage'. Sylvie for her part

regarda très agréablement le colonel: elle rencontrait pour la première fois de sa vie un homme à qui l'idée qu'elle aurait pu se marier ne paraissait pas absurde.

But there is an alternative possibility, that of Gouraud marrying Pierrette in the hope of her inheriting her cousins' possessions. The belief that he is making secret advances to her maid-of-all-work brings Sylvie to a high pitch of hatred; her cruelty is aggravated by the fear of the very marriage she is working for, since the malicious Céleste has impressed upon her the dangers attendant on childbirth at the advanced age of forty-two. Pierrette's one ray of hope is due to the presence at Provins of her young Breton sweetheart, the joiner Jacques Brigaut, one of the few 'proletarians' who play an important part in a 'Comédie Humaine' novel. He knows of her plight and is preparing to elope with her. But this fact hastens her destruction, for Sylvie knows nothing of Jacques, and suspects Pierrette's clandestine communications with him to be in reality an intrigue she is conducting with Gouraud. From that moment her relations with Pierrette are those of a cat torturing a mouse.

Pour une fille de cette trempe, la jalousie était moins un sentiment qu'une occupation: elle vivait, elle sentait battre son cœur, elle avait des émotions jusqu'alors complètement inconnus pour elle: le moindre mouvement la tenait éveillée, elle écoutait les plus légers bruits, elle observait Pierrette avec une sombre préoccupation.

Cette petite misérable me tuera! disait-elle.

In the upshot it is she who kills the 'little wretch'. Pierrette's health is already impaired by neglected chlorosis. Sylvie's brutality to her results in a serious injury to her head, and a final nocturnal scene between the two, a struggle for the possession of a letter from Brigaut, in which the infuriated Sylvie falls on Pierrette tooth and nail, brings the girl to death's door. Her rescue from the Rogron clutches by Brigaut and her grandmother, summoned post-haste from Nantes by Brigaut, occurs too late to save her life, even though Bianchon and Desplein are called in and a trepanning operation is performed. The attempt made by Pierrette's grandmother and Brigaut to bring the Rogrons to book for their wickedness is immediately translated into terms of local politics. Even the Tiphaines see in it an opportunity to ruin the anti-monarchical faction. As in *Le Cabinet des antiques*, once public and private interests are intermingled, the claims of justice are likely to go unheard: what matter that in this case a human life has been first mutilated and then obliterated? Vinet's manœuvres save the Rogrons from the punishment they deserve, and Pierrette remains unavenged.

Pierrette is one of those novels in which the action, temporarily suspended after an initial incident while the author gathers his data from the past, moves swiftly once the stage is adequately set. There is a characteristically rapid deflagration of events: Sylvie's bullying interrogation of Pierrette over the identity of her admirer, her viperish outburst against her for giving Gouraud winning advice over a game of boston, the secret exchange of letters between Pierrette and Brigaut, the fight in the bedroom, the gathering of kindly figures round the sick-bed of a girl for so long starved of kindliness, the surrender of the frightened Rogrons to Vinet's purposes in order to stave off legal proceedings, the subterfuges and counter-measures Vinet takes to secure this end, the doctors' efforts to save the dying Pierrette, Brigaut's agony of despair which he can only assuage by setting grimly to work on the making of her coffin, and finally the terrible climax when, arriving at the death-chamber with the coffin, he finds a surgeon, at Vinet's demand, about to perform an autopsy on the corpse in order to ascertain the true cause of death. As Vinet had anticipated, Brigaut's despair turns to violent anger; his threats avert the post-mortem, and the prosecution of the Rogrons has to be dropped.

In narrating the painful story of a helpless and sweet-tempered child's virtual assassination at the hands of an inhuman couple, one of them at first implacable in persecution and then hysterically sadistic, the other spineless and uncomprehending in his toleration of unrelenting cruelty, Balzac gives a memorable example of the unflinching gaze he can direct on human guilt and its motivation. Without effusion of sentiment or exaggeration of pathos, and without allowing himself or his readers any delusions on the score of wrong being righted in this world—the Rogrons and their accomplices live on, prosper, and eventually achieve amity with the Tiphaines—he has equalled if not surpassed the author of *Oliver Twist* and *The Old Curiosity Shop* in the poignancy of his realism. This is so much the more striking because of a sort of inevitability in the sequence of events (the characters of the protagonists being given) to which he evidently submitted in writing the story; and that perhaps despite his original intentions. Indeed his revelation of the criss-cross of local antagonisms and social jealousies may appear insignificant in comparison with the appalling drama the novel so restrainedly unfolds. None the less the aim and achievement of *Pierrette* are to show how closely individual catastrophe is bound up with social behaviour and the play of social passions. As in all his best novels, the moral is left to point itself. Not for him the passionate declamation of a

Dickens as the chased and chivied crossing-sweeper of *Bleak House* breathes his last:

Dead, your Majesty. Dead, my lords and gentlemen. Dead, Right Reverends and Wrong Reverends of every order. Dead, men and women, born with Heavenly compassion in your hearts. And dying thus around us every day.

Instead of the Englishman's generous emotion there is the Frenchman's ironic recording of success for the wicked, and the terseness of a concluding comment:

Convenons entre nous que la légalité serait une belle chose si Dieu n'existait pas.[1]

---

[1] In the 1843 and subsequent editions the force of the sentence is weakened by the insertion after 'serait' of the words: 'pour les friponneries sociales'.

IX

PARIS SCENES OF 1837–8
BUREAUCRACY, BUSINESS AND
BANKING

i. A Trilogy of Novels

Les Employés, *L'Histoire de la grandeur et de la décadence de César Birotteau*, and *La maison Nucingen* form a fairly homogeneous group of 'Scenes'. The first appeared serially in *La Presse* in July 1837 under the title of *La Femme supérieure*. Balzac had been thinking of it or working on it for a year, but only got ahead with it during the month he spent at the Viscontis in June–July 1837. *César Birotteau* had been conceived in 1833. He wrote a first draft of it at Frapesle in April 1834. In November 1837 he was offered 2,000 francs to produce it in haste as a presentation gift which two periodicals, *Le Figaro* and *L'Estafette*, wished to make to their subscribers. It came out in December. At the same time he was writing *La maison Nucingen*, whose subject had already been hinted at in *L'Interdiction*,[1] as well as beginning *La Torpille* and other works. When, in September 1838, *Les Employés* first appeared in book form, it was in conjunction with *La maison Nucingen*, which had *La haute Banque* as its original title, and *La Torpille*. Since the latter belongs to the Rubempré cycle, it may be left out of account for the present. *Les Employés*, *César Birotteau* and *La maison Nucingen* are linked together as 'histoires parisiennes', in which some interesting reappearing characters are conceived. They also have this in common: for practically the first time Balzac gives close and lengthy study to certain clearly defined sections of the Parisian middle classes.

1 And even earlier: *E* I, 240 (11 March 1835)—*La Faillite de M. de Nucingen*.

ii. *Les Employés* (1837)

As a contribution to the political and social history of the early nineteenth century in France, *Les Employés* paints a picture and voices searching criticism of the administrative organization under the Bourbons (*circa* 1824), and, by implication, that also of the Louis-Philippe period. The attitude Balzac adopts is in harmony with his royalist principles and his contempt for parliamentary government. His criticism bears on three aspects of the bureaucratic system which had developed since the Revolution, and indeed had been developing since the reign of Louis XIV, although Balzac tended to ignore the fact. The first aspect is its wastefulness in man-power, its inefficiency and general dilatoriness. The second aspect is the type of persons attracted to the French Civil Service. The third is the injustice and jobbery prevalent in the matter of appointments and promotion: the preference given to third-rate minds and personalities through parliamentary, ministerial and individual wire-pulling. There is even a suggestion that the Church took a hand in these intrigues through the agency of the so-called 'Congrégation', but in the end Balzac virtually rules this out after having quite patently suggested it.

The theme is woven round the person of an Office Director in the Treasury department, Xavier Rabourdin, and his wife. Rabourdin is a man of integrity, energy, talent and statesmanship. For six years he has been working on a scheme of administrative and fiscal reform, and this gives Balzac his opportunity to point out fundamental defects and vices in the administration. Rabourdin's scheme of reform chiefly involves a drastic reduction both in the number of ministries and the number of Civil Servants, with a view to more work being better done by fewer people for more adequate remuneration, and with a better chance of real talent rising to the top. The plan for fiscal reform is less easy to follow, but it involves the suppression of land-tax and all indirect taxation in favour of a curiously conceived personal tax based on the scale of living indicated by expenditure on such things as house-rent, furniture, servants, equipages, etc.; a rational device, according to Balzac-Rabourdin, making for an equitable assessment since standard of living is a reliable guide for estimating capacity to pay. There is no need to dwell upon the economic well-being which in Balzac's idea was to result from such a system. Clearly it is based on the doctrine of a State which is, from the economic point of view, essentially *laissez-faire*, which owns no property, holds no monopolies and does not dabble in production. But over against this apparent economic liberalism is set, as we should expect, the principle of personal rule, personal administration and an eminently personal relationship between ministers, higher officials and the rank and file of the Civil Service.

Unfortunately for his prospects of advancement, the indefatigable Rabourdin has appended to this scheme of reform a register of all the employees of the central administrations in Paris, with an appreciation of their characters, their aptitudes and their weaknesses, and a record of the activities by which they supplement their incomes outside office hours. The scheme itself is sufficiently damaging to vested interests to provoke disapproval. But Rabourdin's downfall is assured by the fact of hostile clerks (one Dutocq in particular) laying hands on the register and divulging its contents at the moment when Rabourdin's succession as Director of the Division to the nonentity La Billardière seems practically certain. His reputation among his colleagues and assistants as a man of honour is compromised by this register, which appears to stamp him as a spy and informer.

But there are other causes for his discomfiture and resignation from the Civil Service. Much depends on Clément Chardin des Lupeaulx, the Secretary-General to the anonymous minister. This man who is destined to frequent appearances in the 'Comédie Humaine' as an intriguer in governmental and administrative circles, makes his first appearance in *Les Employés* and immediately takes an important place in Balzac's imagined world. Morally speaking, he is one more of those shifty schemers of the Du Croisier–Du Bousquier–Vinet–Gouraud type. He is a sort of *touche-à-tout*, an indispensable tool of the minister he serves; a 'vieux beau' just turning forty, indebted, ambitious, aiming at the Chambre des Députés and the Peerage—always a matter, in Balzac's eyes, of fudging the necessary property qualification and corrupting a sufficient number of electors. He is essentially a mediocrity:

> . . . égoïste et vain, souple et fier, libertin et gourmand, avide à cause de ses dettes, discret comme une tombe d'où rien ne peut sortir pour démentir l'inscription destinée aux passants, intrépide et sans peur quand il sollicitait, aimable et spirituel dans toute l'acception du mot, moqueur à propos, plein de tact, sachant vous compromettre par une caresse comme par un coup de coude, ne reculant devant aucune largeur de ruisseau et sautant avec grâce, affronté voltairien et allant à la messe à Saint-Thomas-d'Aquin quand il s'y trouvait une belle assemblée.

Mme Célestine Rabourdin, the 'femme supérieure' of the story —although she has what is in the eyes of the social snobs the disadvantage of being an auctioneer's daughter—is a gracious and cultured woman. At moments Balzac seems to suggest that this 'superiority' is merely assumed. Célestine has been brought up to expectations which cannot be satisfied by a Civil Servant who, however devoted a husband he may be, has so far failed to find his true level in the hierarchy to which he belongs. In this respect alone, although she is no aristocrat, she bears a faint resemblance to the ambitious Émilie de Fontaine in *Le Bal de Sceaux*. But the picture Balzac gives of her does in fact mark her as a woman capable of holding her own in the company of such distinguished ladies as Mme Firmiani and the Marquise d'Espard. She is anxious to make up for her husband's deficiencies by pushing him forward in his profession, and she is intelligent; but not intelligent enough—or rather too virtuous and too loyal to her husband—to play her cards successfully. In order to shine socially she maintains a standard of living above her means, and counts on fascinating des Lupeaulx to the point of making him serve her husband's interests without prejudice to her own chastity. Her chances of success in this delicate operation are destroyed by the play of motives over which she has no control. Xavier's colleague and rival for the post of Director of the Division, the 'imbécile' Baudoyer, has family influences behind him, including that of his wife's uncle, the usurer Bidault, alias Gigonnet, who in collusion with the redoubtable Gobseck brings financial pressure to bear on des Lupeaulx and forces him to make a choice between his pursuit of Mme Rabourdin and the furtherance of his political ambitions.

In Baudoyer's wife Élisabeth, daughter of Saillard, the cashier of the department, all 'superior' qualities are lacking. She is put forward by Balzac as

... une de ces figures qui se dérobent au pinceau par leur vulgarité même, et qui néanmoins doivent être esquissées, car elles offrent une expression de cette petite bourgeoisie parisienne, placée au-dessus des riches artisans et au-dessous de la haute classe [i.e. the upper reaches of the middle class], dont les qualités sont presque des vices, dont les défauts n'ont rien d'aimable, mais dont les mœurs, quoique plates, ne manquent pas d'originalité.

Since the clerks of the ministerial offices are largely drawn from this 'petite bourgeoisie', the originality of *Les Employés* lies in the scrutiny Balzac has made of it. He was to delve even deeper in *César Birotteau*, and from round about 1839 was to form the intention of pursuing this scrutiny in a further work which he began, but which, as with *Le Député d'Arcis*, it became the task of Charles Rabou to finish: *Les petits Bourgeois*. The central interest in *Les Employés*, except of course for the interest of the drama enacted round the upright Rabourdin and his wholly attractive wife, is Balzac's vivacious evocation of the Government offices, their honeycomb of premises, their furniture, the different grades of staff, their outlook, mentality and habits.

He does indeed offer us a whole series of portraits, from the all-observing and critical messengers, and the sweated supernumeraries, hoping like Sébastien de la Roche for permanent employment, to copying-clerks, finance officers, order clerks, deputy-chiefs and chiefs. There are for instance the obsequious but far from glib Saillard, the flabby Baudoyer, the lazy and incapable Dutocq, who intrigues against the perspicacious Rabourdin because he knows he has no chance of promotion with him; the loyal but naïve Sébastien de la Roche; the spinsterish but slovenly Godard; Vimeux, the dandy and would-be lady-killer; the quiet, hard-working, uxorious Minard, a target for the wits at the Office; the stout, jovial Colleville and his slender, handsome crony, Thuillier; the obtuse and gullible Poiret, younger brother of the retired Civil Servant of *Le père Goriot*; the bickering pair of gossips, Paulmier and Chazelle; the aggressive political leftist, Fleury; the humanitarian republican Desroys; the foppish La Billardière junior, relying for advancement on parental and ministerial protection. These and others Balzac shows to us at and away from their desks, with their vices, absurdities, hobbies and manias— Colleville for instance delights in drawing Nostradamus-like prognostications from the anagrams of proper names.

Three others, not yet mentioned, are worth singling out. One is the excellent but pompous Phellion, who teaches at a girls' school in the evenings and writes little scholastic catechisms for the pupils; he, like Colleville and Thuillier, is to have a substantial part to play in *Les petits Bourgeois*. The second is Du Bruel, who under the name of de Cursy[1] collaborates in the writing of vaudevilles, and is making a pretty penny by it. The third and most important is the black-and-white artist Bixiou ('prononcez Bisiou'), on whose delineation Balzac has expended special care: a witty, flippant, cynical observer of men and their foibles, whose aptitude for caricature, mimicry and practical jokes has earned him both admiration and dislike among his colleagues; who supplements his official salary by cartoons, vignettes and book illustrations; a man of the world, dissipated, a popular figure at the gatherings of the theatrical, literary and artistic Bohemias of the time; an artist of great but intermittent talent; vivacious in mind, prodigal of ideas, secretly disenchanted with his lot; hard, trenchant, unable to hold back a devastating *bon mot* even if it wounds his friends; a real judge of worth and discerner of principles, and yet maleficent, for it is he who puts the finishing touch to Rabourdin's discomfiture by producing, at Dutocq's instigation, a caricature of the Office Chief in a butcher's smock gleefully cutting the throats of his colleagues in the guise of chickens, geese and turkeys imprisoned in a cage and awaiting their turn for this 'exécution administrative'.

It is a well-established fact that the artist Henry Monnier, an erstwhile copying-clerk in the Ministry of Justice, who left his post to take up drawing, provided Balzac with a model for this at once amusing and repulsive character. Bixiou is Monnier in almost every detail of his versatile talent and, as regards his physical characteristics, right down to his vague facial resemblance to

[1] This *nom de plume* does not appear until 1840, in *Un Prince de la Bohème*.

Napoleon. We have seen that it is easy, by picking on features of various characters in the 'Comédie Humaine', and on incidents in their history, to identify them in particular respects with known contemporaries of Balzac; but the identification is rarely assured or complete. In the case of Bixiou it does seem more certain. And this is strange in view of the character he gives him, for Balzac and Monnier were old colleagues and friends. Monnier had a part in illustrating many of Balzac's novels. Balzac evidently learned a lot about Civil Service life and habits from Monnier's 1828 album of lithographs, *Mœurs administratives*, and from his *Scènes de la vie bureaucratique*;[1] the latter may even have inspired him to write *Les Employés*. He admired and praised Monnier's wit and talent;[2] he owed something to Monnier for the invention of that type of pompous and unintelligent Philistine whom Monnier immortalized under the name of Joseph Prudhomme, as the examples of Phellion, César Birotteau, Matifat, Philéas Beauvisage and many others may serve to show; he was inspired by Monnier for the idea of several plays in which Joseph Prudhomme was to be the central figure; and at times he even wished to collaborate with him or write parts for him to act—for Monnier was an actor as well as a draughtsman.[3]

Yet there seems to be some malice in the way Balzac has introduced Monnier into the 'Comédie Humaine' and even gone so far as discovering or postulating in him unpleasant traits of character which were at the worst only latent in the original. To explain this, one can only suspect a secret dislike and antagonism between the two men to which Monnier himself was to give some expression later by the absurdities he related of Balzac in his *Mémoires de M. Joseph Prudhomme* of 1857. At any rate a conspicuous fact about *Les Employés* is this bringing of Bixiou, who had already figured in the 1831 edition of *La Peau de chagrin* as an anonymous caricaturist at the 'orgie chez Taillefer',[4] into the limelight.

---

[1] In *Scènes populaires*, edition of 1835.

[2] In *La Mode*, 2 Oct. 1830; in *La Caricature*, 31 May 1832.

[3] This identification of Monnier and Bixiou is discussed anew in Melcher, especially ch. xiii. Also in Marash, ch. viii.

[4] See above, 40 and 97. The guests invite him to give an exhibition of his talent as a mimic. Even in 1831 Balzac clearly had Monnier in mind. In the 1845 edition of *La Peau de chagrin* he makes the now named Bixiou take off Buloz,

Bixiou is without doubt the dominating figure among the group of Civil Servants whom Balzac exhibits in their offices; gossiping, discussing, quarrelling, each cutting his own particular capers, in a series of dialogues which, like Monnier's own 'Scenes', are virtually dramatized.

It would of course be rash to infer that Monnier was Balzac's sole source of information. In any case *Les Employés* stands out as the classic satire on the French bureaucracy and the bureaucratic habit of mind; and we may note that André Gide gave the work unstinted admiration.[1] Furthermore it is impregnated with Balzac's typical blend of censure and sympathy, of humour and sarcasm. The pungency which Flaubert referred to in Voltaire's *Candide* as 'la griffe du lion' is present in *Les Employés*—and in how many side-glances and *obiter dicta*! Three instances may well be quoted. One is the comment of the sanctimonious Abbé Gaudron on hearing of Baudoyer's appointment in preference to Rabourdin: 'Dieu protège ceux qui songent à ses autels!'—Baudoyer, or rather his wife, had made a timely gift of a monstrance to the parish church of St. Paul. Another is the affirmation of Saillard, as he gloats over the triumph of his son-in-law: 'Et l'on peut bien dire que c'est sans intrigue . . . Nous ne sommes pas intrigants, nous autres!' The third is the piece of information vouchsafed by an office servant at the end of the novel: the victorious Baudoyer and his underling Colleville, promoted also—to the rank of Office Chief—proved their incompetence within six months and were diverted to the function of tax-collectors. It is true that this conclusion was not added to the story until *Les Employés* was incorporated in the 'Comédie Humaine' in 1844.[2]

According to Balzac's own testimony,[3] the readers of *La Presse* found *Les Employés* boring and insipid.

whom Balzac so detested since the lawsuit over *Le Lys* in 1836. See *Biography*, 83–5, 107.

[1] *Journal* II, 147.

[2] The pre-original version ends at p. 262 in the Conard edition (vol. xix—*Recevez nos compliments? il est joli celui-là*). The final version runs on to p. 280. Lovenjoul (1), 132–3, is in error about the date of this change.

[3] *E* I, 410.

iii. *Histoire de la grandeur et de la décadence de César Birotteau* (1837)

It is certain that, at the time when *Le père Goriot* was being written, Balzac intended to peer into the life of the 'petite bourgeoisie' in order to give a closer and fuller view of the shopkeeper and small-scale manufacturer type than the study of the long-retired maker of vermicelli could afford. He does so at last in the person of César Birotteau, 'marchand parfumeur établi près de la Place Vendôme'; the son of a Chinon small-holder and younger brother of the Abbé Birotteau, whose tranquil existence as a 'curé de Tours' was not to be shattered until 1826. About 1793 César came up to Paris 'with a louis in his pocket', to make his fortune slowly, first as assistant of the perfumer Ragon, then as his successor by purchase of the latter's establishment, 'La Reine des Roses'; he married the beautiful, good-hearted Constance Pillerault, the chief assistant in a large draper's shop, and set up a small cosmetics factory. Thanks to the recipes furnished by a benevolent chemical researcher Vauquelin (a real person), and thanks also to specious advertisements and skilful marketing tactics proposed by his wife, he prospered, became a prominent figure in his quarter during the early Restoration, reached the height of his 'grandeur' in 1818, and decided to cut away from his shop-serving past and push forward 'dans les hautes sociétés'. So that the beginning of the novel shows this excellent but unlettered and ingenuous man pondering and preparing his ambitious schemes, with his sensible and apprehensive wife, a Mme Jourdain of the nineteenth century, trying in vain to put a drag on his enthusiasm. He embarks simultaneously on several projects: the enlargement and embellishment of his house and premises; the launching of a factory for the production of a new hair-oil, 'l'huile céphalique', under the management of his keen and able assistant, Anselme Popinot, who hopes to wed Birotteau's daughter, Césarine; and the attempt to achieve a spectacular increase in his fortune by entering into a partnership for the purchase of certain undeveloped sites in the region of the Madeleine and waiting for them to appreciate in value.

This novel affords perhaps the best example of a favoured technique of Balzac, inherited from Scott, for embarking on a story: he plunges *in medias res* by showing Constance Birotteau waking up from a bad dream in the small hours to find that her lord and master has deserted the connubial bed. 'Aurait-il une maîtresse? Il est trop bête . . . et d'ailleurs, il m'aime trop pour cela.' She finds him pacing out the premises with a view to the costly alterations he is going to make; and in a heart-to-heart talk between husband and wife we learn of César's intentions. After which there is the usual dip into the past to reveal the antecedents, status and character of the Birotteau couple: admirable pages. Then the narrative proceeds in accordance with Balzac's customary methods—the following-out of a central thread, with pauses here and there to take up subordinate ones, and the weaving of all of them together to produce a texture which gives a convincing impression of real life in all its complexity.

The central thread in question is the theme of César rashly turning from honest and straightforward commerce,[1] for which he has flair and competence, to the hazards of speculation, for which he has sufficient knowledge neither of men nor of affairs: 'il n'est pas de force', as the usurer Gigonnet says of him later in the story. The man who pulls the strings while remaining in the background is the 'faiseur' du Tillet, a former employee of César, who had not only made improper advances to Constance (of this César remained ignorant), but had also been caught one day with his hands in the till. Thereupon, in league with a rascally notary, Maître Roguin, he had taken to banking and speculation under the patronage of Gobseck. The creation of du Tillet is, after the invention of Nucingen in 1834, a major event in the history of the 'Comédie Humaine'. According to Spoelberch de Lovenjoul,[2] Émile de Girardin[3] thought Balzac had him in mind when conceiving this able scoundrel. M. Maurice Serval, to whom we are indebted for an excellent study of this novel,[4] believes that

---

[1] This view depends of course on the reader's political and social leanings. André Wurmser regards César as an immoral bourgeois capitalist, no better than the other 'fripons', du Tillet, Nucingen, Roguin, etc.

[2] In a comment on the proofs of *La maison Nucingen* at Chantilly (A 125).

[3] Founder of newspapers and husband of Balzac's loyal friend Delphine Gay. See *Biography*.   [4] Serval (6).

William Duckett, of *Chronique de Paris* fame,[1] furnished the model, just as he thinks that Nucingen was based on James de Rothschild. Such identifications are more specious than convincing. No doubt there are other likely models. Du Tillet is of lesser stature than the imperturbable Nucingen, so infallible in his acquisitiveness; but he cuts an important figure among the denizens of Balzac's world as a rapacious financier who by dint of cunning, treachery and ruthlessness rises eventually to that kind of respectability which society always confers on its law-abiding criminals. His aim in drawing César into the Madeleine speculation is to vent his spite on his old employer while increasing his own fortune.

The plot whereby César is entangled in this disastrous affair is one of those combinations which Balzac loved to unfold in all their tortuousness, though readers who are financially inexpert find them puzzling.[2] The crux of the matter is that César is induced to call on all his resources and those of his friends, the Ragon couple and Claude-Joseph Pillerault, the retired ironmonger whom Balzac himself identified with his old friend, Dablin, in order to find the capital for taking up his half-share in the speculation. His assets are still further depleted by the large expenses he incurs by rebuilding and redecorating his apartments in preparation for the splendid ball he intends to give in order to celebrate his accession to the Legion of Honour—the date is somewhere in December 1818[3]—and the liberation of French territory from the occupying forces of the allies of 1815. The ball will also mark his ascent to social brilliance, for his aristocratic and royalist patrons are to be present as well as his mercantile friends and associates. Du Tillet engineers his scheme through the agency of two cat's-paws. The one is Roguin, whose wife is his mistress and the mother of Amélie Tiphaine whose acquaintance we make in *Pierrette*. To Roguin César mortgages some sites and factories in return for a loan of 40,000 francs which turns out to be fictitious, for Roguin has already embezzled the money from a client. The other is the

---

[1] See *Biography*, 83–4, 92–3. [2] See Bouvier, ch. iii, 61–87.
[3] The chronology of *César Birotteau* is uncertain. The more Balzac seeks to bind his episodes and characters together in accordance with the principle of reappearing characters, the more embarrassed his dovetailing tends to become. at any rate in regard to minor details.

dissipated, down-at-heel man of straw Claparon, passed off by du Tillet as a reputable banker with whom César is to deposit an even larger sum—140,000 francs in bills of exchange. Thus Claparon enters the 'Études de Mœurs' as the mean and sorry tool of the high-class swindlers Nucingen and du Tillet. Immediately after the ball Roguin decamps, swarms of creditors clamour for payment, and we are confronted with a 'César aux prises avec le malheur'.

All these events move swiftly in point of time. Even the alteration of César's premises is a precipitous affair. But the main interest of *César Birotteau* as a study of manners and a gallery of type-portraits lies in the description of César's activities while he is still aspiring to 'greatness'. We are regaled with a multitude of vivacious scenes—César negotiating for the enlargement of his domicile with Cayron the umbrella-merchant, and with the fussy, grasping and litigious landlord, Molineux, whose supreme aphorism on the sacredness of lucre is that

. . . l'argent ne connaît personne; il n'a pas d'oreilles, l'argent; il n'a pas de cœur, l'argent.

—César making arrangements with the supercilious architect, Grindot,[1] to the consternation of his wife, appalled at the thought of so much money squandered; haggling with Mme Madou, the rough-tongued, aggressive but not unpleasing dealer in 'le fruit sec', for the sale of the hazel-nuts which are to form the chief ingredient for the 'huile céphalique'; discussing the Madeleine transaction with the rugged republican Pillerault, shrewd, blunt and honest; interviewing (and naïvely admiring) the detached but kindly Vauquelin about the possible efficacy of the hair-oil and its process of manufacture. All this is punctuated with vivid evocations of localities and domiciles, with portrayals of Césarine and her adoring suitor Anselme Popinot, with accounts of the latter's preliminary activities before putting the hair-oil into production, his recruitment of 'l'illustre Gaudissart', that expert salesman to whom it falls to advertise the product in collaboration with the needy but resourceful journalist, Andoche Finot, and

[1] In the 1838, 1839 and 1844 editions he is called Rohault—a real contemporary of Balzac.

the drawing-up of the perfect example of the persuasive, pseudo-scientific puff typical of an age in which the art of publicity was making gigantic strides. In the meantime preparations for the ball continue, and also for the completion of the Madeleine contract, signed at a supper-party given by César, in the course of which the vulgar and drink-addled Claparon all but gives the game away by overplaying his part as an important man of affairs. Other scenes are interspersed with these: Anselme's house-warming party in honour of the hair-oil project; the appearance of Anselme's uncle, Judge Popinot, whose future dealings (in 1828) with the d'Espard family have already been recounted in *L'Interdiction*, and who draws up the contract between César and Anselme; the family discussion over the list of celebrities to be invited to the ball, and finally the ball itself. We should expect Balzac to be more than ever in his element here, especially in contrasting the embarrassment of the middle-class guests, such as the simple-minded Ragons and the coarse Matifats, with the gracious or ironic *savoir-faire* of such social stars as Émilie de Fontaine, Mme Jules Desmarets and Mme Rabourdin.

'Comme ils s'amusent!' exclaims the radiant César when, in the later stages of the ball, the dancing of the middle-class couples reaches a paroxysm of vulgar exuberance. 'Pourvu qu'ils ne cassent rien!' is Constance's worried comment. Mindful of his initiation in the mysteries of musicography, between the manuscript and the first edition Balzac works in a dithyramb on Beethoven's C minor Symphony as a means of conveying César's ravishment at this supreme moment of his career.

Analysis cannot do justice to the multiplicity of traits which in this novel illustrate both the author's fertility of invention and the acuteness of his observation. The first half of the work in particular is unparalleled for its pervasive but good-humoured satire. César himself is one of Balzac's greatest creations. Some tribute must be paid to Henry Monnier for the clues his Joseph Prud-homme gave to Balzac in the conception of César Birotteau. But Joseph Prudhomme is predominantly a caricature who never attains three-dimensional humanity. Outside his commercial competence César is the very incarnation of lower middle-class ignorance and illiteracy; but he is not only life-size, he is living: a ridiculous but likeable noodle, as immortal as any of the great comic figures of Dickens. Everything Balzac tells us about his hero—the minutest details of his physical appearance, his demeanour and characteristic gestures—is a joy to read; largely because the tone of superiority which can so easily harden into derision, as I think it does for instance with Rose Cormon, is much less perceptible in this more mellow novel. Indeed César is likeable because and not although he is ridiculous. He can be fatuous:

Quand il croyait avoir dit quelque chose de galant ou de saillant, il se levait imperceptiblement sur la pointe des pieds, à deux reprises, et retombait sur ses talons lourdement, comme pour appuyer sa phrase.

He can be pompous—'je ne me nomme pas César pour rien'—and self-important; as he is, for example, whenever he thinks of his display of martial valour, back in 1795, on behalf of the monarchy, when he had made his one and only incursion into street-fighting activities, which eventually helped to earn him the cross of the Legion of Honour. The satisfaction which this memory affords him is expressed again and again in a grandiloquent refrain:

Peut-être me suis-je rendu digne de cette insigne et royale faveur en siégeant au tribunal consulaire et en combattant pour les Bourbons sur les marches de Saint-Roch, au 13 vendémiaire, où je fus blessé par Napoléon.

He has few ideas or opinions beyond those of his fellow-shopkeepers, and in enumerating these Balzac foreshadows the *sottisier* which Flaubert many times thought of compiling.

Il épousa forcément le langage, les erreurs, les opinions du bourgeois de Paris, qui admire Molière, Voltaire et Rousseau sur parole, qui achète leurs œuvres sans les lire; qui soutient que l'on doit dire *ormoire*, parce que les femmes serraient dans ces meubles leur *or* et leurs robes autrefois presque toujours en moire, et que l'on dit par corruption *armoire*. Potier, Talma, Mlle Mars[1] étaient dix fois millionnaires et ne vivaient pas comme les autres humains: le grand tragédien mangeait de la chair crue, Mlle Mars faisait parfois fricasser des perles, pour imiter une célèbre actrice égyptienne. L'empereur avait à ses gilets des poches en cuir pour pouvoir prendre son tabac par poignées, il montait à cheval au grand galop l'escalier de l'orangerie à

---

[1] Contemporary theatrical stars.

Versailles. Les écrivains, les artistes mouraient à l'hôpital par suite de leurs originalités; ils étaient d'ailleurs tous athées, il fallait bien se garder de les recevoir chez soi . . . Les astronomes vivaient d'araignées. . . .

His utterances *à la* Joseph Prudhomme are numerous:

En voyant la gravure de *Héro et Léandre*, je me suis dit: 'Si les anciens usaient tant d'huile pour leurs cheveux, ils avaient une raison quelconque', car les anciens sont les anciens! Malgré les prétentions modernes, je suis de l'avis de Boileau sur les anciens. Je suis parti de là pour arriver à l'huile de noisette. . . .

His anticipations of the platitudes of Flaubert's middle-class types, the odious Homais and the naïve Bouvard and Pécuchet, are only outrivalled by those of the ex-druggist Matifat. But there is never anything odious or contemptible about César. His stupidity is always redeemed by goodness of heart. He can even be delicate on occasion, as he is when his gratitude to Vauquelin inspires him with a gracious speech persuading the scientist to accept the gift of a picture in return for his advice.

But, if César is laughable during the period of his 'grandeur', he becomes noble and heroic during the period of his 'décadence'. The second half of the novel brings out to the full this aspect of his character. After the ball comes the reckoning: *le quart d'heure de Rabelais*, as Ragon puts it. At a moment when he has heavy bills to meet, Maître Roguin's defection puts him in a terrible position, so that du Tillet and Claparon can set in operation their plan to squeeze him out of the Madeleine affair. He has first of all to face the hard egoism of lesser and greater creditors, an onslaught of Shylocks. In spite of Pillerault's warning that all is lost, he battles on. In a desperate attempt to get his credits renewed, he makes a round of visits to influential financiers. This *via dolorosa* brings him first of all to the banking-house of the Keller brothers. From them he gets nothing but smooth words, ill-concealed derision and finally a bland refusal; and this gives Balzac his opportunity to denounce unprincipled politicians, naturally of liberal hue, for whom finance serves as a means of anti-monarchical intrigue. The Kellers (modelled, according to M. Serval, on the Périer brothers) form an unholy partnership in which the politician, François, mayor of the arrondissement whose deputy-mayor is César himself, plays the part of the benevolent idealist, and Adolphe that of the hard-headed business man who opposes sound sense to his brother's generous impulses.

César appears to have better prospects with du Tillet, now suave and patronizing, flaunting his wealth and importance, and pretending to have no hand in the conspiracy which is bringing César to his ruin. And indeed du Tillet is disposed to some measure of mercy until César's tactless expression of gratitude—'je te rends toute mon estime'—whereby he reminds his erstwhile employee of his former peculations, revives all the vengeful hatred in the banker's heart. He sends him on to Nucingen, who thus makes his first direct appearance in the 'Études de Mœurs' since *Le père Goriot*, and is now (since the proof-sheets of the novel) accredited with that Alsatian jargon[1] which is all the more tiresome because it is based on a systematic deformation of unpronounced as well as pronounced consonants. Nucingen and du Tillet toss César to and fro like a shuttlecock before handing him over to the lesser fry, the squalid Claparon and the contemptuous Gigonnet. In this unequal battle—'a sheep defending himself against a tiger', or rather against a whole league of Parisian *carnivora*—César stands no chance. He is forced to file his petition.

It is at this juncture that his 'décadence' is transfigured to become true 'grandeur'. He has always been uncompromising in his condemnation of bankrupts, and his determination to pay his creditors in full enables Balzac to make a scathing criticism of the existing law (superseded in 1838) through manipulation of which a dishonest man could turn bankruptcy into a profitable swindle. The technique of such operations is revealed in full and somewhat perplexing detail, for Balzac was able to draw from his legal studies as a young man, from his own experience of 1827, when he had found himself on the verge of bankruptcy and managed to avoid it, and from the more recent experience of his publisher Werdet. Moreover the admiration he could never refuse to financial ingenuity, however reprehensible, inspired him to acquire an expert knowledge of the intricacies of such procedure. But in cooperation with the incorruptible Pillerault César first of all

---

[1] In *Splendeurs et misères des courtisanes* Balzac forgets, and calls it a 'patois de juif polonais' (Conard XV, 144 and 274).

achieves an honourable settlement with his creditors; then his family and his friends rally round him magnificently, and toil and scrape (as he also does) to secure his complete discharge. Four years of retrenchment and application to this single purpose— that of César himself, his wife, his daughter, Pillerault, and above all Anselme, who makes a triumphant success of the hair-oil venture—bring him to rehabilitation at the *Cour de Cassation*, to commendation by the Comte de Granville, the Duc de Lenoncourt and other right-minded royalist statesmen, and obtain for him an ovation at the Bourse where a withering retort of Pillerault to the hypocritical du Tillet establishes a true scale of moral values for weighing the respective merits of the vindicated 'sheep' and the despicable 'tiger'. But the joy of reinstatement is too much for César. At the ball given by Anselme and Césarine in celebration of their marriage-contract he collapses and dies. 'Voilà la mort du juste' is the comment of the Abbé Loraux, a wise and saintly priest whom Balzac now adds to his repertory, as a counterpoise to the trio of unedifying clergyman invented during this period: the Abbé de Sponde, the Abbé Gaudron and the Abbé Habert.

Some years later[1] Balzac wrote that he had been unable to proceed with *César Birotteau*, once conceived, until it had occurred to him to make his hero 'l'image de la *probité*'. This idea must date back as far as 1834, for Félix Davin had referred to it in his Introduction to the 'Études philosophiques'.[2] It explains why Balzac had then intended to include the work among the philosophical studies—as illustrating the 'law' of the destructive power of thought: to quote Davin, 'Birotteau est tué soudainement par l'idée probité.'[3] The inspiration was a brilliant one for another

[1] In a letter of Oct. 1846 to Hippolyte Castille, Conard, *O.D.* III, 649.

[2] Lovenjoul (1), 204.

[3] R. Giraud (103–9) argues that the philosophic intention behind the work was to apply to a different *milieu* 'the major theme of *La Peau de chagrin*, namely the cyclic rhythm of life forces, surging to an apogee and then declining to extinction'; and that the 'idée-probité' caused Balzac to change the purport of the work, and turn the latter part of it into 'a *feuilleton* novel of suspense and sentimentality'. But who can prove that the historical generalization attached to the account of César's rise to 'greatness' (Conard XIV, 56) is anterior to the 'idée-probité' inspiration? Could even the critical edition called for by Dr W. G. Moore solve this problem?

reason: it resulted in this novel becoming Balzac's great epic of commercial integrity. As such it provides an answer to those critics who have maintained that he was convincing only in his depiction of vice and monomania, that his virtuous characters are either chimerical, insipid or stupid. Certainly there is an appreciable element of stupidity in César and the Ragons; Constance is *bornée* rather than stupid, and her native prudence is a sterling quality. Certainly the loyal Anselme is a less subtle figure than the shifty Roguin and the brazen du Tillet; but he is no fool. His shrewdness and energy destine him for great advancement in the future, for a political career which is to make him a minister, a count and a peer of France. Césarine perhaps has a degree or two less of vitality than for instance that equally dutiful daughter and unselfish wife, Ève Séchard, but she is more alive than the bloodless *ingénues*, such as Victorine Taillefer, whom Balzac sometimes created. As for Pillerault and Judge Popinot, no case has to be made out for their viability. Enough has been said of César himself to show that, in his ingenuous 'grandeur', and even more still in his painful and bewildered 'décadence', he can stand erect opposite the sordid villains who have caught him in their toils.

But it is characteristic of Balzac that he was not entirely satisfied with the contrast he had established between the Birotteau circle and his new creations du Tillet, the Keller brothers and Claparon. In the preface to the first edition, he promised another work—*La maison Nucingen*—as the reverse of the medal of which *César Birotteau* was the obverse. 'Les deux histoires sont nées jumelles.' Having shown how the honest man lost his fortune, he felt impelled to show how the financial sharks had laid the foundations of their prosperity.

iv. *La Maison Nucingen* (*La haute Banque*) (1838)

The author, dining in 1836 with a lady companion at Véry's fashionable restaurant, overhears through a partition the conversation of other diners: 'quatre des plus hardis cormorans éclos dans l'écume qui couronne les flots incessamment renouvelés de la géneration présente . . . spirituels *condottieri* de l'industrie moderne'. This conversation turns in the first place on the question of how Eugène de Rastignac acquired capital and a comfortable income under the ægis of Nucingen, whose career is thus illuminated.

The manner of Nucingen's advance to wealth since 1804, when he was comparatively unknown on the Paris Stock Exchange, is clear in its essentials: the thrice-repeated process of suspending payment of his bills of exchange at a well-chosen moment as if he were about to go into liquidation, thereby frightening his creditors into settling for shares of doubtful value; and then resuming payment as if nothing had happened. The device had proved eminently successful in 1804, 1815 and 1826-9. On the first two occasions the 'valeurs' thus unloaded turned out to be good; those of the 1815 operation (accompanied by the cheap purchase of wines in bulk and the profitable sale of them to the occupying allied forces) are named as being mining shares. These fortuitous appreciations had greatly enhanced Nucingen's reputation, and established him in France and abroad as 'le plus honnête homme du monde'. On the third occasion, in 1826, disappointed at having enriched his previous victims,[1] he had taken the precaution of launching beforehand, in conjunction with du Tillet, and with the bogus banker Claparon in nominal control, a joint-stock company which was basically sound, but which he artificially boosted by the payment of an unearned dividend, so that the shares reached a swollen price on the market. Then he played his vanishing-trick, employed Rastignac to persuade his creditors to accept payment in shares of this company while they were at a premium, reappeared more triumphantly solvent than ever, and when the shares had lost their artificial value, left Claparon to go bankrupt and bought them in again at a panic price.[2] Thus he increased his capital by several millions at the expense of many dupes. The moral of the story is the usual one:

Il y a des actes arbitraires qui sont criminels d'individu à individu, lesquels arrivent à rien quand ils sont étendus à une multitude quelconque, comme une goutte d'acide prussique devient innocente dans un baquet d'eau.

[1] 'Il a voulu les rouer, impossible!' says Bixiou, relating the transaction.

[2] Other paper assets of which he disembarrassed himself in the same way include shares in silver-bearing lead-mines. Balzac evidently had his own experiences of 1838 in Sardinia in mind. See Biography, 94-5.

Steal on a small scale and you go to prison. Steal on a large scale and you become a great man.

La maison Nucingen gives more information on Rastignac than Balzac had made available since *Le père Goriot*. We learn how, by hanging on to the skirts of Delphine de Nucingen, he drew her husband's attention upon him as a convenient cat's-paw. Nucingen used him to betray his friends and acquaintances into falling into the financial trap set for them, so that Rastignac came out of the 1826-9 affair with an income of 40,000 francs. He is summed up in this *nouvelle* as a man who

> . . . a tout l'esprit qu'il faut avoir dans un moment donné, comme un militaire qui ne place son courage qu'à quatre-vingt-dix jours, trois signatures et des garanties. Il paraîtra cassant, brise-raison, sans suite dans ses idées, sans constance dans ses projets, sans opinion fixe; mais s'il se présente une affaire sérieuse, une combinaison à suivre, il ne s'éparpillera pas. . . . Rastignac se concentre, se ramasse, étudie le point où il faut charger, et il charge à fond de train. Avec la valeur de Murat, il enfonce les carrés, les actionnaires, les fondateurs et toute la boutique; quand la charge a fait son trou, il rentre dans sa vie molle et inconséquente, il redevient l'homme du Midi, le voluptueux, le diseur de riens, l'inoccupé Rastignac qui peut se lever à midi parce qu'il ne s'est pas couché au moment de la crise.

In this way, during the later years of the Restoration, he laid the foundations of a fortune and was thus able, after 1830, to enter politics under the patronage of de Marsay, occupy a succession of ministerial posts (as later stories were to show) and end up as a peer of France.

La maison Nucingen also gives a great deal of information about the unfortunate wretches duped and ruined by Nucingen's latest operation. The chief victims, besides the ex-druggist Matifat, were the fashionable young noblemen, Godefroid de Beaudenord, a harmless innocent, and the three d'Aldrigger women— the wife and two daughters of a ruined Alsatian banker whose chief clerk Nucingen had once been. Nucingen swindles them all under a mask of benevolence after steering the susceptible Beaudenord into marriage with the younger of the two daughters, Isaure, a beautiful addlepate. The love romance of this pair, and their subsequent reduction to penury, is narrated with an appar-

ently heartless good-humour and nonchalance that leave an unpleasant impression with the reader.

This impression is due to the fact that the story of Nucingen's
machinations is told by Bixiou, with whom readers of *Les
Employés* are already familiar, a Bixiou who by 1836 has become

le misanthrope bouffon à qui l'on connaît le plus de verve et de
mordant, un diable enragé d'avoir dépensé tant d'esprit en pure perte,
furieux de ne pas avoir ramassé son épave dans la dernière Révolution,
donnant son coup de pied à chacun en vrai Pierrot des Funambules,
sachant son époque et les aventures scandaleuses sur le bout de son
doigt, les ornant de ses inventions drolatiques, sautant sur toutes les
épaules comme un clown, et tâchant d'y laisser une marque à la
façon du bourreau.

For the somewhat desultory after-dinner conversation, in which
the above events are related, takes place between him and three
other men who, from 1837 to 1839, are fast becoming members
of the 'Études de Mœurs' community. The least important of
them, though he is to be a recurring figure in other novels, is
Couture, half-journalist, half-banker and speculator, a man who
is involved in one unsavoury venture after another. The other
two, Andoche Finot and Émile Blondet, are much more significant. Their obtrusion in Balzac's consciousness from 1838 to 1839
is symptomatic of the increasing attention he is then giving to
the world of newspapers and journalists. Finot had put in a fleeting appearance in *Les Employés* as a manipulator of the Press at
des Lupeaulx' instigation. While correcting the proofs of *César
Birotteau* in late 1837, Balzac substituted his name for that of
d'Harancourt, the hungry botcher of prospectuses whom Gaudissart calls in to boost the 'huile céphalique'. Evidently the idea of
making Finot a fully fledged character had suddenly come to him;
he therefore added a whole page describing the position in which
this 'gros garçon assez joufflu' finds himself at the end of 1818.
Realizing that he has no literary talent and will never make a
successful career as a journalist, he decides to make a living by
exploiting the literary talents of others. From then on his career
is clearly marked as one who is to found ephemeral newspapers—
petits journaux as they were called—as a weapon for blackmail
and political intrigue. So that in *La maison Nucingen* he is shown

203

at the height of his career, the type of unscrupulous newspaper-owner of whom there were living examples in the persons of Le Poitevin Saint-Alme, Amédée Pichot and Victor Bohain, with all of whom Balzac himself had had much to do or from whom he had had much to suffer. One might plausibly add the name of François Buloz and that of Émile de Girardin, unacknowledged son of the Count Général de Girardin, who was a newspaper-proprietor on a larger scale; for one of Balzac's remarks about Finot is suggestive: 'Semblable à l'un des grotesques de Gustave, il est marquis par derrière et vilain par devant.' Naturally enough, Finot's character has taken a turn for the worse from *César Birotteau* to *La maison Nucingen*, that is, according to the chronology of Balzac's fictitious world, from 1818 to 1836. He has become taciturn, cold and stiff. He is devoid of wit. He is servile to anyone of whom he requires a favour, insolent to those he no longer needs. In *La Torpille*, published contemporaneously with *La maison Nucingen*, similar traits are emphasized in the Finot of 1824: he is heavy of demeanour, brutal in determination, an indefatigable gleaner of ideas and crown-pieces, the taskmaster of irresponsible writers and journalists. But all these are general characterizations. At last, in June 1839, in *Un grand Homme de province à Paris*, Balzac was to show him at work at a decisive moment, in 1821: the central cog in the ingenious machine of journalistic graft.

It goes without saying that in course of time Finot was to be insinuated into new editions of previous fictions: into *L'Illustre Gaudissart* in 1843 as the commercial traveller's prosperous newspaper-owning friend; and even, in 1845, into *La Peau de chagrin*, where he replaces, rather incongruously, the hack writer Marivault for whom, in the original edition, Rastignac persuades Raphaël de Valentin to compose pseudo-memoirs in the name of his defunct aunt. But in *La maison Nucingen* the chief fact that is brought out about him, apart from a certain slow-wittedness in the give and take of repartee, is the hold he has on Blondet, the 'train-bearer' to this 'industrial prelate'—

. . . rédacteur de journal, homme de beaucoup d'esprit, mais sans conduite, décousu, brillant, capable, paresseux, se sachant exploité, se laissant faire, perfide comme il est bon, par caprices; un de ces hommes que l'on aime et que l'on n'estime pas; mais fin comme une soubrette de comédie, incapable de refuser sa plume à qui la lui demande, et son cœur à qui le lui emprunte; enfin le plus séduisant de ces hommes-filles de qui le plus fantastique de nos gens d'esprit a dit, —'Je les aime mieux en souliers de satin qu'en bottes.'

That is, chronologically speaking, Blondet's first appearance in the 'Études de Mœurs'. It is true that he resembles the Émile of the original *Peau de chagrin* like a twin—that author, poet and critic who met Raphaël de Valentin as he emerged from the old curiosity shop, who tried to recruit him for the running of a bogus opposition journal, and who was the life and soul of the orgy which followed their meeting. But from a proof correction of *La maison Nucingen* onwards, Blondet was provided with the Christian name of Alfred and kept it until Balzac altered it to Émile by a correction inserted in the manuscript of *Un grand Homme de province à Paris*. His character as a 'condottiere de plume' is repeated in *La Torpille*; but almost simultaneously *Le Cabinet des antiques* (September–October 1838) shows him as a man-about-town in 1822, consorting with de Marsay and his like, a native of Alençon whose life-long friendship with Virginie de Troisville has won him access to elegant circles. A year later the Souverain edition of *Le Cabinet des antiques* was to credit him with a putative father in the person of Judge Blondet. Balzac was already planning, in 1838–9, to give him the prominent place he enjoys in *Les Paysans* as the lover of Virginie, now wife of General de Montcornet. At the turn of the year 1838 he is to figure again in *Une Fille d'Ève*—this time as a social cicerone. And again, as with Finot, *Un grand Homme de province à Paris* takes him back to his beginnings as a journalist on the staff of *Le Journal des Débats*, and assigns him a considerable role among his brother journalists. In the meantime we may note that one of these latter, Lousteau, seems like him to have stemmed from the 'Émile' originally conceived in *La Peau de chagrin*. We shall learn more of Lousteau hereafter, but he has his beginnings in that portion of *La grande Bretèche ou Les trois vengeances*, of February 1837, which is a sort of preliminary sketch of *La Muse du départment* of 1843. There was undoubtedly some hesitation in Balzac's mind. In *La grande Bretèche* Lousteau is alternately Émile and Jules— as prototypes of this second irresponsible journalist and literary mediocrity Jules Sandeau and perhaps Jules Janin leap to the mind, and M. Adam would bring Hyacinthe de Latouche also into the picture.[1] In *Une Fille d'Ève* he is still Émile Lousteau; but at last, in *Un grand Homme de province à Paris* he achieves stability as Étienne Lousteau, though here and there, both in the manuscript and the edition of 1839, Balzac still calls him Émile.[2]

The mystery of initial twinship between Lousteau and Blondet —it was under this cognomen, by the way, that Lhéritier de l'Ain, Balzac's collaborator in 1830 for the *Mémoires de Sanson*, sometimes wrote—is an intriguing one. But as far as *La maison Nucingen* is concerned, out of all the swarm of journalists that are to come, we have only to deal with Finot, Blondet and Couture. And Bixiou eclipses all three of these birds of a feather in this exchange of gibes and sarcasms. Bixiou is the chief spokesman of the story. His versatility, irony, bitter humour and vivacity in this restaurant scene call to mind the exhibitionism of the ne'er-do-well in Diderot's *Neveu de Rameau*; and indeed this work is mentioned in *La maison Nucingen*. It is Bixiou who hits off the characters of Rastignac and Nucingen, calls up the figures of Beaudenord and the Alsatian women, and, into the bargain, launches upon his denunciation of English prudishness in a disquisition on the meaning of the term 'improper' which is one of the Anglophobe Balzac's most famous sallies.[3] Nevertheless it is Finot and Blondet who bring us almost to the threshold of the second part of *Illusions perdues*. For years Balzac had been brooding over the misdeeds and treacheries of the cut-throat journalistic confraternity. His memories of quarrels with Latouche, Janin, Bohain, Pichot, Buloz and Émile de Girardin must have rankled still more after his lawsuit over *Le Lys dans la vallée* and the failure of his *Chronique de Paris* in 1836. From as early as 1837 we can feel him working up to his startling offensive of June 1839. He was burning with indignation at the thought that the work of scrupulous and inspired artists should be at the mercy of profane, envious and greedy adventurers. And this indignation is already perceptible in the following passage which concluded the manuscript version of *La maison Nucingen*, but which he suppressed

[1] Introd. to Garnier edition of *Illusions perdues*.
[2] Hunt (6).   [3] Hunt (4).

as superfluous. It reveals the reaction of his fair companion after hearing the conversation of the 'quatre hardis cormorans'.

—Quelle effroyable jeunesse! s'écria-t-elle.

—Le journalisme est l'alchimie de l'intelligence, dis-je à ma voisine étonnée; vous venez d'en voir les plus beaux *précipités*. Est-ce à dire que ni la *vertu* ni l'*art* n'existent, parce qu'il y a des gens qui passent devant Raphaël en causant d'affaires, ou qui ne saluent pas un homme dans le malheur? Il est en nous un sentiment du beau idéal; moralement il produit la vertu, physiquement il produit l'art. Chez ces gens-là, l'esprit a tout tué. Ils n'ont pas un ami, pas une maîtresse. Ils dînent au Rocher de Cancale quand on se bat dans Paris; ils suivent en tilbury les tapissières chargées de morts pendant le choléra; ils ne savent pas ce qu'on trouve dans Raphaël. . . .

—Les pauvres gens! dit-elle.

—Eh bien! Tu les plains?

X

'L'ORDRE GENDELETTRE'[1]

i. The works of 1839

THIS WAS A YEAR of remarkable productivity. To it belong, in addition to the works about to be considered, *Massimila Doni*, the first version of *Le Curé de village* and portions of *Petites Misères de la vie conjugale*, as well as some miscellaneous writings. But *Un grand Homme de province à Paris* is the most important novel of that year. Much of its substance is presupposed in *La Torpille* of 1838. Around it we may group a series of works, chiefly *nouvelles*, which are heterogeneous as far as the official categories are concerned, but which all have men of letters as their principal or subsidiary figures. The year 1839 is the one in which Balzac is occupied to the point of obsession with those who make their living by the pen. It is impossible to assign to any of these an assured priority of date of composition, for he was working on most of them simultaneously. *Une Fille d'Ève*, classified in 1842 as a 'Scene of Private Life', was first offered to the public in *Le Siècle* of December 1838–January 1839: it relates the thwarted love-affair of Raoul Nathan, poet, novelist and dramatist, with the wife of Félix de Vandenesse. Next came what are now the first two parts of *Béatrix*, which also went into the Private Life category in the 'Comédie Humaine' of 1842, but which first appeared in *Le Siècle* in April–May 1839. There the great 'femme de lettres', Félicité des Touches, alias Camille Maupin, and the critic Claude Vignon make their first bow to Balzac's public. *Béatrix* was followed in book-form by *Un grand Homme de province à*

---

[1] This title is borrowed from Balzac's *Monographie de la Presse parisienne*, written 1842, published 1843, as part of a composite work, *La grande Ville, Nouveaux Tableaux de Paris*. The satire professes to be a fragment from 'L'Histoire naturelle du Bimane en société'.

Paris, the second part of *Illusions perdues*, in June of that year.[1]
At the end of August *La Presse* serialized *Les Secrets de la Princesse de Cadignan*, or *La Princesse parisienne*, as it was then called.
It relates the love-story of one of Balzac's high-principled writers,
Daniel d'Arthez, and went naturally into the Parisian category
in 1844. Equally destined for that category are two short stories
of 1840: *Les Fantaisies de Claudine* (later *Un Prince de la Bohème*)
and *Pierre Grassou*. They may conveniently be regarded as appendages to the 1839 stories. The first-mentioned evokes a *milieu*
in which many of the writers invented in 1838–9 find their
spiritual home; the second, of minor importance, turns from the
study of writers to that of painters.

It will be noticed that the newspaper-owners and journalists
who were Balzac's constant target at this time are for the most
part shown at moments in their career subsequent to the Revolution of July 1830. That is so in *La maison Nucingen*. It had been
so in *La Peau de chagrin*. It is so in *Une Fille d'Ève*, *Les Secrets
de la Princesse de Cadignan* and *Un Prince de la Bohème*. In
Balzac's view the Press rose to its highest point of power and
maleficence after July 1830. Even in 1831 he had embroidered on
that theme. But this evil, like all those from which public life was
suffering under Louis-Philippe, had its roots in the intrigues and
manœuvres by which the liberal opposition of the early eighteen-
twenties sought to undermine the authority and prestige of the
more or less reactionary ministries of the Restoration period. By
1838 Balzac had done a lot, in such novels as *Le Médecin de
campagne*, *L'Histoire des Treize*, *La vieille Fille*, *Le Cabinet des
antiques*, *Les Employés*, *César Birotteau* and *La maison Nucingen*,
to show how the anarchy of individualism and the spirit of 'Ôte-
toi de là que je m'y mette' had sprung, partly from the inertia and
class prejudice of the old aristocracy, but more patently still from
the heresy of constitutionalism and parliamentary institutions.
This meant that he had perforce turned the searchlight of his
criticism on the reign of Louis XVIII and more especially on the
years 1818–24. In *Un grand Homme* . . . his scrutiny bears on the
same significant years as having witnessed the beginnings of

[1] As a continuation of *Les deux Poètes*, it had officially to rank, from 1843,
among the Provincial Scenes.

journalistic corruption.[1] The adventures of Lucien de Rubempré in Paris, whither *Les deux Poètes* had shown him proceeding with Mme de Bargeton in 1821, serve as a basis for Balzac's savage on-slaught on nineteenth-century journalism at the start of its ignoble career. This is what makes of *Un grand Homme . . .*, to use his own words, 'l'audacieuse peinture des mœurs intérieures du journalisme parisien, et qui est d'une effrayante exactitude',[2] ' . . . une grande action, courageuse surtout'.[3]

ii. *Illusions perdues* II (*Un grand Homme de province à Paris*)[4]

Spurned by Mme de Bargeton and the 'smart set', and having no resources but those he can borrow from his hard-up family at Angoulême, Lucien takes to a frugal and studious life in a garret. He has lost no illusions about his genius:

> Les hommes illustres d'une époque sont tenus de vivre à l'écart. Ne sont-ils pas les oiseaux de la forêt? Ils chantent, ils charment la nature, et nul ne doit les apercevoir.

This 'forest-warbler' takes his historical novel, *L'Archer de Charles IX*, to two publishers, the partners Vidal and Porchon, and Doguereau. The former refuse the novel while Doguereau offers a ludicrous price for it. Full of despondency, Lucien falls in with Daniel d'Arthez, a budding literary genius who has chosen the hard way of getting on: austerity, virtuous independence, patient study, apprenticeship to his writer's vocation envisaged as a 'sacerdoce', a priestly function. D'Arthez admits him to the 'Cénacle de la Rue des Quatre-Vents', a group of young idealists who have adopted his principles, each in his particular sphere of activity. We are not surprised to find Louis Lambert and Horace Bianchon among them, though the former does not appear in this story. Others are the scientist Meyraux (in real life Meyranx), the

[1] 'En 1821, le journal était dans sa robe d'innocence, comparé à ce qu'il est en 1839.'
[2] *E* I, 512.   [3] *E* I, 522.
[4] Apart from the excellent critical edition in Garnier (M. Antoine Adam, 1956) the following articles may be consulted: Merlant (3), Nadeau, and Hunt (6).

painter Joseph Bridau, the republican with Saint-Simonian tendencies, Michel Chrestien, the humanitarian philosopher, Léon Giraud, and the dramatic genius disdainful of fame, Fulgence Ridal.[1] D'Arthez tries to instil his own principles into Lucien, and teaches him, after Buffon, that 'le génie, c'est la patience'. He gives him advice on the writing of historical novels; he and his friends touch up and transform *L'Archer de Charles IX*.

D'Arthez thus assumes the role of Lucien's guardian angel, one whose mission it is to keep him in the strait path of modest and uncomplaining endeavour. But Lucien soon tires of this, and after a vain attempt to get on the staff of Andoche Finot's 'petit journal', falls in with the tempting demon, Étienne Lousteau, to whom he reads his collection of sonnets, *Les Marguerites*.[2] In a long autobiographical and cynical discourse on literature and its devotees, Lousteau opens Lucien's eyes to the servility and treachery by which a writer must demean himself before he can hope to live by his pen; and having failed to warn Lucien off the literary career, becomes his mentor and guide through the underworld of journalism. D'Arthez and Lousteau are really at one on this issue. For d'Arthez newspapers are 'the brothels of thought'. For Lousteau journalism is nothing but the prostitution of talent; but he is glad to lead an innocent soul into his own particular hell.

Under Lousteau's tutorship Lucien's education proceeds apace. With him, in due course, he visits the various kinds of publishers and publisher-booksellers. Balzac brings five kinds of these on to his stage. He has already introduced us to Vidal and Porchon, the 'libraires-commissionnaires', whom he condemns as being unnecessary middlemen between publishers and booksellers, and Doguereau, the exploiter of incipient talent. Now he gives us the

---

[1] Naturally real models have been found for each of these characters. D'Arthez is, according to diverse opinions, Balzac's schoolfellow, Barchou de Penhöen, the parliamentary orator Berryer, the novelist Félix Pyat, Alfred de Vigny, and the Saint-Simonian philosopher Buchez. More obviously still, he is the embodiment of Balzac's own ideal. Bianchon is Émile Regnault and Mardochée Marx. Bridau is Delacroix. Chrestien is Armand Carrel. Giraud is Pierre Leroux. Ridal is the vaudevillist Merle. In actual fact, like all Balzac's characters, they are creatures of his own imagination enriched with traits from living people.

[2] The sonnets quoted were furnished by Théophile Gautier, Delphine de Girardin and Ch. Lassailly.

large-scale publisher Dauriat, some of whose traits and methods are borrowed from actual publishers such as Ladvocat and Renduel; he is a mendacious, evasive and intriguing speculator in *chefs d'œuvre* with whom Finot, a kindred spirit, remains hand in glove—so long as their interests coincide. We are also introduced to the 'libraire-escompteur' Barbet, who preys upon authors by discounting the bills of exchange with which publishers pay them for their manuscripts, and upon the publishers themselves by purchasing their publications with these bills and also by buying the review copies (mostly unread) from the journalists at reduced prices; and finally the firm of Fendant and Cavalier which lives on credit from paper-makers and printers, pays in bills of exchange which rapidly lose value, and is constantly on the edge of bankruptcy.

During the eight months or so that he spends in Paris—from November 1821 to August 1822—Lucien is made wise to all the shifts and rogueries of these speculators in the printed word, and those of other parasites such as the discounters Chaboisseau and Samanon—the latter being a worthy addition to Balzac's gallery of squalid and grasping misers. But these give only one aspect of the thieves' kitchen into which, after abandoning the Cénacle and its members, who make fruitless efforts to bring him back to the fold, Lucien finds himself plunged through the questionable benevolence of Lousteau. Dauriat has his headquarters in the Galeries de Bois at the Palais-Royal—that erstwhile haunt of publishers, booksellers, milliners and prostitutes whose description, like that of Flicoteau's restaurant in the Latin Quarter, forms one of the *bravura* pieces of *Un grand Homme*. . . . It is there that Lucien is introduced to Finot and his satellites. Some of them are men of superior talent, like Raoul Nathan, the author of a brilliant novel which Dauriat has just brought out, and whose play, *L'Alcalde dans l'embarras*, written in collaboration with du Bruel, is even now awaiting its first night at the Panorama-Dramatique, having as its chief interpreters the actress Florine, kept by the druggist Matifat, but intimate with Lousteau, and the eighteen-year-old Coralie, kept by the silk-merchant Camusot, but soon to fall madly in love with the handsome Lucien. Émile Blondet is equally outstanding; he writes for the *Journal des Débats*. As we have seen,[1] through the good graces of Virginie de Montcornet, he has his feet firmly planted in Faubourg Saint-Germain circles, and frequents the salons of the Marquise d'Espard and the illustrious writer, Félicité des Touches. There is also Claude Vignon, a talented but destructive critic, who belongs to the journalistic confraternity, but reluctantly and ashamedly, and inveighs with Balzac against the corruption of the Press. Among the less talented figures we see Lousteau himself, once an idealist but now a time-server, well-trained and well-equipped for any task of perfidy or malevolence which Finot may assign him; Félicien Vernou, envious, jealous, his spirit galled by domestic chains from which he has not the courage to free himself, and regarding all other people's success as an insult to himself; and Hector Merlin, attached (but not by the sincerity of his principles) to a Right-Centre newspaper, a venomous and dangerous person. The tale of these journalist-bandits will be complete when, later, the conservative journalist, Théodore Gaillard, makes his appearance as one of those through whose agency Lucien comes to grief.[2]

Finot is the ring-master of this circus. He owns a 'petit journal'

[1] See above, 205.

[2] As with the members of the Cénacle, critics and historians have busied themselves trying to discover the real persons who have lent traits to these invented ones. Finot has his prototype in such men as Le Poitevin Saint-Alme and Latouche (inevitable identifications since Finot's 'petit journal' is so evidently *Le Figaro* in its manifold vicissitudes—but it could equally well be *Le Corsaire* or *Le Miroir* or many others); he has also affinities with Véron, Amédée Pichot, Victor Bohain, and perhaps Émile de Girardin. Balzac owes his conception of Nathan to Léon Gozlan, or Eugène Sue, or Théophile Gautier, or Latouche, or even Charles Nodier. There has been less speculation about Blondet, though the name of Lhéritier de l'Ain has been put forward. Jules Sandeau may have contributed something to his formation, as he undoubtedly did to that of Étienne Lousteau; but on the latter Jules Janin can also stake solid claims. To Gustave Planche, as we shall see, goes the doubtful honour of having posed for Claude Vignon. The question is not worth pursuing. It is insoluble even in the case of Lucien himself. According to the different moments at which we take him, he too may be likened to Jules Sandeau or Jules Janin; and also to Jules Lecomte, the defaulting secretary of Alexandre Dumas, and Albéric Second, whom Balzac had first known as an admiring youth at Angoulême. Again, if any identification is to be attempted, it is with Balzac himself—as he was at certain moments, and as he might have been had he not possessed real genius and staying-power, instead of Lucien's spurious talent and lack of perseverance.

of liberal hue (*Le Courrier des Théâtres*), which pays its way by intimidation and blackmail. At a time when regularly paid advertisement ('l'annonce payante') has not yet come into fashion, it extracts perquisites in kind or a certain number of subscriptions from tradespeople who want their wares to be puffed. Through the power of its reviews to fill or empty theatres it holds theatre-directors, actors and actresses and opera singers to ransom: the payment taking the form of subscriptions to the newspaper, free boxes and free theatre-tickets. So that the theatres have to placate such newspapers as well as satisfying the demands of the professional 'claque' organized by such men as Braulard. Finot's 'petit journal' is a thorn in the flesh of politicians, ministers and even the Crown itself through the malicious audacity of its epigrams and gossip-columns. Each of its numbers is thrown together late at night by wine-heated redactors who pause between their orgies to offer pabulum to a public avid, not for news, but for spicy scandal and invented anecdotes. 'Le journal . . . tient pour vrai tout ce qui est probable. Nous partons de là . . . la justice criminelle ne procède pas autrement.'

Finot's projects are expanding, and he is on the point of taking a share of one-third in a weekly (*Le Mercure*, the manuscript of the novel tells us) which Dauriat is buying up—on condition that Lousteau, in return for being made chief editor of *Le Courrier des Théâtres*, shall induce Florine to work on Matifat to buy from him a half of the share he is taking—at the price he is paying for the whole share.

'. . . je te donnerai la rédaction en chef de mon petit journal. . . . Tu seras mon prête-nom, je veux pouvoir toujours diriger la rédaction, y garder tous mes intérêts et ne pas avoir l'air d'y être pour quelque chose . . . je veux rester maître de faire attaquer ou défendre les hommes et les affaires à mon gré dans le journal, tout en te laissant satisfaire les haines et les amitiés qui ne gêneront point ma politique. Peut-être serai-je ministériel ou ultra, je ne sais pas encore; mais je veux conserver, en dessous main, mes relations libérales . . . dans un an le recueil vaudra deux cent mille francs à vendre à la Cour, si elle a, comme on le prétend, le bon sens d'amortir les journaux.'[1]

[1] It was in 1824 that the Prime Minister Villèle decided to silence opposition by the process of *amortissement*, i.e. by buying up hostile newspapers and converting them into ministerial ones.

Entering wholeheartedly (though without any love for Finot) into this scheme, Lousteau proposes to recruit Lucien for it as well. In one of the heart-to-heart talks they have together he enlarges on the advantages that will accrue to him if he abandons ideals and scruples.

'N'avez-vous pas un immense avenir si vous obéissez aveuglément aux haines de position, si vous attaquez quand Finot vous dira: Attaque! si vous louez quand il vous dira: Loue! Lorsque vous avez une vengeance à exercer contre quelqu'un, vous pourrez rouer votre ami ou votre ennemi par une phrase insérée tous les matins à notre journal en me disant: Lousteau, tuons cet homme-là! Vous réassassinerez votre victime par un grand article dans le journal hebdomadaire. Enfin, si l'affaire est capitale pour vous, Finot, à qui vous vous serez rendu nécessaire, vous laissera porter un dernier coup d'assommoir dans un grand journal qui aura dix ou douze mille abonnés.'

This Lousteau tells Lucien in a box of the Panorama-Dramatique where he and his associates are watching the opening performance of du Bruel's and Nathan's play before proceeding to a supper given by Matifat and Florine. At that supper, which recalls the 'orgie chez Taillefer' in *La Peau de chagrin* for its boisterousness and the freedom of its discussion, both Blondet and Claude Vignon speak out, the one cynically, the other trenchantly, against the power of the Press and its misuse.

—Aussi, dit Blondet, si la Presse n'existait pas, ne faudrait-il pas l'inventer; mais la voilà, nous en vivons.

But, even before the meal, the opportunity has come to Lucien to prove his mettle by dashing off a vivacious article in praise of *L'Alcalde dans l'embarras*. Having thus won his spurs he soon finds himself on the best of terms with Finot, who paints a glowing picture of the financial prosperity that waits him: 150 francs a month for his work on the 'petit journal', 200 francs for his articles in the weekly newspaper; 40 francs from the sale of his perquisites—boxes and tickets—as a dramatic critic, and 60 francs for the sale of the books he reviews. A grand total of 450 francs a month, worth well over £80 in our currency of 1958. Lucien is not slow in stifling the voice of conscience, and before long we find him joining with gusto in the journalistic mêlée. 'Tu es né journaliste', Lousteau assures him. Easy money and the sense of power go to his head. Lousteau has leapt at the opportunity of avenging him on Mme de Bargeton and Sixte du Châtelet by a series of articles replete with cruel epigrams and innuendoes. And Lucien discovers how easy it is to force Dauriat to pay 3,000 francs for *Les Marguerites* (which however he never publishes) by damning Nathan's novel in one newspaper and then, when the price is paid, lauding it to the skies in another. Just as he had previously learnt from Lousteau how easy it is to review a book without reading it, now he learns from him the art of demolishing a book in the name of lofty æsthetic and patriotic principles; and from him and Blondet the art of eating his own words in the name of equally lofty, but diametrically opposed principles:

> Tout est bilatéral dans le domaine de la pensée. Les idées sont binaires. Janus est le mythe de la critique et le symbole du génie. . . . La critique doit contempler les œuvres sous tous leurs aspects.

Lucien proves an apt pupil. But other influences have also entered his life. The evening at the Panorama-Dramatique and the supper at Florine's have brought the entrancing and impulsive little Jewish actress Coralie to his feet. Coralie had been 'sold' to de Marsay and had passed from hand to hand until Camusot had taken her over and set her up in an expensive way. When she meets Lucien she falls in love for the first time: violently, for Balzac was ready to allow an unlimited capacity for genuine passion and selfless devotion to the soiled dolls of the theatre and the opera-house. Contemptuous as he was of Victor Hugo's plays, he heartily concurred with the courtesan's statement in *Marion Delorme*: 'Et ton amour me fait une virginité'.

On that evening Coralie's acting, responsive then as later to emotion and atmosphere, has suffered from her infatuation. At Florine's dinner she throws herself at his head, takes him home that night, drunk, to her apartment and gives herself to him without regard for her dependence on Camusot, who indulgently accepts the situation in the hope of eventually regaining her. She installs Lucien in her flat, caresses, cossets and spoils him, encourages him in his self-conceit and love of luxury, aids and abets him in a course of extravagance and improvidence which in due time brings them both to ruin. Lucien, flattered and gratified, yields promptly to the seduction of what Balzac again calls 'la poésie des sens'. Provided by Coralie with fine clothes, he flaunts about Paris on horseback or in her coupé (soon to be seized by the bailiff's men with her furniture and jewellery) and becomes one of the group of Parisian 'viveurs' to whom Balzac devotes a memorable chapter.

But older ambitions are stirring within his breast. By his pen he has won a respect born of fear. He has gained admission to the salons of Mme d'Espard, Mme de Montcornet and Félicité des Touches. He again meets the now widowed Louise de Bargeton, who this time would have been an easy conquest had his off-hand response to her advances not infuriated her. There is even talk of his winning the hand of Félicité des Touches. But Blondet, Virginie, Mme d'Espard, du Châtelet, the Duc de Rhétoré,[1] Rastignac and des Lupeaulx set a snare for the overweening poet: luring him with the hope of obtaining royal sanction for assuming his mother's name of Rubempré, they draw him away from Finot and liberal journalism, and induce him to join Théodore Gaillard and Hector Merlin in the launching of an 'ultra' journal and so win the favour of King and Court. Fatuously, Lucien falls into the trap. His break with the liberals has made them his inexorable foes. Misfortunes fall thick and fast on him and Coralie. Called upon by his new collaborators to write a scathing attack on a book which d'Arthez has just brought out, Lucien does so 'la mort dans l'âme', after confiding in d'Arthez, who treats him with infinite compassion. Coralie's dramatic career is smashed by the intrigues of Florine, Nathan and Lousteau. Fendant and Cavalier publish *L'Archer de Charles IX* and then go bankrupt, leaving nothing but the prospect of remaindered sales for this unhappy lucubration.

But it is Finot, in combination with des Lupeaulx[2] in spite of their opposing political 'principles', who administers the final blow. Taking advantage of the fact that Lucien is still bound to him by

[1] The Duc de Rhétoré's frequentation of Florine's 'salon' and the nature of the advice he gives to Lucien—to turn over to royalism—remind one of the Duc de Fitz-James' visits to the salon of Olympe Pélissier and his influence in helping to 'convert' Balzac in 1831–3.

[2] See above, 185–6.

contract, he fathers him with a scandalous article in which the King, the Keeper of the Seals and his wife are held up to ridicule. Lucien is overwhelmed, though he still does not know that the royal ordinance which was to have ennobled him is a figment of his enemies' imagination. His fall is dramatically swift. Michel Chrestien, outraged at his attack on d'Arthez, challenges him to a duel and inflicts a wound which incapacitates him for two months. On his recovery the faithful Coralie falls into a mortal illness; in a desperate effort to find money, Lucien forges the signature of David Séchard on a bill for 3,000 francs. He is now held in execration by royalist and liberal journalists alike, and can get no articles accepted. Coralie dies a Christian death, and he is obliged to write libertine verses beside her corpse in order to pay for her funeral. No resource is left to him but to return to Angoulême, and Coralie's ugly but adoring servant Bérénice goes on the streets to earn the wherewithal for his journey.

This grim and pitiful story of the brief grandeur and rapid decadence of Lucien Chardon is of absorbing interest; in the main, perhaps, because of its uncompromising denunciation of the Parisian Press. As such it is a piece of history; but it is also a piece of prophecy, for the evils which Balzac exposed by no means diminished as the century wore on. *Un grand Homme . . .* aroused a furious storm which raged for several years, with Albéric Second, Jules Janin, Buloz and Sainte-Beuve taking sides against Balzac; with Granier de Cassagnac defending him in *La Presse*, and the gentle and witty Delphine de Girardin intervening in October 1839, with her play, *L'École des Journalistes*, which was published but never performed. Nor had Balzac himself said his last word. In 1839 and 1840, as President and then Vice-President of the Société des Gens de Lettres, he not only fought a vigorous battle for the protection of authors against piracy and the iniquities of publishers, but also, in his *Code Littéraire*, demanded that writers should be protected by law from the attacks of unscrupulous critics. His *Revue Parisienne* of 1840 was in part inspired by the desire to set his compatriots an example of respectable and high-principled journalism, though his own attack on Sainte-Beuve's *Histoire de Port-Royal* and the articles on Thiers and his mother-in-law, Mme Dosne, have much of the 'petit journal' spirit in them. In 1842 he resumed hostilities with his *Monographie de la Presse parisienne*, in which such of his *bêtes noires* as Jules Janin and Sainte-Beuve, and apparently Gustave Planche into the bargain, felt the full weight of his sarcasms and parodies; in which also Blondet's epigram quoted above[1] serves as a concluding judgment.

Thanks to this crusading spirit, *Un grand Homme de province à Paris* contains a vast number of vivid and penetrating sketches of types and *milieux*. But it would be a mistake to refuse primary importance to the fiction itself: this work is, after all, the second instalment of *Illusions perdues*. The limelight is in fact centred on the impressionable Lucien, grieved and bruised as he realizes the hardness of mundane society and sees his protrectress won over to their snobbery; moved to admiration and emulation of the austere purity of life to which d'Arthez and his friends adhere; bewildered, horrified, then impressed and corrupted by the brilliance, versatility and resourcefulness of Finot's associates; thrilled, charmed and captured by the depth of Coralie's devotion, and evincing a sort of loyalty to her which is surprising in this vain and effeminate opportunist; and achieving a pathetic if not tragic dignity when, his head bowed under the buffets of fortune, he comes—for a time—to understand what a sorry figure he has cut.

And Coralie? She is vulgar, uneducated, unintelligent; she is petulant and cruel to Camusot, though perhaps he deserves no better treatment; yet Balzac has made her unreflecting forthrightness a corrective to her amorality. Her passionate and humble attachment gives her something which might be called saintliness, if it were manifested in a better cause and with less sensual gusto.

'Et quand il ne sera séparé de quelque sceptre que par l'épaisseur d'un cadavre' [she exclaims] 'il pourra se faire un marchepied du corps de Coralie.'

Balzac's data are absurd: a rich man's light-of-love, hard and mercenary in her outlook—'sois méchant avec les hommes, c'est bon genre'—becomes the Juliet of a flabby and self-adoring Romeo who has even spilt his drunken vomit on her frock,

[1] See above, 215.

which henceforth she keeps as a sacred relic. All her subsequent acts and thoughts are in conformity with this self-abasement. And yet we like her, accept her and believe in her. The fact is that formal logic here yields to a more subtle one, and reasoned psychology to psychology in depth. *All is true*, said Balzac in *Le père Goriot*. At his best he is able to persuade us of anything. And perhaps the more readily here because Coralie stands out in welcome relief against the harder-headed Florine, against the refined and self-possessed women of the Faubourg Saint-Germain, and against the lynxes and jackals of the journalistic Bohemia whose rule of life is summed up by Hector Merlin:

> Si vous êtes bon, faites-vous méchant. Soyez hargneux par calcul. . . . Pour être aimé, ne quittez jamais votre maîtresse sans l'avoir fait pleurer un peu; pour faire fortune en littérature, blessez toujours tout le monde, même vos amis, faites pleurer les amours-propres: tout le monde vous caressera.

iii. *Une Fille d'Ève*

The story of Raoul Nathan's almost successful attempt to seduce Marie-Angélique de Vandenesse has the dimensions of a shortish novel—it occupies 136 pages of the Conard edition. It is an interesting example of that type of work which is a meeting-house for persons and groups from different kinds of 'Scenes'. Raoul Nathan, of course, lives and moves in the *Illusions perdues* atmosphere. *Un grand Homme* . . . shows him in 1822 in the act of displacing Étienne Lousteau in the affections of the actress Florine. In 1834, the date at which the events of *Une Fille d'Ève* take place, he has for ten years been her accredited lover, living with her in those 'Bohemian' circles—the term 'Bohème' is already used in *Un grand Homme* . . .—of which Olympe Pélissier, her lovers such as Eugène Sue and Rossini, and her mixed crowd of satellites, seem to have furnished the preliminary model.

When we think of 'Bohemia' today, we are influenced by Murger's *Scènes de la vie de Bohème* (1851) and similar writings. We think of needy painters and down-at-heel apprentice scribblers congregating in studios and garrets of the Latin Quarter. No doubt the 'Petit Cénacle' of 1830–3, as advertised later in the writings of Théophile Gautier, set the first example of this way of living. Camille Roger, Gérard de Nerval and Arsène Houssaye continued it in the late eighteen-thirties in the Impasse du Doyenné, and normally this grouping is known as the 'First Bohemia'. Many of its members were well-to-do and were in contact with elegant society. Perhaps Balzac had such circles in mind, and his application to them of the term 'Bohemia' probably gave Murger his first clue for its use in connection with the more bedraggled section of the community he wrote about.[1] But Balzac's conception of 'Bohemia' is quite distinctive. It is centred round the irregular life of actresses and opera-singers; it includes journalists, writers and artists among its denizens, but also fast-living upper-class rakes, financiers and rising politicians.

Quoique la vie de la Bohème se déployât chez elle [Florine] dans tout son désordre, au milieu des rires de l'artiste, la reine du logis avait dix doigts et savait aussi bien compter que pas un de tous ses hôtes. Là se faisaient les saturnales secrètes de la littérature et de l'art mêlés à la politique et à la finance. Là le Désir régnait en souverain; là le Spleen et la Fantaisie étaient sacrés comme chez une bourgeoise l'honneur et la vertu. Là venaient Blondet, Finot, Lousteau son septième amant et cru le premier, Félicien Vernou le feuilletoniste, Couture, Bixiou, Rastignac autrefois, Claude Vignon le critique, Nucingen le banquier, du Tillet, Conti le compositeur; enfin cette légion endiablée des plus féroces calculateurs en tout genre; puis les amis des cantatrices, des danseuses et des actrices qui connaissaient Florine.

This then is the spiritual home of Raoul Nathan, to whose physical and moral description Balzac devotes many pages of *Une Fille d'Ève*. This 'Byron mal peigné, mal construit', with his penetrating Napoleonic glance, his wild and slovenly exterior, has links with the Jeune-France movement, is a sectary of 'Art for Art's sake', has produced brilliant novels and plays, and some poetry of the nebulous kind. He has political ambitions, but vacillating political principles. His literary effort is dissipated and inconsistent. He is an egoist, 'paresseux au superlatif', and thoroughly insincere. In a word, Balzac makes of him the type of unfulfilled and ineffectual talent straining to show itself as genius.

[1] This difficult question of influences and succession has been discussed in the as yet unpublished thesis of M. F. Easton.

. . . Nathan offre une vraie image de la jeunesse littéraire d'aujourd'hui, de ses fausses grandeurs et de ses misères réelles; il la représente avec ses beautés incorrectes et ses chutes profondes, sa vie à cascades bouillonnantes, à revers soudains, à triomphes inespérés. C'est bien l'enfant de ce siècle dévoré de jalousie, où mille rivalités à couvert sous les systèmes nourrissent à leur profit l'hydre de l'anarchie de tous leurs mécomptes, qui veut la fortune sans le travail, la gloire sans le talent et le succès sans peine.

In 1833, when the salons of the Faubourg Saint-Germain began to reopen after the intransigeant aristocracy had decided to emerge from its period of 'mourning' for the fate of the legitimate dynasty, Nathan is able, through the good offices of Émile Blondet, to parade his Byronic eccentricity and iconoclasm at the soirées of the Comtesse de Montcornet and other brilliant ladies. It is here that he takes notice of the naïve and impressionable wife of Félix de Vandenesse. So *Une Fille d'Ève* comes into the wake both of *Le Lys dans la vallée* and of *Une double Famille,* for Marie-Angélique and her sister Marie-Eugénie du Tillet are daughters of the saddened and disillusioned Comte de Granville. Moreover, the presence in this novel of Nucingen, his wife Delphine, and du Tillet, binds it up as well with *La maison Nucingen.* Marie-Angélique is one of those innocent and unsophisticated wives for whose ignorance of the world and its dangers the author of *La Physiologie du mariage* blames the hot-house conventual system of education. By implication he also blames the shortsightedness even of such fathers as Granville. For if the latter has given Marie-Angélique to a steady, reliable husband, the erstwhile platonic lover of Henriette de Mortsauf, he has married off Marie-Eugénie to a successful but thorough-paced rogue. But even Félix de Vandenesse incurs his share of blame for making conjugal life a synonym for respectable boredom and withholding from Marie-Angélique the pleasures and excitements for which a wife may legitimately crave.

As a consequence, Marie-Angélique, full of yearning romanticism and a desire to taste the exhilarating nectar of love inspired and reciprocated, is ripe for the seducer's blandishments. She falls ingenuously in love with the misunderstood and melancholy genius that Nathan makes himself out to be. Elegant mischief-makers like Mme d'Espard, Félix's own sister-in-law Mme Charles de Vandenesse,[1] Natalie de Manerville and Lady Dudley, are there to help the affair along in its progress from soulful idealism to its hoped-for consummation in marriage-wrecking adultery. As is usual with Balzac's heroes, Nathan combines his scheme of conquest with a plan for using his high-society liaisons as the avenue to a political career—with a daily newspaper and a 'petit journal' at his command. But he reckons without the tortuous cunning of du Tillet, who has his own financial and political fish to fry;[2] and also without the patient understanding and strata-gems of Félix de Vandenesse, who brings his wife to her senses when, through her idealization of Nathan, she stands on the brink of the abyss. Nathan has also failed to reckon with the tenacity and resentfulness of Florine, who helps Félix to unmask her lover when she learns of his proposal to desert her after all the sacrifices she has made for his sake. Foiled in every one of his undertakings, Nathan resigns himself to the lot which he deserves and which Balzac is always happy to assign to his opportunist scribblers: a mediocre career as a pro-government journalist instead of the meteoric career he had hoped for as an emulator of Talleyrand. Marie-Angélique is cured of her folly through the gentle and self-accusing sympathy of her husband. Thus Balzac fulfilled the promise of 1837[3] and 're-established' the character of Félix de Vandenesse by endowing him with the firm manliness he had lacked in Le Lys dans la vallée.

Une Fille d'Ève is a clever and subtle study. Balzac's analysis of Marie-Angélique, the motives and the stages of her infatuation, is an able piece of work. Nor is the novel lacking in variety of scene and action. The rogues in the background, du Tillet, the barrister Massol and the usurer Gigonnet run true to form. The imperious, clever and calculating Florine has her past unveiled as well as her physical charms and her mastery of the meretricious arts. Marie-Angélique's indiscreet activities to save her admirer from ruin and suicide are narrated with that sense of the dramatic which always serves Balzac well when he is describing the frantic

---

[1] Our old acquaintance Émilie de Fontaine, heroine of Le Bal de Sceaux.
[2] His dealings with Nathan are reminiscent of those of William Duckett with Balzac over the Chronique de Paris affair.   [3] E I, 377. See above, 117.

expedients of those who need money as an anæmic person needs blood-transfusion. Certain old-stagers of the 'Études de Mœurs' move forward to their appointed destinies; the Prime Minister de Marsay to his death, Rastignac to his wedding with Augusta de Nucingen. His brother has become a bishop. A new figure appears in the shape of the kindly, unworldly musician Schmucke, who has yet to wait six or seven years before he can play his major part in *Le Cousin Pons*.[1] And the theme of Balzac's forthcoming novel *Béatrix* is foreshadowed. Marie-Angélique had fancied herself in the poetic role of a Beatrice. The curtain is ready to go up on the tragicomedy in which the Marquise de Rochefide comes nearer to making a success of the part with Calyste du Guénic as an unliterary Dante.

iv. The first instalment of *Béatrix*

This work owes its conception to a short visit Balzac paid to George Sand at Nohant in February–March 1838, and its localisation around Guérande, at the mouth of the Loire, to his sojourn there with Mme de Berny in 1830. This visit to the marshy regions of Le Croisic had already given him a setting for *Un Drame au bord de la mer*. Until recently, it was supposed that Balzac revived his topographical memories by a new holiday spent in this area with Hélène de Valette in 1838. He needed no such stimulus. It is now established that he did not meet Hélène until early in 1840.[2]

The visit to Nohant restored and sealed Balzac's former friendship with George Sand. He heard and accepted her version of the break with her lover, Jules Sandeau, in 1832; hence a noticeable hostility to Sandeau and the incorporation of some of his traits into 'Conti le musicien', who has the villain's role in *Béatrix*. But Balzac and Sand also had long talks over the love affair between the pianist Franz Liszt and the Countess Marie d'Agoult, later known as the novelist and memorialist 'Daniel Stern'. These two,

---

[1] He figures also in *Ursule Mirouët*.

[2] See M. Regard's edition of *Béatrix* (Classiques Garnier, 1962), xxxix-xlii, and 395–422, for a demolition of the legends about Balzac's relations with Hélène.

who had met towards the end of 1832, had advertised their relationship to the world by running off to Geneva together in 1835.
George Sand had consorted with them in Switzerland, and on
their return to France in 1837 gave them hospitality at Nohant in
May and July, before they departed for Italy. She seems to have
watched the course of their liaison with some sourness. Both then
and afterwards she took pleasure in detecting symptoms of their
eventual separation. There was a great deal of idealism in Marie's
love for Liszt, whom she endeavoured—unavailingly—to wean
from his vanity and charlatanry as a virtuoso. But Sand, in
whose heart jealousy probably rankled—a celebrated musician
was something of a catch—was not likely to give her much credit
for this. And so Balzac came away from Nohant in 1838 with the
subject whose original title was the significant one of *Les
Galériens ou Les Amours forcés*, with Marie d'Agoult as Béatrix
de Rochefide (initially Rochegude) and Félicité des Touches, or
Camille Maupin, more or less taking the part of George Sand.

'Sauf quelques variantes, *l'histoire est vraie*', he averred.[1] In
actual fact the theme of *Béatrix* is not so much that of waning love,
envisaged as a form of penal servitude, as the rivalry between
Félicité des Touches and Béatrix de Rochefide over an entirely
invented personage, the frank and ingenuous Calyste du Guénic,
only son of the Baron du Guénic: 'type essentiel . . . du jeune
homme dans toute sa gloire, offrant à la fois beauté, noblesse et
sentiments purs'.[2] But to keep for the moment to the 'Galériens'
aspect, naturally Balzac saw the matter through George Sand's
eyes. His Béatrix figures as an affected and pretentious woman
who, finding her own class effete, had taken to the new literary
fashion, and aspired to become an important person among the
intelligentsia. Anxious to be the Egeria of some great artist, she
more or less filched Conti from Félicité des Touches, and braved
the social conventions by going off with him to Italy. Marie
d'Agoult had a good reason for her flight to Geneva—the impending birth of a child of whom Liszt was the father. A much more
shallow motive is attributed to Béatrix de Rochefide:

. . . L'éclat de sa chute n'était pas nécessaire, elle n'eût rien été sans
ce tapage, elle l'a fait froidement pour se donner un rôle. Elle était

[1] *E* I, 527.   [2] Preface of 1839 edition, *Éd Déf.* XXII, 536.

rongée de vanité. Sa fortune, son esprit, n'avaient pu lui donner la royauté féminine qu'elle cherchait à conquérir en trônant dans un salon. . . .

So speaks Félicité des Touches. On this conception, and on the postulate that during their two years' stay in Italy whatever ardour there had been between the two lovers had cooled down considerably, Balzac's novel is built. When she read the novel, Marie d'Agoult was indignant at the travesty Balzac had made of her. Liszt, although he too must have divined something of himself in Conti, took the matter lightly. He was at that time—and until well on in 1843—still friendly with Balzac, and contrived to reconcile Marie with the novelist in 1840. But the novel put an end to any real friendship that may have subsisted between her and Sand, who no doubt got some satisfaction out of the affair— 'elle prend là une petite vengeance sur son amie'[1]—while taking up a hypocritical attitude over it.

The history of 'l'affaire *Béatrix*'[2] is amusing in its details, though this bare outline must suffice. It is also particularly interesting for students of Balzac, since it shows him taking much more from real life and real persons than he was wont to do. In addition to the Marie-Béatrix, the Sand-Maupin and the Sandeau-Conti or the Liszt-Conti equations, we have Balzac's further avowal that Claude Vignon, the disgruntled critic who, at the beginning of the story, is Camille Maupin's official lover, is a portrayal of Gustave Planche, who had at one time been enamoured of George Sand, had for a short time been on the staff of Balzac's own *Chronique de Paris* and had already established himself, by his murderous articles in *L'Artiste* and *La Revue des deux mondes*, as what Balzac himself was later to call 'l'Exécuteur des Hautes Œuvres'. So, in the persons of Camille Maupin and Vignon, the novel not only puts us again in touch with the 'ordre gendelettres', but also gives us an opportunity to see what Balzac does with living models admittedly selected from among them. What light do we get from this? The initial description of Claude Vignon is not a flattering one. 'Écrivain dédaigneux et superbe', he has abandoned any attempt to develop his creative genius and

---

[1] *E* I, 527; Feb. 1840.
[2] See Pourtalès, Marix, M. O. Monod, Vier (1), (2) and (3), and Beckett.

sought to prove his superiority by acid and destructive criticism. Planche can scarcely have felt gratified when he read of his 'caractère sans ressort, sa paresse, sa profonde misère, son incurie et son dégoût de toutes choses'. But M. Maurice Regard has shown that, in the manuscript of *Béatrix*, the above description was at first intended to fit Raoul Nathan; that Balzac changed his mind and, at a later moment in the story, paints a life-like portrait of Planche as Vignon; that, in subsequent retouches, Claude Vignon begins to 'vivre de sa propre vie'.[1]

In the much more complete and much more important picture we get of that first-rate literary (and musical) genius Camille Maupin, fiction claims its rights from the start. She is an idealized figure, though many traits of Sand are recognizable. Camille's aristocratic origins, her impressive personality and the details of her brilliant career are developed at great length. So are her early liaisons, which are a compound of those which Sand had had with Sandeau, Mérimée, Musset and others. Like Sand, she is a tobacco addict. The virile element which Balzac discerned in Sand's character, and on which he enlarged in a letter to Mme Hanska—

Son mâle était rare . . . elle n'est point aimable . . . elle ne sera que très difficilement aimée. Elle est garçon, elle est artiste, elle est grande, généreuse, dévouée, *chaste*; elle a les grands traits de l'homme; *ergo*, elle n'est pas femme[2]

—is transferred to Camille, and given prominence as a trait which weakens her power to be the sort of woman a man wants. 'On a peur de trouver en elle', he writes of Camille as she was in 1836, 'je ne sais quoi de vierge, d'indompté.'[3] But in this delineation a series of divergences are immediately perceptible. Camille is a celibate whom the idea of maternity disgusts; she dislikes children. Her physical traits are borrowed from those of the actress,

[1] Regard (3), t. I, 244–54.

[2] *E* I, 463. Of course we must allow for the likelihood of Balzac exaggerating this masculinity in Sand, so as to convince Mme Hanska that he looked on her as a 'camarade' and not as a possible mistress.

[3] In the choice of a pen-name for Félicité des Touches, it is obvious that two patronymics are involved: that of George Sand herself (Dupin), and that of the hermaphrodite heroine of Gautier's novel of 1835: *Mademoiselle de Maupin*. The Christian name is that of the androgynous Camille in Latouche's *Fragoletta* (1829).

Mlle Georges.[1] 'Comme l'abeille, Balzac picore partout.' Camille emerges as a distinctly independent personality whom a kind of Olympian superiority detaches from the ordinary pettiness of life, capable of submitting her own emotions, no less than those of others, to a clairvoyant scrutiny, and of sacrificing them to the urge of calculated benevolence. Be it said however that, as a writer of genius, she rejoins George Sand in the company of those 'monstrous exceptions' whom, in his preface at least, Balzac warns young women not to set up as an imitable ideal.

Naturally, if we wish to do full justice to the work, we shall think of Camille Maupin in detachment from her model, especially since her position with regard to the Béatrix–Conti–Calyste imbroglio bears little relation to the actual history of the Agoult–Liszt–Sand situation. The imbroglio in question does not show Balzac at his best in any case, and that is perhaps why in February 1840 he wrote to Mme Hanska: 'Non, je n'étais pas *heureux* en faisant *Béatrix*.' It was no doubt an embarrassing affair to incorporate so much approximate reality in a work of fiction, and to interpret it in the light of his own psychological intuition and experience. As Joachim Merlant shows, although he does not go so far as to infer therefrom the relative inferiority of the work as a piece of fiction, Balzac's manner of composition enabled him to achieve only bit by bit anything like clarity and consistency in his essential data.

It is true that the position of Calyste is clear enough. He is a green youth, brought up away from the world by his doting mother, his feudal-minded father, and his careful, scraping aunt Zéphirine du Guénic. He first falls in love with the overwhelmingly intellectual Camille, is introduced by her into a new and unknown world—that of art, literature and music—but is held at arm's length. In consequence, when Béatrix comes with Conti to visit Camille at her country-house near Guérande he falls madly in love with Béatrix. The latter's motives are also fairly clear. Weary of Conti, she is flattered by Calyste's adoration, and would be inclined to love him in return but for worldly motives. Balzac takes us back here to the idea behind *La Femme abandon-*

[1] See Merlant (2). Balzac used a series of articles by Gautier in *Le Figaro*, 1837–8.

née. A woman who has once flouted the social conventions may arouse sympathy and even admiration, whereas a second fall puts her beyond the pale. So, as the first title had hinted and the preface of 1839 melodramatically states, Béatrix feels herself 'attachée à jamais à l'auteur de sa ruine, comme un forçat à son compagnon de châine'. But, lacking Camille's altruism, she is not averse from binding Calyste to herself as an all-absorbing but intangible ideal—'ce qu'était Béatrice pour Dante, une éternelle statue de marbre aux mains de laquelle il suspendrait ses fleurs et ses couronnes'. When Calyste was still only in love with the verbal picture Camille had painted of Béatrix, to kneel thus at her feet seemed the consummation of happiness. In this attitude he is not without some affinity with Félix de Vandenesse in *Le Lys dans la vallée*, not only because in his inexperience he falls an easy prey to the wiles and graces of a 'femme du monde', but because he is in love with love. Nevertheless he is an improvement on the Félix of 1836. Balzac casts aside the sickly notion of a youth remaining docile when fobbed off with the counterfeit coin of platonic affection, and Calyste's sudden impulse to fling Béatrix from the summit of the rocks of Le Croisic when she has cast too great a chill upon his ardour enables us to credit him with a modicum of virility. Even Béatrix is impressed. But for her, a person fundamentally insincere with herself, the pull of social convention decides the issue—at least in so far as the 1839 instalment of the novel is concerned. Conti returns to Guérande after a temporary absence, and Béatrix goes back to Paris with him.

It is the part played by Camille Maupin in this affair that is ambiguous; it is her motivation that is hesitant. Her half-hearted continuation of her liaison with Claude Vignon appears to be prompted by the feeling that she ought to discourage the advances which, in the first place, Calyste has made to herself. Why does she adopt this plan of action? Because she is aware of the intellectual 'superiority' in which she stands over against Calyste. Because she has reached the age of forty-five, though her judicious responses to masculine homage have, through some secret of hygiene which Balzac does not divulge, kept her wonderfully youthful in looks. Being a 'sorte de Don Juan femelle', she can read men like a book, and she foresees her inability to hold for

long the affections of the susceptible Calyste. So she practically
throws him at the head of Béatrix, after preparing his mind for
infatuation with her in a singular way—by giving him a long
account of her life-story in which the defects in her beauty and
character are brought into relief no less than her charms. And
then she remarks by way of conclusion: 'Eh bien, n'allez-vous
pas tomber amoureux de Béatrix sur le portrait que je vous en
fais?' She acts more or less like a high-minded procuress; yet she
is jealous, and loves Calyste herself, albeit for his sake, and not
for her own. As the novel progresses, her real intention becomes
more evident: it is to help Calyste in winning the slender, long-
faced, green-eyed Béatrix so that he may get her out of his system.
But since Calyste is too impetuous and too impatient to play the
game of a calculating seducer, she finds it impossible to disillusion
him about Béatrix. At the same time Balzac has sought to trace in
the free-thinking Camille a progress towards religion. She turns
from the love of men—here Balzac is conventionally, and even
absurdly romantic—to the love of God. 'Dieu, c'est l'inconnu.
Je m'y jetterai comme dans un abîme.'[1] So the solution of her
problem is found in her taking the veil and making over to
Calyste enough of her property to facilitate his marriage, not
indeed with his boyhood sweetheart, Charlotte de Kergarouët, as
Calyste's family had wished, but with Sabine de Grandlieu. After
the departure of Béatrix, this ineffectual Romeo has fallen into a
decline; but he allows himself to be weaned of his infatuation by
the masterful Camille. The cure is only temporary, as later events
are to show.

The trouble about Balzac in his more sentimental fictions—in
Béatrix on the whole the sentimental prevails over the sardonic,
that other dominant element in his make-up—is that cold analysis
provokes objections that seem less cogent as one glides down the

[1] Her reasons for abandoning free-thought are naïve enough to recall those
of Bernardin de Saint-Pierre or Chateaubriand. During the excursion which
she, Béatrix and Calyste make to the rocks of Le Croisic, she refreshes herself
with some strawberry-flavoured pastilles. '. . . tout en les savourant, elle ne
put s'empêcher de remarquer que les fraises, qui n'existaient plus, revivaient
complètement dans leurs qualités. Elle conclut de là qu'il en pouvait être ainsi
de nous. La mer lui offrait alors une image de l'infini. Nul grand esprit ne peut
se tirer de l'infini, en admettant l'immortalité de l'âme, sans conclure à
quelque avenir religieux.'

stream of his imaginative creation. Then, when one yields to the influence of general impressions, the difficulties have a curious knack of smoothing themselves out. The data given above are relatively clear when deduced from the general drift of the novel. But they are not well worked-out. The imbroglio is imperfectly conceived and carried through gropingly. There are other uncertainties of motivation. Balzac is not only hesitant about Camille Maupin. He blows hot and cold over Béatrix, at one moment— especially in the preface—sympathizing with her, at another condemning her as one of those heartless women who, like Fœdora and Antoinette de Langeais, are interested in a man only in order to play with him. Claude Vignon's position, though a subordinate one, is also ambiguous. In the first manuscript redaction, as M. Merlant has shown, Balzac credited Camille Maupin with a violent passion for him—which would make her passion for Calyste improbable—but did not eliminate all traces of this from the printed version. His resultant role, after revision, is not much more than to further the action by the cynicism he exudes, and to aid Camille to see more clearly within herself. Conti's role on the other hand is a consistently odious one. He is a second-rate artist compounded of vanity and perfidy: a dog-in-the-manger, who pulls Béatrix from Calyste's grasp in the end, not because he still loves her, but because it would injure his self-esteem to have her escape him. But rational criticism cannot remain silent even in regard to Calyste's mother, the dainty and beautiful Fanny O'Brien, with whom the Baron du Guénic had fallen in love when exiled in Ireland, the home of 'ces filles pétries de lait, à chevelure dorée, dont les boucles sont tournées par la main des anges'; with whom Balzac himself had fallen in love, for some of her traits are modelled on those of the Countess Guidoboni-Visconti to whom he dedicated the work.

The Baronne du Guénic is a dutiful and loyal wife to a man some thirty years her senior. She is pious, ingenuous, one to whom the torments of romantic passion and illicit relationships are a closed book, and for this reason a person unfulfilled, as Balzac is inclined to hint with a sort of regretful admiration; but revealing even in her physiognomy 'l'inaltérable douceur, la tendresse infinie des anges'. It is her motherly virtues that are open to rational question. She is first of all suspicious, then jealous of Camille Maupin, especially when she discovers the maternal element in Camille's love for Calyste. But her fondness for Calyste makes her easily convinced that he must have a soul-shattering love-affair before he settles down to marriage. She sympathizes with him, consoles him, and is, by her sympathy, as much of an *entremetteuse* as Camille is by virtue of her unselfish passion. 'Mon rôle n'est pas de te tourmenter.' Balzac complained[1] of the expurgations which *Le Siècle* imposed upon the novel in its serial form. He attributed them to a puritanism which strained at words and harmless jests, and from which the first printed version emerged 'mauvaise et châtrée'. More severe moralists might find a real grievance in this picture of a mother so anxious for her son to find satisfaction in 'belles et folles amours' that she solici-tously watches every stage in his wooing of Béatrix; a mother of whom Balzac records that, when she is wheedling the latest news out of him, '[elle] eut en ce moment la grâce d'une courtisane qui vent obtenir une concession'.

Fanny O'Brien's amiable weaknesses are perhaps an expression of Balzac's yearning for a complaisant maternity which he never himself experienced. In any case *Béatrix* is not one of his most successful explorations of the psychology of love. Thanks to his habit of composing in successive drafts and proofs, of sketching his portraits and developing his analyses as he goes along, a pro-cedure made more harmful here by his failure to co-ordinate and erase, the work has too much of the palimpsest about it. Here, above all, a little of Flaubert's meticulous care for the homo-geneity of a work of art would have served him better. Only a collation of such part of the manuscript as is extant with the proofs (if available), the *Siècle* serial, and subsequent editions, could disentangle Balzac's earliest and latest intentions, and so explain the ambiguities; though of course it could not abolish them. Yet the novel has many excellent features. One of them is the after-dinner scene in which Camille and Béatrix throw off the masks under which each has dissimulated her true intentions, and take to fighting with the stilettos of honeyed or envenomed phrases, not for the possession of Calyste, but over the question

whether Béatrix shall yield herself sincerely to Calyste or continue to pose as the unapproachable goddess. Balzac may strike
false notes when sentimentalizing about love, especially when
making his characters indite such letters as those which pass between Béatrix and Calyste in the course of the 1839 novel. But
his insight into the subtleties of feminine rivalry remains unim-
paired.

Another excellent feature is the renewal here of the theme
already treated in *Le Bal de Sceaux* and *Le Cabinet des antiques*:
the study of the static aristocracy which emerged from Revolution
and Empire. In this work it is exemplified by the du Guénic
family, the Baron, his sister Zéphirine, their family retainers,
Gasselin and Mariette, and their kinsfolk—the economical, matchmaking old spinster Jacqueline de Pen-Hoël, the Vicomtesse de
Kergarouët and her daughter Charlotte, the hypochondriacal but
still robust Chevalier du Halga, who subsists on the memory of
his exploits as a sailor and his conquests as a gallant. Before the
reader can get into the swing of the story he has to do a good deal
of what George Saintsbury called 'literary mountaineering' and
absorb the atmosphere in which the little town of Guérande is
steeped. It is as feudal and antiquated in its structure as the du
Guénics are in their ideas and outlook. To Guérande as a setting
for the story is added that of the arid but picturesque salt-
marshes of the mouth of the Loire, and sometimes they are
evoked with a delightful vividness. So also is the human background of peasants and salt-marsh workers who, by the peculi-
arity of their staple occupation, by their adherence to the conventional Breton costumes, and also by the unchangeableness of their
manners and mode of living, are as spiritually remote from nineteenth-century ideas as they are physically so from the French
capital.

Against this background the du Guénics live out their life
oblivious of the changing times. The decrepit and illiterate Baron
—'il n'avait pas lu trois volumes dans sa vie'—and his com-
panions are incarnations of the throne-and-altar allegiance. Pending the 1845 edition of *Les Chouans* in which the Baron was to
oust the Chevalier de Renty as a model of Chouan loyalism, he
stands as another of those unswerving noblemen always ready to

233

expend themselves, without looking for any reward, in the service of the legitimate dynasty. He and his son have ridden out unhesitantly in 1832 to rally round the adventurous Duchesse de Berry. Balzac gives an amusing and pleasant picture of this family group—'les chefs du petit faubourg Saint-Germain de l'arrondissement'—whose major concern is to maintain their purity of race and regild their escutcheons by modest economy and carefully planned marriages within their own class. The climax of their uneventful day is the evening game of 'mouche', in which all their capacity for emotion is called into play, and which Balzac describes with much humour and skill, in such a manner that the conversations punctuating the tactics with which they pursue this absorbing game further the development of the story. They regard the emancipated Félicité des Touches, herself of good Breton stock, with scandalized incomprehension: 'une gaupe, une gourgandine' is the Abbé Grimont's opinion of her. Balzac's admiration for the old aristocracy as the champions of a lost cause and the defenders, however ineffective, of old-world values, appears to be waxing. There is none of the severity which inspired his recriminations against the Faubourg Saint-Germain in *La Duchesse de Langeais*; and the du Guénics, especially the erstwhile Fanny O'Brien who is a graceful and attractive figure in spite of her strange conception of the lengths to which indulgent motherhood may go, have a human appeal of which the d'Esgrignons are to some extent deprived through the ceremonious rigidity of their pride of caste.

That is why Calyste du Guénic is presented as a much more likeable youth than the arrogant Victurnien d'Esgrignon. Fond as his mother is, she has not spoilt him as Armande d'Esgrignon spoilt her nephew. He has not recoiled before the risks involved in a royalist insurrection. And he has Camille Maupin to educate him and wean him from his parochial tastes and habits of mind. The latter thus plays her part as an intermediary between the sophisticated world of Paris and the simple world of Guérande. She is also put forward as one who might have made a great writer of the embittered Claude Vignon had his degeneration as a member of the literary confraternity which Balzac pillories in *Un grand Homme de province à Paris* not gone too far. By a cus-

234

tomary swing of the pendulum, Balzac now brought his attention back to the frivolous society of the Faubourg Saint-Germain. In obedience to a noteworthy instinct for symmetry, he took up anew the history of Diane de Maufrigneuse, the coquette who had driven Victurnien d'Esgrignon to the verge of ruin and disgrace. And by an ironic twist, her new victim is not an unintelligent young fop, but that paragon of literary virtue, Daniel d'Arthez.

Not that he had finished with Béatrix de Rochefide. In February 1840[1] he announced to Mme Hanska that he had a fourth[2] part of *Béatrix* in store. It was only to materialize in the December and January of 1844-5.[3] Here the tragicomic idyll of this 'Scene of Private Life' which had begun on the shores of the Atlantic was to find its predominantly comic sequel in a wholly Parisian setting, with the mundane interests of Paris, its material calculations, its lofty families, its Bohemians and *demi-mondaines* fully involved.

v. *Une Princesse parisienne (Les Secrets de la Princesse de Cadignan)*

This sprightly *nouvelle* offers a situation which is almost the complete reversal of that in *Une Fille d'Ève*: a man of letters who becomes the prey of a society woman. In *Un grand Homme . . .*, that is to say in 1821, d'Arthez is at the *per ardua ad astra* stage of his career. In *Une Princesse parisienne*, that is to say in 1835,[4] at the age of thirty-eight, he is at the peak of his career as a great writer, and, as a rising politician, has a seat in the Chamber of Deputies. He has inherited a fortune, but still lives as an ascetic recluse, though now he has taken to satisfying the demands of nature by a liaison with a woman of low class and no education—partly through natural timidity, and partly, Balzac suggests, because he has too high an ideal of true love to deliver his heart over to a 'femme comme il faut'. Nor has he yet come to realize that

[1] *E* I, 532.

[2] The instalment of 1839 was divided into three parts. They are now reduced to two.

[3] In *Le Messager: Un Adultère rétrospectif*. See below, 333 ff.

[4] After 1844 Balzac moved the action from 1835 back to 1832 (see Jackson in Dargan and Weinberg, 412), but forgot to make all the necessary chronological changes, so that d'Arthez' age is put at 38 even at the earlier date.

... L'une des gloires de la Société était d'avoir créé *la femme* là où la nature avait fait une femelle, d'avoir créé la perpétuité du désir là où la nature n'avait pensé qu'à la perpétuité de l'espèce, d'avoir enfin inventé l'amour, la plus belle religion humaine.

But one of Society's most exquisite creations is lying in wait for him. Blondet and Rastignac (incompatible friends for the d'Arthez of 1821), with Mme d'Espard, take a malicious pleasure in throwing him in her way. Diane de Maufrigneuse, who has now become Princesse de Cadignan through the death of her father-in-law, is shown 'swigging off' Balzac's high-minded hero with more difficulty, it is true, but also with much greater skill, than she had 'swigged off' d'Esgrignon in 1822.[1]

In *La Princesse parisienne* Balzac much enriches his previous portrait of Diane. Out of the thirty-odd lovers with which public gossip credits her, some ten are named as authentic cases.[2] Inordinately expensive as a mistress, she has also dissipated her own resources; moreover the Cadignan fortunes have drooped as a result of the Revolution of July. Her husband has gone off into voluntary exile with Charles X, leaving her, as he had in fact always left her, to continue sowing her wild oats as the fancy takes her. But her reduced circumstances have forced her to adopt a modest scale of living, and she has made a virtue of necessity by interesting herself in the upbringing of her adolescent son, Georges de Maufrigneuse. As she is nearing the age of thirty-seven (in the later editions thirty-six), something resembling resipiscence is taking hold of her, but of a curious kind. She regrets never having known real love, and in a heart-to-heart talk with her bosom friend Mme d'Espard—we expect Balzac to expend some irony over the poisoned-dagger quality of a friendship between two society queens—she remembers that the noble-hearted republican Michel Chrestien had worshipped her at a distance before losing his life in the Saint-Merri insurrection of 1832. The two women agree that only one man is likely to offer her the same

[1] See above, 164.

[2] Balzac puts the figure at thirteen (not counting d'Arthez) in *E* I, 519. Those mentioned in the text are de Marsay, de Trailles, Rastignac, d'Esgrignon, General de Montriveau, Ajuda-Pinto, Prince Galathionne, the Duc de Rhétoré, the Duc de Grandlieu, the Vicomte de Sérisy, and, in later editions, the Marquis de Ronquerolles and Lucien de Rubempré.

passionate idolatry, provided that she can sufficiently whitewash
her past: and that man is Chrestien's friend d'Arthez. 'La plus
grande comédienne de ce temps', Diane sets out to entice, hood-
wink and conquer him, but with the genuine intention of fidelity
to her last love; and the application to this task of the arts and
graces of this 'femme douce et simple . . . pleine d'âme et
calomniée . . . cet ange meurtri' inspires Balzac with some of his
most brilliantly ironic pages. Within fifteen days,[1] by tactics
which naturally include long hours spent in conning and then
discussing his literary works, she has brought him to the stage at
which he is ripe for the crowning deception—her 'roman préparé
de longue main', the account of herself as an innocent young wife
married in 1815 (or 1814) to a profligate who is the lover and
accomplice of Diane's own mother, the Duchesse d'Uxelles.

This is a fact, but Diane exploits it with wicked ingenuity.
Her escapades are represented as being the high-spirited indiscretions, born of forced gaiety, natural to an injured child-wife. They
have compromised her reputation and provided universal scandal
but left her virtue intact.

> Innocente comme un enfant, je passais pour une femme perverse,
> pour la plus mauvaise femme du monde, et je n'en savais rien. . . .
> Qui pouvait croire que la vie se traduit, pour la princesse de Cadignan,
> par une mauvaise nuit de mariage; et toutes les aventures qu'on lui
> prête, par un défi de petite fille à deux épouvantables passions? Mais
> personne.

All this d'Arthez laps up with sublime credulity:

> D'Arthez rebaisa la main de cette sainte et céleste femme qui, après
> lui avoir servi sa mère hachée en morceaux, avoir fait du prince de
> Cadignan . . . un Othello à triple garde, se mettait elle-même en
> capillotade et se donnait des torts, afin de se donner aux yeux de ce
> simple et candide écrivain cette virginité que toutes les femmes essaient
> d'offrir à tout prix à celui qu'elles aiment.

It only remains to put him to the final test by contriving that
her 'friend' the Marquise d'Espard shall—albeit with intentional
perfidy—arrange a social occasion at which d'Arthez brushes aside
the 'calumnies' directed against Diane by a carefully selected

---

[1] Balzac later lengthened this softening-up process to sixty days.

company, which includes de Marsay, Eugène de Rastignac, and Victurnien d'Esgrignon, characteristically ungrateful to the woman who had after all saved him from the galleys. D'Arthez does so with a mocking serenity which proves that his delusion is incurable. He has his reward. Diane has duped him but, if we can believe Balzac, she has found true love in so doing.[1] Henceforward the two live for one another. As writer and potential statesman d'Arthez no longer counts.

It is a disconcerting conclusion to a career which, in 1821, had seemed so promising; Balzac has broken his own idol with a vengeance. However consummate the agility and artfulness he accorded to the Princess, it was a bold venture to make a man of mature age and profound intelligence so gullible. Mme O'Donnel, the sister of Delphine de Girardin, was unable to accept such a postulate. 'Ce n'est qu'à vingt-sept ou vingt-huit ans qu'on se laisse duper sans être ridicule. . . . Mais à trente-huit! C'est un imbécile s'il ne se doute pas de tout.'[2] But in order not to make d'Arthez appear an imbecile, Balzac laid stress on his unworldliness and the youthful naïvety which, in spite of his penetration as a psychologist and a poet, his retired mode of life had preserved in him. 'Le génie seul', Mme d'Espard observes, 'a la foi de l'enfance, et se laisse volontiers bander les yeux.' Balzac took care also to show how Diane realizes that she must surpass herself if she is to make her capture. For although after her first talk with him she confides to Mme d'Espard: 'mais c'est un adorable enfant, il sort du maillot', she measures out her seduction of him in carefully graduated doses; and even after her well-timed 'confession' perceives that it would be dangerous to rush her fences.

Ce sera bien long, pensait-elle en regardant Daniel le front haut et la tête sublime de vertu.

In short, whatever difficulty the reader may have in arriving at the 'suspension of disbelief' necessary for the acceptance of d'Arthez' gullibility, he will scarcely refuse admiration for Bal-

---

[1] See *E* I, 519 (15 July 1839) '. . . C'est, comme le disait Mme de Girardin, *Célimène amoureuse* . . . le chef-d'œuvre est d'avoir fait voir les mensonges comme justes, nécessaires, et de les justifier par l'amour. C'est un des diamants de la couronne de votre serviteur.'

[2] Malo (2), 162.

zac's skill in putting Diane de Cadignan and Mme d'Espard, 'ces deux fines couleuvres', through their serpentine convolutions. He may even be brought to feel that the most perspicacious of men might enjoy being fooled by such a 'comédienne' as Diane, especially when the deception ends with the soft avowal: 'O niais illustre! ne vois-tu pas que je t'aime follement?'

This drawing together of two apparently incompatible personalities is the foremost interest in *Les Secrets de la Princesse de Cadignan*; but as a scene of 'high life', with its surface of suave and tolerant politeness, its staid-seeming *galanterie* and its undercurrents of envy, hatred, and malice, and all uncharitableness, it gave great pleasure to Marcel Proust, that chronicler of a later but even more decadently artificial society.

vi. *Les Fantaisies de Claudine*[1] (*Un Prince de la Bohème*); *Pierre Grassou*[2]

The first of these *nouvelles* is closely connected with the 1839 group of fictions. The story it contains is narrated in the first instance, and, in its opening pages, in a style which is intended to parody that of Sainte-Beuve, by Raoul Nathan to the young wife of Rastignac. After 1844, in marginal corrections on the 'Comédie Humaine' addition, Balzac replaced her by the Marquise de Rochefide, and thus tied the work up with the last part of *Béatrix*.[3] The tale is concerned both with Nathan and du Bruel, but introduces a new personage, the central one, the 'Prince de la Bohème' of the later title: Charles-Édouard Rusticoli, Comte de la Palférine. The definition of the 'Bohemia' to which La Palférine belongs, already made in *Une Fille d'Ève*, is now expanded. It is a loose grouping of *viveurs* and iconoclasts in revolt against the respectability of normal society:

La Bohème est la Doctrine[4] du Boulevard des Italiens. Elle se compose de jeunes gens qui ont plus de vingt ans, mais qui n'en ont pas

[1] *Revue parisienne*, 25 Aug. 1840.
[2] Published in *Babel*, a collective work, 1840.
[3] Also Mme de La Baudraye is credited with having written up the story. Connection is thus made with *La Muse du département* of 1843.
[4] That is, a social opposition, likened to the 'Doctrinaires' of the Restoration period who had formed a political opposition.

trente, tous hommes de génie dans leur genre, peu connus encore, mais qui se feront connaître, et qui seront alors des gens fort distingués; on les distingue déjà dans les jours de carnaval, pendant lesquels ils déchargent le trop-plein de leur esprit, à l'étroit durant le reste de l'année, en des inventions plus ou moins drolatiques.

Balzac attributes their existence, and their indiscipline, to the failure of Louis-Philippe's government to attract and promote youthful talent as Napoleon had done, and he emphasizes their rakishness and libertinism—

Il s'y trouve des écrivains, des administrateurs, des militaires, des journalistes, des artistes: il y a de tous les genres d'esprit et de capacité. C'est un microcosme. . . . Ce mot de Bohème vous dit tout. La Bohème n'a rien et vit de ce qu'elle a. L'Espérance est son code, la Foi en soi-même est son gouvernement, la Charité est à l'état de théorie. Tous ces jeunes gens sont plus grands que leur malheur, au-dessous de la fortune, mais au-dessus du destin. Toujours à cheval sur un *si*, spirituels comme des feuilletons, gais comme des gens qui doivent, oh! ils doivent autant qu'ils boivent! Enfin . . . ils sont tous amoureux, mais amoureux! . . . ils sont éclectiques par excellence en amour, ils vous servent une passion comme une femme peut la vouloir; leur cœur ressemble à une carte de restaurant, ils ont mis en pratique, sans le savoir et sans l'avoir lu peut-être, le livre *De l'Amour* par Stendhal; ils ont la section de l'amour-goût, celle de l'amour-passion, l'amour-caprice, l'amour cristallisé, et surtout l'amour passager.

As for the Beau Brummel of this Bohemian society, Balzac has done his best to make him a worthy accession to the Marsay-Trailles brotherhood by parading his insolence and passing off his aristocratic caddishness as a demonstration of original and scintillating wit. It is a sorry creation, but the story has some point of savour in so far as it evokes the figure of yet another courtesan, the one-time opera-singer Claudine Chaffaroux, known as Tullia. In this respect the *nouvelle* has affinity with Diderot's *Ceci n'est pas un conte*. Claudine, though she has a promiscuous past behind her, plays the part of Diderot's Mlle de la Chaux as a woman infatuated to the point of servility with a rake, in this case La Palférine himself. In order to satisfy a whim of this arrogant hoaxer, she marries, exploits, bullies and caresses a man who is as much her dupe as she is La Palférine's dupe: the dramatist du

Bruel, whom she pushes on in his career so that through him she may acquire the wealth and social prestige which La Palférine professes to demand of the women who would win and keep his favour.

Were it not for this ingenious variation on one of Balzac's favourite themes—the blend of good and evil, of unscrupulousness and self-abasing fidelity in the heart of a light-of-love—*Les Fantaisies de Claudine* as a tale would be of little worth. Balzac takes his usual pleasure in contemplating the twists and turns of human, or rather of Parisian dupery. It is not easy to deny that he can be indiscreet and clumsy in the two opposite extremes—of sentimentality and would-be comic cynicism—to which he sometimes goes. *Un Prince de la Bohème* in particular illustrates what we may legitimately call the cheaper side of Balzac's humour, which on other occasions can be rich and even subtle.

Since *La Vendetta*, in which the drawing-master Servin had appeared, *Le Chef d'œuvre inconnu* and *La Bourse*, Balzac had not given any specific attention to the world of painters, though in *Un grand Homme . . .* he had invented the future genius Joseph Bridau and made him a member of the d'Arthez Cénacle. Bridau was not to appear in an important role until *La Rabouilleuse*. But in *Pierre Grassou*, one of his shortest stories, Balzac creates the opposite of the Hippolyte Schinner–Joseph Bridau type of artist: the dauber who, against expert advice, persists in painting uninspired pictures, has the luck to obtain royal patronage by an impressive pastiche, and wins success through the appeal of his canvasses to the taste of the undiscerning. This success is crowned by marriage with the daughter of a rich bottle-manufacturer who has brought himself, his wife and the girl to Grassou to have their portraits painted. The reappearance from *Le Contrat de mariage* of the Jewish art-dealer, Élie Magus, as Grassou's patron and exploiter, gives further light relief to the story, for when Grassou visits his future father-in-law's much vaunted picture-gallery, stocked with old masters, he finds that these same 'old masters' are his own daubs which the apparently benevolent Magus had bought from him for a song and faked. But the main interest of the story is the illustration it gives of Balzac's transference, to the realm of painting, of the æsthetic principle which, in all scrupulousness, he applied to his own art of writing: scorn for mediocrity and pot-boiling. *Pierre Grassou* is permeated with that contempt for the Philistine, that mockery of middle-class taste, which the artistic and literary vanguard of those years first brought into fashion. Henri Murger had but to combine two elements—the wider Bohemia of *Les Fantaisies de Claudine* and the conception of art as a religion cultivated by needy hierophants—and the basic theme of *Les Scènes de la vie de Bohème* was his for the using.

XI

NEGLECTED CATEGORIES

i. Political, Military and Country Life

THREE CATEGORIES of the 'Études de Mœurs', the Scenes of Private, Provincial and Parisian Life, had by now received ample attention. The other three were still hanging fire. Nowhere in his works had Balzac made a secret of his political theory. It had been trenchantly expressed in *Le Médecin de campagne* and was at least implied in Parts II and III of *Sur Catherine de Médicis* before being fully expounded in the Preface of that work.[1] But it had not been systematically applied to nineteenth-century history in specific studies of political life. *Z. Marcas*, printed in July 1840, in the opening number of *La Revue parisienne*, is a first contribution. As early as April 1839 Balzac had in mind a novel which should show up the weakness of the French electoral system borrowed from English constitutionalism. This project only materialized in 1847 in the unfinished *Député d'Arcis*. But in 1840 he set to work on *Une ténébreuse Affaire*, and published it in serial form during the first two months of 1841. It would have served as an appropriate introduction to a series of political studies covering the period of Balzac's lifetime, since its theme is the antagonism between the old aristocracy and Napoleon, as First Consul and then as Emperor. His sympathy for the dispossessed nobility is evident throughout the work, but he does not disguise his admiration for Napoleon. In fact this novel by no means cancels out what he had written in 1832, in one of his contributions to the composite work *Contes Bruns*. There, in the 'Conversation entre onze heures et minuit',[2] he makes one of his characters embark on a panegyric of Napoleon.

[1] See above, 153.
[2] pp. 14–16. Reprinted in 1844, together with *Splendeurs et misères des*

. . . Un homme qu'on représente les bras croisés, et qui a tout fait, qui a été le plus beau pouvoir connu, le pouvoir le plus concentré, le plus mordant, le plus acide de tous les pouvoirs; singulier génie, qui a promené partout la civilisation armée sans la fixer nulle part; un homme qui pouvait tout faire parce qu'il voulait tout; prodigieux phénomène de volonté . . ., un homme qui avait dans la tête un code et une épée, la parole et l'action; esprit perspicace qui a tout deviné, excepté sa chute; politique bizarre qui jouait les hommes à poignée, par économie, et qui respecta deux têtes, celles de Talleyrand et de Metternich, diplomates dont la mort eût évité la combustion de la France, et qui lui paraissaient peser plus que des milliers de soldats; homme auquel, par un rare privilège, la nature avait laissé un cœur dans son corps de bronze; homme, rieur et bon à minuit entre des femmes, et, le matin, maniant l'Europe comme une jeune fille fouette l'eau de son bain! . . . Hypocrite, généreux, aimant le clinquant, sans goût, et malgré cela grand en tout, par instinct et par organisation. . . . Homme qui, toute pensée et tout action, comprenait Desaix et Fouché. . . . Tout arbitraire et toute justice!—le vrai roi! . . .[1]

The sort of king, in fact, that Balzac would have liked to see occupying the throne of France instead of Louis-Philippe.

His penultimate category in the 'Études de Mœurs', the Scenes of Military Life, was ill-fated. That grim episode of the Peninsular War, *El Verdugo*, had originally been proffered in *La Mode* (29 January 1830) as an extract from *Scènes de la vie militaire*, but had been relegated to the philosophical studies. Other tales of military life, or having a military background, like *Adieu*, *Le Réquisitionnaire*, *L'Auberge Rouge*,[2] *Un Grand d'Espagne*,[3] *La Maîtresse de notre colonel*,[3] found their way into other categories. In 1835[4] Félix Davin had been able to cite *Les Chouans* as a Scene of Military Life, and it was indeed incorporated in the 'Comédie Humaine' as such in 1845. He also promised, in Balzac's name, a novel *Les Vendéens*, which, as an account of open civil

courtisanes, as *Échantillon de causeries françaises*. Two stories contained in it were transferred in 1842 to *Autre Étude de Femme*, but the *Échantillon* itself was dropped from the 'Comédie Humaine'.

[1] See in *Autre Étude de femme* (1842) the expansion of this eulogy. Conard VII, 395–6.

[2] For reference to these three titles, see above, 32 and 36.

[3] Extracted from *Contes Bruns*.

[4] See above, 127 ff., and Lovenjoul (1), 49.

war, was to be set off against *Les Chouans*, a tale of guerrilla warfare; and he made grandiloquent advertisement of the long-
projected work *La Bataille*, which was to deal with one of the
Napoleonic campaigns culminating in Wagram and Essling. The
friend of the Carrauds, Commandant Périolas, was to have furnished Balzac with the necessary data. But neither of these works
ever saw the light, and therefore the sole concomitant of *Les
Chouans* is the relatively trivial *Une Passion dans le désert*.[1] But
we shall see that *Une ténébreuse Affaire* is a worthy sequel to
Les Chouans, and has in it features which give it something of the
flavour of a Scene of Military Life.

The Scenes of Country Life fare better. *Le Médecin de campagne* had existed since 1833 to justify Davin's account of their
scope and purpose. *Le Curé de village* belongs essentially to the
annus mirabilis, 1839. We shall therefore consider it before
Z. Marcas and *Une ténébreuse Affaire*.

ii. *Le Curé de village* (1839)

When in the beginning of 1834 Balzac was staying at Geneva,
Mme Hanska and her husband encouraged him to plan and write
two novels: *Le Prêtre catholique* and *Le grand Propriétaire*. The
Abbé Bertault[2] has given an interesting account of the fate of the
former project, which resulted only in a few fragmentary pages.
After his return from Geneva Balzac became too concerned with
Séraphita, as an expression of his religious belief, to make head-
way with *Le Prêtre catholique*. *Le grand Propriétaire* has a long
history, which Lovenjoul traced out.[3] Through various stages of
metamorphosis it eventually materialized as *Les Paysans*, which
we reserve for later study. An intermediate study of this great
Country Life Scene is *Qui a terre, a guerre*, announced several
times in 1836. During the years 1838–9 Balzac was negotiating
its publication with various editors and publishers, and he probably sent the manuscript of the first draft to the printers early in
1839, in order, as was his custom, to have a rough proof to work
on. But by that year, he was already preoccupied with what was
to appear as his second Country Life Scene: *Le Curé de village*,

[1] See above, 36.   [2] Bertault (7).   [3] Lovenjoul (4).

which in many respects can be regarded as the implementation of his *Prêtre catholique* project. This novel also went through many stages of composition and rearrangement. It originally appeared in *La Presse* in three instalments: *Le Curé de village* (1–7 January 1839), *Véronique* (30 June–13 July 1839), and *Véronique au tombeau* (30 July–1 August 1839). In 1841 Souverain published it in two volumes, but it had already been rearranged and enlarged for his edition. When it took its place in 1846 in the first edition of the 'Comédie Humaine', further alterations had been made. The definitive version therefore gives an imperfect idea of what the work was in 1839. From the Souverain edition onwards, the two first instalments of the original serial novel were, roughly speaking, interchanged, presumably to give greater consecutiveness to the narrative.

In both of these arrangements the work consists of two apparently unrelated parts, followed by a third part which links them together in a more or less satisfactory way. Hence W. S. Hastings' judgment of the work in his *Balzac and Souverain*: 'Perhaps of all the works from the pen of this realist none is more shapeless and ill-proportioned . . .; perhaps none cost the author such infinite pains to compose; nor was the object of such superhuman creative activity.'[1]

Superhuman indeed, when we consider how many other irons Balzac had in the fire in 1839. The expression 'shapeless and ill-proportioned' may seem too harsh to a reader of the final version, but a certain lack of co-ordination between the parts is still sensible. The first chapter of the final version (*Véronique*), which had Part II of the serial novel as its nucleus, is a piece of close, direct narration. It is the history of a scrap-iron merchant of Limoges, his wife and daughter. Balzac had not made such a study of provincial acquisitiveness and the patient building-up of wealth since *Eugénie Grandet*. Sauviat and his wife are a pair of honest misers, careful, shrewd, parsimonious, but they lack the boa constrictor voracity of old Grandet; and the birth of a daughter humanizes them as the cooper of Saumur is never humanized. The parsimony of their lives is not allowed to touch Véronique, on whose behalf they are even lavish according to their lights.

[1] Hastings (1), 35.

The result is that Véronique, although brought up with religious care, is set on the road towards disaster by an incompatibility between her restricted experience and the romantic world which a precocious reading of *Paul et Virginie* opens up to her imagination.

In this respect Balzac's heroine is not without a point of resemblance with Emma Bovary. But Véronique is intelligent, while Emma is not. And instead of being tied to a booby of a country doctor, Véronique is married to a rich banker of Limoges, one Pierre Graslin. The considerable dowry which her parents have accumulated for her, her husband's social standing, and her own intelligence and personal charm bring her into high middle-class circles at Limoges. She has an affectionate friend and counsellor in another and richer banker, Grossetête. The local Avocat-Général,[1] the vicomte de Grandville, son of the hero of *Une double Famille*, pays court to her. And her salon is also visited by ecclesiastical notables: the Bishop of Limoges; his Vicar-General the Abbé Dutheil, whom Balzac depicts as a potential Lamennais, but a Lamennais who never strayed from the orthodox fold; and his chaplain, the affected and elegant Abbé de Rastignac, younger brother of Eugène. The action begins in earnest in the year 1828.

The 'Curé de village' part, which in 1839 had opened the narrative, now follows the chapter devoted to Véronique and her origin. It begins as a murder story, and has some of the stock features of the detective novel—footprints, a watch stopped at the moment of a crime of violence, and so forth. Jean Tascheron, a young workman from Montégnac, a poverty-stricken village in a desolate district of the Limousin province, is accused and brought to trial for murder. Pingret, an old skinflint of Limoges, had kept his hoard of money (100,000 francs) buried in his garden, and Tascheron, surprised in the act of rifling it, had killed both him and his housekeeper and made off with his booty. Investigation had shown that he had an accomplice for the theft and disposal of the stolen money: a woman with whom he was evidently planning to elope. The magistrates were anxious to discover the identity of this accomplice, but Tascheron maintained a stubborn

---

[1] The equivalent of 'Public Prosecutor' in England.

silence. Naturally the crime had become the talk of the town. It is discussed in Véronique's salon, and she formulates a theory about the status and motives of the woman in an attempt to persuade the Public Prosecutor to accept the crime as unpremeditated and so to save the criminal from death.

The reader does not need to await the solution given at the end of the novel to realize that the mysterious woman is Véronique herself. She had fallen in love with the young workman, in whom her husband had taken a kindly interest, yielded to his entreaties to run away with him, been an involuntary and horrified witness of the murder, and helped him to hide the stolen money in an island of the river Vienne. The Public Prosecutor remains obdurate, and Tascheron is condemned to die at the very time when Véronique is due to give birth to the child who is the fruit of their passion. Her efforts to soften the Public Prosecutor's heart, her apparently disinterested pleas on behalf of Tascheron, and the long illness which attacks her after Tascheron's execution and her own confinement, are so many clues whose significance is only made fully clear at the end of the novel. In the meantime the interest moves in another direction. The civil authorities are anxious, not only to bring the murderer's accomplice to justice, but also to recover the stolen money for Pingret's heirs. The clergy of Limoges are intent on bringing Tascheron to repentance so that the cause of religion may not suffer by the example of a murderer going to his account in a state of obstinate unconcern for his fate beyond the grave. To avert such a victory for the forces of unbelief, the Bishop of Limoges dispatches the Abbé de Rastignac to Tascheron's native village to call in the aid of the parish priest, the Abbé Bonnet. Thus we meet a new character who stands with Dr Benassis, Judge Popinot and others among Balzac's most exemplary champions of virtue and beneficence. The Abbé Bonnet is the 'Prêtre catholique' incarnate.[1]

Gabriel de Rastignac's journey to Montégnac gives occasion for a description of the bleak and rugged nature of the countryside. As in *Le Médecin de campagne*, Balzac connects physical and spiritual well-being, but is here so anxious to pay tribute to the Church and its ministers that he tells how this ardent and ascetic

---

[1] See Bertault (2), 237–49.

priest has brought back an impoverished community to religion and virtuous living, in spite of its desperate economic plight. The Tascheron family, austere and pious, is akin to those which Balzac had already evoked in *Le Médecin de campagne*. There is a well-painted scene in the little village church where Bonnet is saying mass for that member of the Tascheron family who has gone astray, and whom his relatives suppose even now to be undergoing execution. But it has been postponed so that the visiting priest may summon Bonnet to the gaol in Limoges. Jean Tascheron's sister Denise goes with him; and another striking scene shows Bonnet softening Tascheron's heart. The latter dies having made his peace with God and taken steps for his sister to retrieve and restore the stolen money. But he still refuses to name his accomplice. Denise and her family emigrate to North America, to withdraw from the shame that has come upon them.

Henceforward the broken-hearted Véronique Graslin is the central figure. Her only thought is to go to Montégnac and make what amends she can for her part in the Tascheron tragedy. Balzac here forces events to suit his purpose. The only task reserved for Graslin, before he conveniently dies, is to satisfy his wife's whim by buying the derelict castle and estates of Montégnac, whither Véronique retires with her infant son. She quickly falls under the spell of the Abbé Bonnet, who opens her heart to true repentance and, in the expanded versions of 1841 and 1846, unfolds to her a grandiose scheme whereby the wasted waters of a river may be diverted and used to irrigate a large area of barren land and thus bring prosperity to Montégnac and its environs.[1] Need we say that Balzac goes into the details of this scheme with his usual zest? It is for Véronique to discharge her duty as a rich landowner by raising the capital needed. The local inhabitants are eager to second her and the Abbé with their labour. The only person lacking is an expert technician. So Véronique's elderly friend, Grossetête, is consulted, and calls in a civil engineer from Paris, Grégoire Gérard.

His case is similar to that of Dr Benassis. But Gérard's reason for throwing up his government post and devoting himself to the

---

[1] In *La Presse* (13 July 1839) the Curé merely tells Véronique of the need for irrigating the Montégnac district, and she guarantees that it shall be done.

Montégnac project is not that he has been crossed in love. Balzac is not directly interested in Gérard, as he had been in Benassis, with whom he had in some respects identified himself. He makes Gérard the mouthpiece of his own disgust with the administrative incompetence of post-Napoleonic governments. So Gérard inveighs against a system which trains its engineers and then lets them stagnate. A letter he writes to Grossetête is one long complaint against the regime for the frustration it imposes on genius and talent. It is virtually a short treatise on technical education.[1]

In fact the novel develops henceforth into a thesis. Again Balzac states views already expressed in *Le Médecin de campagne* and elsewhere. Once more he stages a meal-time debate, bringing the local notables together at Véronique's table and making them discuss the causes of present discontent. In one respect he here anticipates the theme of *Les Paysans* and expatiates on the ruin brought to agriculture and the countryside by that splitting up of large estates which Revolutionary confiscation and the law of equal inheritance had caused. Also he embarks upon a fresh denunciation of the individualism of the times—*Chacun pour soi, chacun chez soi*—which was expressing itself in the so-called liberal forms of government. Balzac has nothing new to offer us here.

But *Le Curé de village* unfolds his thoughts about the Catholic religion much more cogently than *Le Médecin de campagne* had done. It is, as he said to Mme Hanska, the religious counterpart of the earlier novel. Religion is the great antidote to the individualistic poison that is sapping the vitality of France. At this meal-time discussion in particular, and in general through his ministrations to Véronique, the Abbé Bonnet is the dominant spirit. Gérard and the villagers set to work, the great scheme of irrigation is carried through in the course of many years (Balzac extends the period to 1843 in his final version), and then the personal drama of Véronique is brought to its climax and conclusion.

For although Balzac has yielded to his passion for propaganda, he has not forgotten that he is writing a novel. Its fictional and psychological value is to some extent saved by the invention of a picturesque figure—that of the refractory conscript and outlaw,

---

[1] In *Le Cousin Pons* (1847) he was to chide the State for its similar neglect of young artists after awarding them public prizes.

Farrabesche, a good-hearted rebel whom Bonnet and Véronique befriend. But even here the thesis is not forgotten. The influence of religion on Farrabesche is potent enough to make him surrender willingly to the authorities and accept the ten years' penal servitude his brigandage has earned him. Another episode is the return of the Tascherons from the American town of 'Tascheronville' which they have founded and in which they have prospered. But this return precipitates the crisis. Denise's exclamation—'Dear brother'—on catching sight of Véronique's child puts the mother into emotional turmoil once more, and this brings her to her death. The last act of her long expiation, now that her task of regenerating a whole countryside is almost completed, is to make public confession of her share in Jean Tascheron's guilt.

Never before had Balzac made so thorough an attempt to edify his readers; for this time he was arguing, not for illuminism, as in *Séraphita*, but for orthodox Catholicism. He assembles Véronique's former friends, Grossetête and the Vicomte de Grandville, the one person against whom she had continued to nourish resentment for the part he had played in Tascheron's conviction and execution. Dutheil, now an archbishop, and Bianchon, as medical consultant, are also summoned, and Véronique's last days on earth, her avowal of her sin in the presence of clergy, notables and peasants, her reception of the last sacraments and her saintly death, are intended to bring the story to an overwhelmingly moving conclusion. Again Véronique's end, like her beginnings, puts one in mind of Emma Bovary. Flaubert indeed may owe to Balzac the idea of describing the ceremonies and formulas of extreme unction, though he could also have borrowed it from Sainte-Beuve's *Volupté*. But the difference between the two writers comes out strongly when we consider that whereas Flaubert handles this theme with ironic pessimism, Balzac is concerned only to advertise the majesty and consoling power of the Catholic ritual. The work looks back to *Le Génie du Christianisme* rather than forward to *Madame Bovary*.

This contrast, no less fundamental than the contrast between the two erring women, may well serve to measure the vastness of the gulf which separates these two men of such divergent genius. *Le Curé de village* may indeed have helped to strengthen Flaubert's conviction that art must not be put to the service of a cause. Balzac was too impetuous, too lacking in the æsthetic tact needed, that kind which for instance François Mauriac evinces in his best works, to write a great religious novel. Moreover by 1839 he had scarcely attained to that depth of personal religious feeling which sympathetic readers may discern in his last edifying novel: *L'Envers de l'histoire contemporaine*. In *Le Curé de village* the author's motives are at once too political and too transparent. The Tascheron crime,[1] in spite of its intrinsic interest as a murder mystery and the ingenuity with which Balzac lets the reader into the secret of Véronique's guilt while keeping it from the people in the story, including the redoubtable Grandville, serves too ostensibly as a pretext for and a prelude to the beneficent collaboration between Bonnet and Véronique at Montégnac.

Also Véronique's psychology is insufficiently developed. Her fall and repentance have too much melodrama in them.[2] The part she has played in Jean Tascheron's crime remains obscure. We are never allowed to enter closely into her thoughts or to gain an intimate understanding of her passion. Nor is it clear why, once the lovers had decided to elope, theft was the only resource open to them. During the torment of his interrogation and trial she is presented as being too self-possessed, and even too hypocritical, for her subsequent collapse and remorse to be unquestioningly accepted. It is true that her death-bed confession, although it is unctuous and edifying rather than introspective, helps to explain her conduct at the time of the trial. She might perhaps have saved her lover from the guillotine had she come forward as his accomplice and borne witness that the murder was unpremeditated. But she was deterred by the thought of the stigma which her revelation would have put upon her unborn son.

'Cent fois, j'ai voulu me livrer pour le sauver, et cent fois un horrible héroïsme, nécessaire et supérieur, a fait expirer la parole sur mes lèvres.'

---

[1] It is interesting to see Balzac inventing a sensational murder case only a few months before he so passionately espoused the cause of Sébastien Peytel. See *Biography*, 100–2.

[2] See Bertault (2), 269–70, for a criticism of the conception of repentance revealed in this novel. But Balzac himself draws attention to the persistence of 'l'homme charnel' in the penitent Véronique.

Unfortunately these words seem to come rather from Balzac's pen than from her lips, and one does not readily equate the Véronique of Chapter II with the self-revealed Véronique of the final pages.

Henry James, for whom the work is 'so nearly a masterpiece yet so ultimately not one', sees it as a perfect illustration of 'Balzac's monstrous duality', a case of the artist 'handing over his data to his twin-brother the impassioned economist and surveyor'.[1] On the other hand, Mr. S. Rogers believes that the apparently imperfect co-ordination to which we have referred constitutes one of the novel's most fascinating features. 'Its structure gives the effect of two stories, one fully lighted, one that never emerges from the shades.'[2] He is satisfied that 'the extraordinary drive of the central theme holds the novel together'. Whether we share this view or not, it is fair to add that *Le Curé de village* is a work of wide and varied interest, psychological and topographical as well as sociological, while its portraits of ecclesiastics are comparable with those to be found in Trollope's novels.

iii. Z. Marcas (1840)

This little work may be regarded as stemming from *Les Employés*, since the narrator of the story is the son of Xavier Rabourdin, and since its hero represents in the political sphere what Rabourdin represents in the administrative sphere: a man of integrity and talent, even genius. Marcas' gifts as a profound and far-seeing politician are wasted in the service of a mean and jealous deputy whose reputation he makes, whose career he advances, and who reciprocates by dropping him after he has climbed to office on his shoulders. The work is also a stricture on the mediocrity, short-sightedness and Philistinism of the Louis-Philippe regime and its adherents. Nor does Balzac, always prolific on this subject, fail to develop an ancillary theme—the bitterness of the struggle for life which aspirants to the legal and medical professions must face. But this *nouvelle* is perhaps best known as a special illustration of one of Balzac's obsessions: the belief that a person's name is as eloquent for the revelation of his character and destiny as the

[1] James (3), 28–9. [2] Rogers, 160.

cut of his features and the conformation of his skull. He borrowed this idea from Sterne.

Léon Gozlan, in his amusing *Balzac en pantoufles*,[1] gives a vivacious account of the discussion he had with Balzac on this subject in June 1840. Balzac maintained that

On est nommé là-haut avant de l'être ici-bas. C'est un mystère auquel il ne convient pas d'appliquer, pour le comprendre, les petites règles de nos petits raisonnements.

And since he had not been able to invent a significant name for his frustrated genius, he dragged Gozlan with him on an interminable tour of Paris, gazing at all the shopkeepers' signboards in search of the predestined but elusive patronymic. After they had threaded their way through innumerable streets he at last found what he wanted. His ecstasy over his discovery was only momentarily damped by the realization that the bearer of the name was a mere tailor. The result of this curious research is embodied in the opening page of the *nouvelle* he was writing for the *Revue Parisienne*:

MARCAS! Répétez-vous à vous-même ce nom composé de deux syllabes, n'y trouvez-vous pas une sinistre signifiance? Ne vous semble-t-il pas que l'homme qui le porte doive être martyrisé? Quoique étrange et sauvage, ce nom a pourtant le droit d'aller à la postérité; il est bien composé, il se prononce facilement, il a cette brièveté voulue par les noms célébres. N'est-il pas aussi doux qu'il est bizarre? mais aussi ne vous paraît-il pas inachevé? . . . Entre les faits de la vie et le nom des hommes, il est de secrètes et d'inexplicables concordances ou des désaccords visibles qui surprennent; souvent des corrélations lointaines, mais efficaces, s'y sont révélées. Notre globe est plein, tout s'y tient. Peut-être reviendra-t-on quelque jour aux Sciences Occultes.

Ne voyez-vous pas dans la construction du Z une allure contrariée? ne figure-t-elle pas le zigzag aléatoire et fantasque d'une vie tourmentée? Quel vent a soufflé sur cette lettre qui, dans chaque langue ou elle est admise, commande à peine cinquante mots? . . . Examinez encore ce nom: Z. Marcas! Toute la vie de l'homme est dans l'assemblage fantastique de ces sept lettres. Sept! le plus significatif des nombres cabalistiques. L'homme est mort à trente-cinq ans, ainsi sa

[1] Ch. ix.

vie a été composée de sept lustres. Marcas! n'avez-vous pas l'idée de quelque chose de précieux qui se brise par une chute, avec ou sans bruit?

Z. *Marcas* may be felt to have only subsidiary value, since it is yet another account of the misery which Paris inflicts on sanguine youth in quest of fame and success, and of the despair which drives resentful spirits to emigration—a last resource which Balzac himself was inclined to contemplate at times. But as a vehicle for a characteristic Balzacian whimsy it is bound to provoke curiosity. Is this notion seriously proposed as an extension of the 'physiognomy' theory, or is it the proof of a wayward sense of humour? Is it mysticism or mystification? Many names in the 'Comédie Humaine' are no doubt expressive of character: Gobseck, Gigonnet, Rigou, Lousteau, Finot; but they were invented to suit the person. And yet the idea is quite consonant with the fanciful theory of language outlined in the early pages of *Louis Lambert*.

iv. *Une ténébreuse Affaire* (1841)

As usual, readers of this novel in its definitive version remain in ignorance of the stages of its composition. The proofs on which Balzac worked, once in the possession of Mr Stefan Zweig, were photographed in 1937 at the instance of the late Professor Dargan, and form part of the Balzac collection at the University of Chicago.[1] They were presumably used by Balzac for revising the story previously to its appearance in *Le Commerce*, January–February 1841. The first book-edition was published by Souverain in three volumes, which were dated 1843, but came out in 1842. *Une ténébreuse Affaire* was then incorporated in the first edition of the 'Comédie Humaine' in 1846.

Balzac had long held in reserve the material for this story. It had as its nucleus the mysterious abduction in 1800 of a senator of the Consular regime, Clément de Ris. This abduction, it appears, was arranged by Fouché, then Minister of Police, as a means of laying hands on and destroying some documents which revealed the part

[1] A summary description of it is given in Dargan and Weinberg, Appendix, 427–9. Mr. Wells Chamberlin was in 1942 preparing a critical study of the novel. It exists in typescript at Chicago University 1964.

he had played in conspiring against Napoleon while the latter was conducting the Italian campaign which culminated in the victory of Marengo. Fouché laid this crime to the charge of some Chouan officers whom he caused to be arrested and executed.[1] According to thé Preface of the Souverain edition,[2] it was from his own father ('une personne de sa famille') that Balzac had learnt the facts of the story. He had recounted them in 1823 to the Duchesse d'Abrantès, who had used—and distorted—them in her *Mémoires*. Now at last he drew from them a fiction that was well calculated to illustrate the intention which lay behind the *Scènes de la vie politique* as described by Davin in the 1835 Introduction to the 'Études de Mœurs'.[3]

Jusque-là [in the three first categories of scenes), l'auteur a montré les sentiments et la pensée en opposition constante avec la société, mais dans les Scènes de la vie politique, il montrera la pensée devant une force organisatrice, et le sentiment complètement aboli. Là donc, les situations offriront un comique et un tragique grandioses. Les personnages ont derrière eux un peuple et une monarchie en présence; ils symbolisent en eux le passé, l'avenir ou ses transitions, et luttent non plus avec des individus, mais avec des affections personnifiées, avec les résistances du moment représentées par des hommes.

What this means in reference to *Une ténébreuse Affaire* is that, at the time when the Directory had just been transformed into the Consulate, when Napoleon was feeling his way towards Empire, and when consequently the political situation in France was, or appeared to be, fluid and uncertain, the men ostensibly behind Napoleon—Talleyrand, Fouché, the Abbé Sieyès, and Lebrun—were weighing up his chances of success, and were ready to desert and betray him if at any moment he sustained a major military defeat. Royalists and Republicans were willing to make common cause, however momentarily, to secure Napoleon's overthrow, and were, in fact, hatching plots for his assassination. Balzac therefore wished to portray a typically adroit politician who had made his way successfully through the Revolutionary years, had risen to be a senator under the Consulate, had one foot

[1] See Merlant (1), 349–352.
[2] *Éd. Déf.* XXIII, 550 ff.
[3] Lovenjoul (1), 48.

in both camps, the Bonapartist and the Royalist, and intended to buy up the castle and estate of his former feudal lords and become a member of the new governing aristocracy which was even then making its way to wealth and power. So he replaced the historical Clément de Ris by a character who had already appeared in *La Paix du Ménage*:[1] Malin, an upstart native of Troyes who, by his purchase of the estate of an aristocratic family, the Simeuses, becomes Malin de Gondreville, achieves the title of Count under the Empire, and is made a peer of France under the Restoration regime. An indefatigable intriguer and opportunist, not vicious or vindictive, as the plot of *Une ténébreuse Affaire* shows; but regarded as a despicable and mortal enemy by the family he has dispossessed, in spite of the relations he secretly maintains with Louis XVIII and the emigrant nobles of Coblenz. In fact this cautious and to some extent pusillanimous man stands in sharp contrast to the conspiring nobles who, in their royalist zeal, are ready to risk life and limb in their intransigeant opposition to Napoleon and his agile but unfanatical supporters.

This then is the background against which Balzac sets his fiction. But the political situation is complicated by the existence of an active, all-seeing, all-pervading body of political police organized by Fouché. He has two principal agents, both of whom are destined to be prominent figures in the 'Comédie Humaine'. One is the coarse and blundering Peyrade, a policeman to the fingertips, and the other the coldly subtle and resourceful Corentin who, in *Les Chouans*, had brought Alphonse de Montauran and Marie de Verneuil to their deaths. The part he plays in *Une ténébreuse Affaire* is wholly in keeping with his role in the novel of 1829. 'Qu'a voulu l'auteur?' asks Balzac in his Preface: 'Peindre la police politique aux prises avec la vie privée et son horrible action.' In consequence *Une ténébreuse Affaire* is not only a novel of political life; it is also another of Balzac's early *romans policiers*. In both respects it possesses capital value as a means of soldering together past and future contributions to the 'Comédie Humaine'. It has traces of the Military Life Scene about it in so far as it continues *Les Chouans* and brings the campaigning Napoleon into the picture. Thanks to the fact that the action takes place in and

[1] As the Comte de Gondreville.

around Troyes, in the neighbourhood of the little town of Arcis-sur-Aube, it anticipates *Le Député d'Arcis*. Through the persons of Peyrade and Corentin in particular it glances forward to *Splendeurs et misères des courtisanes* and to another unfinished novel, *Les petits Bourgeois*. Through the person of the Comte de Granville,[1] the foundations of whose brilliant magisterial career are laid in this novel, *Une ténébreuse Affaire* takes us back to *Une double Famille*; and it also prepares the way for Balzac's last Political Life Scene, *L'Envers de l'histoire contemporaine*. Nor does this list exhaust the study of its ramifications through the length and breadth of the 'Comédie Humaine'.

In spite of his representative character as a fisher in troubled waters, Malin plays a fairly passive role as a figure around whom the plot revolves. In it three persons are chiefly concerned. One is the heroine, Laurence, Comtesse de Cinq-Cygne, bereft by the Revolution of her immediate kin and the bulk of her estates, and living in her sole remaining castle of Cinq-Cygne, with two elderly relatives, M. and Mme d'Hauteserre. Her cousins, Paul-Marie and Marie-Paul de Simeuse, have left the emigrant army and clandestinely re-entered France in order to take part in the 1803 conspiracy against Napoleon. They are identical twins; both are in love with Laurence, and she is hard put to it to decide which of them she wishes to marry. But she is heart and soul with them in her Royalist zeal; she keeps in touch with them, supplies them with funds, aids and abets their enterprise. The second important person is her able lieutenant Michu, a supposed Jacobin, former intendant of the Simeuse family, who for fourteen years has worn the mask of a Revolutionary the better to protect the interests of the young Simeuses. The third protagonist is the shifty Corentin, who in the first part of the novel plays a direct part in events, and in the second is no less dangerous because his machinations are sensed but not seen. In their conflict with him, Laurence and Michu win the first round, whereas in the second Corentin's triumph is almost complete.

So the work comprises two major episodes, the one occurring in

[1] In this novel, and sometimes elsewhere in the 'Comédie Humaine', the name is spelt 'Grandville'. In the 1839 and 1841 versions of *Le Curé de village* Balzac had used both spellings for the younger Granville.

1803 and the other in 1806. In the first Corentin and Peyrade are concerned with laying hands on the Simeuse brothers, who with their kinsmen Robert and Adrien d'Hauteserre, sons of the d'Hauteserre who is Laurence's guest, estate-agent and guardian, are making their way clandestinely to Paris. Michu arranges with Laurence to hide them in an underground chamber in the ruins of an ancient monastery. The police agents, with their gendarmes, in vain descend upon the castle of Cinq-Cygne. By the time they have ransacked it Laurence has made her plans for her cousins' security, and returns to flout and defy them.

Balzac's guiding principle is, however, that though the police may be thwarted, their rancour is tenacious and unappeasable. After an inconclusive colloquy between Napoleon and his ministers over the affair, the four Royalists resume normal life under surveillance. But caution and discretion are unknown qualities to Laurence and her four cousins. They refuse to come to terms with Malin, and their expedition into the neighbouring forest to dig up the Simeuse treasure, which Michu had buried and guarded, coincides with the attack on the castle of Gondreville and Malin's abduction by five masked marauders, chosen by Corentin because of their physical resemblance to Michu and the four Royalists. Suspicion falls on them; they are unable to establish their alibi; Malin is not to be found; they are arrested and brought to trial. In spite of the efforts of another kinsman, the Marquis de Chargeboeuf, who brings in two able barristers for the defence, Bordin and Granville, a further intervention by Corentin turns the scales against the accused. They are condemned—Michu to death and the other four to penal servitude.

At this stage Laurence, who has remained insolently intransigeant throughout, is prepared to come to terms with the new regime in order to save the condemned men. Befriended by Talleyrand, and escorted by M. de Chargeboeuf, she goes to Prussia to intercede with the Emperor himself on the eve of the Battle of Jena. In gracious mood, Napoleon pardons the four nobles on condition that they serve in his armies; but Michu must die, as Balzac had prophesied at the beginning where, astride on his hobby-horse, the 'science' of physiognomy, he had averred that people destined for the scaffold have their fate imprinted in their features. Michu was one of these. His face is as prophetic as Zéphirin Marcas' name.[1]

The conclusion of the novel is sad and tense. All of Laurence's young kinsmen perish on the battlefield, except Adrien d'Hauteserre whom she eventually marries. The true meaning of the events narrated is revealed in 1833, in the Princesse de Cadignan's salon, by the then Prime Minister, Henri de Marsay. Malin de Gondreville's abduction is attributed to the same motive as that of Clément de Ris; but the victimization of Michu, the Simeuse and the d'Hauteserre brothers is explained as Corentin's act of personal vengeance.

A flaw in this literary exploitation of a historic episode is the postponement of the abduction from 1800 to 1806, for it is inconceivable that Fouché and his fellow-intriguers should have waited six years before attempting to destroy documents which compromised them. But *Une ténébreuse Affaire* is a brilliant and exciting novel. Although Balzac keeps his readers more or less guessing about this 'labyrinthine affair' until the end of the novel, this mystery story does not suffer from the dichotomy apparent in *Le Curé de village*. Putting aside the political implications, it is an adventure story in a historical setting and with historical figures in the background. By Balzac's own admission, Laurence de Cinq-Cygne is partly inspired by the Diana Vernon of *Rob Roy*. She is a resolute figure, passionate in her loyalty to the throne and her hatred of Napoleon; a refreshing contrast to Balzac's ordinary men and women in that she is a stranger to self-interest and contemptuous of material things. Her heroism stands revealed in the various episodes of which she is the centre. We see her first in the mob-beleaguered house of the Cinq-Cygnes at Troyes, a girl of twelve loading the rifles for her cousins to fire at the besiegers. Her scene with Corentin at the castle of Cinq-Cygne is a vivid one. Her attack on him with a riding-whip, and the verbal duel between this haughty and fearless young woman of twenty-two and the cold, crafty Corentin give one of the best examples of Balzac's vigour in narration. Imperiousness and pride, well exemplified in her congratulation of Michu when she first realizes

[1] Balzac does not seem to have discerned such a mark of fate in the physiognomy of Peytel when, in 1839, he tried to save him from the scaffold.

his fidelity to her cause—'Vous êtes digne d'être noble'—give place to tragic distress for her cousins after their arrest; but even then she is no less attractively dignified, and her exchanges with Napoleon at Jena show a mixture of admiration and scorn for the Man of Destiny which keeps her true to her lofty sense of values. And this confrontation is no less effective for the economy with which Balzac makes Napoleon himself reveal both his greatness as a captain and leader and his lesser qualities as a *parvenu*.

But did Balzac altogether succeed in showing the woman beneath the Amazon? He himself felt doubtful on this point. He gives her no conventional feminine beauty. Her profile 'offrait une vague ressemblance avec une tête de brebis', and she herself confesses that she has 'l'air d'un mouton qui rêve'. It is in the second chapter of the novel as it now stands that Balzac seeks to bring out her feminine traits. In fact, for a moment, heroic adventure gives place to something like a love-idyll. In posing to Laurence the problem of choosing between Paul-Marie and Marie-Paul, both of whom are linked together by that mysterious affinity and sympathy between identical twins on which George Sand was a few years later to found her rustic novel, *La petite Fadette*, Balzac seems to have had the notion of studying an abnormal case of the psychology of love. So great is Laurence's virginal perplexity that she decides that chance shall determine the issue. Then the drama of the abduction intervenes and the love-story is virtually submerged. Her marriage with Adrien d'Hauteserre is a final solution forced on her by circumstances. So, in the case of Laurence, Balzac presents us, unusually, with a heroine whom sexual passion has passed by, and whose melancholy reflection as she contemplates the daughter born to her is that the latter is 'more feminine' than herself.

Michu too is an interesting figure. Less savage and instinctive than Pille-Miche or Marche-à-Terre, he nevertheless gives the impression of having stepped straight out of *Les Chouans*. Masterful to the point of harshness—his lightest word is law to his mother, his wife and his young son François whom he has trained to be an obedient and clever auxiliary—he is put forth by Balzac as the incarnation of undeviating and selfless peasant loyalty. He lives and dies for the Simeuse family without complaining. But he is more than this. In his activities on behalf of Laurence and the Simeuses he shows the skill of the prairie scout, and behind him one may still sense Balzac's addiction to the works of Fenimore Cooper. In fact he gives Michu rather too much ability and resourcefulness. Naturally in a novel of adventure one expects an element of improbability; here it lies in the lightning swiftness with which Michu prepares a hiding-place for the Simeuses and performs prodigies to fetch them to it while all the time, according to the alibi he has contrived, he is deemed to be passing the evening and night bargaining with a farmer over the sale of a messuage and drinking him under the table. For all that, he is a striking creation; and never more so than when he is spurning the advances of Corentin in terms as trenchant as those with which Commandant Hulot had dismissed the foppish police-spy in *Les Chouans*.

Une ténébreuse Affaire abounds in other interesting persons. The brothers Simeuse, perhaps, are not quite flesh and blood. Robert d'Hauteserre is an insensitive, soldierly type, to whom his brother Adrien stands in sharp contrast. The study of the d'Hauteserre parents is useful for the political and social background of the story. M. d'Hauteserre is timorous and prudent. Unlike the four heroes, he bows before the storm, looks after Laurence's material interests and would willingly adopt conformist tactics in the hope of better times to come. Another addition to Balzac's portrait-gallery of priests is the subtle, perceptive, but wholly admirable Abbé Gouget, vicar of Cinq-Cygne, who also has a brush with Corentin and wins on points. Half-way between the elder d'Hauteserres and the group of young aristocrats is the Marquis de Chargebœuf, a sage and benevolent counsellor of Laurence, who, while incurring the contempt of the young conspirators for his prudence, remains a sympathetic example of such noblemen as in those dangerous times tempered principle with a sense of realities.

As for Talleyrand, Fouché and Napoleon, brief as are their appearances in the novel, they are characteristically and authentically sketched. The curt scene at Jena gives a sample of what Balzac might have achieved had his project for *La Bataille* materialized. As for the general action of the novel, nowhere is

Balzac's sense of drama more acute. But one more feature should be noted. No one was more aware than Balzac of the fact that, in Revolutionary and Imperial times as well as later, political manœuvring not only expressed itself in insidious police activity but also had its repercussions in the judicial sphere. *Le Curé de village* had shown political motives imprinting a certain direction on a murder investigation and its sequel. No doubt also the Peytel affair had stimulated his interest in 'causes célèbres'. *Une ténébreuse Affaire* works up to the description of an investigation and trial which provide one of the outstanding scenes of the work. Balzac does not suggest that the trial of the Simeuse group is 'managed' from on high. The magistrates concerned are genuinely perplexed over a case in which unseen influences are suspected. Balzac pays tribute, as we should expect from one holding his undemocratic views, to the reasonableness of experienced judges as opposed to the emotionalism of juries. And he takes us through the peripeteias of the court-scene with minute attentiveness, examining the evidence for defence and prosecution, summarizing the speeches of the rhetorical Granville and the logical Bordin, and adjourning the trial at a critical moment so that the reappearance of Malin may seal the fate of the defendants. Here is no arraignment of the principles of French justice, even though its court-room be shabby and undignified, and its procedure in some respects defective; Balzac's point is that politicians and policemen doctor the evidence, manipulate the facts and confuse the minds of all concerned in order to bring off a flagrantly unjust verdict. Yet, although such criticism is implied and sometimes even stated, there is nothing of a 'roman à thèse' in *Une ténébreuse Affaire*. In its particular sphere it is one of Balzac's most memorable creations.

PART III

1841–8

XII

'LA COMÉDIE HUMAINE': DOCTRINE AND AESTHETICS

i. Title and Publication

THE YEARS 1841–2 bring Balzac to the definitive stage of his projects as the social historian of his times. We have seen how, since the completion of the Béchet–Werdet edition of 'Études de Mœurs' in February 1837, and that of the Werdet–Delloye–Lecou edition of 'Études philosophiques' in July of that year, Balzac had been extending his domain. Novels printed in periodicals were at the first opportunity published in book-form. Souverain for instance published four two-volume collections in the autumn of 1839, and in the same year Charpentier included twelve volumes of Balzac in his popular edition of one-volume novels (at 3.50 francs each). Similar issues of unpublished or republished works went on in 1840 and 1841. But by 1841 the time had come (financial needs providing a further spur) for a reorganization of the extant works. His mind had leapt forward to a more patent unification of the three types of 'Études', and already in 1840 he had found the title by which they were ever afterwards to be known.[1]

There has been much speculation as to how he came by this title. According to Lovenjoul,[2] Balzac's one-time secretary, Auguste de Belloy, whose mind was obsessed with the *Divina Commedia* as a result of travels in Italy, suggested 'La Comédie humaine' as a counterpart to Dante's masterpiece. In Fernand

[1] Bouteron (6) refers to a letter of Balzac, published later in *La Revue hebdomadaire*, 16 Feb. 1924, 369–70, which was addressed to an editor—perhaps Furne—in 1840. See also Chancerel and Le Yaouanc (2). The earliest mention of the title after this is in Balzac's letter to Mme Hanska of 1 June 1841 (*E* I, 557). But see also P. Citron, *RHLF*, janv.-mars, 1959, 91–3.

[2] Lovenjoul (1), 414.

Baldensperger's opinion,[1] Henry Reeve, who visited Balzac in Paris early in 1835, may have set the idea working in the latter's brain—

'If Balzac wants a title . . ., I shall beg to suggest the parody of Dante's "Divina Commedia"—for this modern "commedia" is *tutta diabolica*—"la Diabolique Comédie du sieur de Balzac".'[2]

Balzac himself had written a 'Comédie du Diable' in 1830,[3] and from 'Diabolique Comédie' to 'Comédie Humaine' is perhaps not a large step—but why should Balzac have waited five years to take it? Dante loomed large enough in his consciousness for the idea to have come to him spontaneously. There had been allusions to the Florentine poet in *Le dernier Chouan*. He figures as one of the heroes of *Les Proscrits*. In *La Fille aux yeux d'or*, Balzac writes of Paris: 'nous voici donc arrivés au troisième cercle de cet enfer qui peut-être un jour aura son Dante'. In 1835, in his preface to *Le Livre mystique* (*Louis Lambert, Séraphita, Les Proscrits*), talking of the writings of Swedenborg, he alleges that he had early sensed in them 'comme une nouvelle *Divine Comédie*'. It may well have occurred to him, later, to use the title 'Comédie Humaine' for the 'Études de Mœurs' in contrast to *Séraphita*, a novel he might well have thought of as being more directly Dantesque. Moreover, Reeve's suggestion reads like a bright afterthought, and he never states that he offered it *viva voce* to Balzac himself.[4]

The question is an intriguing, but not an important one. On the 14th of April 1841 Balzac signed a contract (and on the 2nd of October a revised form of it) with a consortium of editors, Paulin and Hetzel, Furne and Dubochet, for the publication of the 'Comédie Humaine'[5] in sixteen octavo volumes, whose issue began in April 1842 and continued until 1846. Publication was to take two years, but it actually proceeded as follows:

Tomes I–III (*S. v. priv.* I–III), 1842.

Tomes V, VI, VIII (*S. v. prov.* I, II, IV), IX (*S. v. par.* I), 1843.

Tomes VII (*S. v. prov.* III), X, XI (*S. v. par.* II, III), 1844.

---

[1] Baldensperger (1).   [2] Quoted by Royce (1), 178.   [3] See above, 38.
[4] Ethel Preston also discusses the question, 220–1. So also Dedinsky, 129 ff.
[5] The title only appeared in the revised contract.

Tomes IV (*S. v. priv.* IV) and XIII (*S. v. mil.* and *S. v. camp.*), 1845.

Tomes XII (*S. v. par.* IV and *S. v. pol.*), XIV, XV (*Ét. Phil.* I and II) XVI (*Ét. Phil.* III and *Ét. Anal.*), 1846 (tt. XIV and XV were dated 1845).

Tome XVII (supplementary volume, published by Furne: *Les Parents pauvres*), 1848.[1]

Naturally enough, by the end of these five years, Balzac had written much more, and the sixteen-volume compass was no longer sufficient. In fact, the publishers of the 'Comédie Humaine' found themselves more or less in the position of Alice at the Queen's croquet-party and had to knock their ball through continually moving hoops. What new accretions occurred during the still fertile years to come will be considered later. But the bare project of publication was coincident also with what may be regarded as final formulations of principle and intention. What advances had Balzac made in theory since he had inspired Félix Davin's Introduction in the winter of 1834-5?

ii. Prefaces

Balzac's prefaces[2] of the 1835-41 period are numerous and often enlightening. As a man who had no scruples in using his text to say anything he wanted to say, he had some distaste for the habit, widespread in his time, of vindicating new works in portentous prefaces. He justified his own recourse to them as a merely provisional means of telling his readers about his ultimate objectives, and he promised to give them up when his task was completed. They were, in fact, withdrawn from new editions at an early date. We have referred to them incidentally for the light they throw upon specific intentions behind his stories. Some of them are perhaps more important still in so far as they prepare the ground for

---

[1] In 1855 Mme Houssiaux bought up the Furne-Hetzel edition and published three 'tomes complémentaires'; vols. XVIII–XX, containing Balzac's works later than 1846: *Petites Misères de la vie conjugale*, *La dernière Incarnation de Vautrin*, *L'Envers de l'histoire contemporaine*, his *Théâtre* and *Les Contes drolatiques*.

[2] Collected in *Éd Déf.*, t. XXII. Also Pléiade XI, and 'Formes et Reflets' XV. For a general study of them see Pommier (2).

a more complete elucidation of his general purposes, those which develop and transcend the particular theory which, through Davin, he had elaborated in order to show a thread of continuity running through his *Scènes* and his *Études*. His periodic defence of or self-felicitation for the device of reappearing characters need not detain us. One example of this has already been cited.[1] What cannot be neglected are the further reflections he makes on the scope and characteristics of the novel envisaged as a form of sociological inquiry or scientific diagnosis.

As regards the sociological aspect, a passage from the preface to *Une Fille d'Ève*[2] is illuminating, since it brings out admirably Balzac's own conception of the revolution he was accomplishing in the realm of the novel. In a disquisition on the complexity of the 'Études de Mœurs', he characterizes the novel before his day as a form that treated of simple issues, and, in the social sphere, issues that Scott had dealt with to the point of exhaustion: opposition between serf or burgher and noble, for instance. The Revolution had changed all that.

Aujourd'hui, l'égalité produit en France des nuances infinies. Jadis la caste donnait à chacun sa physionomie qui dominait l'individu: aujourd'hui l'individu ne tient sa physionomie que de lui-même. Les sociétés n'ont plus rien de pittoresque; il n'y a plus ni costumes ni bannières; et il n'y a plus rien à conquérir. Le champ social est à tous. Il n'y a plus d'originalité que dans les professions, de comique que dans les habitudes. La forme faisant défaut, il a fallu que la littérature se jetât dans la peinture de l'idée, et cherchât les émotions les plus délicates du cœur humain.

We can pass with a smile over the excessive simplicity of this generalization, in so far as it affects to summarize the history of the novel before the advent of Balzac. As if English literature had nothing to show before the historical novels of Scott! As if the French novelists, before and after Mme de la Fayette, had paid no attention to 'the most delicate emotions of the human heart'! But Balzac's essential drift is made clear in what follows—

Voilà pourquoi l'auteur a choisi pour sujet de son œuvre la société française: elle seule offre esprit et spontanéité dans les situations normales où chacun peut retrouver sa pensée et sa nature.

[1] See above, 96.   [2] *Éd. Déf.*, XXII, 518–50 (dated Feb. 1859).

He rules out the possibility of English society offering so rich a subject of study—as if he understood English society, or were capable of basing a 'Human Comedy' on a mode of life of which he was almost completely ignorant! He excludes Italy, too, with a passing compliment to Stendhal for having written the only possible novel on life in that country,[1] but also for having realized to a remarkable degree 'combien les mœurs françaises sont, littérairement parlant, au-dessus de celles des autres pays, comme variété de types, comme drame, comme esprit, comme mouvement; tout s'y dit, tout s'y pense, tout s'y fait'.

In such terms does Balzac unfold what is, no doubt, his primary *æsthetic* motive for constituting himself the historian of his times:

Il s'applaudit de la grandeur, de la variété, de la beauté, de la fécondité de son sujet, quelque déplorable que le fassent, socialement parlant, la confusion des faits les plus opposés, l'abondance des matériaux, l'impétuosité des mouvements. Ce désordre est une source de beautés. Aussi n'est-ce pas par gloriole nationale ni par patriotisme qu'il a choisi les mœurs de son pays, mais parce que son pays offrait, le premier de tous, l'HOMME SOCIAL sous des aspects plus multipliés que partout ailleurs.

It would be idle to deny that Balzac is on solid ground in thus revealing, with a kind of glee whose sincerity only a voracious genius like his could render convincing, the overwhelming urge which drove him to his great purpose. As a novelist he is in quest of the picturesque and the dramatic. He finds it in the clash of individual with individual and of individual with society; he is not dismayed, but rejoices to unravel the subtlety and intricacy of the motives behind this clash. He is a historian rather for artistic and humanistic reasons than by virtue of the historian's zeal for the discovery and reconstruction of past and present. But once the artist's cravings are satisfied, up come the philosopher and the scientist who must also be assuaged. And Balzac's affirmation of a scientific foundation for social history is also illustrated in certain of the prefaces he wrote during this period.

In this regard, we shall do well to recall what previous pages

[1] i.e. *La Chartreuse de Parme*. His admiration for Stendhal was profound, as is shown by his 'Étude sur M. Beyle' in *La Revue parisienne*, 25 Sept. 1840 (Conard, *O.D.* III, 371 ff.). See *Biography*, 107.

of this work have already shown,[1] namely that with Balzac scientism and mysticism had ever gone hand in hand; that his ideology has a determinist ring about it, as when, for instance, in *Louis Lambert* and elsewhere, he tends to give an almost calculatedly mechanistic mode of operation to those invisible fluids which thought, will and emotion are to him. Whatever element of truth there may be in M. Fernandez' contention[2] that the emergence of character and physiognomy from environment is with Balzac a device for casting abstract conceptions into a concrete mould, Balzac never tires of repeating his belief in the enchainment of cause and effect.[3] One is therefore mildly surprised to find, in this same preface to *Une Fille d'Ève*, that Balzac, making one of his frequent apologies for his addiction to preliminary geographical, topographical and archæological description, excuses himself merely on the ground that he is compiling a sort of guide-book.

Il veut peindre le pays, tout en peignant les hommes, raconter les plus beaux sites et les principales villes de la France aux étrangers, constater l'état des constructions anciennes et modernes au dix-neuvième siècle, expliquer les trois systèmes différents qui ont, en cinquante ans, donné une physionomie spéciale aux meubles, aux habitations. Grâce au soin qu'il a eu, peut-être saura-t-on, en 1850, comment était le Paris de l'Empire.[4]

The same excuse is often urged in the novels themselves at the instant when Balzac is about to begin what reads like a long auctioneer's inventory. Perhaps such excuses merely serve to disguise the fact that he loves objects—towns and streets, buildings, rooms and furniture—for their own sake. And his photographic memory rendered easy for him a task whose value only a reader possessing a highly developed faculty for visual evocation can appreciate.

---

[1] See above, ch. ii, section iv, 54–6.   [2] See above, 55.

[3] See in particular the Introduction to *Ecce Homo* (29 May 1837) in *Éd. Déf.* XXII, 489–91. He disbelieves in the fatality of 'tout est écrit', but he also eliminates the possibility of chance. Cf. *Ecce Homo* itself (*Chronique de Paris*, 9 June 1836: Conard, *O.D.* III, 116. Cf. in *Le cousin Pons*, Conard XVIII, 132–3, the well-known passage beginning: 'En effet, tout s'enchaîne dans le monde réel, tout mouvement y correspond à une cause, toute cause se rattache à l'ensemble; et, conséquemment, l'ensemble se représente dans le moindre mouvement . . . tout est fatal dans la vie humaine . . .'

[4] *Éd Déf.* XXII, 524.

But Balzac the philosopher-scientist could not rest content with so homely a motive, or neglect to point out that his attentiveness to material things had a deeper significance. The preface goes on to state that medical specialists have praised him for the aptness of his descriptions of physique and physiognomy, and to show to what great pains of documentation and research he has been put to make these descriptions effective. And then with one bound, quoting a page from his recently published *La Torpille*, he plunges into an exposition of determinist theory that is redolent of Lamarck, although the source of his quasi-transformist fancies is mainly Geoffroy Saint-Hilaire. The debate between the great archæologist, Cuvier, who adhered to the theory of the fixity of species, and Saint-Hilaire, who, with Lamarck, paved the way for Darwinism, had greatly interested Balzac; while respecting both Cuvier and Saint-Hilaire, he favoured the latter.[1] In the passage quoted from *La Torpille*, after toying for a moment with a *cause-finaliste* hypothesis to explain the fascinating eyes of the Jewess Esther van Gobseck, he passes to a much less romantic hypothesis:

. . . ou les êtres humains prennent-ils, comme les autres, quelque chose aux milieux dans lesquels ils se développent, et gardent-ils pendant des siècles les qualités qu'ils en tirent! Cette grande solution du problème des races est peut-être dans la question elle-même. Les instincts sont des faits vivants dont la cause gît dans une nécessité subie. Les variétés animales sont le résultat de l'exercice de ces instincts. ·

This theory of the differentiating power of environment and the transmission of evolving instincts, so heartily adopted by Taine and developed into the *race-moment-milieu* theory, Balzac had for some time been applying to humankind. In 1837 he had reaffirmed his design of embarking on a complete description of society, in all its aspects and phases, 'en partant de ce principe que l'état social adapte tellement les hommes à ses besoins et les déforme si

---

[1] See, in *Scènes de la vie privée et publique des animaux*, a work by a miscellany of authors, published by Hetzel, 1841–2, Balzac's contribution *Guide-Âne à l'usage de ceux qui veulent parvenir aux honneurs*, reproduced in Conard, *O.D.* III, 455–65. Also in *O.D.* III, 618–37, the fragmentary sketches entitled *Entre Savants* (1845). See Pommier (4). It may be observed *en passant* that Hetzel was a writer as well as a publisher, and himself contributed to such miscellanies as the above.

bien, que nulle part les hommes n'y sont semblables à eux-mêmes, et qu'elle [i.e. la société] a créé autant d'*espèces* que de *professions*; qu'enfin l'Humanité sociale présente autant de variétés que la Zoologie'.[1]

By 1842 the time was ripe for a welding together of his æsthetic, sociological and scientific system so that he might offer what in his eyes was the complete justification for the 'Comédie Humaine'. He performed this task by writing the famous *Avant-Propos*, dated July 1842 and published in that year in the first volume of the 'Comédie Humaine'.[2]

iii. *Avant-Propos* to the 'Comédie Humaine'

But he did not at first, it appears, approach the task with great eagerness. In April he was trying to persuade George Sand to write the Preface in atonement for a scathing article on his work which had appeared in *La Revue Indépendante*, a periodical which she financed. This did not materialize,[3] and Balzac would have been content to reproduce Davin's Introductions as a preface. But Hetzel, who was treating with Balzac on behalf of his associates, demurred. To do so, he argued, would be poor publicity,[4] and he urged the novelist to write a less academic, more modest and more succinct preface for himself. A first draft of the resultant *Avant-Propos*, in Hetzel's handwriting, has been found among the latter's papers, and Hetzel's biographers surmise that the publisher himself had a hand in it.[5] This may well be, since it is disjointed and flat in comparison with the finished product, which is couched in Balzac's most vigorous and confident style.

---

[1] Preface to first edition of *Illusions perdues* (*Les deux poètes*), dated 15 Jan. 1837, *Éd. Déf.* XXII, 389. Guyon (1), 290 ff., insists strongly on the presence of this conviction in Balzac's thought from the earliest moment, and hails its formulation in *La Physiologie du mariage*. See in *Pensées, Sujets et Fragmens*, 154 (*circa* 1838), the amusing entry: 'Espèces sociales—Histoire naturelle du Bimane en société (Genre homo).'

[2] It was reprinted in *La Presse*, 25 Oct. 1846, with an Introduction by Delphine de Girardin.

[3] She made amends by writing a 'notice' for the Houssiaux edition of Balzac's works in 1855.

[4] Lovenjoul (3), 239 ff.

[5] A. Parménie and C. Bonnier de la Chapelle, 30–4. This work reproduces the draft.

In the *Avant-Propos* definite approval is given to the theory of *l'unité de composition* whose history Balzac traces back to the eighteenth century and for whose formulation he honours Geoffroy Saint-Hilaire.

Il n'y a qu'un animal. Le Créateur ne s'est servi que d'un seul et même patron pour tous les êtres organisés. L'animal est un principe qui prend sa forme extérieure ou, pour parler plus exactement, les différences de sa forme, dans les milieux ou il est appelé à se développer. Les espèces zoologiques résultent de ces différences.

Balzac claims long since to have perceived that this principle is equally applicable to human society.

La société ne fait-elle pas de l'homme, suivant les milieux où son activité se déploie, autant d'hommes différents qu'il y a de variétés en zoologie?[1] Les différences entre un soldat, un ouvrier, un administrateur, un avocat, un oisif, un savant, un homme d'état, un commerçant, un marin, un poète, un pauvre, un prêtre sont, quoique plus difficiles à saisir, aussi considérables que celles qui distinguent le loup, le lion, l'âne, le corbeau, le requin, le veau marin, la brebis, etc. Il a donc existé, il existera donc de tout temps des espèces sociales comme il y a des espèces zoologiques. Si Buffon a fait un magnifique ouvrage en essayant de représenter dans un livre l'ensemble de la zoologie, n'y avait-il pas une œuvre de ce genre à faire pour la société?

So Balzac formally places his work under the ægis of Science, while showing that the presentation of the human 'zoology' has its special difficulties and complexities. In nature, for instance, distinctions of species are more precise and more rigid. In society, not even male and female (even when mated together) are always of the same 'species'. 'La femme d'un marchand est quelquefois digne d'être celle d'un prince.' Reading between the lines, one can see that Balzac is not perfectly decided over the question of transformism. The phrase in the rough draft

S'il n'est pas encore prouvé que le poisson devient volatile ou que le volatile devient poisson, il est prouvé que l'épicier peut devenir pair de France . . .

---

[1] In the draft of the *Avant-Propos* (Parménie and Bonnier de la Chapelle, 33) the analogy is stated with a closer parallelism of form: 'Dans la nature il n'y a qu'un animal . . . Dans la société il n'y a qu'un homme.'

seems more humorous than scientific in tone. Yet, in the text itself, in the phrase

si quelques savants n'admettent pas encore que l'animalité se transborde dans l'humanité par un immense courant de vie . . .

there seems to be a serious hint of the evolutionary hypothesis. However this may be, his argument is that in the animal world the struggle for life is simple and clear. In the social world it is dramatic and confused, and expresses itself in the crossing of those social barriers which, by his ingenious reckoning, separate one human 'species' from another. Nor have the animals arts and sciences by means of which man puts the stamp of his manners, thought and life on the objects he appropriates to his use. Moreover, the habits of animals are stable; those of men change from period to period and from civilization to civilization.

Ainsi, l'œuvre à faire devait avoir une triple forme: les hommes, les femmes et les choses, c'est-à-dire les personnes et la représentation matérielle qu'ils donnent à leur pensée: enfin l'homme et la vie.

The Scientist has spoken. Now comes the turn of the Historian who is also the Artist. Dismissing in a brief paragraph 'les sèches et rebutantes nomenclatures de faits appelées *histoires*'—he had from 1830 onwards uttered this condemnation often enough in his novels, occasional writings and *obiter dicta*—he unfolds his own conception of what a historian of manners can do, and shows how, while seeking to 'faire concurrence à l'état civil', he can infuse interest into 'le drame à trois ou quatre mille personnages que présente une société'. Again, as in the Preface to *Une Fille d'Ève*, casting a glance at the novel throughout the ages, he renders homage to the genius of Scott for the brilliance and variety of his historical evocations, but finds in him a capital defect: 'il n'avait pas songé à relier ses compositions l'une à l'autre de manière à coordonner une histoire complète, dont chaque chapitre eût été un roman et chaque roman une époque'. At this juncture we may remember that Balzac had arrived at this further stage, still as a result of meditating upon Scott, at an early moment,[1] and that he had many times played with the notion of

[1] See above, 11.

writing the consecutive history of France in a series of novels. *L'Excommunié*,[1] *Les Proscrits* and *Sur Catherine de Médicis*—and even perhaps *Maître Cornélius*, *Le Chef d'œuvre inconnu* and *L'Enfant maudit*—may be considered as isolated pieces of the immense pattern projected. But the idea of novels linking epoch to epoch, except within the narrower space of nineteenth century regimes, has been abandoned in favour of a more feasible project.

La société française allait être l'historien, je ne devais être que le secrétaire.[2] En dressant l'inventaire des vices et des vertus, en peignant les caractères, en composant des types par la réunion des traits de plusieurs caractères homogènes, peut-être pourrais-je arriver à écrire l'histoire oubliée par tant d'historiens, celle des mœurs . . . je réalise-rais, sur la France du XIXe siècle, ce livre que nous regrettons tous, que Rome, Athènes . . . ne nous ont malheureusement pas laissé sur leurs civilisations.

After the Historian, the Thinker, or, to quote de Bonald, the 'Instituteur des Hommes'. To be observer and painter is not enough. The thinker must 'étudier les raisons ou la raison de ces effets sociaux, surprendre le sens caché dans cet immense assem-blage de figures, de passions et d'événements'. He must meditate on natural principles and bring to light the deviations society has made from its true principles. Balzac does not lag behind other Romantics in making the artist 'égal et peut-être supérieur à l'homme d'État';[3] his work is to offer both a diagnosis of and a remedy for social evils.

L'homme n'est ni bon ni méchant, il naît avec des instincts et des aptitudes; la société, loin de le dépraver, comme l'a prétendu Rousseau, le perfectionne, le rend meilleur; mais l'intérêt développe aussi ses penchants mauvais.

---

[1] A historical novel dealing with the Armagnac–Burgundian civil strife of the fifteenth century, partly written by Balzac, and completed for the Souverain edition (1836) of the works of 'Horace de Saint-Aubin' by the Marquis de Belloy.

[2] Cf. *Théorie de la démarche* (Aug.–Sept. 1833), Conard, *O.D.* II 625–6: 'Il y a dans tous les temps un homme de génie qui se fait le secrétaire de son époque: Horace, Arioste, Tacite, Shakespeare, l'Arétin, Machiavel, Rabelais, Bacon, Molière, Voltaire, ont tenu la plume sous la dictée de leur siècle.'

[3] This is no doubt the meaning of the inscription he had put on his statuette of Napoleon in his Rue Cassini flat: 'ce qu'il n'a pu achever par l'épée, je l'accomplirai par la plume'. See above, 72–3.

Christianity, or better still Catholicism, is there to repress these depraved tendencies, and Balzac here weaves into his defence of Christianity ('l'unique religion possible') the central theory of his 'Études philosophiques'—thought and passion as a destructive element, but in this context destructive of society itself. With Catholicism the principle of monarchy is of course linked. 'J'écris à la lueur de deux Vérités éternelles: la Religion, la Monarchie, deux nécessités que les événements contemporains proclament.' Again we read that the enemy of sound laws and good government is the electoral principle 'prise comme unique moyen social', which substitutes mass-tyranny for responsible rule, and which makes the individual, instead of the family, the essential unit of society.

After this condemnation of democracy, though he leaves himself a loop-hole in case the whim again takes him to stand for the Chambre des Députés, he proceeds to defend himself against the many critics who, up to date, have taxed his work with immorality—partly because they have written in ignorance of the general plan of his work, partly because they have been scandalized by the predominance of the guilty over the innocent in his 'fresco' of human society.

Balzac points out that the most conscientious novelists have doubted whether 'la société humaine pouvait offrir autant de bonnes que de mauvaises actions'. But he claims that, in his work, virtuous people are more numerous than vicious ones, and that the latter 'trouvent toujours leur punition humaine ou divine'. After postulating, with reference to the *Scènes de la vie politique*, special criteria for the moral judgments which the historian passes on monarchs and statesmen—here are echoes of his reflexions on political morality to be found in *Sur Catherine de Médicis*—he further defends his own morality by repeating the criticism he had several times made of Scott. The latter, being a Protestant, understood only Protestant women, too marmoreally chaste and orderly, and he emasculated life and reality by banning passion from his work. Not for Balzac such hypocrisy. 'La passion est toute l'humanité. Sans elle, la religion, l'histoire, le roman, l'art, seraient inutiles.' Nor does he accept the epithets of 'sensualiste' (i.e. 'sensationalist' in the Lockian tradition) and 'matérial-

278

iste' which had been attached to him. Repudiating the current doctrine of the indefinite progress of society in favour of 'le progrès de l'homme sur lui-même', he does not regard man as a 'créature finie' (by which he means a mere physical organism with no immortal future). His attachment to Mesmer, Gall and Lavater, his excitement at the possibility that thought may be a quasi-electrical force, are defended as manifestations of spiritual and mystic enthusiasm, not of materialism.

It is no doubt as a further proof of his idealism that he stresses the major attention he has so far accorded, in the 'Comédie Humaine', to spiritual rather than material facts: 'aux actes de la vie individuelle, à leurs causes et à leurs principes'. Mindful perhaps of pleas on behalf of the moral wholesomeness of his work made in 1835 in the Preface to *Le père Goriot*,[1] he adds:

la bataille inconnue qui se livre dans une vallée de l'Indre entre Madame de Mortsauf et la passion est peut-être aussi grande que la plus illustre des batailles connues . . .

In fact, the sufferings he portrays in his works are moral ones. Moreover virtue is soon exhausted as a subject for art.

Lovelace a mille formes, car la corruption sociale prend les couleurs de tous les milieux où elle se développe.[2] Au contraire Clarisse, cette belle image de la vertu passionnée, a des lignes d'une pureté désespérante. Pour créer beaucoup de Vierges, il faut être Raphaël.

And Balzac, with some pride, draws up a list of the irreproachable women and honest men who abound in his work '. . . ne résolvent-ils pas le difficile problème littéraire qui consiste à rendre intéressant un personnage vertueux?' In less solemn mood, in the Preface to *Le père Goriot* just cited,[3] he had compiled an inventory of his 'femmes vertueuses' and his 'femmes criminelles'. He had taken as his criterion of virtue the abstinence from sexual irregularity, and so could sardonically include in the 'virtuous' category such spiteful spinsters as Mlle Gamard, such soured and grasping widows as Mme Vauquer, and such icebergs as Fœdora. The list

[1] *Éd Déf.* XXII, 407–15. Preface to second edition.
[2] An echo perhaps of Hugo's dictum in *La Préface de Cromwell*: 'le beau n'a qu'un type: le laid en a mille'.
[3] *Éd. Déf.* XXII, 413–14.

of virtuous women in this *Avant-Propos* appears to be dictated by the same consideration. The list of good men has more general value.

iv. Further debate on morality

So Balzac establishes his position as scientist, social historian, sociologist, moralist and artist. The rest of the *Avant-Propos* is of less interest to the reader who has studied Davin's Introductions, since it recapitulates, in brief, the scheme of the six types of 'Scenes', adds a perfunctory word about the Philosophical and Analytical Studies, and concludes with an expression of high-minded resignation in face of the calumny and discouragement his work has received from the Press. However, before turning again from Balzac's theory to his practice, we should give some attention to what may be considered as a sort of postscript to the *Avant-Propos*: the letter which, in 1846, he published in *La Semaine* in answer to a courteous but penetrating criticism of his work made by the journalist Hippolyte Castille. Castille's article[1] is largely concerned with the question of morality, to which, as we have seen, Balzac had already given a fair amount of attention in the *Avant-Propos*.

According to Castille, the 'Comédie Humaine' inspires sadness and despair in serious-minded readers, and this he attributes partly to the legacy of doubt and cynicism which Balzac had inherited from Rabelais, and partly to the fanatical zeal for his art which had got the better of his moral sense. In fact he makes of Balzac a leader of the 'Art for Art's sake' school. In painting Vautrin, for instance—'ce beau bronze aux reflets rouges et aux muscles tordus'—he has become so intoxicated with his own talent that he has finished by adoring the monster of his own creation. And the reader is impelled to do the same. Nor can he withhold

[1] It had appeared in *La Semaine* on the 4th October 1846. It is reproduced in Lovenjoul (1), 362–8. Balzac's *Lettre à M. Hyppolite* [*sic*] *Castille* appeared in the issue of 11th October. In 1843 Balzac had even been attacked as immoral in the Chambre des Députés (session of 13th June) by 'un brave Auvergnat, nommé Chapuys Montlaville . . . cela m'a fait rire' (*E* II, 178). *Dinah Piedefer* had occasioned this attack, and indeed had provoked an earlier one in April (*E* II, 139–40). He made a vigorous retort in the Preface to *Illusions perdues* III (dated March 1844).

his admiration from such 'secondary demons' as Ferragus, Bixiou, Lousteau and Eugène de Rastignac: this is the more regrettable because their nefarious enterprises are so often crowned with success. Castille also takes up the question of Henriette de Mortsauf in *Le Lys dans la vallée*, where Balzac has portrayed a life of self-immolation terminated by a paroxysm of erotic regrets. After this Castille's moral censure broadens out into an æsthetic one. Discussing Balzac's place among the novelists of the 'école réaliste', whilst acknowledging his capacity to seize the 'côté dramatique de chaque chose', he accuses him of being immersed in local colour and cultivating a realism that is solely material. Moreover, instead of creating types by the process of generalization, he has made his heroes, and even some of his subordinate characters, gigantic exceptions, standing apart from humanity. This accusation has, of course, often been made since, but, interestingly, Castille traces it to an incoherence in Balzac's technique: in his attention to the minutiæ of detail he emulates the Flemish school of painters, but instead of producing a miniature he enlarges it to colossal dimensions ('de la miniature de grenadier') thereby cutting himself off from all possible comparison with the great masters of literature—Lesage, Cervantes, Molière.

Balzac must have been touched to the quick by the twofold condemnation of his morality and his art. In general, dealing with the moral issue, his letter to Castille reaffirms the necessity of presenting things as they are, and of showing the meaning of life as a struggle between good and evil, now an external conflict between the champions of each, now an internal one between the contending forces in the individual soul. In particular, he defends his presentation of Mme de Mortsauf as an illustration of the internal conflict, being no doubt vexed to see once more called into question what he regarded as a proof of his contention that virtue need not necessarily be boring. As he had said in October 1835, 'Si *Le Lys* n'est pas un bréviaire femelle, je ne suis rien. La vertu y est sublime et point ennuyeuse.'[1] He also insists (irrelevantly, from both the moral and the æsthetic points of view) that Vautrin is modelled on a real person, and that in any

[1] *E* I, 278.

case he proposes to bring him to confusion in *La dernière Incarnation de Vautrin*. He repeats his assertion that there are plenty of 'good characters' in his books, and on two occasions at least gives voice to an opinion that Flaubert was to adopt—a true representation of life contains its own morality, and if his readers are not repelled by the vicious characters and moved to emulate the virtuous ones, the fault lies in themselves: no literature, however edifying, will improve them. This point he had already made in the Preface to *Pierrette*. 'Si, lisant cette histoire vivante des mœurs modernes [*César Birotteau*], vous n'aimez pas mieux, toi boutiquier, mourir avec César Birotteau ou vivre comme Pillerault, que d'être du Tillet ou Roguin . . . le but de l'auteur serait manqué.'[1] And his retort to Castille clearly shows that he is irritated by the implication that vice should be made artificially hideous, and by the suggestion that villains should always come to a bad end.[2] Vice would have no hold on men and women if it were unattractive.

. . . Si, comme dit la Bible, Satan n'était pas le plus beau des anges, qui donc laisserait dévorer sa fortune par une courtisane, sa santé par l'amour, sa vie par la débauche, son talent par la paresse? Les grandes œuvres, monsieur, subsistent par leur côtés passionnés. Or, la passion, c'est l'excès, c'est le mal. L'écrivain a noblement accompli sa tâche, lorsqu'en prenant cet élément essentiel à toute œuvre littéraire, il l'accompagne d'une grande leçon.

Few critics would contest the validity of this point today. Many, however—from Lanson who maintains that 'la vertu comme la grâce réussit mal à Balzac; son génie commence à la vulgarité et au vice', to Alain who asserts that 'Balzac est indifférent devant la vertu . . ., et c'est par là qu'il la peint de ses vraies couleurs'—deny his claim to have made virtue interesting. The explanation no doubt is that the children of his imagination, as opposed to

[1] 1840. *Éd. Déf.* XXII, 544.
[2] That they should prosper is an 'affreuse plaisanterie' which Providence fairly often perpetrates. Nevertheless, Balzac was occasionally to go beyond probability in punishing his wicked characters. The prosperity of the Rogron pair after Pierrette's death is artistically more satisfying than the retribution meted out in later novels: to the Minoret-Levrault family in *Ursule Mirouët*, to Philippe Bridau in *La Rabouilleuse*, to Rosalie de Watteville in *Albert Savarus*, and to Valérie Marneffe in *La cousine Bette*.

those whom his sense of duty inspired him to create, were so vivid to him, and the umbilical cord which still bound them to him so strong, that he could not refuse to them that deep-seated sympathy which we suppose the Divinity to feel for all his creatures, however reprobate. Balzac's morality can be called into question on another score. Whether we consider his attitude to Julie d'Aiglemont in *La Femme de trente ans*, to Marie-Angélique de Vandenesse in *Une Fille d'Ève*, to Calyste du Guénic's amorous yearnings in *Béatrix*, and many other similar cases, we are forced to the conclusion that, in his heart of hearts, Balzac felt that marriage and passionate love were incompatible—'Si vous continuez à parler passion quand je vous parle mariage, nous ne nous entendrons bientôt plus', says the Duchesse de Carigliano to the guileless Augustine de Sommervieux[1]—that passion is the supreme experience of life, and that when conjugal duty and passion are in conflict it is the former which goes to the wall. Judged by puritanical standards, *Béatrix* in particular is immoral; so is *Les Secrets de la Princesse de Cadignan*; so are most of Balzac's novels in so far as they treat of mundane passion.[2] Quite often, one sees Balzac trying to put himself on the side of the angels by using epithets which themselves imply a censure of actions and scenes which he nevertheless thoroughly enjoys, however reprehensible their nature. For example, in the work just mentioned, the Princesse de Cadignan's deception of d'Arthez is qualified as

. . . une de ces comédies inconnues jouées dans le for intérieur de la conscience, entre deux êtres dont l'un sera la dupe de l'autre, et qui reculent les bornes de la perversité, un de ces drames *noirs* et comiques, auprès desquels le drame de Tartufe est une vétille. . . .

It is then characterized as 'un drame *horrible*' . . . 'une *épouvantable* comédie', just as Diane's false confidence to d'Arthez is described as 'cette *atroce*[3] élégie'. He applies the same balm to injured morality by the use of the ironic as by the use of condemnatory adjectives, as when for instance he speaks of Mme d'Espard as being a 'sublime' or 'admirable' creature. Yet, when

---

[1] *La Maison du chat qui pelote.*

[2] No one will be surprised to learn that, of Balzac's works, 'omnes fabulæ amatoriæ' were put on the Roman Catholic Index. Royce (1), 25.

[3] Naturally these epithets are not italicized in the text of this *nouvelle*.

all is said and done, his condonation, whether expressed or disguised, of the passions or foibles of his characters is venial enough when compared with the contemptuous rejection of old-fashioned morality so common in the literature of our day. We can accept the essential fact as stated by the Abbé Bertault—'sa puissance d'imagination est telle que les convictions de ses héros l'entraînent comme dans une seconde existence. Il se livre à eux de toute la vigueur de sa sensibilité.' Yet not everyone will agree with the author of *Balzac et la Religion* when he adds, 'Mais sa préférence accusée va vers les rôles qui traduisent les sublimes grandeurs du Catholicisme et de ses vertus.'[1] One's opinion in this respect depends on the value accorded to such 'romans à thèse' as *Le Médecin de campagne*, *Le Curé de village* and the later *Envers de l'histoire contemporaine*.

Even more vivacious is Balzac's reply, in this letter, to the criticism of his technique that Hippolyte Castille had voiced in an earlier part of his article. To have confessed outright to the charge of building his characters on the exceptional would have been tantamount to condemning himself out of hand, for he had stated emphatically in an article of 1840: 'Les héros de roman ne doivent pas être des exceptions.'[2] His retort here is that Castille's contention—that he chose exceptions and yet accumulated trifles to make his characters gigantic—is self-contradictory.

Mais, monsieur, qu'est-ce que la vie? Un amas de petites circonstances, et les plus grandes personnes en sont les humbles sujettes. Tout est petit et mesquin dans le *réel*, tout s'agrandit dans les hautes sphères de l'idéal.

And, in writing his drama 'à quatre ou cinq mille personnages saillants' (a reference back to his *Avant-Propos*)

. . . comment faire accepter une pareille fresque sans les ressources du conte arabe, sans le secours des titans ensevelis? Dans cette tempête d'un demi-siècle, il y a des géants qui font marcher les flots, ensevelis sous les planches du troisième dessous social. Quand, pour obtenir un si grand résultat, on prendrait quelquefois une exception, où serait le tort? Croyez-vous que Lovelace existe? Il y a cinq cents dandys par génération qui sont, à eux tous, ce Satan moderne.

[1] Bertault (2), 498.   [2] In *La Revue parisienne* (Conard, *O.D.* III, 321).

In the *Avant-Propos* the case of Lovelace had been quoted to illustrate the picturesque variety of vice. Here it is used to justify Balzac's own special method of 'typisation'. He continues:

Croyez-vous qu'un pareil ouvrage serait lisible, s'il fallait scrupuleuse-ment y faire occuper la place réelle qu'occupent, dans l'état social, les honnêtes gens dont la vie est sans drame?

The debate between Castille and Balzac has been considered worth recording because nothing could throw greater light on the vexed question of Balzac's 'realism',[1] or show how far he would have been, in theory as well as in practice, from favouring the attitude of the official sponsors of 'realism' in the eighteen-fifties—Duranty and Champfleury. One cannot help noticing how obsessed he seems to have been, at least when confronting his critics, with the necessity of making his 'social history' enlivening if not startling: no doubt because he felt the need for giving artistic justification to that melodramatic, one might even say Manichæan view of things, which had been his from his earliest beginnings. Is the explanation he gives of his own technical pro-cedure coherent or correct? Probably not. It is not a fact that his colossi are compounded of a thousand insignificant details. They stand out as independent conceptions against a background created from material minutiæ. The originality of Balzac resides to a large extent in the vivid and striking effects he draws from this opposition, though no doubt more still in the compelling vitality of these creations born of his continuous hallucination. George Sand, in her *Histoire de ma vie*,[2] puts into his mouth an account of his technique and motives which, second hand as it is, is per-haps nearer the mark:

Vous cherchez l'homme tel qu'il devrait être; moi, je le prends tel qu'il est. Croyez-moi, nous avons raison tous deux. Ces deux chemins conduisent au même but. J'aime aussi les êtres exceptionnels; j'en suis *un*. Il m'en faut d'ailleurs pour faire ressortir mes êtres vulgaires, et je ne les sacrifie jamais sans nécessité. Mais ces êtres vulgaires m'intéressent plus qu'ils ne vous intéressent. Je les grandis, je les

---

[1] See above, 54–8, my remarks on this question envisaged from the philo-sophical and scientific, rather from the æsthetic angle.

[2] Sand (1), vol. IV, 136.

idéalise en sens inverse, dans leur laideur ou leur bêtise. Je donne à leurs difformités des proportions effrayantes ou grotesques.

The *Lettre à M. Hippolyte Castille* concludes with an appeal to the history of all great writers who, though considered immoral in their time, were the builders of the future. Also with a return to a major assertion of the *Avant-Propos*. After literature has performed its task in exposing the evils of society, it is for religion to step in and correct them. 'La religion est à la société ce que l'âme est au corps. Notre corps est immoral, en le regardant comme l'antagoniste éternel de l'âme. Nous ne pouvons donc que procéder par contrastes.'

XIII

WORK FROM 1841 TO 1844

i. Generalities

AFTER AS BEFORE the contract of 1841, which put upon him the extra obligation of preparing for republication the already extant works of the 'Comédie Humaine',[1] Balzac gave out his novels and stories pell-mell. His creative energy may be likened to a cataract feeding simultaneously a network of streams, though the volume of its water varies. Now it is as tumultuous as Niagara, now a diminished flow, now a tired trickle, according to the vagaries of health, preoccupations and distractions. How interesting it would be to trace in detail, from week to week and from month to month, the course of Balzac's productivity, to watch him reach from subject to subject, to measure the span of his embrace, to see him at work, simultaneously or consecutively, on new themes in proportion as they fired his eager imagination, on projects conceived long since and, after slow gestation, piercing through to the light of day, on schemes half-executed and partly published, seized on anew, resurrected or reshaped in order that he might swell out a half-filled category, pay an urgent debt, or pacify an impatient publisher or editor! How fascinating it would be to surmise the reasons and motives, the obscure determinations, caprices and inspirations which drove him precipitously in one direction or another; to discover what incentives other than the accidental and the fortuitous, the need or impulse of the moment, urged him to one or other of his fictions and explorations! 'J'ai à remplir les cadres', he wrote in September 1841.[2]

[1] See *Biography*, 122–3. A noteworthy point about the Furne collection, repeated in the subsequent editions of the collected works of Balzac, is the suppression of the numerous chapter divisions to which Balzac was addicted—either to save space, or to give a better impression of the unity of each 'Scene'.

[2] *E* I, 565.

But it is impossible to discern any steady plan of advance or systematic strategy for the conquest of his domain, any thought-out method presiding over his activity.

Very often the motives which preside over the composition of certain individual works are as difficult to detect as the rhyme and reason behind the succession of novels. M. Guy Robert has pointed out that a novel of 1842, *Un Début dans la vie*, 'ne ramasse pas le récit autour de quelques faits logiquement sortis les uns des autres, mais juxtapose trois épisodes, dont la communauté des personnages constitue le principal lien'. And he adds:

Le cas est loin d'être isolé dans la *Comédie Humaine*: pour nous en tenir aux années voisines de 1840, l'intrigue de *Béatrix*, d'*Illusions perdues*, de *la Rabouilleuse*, de *la Muse du département* elle-même offrent, à des degrés divers, cette sorte de discontinuité; Balzac en écrivit les diverses parties à plusieurs mois, parfois à plusieurs années d'intervalle. Indigence ou fatigue d'imagination? Le reproche serait étrange, adressé à l'auteur de la *Comédie Humaine*: au moment même où il écrit le *Voyage en coucou*,[1] il ramasse le récit d'*Albert Savarus* autour d'une seule intrigue, comme peu auparavant celui de *la Fausse Maîtresse*, comme quelques mois plus tard celui d'*Honorine*. Tantôt les récits de Balzac affectent une continuité rigoureuse, tantôt ils paraissent refléter certains caprices de l'imagination—ceux de la vie elle-même.[2]

So it is with the mosaic pattern of the works *in toto*: replaced in the periods of time which witnessed their appearance, they form a kaleidoscopic picture whose background is Balzac's own life: 'Les grands événements de ma vie sont mes œuvres.' It would then be absurd to imagine Balzac directing his attention, especially during the period under consideration, to the completion of a particular category, to the exhaustive evocation of a single *milieu* or the illustration of a single conviction. Yet a preliminary glance at Balzac's production from 1841 to 1844 may enable us to draw some impression of order from apparent chaos.

Chronological priority could easily be accorded to certain works. *La Rabouilleuse* had been simmering in Balzac's mind as far back as 1833. He referred to it spasmodically in 1835 and 1836. In July 1839 he told Mme Hanska that the first portion of it, *Le*

[1] First part of *Un Début dans la vie.*   [2] Droz edition, Introduction, lx.

bonhomme Rouget, was being set up in print.[1] In January 1840
he was 'finishing' it—no doubt a case of wishful thinking rather
than a statement of fact, since the first part, then entitled *Les deux
Frères*, only appeared in *La Presse* from 24th February to
4th March 1841. The second part, *Un Ménage de garçon en
province*, did not materialize until October–November 1842, and
the two parts were not put together until 1843.[2] *Ursule Mirouët*
came next to *Les deux Frères* in order of publication.[3] He had
agreed in June 1840 to write it for *Le Messager*. 'Je l'ai là', he
might well have said of it as he said of an unwritten article of
1836, while tapping his forehead, 'je n'ai plus qu'à l'écrire'; but
it really only came into existence—in twenty days[4]—in July–
August 1841. *La fausse Maîtresse* is a rapid composition of a few
months later.[5] *Les Mémoires de deux jeunes mariées*, given to *La
Presse* from November 1841 to January 1842, is a work with a
long history behind it: its first conception goes back to 1834, but
Balzac only appears to have given serious thought to it in the
course of 1838 and 1839; as we shall see, it underwent serious trans-
formations before it took definite shape in late 1840 and in 1841.

The next works on our chronological list would be *Albert
Savarus*, a product of the summer of 1842;[6] *Autre Étude de
femme*,[7] a conversation piece of older provenance now re-edited
for gap-filling purposes; *Un Début dans la vie*,[8] based on a *nouvelle*
by Laure Surville, but belonging essentially to the year which
witnessed its publication; and, as stated, the second instalment of
La Rabouilleuse.[9] Then came *Honorine*,[10] a work quickly conceived and quickly written—in three days, according to Balzac
himself.[11] *La Muse du département*,[12] whose origins date back to
1837, only achieved the dimensions of a novel in 1843. The third
part of *Illusions perdues*[13] had been on the stocks since 1837 or

---

[1] *E* I, 517.
[2] The final title was only attributed to it in Balzac's posthumous notes.
[3] *Le Messager des Chambres*, Aug.–Sept. 1841. Then in two volumes by
Souverain the same year.
[4] *E* I, 568.   [5] *Le Siècle*, 24–8 Dec. 1841.
[6] *Le Siècle*, 29 May–11 June 1842.   [7] June 1842, 'C.H.', *S. vie privée* II.
[8] *La Législature*, 26 July–4 Sept. 1842.
[9] *La Presse*, 27 Oct.–19 Nov. 1842.   [10] *La Presse*, 17–29 Mar. 1843.
[11] *E* II, 100.   [12] *Le Messager*, 20 Mar.–29 Apr. 1843.
[13] *L'État*, 9–19 June 1843, and *Le Parisien-L'État*, 27 July–14 Aug. 1843.

earlier, but he never found time to write it until this year. As for its sequel, *Splendeurs et misères des courtisanes*, begun in 1838, further instalments of it appeared at intervals, one in the summer of 1843, another in November 1844, but it was not to be completed until 1847.[1] *Modeste Mignon* is solely a creation of 1844.[2] So is the little sketch, *Gaudissart II*.[3] Finally we may list the first part of *Les Paysans* and the last instalment of *Béatrix*, both printed at the end of the year.[4]

In addition to the above works, and *Les Lecamus*,[5] and *Les petites Misères de la vie conjugale*, whose composition sprawls over the years 1839–46,[6] it should not be forgotten that from 1841 to 1844 Balzac had other important projects in view, and that at times he was much exercised with their execution: portions of *L'Envers de l'histoire contemporaine* and, besides *Les Paysans*, two more novels which he himself was never able to finish—*Les petits Bourgeois* and *Le Député d'Arcis*. But a study of this list suggests that, during this circumscribed period, his inspiration moved chiefly, though not exclusively, in the domains of private and provincial life; and that, although the frontiers between the two remain, as always, ill-defined and shifting, the former on the whole dominated his inspiration before giving way to the latter. Then, from the middle of 1843, his interest appears to become more and more centred on Paris as the scene of human effort and drama, while all this time he does not lose sight of another purpose, that of vindicating his political doctrines by eulogizing the politically elect and satirizing the politically reprobate. From this analysis it follows that no violence will be done to our historical principle if in the succeeding chapters we examine groups of works in conformity with Balzac's own sequence of scenes, namely, Private, Provincial and Parisian.

But one Scene of Provincial Life—*Ursule Mirouët*—stands by itself as representing a notable return on Balzac's part to the occultist fantasies which had inspired *Les Proscrits, Louis Lam-*

---

[1] See below, 358.

[2] *Journal des Débats*, 4 Apr.–21 July 1844 (with interruptions).

[3] *La Presse*, 12 Oct. 1844.

[4] In *La Presse* (3–21 Dec. 1844) and *Le Messager* (24 Dec. 1844–23 Jan. 1845) respectively.

[5] See above, 147. [6] See below, 415–16.

bert, Séraphita and *Maître Cornélius.* It therefore claims immediate attention.

ii. *Ursule Mirouët* (1841)—postscript to *Séraphita*

The first allusion to *Ursule Mirouët* in the letters to Mme Hanska occurs on the 16th of July 1841.[1] 'Je viens de faire *Ursule Mirouët,* une de ces histoires privilégiées que vous lirez . . .'

In what sense is it an 'histoire privilégiée'? In the first place because it represents a return to Balzac's own special brand of mysticism, and also because this mysticism is proposed as an avenue to orthodox faith, so that *Ursule Mirouët* looks forward to the later *Envers de l'histoire contemporaine,* an apologia for practical Christianity. Even in 1841 he was planning the first part of that work, in the hope that he might thereby obtain what in 1832–3 he had hoped to obtain for *Le Médecin de campagne*—the 'Prix Montyon'.

Balzac was permanently curious about occultism in its manifold forms. In July 1841 he visited Balthazar, a 'très fameux sorcier', was astonished by the accuracy of certain details about his past life and future prospects which this fortune-teller 'read' in the cards, and was impressed by his prophecy that in six weeks' time he would receive news which would 'change his life'.[2] Such a piece of news did in fact come, though nearly six months later; it told him of the death of M. Hanski. His accounts of this consultation show a mixture of credulity and amusement. In 1843 the unfortunate prophet was in prison for the practice of abortion, but Balzac was not disillusioned.[3] He recorded in January of that year that he had gone to consult the 'magnétiseur' du Potet[4] with Mme de Girardin. It was usual for these magnetizers to employ a woman 'somnambulist' at their seances, and on this occasion du Potet's somnambulist, after placing Balzac's hand on her chest, exclaimed:

Qu'est-ce que cette tête-là? C'est un *monde.* Cela me fait peur!

[1] *E* I, 560. [2] *E* I, 562–4; *E* II, 137 and 146. See *Biography,* 116, 135.
[3] Léon de Lora makes a mocking reference to Balthazar in *Les Comédiens sans le savoir* (1846; Conard XIX, 350–1), but this is in keeping with his character. See below, 371.
[4] On this 'quatrième Pape des magnétiseurs', see Viatte (2), 24 ff.

On another occasion, recounted by Théophile Gautier,[1] Balzac and Delphine de Girardin went off together in search of a fortune-teller, but arrived at the wrong address. Such excursions may have been frequent, for the occult fascinated Delphine. Later she took up the new vogue of table-tapping, and in a visit to the Hugos at Jersey in 1853 she initiated them in this exercise: hence Victor Hugo's communications with the 'spirit-world' in 1853 and 1854.

So then the composition of *Ursule Mirouët* coincided with a renewal of the preoccupations which, during a period of greater mystic fervour it is true, had inspired *Louis Lambert* and *Séraphita*; and Balzac's visit to Balthazar in July 1841 was prompted no less by superstitious curiosity than by the desire to get atmosphere and local colour for certain episodes in the novel. Yet its primary point of interest is the study of the solidarity through greed of a middle-class family in the little town of Nemours; a study which justifies the insertion, in 1843, of the novel into the category of the 'Scenes of Provincial Life'. Balzac had no doubt obtained his first-hand knowledge of that town during his visits, in the early eighteen-thirties, to Mme de Berny's house of La Bouleaunière. *Ursule Mirouët* affords an excellent example of his favourite method of developing a story, since it begins (in the year 1829) with an initial incident—the Nemours 'postmaster',[2] François Minoret-Levrault, awaiting the arrival of his son Désiré at Nemours by stage-coach—and then proceeds to a series of portraits—physiognomies and antecedents—of the chief protagonists; thereby pushing the preparatory action on step by step until the whole scene is illuminated and the essential action can be set in motion. Out of 205 pages in the Furne edition of 1843, 107 are, by Balzac's own admission, devoted to the 'exposition'. No better illustration could be given of the aptness of M. Bardèche's formula which defines a Balzacian novel as 'la combinaison d'une crise relativement courte et d'une longue phase de préparations'.[3]

The action derives from the opposition of two groups of people. The central personage in the first group is the rich

[1] *Portraits contemporains* (ed. of 1874, 125–6).

[2] In the nineteenth-century sense, the person in control of the local passenger as well as the parcel service.   [3] Bardèche (1), 384.

octogenarian doctor Denis Minoret who, having retired to his home-town, has devoted fifteen years to the task of bringing up his orphan niece, the affectionate and pious Ursule, with the aid of the curé (the Abbé Chaperon), the *juge de paix* (M. de Bongrand) and other elderly friends. Against them are arrayed Minoret's expectant heirs, who go about their daily business in constant fear of being cheated of their hopes by this girl, whom they regard as an intruder, since she is the child of an illegitimate father and has no blood connection with the Minoret family. The more immediate heirs are three: Minoret's nephew, the postmaster, Minoret-Levrault, a huge, ungainly, covetous, unintelligent man who is under the heel of his harsh, waspish, acrimonious wife Zélie; a niece, Mme Crémière, wife of the tax-collector and a minor Mrs Malaprop; and a great-niece, Mme Massin, wife of the Clerk to the Justices. These avid and anxious persons are supported by their numerous kinsfolk who appear to constitute the bulk of the middle-class population of Nemours. They are a veritable clan which has sprung from a ramification of intermarriages begun in the fifteenth century.

After working out the bewildering pattern of these genealogical permutations and combinations, Balzac embarks upon a long-planned theme, the study of a family 'succession', which he was almost simultaneously treating in *La Rabouilleuse*.[1] The clan, egged on by the acid Zélie, and legally advised by the notary Crémière-Dionis, hates Ursule, suspects Dr. Minoret's intentions, although he merely wants to make a reasonable provision for Ursule's future, and conducts a campaign of silent espionage and intrigue which becomes more intense when Minoret, an erstwhile 'philosophe' and atheist, is converted to Catholicism. He dies in 1835, and even before the breath is out of his body the scramble for the succession begins. Ursule is driven from her uncle's house and reduced to penury, for the postmaster brings

---

[1] In Oct. 1835 he had mentioned *L'Inventaire après décès* (*L.F.*, 184); in Mar. 1836 *Les Héritiers Boirouge* (*E* I, 316). This seems to have been the original title for *Ursule Mirouët*, but its connection with *La Rabouilleuse* is also evident, and part of the material for *U.M.* was transferred to the latter. A fragment of the original twelve pages of *Les Héritiers Boirouge* was printed by Lovenjoul in *La Revue des deux mondes*, 15 Dec. 1917. It is also included as an Appendix in the Garnier edition of *U.M.* See also Guyon, *MF*, July 1958, 477–8.

to naught the financial precautions which Minoret had taken by purloining and destroying his will, and by making off with the bonds that had been reserved for Ursule. In the meantime a love interest has cropped up. A young noble of Nemours, the Vicomte Savinien de Portenduère, a replica of Victurnien d'Esgrignon in so far as he has wasted his substance with riotous living in Paris, but quite unlike him in being at bottom an upright and sensible youth, has entered Ursule's life. The lovers' happiness is menaced by the class prejudice of Savinien's obstinate old mother, and the scenes in which Minoret's dignified generosity is contrasted with her snobbery give further variety to the story.

Deprived of her uncle's protection, Ursule meets with systematic persecution. Her presence in Nemours is a constant goad to the conscience of the weak-willed postmaster, who avails himself of the interested services of Crémière-Dionis' clerk, Goupil, a sort of Uriah Heep in whom fawning servility is replaced by a gift for trenchant utterance, but who is no less resentful of slights put upon him, and much more resourceful in securing the funds he needs in order to set up as a notary. This man, morally as well as physically deformed, is one of the most effective minor scoundrels of the 'Comédie Humaine'. His plan, implacably pursued, is to drive Ursule away (or to force her to marry him) by means of anonymous letters, nocturnal serenades and other annoyances. His campaign only ceases when the postmaster cheats him by refusing him the reward of his villainies.

There is nothing in the situation and train of events, as thus outlined, to stamp *Ursule Mirouët* as being anything but a good example of Balzac's penetrating scrutiny of everyday life in a provincial backwater. But he gives equal if not greater prominence to the supernatural element in the novel. The immediate cause of Minoret's conversion is the intervention of an old medical friend, Dr Bouvard, who in 1829 has summoned him to Paris in order to offer him proof of the genuineness of mesmerism, which up to now Minoret has violently condemned. Balzac thus creates for himself the opportunity to give a history of Mesmer and his discoveries; to define and extol 'magnetism' as 'la science favorite de Jésus'; to explain it as a means of controlling those 'fluides humains qui donnent le pouvoir d'opposer assez de forces intérieures pour annuler les douleurs causées par des agents extérieurs'; to declaim against the materialism of the Encyclopædists and their successors; to link up magnetism with the 'second sight' of Scott and his own favourite 'sciences', phrenology and physiognomy; to insist that palmistry, cartomancy and astrology also have a scientific basis; and finally to transform the Balthazar of real life into a grave, austere and disinterested healer of sickness. Bouvard arranges for this magnetizer, this disciple of Swedenborg, to hold a seance which confounds Minoret's scepticism, so that he offers no more resistance to Ursule's ardent desire to make a Christian of him—she is working in pious collaboration with the Abbé Chaperon, who is destined after Minoret's death to take his place with Bongrand as her tutelary genius.

This is only the prelude to *Ursule Mirouët* considered as a tale of the occult. After Goupil's infamous campaign, by which Ursule has been reduced to a state of extreme nervous tension, she has three dreams in which the defunct doctor summons her from her bed, leads her to the summer-house where the will and documents had been hidden, and actually shows her Minoret-Levrault in the act of stealing and burning them. The Abbé Chaperon forthwith takes the matter in hand and eventually obtains evidence of the postmaster's guilt; but not before Ursule has suffered a fourth dream in which Minoret has again risen from his grave and foretold the punishment of the Minoret-Levrault couple through the person of their son Désiré, the clever, dandyish, but fundamentally honest young attorney who is in fact fatally injured at the precise moment when, informed by the magistrates of his father's crime, he is taking steps to make restitution. Needless to say, such a sequence of events, however unplausible, is sufficient to inspire Balzac with many impressive and vigorous scenes which picture the conflict ranging Chaperon, Bongrand and Savinien de Portenduère against Goupil, the postmaster and his wife.

This is the last occasion on which Balzac intimately wove the occult into the texture of a novel, though he was to introduce another fortune-teller, Mme Fontaine, into *Le cousin Pons*, and to exhibit her as a Paris curiosity in *Les Comédiens sans le savoir*. But he did not abandon his belief in magnetism. He even claimed magnetic powers himself.[1] *Ursule Mirouët* exists as a challenge to such critics as would see in the later Balzac a mere positivist, or a 'naturalist'. It exists as an irrefragable proof that the unflinching observer and the speculative dreamer continued their collaboration throughout. Is it the former, the latter, or the avuncular moralist of 1829–30, the author of such works as *Le Bal de Sceaux* and *La Vendetta*, who distributes rewards and punishments at the end of *Ursule Mirouët*, who kills off Désiré Minoret-Levrault, sends his mother into a madhouse, turns his repentant father into a dispenser of alms and a churchwarden, awards prosperity to Goupil, but gives him an ugly wife and rickety, hydrocephalous children, and makes up for the pains that Ursule and Savinien have endured by parading them as the happiest and most loving couple in his fictitious world?[2] Possibly it was the combination of the realist and idealist themes in this novel that prompted him to claim it as 'le plus bel ouvrage' he had written in 1841.[3]

But *Ursule Mirouët* holds further interest as a study of love in its beginnings and growth: love at first sight, whose force and validity Minoret himself recognizes even while he sees the dangers that attend on it and foresees the shipwreck of conjugal happiness to which it may possibly lead:

J'ai bien observé les femmes, et sais que, si, chez la plupart l'amour ne s'empare d'elles qu'après bien des témoignages, des miracles d'affection, si celles-là ne rompent leur silence et ne cèdent que vaincues; il en est d'autres qui, sous l'empire d'une sympathie explicable aujourd'hui par les fluides magnétiques, sont envahies en un instant. . . . Y a-t-il en amour une seconde vue?

This thought Balzac was to reiterate, in 1846, in *La cousine Bette*:

Les passions vraies ont leur instinct. Mettez un gourmand à même de prendre un fruit dans un plat, il ne se trompera pas et saisira, même

---

[1] See *Biography*, 148. We are given another glimpse of Dr Bouvard in *Splendeurs et misères des courtisanes* (Conard XVI, 142–3), apropos of the superhuman strength which passion can confer—another instance of 'animal magnetism'.

[2] 'C'est le plus joli bonheur que j'aie jamais vu.' Such is the testimony of Renée de l'Estorade, that model of wifely virtue who figures so largely in *Mémoires de deux jeunes mariées*.

[3] *E* I, 574—'Une des "scènes" les plus révélatrices de la *Comédie Humaine*', writes Gide (*Journal* II, 144).

sans voir, le meilleur. De même, laissez aux jeunes filles bien élevées le choix absolu de leurs maris, si elles sont en position d'avoir ceux qu'elles désigneront, elles se tromperont rarement. La nature est infaillible. L'œuvre de la nature, en ce genre, s'appelle: aimer à la première vue. En amour, la première vue est tout bonnement la seconde vue.[1]

Such 'second sight', that intuitive vision which is a faculty of 'spécialistes' like Louis Lambert,[2] is then infallible. Was it in unguarded moments that Balzac, the champion of reasonable partnership in matrimony, made such assertions, such concessions to current sentimentality? It does not seem so. In *Ursule Mirouët* he draws a careful distinction between love and irresponsible passion.[3] The love of Ursule and Savinien is not consummated in a hasty marriage. It has to pass through the fires of adversity, and it calls for the virtues of patience and self-sacrifice. Moreover Balzac makes their love an admissible avenue to marriage by postulating in his Ursule, 'la sœur heureuse d'Eugénie Grandet',[4] what he postulated in few of his feminine creations, an 'angelic' goodness akin to that of Séraphita; and also by imposing on Savinien a long course of repentance and amendment for his indisciplined past. This gives us yet another explanation of Balzac's motives in referring to *Ursule Mirouët* as 'une histoire privilégiée'. His lovers here are privileged persons. That is why he was able to dedicate the work to his niece, Sophie Surville, as one which 'ne transige avec aucun des nobles principes d'une sainte éducation', as one of the books which are 'pure comme votre âme est pure'. Our next chapter will show that, in the ordinary course of things, Balzac was no more disposed now than he had been in 1830 to sanction sentimental or passionate attraction as a normal prelude to matrimony.

[1] *La cousine Bette*, Conard XVII, 112–13. [2] See above, 50.
[3] See Savinien's letter to Ursule, Conard VIII, 155–6. [4] *E* II, 67.

XIV

PRIVATE LIFE:
LOVE, COURTSHIP, MARRIAGE

i. *Mémoires de deux jeunes mariées* (1841–2)

THESE *Mémoires* were written and committed to the press before
Balzac learnt of the death of M. Hanski; but his relations with
Mme Hanska, which had been chilly for some time, were warmer
during the latter half of 1841.[1] From then on, and for several
years while he was aspiring to union with her as being at once
the consummation of an enduring passion and an alliance founded
on reason and fraught with solid advantages, the novelist's mind
frequently returned to the problems of love, courtship and marriage, and to reflection on the difficulties and disillusionments that
may follow matrimony. *Les Mémoires de deux jeunes mariées*,
alleged, in the Souverain edition of 1842, to be based on a real
correspondence between two women, states the pros and cons of
diametrically opposed types of marriage: the romantic and the
common-sense types, marriage for love and marriage envisaged as a rational partnership.

Louise de Chaulieu and Renée de Maucombe are two aristocratic girls, close friends, who have been brought up together in
the Carmelite convent at Blois, where it has been their parents'
intention that they should take the veil. Neither of them has the
religious vocation, and in 1823 they return to their families,
Louise to Paris, and Renée to her father's estate near Marseilles.
Louise takes two husbands in succession. Her first choice falls upon
a man whom chance throws in her way as her tutor in Spanish—
an exiled grandee of Moorish descent, the noble, melancholy,
single-minded Felipe Henarez, baron de Macumer, formerly Duke

---
[1] See *Biography*, 115–18.

of Soria. Her egoistical monopolization of him brings him to an early grave. Her second match ends fatally for herself. Meanwhile her friend Renée has accepted a *mariage de convenance* with an ex-prisoner of war, Louis de l'Estorade, whose unhappy experiences have robbed him of the zest and initiative which would have enabled him to make his way in the world. She pushes him on in his political and administrative career and makes a successful public figure of him; she also bears him three children. Louise and Renée exchange confidences and relate their experiences to each other in a series of letters. Their continued debate on the meaning and purpose of marriage forms the substance of this novel in letter form, for which *La nouvelle Héloïse*, *Clarissa* and Pope's *Eloisa* provide the more obvious models.

Les Mémoires de deux jeunes mariées had hung fire for many years and the work has a chequered history. A *Sœur Marie des Anges*, conceived in 1834, was to have shown a 'Louis Lambert femelle' disillusioned about religion by convent life;[1] and a novel of similar if not identical inspiration, *Les Mémoires d'une jeune mariée*, was in Balzac's mind during the same period.[2] When at Milan in May 1838, after his visit to Sardinia, he wrote to Mme Hanska about a book in which 'happy love' should be depicted. Rousseau, Richardson, Pope and others he criticized as having failed in such a purpose.

Nul n'a décrit les jalousies hors de propos, les craintes insensées, ni la sublimité du don de soi-même. Enfin je veux terminer ma jeunesse par toute ma jeunesse, par une œuvre en dehors de toutes mes œuvres, par un livre à part qui reste dans toutes les mains, sur toutes les tables, ardent et innocent, avec une faute pour qu'il y ait un retour violent, mondain et religieux, plein de consolations, plein de larmes et de plaisirs; et je veux que ce livre soit sans nom [i.e. anonymous] comme l'*Imitation de Jésus-Christ*.[3]

In view of the fact that Balzac had just been exploring Sardinia

---

[1] *E* I, 224; 16 Jan. 1835. It was perhaps intended as a warning to Mme Hanska against the religious mysticism to which she was at times prone.

[2] *E* I, 201; 26 Oct. 1834. In a letter of July 1834 to Auguste Borget ('Formes et Reflets edition, XVI, 159) there is mention of *Mémoires d'une jeune femme*. Lambinet avers (Léger (2), 196 ff.) that Balzac asked Mme. Visconti to help with the *Mémoires* in 1835, but did not use what she wrote.

[3] *E* I, 476.

and that the Baron de Macumer of the finished *Mémoires* has estates in Sardinia, whither he has momentarily repaired after his retreat from Spain as a political refugee, it seems likely that this was the moment when the *Mémoires* began definitely to take shape. In August 1838,[1] however, he stated that the object of his 'livre d'amour' was to show a young person revolting against convent life, plunging into Paris society, judging it and depicting it, and then returning to the convent after the experience of a violent love-affair. A reminiscence of this second intention is perhaps to be found in the definitive *Mémoires*, in the farewell speech which Louise's aunt, the Abbess, makes to her before she goes out into the world: 'cet adieu n'est pas le dernier, nous nous reverrons: Dieu t'a marquée au front du signe des élus . . .'

For a long time Balzac was still thinking of this work as having for its title *Sœur Marie des Anges*, although right up to November 1839 its subject was to be 'l'amour *humain* conduisant à l'amour *divin*'—a direct reversal of the intention of 1834.[2] It was not until February 1840[3] that he decided to detach this 'roman par lettres' from *Sœur Marie des Anges* and give it another and perhaps shorter title. On the 16th December 1840[4] he claimed to be finishing *Les Mémoires de deux jeunes mariées*, but he did not really do so for nearly another year. By then the idea of sending his heroine back into a convent had disappeared; and that is probably the real reason why the title *Sœur Marie des Anges* had disappeared also.

There seems to be little doubt that the *Mémoires d'une jeune mariée*, and subsequently the *Mémoires de deux jeunes mariées*, had for basis the equations Balzac = Macumer (or his archetype), and Louise = Mme Hanska. 'Il y a là [in the *Mémoires*] une lettre inspirée par une jalousie à faux à Vienne . . . C'est la seule lettre de Louise à Felipe'[5]—the letter, in fact, in which Louise de Chaulieu reprimands Felipe de Macumer for a too ostentatious display of his happiness in knowing that he is loved. When Balzac had stayed at Vienna near the Hanskis in May 1835, 'Ève' had given various manifestations of jealousy, but she had also told him: 'Je sais combien vous avez l'âme noble et grande, et je sais

[1] *E* I, 486.
[3] Ibid., 532; 14 Feb. 1840.
[2] Ibid., 522; 2 Nov. 1839.
[4] Ibid., 549. [5] *E* II, 76.

où vous atteindre. . . .'[1] Balzac had stored up this saying in his heart, and it is clear that he conceived himself as playing the part of Macumer to her Louise. In October 1838, at a period when he was receiving much admonishment and advice from her, he referred to her, with tender jocularity, as 'une grave et sérieuse abbesse';[2] Macumer receives similar admonishments and dictatorial counsels from the girl whose slave he has become.

What then induced Balzac to introduce Renée de Maucombe and provide his *Mémoires* with a second 'jeune mariée'? It can only be because, round about 1838, when he was still brooding over the form the novel was to take, he had Zulma Carraud much in mind. He mentioned her to Ève on more than one occasion. Zulma's marriage had been a typically reasonable one. Like Renée, she had wedded an ex-prisoner of war, whom privations in a prison camp had left with a certain 'atonie morale',[3] although Major Carraud was a far sturdier and more independent character than Louis de l'Estorade was allowed to be. She had borne her husband two children and was wrapped up in them. Her correspondence with Balzac, less regular in 1838 and 1839 than it had been of yore, was still full of sage advice. At moments when Ève's changes of mood tormented him and served to show him how little return life might give him for staking all on a romantic love-match, what could be more natural than that he should have reflected upon Zulma's position and contrasted her steadiness with Ève's changeableness?

Moreover, although he told Ève that he was angry with Zulma for trying to get him married,[4] both in the autumn of 1838 and of 1839 he was asking Zulma to find him a well-to-do girl who would marry him and pay off his debts[5]—just as, by a sort of wish-fulfilment, he makes Louise pay off her second husband's debts in the *Mémoires*. In November 1839 he was momentarily despairing of love. 'Je ne veux plus avoir de cœur', he wrote to Zulma:

Aussi pensé-je très-sérieusement au mariage. Si vous vous rencontrez vous-même, jeune fille de vingt-deux ans, riche de deux cent mille

[1] *E* I, 515. [2] Ibid., 491–2.
[3] Z.C., 90. [4] *E* I, 501.
[5] See *Biography*, 114–15.

francs ou même de cent mille francs, pourvu que la dot puisse s'appliquer à mes affaires, vous songerez à moi.[1]

Grieved at this mercenary attitude, Zulma pointed out to him what a serious matter marriage was.[2] It is amusing to see how Balzac, making literary capital of her disapproval, works up his knowledge of her as wife and mother—also no doubt his know-ledge of his sister Laure Surville—and creates the exemplary Renée de Maucombe, so liberal of salutary advice that we should not be rash in establishing a secondary equation in the *Mémoires*: as Zulma is to Balzac, so is Renée to Louise.

So then a detailed study of the *Mémoires* in reference both to the Zulma Carraud correspondence and the *Lettres à l'Étrangère* might well throw fascinating light on the arcana of Balzac's creative processes. But the thesis of rational marriage is his as well as Zulma's. He had preached it in 1830 and 1831. From 1838 to 1841, torn between the desire to live in the atmosphere of a 'belle passion' and the desire to make marriage an avenue to security and tranquillity, he returns to the austere doctrine of *La Maison du chat qui pelote*, *La Vendetta*, and 'Premières Fautes' in *La Femme de trente ans*.

The psychology of the *Mémoires* is interesting. The men of course (as seen through the eyes of the two letter-writers) are abstract ideas rather than flesh-and-blood characters, with the exception of the rarely seen Duc de Chaulieu, Louise's father. Among the women, the worldly Duchesse de Chaulieu, wrapped up in her love intrigue with Saint-Héréen (later to be transmuted into the 'angelic' poet, Canalis), has some vitality. But naturally the two heroines steal the limelight, and they are subtle creations. Louise de Chaulieu, a 'blonde méridionale et pleine de sang',[3]

---

[1] Z.C., 261. Should the text read: 'Si vous rencontrez vous-même une jeune fille . . .'? Probably not: Balzac wishes to find another (but younger) Zulma!

[2] Z.C., 263.

[3] Abraham (2), ch. v and vi, studies Balzac's ideas about pigmentation. In the 'Comédie Humaine', blonde, blue-eyed women, the decisive ones (more passive ones are dreamy and ineffectual), are those who love love rather than men; whereas dark, brown-eyed women are capable of passionate devotion to a man—the dark-complexioned Renée brings her reasoning powers to the service of this devotion. But, as M. Abraham shows, Balzac was quite ready to change the colour of a woman's hair and eyes when it suited him, if he wished her to change from a passive into a passionate one, or vice versa (Honorine de Bauvan,

seems to start as a sort of Marianne (the heroine of Marivaux'
famous novel) coming into contact with the world and judging it
—as Balzac had promised—with some self-assurance; but of
course she is a Marianne whose lineage and status are not in
question. She is presented as naïve but perceptive, waking up to
life, forming her opinion of it, and choosing her way with resolution. It is the way of love—dominating love, a passionate partnership of which it is for her to determine the ruling principles and
of which she is to set the pace.

Que celui que je daigne aimer s'avise de faire autre chose que de
m'aimer! . . . Oh! comme j'aurais dominé Napoléon!

Once Louise sees a possible husband in Macumer, whose divorce
through circumstances from his real vocation, that of a statesman,
leaves him nothing to fill his life but the hope and experience of
an overwhelming romantic passion, his doom is sealed. She
watches, schools and trains him; encourages, discourages, scolds
and corrects him until she has made of him exactly what she
wants him to be: a submissive lover who will live for her alone.
This verges on the ridiculous in its manner of expression:

Votre visage sublime [in fact Macumer is ugly, but this gives Louise an
absolute advantage over him] n'a son caractère, son langage, sa physionomie que pour moi. Moi seule, j'ai le pouvoir de vous transformer, de
vous rendre le plus adorable de tous les hommes; je ne veux donc point
que votre esprit échappe à ma possession.

In real life a man of Macumer's maturity might be expected to
send such a presumptuous little person of eighteen packing; but
his docility is complete. Once he has passed the tests she puts him
through, she marries him promptly and competently, securing
her parents' co-operation by the simple means of forcing Macumer
to marry her without a dowry. This suits them, for they want to
use her personal inheritance in order to provide for her brother,
the Duc de Rhétoré. Although her mother tries to instil in her
some fears about the physical side of marriage, she finds delight
in it. To Renée, who knows not such joys, she exclaims: 'Tu
restes sur la terre, je suis dans le ciel!' On her protracted honey-

in *Honorine*; Esther van Gobseck, in *Splendeurs et misères des courtisanes*).
Pommier (8), 65, rejects this explanation of Balzac's inconsistency.

moon, and during the whirl of social life in Paris which follows, she remains absorbed in enjoyment of her husband's adoration. Renée sees clearly into the situation, especially when, during a visit to the de l'Estorade mansion, Louise shows jealousy over the sympathy existing between Macumer and her friend.

'Dans un temps donné, tu auras réduit Macumer à n'être que l'ombre d'un homme: il n'aura plus sa volonté, il ne sera plus lui-même, mais une chose façonnée à ton usage . . . tu aimes Felipe pour toi, et non pour lui-même.'

Unperturbed, Louise continues her role of praying mantis, and within four years of his wedding day Felipe is dead, stifled by her possessiveness. In its way, Louise's mania is of the *Père Goriot* type. Two years later a young poet, Marie Gaston,[1] as handsome as Macumer was ugly, the friend and protégé of Daniel d'Arthez and Joseph Bridau, begins to fill her life. She builds a chalet in Ville d'Avray—modelled on Les Jardies—as a love-nest in which they may live for each other in isolation from the world. Although she proclaims herself as much a slave to Gaston as Macumer had been to her, her 'assimilation' of him is no less complete, and she leaves him no refuge into which he can retire from the surfeit of physical and sentimental love: she even participates in his literary activity. Renée-Cassandra multiplies her warnings and forebodings, but Louise persists in her wilful and ecstatic blindness, until catastrophe comes. Unjustly persuaded of Gaston's infidelity, she courts and finds death in rapid consumption. Comprehension and reconciliation return at the end, but serve only to sweeten her last moments. So ends the tale of 'happy love' on which Balzac had decided in 1838. Louise dies before reaching thirty, as she had once wished—though not as she had hoped, 'dans toute la splendeur de la vie, dans les roses de l'amour, au sein des voluptés'.

In her choice of a philosophy of life diametrically opposed to this 'égoïsme féroce', Renée de l'Estorade stands in danger of emerging as a prig. But we are not brought to think of her as such. There is resilience behind her apparent rigidity. She enters the married state with calm deliberation, giving herself to a man

[1] He is the second son of Lady Brandon, the forlorn woman of *La Grenadière*. See above, 63.

who evokes no passion in her—but on her own terms, and in such a way as to remain 'absolute mistress of herself', until such time as her duty to the family she has entered and her devotion to her offspring infuse joy and satisfaction into her self-abnegation. In the carrying-out of her resolve to 'make' her husband and rear and educate her children, reason remains her guide; but in due course she fully espouses her husband's life and cause, and confesses that her second child is the fruit of love as well as of duty: 'je suis pour quelque chose dans la façon de cette petite fille'.

In thus unveiling the innermost thoughts and motives of his two heroines—as bosom friends they reveal to each other the secrets of their conjugal life with an abandon which any husband might well find indiscreet—Balzac markedly displays that capacity for intimate sympathy, that ability to run with the hare and hunt with the hounds which constitutes a large part of his genius. In the course of her letters Louise becomes what she bade fair not to be at the outset—a real woman. So does the sage Renée. It is true that this 'docteur en corset' has something of the Julie de Wolmar in her. But since Balzac elected to eschew the triangle theme in his story, she has none of the ambiguity which the heroine of *La nouvelle Héloïse* acquires through the fact of being divided between two men. Balzac has gone even farther than Rousseau in applying his reflexion and experience (a vicarious one) to the depiction of the ecstasies and pains, the sorrows and fears of a wife and mother. Nothing escapes his scrutiny: the misgivings and caprices of impending maternity, the anguish of childbirth, the delight of a mother in suckling, bathing and tending her child; her terrors too when unexpected crises, such as convulsions, seize her first-born; her care for her children's future, her concern over their education, and the reward she reaps in their adoration and that of the husband she has come to regard with an affection akin to the maternal one. Henry James has paid tribute to the highly developed faculty for identifying himself with his characters which Balzac so strikingly displays in this novel. 'He bears children with Madame de l'Estorade . . . Big as he is he makes himself small to be handled by her with young maternal passion, and positively to handle her in turn with infantile innocence. These things are the very flourishes, the little technical amusements of his penetrating power.'[1]

In this work, by contrast with *L'Enfant maudit* and *La Grenadière*, Balzac has shown not only a tenderness for children, but also an understanding of them which is more human, more convincing, because less pedantic and ideological, than anything Rousseau could show. Even his Anglophobia yields to admiration for the superiority of the English nursery system. If *Le Lys dans la vallée* is Balzac's *Nouvelle Héloïse*, *Les Mémoires de deux jeunes mariées* is his *Émile*, for Renée de Maucombe's justification as a creature of fiction is, in the main, that she stands for the principle that the procreation and nurturing of children are the real end of marriage, as even the childless Louise admits at times. And so two ideals of womanhood, to both of which Balzac felt himself drawn, are unfolded. This is how Louise puts it to her friend: 'beaucoup de philosophie et peu d'amour [*scilicet* sexual], voilà ton régime; beaucoup d'amour et peu de philosophie, voilà le mien'. Renée's point of view, so forcefully stated and repeated, so justified by events that we must believe it to be also the fundamental viewpoint of the author himself, is never in doubt. In her opinion Louise has debased the institution of marriage. The exclusive felicities for which she has striven are condemned both by nature and society, and Heaven itself looks askance at them.

L'amour est un vol fait par l'état social à l'état naturel, il est si passager dans la nature, que toutes les ressources de la société ne peuvent changer sa condition primitive. . . . La Société, ma chère, a voulu être féconde. En substituant des sentiments durables à la fugitive folie de la nature, elle a créé la plus grande chose humaine: la Famille!

Man as well as woman is sacrificed to this end, for self-abnegation is not confined to the latter. None the less, there can be no real equality between husband and wife; 'le viatique du mariage est dans ces mots: résignation et dévouement'. Louise herself confesses at the end:

Oui, la femme est un être faible qui doit, en se mariant, faire un entier sacrifice de sa volonté à l'homme, qui lui doit en retour le sacrifice de son égoïsme. Les révoltes et les pleurs que notre sexe

[1] James (3), 46–7.

a élevés et jetés dans ces derniers temps avec tant d'éclat sont des niaiseries qui nous méritent le nom d'enfants que tant de philosophes nous ont donné.

A firm and formal condemnation of the Romanticism into which Balzac himself, elsewhere, has often fallen and is again to fall. The *Mémoires* may be regarded as giving the positive side of what he had negatively and jocularly expressed in *La Physiologie du mariage*. We may therefore feel some surprise because, on those many occasions when he defended himself against the charge of immorality, and especially in 1846, when he met the accusations of Hippolyte Castille, he did not urge this novel, this 'livre à part', rather than the sickly *Lys dans la vallée*, as a proof of the bracing moral tone of his works. Was it because, in spite of his award of the palm to Renée de l'Estorade, his heart remained after all with Louise de Macumer in her pursuit of the chimæra of a passion ever-satisfied and ever-renewed? However consuming Louise's folly may have been, Balzac seems to be at one with Renée in lamenting the untimely end and admiring the beautiful death of 'l'ange le plus charmant que nous pourrons voir jamais sur cette terre'. 'Ce livre a brillé', he wrote in October 1842, 'en éclipsant tous les autres.'[1] But he had much more to say yet on the subject of love and marriage.

ii. *La fausse Maîtresse* (1841-2): *Albert Savarus* (1842)

The first of these works is a short story, and the second almost a novel. They have two features in common: both owe their inspiration to Balzac's relationship with Mme Hanska and her entourage; each of them, though in different ways, evokes the picture of an ideal lover. The scene of *La fausse Maîtresse* is set in Paris. Its hero, a Polish exile, Captain Thaddée Paz, friend and steward of another Polish exile, Count Laginski, falls in love with the latter's French wife, Clémentine du Rouvre, allied to the Ronquerolles and Sérisy families. Out of loyalty to his friend, on perceiving that Clémentine is on the verge of becoming emotionally interested in him, Thaddée deliberately demeans himself in her eyes by keeping

[1] *E* II, 67. Gide (*Journal* I, 198) calls it a 'livre confus, pâteux', but finds in it 'les linéaments d'un chef-d'œuvre'.

an official mistress to whom he is not in the least attracted, the circus equestrian Malaga. Furthermore, when a grave illness contracted by Laginski seems to hold out some hope of his eventually obtaining Clémentine for a wife, he gives all his energies to the task of saving his friend's life and then stages a fictitious expedition to Russia (while actually contriving to live incognito in Paris) in order to keep out of her way. This perfect example of a selfless passion was apparently inspired by the silent adoration which a real person, Thaddaeus Wylezinski, accorded to his cousin, Mme Hanska.

One of Balzac's motives in writing the story was evidently the desire to arouse interest and sympathy for the Polish exiles in Paris, driven from their country after the failure of their struggle for independence of Russia in 1830–1; also to show the consequent disorganization in the lives of these frustrated patriots, in whom mysticism and a childish indiscipline were equally blended. Adam Laginski is fairly representative of these; but his demoralization is arrested, in part by the responsibilities of matrimony, in greater part by the zealous thrift of the friend who has chosen to become his major-domo. Moreover, this *nouvelle* affords us a brief but vivid glimpse of a Parisian 'femme à la mode' in the person of Clémentine: of captivating beauty, frail and delicate, but a hardened campaigner when it comes to the preservation of her looks and the application of all her waking hours to the business of 'reigning over that inconstant Paris'; attached to her husband, but capable of allowing feminine curiosity to deepen into passion, if, by his pretended infatuation for Malaga, Paz had not kept her self-esteem on the simmer and used it as a check to her sentimental proclivities. As for Paz himself, as a picture held up for our admiration, the sublimity of his heroism leaves us a little unconvinced.[1]

At first glance *Albert Savarus* also is a work of dubious value. The story of the Brabantine Albert Savaron de Savarus' passionate loyalty to an Italian princess, his twelve years of single-minded efforts to become a great man, first in industry, then in politics, so that he may be worthy of marrying the lady when her elderly husband, the Duc d'Argaïolo dies, savours much of the

[1] See above, 102.

novelette type of fiction to the reading of which, in the past, chambermaids were reputedly addicted. So also does the *nouvelle* embedded in the story, *L'Ambitieux par amour*, written by Savarus for a newspaper he has founded and which tells the same tale in disguised form. But this sentimental and romantic theme derives real interest from the fact that it is a transcription of Balzac's own experience—his long courtship of Mme Hanska. He wrote it in the spring of 1842, after having at last learned that his Éveline was free. Its first and most obvious purpose therefore was to present his own case before her, embellished by the ornaments of contemporary fiction: to recall the incidents of their first meetings and love-making in Switzerland, in 1833 and 1834,[1] the date at which Albert Savarus' own drama reaches its climax; to keep her in mind of the promise she had then made to marry him when her present husband died; to show her how, through seven years of separation, his life had been planned and his gigantic tasks pursued in the hope of that bargain being fulfilled; in a word, to plead in a more sustained and eloquent manner the cause which he so often pleaded, and was yet for many more years to plead, in his letters to Ève.

That being so, it follows that there were many touches of Ève in the character of the Duchesse Francesca d'Argaïolo, and also a discreet note of criticism of her exacting idealism— '. . . il y a bien de la fierté sur ce front, il est implacable, elle ne pardonnerait pas une injure! C'est un archange Michel, l'ange des exécutions, l'ange inflexible . . .'[2] But the Duchess remains too much in the background of the novel for it to be possible to equate her definitely with Ève. On the other hand, allowing for the necessary alterations of fiction, one can assert that Albert Savarus is compounded almost totally of Balzac. Just as the hero's conversations with the Duchess and his letters to her are replete with protestations and sentiments whose parallel can be found everywhere in the *Lettres à l'Étrangère*, so his physical and moral conformation, even including his 'belles mains de prélat', corresponds with that of Balzac as he sees himself.[3] Aspects and events in

[1] See *Biography*, 60–1.
[2] Conard III, 112: the Abbé de Grancy's reflexion before the Duchess's portrait.   [3] See Abraham (2), 54 ff.

Albert's chequered career are the transmutations of innumerable ones in Balzac's own life from his days as publisher-printer onwards. 'Here, then,' we can divine Balzac saying to his Ève, 'is the story of my life as it has been since you came into it. Judge if I have not merited the reward for which I have been striving and to which all my efforts have tended.'

The tragic ending to the story of Albert's long wooing, impeccable from the artistic viewpoint, is curious in the circumstances. Albert has come from Paris to Besançon in order to use his skill as a barrister and build up for himself the electoral support he needs so that he may launch out on a political career. He counts on this alone, not on personal charm or social brilliance, for he knows that in this self-centred city strangers are suspect, and that the goodwill of its voters can only be founded on gratitude for services rendered.[1] He has the misfortune, though unwittingly, to inflame the heart of a headstrong girl of seventeen, Rosalie (originally Philomène[2]) de Watteville, the daughter of a dull-witted but indulgent father and a domineering mother who combines narrow piety with much worldly calculation and, as later appears, the more primitive urges of an unsatisfied female. The girl herself is presented to us as a throw-back: she has inherited the ruthless and restless egotism of a seventeenth-century Watteville, 'le plus heureux et le plus illustre des meurtriers et des renégats'. Balzac traces with great skill the growth of infatuation and jealousy in the mind and heart of this wilful and selfish girl. Her secret resolve to supplant the Duchesse d'Argaïolo and steal Albert for a husband, though weakened at times by moral and religious scruples, inspires her with the idea of blackmailing the family servant to intercept Albert's correspondence, of purloining his letters to Francesca and, at the moment when the Duc d'Argaïolo's death makes the way clear for the lovers, of forging Albert's handwriting in order to persuade Francesca that he no longer wishes to marry her. At the same time, by ingenious intrigue, she ruins Albert's chances of being elected as deputy for Besançon. Believing her lover false, Francesca makes a match with

[1] On Balzac's interest in Besançon through his relations with the novelist Charles de Bernard, see Léger (1).

[2] A change effected after 1842 for a purely incidental reason. See Lovenjoul (1), 10–11.

310

the Duc de Rhétoré. Albert throws up his parliamentary candidature and goes off in a vain endeavour to placate her; finally he retires from the world and enters the Grande Chartreuse.

What were Balzac's motives for bringing Albert's plans to such disaster? This is how he explains his purpose in a letter to Ève:

Je veux mettre dans mon premier volume de *la Comédie Humaine* une grande leçon pour *l'homme*, sans y mêler de leçon pour *la Femme*, et je veux montrer comment en donnant à la vie sociale un but trop vaste, et en fatiguant le cœur et l'intelligence, on arrive à ne plus vouloir ce qui avait été l'objet de toute la vie, au début. Ce sera *Louis Lambert* sous une autre forme.[1]

If we take this assertion at its face value, Balzac's intention was to formulate and illustrate a truth of universal application. But the terms of this passage scarcely disguise a more personal motive. If there was to be no lesson for 'la Femme', there was certainly one for 'une femme'. Balzac wanted to make Ève see, not only that a secondary and subsidiary ambition could supersede and frustrate a primary one, but also that a man could wear himself out if he pursued that primary one too long without reaping the deserved reward. How often, in the *Lettres à l'Étrangère*, does he insist that this is precisely what is happening to him! In the novel Albert Savarus utters the same complaint in a letter to his friend, Léopold Hannequin, enlarging on the damage done to his health by his continual toil and effort:

Ce combat avec les hommes et les choses, où j'ai sans cesse versé ma force et mon énergie, où j'ai tant usé les ressorts du désir, m'a miné, pour ainsi dire, intérieurement.

This lament, which is also a veiled reproach, could be reconstructed from the *Lettres* in almost the same words, and on how many occasions![2] It is followed in the novel by a passage whose poignancy—for us—is due to the fact that it is virtually a prognostication:

Atteindre au but en expirant, comme le coureur antique! voir la fortune et la mort arrivant ensemble, sur le seuil de la porte! obtenir celle qu'on aime au moment où l'amour s'éteint! n'avoir plus la faculté de jouir quand on a gagné le droit de vivre heureux! . . .

[1] *E* II, 33, 21 Apr. 1842. See Korwin-Piotrowska, 350 ff.
[2] See *Biography*, ch. iv, and especially 130 ff.

Nowhere in his other fictions does Balzac bring us so close to his own personal tragedy. *Albert Savarus* thus acquires a pathos which eliminates any objections we might urge against what, otherwise, might seem a rather absurd romance—and not less so because Balzac himself, with a wry smile, introduces Albert's own *nouvelle* as an imitation of the work of some modern writers 'qui, faute d'invention, racontent leurs propres douleurs ou les événements mystérieux de leur existence'.

As usual the story becomes more gripping as it gathers momentum. Once the climax is reached, and the fiction is carried through to its rapid and pitiful dénouement, the reader no longer struggles against the spell cast on him. Also, *Albert Savarus* is more than an unhappy love-story. Though it belongs to the Private Life category, it is a lively and observant sketch of life in a stagnant provincial town. It gives yet another view of the conflicts of interests in a small closed community. It is a revelation, in a similar vein to Stendhal's *Lucien Leuwen*, and Balzac's own *Député d'Arcis*, of the intrigues and manœuvres which characterized parliamentary elections under Louis-Philippe, the shufflings and bargainings and shifts of front between individuals and parties, and the unprincipled tactics indulged in without compunction by even the high-minded Savarus and his friend the Abbé de Grancy. In the latter character, moreover, we have an interesting addition to Balzac's picture-gallery of priests, in this case a good and benevolent one, but wily and supple. There are other well-drawn figures as well: the Watteville parents, the local 'lion', the fatuous Amédée de Soulas, whom the Baronne de Watteville first tries to marry to Rosalie and then, when widowed, takes for herself, at her daughter's sharp-tongued suggestion, and to his discomfiture, for this second marriage rejuvenates her and ages her new husband—'Pour bien connaître une dévote, il faut malheureusement l'épouser!'

But Rosalie herself is the most striking creation. This jealously passionate and vengeful girl recalls Mme du Gua Saint-Cyr in *Les Chouans* and looks forward to Lisbeth Fischer in *La cousine Bette*. She ranks high among Balzac's wicked women, the more so because, like Anne Gérard in Balzac's drama *L'École des Ménages*, she combines the apparent fragility of adolescence with the un-hesitant criminality which one would only expect to find, if at all, in a woman of riper age. Perhaps, in inventing her, Balzac was minded to show how easily the trustful harmony existing between two lovers may be shattered by the malevolent intervention of third parties—in the case of Honoré and his *louloup* the persistent calumnies of the latter's aunt by marriage, Rosalie Rzewuska. Nevertheless she stands on her own feet. She is at once the victim of heredity, of her environment and of the petty-mindedness of her upbringing. Trained in the habit of regular confession, she has learned how to strain at a gnat and swallow a camel. Her warped and vicious nature is only fully revealed after she has caused disaster to Albert. Remorse at the harm she has done is still subordinated to the hope of netting him after all. Her asperities to her mother are equalled only by her obstinate determination, when all hope is lost, to inflict on Francesca the pain of knowing that her lover had not betrayed her. Her future development is in harmony with her beginnings. She becomes a notorious eccentric, burying herself on the estate her father has left her, and refusing all offers of marriage. Five years later, she is horribly mutilated and crippled in an accident which condemns her to lifelong suffering.

'Quoique de tels caractères soient exceptionnels, il existe malheureusement trop de Rosalies, et cette histoire contient une leçon qui doit leur servir d'exemple.' Perhaps Balzac sinned against art and verisimilitude when, in order to disarm some of his critics, he awarded Rosalie so cruel a punishment for her misdeeds. More important than this chastening conclusion[1] is the idea implied throughout the work, that such invincible selfishness is not corrected but encouraged by a training in conventional, hair-splitting piety. Rosalie de Watteville is a nineteenth-century Agnès whom a narrow kind of education has turned, not into a charming simpleton, but into a viperish egocentric. Balzac intended to write three novels about education.[2] What a pity that he was never able to do so!

Mme Hanska had no high opinion of *Albert Savarus*. She called it 'un ouvrage d'homme'.

---

[1] It was added in the Furne edition of the same year (*S. vie priv.* I, 1842.)

[2] *Les Enfants*; *Un Pensionnat de demoiselles*; *Intérieur de collège*. See below, 421–2 on the 'Catalogue' of 1845.

iii. *Autre Étude de Femme* (1842): *Un Début dans la vie* (1842)

These are both, in principle, 'Scenes of Private Life', but the variety of their subject-matter and interest makes a break between *Albert Savarus* and Balzac's next study of love and marriage, *Honorine*.

Autre Étude de Femme draws its inspiration and many features from earlier writings,[1] and had not reached its final form even in 1842. Its setting gives it the flavour of a scene of Parisian life, since it is an account of conversations that take place, a year or two after the July Revolution, in the salon of the Marquise d'Espard—or perhaps in that of Mlle des Touches[2]—where many of the élite of the 'Comédie Humaine' are assembled. Balzac's intention is to give a vivid picture of the 'raouts' and 'soupers intimes' (the latter, he regrets, have become more rare since 1830) which for him represented the quintessence of cultured life at Paris. Part of the discussion turns on the revolution in social manners which, since 1789, had replaced the great lady of the Old Regime, the flower of a monarchical and aristocratic civilization, by the dynastically more dubious but yet graceful figure of 'la femme comme il faut', the nineteenth-century feminine counterpart in France of the English gentleman. Émile Blondet paints a full-length portrait of this woman for the benefit of the Polish Count Laginski, and brilliantly draws the distinction between her and the less artificial but also less exquisite *bourgeoise* who is becoming the prevalent feminine type. Disquisitions on Napoleon,[3] on literary women and on women in general are interspersed with anecdotes on female inconstancy. Henri de Marsay's account of

---

[1] One of Balzac's contributions to *Contes Bruns* (1832): *Une Conversation entre onze heures et minuit*; and a fragment of 'La Femme comme il faut', from another composite work by different authors: *Les Français peints par eux-mêmes* (1840–2). *Une Conversation . . .*, relieved of two episodes, was reprinted in 1844 as *Échantillon de causeries françaises*. The *Autre Étude* of 1842 was also republished in 1845 as *Les premières Armes d'un lion*, the 'lion' in question being Henri de Marsay.

[2] There is some ambiguity about this, at any rate in the Conard text. This is due to an alteration Balzac made on his copy of the Furne edition.

[3] See above, 244, for the original nucleus (in *Contes bruns*) of an eulogy attributed in 1842 to d'Arthez and, in the Furne corrections, to Canalis.

his first love affair, the disillusion it brought him, and the training
it gave him in the urbane but cynical self-mastery which a would-
be statesman needs, is worth setting beside *Les Secrets de la
Princesse de Cadignan* as a revelation of feminine deceitfulness
and histrionic talent. The conversation soon turns to reflexions
on the punishment fate sometimes inflicts on inconstant women,
and Balzac puts into the mouth of General de Montriveau that
story from *Contes bruns—La Maîtresse de notre colonel*—which
tells of the terrible vengeance taken by an Italian captain of the
Grande Armée, during the retreat from Moscow, on his guilty
wife and her lover, his superior officer. The horrors of the Beresina are thus again evoked, as they had been in *Adieu* (1830). The
story does, of course, belong to the same early period as *Adieu*.

Such stories had been one of Balzac's specialities round about
1832, and he was very apt to shuffle them about in his collections.
In 1837 he had republished *La grande Bretèche*[1] under a more
comprehensive title—*La grande Bretèche ou Les trois Vengeances*
—justified by the addition of two others stories from *Contes
bruns*. One of them, *L'Histoire du Chevalier de Beauvoir* (a fragment from *Une Conversation entre onze heures et minuit*), tells how
a captured Chouan officer narrowly escapes death at the hands of
his jailer, a jealous Corsican. The other, *Le Grand d'Espagne*,
recounts with what brutality a Spanish nobleman of the Peninsular War period wipes out the slur cast on his name by his wife's
adultery. In 1843 this trilogy of stories was to be broken up to
provide material for *La Muse du département*, and since henceforth *La grande Bretèche* alone remained unused Balzac decided,
in 1845, to tack it on to *Autre Étude de femme*. It is in fact in the
modern editions of the latter that it can now be read.

So *Autre Étude de femme*, composed as it is of disparate elements,
does at any rate preserve for us some good samples of Balzac's
early art as a *raconteur*, as well as giving coherence to the device
of reappearing characters by bringing the prominent ones out of
their relative isolation and throwing them together in the com-
municative promiscuity of a 'souper intime'. And if it takes us
far away from the themes so minutely explored in the novels
considered in the earlier sections of this chapter, a reminder of

[1] See above, 32–3.

Balzac's abiding contention occurs in a passing—and savage—comment made by de Marsay on the anti-social effects of passion. 'Les deux sexes doivent être enchaînés, comme des bêtes féroces qu'ils sont, dans les lois fatales, sombres et muettes.' *Un Début dans la vie*[1] also continues the studies of love and marriage only in one respect. It brings into prominence the Comte de Sérisy, a dignified and saddened statesman and administrator of fifty-seven. At the moment when the story begins (1822) he has been married for sixteen years to a woman whose addiction to passionate intrigues has occasionally been alluded to in earlier novels. Despite her infidelities, his love and patience are inexhaustible. The main reason—so Balzac implies—why the Comtesse de Sérisy seeks satisfaction outside marriage is that the Count suffers from a scrofulous disease due to his overwork as an administrator.

The chief interest of *Un Début* lies elsewhere. It begins with a journey made by a handful of travellers in a *coucou*[2] plying from an inn in the Faubourg Saint-Denis to l'Isle-Adam. This episode was closely modelled on an edifying *nouvelle* written for children by Laure Surville;[3] but at Balzac's hands it has become a swift and vigorous story with many themes interwoven. The nucleus of the plot is the action taken by Sérisy when he discovers the dishonesty of Moreau, who has for long years been in charge of his château and estate at Presles, has amply feathered his own nest and is in collusion with a rich farmer, Léger, over the sale of a farm contiguous to the Presles estate which Sérisy intends to buy. From this stems another interest. In Revolutionary times Moreau had been saved from the guillotine by an 'Aspasia' of those days, a Mme Husson whom he now befriends and protects, with the disapproval of his pretentious wife, a former chambermaid of Mme de Sérisy. This protection extends to Mme Husson's son,

---

[1] Its title in *La Législature* (July–Sept. 1842) was *Le Danger des mystifications*. Balzac probably began it in May 1842, and appears to have had only the first episode of it—the account of the omnibus journey—ready for publication in *La Législature* in August; he wrote the rest as the serial was appearing.

[2] A small, uncomfortable horse-omnibus in use before transport between Paris and its environs was more efficiently organized.

[3] Published in 1854, in a collection of tales, *Le Compagnon du Foyer*, as 'Le Voyage en Coucou'. There are two more or less 'critical' editions of *Un Début*: one of 1949, edited by Gilbert Mayer (Nizet); the other of 1950, edited by Guy Robert and Georges Matoré (Droz). The latter has more value.

Oscar, for whose education Moreau has provided. It is Oscar's 'start in life' that forms the substance of the story.

It has been suggested that it is chance which brings together the persons concerned in the action of the novel. This is inexact: it is rather a chain of circumstances closely connected with the Sérisy-Moreau imbroglio which determines that the following persons make the journey in the carrier Pierrotin's crowded and creaking *coucou*: the Comte de Sérisy, who is travelling incognito in order to arrive unexpectedly at Presles and so nip Moreau's intrigues in the bud; Georges Marest, the flippant, elegant, handsome second clerk of Sérisy's notary, Maître Crottat; two painters, Joseph Bridau,[1] who since *Les deux Frères*[2] has become a prominent member of the 'Comédie Humaine' repertory, and Léon de Lora, nicknamed Mistigris, who are going to the Presles château to assist in its decoration; and Oscar himself, a silly, vain, discontented, imprudent youth, with no native flair to make up for his inexperience of life, who is going to stay with Moreau in the hope of succeeding him as Sérisy's steward. The novel begins with a short history of the omnibus services running in Paris and the neighbourhood and shows the anxious and ambitious Pierrotin, a well-sketched figure, at the beginning of his rise to prosperity as a provider of transport. It also stages an interesting clash of personalities and tells how, after the first few miles, the travellers unbend and while away the time with talk and mystifications. Marest begins by spinning yarns about his fictitious adventures in Egypt and Turkey; Bridau passes himself off as the illustrious painter, Hippolyte Schinner,[3] and relates no less fictitious adventures in Dalmatia. Mistigris, a pert little cad, regales the company with distorted proverbs which Balzac, regretful at not being able to make telling puns, thought extremely witty, and with the invention of which he sometimes amused himself. The sorry, shabby little Oscar, after being seen off on his journey by the devoted mother of whom he is ashamed, tries to compete with the others, fired as he is by the verve of Marest and the wine he has taken during a halt. Devoid of discretion, he tells the tale of Sérisy's conjugal misfortunes, not knowing that the severe 'bourgeois'

[1] See above, 211 and 241.   [2] See below, 339 ff.
[3] See *La Bourse*, cf. above 30.

who is travelling with them is Sérisy himself. His blabbing leads to the discomfiture of Moreau and his own ignominious dismissal once he arrives at Presles.

Such is the first phase in Oscar Husson's 'début dans la vie'.[1] In despair his mother, already bowed down by the misery of her life with her unpleasant, querulous, sneering nonentity of a husband, Clapart (Oscar is her son by a former husband, or perhaps by Moreau himself), enlists the support of the rich *viveur*, the retired silk-merchant, Cardot, a relative by marriage. And so Oscar makes a new beginning as a junior clerk of the solicitor Desroches, and spends an irreproachable three years—until 1825, when he reaches his majority—under the firm but benevolent rule of Desroches' chief clerk, Godeschal. This gives Balzac an opportunity to recall his own experiences of 1816–19 as a clerk in the offices of Guyonnet-Merville and Passez, as he had previously done in *Le colonel Chabert*; also to draw a lively sketch of the frivolities and relaxations with which the *basochiens* of those times punctuated their long bouts of hard work. As Oscar gains experience and acquires some sense of responsibility, Godeschal's control of him is relaxed; and the revival of an old custom which obliged a newly admitted clerk to stand his fellows a banquet brings him into new disgrace. An orgy arranged by Georges Marest, whose second appearance, like the first, spells disaster to Oscar, ends up in a gambling-party in the 'salon' of Florentine Cabirolle, Cardot's mistress, where Oscar, sodden with drink, loses money entrusted to him by Desroches.

He has now no protector to buy him out from impending conscription, and is drafted into the army. Years of service with the colours make a man of him, and after the Revolution of July he rises to officer-rank, distinguishes himself in the African campaigns, heroically rescues his wounded colonel (Sérisy's son) from death at the hands of the Arabs, losing his left arm in the encounter, and is invalided out of the army a lieutenant-colonel.[2] Having thus regained the favour of the Comte de Sérisy, he is appointed collector of taxes in the Oise district, so that the story

---

[1] There is much about him of the immature Balzac of eighteen. See Lovenjoul (2), 159–79.

[2] A *chef d'escadron* until the 'Comédie Humaine' edition of 1845.

can end up symmetrically with the description of the journey he once more makes from the Lion d'Argent, this time with his proud mother by his side, in the now well-to-do Pierrotin's rich and gaudy stage-coach. His fellow-travellers are the ex-farmer Léger and Moreau, who have become millionaires as a result of their partnership in estate speculation, the now illustrious Joseph Bridau, and Georges Marest. He has the satisfaction of seeing himself respected as a dignified citizen, while the once smart and cocksure Marest, having run through an inheritance, has become bald, fat, dissipated and down-at-heel and is reduced to eking out a living as an insurance agent.

L'aventure du voyage de Presles avait donné de la discrétion à Oscar, la soirée de Florentine avait affermi sa probité, les duretés de la carrière militaire lui avaient appris la hiérarchie sociale et l'obéissance au sort; il était devenu sage, capable, et fut heureux.

So Balzac enriches and rounds off the story, invented by his sister, of the young man who meets disaster for being ashamed of his mother. The passage of time involves for many persons concerned the change in fortune, the enrichment to which Balzac saw the plebeians of his time reaching out as a result of the social and economic revolution. Irony tinges his final comments on the prosperity of this 'homme ordinaire, doux, sans prétention, modeste et se tenant toujours, comme son gouvernement [the government of Louis-Philippe], dans un juste milieu . . . il n'excite ni l'envie ni le dédain. C'est le bourgeois moderne.' Oscar's transformation and rehabilitation, though more swiftly narrated than his career of weakness and vanity, do not lack plausibility. But the value of the story does not lie solely in the account of a young fool making good. It is an amalgamation of various types of scene. True to its label as a scene of private life, it is also one of provincial, country and Parisian life. It is a good-humoured novel of considerable comic value, the latter being diminished only by the supposed witticisms of Mistigris. It is, more conspicuously even than *Autre Étude de femme*, a meeting-house for characters of the 'Comédie Humaine'. M. Gilbert Mayer[1] computes that *Un Début* reintroduces forty-six known

[1] Nizet edition, Introduction, xxxiii.

characters and invents fourteen new ones, including of course Oscar Husson. It gives the life-story of the Comte de Sérisy, only heretofore casually mentioned in *Le Contrat de mariage*. It presents Moreau as a type of the unjust steward, not devoid of good qualities, who finds his way to wealth and eventual respectability. As for the two retired silk-merchants, the elder Cardot and his son-in-law Camusot, the former appears for the first time, while the latter acquires fuller dimensions. They are true to type as middle-aged roués, at once the patrons and dupes of such voracious courtesans as Florentine Cabirolle and Fanny Beaupré. We renew acquaintance also with Tullia,[1] Mme du Val-Noble,[2] and the Bohemian circles frequented by such as Finot, Nathan, du Bruel and Giroudeau, as well as meeting a new 'rat d'opéra', Maria Godeschal. Derville's former clerks from *Le colonel Chabert*—Desroches and Godeschal—are among others who come to life more fully in this novel. And a welcome new arrival is the Baron de Canalis, whom *Modeste Mignon* is to bring into the front rank. Joseph Bridau, since his introduction in *Un grand Homme de province à Paris* as a 'talent inégal' and his appearance in *Pierre Grassou* as a wayward genius, had already achieved major status in *Les deux Frères* and been transformed into a devoted son and a persevering craftsman; but more light is here thrown on his character and career. *Un Début dans la vie* cannot stand beside *Les Employés* and *César Birotteau* as a novel; but like them it plunges us agreeably into certain non-aristocratic circles of Balzac's world. And the exchange of false reminiscences in the *coucou* brings us again into contact, through the transparent figures of Georges Marest and Joseph Bridau, with the inexhaustible spinner of wild tales who, in 1828, had astonished the Pommereul couple at Fougères: *du Balzac tout pur*!

iv. *Honorine*[3] (1843)

'J'ai peur d'avoir écrit une sottise.' So Balzac wrote[4] of this work —a long *nouvelle* rather than a novel, though originally divided

---

[1] See above, 240–1.   [2] See above, 160 and 162.

[3] It is included in the Garnier edition with *Le colonel Chabert* and *L'Interdiction*, with introduction, notes and variants by M. Allem.

[4] *E* II, 119; 2 Mar. 1843.

into forty chapters—on the eve of its publication in *La Presse*.
A few weeks later,[1] informing Mme Hanska of the success it was
obtaining, he wrote:

> Tout cela veut dire qu'un *ouvrage de femme* est une bien meilleure
> spéculation de gloires, qu'un ouvrage viril.

Ouvrage de femme: a curious phrase. Perhaps he was playfully
comparing *Honorine* with *Albert Savarus*, which Mme Hanska
had disparaged as 'un ouvrage d'homme'. Or perhaps he was
thinking of *Honorine* as a work in which he had looked with
unusual insight and sympathy into the heart of a woman; one
especially interesting in so far as she incarnates that deep-seated
repugnance for the possessive male which sometimes, perhaps
always, resides in the female alongside of the procreative urge and
the social docility which normally correct or submerge it. In our
century, Jean Giraudoux has treated the subject at much greater
length and no doubt with greater sophistication and perceptive-
ness, especially in *Le Choix des élues*. But Balzac has made a good
and well-told story of the theme.

In one of its episodes, *Honorine* brings three unhappy men into
dinner-time conversation, the Comte de Granville, who is unable
to endure life with a bigoted woman; the Comte de Sérisy, an
enamoured husband unable to win and retain his wife's love;
and the husband in this new story, the Count Octave de Bauvan,
like them a magistrate and statesman,[2] but whose case is more
curious and more unusual than theirs.[3] His wife is the heroine of
the story. As a girl of nineteen, fresh, innocent, confident,
Honorine has married Bauvan of her own free will—'à la fois un
mariage d'inclination et de convenance'—and has received from
him all the devoted attachment that could be desired. Yet, after
three years, she has left him for a worthless lover who, eighteen
months later, has deserted her when she is penniless and pregnant.
For over five more years, that is to say until 1827, according to the
chronology of the story, she has lived in solitary obscurity while

---

[1] *E* II, 130; 25 Mar. 1843.
[2] His relationship to the Comte de Bauvan in *Les Chouans* (see above, 18) is
never stated in the 'Comédie Humaine'.
[3] The case of Félix de Vandenesse in *Une Fille d'Ève* does not appear to have
been in Balzac's mind as he wrote *Honorine*.

Bauvan has secretly watched over her like a guardian angel and, without her realizing it, has provided her with a means of livelihood. He only succeeds in breaking down the barrier of guilt-consciousness mingled with repugnance that separates her from him by using the offices of his young secretary, Maurice de l'Hostal, who poses as a melancholy misogynist with a taste for horticulture in order to live near her and prepare the ground for a reconciliation. By a combination of ruse and kindness, and with the help of Maurice's saintly uncle, the Abbé Loraux, whom we have first met with as the confessor of César Birotteau,[1] she is prevailed upon to return to Bauvan, but dies of despair at being unable to requite him with the love he has so nobly earned. The memory of her surrender to the rogue who seduced her and that of the child, now dead, she had borne him, still mean more to her than her husband's loyal and forbearing adoration. The story is related by Maurice de l'Hostal in 1836, at Genoa, where he has become French consul, to a group of visitors: Mlle des Touches, Claude Vignon, and the now famous landscape-painter, Léon de Lora. The presence of the first two reminds us that, by the chronology of the 'Comédie Humaine', we are now on the eve of the drama of *Béatrix*.

Throughout the *nouvelle* the reader is brought to speculate, in company with Balzac himself and his characters, over the secret cause of Honorine's inability to love Bauvan as a man, in spite of the fact that she had married him in all affection and confidence and that she admires and reveres him. Is it due to horror born of a tactless sexual initiation or to an excess of passion on her husband's part? Or on the contrary, is it due to his quasi-paternal possessiveness, to his failure to cast off the mantle of marital superiority this grave young magistrate has worn while guiding his bride through the ways of social life which marriage has opened up to her? 'Par quelle poésie', Bauvan asks himself, 'ma femme était-elle séduite? Était-ce les sens? était-ce le magnétisme du malheur et du génie?'

All that Honorine can convey to Maurice about her surrender to the seducer is that it was spontaneous and uncompromising; that 'l'amour pour certaines âmes ne s'essaye pas: ou il est, ou il

[1] See above, 199.

n'est pas!' The explanation which Balzac entrusts to Mlle des Touches is a romantic and somewhat insipid one. Honorine is the victim of an unrealizable ideal which prevents her from submitting to married life in its everyday duties and routine:

C'est une des plus rares exceptions et la plus douloureuse[1] de l'intelligence que cette femme—une perle! La vie se compose d'accidents variés, de douleurs et de plaisirs alternés. Le paradis de Dante,[2] cette sublime expression de l'idéal, ce bleu constant ne se trouve que dans l'âme, et le demander aux choses de la vie est une volupté contre laquelle proteste à toute heure la nature. À de telles âmes, les six pieds d'une cellule et un prie-Dieu suffisent.

The impending crisis in Mlle des Touches' own life and her eventual retreat into a convent suggest that her explanation is determined by reflections on her own situation.[3] But evidently Balzac thought it valid for Honorine's case as well. It is a disappointingly banal solution of the problem, one which does not take us beyond the sentimentality of Balzac's period, unless we are willing to credit the work with a psychological subtlety which the conventional language of the age is inadequate to express. This woman who, unlike Mme de Sérisy, has nothing of the sensualist or the passionate adventuress about her, who runs away from the most attentive and unselfish of husbands, who even punishes him cruelly by clinging for so many years to the loneliness which her own sin has brought on her, whose sense of guilt is profound, comes to an early death for submitting to the violation of a strange *pudeur* which seems to confer on her an indefinite kind of immaculateness. In Balzac's language this *pudeur* is presented as the shrinking of a woman, still virginal of soul, from the mere thought

---

[1] From the edition of 1844 onwards the epithet is *monstrueuse*.

[2] Balzac has in mind the line from the *Paradiso* (Canto XXVII): *O senza rama sicura richezza!* The phrase often occurs, misquoted, in his correspondence with Mme Hanska. In *Modeste Mignon* (Conard II, 98), Ernest de La Brière refers to '*cette félicité sans trouble* dont parle Dante', and hopes for such with Modeste as a wife.

[3] Cf. Claude Vignon's appraisal of her outlook as regards love in *Béatrix* (Conard V, 143): 'Pour vous l'amour n'est pas ce que la nature l'a fait . . . vous le voyez tel que l'a créé le christianisme: un royaume idéal, plein de sentiments nobles, de grandes petitesses, de fleurs morales, d'harmonies enchanteresses, et situé bien au-dessus des grossièretés vulgaires', etc.

of belonging to any man with whom she does not feel herself to be supremely, ecstatically identified by love.

At the end of the story Mlle des Touches is made to hint that Honorine had not been far from falling in love with Maurice de l'Hostal. There is no other foundation for this supposition except that Honorine is shown to have divined Maurice's love for her. Indeed, as Balzac and probably most men would do, Maurice finds the complex Honorine, the 'pécheresse à relever', more attractive than the straightforward Amélie de Courteville whom he could have married. His wedding to an Italian girl with the Christian name of Onorina is an attempt to cheat his longing for the inaccessible Honorine de Bauvan.

But what is to be done in real life with women like her? It is not surprising that Balzac, the man of commonsense, repeats a conviction he had so many times expressed before: '. . . le mariage exclut la passion . . . la famille ne saurait avoir les orages de l'amour pour base.' It is Honorine herself who, with almost brutal frankness, in a final letter to Maurice, propounds the practical solution:

Que votre femme soit promptement mère! Jetez-la dans les matérialités les plus vulgaires du ménage; empêchez-la de cultiver dans son cœur la mystérieuse fleur de l'idéal, cette perfection céleste à laquelle j'ai cru, cette fleur enchantée aux couleurs ardentes, et dont les parfums inspirent le dégoût des réalités. . . .

It may be observed by way of conclusion that this metaphor of the 'fleur enchantée' forms as it were the decorative theme of the book. In the original serial published in *La Presse* he had quoted, under the title, a passage from what at this time must have been his favourite novel, Gautier's *Mademoiselle de Maupin*: 'Idéal! fleur blanc au cœur d'or . . . dont les racines fibreuses, mille fois plus déliées que les tresses de soie des fées, plongent au profond de notre âme . . . pour en boire la plus pure substance!'[1] It is clear that Balzac was consciously indulging in symbolism when he made Honorine, during the years of her protected seclusion, take up the manufacture of artificial flowers, and discuss with the supposed horticulturist Maurice the subtleties of the 'language' they speak.

[1] *Mademoiselle de Maupin*, Garnier, 266.

LOVE BY POST

v. *Modeste Mignon* (1844)

During his stay at St Petersburg from the end of July to October 1843, when he enjoyed the felicity of reunion with Mme Hanska after long separation, Balzac read the *Bettina* of Frau von Arnim, formerly Bettina Brentano. This example of a romantic friendship (by correspondence) between a girl of twenty and a venerable poet of sixty-two inspired him with some satirical observations which he confided to Mme Hanska.[1] He found the relationship ridiculous rather than moving, since Bettina was not really in love with Goethe, who served merely as 'un prétexte à lettres'. Nor did Goethe love Bettina. He liked the woollen waist-coats and slippers she knitted for him, and appreciated her needle-work more than her rhetoric.

'Qui dit amour dit souffrances: souffrances d'attente, souffrances de combat, souffrances de séparation, souffrances de désaccord. L'amour est par lui-même un drame sublime et pathétique.'[2] Balzac and Ève no doubt discussed the differences between their case and that of Goethe and Bettina, and Ève drew from it a *nouvelle* which she first of all tore up, and then, at his request, sketched out anew and forwarded to her lover. His letters to her[3] show with what enthusiasm this *nouvelle* filled him, and with what fervour he set about expanding it into a novel. When at last it was finished and the new work was appearing,[4] he exclaimed: 'J'ai la conscience d'avoir fait un chef-d'œuvre pour moi, pour vous, et que m'importe le reste!'[5] Not all critics are agreed as to the excellence of the work, but it has a great deal to recommend it, and M. Hubert Gillot wrote a very eulogistic study of it in 1945.[6]

The scene is set at Le Havre, and as usual Balzac gives a lively impression of that town with its commercial interests and social types. The heroine's father, Charles Mignon, is a Comte de la Bastie, but no longer uses the title. After passing through the

[1] *E* II, 186–9.   [2] *E* II, 188–9.   [3] Notably *E* II, 325, 336, 351, 387, 391.
[4] In *Le Journal des Débats*, April to July 1844.
[5] *E* II, 391; 15 July 1844.
[6] Gillot (2). See also Korwin-Piotrowska, 361–83; and Baldensperger (2), 205–8.

Napoleonic wars as a soldier, he has enriched himself as a ship-owner at Le Havre, lost his fortune, and, in 1826, set off to the East to make a new one. He does so in the course of three years by such brilliant commercial operations as often provide a fairy-tale element in Balzac's novels, and returns to find his daughter, Modeste, whom he has entrusted to the jealous surveillance of his friend, assistant and former war-time comrade Dumay, involved in a romantic love-affair. Mindful of the fact that her elder sister had been brought to misery and death by a blind infatuation, Modeste intends to be circumspect in love. But her mother is German, and from her she inherits not only the 'celestial' blond-ness of the race, but also the nebulous idealism with which the French of those days so generously credited the Germans. Since Heaven has been slow to provide her with the man of her dreams, she has fallen in love with a man she has never seen, the 'Angelic poet', Melchior, Baron de Canalis, on the strength of his soulful verse, which is lacking in real power, but is well calculated to appease the sufferings, real or imagined, of a young girl's heart. 'Avoir de l'amour toutes les poésies sans voir l'amant! quelle suave débauche! quelle Chimère à tous crins! à toutes ailes!' She begins a correspondence with him. Canalis, sated with anonymous admiration, hands on her first letter to his secretary, Ernest de La Brière. Ernest's first replies to her are of a damping nature. But the blend of maidenly dignity and self-sacrificing enthusiasm in Modeste, reinforced by the effect of a clandestine meeting in a church at Le Havre, conquers his heart; and Ernest woos her for himself.

When this romantic but high-spirited and intelligent girl learns from her father, now returned, of the trick that has been played upon her, although Ernest has made full and honest confession to Charles Mignon and asked for her hand, she is naturally indignant. Canalis, learning that marriage with her is now a good financial proposition, and minded to escape from the clutches of a tyran-nical mistress, the Duchesse de Chaulieu,[1] if he can make his way in life without her, also comes forward as a suitor. He is a formid-able one, since the enamoured and penitent Ernest is now in disgrace. Canalis is a *poseur*, and easily able to fascinate Modeste by

[1] Mother of Louise de Chaulieu (*Mémoires de deux jeunes mariées*).

the specious brilliance of his conversation, while Ernest remains silent and crestfallen. The entrancing Modeste already has an ardent admirer in the person of the family lawyer's hunchbacked clerk, Butscha; but he has no chance, and knows it. Now a third eligible suitor appears, the Duc d'Hérouville, Master of the King's Horse and Peer of France, a diminutive and frail descendant of the d'Hérouville who has figured as such a brutal father in *L'Enfant maudit*.[1] He does not disguise the fact that he wants the marriage as a means of restoring the family fortunes, but he is a modest, sensitive and likeable person. Nothing stamps him better than the quiet remark he makes when Modeste eventually refuses him: 'mon peu de mérite m'a donné l'habitude de ces refus'.

The remainder of the story, whose original sub-title, *Les trois Amoureux*, was appropriate enough, is concerned with Modeste's hesitation between these three suitors. The devoted Butscha is able by a well-devised stratagem to convince her of Canalis' mercenary motives. Her decision is finally made at a hunting-party at the château of Rosembray, attended by a galaxy of great lords and ladies. This is one of the rare occasions when Balzac showed any interest in out-door recreations; but although there is an amusing sketch of an English groom, the details of the hunt are neglected in favour of a task in which Balzac takes evident pleasure—that of showing off this social élite in their refinement of manners, deportment and conversation; and also, to some extent, in their physical degeneracy and their occasional bad taste. Balzac is never too much of a snob to let the observer lie dormant in him. Particularly interesting is the way in which the Duchesse de Chaulieu, indignant at her lover's efforts to slip from her grasp, brings Canalis to heel and ruins his chances of regaining Modeste's favour. In the end, Modeste, far from being dazzled by the brilliance and dignified condescension of the great ladies around her —being of noble blood herself she easily adapts herself to their elegant and gracious ways—forgives her real lover, Ernest, and marries him. The fairy-tale conclusion which befits this story— *they lived happily ever afterwards*—is translated by Balzac into terms of estates, income and titles.

[1] See above, 146–7.

The novel is studded with reminiscences of Goethe; but the tale is pulled vigorously into the Hanska orbit. So strong is the parallel between Modeste and Ève that, on reading the first part of the novel, Ève was inclined to take as a criticism of herself the passage where Charles Mignon scolds his daughter for her brazenness in writing to a strange man. To placate her, Balzac had to expatiate on the joy and happiness Ève's own audacity of 1832 had brought to him. His business in writing this novel, despite the fictitious elements, the details of background, character and plot which his transformation of theme imposed, is to make Modeste an ideal equivalent of Ève, the object (*via* Ernest) of the admiration and adoration he felt for Ève, and also, through Modeste's chosen role as champion of the man of genius, a further means whereby he could plead his cause with Ève. The letters that pass between the young couple are intended as a model of pre-conjugal correspondence.

In addition, the general problem of marriage is again debated —between Modeste and Ernest in their letters, between Modeste and her father in conversation. Ernest's task at the beginning is to urge Balzac's own thesis on the claims of society and the family, on the sacrifice an intending bride must make to them. He voices Balzac's usual objections against the folly of making love and passion a constituent part of marriage. In due course Modeste retorts by giving her views on the preparation of youth for marriage and mocking at the bourgeois conception of it. To the uncertain but impetuous aspirations of an ingenuous girl she opposes the formal and mercenary arrangements of parents convinced that they are doing their best for their child.

Si le Léandre fourni par la voisine ou pêché dans un bal n'a pas volé, s'il n'a pas de tare visible, s'il a la fortune qu'on lui désire, s'il sort d'un collège ou d'une école de droit, ayant satisfait aux idées vulgaires sur l'éducation, et s'il porte bien ses vêtements, on lui permet de voir une jeune personne, lacée dès le matin, à qui sa mère ordonne de bien veiller sur sa langue, et recommande de ne rien laisser passer de son âme, de son cœur sur sa physionomie, en y gravant un sourire de danseuse achevant sa pirouette, armée des instructions les plus positives sur le danger de montrer son vrai caractère, et à qui l'on recommande de ne pas paraître d'une instruction inquiétante.

Disgusted with the idea of taking part herself in such a 'pitoyable comédie', Modeste stands up in full revolt.

> . . . Je veux faire succéder le mariage légitime à quelque long mariage des âmes. . . . Une jeune fille n'a, dans toute sa vie, que ce moment où la réflexion, la seconde vue, l'expérience lui soient nécessaires. Elle joue sa liberté, son bonheur, et vous ne lui laissez ni le cornet, ni les dés; elle parie, elle fait galerie. J'ai le droit, la volonté, le pouvoir, la permission de faire mon malheur moi-même.

She is making the same claim as Balzac had made in *La Physiologie du mariage*,[1] except that there is here, naturally enough, no plea for the right to make pre-conjugal physical experiments as well. The fact that a wide-awake young woman is defending this opinion shows that Balzac still felt how strong were the arguments against Ernest's contention. In the discussion that Modeste has with her father, it of course falls to him, indulgent though he is, to uphold the middle-class point of view which is also the normal French one, against that commonly held and acted upon in England, Germany and Switzerland. Modeste believes that hers is the viewpoint of the aristocracy to which she never forgets she belongs. Is it for this reason that Balzac half-condones it and allows events to justify it? Probably not, for what redeems the situation in Balzac's conception is the fact that, unconventional and romantic as Modeste may be, she has shrewdness and a power of judgment which, in the long run, and with the aid of circumstances, rectify and justify her dangerous procedure. In any case her demand for love and harmony of outlook in marriage is in no way comparable to the self-centred exigency of Louise de Chaulieu or the pathetic idealism of Honorine de Bauvan. She has been able to discern in Ernest a like-mindedness with herself as regards the essentials of married partnership. Her witty persuasiveness brings him to recantation, and he defines happiness as

> une fusion complète des sentiments, une parfaite concordance d'âme, une vive empreinte du beau idéal (ce que Dieu nous permet d'en avoir ici-bas) sur les actions vulgaires de la vie au train de laquelle il faut bien obéir, enfin la constance du cœur plus prisable que ce que nous nommons la fidélité.

[1] See above, 23.

329

Balzac's own letters to Ève contain many similar definitions. And Modeste's conception of her role, one might say mission, as a wife is as follows:

> Oui, je veux être une source, inépuisable comme un beau pays, pendant les vingt ans que nous accorde la nature pour briller. Je veux éloigner la satiété par la coquetterie et la recherche. Je serai courageuse pour mon ami, comme les femmes le sont pour le monde. Je veux varier le bonheur, je veux mettre de l'esprit dans la tendresse, du piquant dans la fidélité. Ambitieuse, je veux tuer les rivales dans le passé, conjurer les chagrins extérieurs par la douceur de l'épouse, par sa fière abnégation, et avoir, pendant toute la vie, ces soins du nid que les oiseaux n'ont que pendant quelques mois.

Clearly, then, Modeste's preoccupation is with what she can bring to marriage rather than what she can get out of it, and this is her saving grace. In March 1844 Balzac had described the novel as one which staged 'le combat de la réalité et de la poésie, de l'idéal et du positif, de la poésie physique et de celle qui est un effet d'âme, une faculté'.[1] Yet the issue of the combat seems to be a reconciliation between these two opposites. It is Modeste's judgment of positive values—poetry and idealism are not excluded from them—which determines her eventual choice. Hers is no case of a silly, wilful girl obeying the dictates of a heady passion. It is true to say that her marriage with Ernest is as much one of reason as it is of inclination.

In that sense the dénouement of *Modeste Mignon* represents the triumph of the ideal, but it is an ideal founded in reality. Balzac said of the work, while still writing it, 'Ce sera la dernière *Scène de la vie privée* dans l'ordre et le classement définitif des idées que chacune présente.'[2] He had still *Béatrix* to finish, and the Catalogue of 1845 shows that he hoped to write still more Scenes of Private Life. But he means here that *Modeste Mignon* takes the study of marriageable youth, the dominant theme of his *Scènes de la vie privée*,[3] to its conclusion, since, in spite of the romantic nature of the fiction, it shows how a young couple may steer to the haven of happiness through the reefs and shoals of courtship.

[1] *E* II, 325.   [2] *E* II, 331; 16–17 Mar. 1844.   [3] See above, 128.

Modeste Mignon is not without its minor absurdities, one of which is the heroine's untutored musical ability. But we should not suppose that it offers nothing but the discussion of a social and moral problem. It paints two *milieux*: the semi-bourgeois one of the Mignons, with their satellites and rivals, and the 'high-life' one of the château of Rosembray. The etching of the subordinate figures, the notary Latournelle in particular, is sharp; while the more important ones, Modeste herself, Charles Mignon, Dumay, Butscha, Canalis, d'Hérouville and Mme de Chaulieu, are fully alive. Butscha is a special case. He comes originally, so Balzac hints, from Scott's *Black Dwarf*. He seems like a concession to Victor Hugo's theory about the opposition of the grotesque and sublime, and appears to have some affinity with the Quasimodo of *Notre-Dame de Paris*. But whereas Hugo's dwarf is almost sub-human, Butscha's intelligence, like his altruism and his sensibility, is far above the average. In philosophic mood, Balzac makes of this a law of compensation.

La courbure ou la torsion de la colonne vertébrale produit chez ces hommes, en apparence disgraciés, comme un regard où les fluides nerveux s'amassent en de plus grandes quantités que chez les autres.... Il en résulte des forces, quelquefois retrouvées par le magnétisme, mais qui le plus souvent se perdent à travers les espaces du monde spirituel. Cherchez un bossu qui ne soit pas doué de quelque faculté supérieure, soit d'une gaîté spirituelle, soit d'une méchanceté complète, soit d'une bonté sublime....

In *César Birotteau*, with reference to the club-footed Anselme Popinot, he had attributed these extremes of benevolence or malevolence not to physical causes or 'magnetic fluids', but to a decision of the will: 'il ne lui est pas permis de flotter entre les moyens termes habituels à la plupart des hommes'. Butscha's physical conformation urges him to a benevolence which sagacity and goodwill strengthen, especially where Modeste is concerned. Three or four years earlier, Charles Dickens, in *The Old Curiosity Shop*, had gone to the other extreme and infused the pure spirit of malignity into his hunchback Quilp. Almost simultaneously, in *Ursule Mirouët*, Balzac himself had done likewise in inventing Goupil, the notary's clerk at Nemours.[1] There however the

[1] See above, 294.

gibbosity is a sort of internal, invisible one, due to over-development of the bust. This coincidence with Dickens is noteworthy. In *The Mill on the Floss* (1860), George Eliot, with Balzac's observations on Butscha probably in her mind, reflected on the similar case of Philip Wakem and suggested that 'ugly and deformed people have great need of unusual virtues, because they are likely to be extremely uncomfortable without them; but the theory that unusual virtues spring by a direct consequence out of personal disadvantages, as animals grow thicker wool in severe climates, is perhaps a little overstrained'.[1]

More important, however, for readers of the 'Comédie Humaine' than the presence of Butscha is that of the vain, pretentious and fatuous Canalis. As a poet with political ambitions, but as yet anonymous, he had already made a momentary appearance in the 1839 version of *Un grand Homme de province à Paris*, and then, by name, in *Un Début dans la vie*; but only as a politician. In *Modeste Mignon* these data are combined, and he is now shown at an intermediate phase in his career, as a poet whom inability to invent a new fashion in poetry, after he has fully exploited the particular vein made popular by Lamartine, 'le chef de l'École Angélique',[2] is driving in the last years of the Restoration to a political or ambassadorial career. He already holds an administrative post as *maître des requêtes*. He is

. . . un petit homme sec, de tournure aristocratique, brun, doué d'une figure vituline,[3] et d'une tête un peu menue, comme celle des hommes qui ont plus de vanité que d'orgueil. Il aime le luxe, l'éclat, la grandeur. . . . Fier de sa noblesse, il a tué ses ancêtres par trop de prétentions dans le présent.

Balzac professes a very poor opinion of his poetic gifts, as we have seen. He mocks at him as being shallow, conceited and mercenary. His only real ability is to strike attitudes and impose his Olympian personality in the ladies' drawing-rooms, where he talks loftily of æsthetics, anticipates Flaubert's theory of impersonality in art,

---

[1] *The Mill on the Floss*, Nelson, 370.
[2] The reference is of course to the melancholy, personal, religious kind of lyricism for which Lamartine is illustrious, that of the *Méditations poétiques* (1820), and *Harmonies poétiques et religieuses* (1830).
[3] i.e. *calf-like*.

and echoes the doctrine of Théophile Gautier: 'tout ce qui est utile est affreux et laid'. But even in his defence of this thesis he is insincere and inconsistent; 'au moral une espèce de Narcisse'.

It goes without saying that, in subsequent years, Balzac worked Canalis back into earlier novels, and, unlike other poets of the 'Comédie Humaine', he always falls victim to Balzac's sarcasm. Why? Much discussion[1] has taken place on the subject of Canalis' possible prototype. As a 'seraphic poet' who abandoned poetry for politics, Lamartine comes nearest to him. Canalis' winning of royal favours for a patriotic poem recalls the early success of Victor Hugo for his *Odes* of 1822. Other candidates are Chateaubriand, Eugène Sue, Adolphe Thiers and Franz Liszt. If we look forward to *Splendeurs et misères des courtisanes*[2] we can even think of Canalis in connection with Alfred de Vigny, for there he is credited with a poem on the theme of 'un démon possédant un ange attiré dans son enfer pour le refraîchir d'une rosée dérobée au paradis'; this points clearly to Vigny's *Éloa*.

Such an inquiry is fruitless. But one fact may serve to explain Balzac's distaste for this particular creation of his. Like Lamartine, and also like Victor Hugo in the eighteen-forties, Canalis was making poetry the avenue to a political career: 'la poésie était la préface de l'homme d'état'. Balzac had failed in a similar purpose, but never entirely gave up hope of achieving it in the future. There was some envy in this, as well as disgust. Believing that he had in him the stuff of which realist and practical statesmen are made, he could not help feeling vexed and scornful when he saw men he considered as windbags making their way as political orators.

vi. The conclusion of *Béatrix* (1844–5)

Balzac's last contribution to the Private Life series, the third part of *Béatrix*, had two other titles[3] before it settled down to the

[1] Inaugurated by Lovenjoul (5).

[2] *La dernière Incarnation de Vautrin*, Conard XVI, 146.

[3] In the original serial (*Le Messager*, 24 Dec. 1844–23 Jan. 1845) it was *Les petits Manèges d'une femme vertueuse*. In the Chlendowski edition of 1845 it was *La Lune de miel*. The first pages of the continuation contain a criticism of the honeymoon convention which, in *La Physiologie du mariage*, Balzac had blamed as an importation from England.

definitive one: *Un Adultère rétrospectif*. This title was inspired by the fact that Mlle des Touches, in the conclusion of Part II, had used the device of making Sabine de Grandlieu dress like Béatrix de Rochefide for the signing of the marriage contract, in order to conquer Calyste du Guénic's reluctance. He weds Sabine as a substitute for and a faint replica of Béatrix. During the honeymoon spent in Brittany, his relations with Sabine are based upon this mental substitution. When Sabine realizes this she comes to regard herself as being degraded to the role of a prostitute.

Une Fille d'Ève had described the stratagem by which a tempted wife was brought back to the path of reason and duty. In *Un Adultère rétrospectif*, it is the husband who goes astray. Sabine du Guénic is a vivid, forthright, passionate little person, and her trouble with 'le beau Calyste', that impressionable ninny, comes from her failure to follow the advice formerly given to Augustine de Sommervieux by the Duchesse de Carigliano in *La Maison du chat qui pelote*,[1] repeated here by Sabine's mother, the Duchesse de Grandlieu, and more frankly by Mlle des Touches in her convent:

> 'Dans votre intérêt à tous deux, essaie d'être capricieuse, sois coquette, un peu dure, il le faut. . . . Sache prendre honnêtement un peu d'empire sur Calyste.'

Unfortunately for her, Sabine is too enamoured, too loyal of nature to play such a part. Her experiences as a young bride are similar to those which Delphine de Girardin had had with her philandering husband during the first three years of their married life—and, it seems, more recently still, thanks to his infatuation with Marie d'Agoult.[2] Sabine's situation remains tolerable until the couple return to Paris in December 1838. Then she bears a son, gives all her attention to him, and so leaves Calyste unoccupied. Béatrix de Rochefide has now been abandoned by Conti. Her pretence of Platonic idealism has worn thin, and when Calyste falls in with her again, he becomes an easy prey. Before long his deceit and disloyalty have reduced Sabine to despair, and also to panic, because she is still the adoring wife and makes frantic efforts to win her battle with the experienced, cunning and now vindictive Béatrix.

[1] See above, 29 and 283. [2] *E* III, 8; 3 Jan. 1845. Cf. Regard, *Béatrix*, xlix.

The first phase of the continued story has taken the form of a subtle description, mostly through letters, of Sabine's endeavour to wean her husband from his sentimental attachment to Béatrix. Now the main interest turns momentarily to Béatrix herself, and Balzac gives a masterly study of the wiles and manœuvres of a woman bent on stealing a man. The third phase begins when the Duchesse de Grandlieu, with the complaisant but discreet approval of the Abbé Brossette, imported from the unfinished pages of *Les Paysans*, decides that desperate ills need desperate remedies. She calls upon the services of 'le chef des aventuriers parisiens', Maxime de Trailles, who also enlists those of La Palférine, his successor in dandyism. The conspiracy which he hatches is more tortuous than that of Félix de Vandenesse in *Une Fille d'Ève*. It involves the extrication of Béatrix' husband, Arthur de Rochefide, from his liaison with an enterprising courtesan, 'Madame' Aurélie Schontz; a bid on La Palférine's part to cut out Calyste with Béatrix; an arranged humiliation suffered by Béatrix at the Théâtre des Italiens, whereby she is made to realize the danger she runs of finally losing caste by the pursuit of her irregular *amours*; and the ultimatum which La Palférine delivers to Béatrix—that she shall return to her husband—as a condition to be fulfilled before he consents to bestow his (delusive) favours upon her. The plot is successful. Maxime de Trailles and La Palférine 'operate' on Calyste to cure him of his illusions—it is amusing to read the sermon on marital fidelity which, at the end, that accomplished profligate Maxime preaches to Calyste—and the chastened husband, who has paid a physical penalty for his aberration, is welcomed back by his still adoring and now radiant wife.

Naturally the efficient intriguers who bring off this happy coup do so for tangible rewards. Maxime de Trailles in particular stipulates that the Duchess shall launch into society the 'héritière d'une famille riche mais excessivement bourgeoise' he is about to marry: as the year is now 1840 or 1841 we can guess that the heiress in question is Cécile Beauvisage, heroine of *Le Député d'Arcis* and a prize in the election stakes of 1839 which was to be the subject of that novel.[1] Aurélie Schontz in her turn is helped

[1] See below, 406–7.

towards the goal after which she has been striving for five years or more—a respectable and legal marriage in place of the 'mariage au treizième arrondissement'[1] which has bound her hitherto to Arthur de Rochefide. So then the third and final phase of the conclusion to *Béatrix* takes us far from the close contemplation of the tribulations of a deserted wife. Maxime de Trailles, hitherto only a fleeting silhouette, becomes more solid as a character of the 'Comédie Humaine' and actually does give valid samples of that wit and resourcefulness with which Balzac had always credited him. So does La Palférine, 'un soleil à son lever', whereas Maxime is presented as 'un astre à son déclin'. The Abbé Brossette is a good example of the qualities Balzac found, and liked to find, in a competent priest: a fundamental saintliness not unmixed with an aptitude for delicate casuistry:

> Sans doute [he says to the Duchesse de Grandlieu] le rôle d'une Chrétienne est bien plutôt de retirer la femme perdue de la mauvaise voie que de l'y pousser plus avant;[2] mais quand on s'y trouve aussi loin qu'y est Madame de Rochefide, ce n'est plus le bras de l'homme, c'est celui de Dieu qui ramène ces pécheresses; il leur faut des coups de foudre particuliers.

This accommodating sympathy is all the more timely because Balzac lends to his great lady, Sabine's mother, a naïve piety which fears to take drastic action without consultation with a confessor. But the attention Balzac gives to new figures in his Bohemia, 'le faubourg Saint-Germain du treizième arrondissement', is detailed and skilful. Arthur de Rochefide, 'l'Homme abandonné', 'ce loyal, ce brave et très sot gentilhomme' who likes to be economical in the consolations he offers himself for his wife's desertion, who cuts a passable figure by borrowing other people's *bon mots*, including those with which Aurélie Schontz provides him, is an excellent creation. Even more so is Aurélie Schontz. She is a new entry in Balzac's list of loose-living females, a real specimen of

[1] Until 1860 there were twelve arrondissements in Paris. Marriage in the 'thirteenth' was therefore an ironic euphemism for concubinage. Nowadays there are twenty, so the term 'mariage au vingt-et-unième arrondissement' is current.

[2] The Duchess's first plan was merely to extricate Calyste by putting another man in Béatrix' path.

those 'demi-mondaines' whom the younger Dumas was to de-fine.[1] Balzac expends much verve and humour in describing the rise of this sprightly and clever 'Aspasia' through the four stages of her unsanctified 'marriage' with Arthur, by means of a care-fully executed five-year plan, to such a position that she can terminate her calculated fidelity to Arthur and bargain for a husband whom she can rule, school, and push to social heights.

Other 'Bohemians' also appear again as the satellites of Aurélie or the instruments of Maxime de Trailles; among them is Raoul Nathan who, with a fine touch of irony, is also enrolled among those whose task it is to restore harmony between an estranged couple. Thus the final pages of the novel form a vivacious appen-dage to *Un Prince de la Bohème*. But the essential drama of the story lies in the duel between an injured wife and the Béatrix who has become the incarnation of that supple, ferocious felinity to be found in husband-stealers. Calyste himself, although he is not much more than a pawn in the game, excites Balzac to musings on the vagaries of human passion and the strange tendency of husbands to flee from the easy security of domestic happiness and hurl themselves into the mill-race of passionate adventure.

[1] In the Avant-Propos of *Le Demi-Monde* (1855). Mme Schontz is supposed to be modelled on Countess Merlin, that prominent society hostess of the eighteen-twenties and eighteen-thirties.

XV

THE LAST PROVINCIAL SCENES

i. Issoudun. *La Rabouilleuse*[1] (1841–3)

WE HAVE SEEN that *La Rabouilleuse* and *Ursule Mirouët* both
spring from the desire to write a novel on the subject of family
inheritance; a theme 'où l'horrible se mêle si souvent au comique'.[2]
La Rabouilleuse also forms a pendant to *Le père Goriot* as a study
of parental infatuation. The case of the widow Agathe Bridau
repeatedly sacrificing herself and her younger son in order to save
her elder son from the consequences of his crimes was born to
some extent of Balzac's frequent broodings on the love and money
his own mother squandered on his feckless brother Henri while
holding Honoré himself, the genius of the family, to the strict
settlement of the debt he had contracted to her in 1826–8. But
the parallel is not exact, for Henri was Mme Balzac's younger son,
and probably fathered by M. de Margonne. Moreover, under the
stress of debt and uncertainty about his future with Mme Hanska,
Balzac, unlike Joseph, was often deplorably unjust to his mother.
'Ma mère est l'auteur de tous mes maux.'[3] 'Je n'ai jamais eu de
mère.'[4] This personal grievance did not prevent him from portraying Agathe Bridau with all the insight and sympathy her weakness deserved, but, as with Goriot, this weakness is magnified into
an obsession. 'C'est ta passion, à toi, ce garçon', says the always
tenderly affectionate Joseph Bridau to his mother, 'et nous avons
tous notre passion malheureuse.' That of Joseph is for his art,
that of his brother for gambling and dissipation, that of his
mother's aunt, the aged Mme Descoings, for obstinate persistence
in a system which she expects to win her a substantial prize in the

---

[1] For details of publication see above, 288–9.
[2] See above, 293 n. i.   [3] *E* II, 72; 17 Oct. 1842.
[4] *E* III, 176; 2 Jan. 1846. See *Biography*, 131–2 and 163.

National Lottery. But Joseph's passion for his art is subordinated to his duty towards his mother, that of Philippe Bridau to his determination to destroy all those who stand between him and wealth, while that of Mme Descoings is frustrated by Philippe's pilfering of the sum which, had she followed out her system, would have made her rich. The mania of the 'imbécile de mère' persists to the end, and is the cause of her long martyrdom.

La Rabouilleuse is half Parisian, half provincial in its setting. The first part, originally *Les deux Frères*, revolves round Agathe, living in the Rue Madeleine, 'un des plus horrible coins de Paris', with her aunt and her two sons. She is the daughter of a now defunct Issoudun doctor, Rouget, who had suspected her of being really the child of a local official, Étienne Lousteau's father,[1] and had therefore cut her out of his inheritance. This part of the novel is chiefly concerned, in the years 1814–24, with the early history of the two brothers. Philippe is a Napoleonic veteran, a valiant cavalryman and officer of the Legion of Honour, thrown out of the only employment for which he is competently trained—that of killing—by the restoration of the Bourbons; gamester, profligate, thief and conspirator, having physical courage as his only virtue; the most selfish, ungrateful, cynical and black-hearted but vigorous and pertinacious scoundrel that Balzac ever invented, a 'monstrous being' who well illustrated what dire effects may result from the absence of a father's controlling hand.[2] It is part of the irony of things that, while his mother dotes on Philippe, she misunderstands Joseph and, at the beginning, when his inborn talent is urging him forward as a draughtsman and colourist, does her best to thwart him. The story of his efforts to prove his vocation, in the studios of such masters as Chaudet, Regnault and Gros, is by no means an uninteresting aspect of the work. No doubt Balzac had in mind his own analogous endeavours to establish himself as a writer from 1819, though the figure of Eugène Delacroix looms behind his conception of the struggling and eventually triumphant artist,[3] whom the love of his craft and earnest

[1] An interesting transference of the dubious paternity of Henri Balzac?

[2] See Balzac's *Dédicace*, addressed to Charles Nodier in 1842.

[3] In *Ursule Mirouët* Joseph is credited with a picture of Goethe's Mephistopheles, a subject Delacroix had painted. In *Entre Savants* (1845) Joseph is inadvertently referred to as Eugène Bridau. (Conrad, *O.D.* III, 635.)

application to it made a worthy member of d'Arthez' Cénacle. The impression which Balzac, in *Un grand Homme de province à Paris*, had left of Joseph as a somewhat temperamental and wavering genius is here effaced.

The minute attention, half sardonic, half sympathetic, with which Balzac traces Philippe's history, that of a typical demobilized soldier who can equip himself for no honourable career in civil life, prompted M. Ramon Fernandez to suggest 'l'Art d'accommoder les restes de l'Empire' as a sub-title for *La Rabouilleuse*.[1] And indeed the figure of the Emperor overshadows the novel. There are other and similar misfits. A minor figure is that of the ex-soldier Giroudeau, already sketched in *Un grand Homme de province à Paris*, as cashier and general assistant in the office of his nephew Finot's 'petit journal'. Giroudeau's swordsmanship is useful as an *ultima ratio* for intimidating indignant victims of journalistic satire when they arrive to demand satisfaction. It is in fact he who recruits Philippe for this occupation—a temporary one, for Philippe's peculations soon oust him from it. Another Imperial 'remnant', and one far more important than Giroudeau, is the ex-captain of the Guards, Maxence Gilet, a turbulent spirit with a long history of black and heroic deeds behind him, now the acknowledged leader at Issoudun of a set of officers on half-pay and indisciplined young bullies who, in the early years of the Restoration, are scandalizing or terrifying the inhabitants with the practical jokes they perpetrate as 'les Chevaliers de la Désœuvrance', that is to say, as a set of local gangsters who have nothing better to do than to create disturbances. The conflict between these two swashbucklers, Philippe and Max Gilet, constitutes a major theme in the second part of the novel, originally *Un Ménage de garçon en province*.

The bachelor[2] concerned is Jean-Jacques Rouget, brother of

[1] Fernandez, 203. Like his fellows, Philippe is in some sense the victim of his times. In 1817, in an effort to make a new life for himself, he had joined the colony of proscribed Bonapartists and liberals in Texas, the so-called 'Champ-d'Asile'. Balzac qualifies the foundation of this colony, which soon failed, as a 'terrible mystification'; and he attributes Philippe's moral deterioration to his experience of life in America.

[2] 'C'est la troisième histoire des *Célibataires*, et avec *l'Abbé Troubert* (*Le Curé de Tours*) et *Pierrette*, cela complète ce que je voulais écrire sur le célibat'. *E* II, 73. See above, 131.

Agathe Bridau, a perverted and stupid weakling who, to Agathe's disadvantage, has inherited his father's property, and, to his own detriment, has succeeded to his father's mistress, Flore Brazier, whom the latter had coveted and appropriated after surprising her, as a girl of twelve, muddying the local stream in the search for crayfish. This occupation, *rabouiller*, is the origin of her nickname 'La Rabouilleuse' and of the title eventually given to the novel. Flore Brazier takes her place in the 'Comédie Humaine' as a classical example of the 'servante–maîtresse' type, ignorant, unintelligent, sensual, callous, but servile at bottom, skilled in the art of tyrannizing over the squalid bachelor who will put up with any ignominy rather than forgo the limited satisfactions he can enjoy with her. Max Gilet is reputedly the bastard half-brother of the 'bonhomme Rouget'. Having easily established a firm hold on Flore, he has installed himself in the Rouget household; and this pretty pair look forward to laying hands on the Rouget fortune once their imbecile victim has debauched himself into his grave. But Agathe and Joseph Bridau have already visited Issoudun and made an abortive attempt to establish their claim to a share of the Rouget inheritance. Now a more formidable claimant appears, Philippe Bridau himself, released from prison after condemnation for the part he has played in a Bonapartist plot, and conveniently relegated to police-supervised residence at Issoudun.

It is an easy matter for him to pick a quarrel with Max Gilet and kill him in a sabre-duel which Balzac graphically describes; to acquire complete domination over Jean-Jacques Rouget and a contemptuous mastery of Flore; and to arrange the marriage of these two—a triumph for virtue and religion, so think the pure-minded among the inhabitants of Issoudun. He then drags the unhappy pair off to Paris, sees to it that Jean-Jacques shall rapidly succumb to the ravages of dissipation—'il suffit', as Bixiou says to Desroches later on, 'de livrer un homme à un vice pour se défaire de lui'—marries the widow, flings her also into a career of debauchery, and leaves her to die of a dipsomaniac's disease which even the skill of Bianchon cannot cure. Philippe's treatment of his destitute mother is equally heartless: 'le seul service', he tells his brother, 'que puisse me rendre la bonne femme est de crever le plus tôt possible'. This service she does indeed render, and Balzac disposes of the too maternal saint in another of his harrowing death-bed scenes. The attainment of riches has helped Philippe to rehabilitation; he has resumed his military career and become the Comte de Brambourg. But Balzac does not let his most accomplished villain escape retribution. Philippe's hopes of an aristocratic marriage are foiled by Bixiou, whose self-esteem Philippe has wounded, and whom he has outraged by his behaviour to his mother; and in 1839 he meets with a painful death at the hands of the Arabs in Algeria.

La Rabouilleuse is the grimmest story of human wickedness that Balzac ever wrote; so much so that the attitude of moral censure which he maintains throughout the book, reinforced by the frequency of the epithet 'horrible' which he applies to his villain's exploits, scarcely attenuates the impression of black pessimism which remains with the reader after he has closed the book. Yet this long work contains enough incidents and scenes to lighten the sombre tone of the 'rake's progress' with glimpses of normal existence, including those of the Bohemian life in which Philippe Bridau mixes as his increasing depravity reduces his mother to despair and rouses his brother to fury or contempt. In Paris there is, on the credit side of human morality, the constant readiness of the elder Desroches to befriend the Bridau family and avert the worst consequences of Philippe's escapades. At Issoudun there is the generous sympathy which Madame Hochon shows to her old friend and temporary guest, Agathe Bridau, although she herself is a martyr to the cheese-paring niggardliness of her aged husband. There is comic relief in the exploits of the 'Chevaliers de la Désœuvrance', though these are overshadowed by sinister incidents: the attempted assassination of Max Gilet by a victim of his practical jokes (for a few days the honest Joseph runs the risk of paying the penalty for this crime), the fight in the café between royalists and liberals, and the duel to the death in which the Issoudun drama culminates.

Has Balzac forced the tone, yielded to his craving for the melodramatic, and made his villain too competent and too promptly triumphant? We should remember that Balzac's aim was not only to emphasize the weakness of maternal authority and the impotence of human justice, unsupported by religion, to curb individual rapacity,[1] but also to show how the real qualities of a man of action may be misapplied in a society which has no use for them. When action is needed Philippe is alert, resolute and fearless. It may also be felt that Jean-Jacques Rouget is too spineless and Flore Brazier at once too domineering and too malleable; that the scenes of the successive *ménages à trois* (the Rouget–Flore–Gilet association followed by the Rouget–Flore–Bridau combination) are too lurid and too nauseating to count as scenes from real life. Yet the addition of Flore Brazier to Balzac's tribe of harpies is an interesting one. Hitherto the novelist, seasoning reprobation with more than a pinch of admiration, had shown such creatures using their charms and wiles victoriously and to their own advantage. The fact that Flore Brazier's technique in reducing Rouget to pathetic submissiveness is the technique of all women, from the duchess to the prostitute, is urged as an excuse for what Balzac calls 'la crudité de cette peinture'; but he had never before gone so far, not even in *Un Prince de la Bohème*, in studying the victimizer in her alternative role of victim. Philippe Bridau bends Flore to his will with the utmost cynicism.

'Les femmes sont des enfants méchants; c'est des bêtes inférieures à l'homme, et il faut s'en faire craindre, car la pire condition pour nous est d'être gouvernés par ces bêtes-là.'

It is true that 'la Rabouilleuse' is nothing better than a peasant drab, who in happier circumstances might have been harmless and even blameless; she cuts a poor figure in comparison with her vivacious and resourceful Parisian sisters.

Balzac's setting of the main scenes at Issoudun, a Berrichon town half-way between Bourges and Châteauroux, is due to the idea that a situation like that of the Rouget household, and a besotted character like Rouget himself, could only arise in conditions of social stagnation. He went several times to Issoudun when staying with his friends the Carrauds after their retirement to Frapesle in 1834. Research has been made[2] into the circumstances of these visits, the local history of Issoudun and the types of people he met or heard of there. Some of the characters in the

---

[1] See the *Dédicace* of this work.

[2] See Serval (1). M. Allem resumes his findings in the Introduction to the Garnier edition of *La Rabouilleuse*. See also Guignard.

story, including Max Gilet, had their counterpart in real life. The
'Chevaliers de la Désœuvrance' really existed. Some of the practical jokes played by them in the novel are authentic, and 'La
Cognette', the proprietress of the tavern where they foregather in
the story, has been identified. But behind local anecdotes and
rakish prototypes Balzac discerned a more commonplace reality.
Issoudun was for him—and assuredly was so for the Carrauds as
well—a town where nothing interesting happens, where economic
and commercial life are moribund, where social and intellectual
life are non-existent. It was an administrative and political backwater whose inertia was disturbed only by the quarrels and
pranks of irresponsible ruffians and by domestic dramas such as
the Rouget one. 'Issoudun aurait engourdi Napoleon.'

Of course Balzac blames the hegemony of the middle class for
this stagnation, and promises a like fate for the rest of French
towns, including Paris itself, if the present regime continues. We
have already seen that, except when his own local patriotism
comes into play—as for instance in *L'illustre Gaudissart*, where
cunning natives of Vouvray get the better of a smart Parisian—
his interest in the provinces is tinged with disdain, especially
when he turns his attention to the inept imitations of Parisian
social brilliance in which the would-be intelligentsia of towns like
Angoulême indulged. In his next 'Scene of Provincial Life', *La
Muse du département*, this disdain reappears, and is heightened
by the sense of superiority with which the Parisian man of letters
is filled when he thinks of the literary flounderings of provincial
poetasters and connoisseurs. In that volume of the 'Comédie
Humaine' in which the two parts of *La Rabouilleuse* were united,
he also collected *L'illustre Gaudissart* and *La Muse du département* under the title 'Les Parisiens en province'. In the second of
these works Gaudissart's humiliation of 1831 is more than
avenged by the victorious aplomb of Étienne Lousteau and Horace
Bianchon when in 1836 they visit their native Sancerre,[1] another
Berrichon town not fifty miles north-east of Issoudun.

[1] The connection of these two with Sancerre points to Latouche and Émile
Regnault as having contributed something to their make-up. Both had been
educated at the Collège de Bourges. Latouche was in fact a native of La Châtre;
but Regnault had been a medical student at Sancerre. See above, 138 n. i,
and 205–6.

ii. Sancerre. *La Muse du département* (1843)

The 'Muse' in question, the 'femme supérieure' of her province, is a young woman of bourgeois stock, Dinah Piedefer, married since 1823 (the action of the story begins in 1836) to a Baron de La Baudraye, in whose person, through the course of the novel, Balzac illustrates the climb of a dubious 'petite noblesse' to greater social heights by means of a careful accumulation of estates and a no less careful utilization of such claims as it could make to the benevolence of the monarch. A frail undersized person—'avorton' and 'insecte' are terms frequently applied to him —and twenty-seven years older than his wife, La Baudraye is unable to give her the children he needs in order to qualify for the desired status of count and peer of France. He is too stingy to allow her the social joys of life in Paris: she compensates herself by taking to poetry and fiction and by founding a literary society at Sancerre. This provincial muse, who writes under the Spanish pseudonym of Jan Diaz and whose poetic effusions Balzac analyses with a blend of sympathy and disparagement, covets the laurels of a Mme de Staël or a George Sand.

We have seen that Balzac has a prejudice against literary women.[1] In *Autre Étude de femme* Blondet speaks caustically of the 'femme de lettres': in contrast with the 'femme comme il faut', 'quand elle n'a pas de génie [a sop to Camille Maupin], c'est une femme comme il n'en faut pas'. Firm as Balzac's friendship had now become with Sand, much as he admired many of her works, it is doubtful whether, as an authoress, she entirely escaped his disapproval. *La Muse du département* contains adverse comments on the 'Sandisme' of the century; nor can one fail to notice the parallel between the history of the Berrichon Aurore Dudevant leaving her husband in 1831 to set up in Paris with a Berrichon journalist, Jules Sandeau, and the similar history of the fictitious Dinah. In fact we may be sure that *La Muse*, as well as *Béatrix*, bears traces of the confidential talks between Sand and Balzac at Nohant in February 1838,[2] and that from them Balzac drew data for the portrayal not only of Lousteau, the villain of the story, but also of its heroine. But the analogy between the two

---

[1] See above, 173 and 228. [2] See above, 224–6.

women must not be pressed. Dinah is no genius like Camille Maupin. Certainly she is intelligent and attractive, 'adorée pour sa beauté sans rivale, admirée pour son esprit par les hommes *les plus comme il faut* de Sancerre'; but her literary knowledge and general erudition are artificially acquired, her wit and brilliance somewhat strained. Of course marriage has brought her no satisfaction; it has merely added an irritating subordination to the inferiority in which, according to Balzac, a provincial woman, however honourable her status, inevitably finds herself by comparison with the more emancipated ladies of Paris.

An admirable page serves at once to convey the incompleteness of the social satisfactions which Dinah creates for herself and to measure their value in terms of an unappreciative husband's reactions:

Aussi, de Cosne, de La Charité, de Nevers sur la rive droite, et de Léré, de Vailly, d'Argent, de Blancafort, d'Aubigny sur la rive gauche, venait-on se faire présenter à madame de La Baudraye, comme en Suisse on se faisait présenter à madame de Staël. Ceux qui n'entendaient qu'une seule fois les airs de cette tabatière suisse, s'en allaient étourdis et disaient de Dinah des choses merveilleuses qui rendirent les femmes jalouses à dix lieues à la ronde.

Il existe dans l'admiration qu'on inspire, ou dans l'action d'un rôle joué je ne sais quelle griserie morale qui ne permet pas à la critique d'arriver à l'idole. Une atmosphère produite peut-être par une constante dilatation nerveuse fait comme un nimbe à travers lequel on voit le monde au-dessous de soi. Comment expliquer autrement la perpétuelle bonne foi qui préside à tant de nouvelles représentations des mêmes effets, et la continuelle méconnaissance du conseil que donnent ou les enfants, si terribles pour leurs parents, ou les maris si familiarisés avec les innocentes roueries de leurs femmes! Monsieur de La Baudraye avait la candeur d'un homme qui déploie un parapluie aux premières gouttes tombées. Quand sa femme entamait la question de la traite des nègres, ou l'amélioration du sort des forçats, il prenait sa petite casquette bleue et s'évadait sans bruit avec la certitude de pouvoir aller à Saint-Thibault surveiller une livraison de poinçons,[1] et revenir une heure après en retrouvant la discussion à peu près mûrie. S'il n'avait rien à faire, il allait se promener sur le Mail d'où se

[1] La Baudraye is patiently increasing his fortune by cultivating his vineyards and selling the wine from them.

découvre l'admirable panorama de la vallée de la Loire, et prenait un bain d'air pendant que sa femme exécutait une sonate de paroles et des duos de dialectique.

Dinah receives much amorous attention from the notables who frequent her 'Cénacle' and who help her to raise its tone above the small-talk and petty scandal to which their womenfolk would willingly reduce it. Such courtship she accepts but does not greatly encourage; she is a likely prey for more brilliant advances. They come in the shape of Lousteau and Bianchon. When these two, invited by Dinah as Parisian celebrities, arrive at her husband's château of Anzy, it is to them that Balzac assigns the role of dazzling and mystifying the local élite, of showing up, as in *Les deux Poètes*, the inferiority of the local culture, and of drawing out, with malicious ingenuity, the conversational talent and literary accomplishments of the local 'Sappho'.

Also of seducing her. Lousteau decides to supplant Dinah's most favoured admirer, the public attorney, M. de Clagny. With the aid of Bianchon, that benevolent but too scientifically curious Æsculapius of the 'Comédie Humaine', whom we are mildly surprised to see here playing the part of a pander, he is successful, and before the end of his stay has become her lover. A few months after his return to Paris, being pregnant, she takes the decisive step of leaving her husband, joining Lousteau in his Paris abode, and setting up with him there. By so doing she thwarts his plan, furthered by Bixiou, for an advantageous marriage with a young member of the Cardot family, 'presque vierge', as Dr Lotte puts it.

An interesting first sketch of *La Muse du département* is to be found in *La grande Bretèche ou Les trois Vengeances* of 1837.[1] The opening pages of this little work introduce the essential personages of *La Muse*, and comment on the vulgar persistency with which provincial curiosity, avid for signs of secret liaisons, peers into private lives.[2] In this case it suspects a lapse from virtue on the part of Mme de La Baudraye; and the visitors from Paris,

[1] See above, 315. His later expansion of it into a full-blown novel was due to pressure put upon him by the publishers of the 'Comédie Humaine'; an unusual event, for Balzac normally let his inspiration dictate the length of his works.

[2] Lovenjoul (1), 33.

Bianchon and Lousteau, are no less curious than some of the lady's satellites. The purpose then of the conversation in Mme de La Baudraye's salon, and of the anecdotes related, is to sound or divine her secret inclinations. She does not here figure as a local muse. The inquisitive guests draw a blank. The lady's virtue is proved unimpeachable, and the concluding paragraphs of the opusculum give a rapid sketch of the vegetative existence to which she is doomed for the rest of her days.

The definitive *Muse du département* incorporates a good deal of this material, while cutting out the third of the 'vengeance' stories, *La grande Bretèche* itself, and expanding the conversations which take place in Dinah's 'Cénacle'. The description of them, together with the visitors' satirical comments on a melodramatic *nouvelle*[1] attributed to a writer of the First Empire, takes up a considerable amount of space. Another previous sketch, *La Femme de province*[2] is utilized and expanded in *La Muse du département*; it gives a clue for the development of the study of 1843. 'La femme de province n'a que deux manières d'être: ou elle se résigne, ou elle se révolte.'[3] In *La grande Bretèche* of 1837 Mme de La Baudraye had resigned herself. In *La Muse du département* she rebels. '. . . Sa révolte consiste à quitter la province et s'établir à Paris . . . Celle qui s'y établit en abandonnant tout ne compte plus parmi les femmes.'

The second half of *La Muse du département* shows the disillusion and misery that await Dinah at Paris as the mistress of Lousteau, who has seduced her for the fun of the thing,[4] and who comes out in his true colours as the years plunge him into idleness, inconstancy, orgy and debt. But Dinah is far from 'no longer counting among women'. There are very few daughters of Eve whom Balzac cannot forgive when it is a case of 'the world

---

[1] *Olympia, ou les Vengeances romaines*, another excerpt from a previous work, published in 1833 in a collection called *Les Causeries du monde*. See Lovenjoul (1), 85–8.

[2] From *Les Français peints par eux-mêmes*, a large collective work published in eight volumes by Curmer, 1840–2. See Lovenjoul (1), 88–93.

[3] Ibid., 91.

[4] A preliminary incident in this seduction, his deliberate crumpling of Dinah's muslin dress (during a carriage journey) in order to compromise her, roused moral indignation in the Chamber of Deputies. See *E* II, 139–40. So also did the general tone of the work. See *E* II, 178.

well lost for love'. Dinah's redeeming virtue is that an idealism similar to that of Honorine de Bauvan has flung her into her lover's arms: the craving to sacrifice herself to an artist's welfare, the ambition to become his inspiration as well as his drudge. 'Mon abnégation', she says to her still faithful friend and admirer, M. de Clagny, whom she meets at the theatre in Paris at a moment when her eyes are already opened, 'est si complète que j'aurais voulu tout abattre autour de moi pour faire de mon amour un vaste désert plein de Dieu, de *lui* et de moi.' This saves her from falling to her lover's level, and her fall itself is the occasion for rehabilitation.

She has borne two sons to Lousteau, and thanks to M. de Clagny's intervention they have been duly registered as children of M. de La Baudraye.[1] For all his lack of understanding and sympathy towards Dinah, whose newly inherited fortune he has annexed for his own purposes, La Baudraye proves to be one of those husbands who do not let personal grievances weigh against plans for worldly advancement. It suits him to acknowledge Lousteau's children as his own and to take his wife back again so that she may play her part as hostess in the house he has bought in Paris now that his accumulation of wealth has enabled him to reach the height of his ambitions. With M. de Clagny's continued help, Dinah's reinstatement in the ways of virtue and respectability is thus successfully accomplished and seems to be complete. Nevertheless, she does not refuse herself again to Lousteau on a later occasion, when he comes to her begging for the money to save him from the bailiffs. Perhaps she does this, as M. Léon Émery suggests, out of a confused sense of gratitude to the man who has given her the full experience of life:

La misère, le travail et la honte, la joie du corps, l'orgueil de souffrir, la passion de se donner, l'alternance fortifiante des peines et des plaisirs. Par lui, elle s'est épanouie comme une plante vigoureuse, par lui elle est devenue femme et mère.[2]

[1] Lousteau has had the execrable taste to print in his own name cards announcing the birth of their first child. Such an act would be incredible had Jules Janin not done the same thing when a child was borne to him by the Comtesse de la Carte, a mistress he had stolen from Alfred de Musset.

[2] Émery, 105–6.

In what proportions are sentiment and irony mingled as Balzac narrates the career of this woman who has remained 'à peu près honnête'? Measured by ordinary standards, Dinah is at once ridiculous and sublime. She is a provincial, and yet so adaptable as to acclimatize herself rapidly to the animation and brilliance of life in Paris: a blue-stocking, and yet able to use her pen in support of Lousteau's tottering ménage.[1] She is a woman of perception and feeling who reaches the limits of self-abandon, of domestic slavery, and yet whose 'probité virile' can lift her again, after many years, out of such degradation. Is this naïvety and inconsequence on Balzac's part? Or is it, as Mr. S. Rogers would have us believe, an instance of the depth of his psychological perception, his ability to conceive a character *in toto*, to know all the hidden resources a human soul can command while only showing them to us in part, but leaving them free as organic beings, undetermined, inexplicable, to undergo unexpected metamorphoses and to develop in ways unforeseen?[2]

If we accept this view, we may well conclude that Balzac is sometimes unwilling, rather than unable, to bridge over sensible gaps[3] and, if we may use Henry James' expression, to 'go behind', that is, to delve continuously into the inner consciousness of a character and show the sequence of feeling, thought and motive that can make a deviation or a revulsion completely convincing. If his revelation of such inner coherence seems on occasion to stop short just at the moment when it might be most useful, it is perhaps because he feels that human actions can be, at critical moments, so incalculable that a patient explanation of them would make them seem impossible.[4]

In the absence of such Proustian subtleties, *La Muse du département* has much to offer the reader. Not to be despised is the intermittent study of the pertinacious 'avorton', La Baudraye,

---

[1] In later editions of *Un Prince de la Bohème* she is credited with making a *nouvelle* of the material thus given to her by Raoul Nathan.

[2] Rogers, 115–16. Cf. above, 55–6 and 169 n. i.

[3] One of these is in the career of Lousteau. *Illusions perdues*, including its third part, whose publication was only a few months posterior to that of *La Muse*, continues the Lousteau of 1821–2. *La Muse* gives us the Lousteau of 1836–43. What are we to suppose has happened in between? He appears just to have marked time. No novel in the 'Comédie Humaine' fills this gap.

[4] Cf. above, 161.

thwarting all calculations based on his physical fragility, making
his way to establishment as a peer of France and a Commander of
the Legion of Honour. The elderly and ugly M. de Clagny
furnishes one of the best examples of a disinterested and intelligent attachment to be found in the 'Comédie Humaine'. Balzac's
analysis of the frustrating conditions of provincial life has its
merits; so also has the new picture he gives us of the irregularities
and vicissitudes of the life lived in Paris by artists and men of
letters. Such figures as Bixiou and Raoul Nathan are again
mingled with the action; Aurélie Schontz, born in Balzac's imagination in the course of 1843, and destined to play a larger part in the
1844 instalment of *Béatrix*,[1] appears as Lousteau's unofficial con-
sort before she transfers her attentions to Arthur de Rochefide.

To this we may add a feature which is not without relevance to
Balzac's own personal history. References to Benjamin Constant's
Adolphe occur here and there. Dinah is alive to the parallel between her case and the heroine of the story, Éléonore, tortured by
the knowledge that the man who has seduced and compromised
her is anxious to escape from the toils of a now wearisome liaison.
Adolphe has become Dinah's 'Bible', and at the moment when
she has decided to break with Lousteau a discussion arises between
the two lovers about the applicability of the novel to their case.
It is usual for readers of *Adolphe* to accord most of their pity to
Éléonore. Lousteau has the effrontery to stand up for Adolphe,
and to accuse Éléonore of ruining his career. So, Lousteau avers,
has Dinah done to him. She has taken to herself the role both of
Adolphe and Éléonore.

Vous ressentez la douleur que cause une position perdue, et vous vous
croyez en droit d'abandonner un pauvre amant qui a eu le malheur de
vous croire assez supérieure pour admettre que si chez l'homme le
cœur doit être constant, le sexe peut se laisser aller à des caprices.

A characteristic display of egoism on the part of this incorrigible
drifter. And yet Dinah finds some reason in his argument since, at
the beginning of their liaison, she had recognized that Lousteau
might dally with other women without their union being irrepar-
ably damaged. The distinction Balzac puts into Lousteau's mouth

[1] See above, 335-7.

between deep-seated constancy of heart and mere physical infidelity is precisely the one he himself urged when Mme Hanska
pressed too far her reproaches for his occasional adventures with
other women.[1]

iii. Angoulême. *Illusions perdues* III (*Les Souffrances de l'inventeur*, 1843)

Balzac completed only one more 'Scene of Provincial Life', *Les
Souffrances de l'inventeur*.[2] This work serves the perhaps primary
purpose of continuing the life-story of Lucien Chardon, but it is
no less important in taking the reader back to Angoulême to
relate the business misfortunes of the young printer David
Séchard and his loyal wife and helpmate Ève, sister of Lucien.
We should remember[3] that David had, in 1819, bought his
father's antiquated printing-press at an exorbitant price, and that
the mean and bibulous old man had retired into the country on
the proceeds. The cunning and short-sighted greed with which
Séchard senior continues to treat his son, and his incapacity to
appreciate his son's inventive genius, have much bearing on the
tale of the young couple's misfortunes. Their money troubles are
increased by the fact that Lucien, whilst still in Paris, had forged
his brother-in-law's signature to a bill of 3,000 francs. For his sake
they honour this obligation, and Balzac shows up the injustice of
the current legal procedure for the recovery of debts when unscrupulously manipulated.[4] By the accumulation of legal expenses
and lawyers' pickings, the Séchard debt rises from 3,000 to over
10,000 francs.

David, the 'inventor' whose sufferings are thus explored, has
found a way out of his troubles: the process he had discovered for
the manufacture of cheap paper is likely to make his fortune. But

[1] See *Biography*, 132–3.

[2] In serial form in *L'État* and *Le Parisien-L'État*, from June to August 1843.
First title: *David Séchard ou les Souffrances d'un inventeur*. Incorporated also in
1843 in the 'Comédie Humaine' (*S. vie prov.* t. IV) with the other two parts of
Illusions perdues, as *Ève et David*. Published again in 1844 in two vols. by Dumont.

[3] See above, 171–2.

[4] A clerk in the office of Balzac's lawyer and friend, Gavault, has recorded
with what assiduity Balzac supplemented his knowledge of this procedure
during visits to the office. See Bouvier et Maynial (1), 369.

he is not able to exploit it for his own profit, for he gets caught in a web of knavish intrigue similar to that which had brought César Birotteau to ruin. The brothers Cointet, his competitors as printers, conspire to drive him out of business. For this purpose they form an alliance with one of the most foxy lawyers to be found among the characters of the 'Comédie Humaine', the solicitor Pierre Petit-Claud, a former school-friend of Lucien: a cold, sallow, wiry, wily 'vipère gelée', with magpie eyes,[1] who hides disloyalty and ably directed ambition under a mask of benevolence. The brothers Cointet and Petit-Claud have in their pay the compositor Cérizet, a traitor in the Séchard camp; and against this combination the unsuspecting David, the indefatigable and business-like Ève, the faithful Alsatian Kolb and the devoted servant Marion stand little chance. Remorselessly exploiting his financial embarrassments, the Cointets force him to sell the paper-making process to them, and, once the venture is floated, to renounce his share in the profits. David is upright and intelligent, but feeble in affairs. In the end he is only too glad to extricate himself from imprisonment for debt, to sell out all his interests, to go into retirement with his wife and child and live in domestic harmony and tranquillity on the modest competence he has been able to retrieve. However great his misfortune, his happiness is founded on solid rock. He and Ève form the ideal couple: the secret of their happiness lies in perfect understanding and esteem, and contentment with enough money to make both ends meet; though when David's father dies they inherit his substantial property.

In thus returning to the theme of an honest tradesman delivered over to a set of commercial and legal sharks, Balzac is of course in his element, the more so because, when recounting the tribulations that beset the Séchard couple, he must, ruefully, have lived over again many a moment in his own career.[2] The picture of David going into hiding to avoid arrest by the bailiff's men was an easy one for him to paint from first-hand experience.

---

[1] A sign of dishonesty, according to Napoleon; so Balzac avers.

[2] David's workshop at Angoulême is exactly like that of Balzac in his printing-press of 1827, in what is now the Rue Visconti. Cérizet succeeds to David's press just as, in 1828, Balzac's partner Barbier had bought up his. In 1833, too, Balzac too gave much thought to a project for the manufacture of a cheaper kind of paper.

David's troubles are enhanced by the return of the prodigal Lucien to his native town. As an early nineteenth-century 'hitch-hiker' Lucien cuts a sorry and crestfallen figure as he makes his way back to Angoulême. He even suffers the humiliation of filching a ride behind the barouche of the former Louise de Bargeton, as she returns to her native city with her new husband, Lucien's erstwhile rival, Sixte du Châtelet, now a count and the prefect of Angoulême. This is for Lucien an ironic reverse of fortune seeing that, on his journey to Paris a year before, he had sat by her side in a similar carriage. Needless to say, his tribulations have done nothing to make a man of him. He even feeds his self-complacency on the thought of returning home down at heel: 'je suis héroïque!' Received by the Séchard couple with loving forgiveness, he soon lets his volatility get the better of his depression and remorse.

Before many days we find him nursing the idea of his superiority over his mother and sister. 'Elles sont bourgeoises, elles ne peuvent me comprendre.' It is part of Petit-Claud's strategy to get Lucien hailed as a genius by his fellow-citizens, to have him readmitted into polite society at Angoulême, but only in order that Louise du Châtelet may feed his vanity and encourage his indiscretion so that Angoulême may be rid of him for good and all. He is fatuous enough to be taken in once more. Patronizingly benevolent to his brother-in-law, he unwittingly lends himself to the schemes of David's enemies, so that the latter is beguiled into leaving his hiding-place and is flung into prison, from which only virtual surrender to the Cointets can rescue him. Aware of the disaster he has caused, Lucien writes a farewell letter in which the need to dramatize himself is still stronger than genuine repentance, and goes off intending to drown himself: suicide 'par désespoir et par raisonnement', as Balzac puts it. He merely argues himself into a suicidal frame of mind; which means that it will not be difficult for another person to argue him out of it. In fact, just after he has chosen a convenient pool in the river Charente, his last meditations are interrupted and his zest for life renewed by a travelling Spanish ecclesiastic, a self-styled canon of Toledo Cathedral, the 'Abbé Carlos Herrera'. The reader will eventually learn, even if he does not immediately guess, that this benign and potently persuasive clergyman—'gros et court, de larges mains, un large buste, une force herculéenne, un regard terrible, mais adouci par une mansuétude de commande'—is no other than Jacques Collin, alias Vautrin or Trompe-la-Mort, the master-criminal from *Le père Goriot*. Not unnaturally, Balzac had been keeping this startling personality in reserve for future use— witness the mention which a letter of de Marsay makes, in *Le Contrat de mariage* (1835), of Vautrin's escape from the hulks.[1] From 1836 onwards Balzac had been thinking of bringing him back into circulation in *La Torpille*. This fragment, when published in 1838, leapt over the gap in Lucien's life-story which the second and third parts of *Illusions perdues* had yet to fill. Also he had brought him on to the stage in the play, *Vautrin*, of 1840. Now, in these final pages of *Les Souffrances de l'inventeur*, we learn details about the versatile gangster at which *La Torpille* had only hesitantly glanced.[2] Having taken over the identity and papers of the real Herrera, whom he has murdered, he is on the way to Paris to discharge the diplomatic mission which had been entrusted to his victim. In a flash he decides to take Lucien with him as his secretary, with the intention of making a great man out of him by showing him how to act on the cynical principles which had brought the Medicis, Richelieu and Napoleon to the peak of greatness.

A fuller insight into Lucien's character might have made 'Carlos Herrera' realize that Lucien was not of the stuff of which great men are made; but Vautrin has unbounded confidence in his ability to turn a still ingenuous, and very handsome young man, into the instrument of his vengeance against society. He discerns in him what he had not found in Eugène de Rastignac, a malleable and impressionable mind open to specious reasoning and immoral suggestion. D'Arthez had hit the nail on the head in a letter to Ève, written while Lucien was still in Paris: '. . . une

---

[1] This letter is deemed to be written in 1827; but since in *Les Souffrances de l'inventeur* we are in the autumn of 1822, while *La Torpille* is to take us on to 1824, we must assume that when de Marsay wrote about Vautrin the latter had been at large for six or seven years! Obviously Balzac had merely intended, by this insertion in *Le Contrat de mariage*, to keep the memory of Vautrin alive without having yet decided at what date in his complex fiction he was to bring him forward again.

[2] For the development of Vautrin in Balzac's conception from 1838 see Pommier (8), 50–5 and 92–9 ('Les quatre Vautrins').

femmelette qui aime à paraitre . . . Il signerait volontiers demain un pacte avec le démon, si ce pacte lui donnait pour quelques années une vie brillante et luxueuse.' Such a pact Vautrin now proposes, after developing at length the same criticisms of men and society he had made to Rastignac and drawing the same distinction between unskilled and legalized crime. Success, he says, and not morality is what justifies doubtful deeds; a brilliant appearance, not inner virtue, is the criterion by which society measures worth. Lucien has been too frank and too honest in flouting the conventions of society.

Si vous aviez laissé Coralie à ce monsieur Camusot, si vous aviez caché vos relations avec elle, vous auriez épousé Madame de Bargeton, vous seriez préfet d'Angoulême et Marquis de Rubempré.

Lucien listens to all this, and much more besides, horrified but fascinated. Once convinced of Vautrin's benevolence and the strange capacity for vicarious enjoyment of a protégé's triumph which Vautrin puts to the account of 'une amitié d'homme à homme' as strong as that existing between Pierre and Jaffier in Otway's *Venice Preserved*, he is ready for the proposed adventure. How should he refuse so easy a bargain?

'Je veux aimer ma créature' [says Herrera], 'la façonner, la pétrir à mon usage afin de l'aimer comme un père aime son enfant. Je roulerai dans ton tilbury, mon garçon, je me réjouirai de tes succès auprès des femmes, je dirai: —Ce beau jeune homme, c'est moi! ce marquis de Rubempré, je l'ai créé et mis au monde aristocratique; sa grandeur est mon œuvre, il se tait ou parle à ma voix, il me consulte en tout.'

So the way is open for the final adventures of Lucien as related in *Splendeurs et misères des courtisanes*. A few concluding pages suffice for Balzac to wind up the affairs of David Séchard and to point a finger towards the *Scènes de la vie parisienne* which in fact are to be his major concern during these last years of literary creation. He has given good value in this final Provincial Scene: a detailed but not wearisome account of the manœuvres involved in the commercial strangulation of a master printer by his rivals; a further scrutiny of high-class provincial society in which the law of the human jungle is no more compassionate for being wrapped up in polite formalism; some close portraits of such local 'loups-cerviers' as the Cointet brothers and Petit-Claud, of such jackals as Cérizet, of such crapulous fauna as Séchard senior; and to brighten this dark picture, the underlying theme of an ideal matrimonial partnership, supported by two loyal servants, which no tribulation can endanger. To which we may add an ironic twist of events at the conclusion of the story which well characterizes Balzac's sense of the power of the seemingly fortuitous in human affairs: David's surrender to the Cointets occurs only a few moments before the arrival of 15,000 francs, furnished by 'Carlos Herrera', which would have saved the situation for him. A like tardiness in the benefits capriciously bestowed by chance was later to bring Lucien to a sorry end.

XVI

THE LAST PARISIAN SCENES

i. The *Esther* cycle: *Splendeurs et misères des courtisanes*
(1838–47)

THE WORK eventually to be known as *Splendeurs et misères des courtisanes* is one to which Balzac applied himself intermittently over a long period. Even the 1838 instalment of it, *La Torpille*, had been in his mind since at least 1835.[1] The 1843 contribution, *Esther ou Les Amours d'un vieux banquier*,[2] completes Part I, now entitled *Comment aiment les filles*, and adds most of Part II— *À combien l'amour revient aux vieillards*. An interim publication of November 1844—*Splendeurs et misères des courtisanes: Esther*[3] —brought Part II to completion. *Une Instruction criminelle*, constituting Part III, whose final title was to be *Où mènent les mauvais chemins*, was printed after an interval of nearly two years.[4] Part IV, *La dernière Incarnation de Vautrin*, appeared in the spring of 1847.[5] There could be no better example of unmethodical composition. No doubt Balzac had a general plan in

[1] See Pommier (8) for the complicated history of this fragment, as well as for a minute study, not only of its relationship to *Illusions perdues*, but also of the modifications it underwent before the *Esther* cycle attained its final form. The Garnier edition of *Splendeurs et misères* [Adam (2)] did not appear until this book was in print. The Introduction gives useful information about the many sources Balzac used for his study of prostitution and criminality.

[2] *Le Parisien*, 21 May–1 July 1843.

[3] De Potter, Nov. 1844. Parts I and II were incorporated in the 'Comédie Humaine', *Scènes de la vie parisienne*, t. III, 1844.

[4] *L'Époque*, 7–29 July 1846. Also collected in the 'Comédie Humaine', *S. vie par.*, t. IV, 1846, and published separately by Souverain in 1847 as *Un Drame dans les prisons*.

[5] *La Presse*, 13 Apr.–4 May. Published the same year by Chlendowski. Collected into t. XVIII of the 'Comédie Humaine', one of the 'tomes complémentaires' added when Mme Houssiaux republished Balzac's works in twenty volumes in 1855. The four parts were only united in the *Éd. Déf.*

his head, but modified it as he added part to part. The collective title itself fits only the first two parts.

'Ne voyez dans les hommes, et surtout dans les femmes, que des instruments; mais ne le leur laissez pas voir.' The new novel (or novel-cycle) shows how Lucien Chardon, once more in Paris from late 1822 to 1830, fares when he tries to apply this maxim under the guidance and management of that superb devil's advocate, the false Abbé Carlos Herrera, who maps out the preliminaries to a political career on the lines we should expect: Royal sanction for Lucien's assumption of his mother's name of Rubempré, the engineering of his re-entry into polite society, his marriage into the highest aristocracy (the choice falls on Clotilde de Grandlieu, elder sister of the Sabine we already know), and the repurchase of the Rubempré estates as a condition of the match and a prelude to a marquisate and ministerial office. For this a million francs are needed: they are to be provided by Esther van Gobseck, great-grand-niece of the usurer Gobseck, a prostitute whose paralysing beauty has earned her the nickname of 'la Torpille'.[1] She has but to capture a rich financier, although the task is complicated by the passion this successor of Coralie[2] has conceived for the handsome Lucien and he for her. Vautrin's indulgence towards Lucien, who soon learns his true identity, prompts him to tolerate this liaison while preparing her for the kill. The selected prey turns out to be the sexagenarian banker, the 'pot à millions', Nucingen. A romantic nocturnal encounter with Esther transforms him into an extreme example of the classical *vieillard amoureux*, 'un de ces phénomènes sociaux que la physiologie peut le plus facilement expliquer'. Vautrin's concealment of Esther after this encounter is meant to bring Nucingen to such a frenzy of desire that he will be willing to disgorge the million francs which Lucien needs—a fantastic price to pay for venal love! 'Être amoureux à mon âge, je sais bien que rien n'est plus ridicule; mais que voulez-vous? ça y est.'

All this is tied together by a rapid and vivacious succession of 'scenes'. The initial scene—the Opera Ball of February 1824—is one of those which Balzac loved to stage for bringing his promi-

---

[1] Electric ray or numb-fish.

[2] She may well be Coralie's precursor as regards priority of invention, since Balzac got *La Torpille* off his hands before really settling down to *Un grand Homme . . ..* On Esther's origins and genesis, see Pommier (8), 55–67.

nent characters together. Lucien again meets his former journalist associates,[1] and his old enemies, du Châtelet and Mme d'Espard. He floors them by his wit and aplomb, while his masked protector, Herrera-Vautrin, terrifies Rastignac, who recognizes him as his former fellow-lodger at the Pension Vauquer, into becoming an ally. Esther has unintentionally compromised Lucien at the ball, hence her attempted suicide, her rescue by Vautrin, her relegation to a convent school so that she may be educated, refined and 'converted' to religion before Herrera flings her back into Lucien's arms[2] for a long period of virtual claustration—for the lovers it is 'une symphonie de quatre ans'. Then, once Nucingen has been stung by the 'Electric Ray' and has hired police spies to get on the elusive Esther's track, the novel develops into a thriller whose substance is a savage underground battle between three of Balzac's sinister policemen and Vautrin's assistants. On the one side are Corentin and Peyrade, whom we already know,[3] and Contenson, a turncoat aristocrat whose real name is Baron Bryond des Tours-Minières, and whose earlier career in Revolutionary and Imperial times (as an agent both of Louis XVIII and of Fouché) Balzac was outlining, almost simultaneously, in *L'Envers de l'histoire contemporaine*. On the other side are Vautrin, his lieutenant Paccard, his sinister aunt 'Asie', alias Jacqueline Collin, and Esther's personal maid 'Europe', alias Prudence Servien; all of them criminals or involved with the criminal world.

We might well suppose that Balzac had resolved to devote the mastery he had acquired in twenty years to the feat of eclipsing his own *Vicaire des Ardennes* and delivering himself over to the improbable and the horrible. Masquerades—both Peyrade and Vautrin are experts at disguising themselves, and Vautrin has long since used chemical reagents to alter his facial appearance—kidnapping, blackmail, rape, poisoning and fights on roof-tops provide seasoning for this extraordinary tale of an underworld in

---

[1] In the original *Torpille* he meets the 'quatre hardis cormorans' of *La maison Nucingen*—Finot, Blondet, Bixiou and Couture. Also Vernou. In 1838 this influence of the contemporaneous novel, *La maison Nucingen*, was natural. In revisions (from 1843 onwards) Balzac saw how necessary it was to draw this episode into the orbit of *Un grand Homme* . . .. So Couture disappears, while Lousteau and Nathan are introduced into the Opera Ball scene.

[2] It is at this point that the *Torpille* instalment ended.   [3] See above, 257 ff.

turmoil, in which the policemen are as criminal as the malefactors they pursue. But when Vautrin has murdered Peyrade and Contenson, and outwitted Corentin, so that at last Nucingen is willing to pay up, his scheme is shattered by Esther herself. Revolted at the thought of giving herself to anyone but Lucien, she poisons herself, unaware of the ironical fate which decrees that, at the moment of her death, she shall be identified as the heiress of Gobseck and his millions. So now we see Lucien and the supposed Abbé arrested on suspicion of having murdered her, and flung into the Conciergerie. No less formidable in prison than he is out of it, Vautrin engages on a protracted duel with the representatives of justice—the time-serving *juge d'instruction* Maître Camusot, dominated by his ambitious wife, and the noble, austere Attorney General, the Comte de Granville. Camusot has no difficulty in making out a case against the weak and bewildered Lucien, but learns that political strings are being pulled to quash the proceedings.

We are now in 1830. Charles X is anxious to stifle any scandal which may bring the higher nobility into contempt, and Lucien, as well as being the prospective husband of Clotilde de Grandlieu, has had affairs with Diane de Maufrigneuse and the Comtesse de Sérisy. It is here that the latter's unashamedly passionate temperament, indicated in *Un Début dans la vie*, is fully revealed; and not least in the violence with which she seizes Lucien's self-incriminating testimony from Camusot's hands and throws it into the fire, to the horror of that formalistic magistrate. But while steps are being taken to hush the matter up, despair has driven Lucien to write his second suicide letter—an apology to Vautrin for having unintentionally betrayed him and a grandiloquent assessment of his patron's character and ability. This time there is no one to intervene and save him, though the fatal act is delayed for a moment while this poetic dreamer enjoys his last view over the Conciergerie precincts and the Palais de Justice: a sort of inspired vision, since he sees it as it once was in all its medieval beauty. Mme de Sérisy arrives at the prison to find him hanging from the window-bar of his cell, and goes frantic. Vautrin, too, is utterly overwhelmed. His vengeance against society has failed and his purpose in life has gone. *Le fer est roui!*

361

The rest of the book is concerned with his 'last incarnation', and the thriller element is no less to the fore. Though still a prisoner in the Conciergerie and though his identity as Jacques Collin is strongly suspected, he holds trump cards up his sleeve—a packet of indiscreet letters written to Lucien by his women admirers. These he uses as a means of bargaining with the Attorney General—but no longer as a mere blackmailer. He unveils himself to M. de Granville. He is the acknowledged leader of the criminal world—above all in his function as treasurer to the thieving confraternity of the 'Grands Fanandels'—as his easily re-established prestige over the gangsters in the Conciergerie has shown. He is able, thanks to the information which he extracts by threats and promises from a candidate for the guillotine, to expose Bibi-Lupin, the *chef de sûreté*, as the blackest of scoundrels: he coolly proposes to take his place. The scene in which Granville and Vautrin measure forces and weigh each other up—Granville is genuinely impressed by the tragic sincerity of this terrible energumen—and the scenes at the Conciergerie in which 'Carlos Herrera' manages to communicate and hatch plots with his 'Fanandel' confederates, in the convicts' slang which Balzac took pains in mastering for this purpose,[1] are forceful features in this strange novel. Vautrin gains his end, and his 'reincarnation' is complete.

One of Balzac's astonishing qualities is that, however restive his readers may become as intricacies of plot and improbabilities of situation develop, he can, like the Ancient Mariner, hold their attention to the end. This quality helps to make up for the many flaws in *Splendeurs et misères*. Undeniably the action of the story is extravagant. What of the characterization—that of Lucien, for example? With all his effeminate beauty, with all the wit and power of fascination Balzac would persuade us he possesses, he is a mere cat's-paw, whose role in the novel is little more than to parade his charm, arouse feminine sympathy and passion, submit unprotestingly to Vautrin's schemes, and inspire in Esther van Gobseck the passionate fidelity which leads her and him to their deaths. Yet Théophile Gautier writes:[2]

[1] In Dec. 1845 he visited the Conciergerie to get local colour. *E* III, 152.
[2] Op. cit., 160.

Malgré tous ses vices . . . Lucien est séduisant; Balzac l'a doté d'esprit, de jeunesse, d'élégance; les femmes l'adorent.

Can we agree with Gautier? Certainly Balzac himself finds Lucien seductive, and brings in the consensus of many of his other characters to support him. But does Lucien's presence in this work, or even in *Illusions perdues*, enable the reader to feel his charm? There is sometimes a discrepancy between what Balzac alleges certain of his characters to be and what they reveal themselves to be by their words and actions. Is Lucien as poet, wit and ladies' man anything but a postulate?

I think that only the view we obtain of him through Esther, that embodiment of the 'rehabilitation' thesis, would enable us to decide in his favour. As the plot of the novel depends on her, it was right that Balzac should take great pains at the start to show this unhappy girl in all her pathetic naïvety. The scene in which the false Abbé remonstrates with her after saving her from asphyxiation in her shabby and untidy lodgings is a memorable one. It affords a vivid insight into the feelings of a degraded creature who is only too conscious of her degradation and has vainly attempted to lift herself from the mire. And it is she who gives us the clearest glimpse of what Balzac would like us to see in Lucien:

—Je priais le bon Dieu tous les matins, et lui demandais de permettre que jamais Lucien ne connût ma vie antérieure. J'ai acheté cette Vierge que vous voyez: je la priais à ma manière, vu que je ne sais point de prières; je ne sais ni lire ni écrire, je ne suis jamais entrée dans une église, je n'ai jamais vu le bon Dieu qu'aux processions, par curiosité.

—Que dites-vous donc à la Vierge?

—Je lui parle comme je parle à Lucien, avec ces élans d'âme qui le font pleurer.

—Ah! il pleure?

—De joie, dit-elle vivement. Pauvre chat! nous nous entendons si bien que nous avons une même âme! Il est si gentil, si caressant, si doux de cœur, d'esprit et de manières! . . . Il dit qu'il est poète, moi je dis qu'il est Dieu. . . . Pardon! mais, vous autres prêtres, vous ne savez pas ce que c'est que l'amour. Il n'y a d'ailleurs que nous qui connaissions assez les hommes pour apprécier un Lucien. Un Lucien, voyez-vous, est aussi rare qu'une femme sans péché; quand on le rencontre, on ne peut plus aimer que lui: voilà. Mais à un pareil être, il faut sa pareille. Je voulais donc être digne d'être aimée par mon Lucien. De là est venu mon malheur. Hier, à l'Opéra, j'ai été reconnue par des jeunes gens qui n'ont pas plus de cœur qu'il n'y a de pitié chez les tigres; encore m'entendrais-je avec un tigre! Le voile d'innocence que j'avais est tombé; leurs rires m'ont fendu la tête et le cœur. Ne croyez pas m'avoir sauvée, je mourrai de chagrin.

—Votre voile d'innocence? ... dit le prêtre, vous avez donc traité Lucien avec la dernière rigueur?

—Oh! mon père, comment vous, qui le connaissez, me faites-vous une semblable question! répondit-elle en lui jetant un sourire superbe. On ne résiste pas à un Dieu.

—Ne blasphémez pas, dit l'ecclésiastique d'une voix douce.

As for Esther herself, it is impossible not to admire the skill with which Balzac shows the *fille de joie* peeping out under the veil of the repentant sinner. Later on she reverts momentarily to type when she exhibits the vulgar vivacity and *savoir-faire* needed for the purpose of working on Nucingen and finally states her terms with professional candour. Nucingen, though he keeps his recognizable features as a ruthless financier—'comme on a raison d'avoir beaucoup d'argent!' he exclaims in his Germanized patter—is amusing, but hardly acceptable in his role of impassioned wooer.

... Si en vous donnant tout ce que je possède, je pouvais, pauvre, obtenir votre affection, j'aimerais mieux être pauvre et aimé de vous que riche et dédaigné. Vous m'avez si fort changé ... que personne ne me reconnaît plus.

This letter to Esther is out of character, as well as the pitiable childishness with which, while still in search of her, he makes wide advertisement of his state of mind. Balzac was so well aware of the discrepancy that he devoted three pages to asserting and explaining the stupidity of even Napoleons of finance once they wander out of their special domain: 'un banquier est très mal mené quand il aime, et très embarrassé dans le manège de la femme'.

What shall we say of Vautrin, as the adoring patron of a young man whose spinelessness any intelligent person must needs descry, and as the miraculously efficient, omniscient and omnipotent demon of criminality? Is he anything but a model for the writer of gangster stories?

There has been much speculation over the nature and extent of his homosexuality. M. Marceau supposes the worst about his relations with Lucien,[1] but without any evidence from Balzac's text. The only hint of turpitude in Vautrin's relations with men is made in regard to Théodore Calvi, one of his galley-associates whom he saves from execution in *La dernière Incarnation*.[2] Vautrin has a mania for devoting himself to handsome young men —Franchessini, Rastignac, Raoul de Frescas (if we may take the play *Vautrin* into account). He is a woman-hater. His contempt for Esther is scarcely mitigated by his recognition in her of a serviceable tool. 'La femme est un être inférieur, elle obéit trop à ses organes. Pour moi la femme n'est belle que quand elle ressemble à un homme.' Yet it is precisely the feminine weakness in Lucien, his dependence on others, that most attracts Vautrin: Lucien is 'une femme manquée'. This, as well as his vendetta against society, is what has called forth all his protective instincts. Not that there is anything jealous or possessive in his love for Lucien. The feeling he has for him is at once paternal and maternal: 'mon fils' is his favoured mode of address to him; but '. . . je suis *mère*, aussi'. His paroxysm of grief on learning of his suicide resembles Goriot's ravings for his daughters on his death-bed. All this is significant enough, but it is gratuitous to suppose that it was only Balzac's discretion that prevented him from suggesting physical depravity between the two.

Vautrin is much more interesting in his role of converted rebel. In this connection there leaps to the mind a comparison between Vautrin as an enemy, then as a guardian of society, and Victor Hugo's Javert in *Les Misérables*—the inexorable bloodhound driven to suicide by the realization that there is a law of love and mercy superior to the penal code. From *Splendeurs et misères* can be culled many pages which are not less gripping and graphic than those of his great contemporary, and of which Hugo may

[1] Op. cit., 279–80. The interest Proust's pervert, M. de Charlus, takes in the Rubempré cycle of novels, and his special interest in Lucien, are motivated by his own abnormality. So is that of Oscar Wilde, to whom he refers (*Sodome et Gomorrhe*, N.R.F. II, iii, 127 ff.). See article by H. Levin.

[2] Conard XVI, 178–9, apropos of Lord Durham's visit to the Conciergerie. Calvi is Vautrin's 'tante'. See also in *Béatrix* (Conrad) V, 321 a pun on 'tante' and 'tente' which further clarifies the allusion.

well have taken stock.[1] They are those in which Balzac gives picturesque descriptions of prison-life and types of criminal, suggests ideas for the revision of criminal procedure and the reform of prison conditions. Vautrin's denunciation, in conversation with Granville, of the harshness of society to a law-breaker, once condemned, is well in harmony with the ideas which inspired the creator of Jean Valjean:

'La société dit à ce misérable: Paris, le seul endroit où tu peux te cacher, et sa banlieue sur telle étendue, tu ne l'habiteras pas! . . . Puis elle soumet le forçat libéré à la surveillance de la police. Et vous croyez qu'il est possible dans ces conditions de vivre? Pour vivre, il faut travailler, car on ne sort pas avec des rentes du bagne. Vous vous arrangez pour que le forçat soit clairement désigné, reconnu, parqué, puis vous croyez que les citoyens auront confiance en lui, quand la société, la justice, le monde qui l'entoure n'en a aucune. Vous le condamnez à la faim ou au crime. Il ne trouve pas d'ouvrage, il est poussé fatalement à recommencer son ancien métier qui l'envoie à l'échafaud. Ainsi, tout en voulant renoncer à une lutte avec la loi, je n'ai point trouvé de place au soleil pour moi.[2]

Vautrin thus acquires additional symbolic value as a criminal whom society discourages from the amendment of his ways. Such reflexions had of course been common since the time of Ballanche;[3] from the eighteen-twenties onwards Hugo himself had often given voice to them; but they do not lose authority in coming from so powerful a pen as Balzac's. It is worth noting however that this occurs in the 1847 instalment, and that in 1844 he had been less disposed to take such a sympathetic point of view about criminals. He had scolded the philanthropists for doing so. 'Il faut présenter ces êtres-là ce qu'ils sont, des êtres mis à toujours *hors la loi.*' And he had quoted his play *Vautrin* in support of this.[4] No doubt his aim at that earlier date was to pacify such readers as might be scandalized by his picture of the underworld.

[1] Hugo had his great social novel in mind for many years, but he seriously set to work on *Les Misères* in 1845. Needless to say, Sue's *Mystères de Paris* also attracted his attention.

[2] *La dernière Incarnation de Vautrin*, Conard XVI, 282–3. According to Savant (2) Balzac is here echoing Vidocq.

[3] See Savey-Casard.

[4] *Éd. Déf.*, XXII, 576, Preface of *Splendeurs et misères des courtisanes: Esther.*

One lays down *Splendeurs et misères* with mixed impressions. So vast a work could scarcely fail to illustrate some of the great novelist's weaknesses—errors of taste, life presented in too glaring colours, and some inconsistency in the scale of moral values. Nevertheless two considerations may be put forward in its defence. One is the fact that, in the eighteen-forties, Balzac's contemporaries were inclined to regard this kind of subject as lending itself to objective and 'realist' treatment. Eugène Sue's novel of criminal life, *Les Mystères de Paris*, had created a sensation in 1842. His later novels, *Le Juif errant* (1843-4) and *Martin l'enfant trouvé* (1847), were to do the same. Although the first one specially was convicted of crudity and exaggeration, certain critics claimed to see in his works a progress towards detached and scientific observation. Such a judgment must surprise us, but such was the trend in those years.[1] The way for the 'realism' and 'naturalism' of the second half of the century was prepared by such excesses. Now it would be an insult to Balzac to equate him with Eugène Sue. Even his most lurid imaginings are redeemed, if not transfigured, by his gift for evoking personages (however improbable they may be), by his brilliance in dialogue and by a style which, though not impeccable, is that of a great writer. But while Balzac despised Sue, he also envied his success, and was not averse from the idea of trying to eclipse him in his chosen domain. At the same time the years 1843-6 are those of his supreme anguish as a creator. His health was failing, his debts were as great an embarrassment as ever and his literary commitments more formidable than ever. The later months of 1842 and the early ones of 1843 when, until July, he was tied to the printing-press at Lagny[2] and working frantically in order to be free to go to Mme Hanska at St Petersburg, were a period of maximum effort accompanied by excessive worry and fatigue. In consequence he may many times have realized that his attempts to outbid Sue were threatening to bring him down to Sue's level. *Je fais du Sue tout pur*, he groaned to Mme Hanska at the end of May.[3] Yet in June he wrote to her as follows:

. . . *Esther* est une horrible peinture. Il fallait la faire, et elle me sera

[1] See Hunt (1), 158-60.   [2] See *Biography*, 124-5.
[3] *E* II, 171; 31 May 1843.

reprochée comme on m'a reproché *La Fille aux yeux d'or*. Mais il faut bien faire *Paris vrai*.[1]

Did he really believe he was describing the 'true Paris'? He was only just approaching the thick of his imbroglio. Later, in *La dernière Incarnation de Vautrin*, he thought to justify himself as a historian of manners with the following remark:

La nature sociale, à Paris surtout, comporte de tels hasards, des enchevêtrements de conjectures si capricieuses, que l'imagination des inventeurs est à tout moment dépassée. La hardiesse du vrai s'élève à des combinaisons interdites à l'art, tant elles sont invraisemblables ou peu décentes, à moins que l'écrivain ne les adoucisse, ne les émonde, ne les châtre.

Was he persuaded of this, or is it a case of 'qui s'excuse s'accuse'?

The other consideration which may be urged in defence of *Splendeurs et Misères* is a matter of general rather than literary history. When criticizing Balzac's policemen we should remember that they are all more or less modelled on the Vidocq type of ex-convict,[2] emerging from a period when the clever criminal was a useful if not indispensable asset to rulers and regimes. Balzac shows Louis XVIII following the example of Napoleon in this respect, and even employing a counter-police to keep him informed of the activities of the official police. The fact that extensive use was made under Louis-Philippe of 'mouchards' and 'agents provocateurs' is moreover corroborated—in so far as fiction can corroborate—by the illustrations Stendhal gives of it in *Lucien Leuwen*. Balzac's sinister officials of the judicial and the political police also derive greater plausibility from the history of twentieth-century totalitarianism. We have reason in our century to be less incredulous than our immediate forebears about the lengths to which human atrocity can go when inspired by greed and the lust for power. Furthermore, if English consciences still stand aghast at the idea of thieves and murderers like Vautrin and Théodore Calvi eluding the scaffold and becoming pillars of the law—the analogy of the poacher turned gamekeeper is a

[1] Ibid., 175; 13 June 1843. Cf. Preface of 1844 (*Éd. Déf.*, XXII, 576): '. . . ce roman, composé de détails profondément vrais, et pour ainsi dire historiques, pris enfin à la vie privée . . .'
[2] See above, 91.

specious one—the reply is that the French, particularly in their periods of trouble and turmoil, do not seem ever to have had our nice sense of propriety, our feeling, perhaps our delusion, that the heavens will fall if strict justice is not done, if malefactors are not brought to book by the application of an ineluctable code. There has been in France from time immemorial a political justice existing side by side with the civil and criminal justice, capable of overriding them at need. Balzac even advocates, in *À combien l'amour revient aux vieillards*, a preventive justice to forestall crime.[1] In fact, adhering to his oft-expressed view that political expediency rises above private morality, he regrets the disappearance of arbitrary power since the establishment of constitutional government. There can be no doubt that, in writing *Splendeurs et misères des courtisanes*, one of his purposes was to show what anarchy under the apparently calm surface of social life can result from the inability of the executive to go beyond the formalities of the law.

ii. Parisian background: *Gaudissart II* (1844); *Un Homme d'affaires* (1845); *Les Comédiens sans le savoir* (1846); *Les petits Bourgeois* (1845–54)

We should be tempted to classify as Parisian studies of minor importance a certain number of works which appeared between 1844 and 1846, if they had less value as contributions to the background of Balzac's canvases. Three of them—*Gaudissart II*,[2] *Un Homme d'affaires*,[3] and *Les Comédiens sans le savoir*[4]—consist

[1] Conard XV, 200. Also, in *La cousine Bette*, a police empowered to intervene in family troubles (Conard XVII, 425).

[2] Dated Nov. 1844. Written for a miscellaneous collection, *Le Diable à Paris*, published by Hetzel in two volumes, 1844–6; but printed previously in *La Presse*, 12 Oct. 1844, under the title *Un Gaudissart de la rue Richelieu; les comédies qu'on peut voir gratis*. Incorporated in the 'Comédie Humaine', t. IV of *Scènes de la vie parisienne*, 1846, with its definitive title.

[3] *Le Siècle*, 10 Sept. 1845, as *Les Roueries d'un créancier*, part of a series of 'Études de mœurs' written for that journal. Incorporated in the 'Comédie Humaine', t. IV of *Scènes de la vie parisienne*, 1846, as *Esquisse d'un homme d'affaires d'après nature*. It took its final title in *Éd. Déf*.

[4] *Le Courrier français*, 14–24 Apr. 1846. In the same year, 'Comédie Humaine', t. IV, *Scènes de la vie parisienne*. Published again in 1848, by Gabriel Roux, with other opuscula, as *Le Provincial à Paris*.

rather of fragments and sample pieces. The 'second Gaudissart' is, as regards the art of counter salesmanship in one of the Parisian 'grands magasins', what the first, the 'illustrious Gaudissart', had been in the art of travelling salesmanship. This humorous sketch shows the patient assistants of this emporium dealing with a 'Mistress Noswell', a caricature of the suspicious but gullible Englishwoman shopping in Paris. 'L'Anglaise', says Gaudissart II to Bixiou, 'c'est notre bataille de Waterloo.' But it is a Waterloo in reverse, for eventually the head of the establishment sells her for 6,000 francs a shawl worth 1,500. *Un Homme d'affaires* gives us another glance at Maxime de Trailles, the 'corsaire en gants jaunes, à cabriolet, à belles manières', as seen through the eyes of the solicitor Desroches: profligate, dandy, duellist, gambler, sponger, inveterate borrower, always in debt, averse not so much from discharging his debts as from settling them too soon after they fall due. Desroches tells us how two of the sorriest tricksters of the 'Comédie Humaine', the banker Claparon[1] and Cérizet,[2] ex-printer, then journalist, then moneylender, extorted payment from de Trailles in 1833 for bills of exchange he had uttered and wished to honour only when it became convenient. Once more Balzac shows his knowledge of the shifts and devices of debtors and creditors and betrays his admiration for slick dealing. *Un Homme d'affaires* also gives us a later view of the now self-assured Malaga, so timid and tongue-tied in *La fausse Maîtresse*,[3] and introduces us to another 'lorette',[4] Antonia Chocardelle. But it is a poor story, for the simple reason that the financial operation involved remains obscure, like much of the humour. One pleasing feature about Maxime de Trailles is that he takes his discomfiture in good part.

Les Comédiens sans le savoir is a nineteenth-century equivalent of Lesage's *Diable boiteux*, a novel of 1707 which had exposed the

[1] *César Birotteau; La maison Nucingen.*

[2] *Illusions perdues* III.

[3] Her appearance in *La fausse Maitresse* is of 1836; the story of *Un Homme d'affaires* is told by Desroches *circa* 1841.

[4] The 'lorette', so called because the quarter of Paris surrounding the church of Notre-Dame de Lorette was the habitat of so many women of easy virtue, is defined both in *La Muse du département* and in *Un Homme d'affaires*. This quarter was for the same reason known as the 'thirteenth arrondissement'. See above, 336 n. i.

seamy side of life in Madrid (that is, of Paris in disguise) by the device of making a genie lift off the roofs of houses in order to reveal the shortcomings of those living in them. Balzac adopts a more plausible device by getting two wags, the ubiquitous Bixiou and the Léon de Lora of *Un Début dans la vie*, to take a greenhorn from Roussillon, Sylvestre Gazonal, round Paris. Hence a series of brief but scintillating sketches of an assortment of Parisians 'on the make': different kinds of Opera singers and dancers, supported by their elderly patrons, other grades of artistes, former police-spies who sell their talent to writ-servers, a fashionable hatter and a hairdresser, both superbly conscious of their artistic skill, a 'revendeuse à la toilette', that is to say, a second-hand clothes dealer who combines that profession with petty money-lending and an even less respectable one;[1] sprightly courtesans like 'Carabine', du Tillet's mistress, Jenny Cadine, and 'Mme du Val-Noble', now the lawful spouse of the journalist Théodore Gaillard;[2] various small-scale usurers, a crack-brained Fourierist painter, a chiropodist who is a fanatical republican, and a fortune-teller, Mme Fontaine, who can gaze into the past and predict the future, but cannot foretell the winning numbers in the lotteries in which she invests. By way of climax Balzac gives a glimpse behind the scenes of the Chamber of Deputies, and shows politicians like Rastignac, Canalis, Maxime de Trailles, and even the one-time member of d'Arthez' Cénacle, Léon Giraud, accommodating the conflicting principles they profess in public to friendly arrangements in private. 'Tous vos originaux ont quelque chose de méridional', exclaims the astonished Provençal. The thread of plot is of the slightest. Balzac, the eternal schoolboy, the lover of tricks and mystifications, as well as the indefatigable producer of 'physiologies', is here in his element.

In 1843 he began to write *Les petits Bourgeois*, which he had conceived in 1839. He had announced it as being almost finished in March 1844. He had had the beginning of it set up in type somewhere about April 1845,[3] but he wrote less than half of it,

[1] Mme Nourrisson, whose name and attributions Jacqueline Collin sometimes takes over in such works as *Splendeurs et misères* and *La cousine Bette*.
[2] See above, 160–2.
[3] Provisional title (until Feb. 1844): *Les Bourgeois de Paris*. In 1843 he had referred to the projected work by the title *Modeste* (E II, 245–6).

and it was not published until after his death, with a continuation and conclusion written, at Mme de Balzac's request, by Charles Rabou.[1] That Rabou was unequal so such a task is proved by the comparison which M. Bouteron gives, in the Conard edition,[2] of the last pages of Balzac's text with those which Rabou substituted for them. The authentic portion of *Les petits Bourgeois* is in some sense a continuation of *Les Employés*, for it deals with the later history, after 1839, of some of Xavier Rabourdin's Civil Service subordinates; or, more particularly, with their families and off-spring. There is the faded, but still pompous ex-beau Louis-Jérôme Thuillier, with his domineering sister Brigitte and his timid wife; the easy-going Colleville whose life-partner, Flavie, has presented him with five children, only one of which is his own; the honest windbag, Phellion senior, generously and gran-diloquently supporting the candidature of Thuillier in a municipal election campaign.

The central theme is the competition between four men for the hand in marriage of the Collevilles' daughter, Céleste. They are Phellion's son Félix, a free-thinking, high-principled teacher of mathematics; Olivier Vinet, a young magistrate, whose father had played such an odious role in *Pierrette*, Minard, the son of a rich merchant who has made his fortune by the sale of adulterated tea; and the hero-villain of the story, the scheming 'poor man's barrister', Théodose de La Peyrade, grand-nephew of the police spy whom Vautrin had liquidated. It is not hard to guess that, of these four, the sincere and unselfish Félix would have triumphed, as indeed he does in Rabou's continuation.

Squalid intriguers like Cérizet, 'un artiste en mal', and Dutocq, once a clerk in Rabourdin's office and an instrument in his senior's undoing,[3] now a clerk to the justices in his Paris arrondissement, take a hand in the affair, and we have a tortuous financial im-broglio analogous to the one in *César Birotteau*. The extant frag-ment has many of the true Balzacian features. There are pains-taking descriptions of the fast-disappearing corners of ancient Paris interspersed with regrets that no municipal action is taken

[1] In *Le Pays*, 26 July–28 Oct. 1854. A book publication by de Potter fol-lowed in 1856–7.

[2] Conard XX, 465–72 and 486–9.　　　　　[3] See above, 185.

to prevent middle-class vandalism. Minute attention is given to material and human background: the den, for instance, in which Cérizet conducts his business as a moneylender, and the carefully regulated queue of his working-class clients. How different had been the benevolent activity of Judge Popinot when, in the same quarter, he had dispensed his alms with shrewd and discriminating charity! And yet, says Balzac, the social effect was much the same.

Popinot prêtait sans intérêt et savait perdre; Cérizet ne perdait rien et forçait les malheureux à bien travailler, à devenir sages. Les pauvres adoraient Popinot, mais ils ne haïssaient pas Cérizet. Ici fonctionne le dernier rouage de la finance parisienne. En haut, la maison Nucingen, les Keller, les du Tillet, les Mongenod;[1] un peu plus bas, les Palma, les Gigonnet, les Gobseck;[2] encore plus bas les Samanon, les Chaboisseau, les Barbet;[3] puis, enfin, après le Mont-de-Piété, ce roi de l'usure, qui tend ses lacets au coin des rues pour étrangler toutes les misères et n'en pas manquer une, un Cérizet!

Naturally *Les petits Bourgeois* offers new and excellent variants of the ubiquitous Joseph Prudhomme type in the persons of Thuillier and his cronies, assembled in his salon, or at his dinnertable, so economically run by his hard-faced but adoring sister, or at the Colleville soirées; the whole is seasoned with yet more illustrations of the fatuity and vacuousness of Civil Servants. Also we meet with new and entertaining personalities thrown up from the most sordid quarters of Paris, like the fish-wife Mme Cardinal and her uncle, the church-porch mendicant Poupillier, whom she feeds on her stale fish, and whose inheritance she covets, for his profession is as lucrative as that of Altamont in Thackeray's *Yellowplush Papers*.

But Balzac's chief motive had been to create a well-drawn nineteenth-century Tartuffe incarnated in Théodose de La Peyrade. The dedication of the novel (to Mme Hanska)[4] shows that the study of an able and resourceful hypocrite, a philanthropical *bien pensant* whose real aim is his own advancement, was to have formed the backbone of the work. The resemblance with Molière's

---

[1] The Mongenods however were honest and reputable bankers, as *L'Envers de l'histoire contemporaine* makes clear.

[2] *Gobseck; Les Employés.*   [3] *Illusions perdues* II.   [4] *E* II, 270.

villain stands out when Théodose makes the same kind of advances to Flavie Colleville, the mother of the girl he is scheming to marry, as Tartuffe had made to Elmire.

'Ma femme, hé! mon Dieu, ce ne peut être qu'une machine à enfants; mais l'être sublime, la divinité, ce sera toi.'

The difference is that Flavie is likely to prove easier to cajole than Elmire. In fact Balzac here returns to reflexions of earlier years about the dismay with which women in their forties see life and love slipping away from them; and it is tantalizing not to know how Flavie would have fared had Balzac finished the novel. In 1848, in Gabriel Roux' edition of *Les Comédiens sans le savoir*, there appeared a eulogistic preface, a high-toned puff in whose concoction Balzac himself might have been suspected to have had a hand if it had not boasted of the princely fortune he had made —the vigilance of his creditors made rumours of his affluence dangerous. The burden of this preface is that Balzac is the Molière of his century, and no praise could have pleased him more.[1] But for us the Molièresque aspect of the work is less noticeable than the agility with which, in this and all the novels he was composing at this time, he reaches ever and ever deeper into the capacious pocket wherein he kept his supply of personages. In particular the reader is amazed to see him spinning with ever greater intricacy the web of complex relationships between the denizens of his lower world as opposed to those of his higher society, the tale of whom is by now almost complete; and multiplying with astonishing verve the number of those fishers in the troubled waters of commercial, legal, administrative and political activity whose maleficence is no less potent for being relatively obscure. But in *Les petits Bourgeois* the presence of the mysterious Corentin, suitably disguised, shows that Balzac was still intending to exploit the more sensational vein opened up in *Splendeurs et misères des courtisanes*.

[1] See Lovenjoul (1), 154 ff.

XVII

THE LAST PARISIAN SCENES
(continued)

i. *Les Parents pauvres*: (1) *La cousine Bette* (1846)

BALZAC'S PERIOD OF INTENSE PRODUCTIVITY was draw-
ing to a close. Always harassed with debts, always struggling to
meet publishers' demands, torn between hopes and misgivings
about his marriage prospects, and now too painfully aware of his
shattered health, he was nevertheless still capable of prodigious
work. In taking up anew the 'poor relations' theme, which he had
already begun to treat in *Pierrette*,[1] his intention was to overturn
'les faux dieux de cette littérature bâtarde', by which he no doubt
meant the popular publications of Dumas and Sue, and to prove
that he was 'plus jeune, plus frais, et plus grand que jamais'.
L'Histoire des parents pauvres is thus his last great challenge to
an insufficiently appreciative public. It was conceived as a whole
and executed between June 1846 and May 1847. *Le cousin Pons*
seems to have been composed in its essentials while *La cousine
Bette* was still only in the embryonic stage.[2] Then for various
reasons the latter took priority; originally planned as 'une simple
nouvelle', it developed into one of his longest novels.[3]

An incidental but interesting point in both of these works, and
indeed in many of those he had been writing since about 1839,

[1] He proposed in June 1846 to group *Le cousin Pons*, *La cousine Bette* and
Pierrette together. But *Pierrette* also belonged to the sub-category of *Les Célibataires*, and moreover was a scene of provincial life.
[2] On the relative speed with which both works were composed, see Hytier.
[3] Lovenjoul (1), 126–7. Both novels appeared in *Le Constitutionnel*: *La cousine
Bette* 8 Oct.–3 Dec. 1846; *Le cousin Pons* (*Les deux Musiciens*) 18 Mar.–10 May
1847. Further editions: Chlendowski and Pétion, 12 vols. 1847–8, and, also in
1848, in the 'tome supplémentaire' (t. XVII) of the 'Comédie Humaine'. For
more detailed information see Allem (2), Introduction.

is the increasing tendency he shows to move his action forward in point of time; or at any rate, if the main action belongs to the eighteen-twenties or eighteen-thirties, to complete both new and republished stories by narrating the subsequent history of the surviving protagonists up to or nearly up to the year in which he is writing. The tendency is a natural one, especially as he was interweaving the lives of his different characters more and more closely, and using more frequent cross-references to send his readers to other works in which those characters appear.[1] In *La cousine Bette* the action covers the period 1838–46, in *Le cousin Pons* the period 1844–5. Having been so long a historian of the Restoration period, he was following the precedent he had already set in *La Peau de chagrin*, and was becoming more and more immersed in the immediate present. He was showing with ever greater persistency how the chickens of the Restoration were coming home to roost during the July monarchy. Not only by his constant criticisms of the Orleans regime and parliamentary government, but also by his exposure of the seamy side of political, social and private life during that regime, he was making an increasingly conscious and determined onslaught on the *juste-milieu* system and its partisans.

This is how Balzac summarized his dual theme:

Le *vieux musicien* est *le parent pauvre* accablé d'injures, plein de cœur. *La cousine Bette* est *la parente pauvre* accablée d'injures, vivant dans l'intérieur de trois ou quatre familles, et prenant vengeance de toutes ses douleurs.[2]

The latter, the Lorraine-born Lisbeth (or Bette) Fischer, is a plain, unobtrusive and seemingly affectionate satellite of the family of Baron Hector Hulot d'Ervy, younger brother of that straightforward soldier of *Les Chouans*, Major Hulot, now a field-marshal and Count of Forzheim.[3] While the latter has had a heroic military career, Hector has made his way in the Commis-

---

[1] *Modeste Mignon* shows this habit strongly. [2] *E* III, 256; 10 June 1846.
[3] An exchange of letters took place between Balzac and a subscriber to the *Constitutionnel* over this place-name in Germany, which should be Pforzheim. See Lovenjoul (1), 121–4. He had passed through it on his way to Vienna in 1835.

sariat and risen to high rank in the War Ministry. The slights which have been put upon Bette are unintentional, but no less galling for that. The crime of Hulot's wife, her beautiful cousin Adeline, is to have made such a brilliant marriage. That of the Hulot family as a whole—it includes a son Victorin, a rising barrister, and an eminently marriageable daughter, Hortense— is the ease and brilliance of their position, and the patronizing kindness they have shown her. Her long-nourished resentment flames up into active hatred when Hortense, with the careless egoism of youth, captivates and marries the young Polish sculptor Wenceslas Steinbock, whom Bette had discovered in a garret, saved from attempted suicide and launched out on a promising career: her creation, her creature, whom she loves enough to abstain from marrying him but not enough to yield him up to another woman, least of all to a Hulot. Hence the implacable fury behind her resolve to bring the whole family to shame and ruin by secretly encouraging Baron Hulot in his favourite occupation, the pursuit of women. She begins by facilitating his liaison with the mercenary Valérie Marneffe, wife of an unsavoury, evil-living Civil Servant, who bleeds Hulot so thoroughly that he disgraces his name and family, and hastens his brother's death, by embezzling Army supplies in Algeria. Then, unsated, Bette connives at his disappearance, so that under various aliases, during two and a half years of ignoble squalor, he glides further and further down the slope of dissipation, passing from one loose woman to another until his long-suffering wife discovers him earning a pittance as a public scrivener and living with a prostitute of fifteen. Bette has watched his downward career with a joy and satisfaction which however have not been unalloyed. Apart from other mortifications, she has suffered acute chagrin through the death of the Count of Forzheim, whose housekeeper she had become and whom she hoped to marry. And though she has continued to live on apparently excellent terms with the Hulot family, Hector's return home reduces her to despair. She dies of consumption, with all her unsuspecting relatives weeping round her death-bed and 'regretting her as the angel of the family'.

This is of course a simplification of the story, which Balzac has built up, with his usual fecundity, into a very ramified plot.

Interest is focused on many points besides the 'poor relation's' pursuit of revenge and the elusive rake's progress. Not less fascinating is the progress Valérie Marneffe makes in the art of fooling and exploiting her lovers. Hector is far from being her only victim. It has been part of Bette's plan of revenge that Valérie shall in her turn filch Wenceslas from Hortense; and the account of a love-marriage for a long time wrecked by the weakmindedness of the husband is also a vivid element in the novel. Balzac has much to say here, as in *La fausse Maîtresse*, about the irresponsibility ingrained in the Polish character. It is well in keeping with Wenceslas' disposition that he should remain for so long under Valérie's spell, estranged from his wife, and sapped of all energy and purpose as an artist.

Valérie has also under her domination the rich ex-perfumer Célestin Crevel, a former employee of César Birotteau who, on the latter's bankruptcy, had bought up his establishment of 'la Reine des Roses'. Crevel is Hulot's rival in debauchery, and the vain attempt he has made at the outset on Adeline Hulot's virtue was prompted by the fact that Hulot had enticed Josépha Mirah, the *prima donna*, from him. His libertinism would have been equal to that of Hector but for his middle-class propensity to run even his pleasures on an economical footing. It is to him that we owe the famous sally about the five-franc piece as the real ruler of France in the age of Louis-Philippe.[1] His daughter is married to Victorin Hulot, and so Bette is still using Valérie to strike through him at her detested kinsfolk. Crevel has few illusions about Valérie's real worth, but is infatuated enough to install her in a luxurious flat and marry her as soon as she becomes a widow. It is at this point that Nemesis overtakes them both. Valérie has yet another lover, the Brazilian Baron Henri Montès de Montéjanos, an early example of the South American *rastaquouère* who after Balzac's time achieved some popularity in certain kinds of French novels and plays. Balzac credits him with a very savage ingenuousness and elemental ideas about love and fidelity. Moreover Valérie as Mme Crevel offers such a menace to the Hulot family that Victorin arranges to have her removed by drastic means. For this Balzac again calls in denizens of the underworld,

[1] See *Biography*, 35.

notably Vautrin's brothel-keeping aunt, the 'Asie' of *Splendeurs et misères*, here operating under the names of 'Madame de Saint-Estève' and 'Madame Nourrisson'.[1] It is sufficient for her to prove that Valérie is deceiving him for the ebullient Montéjanos to plan and carry out a signal vengeance: he arranges to infect Valérie, and through her Crevel, with one of those diseases which Balzac invents at need, like the one he had invented for Auguste de Maulincour in *Ferragus*. Both the courtesan and the roué die a repulsive death, each of them squaring their account with their Maker in a characteristic fashion, she as a *fille de joie*—

'. . . je ne puis plaire maintenant qu'à Dieu! je vais tâcher de me réconcilier avec lui, ce sera ma dernière coquetterie! Oui, il faut que je fasse le bon Dieu!'

—while Crevel breathes his last with the platitudes of a pre-Flaubertian Homais on his lips, but yet with some stoutness of heart:

. . . soyez calmes, mes enfants, la mort regarde à deux fois avant de frapper un maire de Paris!'

Thus Montéjanos has served as 'l'instrument de la colère divine' and a means whereby Balzac, who has related the feats, ruses and turpitudes of these people with the same cynical and joyous appreciation as the wiles and wantonings of some of his heroes and heroines in *Les Contes drolatiques*, can ward off censure from puritans by showing that, if right does not always triumph, wrong can be ultimately worsted.

If we allow for those 'Grand Guignol' features in *La cousine Bette* which put Balzac again in competition with Eugène Sue, we can but recognize that this is one of the outstanding novels of the 'Comédie Humaine'. It has been hailed as the first 'roman naturaliste' of the century. By 'naturalism' is usually meant the unflinching study of human nature at its worst: a function which Taine, the brothers Goncourt and Zola imposed on the novel after 1850. *La cousine Bette* fairly deserves the epithet in the three essential aspects we have mentioned.

[1] The real Mme Nourrisson is the 'revendeuse à la toilette' in *Les Comédiens sans le savoir*. See above, 371.

First there is the turmoil of hatred and rancour stirred up in the heart of a frustrated old maid, forty-two at the beginning of the action, and the potentialities for long-matured and unrelenting malevolence which such frustration may confer.[1] With regard to Bette Fischer, 'ce caractère de Corse et de sauvage', Balzac comments on the driving-power with which virgins are endowed for the accomplishment of their purposes, good or bad:

La virginité, comme toutes les monstruosités, a des richesses spéciales, des grandeurs absorbantes. La vie, dont les forces sont économisées, a pris chez l'individu vierge une qualité de résistance et de durée incalculable. Le cerveau s'est enrichi dans l'ensemble de ses facultés réservées. Lorsque les gens chastes ont besoin de leur corps ou de leur âme, qu'ils recourent à l'action ou à la pensée, ils trouvent alors de l'acier dans leurs muscles ou de la science dans leur intelligence, une force diabolique ou la magie noire de la volonté.

Sous ce rapport, la vierge Marie, en ne la considérant pour un moment que comme un symbole, efface par sa grandeur tous les types indous, égyptiens et grecs.

The comparison is in bad taste, but the theory itself serves well to explain the concentration which holds Bette to her purpose. Not that she is virginal of soul; she is chaste simply because she is unattractive; she enjoys through the instrument of her vengeance, the pretty and vivacious Valérie, whom she loves to the point of arousing scandalous gossip among the neighbours, the power over men which she can never hope to wield directly. 'Ah! si j'avais été jolie, en aurais-je eu, des aventures!' The steel of which Balzac speaks above is in her will, and not her muscles. She remains inexorable even when Valérie on her death-bed implores her to relent:

[1] Curiously enough, Balzac himself asserted (*E* III, 281; 28 June 1846) that Bette was a compound of his mother, the poetess Marceline Desbordes-Valmore, and Mme Hanska's vexatious aunt by marriage, Rosalie Rzewuska, so hostile to her niece's marriage with Balzac. Obviously none of them were spinsters. Balzac nourished resentment against his mother, as we have seen, and rancour against 'Aunt Rosalie'; but none against the poetess. Probably Ève was suspicious of Balzac's relations with her. On the subject of his friendship with Mme Desbordes-Valmore see Fargeaud. Stefan Zweig, 180 ff. and 353, suggests that Henriette Borel, Anna Hanska's governess (see *Biography*, 60, 78, 142–3) provided Balzac with a model for Bette.

Moi! dit la Lorraine; j'ai vu la vengeance partout dans la nature, les insectes périssent pour satisfaire le besoin de vengeance,—pour se venger quand on les attaque! Et ces messieurs, dit-elle en montrant le prêtre, ne nous disent-ils pas que Dieu se venge, et que sa vengeance dure l'éternité! . . .

The second great achievement of Balzac is the study of senile eroticism. The Hulot case is an extreme one: today we should call it pathological. Even at sixty-seven he has years of woman-hunting before him. At the end of his Odyssey as a libertine, minutely recorded in the novel, he has reached seventy-five, and is still incorrigible. 'Mais pourrai-je emmener la petite?' he meekly asks the nobly forgiving Adeline when she arrives to take him from Atala Judici and restore him to respectable life. This prey to the demon of lust is not by intention a cruel husband: all along his follies have been punctuated with repentances and promises of amendment. But his most flagrant betrayal of Adeline is reserved for the end. When reclaimed and reinstated, he finally breaks her heart by seducing her slut of a kitchen-maid on the promise of marrying her after his wife's death: 'ma femme n'a pas longtemps à vivre, et, si tu veux, tu pourras être baronne'. There has, of course, been much debate over possible models for Hector. An article by M. Pierre Saint-Girons has shown that Balzac was, to say the least, careless in choosing the surname Hulot. There were three Hulots, generals and barons, who had distinguished themselves in the Napoleonic wars, and two of them were still alive while Balzac was writing. Another contemporary, Hector d'Aure, may have provided the Christian name.[1] But these persons furnish no data, either for the administrative dishonesty, or for the lasciviousness of Balzac's hero. It was Professor J. B. Barrère who, struck by the similarity in sound of the names Hector Hulot and Victor Hugo, and also those of the Baronne Hulot— Adeline *née* Fischer—and Mme Hugo—Adèle *née* Foucher—put forth the ingenious suggestion[2] that the incident of Hulot being surprised by the police *in flagrante delicto* with Valérie Marneffe

---

[1] Saint-Girons, op. cit. For earlier theories on Hulot and other characters see Allem (2). Also, on the sculptor Elshoëcht (for some time suitor of Mme de Brugnol) as one who may have lent some traits to Wenceslas Steinbock, see Hytier, 424, n. 2.   [2] Barrère (2).

is almost a transcription of Hugo's adventure with Mme Léonie Biard on July 2nd 1845; the difference being that in Hulot's case the Marneffe couple had arranged the whole affair. It is certain that Balzac was scornful, in his correspondence with Mme Hanska, about Hugo's philanderings, and malice may well have prompted him to use this incident. But a surprise by a supposedly outraged husband for purposes of blackmail is an age-old trick.

The third 'naturalist' aspect of *La cousine Bette* is the attention he concentrates on the horde of Parisian women engaged in 'the oldest profession in the world'. His interest in them seems to have been on the increase during these latter years. Hence his description of this novel as 'le pendant d'*Esther*'.[1] According to a passage in *Splendeurs et misères*[2] the social function of such women is perhaps, in accordance with the Fourierist view, 'to repair the ravages of avarice and cupidity' by redistributing the ill-gotten gains of financiers. *La cousine Bette* parades a miscellany of these captivating parasites—Josépha Mirah the opera-singer, Jenny Cadine the actress, Malaga the circus-rider, the dancers Héloïse Brisetout and 'La Carabine', Olympe Bijou and Cydalise, two neophytes who are guided into Hulot's orbit, and that pathetic waif, Atala Judici. One might say to Balzac, concerning courtesans, what William of Ockham said to the metaphysicians concerning entities: *non sunt multiplicanda[e] præter necessitatem*. These, however, are all needed as protégées, or deceivers, of Baron Hulot. Josépha Mirah is the most fully drawn, and no doubt is the most congenial in Balzac's view. At the beginning of the story we see her transferring her favours from Hulot to the Duc d'Hérouville and explaining to the former with jovial frankness that the latter can pay more. After Hulot's disgrace she befriends him with an equally jovial kindness, so impressed is she with the magnitude of his follies:

—Est-ce vrai, vieux . . . que tu as tué ton frère et ton oncle, ruiné ta famille, surhypothéqué la maison de tes enfants et mangé la grenouille du gouvernement en Afrique avec la princesse?

Le baron inclina tristement la tête.

—Eh bien, j'aime cela! s'écria Josépha, qui se leva pleine d'enthousiasme. C'est un *brûlage* général. C'est sardanapale! c'est grand! c'est

[1] *E* IV, 104; 5 Nov. 1846. [2] Conard XV, 238.

complet! On est une canaille, mais on a du cœur. Eh bien, moi, j'aime mieux un mange-tout, passionné comme toi pour les femmes, que ces froids banquiers sans âme qu'on dit vertueux et qui ruinent des milliers de familles avec leurs rails qui sont de l'or pour eux et du fer pour les gogos! Toi, tu n'as ruiné que les tiens, tu n'as disposé que de toi! et puis tu as une excuse, et physique et morale. . . .

Elle se posa tragiquement et dit:

—*C'est Vénus tout entière à sa proie attachée.*

Still later there is a memorable scene between her and the pious, desolate Adeline searching for her husband. Having herself no pretensions to virtue, she is affected by the sight of innocence in distress, and does her best to trace Hector's migrations from one harlot to another.

Balzac makes a clear distinction between these 'brides of the thirteenth arrondissement' and the 'courtisanes mariées qui, de prime abord, acceptent la dépravation dans toutes ses consé-quences et qui sont décidées à faire fortune en s'amusant, sans scrupule sur les moyens'. Mme Marneffe, of illegitimate birth like so many of Balzac's forceful characters, is a superlative example of these 'Machiavels en jupons'. Beside her Flavie Colleville and even her contemporary in English literature, Becky Sharp, are respectable women. Her physical charms are matched by her wit, gaiety and versatility. To cynicism and hypocrisy are added a diabolical skill in fooling and fleecing men, and an adamantine hardness. Valérie's greatest moments occur when, finding herself with child, she persuades her four lovers simultaneously of their forthcoming paternity;[1] when, in an interview with Crevel, she apes the penitent Magdalen in order to dissuade him from taking effective pity on Adeline Hulot; and also when, as she lies dying of a nauseating disease, she makes the best of a horrible predica-ment and decides to take her chances on a death-bed repentance.

The Hulot women, who are also important characters, stand of course in a very different category. Hortense is a positive and attractive girl who faces with dignity the distressing situation in which Bette's machinations put her. As for her mother, Balzac's conception of this model wife, grateful to her husband for raising

[1] 'Les cinq pères de l'Église', says Marneffe, including himself in their number.

her to high social rank, and forgiving 'unto seventy times seven', was dictated by the opposite of 'naturalist' considerations. No doubt his instinct as an artist urged him to unflinching revelation of human depravity, and he was unquestionably sincere in his piquant assertions that the tales he told and the situations he depicted contained in themselves their own morality.[1] Yet his claim to be philosopher and reformer, and the sentimental disposition which he kept on surprisingly good terms with his Rabelaisian humour, would not let him rest content with Olympian objectivity. And so the moralizing intention is well to the fore in this remarkably varied novel. At the time of writing it he was consciously outbidding Eugène Sue, not only as a painter of extreme vice, but also as a self-appointed critic of social and moral evils; while at the same time he took his stand against the latter's new-found Fourierist creed and all other brands of contemporary socialism.

La cousine Bette includes here and there a word about the squalid lives led by the working classes and the special temptations that assailed them. In the 1848 preface of *Les Comédiens sans le savoir*, to which reference has already been made,[2] he is credited with the declaration: 'Je soutenais une lutte insensée, je combattais la misère avec ma plume!' To do him justice we must recognize that pity for the working classes is at least intermittently evident in his works. To quote only a few examples: he has demanded our sympathy for the hard struggle of fishermen in *Un Drame au bord de la mer*; for honest and charitable men like the dairyman Vergniaud in *Le colonel Chabert* and the water-carrier Bourgeat in *La Messe de l'athée*; for Judge Popinot's pauper protégés in *L'Interdiction* and the usurer Cérizet's clients in *Les petits Bourgeois*; for the victims of justices' courts, again in *Le colonel Chabert*; for prisoners and ticket-of-leave men in *Splendeurs et misères*; and, in *Fragments inédits*[3] and elsewhere, for the *concierges* of Paris forced to live in confined and insalubrious lodges. It is certain that his social snobbery and his love of luxury and ostentation did not prevent him from castigating the well-to-

---

[1] 'Cette scène [*La cousine Bette*] porte d'ailleurs avec elle ses moralités qui sont de plus d'un genre.'
[2] See above, 374.   [3] Conard *O.D.* III, 360–1.

do for their selfish indifference,[1] although he did not feel called upon as an artist to take a primary interest in the life of the working-classes.[2] But nearly always his observations on popular distress are subservient to his hatred of the liberal philanthropists and the publicity he accorded to the Catholic religion as a moral and social panacea.

This preoccupation explains the role he assigned to Adeline Hulot, in *La cousine Bette*, as the ideal Catholic wife and mother; and also as a patroness of the poor, for when she is abandoned by her husband and forced to live a hand-to-mouth existence, she joins the band of charitable workers organized by Mme de La Chanterie, the heroine of *L'Envers de l'histoire contemporaine* whose acquaintance we have yet to make. In this connection Balzac permits himself some criticism of the Church as an organization, particularly in its exaction of fees for marriage which, together with the costliness of the legal contracts, often forces the poor to concubinage. Unfortunately Adeline is from a practical point of view a poor advertisement for the Catholicism which, as presented by Balzac, the Fourierist Alexandre Weill judged to be 'quelque peu faisandé'.[3] She is almost as blameworthy as a wife as Goriot is as a father. The limitless nature of her indulgence towards her husband's vice is illustrated in the advice she gives him at one stage:

'Mon ami . . . s'il te faut absolument des maîtresses, pourquoi ne prends-tu pas, comme Crevel, des femmes qui ne soient pas chères et dans une classe à se trouver longtemps heureuses de peu? Nous y gagnerions tous. Je conçois le besoin, mais je ne comprends rien à la vanité. . . .'

Her readiness at one moment in the action to sacrifice her life-long virtue to Crevel's lust—fortunately she is spared this surrender—is comprehensible in view of the calamity which threatens her family. So too is the envy she feels when, during her visit to Josépha, she reflects on the wealth and luxury which prostituted beauty can acquire. So also is the curiosity which prompts her to study 'le charme que possèdent ces sortes de femmes, pour ex-

---

[1] See Bertault (2), 488–91, on Balzac's 'Pitié sociale'; also the article of Gancier.
[2] On this subject see Guyon (1), 353–5.   [3] See Hunt (1), 213.

traire tant d'or des gisements avares du sol parisien'. All this makes a flesh-and-blood woman of her. But there is more imbecility than Christian patience in the long-suffering which only fails as she utters her last words:

Mon ami, je n'avais plus que ma vie à te donner: dans un moment tu seras libre, et tu pourras faire une baronne Hulot.'

More worldly, more scandalizing perhaps, but more sound and sincere is the view Balzac utters elsewhere in this novel on the best means a wife may adopt to keep her husband constant. It is the means adopted by the artful Marianne in Marivaux's novel:[1] a husband must find sufficient novelty and variety in his wife to keep him perpetually interested. As Marianne puts it, 'je savais être plusieurs femmes en une'. As Balzac puts it, 'On doit avoir toutes les femmes dans la sienne'; so that a man will not seek in a mistress the qualities he misses in his legitimate spouse. The lesson is that of the Duchesse de Carigliano in *La Maison du chat qui pelote*,[2] Félicité des Touches in *Béatrix*,[3] and even Modeste Mignon in a letter to Ernest de La Brière.[4] Josépha's homily to Adeline on wifely strategy expresses the same truth with brisk vulgarity:

'Eh bien, si vous aviez eu, voyez-vous, un peu de notre chique,[5] vous l'auriez empêché de courailler . . . le gouvernement devait créer une école de gymnastique pour les honnêtes femmes! Mais les gouvernements sont si bégueules! . . .'

Style apart, the voice of Josépha is the voice of the author of *La Physiologie du mariage* and *Les petites Misères de la vie conjugale*. Such a sentiment comes more appropriately from him than tears shed for the 'angel' Adeline, to whom he professes to have lent some of Mme Hanska's qualities.[6]

Whatever incidental criticisms one may make of *La cousine Bette*, it remains a great novel. The pathos and horror of the story in its broad lines did not prevent Balzac from displaying his gift for satiric and sardonic observation. He gives us yet another variant of the self-complacent bourgeois in the person of Crevel,

---

[1] *La Vie de Marianne*, Garnier, 53–5.
[2] See above, 283.   [3] See above, 334.   [4] See above, 330.
[5] i.e. *chic*: skill, knack.   [6] *E* IV, 121, 127.

and a provincial understudy of Crevel, a stupid one, in Philéas Beauvisage.[1] He keeps himself well in hand over the matter of topographical descriptions; a notable one, though short, is that of the clusters of sordid houses neighbouring the Louvre.[2] The novel contains some 150 characters.[3] Great scenes abound—Balzac himself was very proud of them—and more than ever one notices the predominance of dialogue over flat narration: the action moves on through conversations and interviews. In these later years Balzac was giving more and more attention to the theatre, and one cannot deny his ability to stage, at any rate within the framework of the novel, scenes of decisive power and vividness.

ii. *Le cousin Pons* (1847)

When Balzac took up *Le cousin Pons* again, he had little time to expand it and give it the complexity of *La cousine Bette*, which is generally considered superior to it. Brunetière, for instance, detects in *Le cousin Pons* more signs of improvisation, and thinks that certain of its subsidiary 'biographies' are less perfectly welded to the whole.[4] But the action is more simple and concentrated. It is as powerful in its general conception as *Le père Goriot*. It is one of his most tragic subjects. The wealth and subtlety of observation it contains and the maturity of the moral experience it reveals bear the stamp of his highest genius.

This time the poor relation is not the villain of the piece but a victim, having some affinity with the Abbé Birotteau of *Le Curé de Tours*: the elderly musician Sylvain Pons, allied by birth or marriage to those prosperous commercial or legal families, the Camusots, the Cardots and the Popinots. The two themes around which the story is woven are indicated by two provisional titles of the novel: *Les deux Musiciens*[5] and *Le Parasite*. Pons is the bosom friend of a mild, unworldly German pianist named Schmucke, a copyist of music at the boulevard theatre run by 'the illustrious

---

[1] See below on *Le Député d'Arcis*.

[2] Chap. xiii in the Garnier edition, which professes to follow the edition of 1848, though the chapter divisions were suppressed in that edition.

[3] According to M. Hytier's computation.   [4] Brunetière, 141–3.

[5] Another was *Les deux Amis*, which Balzac abandoned because of La Fontaine's fable having that title.

Gaudissart' of which Pons is the orchestra-conductor. Pons is a newcomer to the 'Comédie Humaine'. Schmucke, modelled on Jacques Strunz,[1] has already appeared in *Une Fille d'Ève* and *Ursule Mirouët* as a music-master. His personality is already definitely outlined in the former of those two works, but here the portrait becomes life-size. In his kindness, simplicity, sentimentality and complete lack of practical sense he conforms to the conception of the Germanic temperament made popular by Mme de Staël in *De l'Allemagne*, although many passing observations in *Le cousin Pons*, and the attention given to two other German characters, the flute-player Wilhelm Schwab and the ex-profligate Fritz Brunner, prove that Balzac was aware of other aspects in the German temperament.

Pons with his outmoded spencer, his 'vaste visage percé comme une écumoire', his 'nez à la Don Quichotte', is phenomenally ugly. It is implied that Schmucke is even more so. They have lived together for years in the Marais quarter of Paris, where they are known as 'the pair of nutcrackers'. Their friendship is of the Orestes–Pylades quality, though Schmucke's devotion, founded in admiration, is by a clever touch shown to be strengthened by his indulgent awareness of Pons' great weakness, his gluttony.

It is this love of good dinners which has brought Pons to his role of 'parasite'. Having shown promise as a composer in his youth, having won the 'Grand Prix de Rome' but failed, as Balzac believed most beneficiaries of state awards generally do, to bring his talent to fruition, he has found solace in two occupations. One consists in going the rounds of his well-to-do acquaintances and kinsfolk and sharing the delights of their table. In the course of time he has worn out his welcome—'chaque famille l'acceptait comme on accepte un impôt'. The other is the collecting of bric-à-brac, pictures and antique furniture: a taste which he brought back with him from Rome and which, between 1810 and 1844, he has developed to such an extent that, by dint of patient search and cheap buying, he has built up for himself a rich museum of antiques whose accumulated value he only comes to realize through the envious eyes cast on it by other people. His dinners at the rich men's tables have dwindled in number, and his depen-

[1] See above, 145.

dence for gastronomic enjoyment on the table of his 'cousins', the Camusots de Marville, is the mainspring of the action. Readers of the 'Comédie Humaine' have seen Maître Camusot, son of the former silk-merchant who is now a baron, winning his way through subservience[1] to important magisterial office. He has taken his territorial surname of Marville from an estate he possesses in Normandy. Like many of Balzac's successful men, he is more or less the creation of his wife, who can claim to be one of the most venomous and intriguing women of the 'Comédie Humaine'.

Pons has already made an enemy in the Camusot camp by scorning the attentions of their matrimonially disposed but acrimonious housekeeper, Madeleine Vivet, a 'Didon d'antichambre'. A joint humiliation at the hands of Mme Camusot, her daughter Cécile and the servants re-awakens his self-respect, and he banishes himself for a time from their table. Then a disastrous attempt to earn their permanent goodwill by finding a husband for the insufficiently dowered Cécile puts him for ever beyond the pale. Overcome by the shock of this unmerited disgrace, he collapses with a disease of the liver, and the second half of the story shows him in a moribund condition, tenderly nursed by Schmucke, but harried to death by the cupidity of those whom the realization of his wealth has made parasites in their turn. In the foreground are Mme Cibot, the porter's wife, who has become the charwoman and cook in the two friends' establishment, Rémonencq, the old metal dealer from Auvergne, and the rich Jewish collector, Élie Magus. Their aim is to lay hands on Pons' best pictures. In the background, supported by a needy, poor man's doctor, Poulain, and the barrister Fraisier, is Mme Camusot, whose purpose is to oust Schmucke and lay hands on the Pons inheritance. Both groups achieve their end. The collection is despoiled of eight of its most valuable pictures. A succession of grim scenes shows how the dying Pons becomes aware of the frauds that have been practised on him through the gullibility of Schmucke. In a spurt of clear-sightedness and resolution he does his best to thwart his persecutors and contrive that Schmucke shall be his sole heir. But after

[1] *Le Cabinet des antiques* (1839 version), *L'Interdiction* (1844 version), *Splendeurs et misères* (see above, 361).

his death the grief-numbed German is as powerless to cope with the plotters as he is with the other birds of prey that hover over him—undertakers, monumental masons and the like. One of Balzac's most striking achievements is the picture he gives of Schmucke's final capitulation and death. With only one true friend to help him—Topinard, his humble, brow-beaten theatre colleague—heart-broken at being accused of having worked on Pons to gain his inheritance, terrified of the complex machinery of the law which Fraisier threatens to call into play, he cedes his heritage for a pittance and totters away to join Pons in the grave.

Such is 'le drame, ou, si vous voulez, la comédie terrible de la mort d'un célibataire livré par la force des choses à la rapacité des natures cupides qui se groupent à son lit'. This 'force des choses' resides chiefly in Pons' two hobbies which have grown, the one into a vice, the other into an exclusive pursuit; both of them a compensation for the sexual experience he has never enjoyed. The progress of the first is described with such skill and pertinence of comment as only Balzac could command. Brillat-Savarin himself could not have waxed more lyrical in the description of exquisite dishes or the voluptuous processes of digestion, or in the expression of Pons' yearning when deprived of such joys.

But the collector's mania lay nearer to Balzac's heart. He had been enamoured of pictures and furniture and trinkets since his Rue Cassini days. He had sprinkled the pages of the 'Comédie Humaine'—more conspicuously *Le Chef d'œuvre inconnu*, *Pierre Grassou* and *La Rabouilleuse*—with comments and judgments on the art of old and new masters.[1] He had lavished his own and Mme Hanska's money on purchases for the adornment of the 'Maison Beaujon' in which he had now begun to live. With him too collecting had become a ruling passion.[2] In describing the Pons collection he had in mind what he thought or would have

---

[1] He has a habit of invoking their pictorial talent in support of his own, as in *Une double Famille* where, after quite graphically describing the street-scene between Granville and Bianchon, he adds: 'Il faudrait qu'un même homme possédât à la fois les crayons de Charlet, et ceux de Callot, les pinceaux de Téniers et de Rembrand, pour donner une idée vraie de cette Scène nocturne' (Conard III, 303). Is this due to modesty about his own talent, or to a desire to display his knowledge of art?   [2] See *Biography*, 137–8.

liked his own to be—one equal in value and completeness to that of Élie Magus in the story, or those of Sauvageot and du Sommerard in reality. And, mindful of obligations and debts, he worked into his text tributes to the talent of such artists and decorators as Liénard, Servais and Moret, whom he himself had employed. The enthusiasm over four old masters which Magus feels as he gazes at Pons' array of pictures is akin to that which such paintings inspired in himself.

With the love of beautifully wrought things, and the pleasure their possession gives, goes the excitement of the chase. With what gusto Balzac describes it in Pons, especially at that early moment in the story when his timid hero presents a fan exquisitely painted by Watteau to the uncultured Mme Camusot[1] and tells her of the wiles and stratagems of bargaining! Her reaction is of course a chilling one:

—Quel original! Ca vous amuse donc? demanda la présidente. Pons, glacé par cette question, éprouva l'envie de battre la présidente.
—Mais, ma chère cousine, reprit-il, c'est la chasse aux chefs d'œuvre! Et on se trouve face à face avec des adversaires qui défendent le gibier! C'est ruse contre ruse! Un chef d'œuvre doublé d'un Normand, d'un Juif ou d'un Auvergnat, mais c'est comme, dans les contes de fées, une princesse gardée par des enchanteurs!

But Pons' zeal for collecting falls short of monomania. It is balanced by his love of good fare and, in the end, eclipsed by his concern for Schmucke's well-being. The complete maniac, the *tableaumane*, is presented in the person of Élie Magus, the retired dealer, whose portrait, originally sketched in *Pierre Grassou*,[2] now receives a development which puts him on a par with Gobseck or Claës as the incarnation of an obsession.

Cette âme vouée au lucre, froide comme un glaçon, s'échauffait à la vue d'un chef d'œuvre, absolument comme un libertin, lassé de femmes, s'émeut devant une fille parfaite, et s'adonne à la recherche des beautés sans défaut. Ce Don Juan des toiles, cet adorateur de l'idéal,

[1] In *La Vendetta*, as Mlle Thirion, she had been an art student! Here she has not even heard of Watteau. But she had replaced a Mlle de Montsaurin in the Furne edition of *La Vendetta* (1842). Her ignorance of art in *Le cousin Pons* may be due either to forgetfulness or to irony on Balzac's part.

[2] He had first been named in *Le Contrat de mariage* and then identified with the hitherto anonymous dealer in *La Vendetta*.

trouvait dans cette admiration des jouissances supérieures à celles que donne à l'avare la contemplation de l'or. Il vivait dans un sérail de beaux tableaux!

Here is the glimpse we get of Magus gloating over his treasures:

C'était un tableau vivant au milieu de ces tableaux immobiles que ce petit vieillard, vêtu d'une méchante redingote, d'un gilet de soie décennal, d'un pantalon crasseux, la tête chauve, le visage creux, la barbe frétillante et dardant ses poils blancs, le menton menaçant et pointu, la bouche démeublée, l'œil brillant comme celui de ses chiens [the mastiffs he keeps to guard his museum], les mains osseuses et décharnées, le nez en obélisque, la peau rugueuse et froide, souriant à ces belles créations du génie! Un Juif, au milieu de trois millions, sera toujours un des plus beaux spectacles que puisse donner l'humanité.

Such a passion, like that of Claës and Gobseck, is not without its sublimity. The ambition and covetousness which animate most of the other people in the novel are exhibited in all their despicable sordidness—in some cases triumphant from the start, in others fighting a winning battle against kindlier impulses. A sharp delineation is given even to the most subordinate characters, such as the fairly conscientious Poulain, the two minor harpies who flutter round Pons' death-bed, and the funereal ghouls avid to profit by the misery of human bereavement. In an ascending order of importance, leaving Magus out of this reckoning, we may first glance at Rémonencq, the prime mover in Pons' despoilment, who hopes for a fine establishment in the Boulevard de la Madeleine, with the virile beauty of Mme Cibot—too virile, since she is obliged to shave—attracting the customers, and who gains his object after cleverly poisoning her husband with doses of verdigris. Next comes Mme Cibot herself, the former oyster-opener at a popular restaurant, a hearty, vulgar, inexhaustibly garrulous woman, in whom some original goodness of heart is stifled by the hope of collecting an annuity from Pons.[1] This 'affreuse Lady Macbeth de la rue' is ruthless and fearful by turns; superstitious too, since she has recourse to the fortune-teller, Mme Fontaine, for prophecies about the success of her schemes. Nowhere has

[1] It is likely that Mme Cibot borrows some traits (travestied) from Mme de Brugnol, Balzac's housekeeper from 1840 to 1847. She was now blackmailing him with purloined letters of Mme Hanska. See *Biography*, 151–2.

Balzac more forcefully illustrated the technique of low cunning, masquerading as gruff but tender benevolence, than he does in the scenes where she wheedles and bullies the two men. Her interminable scoldings, couched in the vigorous language of her class, are calculated, even in their apparent incoherence. She torments and exasperates Pons, first to find out if he has any legal heirs, then to harry him into making a will, and finally and above all in order to aggravate his hepatitis and hasten his death.

It is a nice point whether her wickedness is a degree inferior or superior to the more sophisticated wickedness of Mme Camusot, who is snobbish, sour, envious, spiteful, and remorseless in the pursuit of her ends—the marriage of her daughter, the seizure of the Pons inheritance, and the promotion of her weak-kneed husband. Her feline cruelty to Pons in the fan scene, her sugariness and exultant boastfulness when she thinks that she has laid hands on a rich son-in-law, and her fury when he withdraws, are only matched by the steely efficiency with which she makes her bargain and hatches her plots with the unsavoury Fraisier. They are a well-assorted pair; yet the palm for villainy should perhaps go to Fraisier—a lawyer 'on the make', whose unprofessional conduct at Mantes has brought him disgrace, but who looks to Mme Camusot to get him on the road to advancement again; a worthy member of the Roguin, Vinet, Théodose de La Peyrade confraternity. His one virtue is gratitude to Poulain, who has doctored him in illness and opened the way to the Pons intrigue. This he conducts with unerring skill, using Mme Cibot as a spy and agent, mastering her by intimidation when she threatens rebellion, adjusting his plans to the needs of every new situation, exploiting every incident and using every influence to bring about Schmucke's surrender. A consummate rogue, but a completely credible one.

And yet over all these servants of evil the two innocent victims tower, and by virtue of their innocence. The best in Pons comes out as he lies dying and makes his desperate arrangements to save Schmucke. For all his guilelessness and incomprehension, Schmucke commands special admiration at certain moments: when he welcomes the hungry and humiliated Pons to an improvised dinner; when he stands up for Pons against the calumnies of his relatives; when he pushes aside all thought of practical necessities in his grief for Pons; and when he makes it his last concern to see that Topinard and his family are provided for. There are also other people of normal humanity in the novel to relieve the blackness of the picture. Wilhelm Schwab and Fritz Brunner are amusing figures. The upright Anselme Popinot, who has risen since 1830 to be a statesman and a count, is ineffectual because he is ignorant of what is going on. His protégé, Gaudissart, the 'Napoleon of the boulevard theatres', is good-natured, though not to the extent of spoiling his prospects of new favours from Popinot. The dancer, Héloïse Brisetout, mistress in turn of Crevel, Bixiou and Gaudissart, brisk in argument and repartee, 'bonne camarade', fearless, is a good-hearted courtesan of the Josépha Mirah type, and comes promptly to Pons' aid at a critical moment. Topinard is a sincere and generous soul who, though momentarily intimidated, obeys his conscience, and in the end risks his livelihood by denouncing the conspiracy against Schmucke.

Le cousin Pons then, while it is one of the saddest of Balzac's tales, is in its essence one of the most human, and also one of the most profound. Practically all the pauses in narration are pertinent to the development of the action. Even the long digression on fortune-telling, while affording one more proof of the fusion of scientific determinism with unscientific credulity in Balzac's philosophy, leads to an excellent scene in which Mme Fontaine goes through her tricks with her gigantic toad Astoroth and her black hen Cléopâtre. The account of Pons' funeral and the preparations for it, reminiscent of similar pages in *Ferragus*, are not only entirely relevant, but poignantly pathetic. A wry humour enhances their effect, as for instance when an embalmer tries his chances with Schmucke:

'Monsieur, nous devons au docteur Ganal une découverte sublime; nous ne contestons pas sa gloire, il a renouvelé les miracles de l'Égypte; mais il y a eu des perfectionnements, et nous avons obtenu des résultats surprenants. Donc, si vous voulez revoir votre ami, tel qu'il était de son vivant. . . .
—*Le refoir*! . . . s'écria Schmucke; *me barlera-d-il?*
—Pas absolument! . . . Il ne lui manquera que la parole. . . .

Even more pungent is the observation which Balzac makes in describing the journey of Pons' few mourners to Pére-Lachaise:

Les morts doivent avoir été bien aimés dans leur vie pour qu'à Paris, où tout le monde voudrait trouver une vingt-cinquième heure à chaque journée, on suive un parent ou un ami jusqu'au cimetière. Mais les cochers perdraient leur pourboire s'ils ne faisaient pas leur besogne. Aussi, pleines ou vides, les voitures vont-elles à l'église, au cimetière, et reviennent-elles à la maison mortuaire, où les cochers demandent un pourboire. On ne se figure pas le nombre de gens pour qui la mort est un abreuvoir. Le bas clergé de l'église, les pauvres, les croque-morts, les cochers, les fossoyeurs, ces natures spongieuses se retirent gonflées en se plongeant dans un corbillard.

A rueful pity furnishes the inspiration behind such passages, just as a kindly sympathy is behind the description of the quarter and rooms in which Topinard, his as yet unofficial wife Lolotte and their three children reside. If Balzac had set himself to the task of portraying working-class life, there is no doubt that his genius would have served him well. Seldom has he shown elsewhere greater competence in his conception of character and the depiction of background, greater fertility and variety in conjuring up new figures, greater artistry in preparing and staging his climax, or a greater appropriateness of style. Gide regarded *Le cousin Pons* as Balzac's greatest work.[1] The tribute of Paul Bourget also is worth quoting.

Peut-être y avait-il en lui, dès cette époque, cet obscur pressentiment de l'artiste frappé à mort et qui ne veut pas s'en aller sans avoir donné sa pleine mesure. Il est certain que dans aucun de ses romans son 'faire' n'a été plus libre. La page succède à la page, toute chargée d'impressions, d'observations, de théories. Vous sentez que l'écrivain ne se ménage pas pour un prochain travail, qu'il vous prodigue à pleines mains le trésor complet de son expérience ... un large souffle d'humanité court sur le tout—l'humanité du Shakespeare de *la Tempête* qui ne s'indigne plus, qui ne se moque plus, qui a trop vu l'envers et les dessous de l'existence pour s'attendre à rien sinon à la fourberie et à la cruauté des uns, à la faiblesse et à l'écrasement des autres.[2]

There is humour rather than indignation even in the final distribution of rewards and punishments. But there is some

[1] *Journal*, II, 373.   [2] Bourget (2), t. I, 47–9.

mockery, even with regard to the worthy Topinard, whose fall into melancholy and misanthropy is attributed to possible vexation at having made an honest woman of Lolotte, as Schmucke had wanted him to do. Fraisier prospers, and Mme Camusot remains his patroness. Rémonencq marries Mme Cibot and sets up handsomely as a dealer in antiques, but inadvertently swallows a glass of vitriol which he had put out for his wife to drink. The latter pays a minor penalty for her crimes. She had looked forward to living in the country: Mme Fontaine's prophecy that she would be murdered there by two escaped convicts keeps her chained to Paris. But the cream of the conclusion is the account Balzac gives of the subsequent fate of 'l'héroïne de cette histoire' —the Pons collection. Bought up at Élie Magus' valuation by Count Popinot (in whose son Cécile Camusot has managed to find a husband, purchased by her parents at the price of a rich dowry), the collection gives the Camusots occasion for gushing over the memory of the 'dear cousin' who had left it to them:

'C'était un homme charmant' [Mme Camusot reports in her fluty little voice] 'Il dînait trois ou quatre fois par semaine chez moi. . . . il nous aimait tant! nous savions l'apprécier, les artistes se plaisent avec ceux qui goûtent leur esprit.'

Volumes of moralizing could not so potently castigate the contemptible and hypocritical selfishness of the worldly people who, when Sylvain Pons was alive, gave him no kindly thought and spoke him no kindly word.

XVIII

COUNTRY LIFE AND POLITICS

i. *Les Paysans* (1844–55)

BALZAC HAD IN HAND two more contributions to his studies of Political Life (to which in 1846 he added *Un Épisode sous la Terreur*)[1] and one more to those of Country Life. They are *Le Député d'Arcis*, *L'Envers de l'histoire contemporaine*, and *Les Paysans*. All three were in his mind, and were being worked on intermittently, during very much the same space of years. *L'Envers* alone was completed, though all parts of it were not put together till 1855. As far as any priority in time can be assigned, it goes to *Les Paysans*.

Les Paysans, whose history is inseparable from that of Balzac's relations with the founder of *La Presse*, Émile de Girardin,[2] only assumed something like a definitive form round about 1838, under the title *Qui a terre, a guerre*.[3] After that it was held up by interminable negotiations, by Balzac's other commitments and by his desire to make an eight-volume work of it with an enormous number of characters. What now amounts to Part I was published as a serial in *La Presse* in December 1844. The first number provoked violent criticism in another periodical, *Le Moniteur de l'Armée*; readers of *La Presse* professed to find it boring, and Girardin interrupted its publication to make way for Dumas' *La Reine Margot*. Then there were further troubles and recriminations until, in July 1847, Girardin and Balzac broke off relations altogether. Balzac definitely withdrew *Les Paysans*, four new chapters of which *La Presse* had set up in proof, and paid

[1] See above, 35.   [2] See *Biography*, 126.

[3] See above, 245. Lovenjoul (4) gives the history of the painful stages of its composition, and also the text of *Le grand Propriétaire* (*circa* 1834), with fragments and an analysis of *Qui a terre, a guerre*. Another provisional title for the work was *La Chaumière et le château* (1841).

back most of the advances received. The rest of his debt, a small sum for which Girardin meanly sued him, he settled in December 1848. After Balzac's death, his widow claimed and obtained sole rights in the work, set herself the task of putting the whole novel together, using what material she could find, and had it published in 1855.[1] She had the original serial in *La Presse* for the first part; the four new chapters of Part II as we now have it, and other rough proofs of 1838, giving what M. Bouteron calls 'le canevas du roman'—on these are based chapters VI–X. Mme de Balzac wrote chapter V in its entirety, interpolated a long fragment before the last paragraph of chapter VI, and finished off chapter X. It is generally agreed that she made an intelligent job of it, unlike Rabou with his continuations of *Les petits Bourgeois* and *Le Député d'Arcis*. No doubt this is because she modestly confined herself to her task, and kept to the spirit of the original, whereas Rabou was more concerned with displaying his own skill as a novelist.

We have seen that the Scenes of Country Life are generally reserved for the expression of Balzac's views on rural economy. *Le Médecin de campagne* and *Le Curé de village* had emphasized the stupidity seasoned with guile, the greed and potential criminality of the French peasant when his animal instincts are not corrected by the ministrations of a devoted priest (the Abbé Bonnet); also his economic helplessness unless his activities are guided by intelligent organizers (Dr Benassis and the engineer Gérard) and financed by benevolent capitalists (Mme Graslin) so as to keep him steadily at work and accustom him to a simple but decent way of life. *Les Paysans* shows what happens when the peasant is left to himself, or, as Balzac saw it, what had indeed happened to him in a general way since the Revolution of 1789 had destroyed the feudal organization of landed property—a destruction which had, in fact, been in progress since long before the Revolution. The manorial lords were driven into exile and their lands were sold as 'biens nationaux' to the highest bidders. They were bought by rich plebeians or, as in Balzac's particular instance, by a retired Napoleonic general, the Comte de Montcornet.

[1] In *La Revue de Paris* (April–June), and then in five volumes (de Potter).

Balzac's thesis is that once the new owners tried to exploit their land as if it were indeed their land, they found themselves in conflict with the surly acquisitiveness of neighbouring small-holders. The latter, during the years of social anarchy, had got into the habit of abusing their long-established rights: in this novel it is a question of gleaning, pasturage and the collection of dead wood from the forests. Moreover, with their land-hunger intensified by the elimination of the lords, they were avid for the break-up of the large estates,[1] so that they might buy fragments of them and enlarge their own holdings. This they could only do by borrowing from the local moneylenders, thus exchanging their former masters for new ones infinitely more rapacious: *qui a terre, a guerre*. The resultant strife which Balzac here describes is that sort of guerilla war which Montcornet, an able soldier but a weak administrator, has to wage against a combination of in-satiable peasants who are determined to drive the owner off his domain by desultory, clandestine poaching and thieving, by physical violence and, in the last resort, by murder. George Moore[2] likens the situation to that of the land-war in Ireland during the eighteen-eighties. It is aggravated by the fact that the domain in question had long since passed out of the hands of its hereditary owners into those of upstarts, that Montcornet him-self is of plebeian origin, and that his military campaigns in Spain and Pomerania have left him with little respect for the traditional perquisites of the peasantry. He is supported by his estate-warden, the ex-cuirassier Michaud, in some respects a replica of the faith-ful Michu in *Une ténébreuse Affaire*.

The scene of this conflict is the château and estate of Les Aigues in Burgundy, in the neighbourhood of the little Morvan towns of La Ville-aux-Fayes, Soulanges and Blangy.[3] Having bought Les Aigues in 1816, Montcornet only settles down there

[1] In 1832 (*Du Gouvernement moderne*, Conard, *O.D.* II, 552), Balzac had sounded a different note—he then had seen no danger in the subdivision of estates, not at any rate as a threat to political discipline.

[2] G. Moore (3), 33.

[3] All three are fictitious, although Blangy suggests Joigny, just as the river Avonne suggests the Yonne. In *Le grand Propriétaire* Balzac had situated La Ville-aux-Fayes between Touraine and Berry. The castle of Les Aigues might be that of Cézy, near Joigny, and its owner, Général-Comte Desfourneaux, Montcornet's prototype – Lov. (4), 58. But Donnard (*Paysans*, Garnier liv) says no.

five years later with his wife, the former Virginie de Troisville. We already know her as the friend since childhood of Émile Blondet,[1] who is destined to marry her after Montcornet's death in 1837 or 1838. It is his visit to the château that opens the story. Montcornet has dismissed a dishonest steward, Gaubertin, but has made the mistake of replacing him by Sibilet, who joins Gaubertin in the conspiracy against Montcornet. The loyal Michaud advocates the rigid policy of protecting the domain by the assertion of legal rights and the prosecution of trespassers. In the first place he and Montcornet have to contend with the peasants, 'les Peaux-Rouges de Cooper', as Blondet calls them, united round the alert and slippery innkeeper François Tonsard, proprietor of the Grand I Vert. But Gaubertin and Sibilet are in league also with the middle-class notables of the three towns, in particular Soudry, mayor of Soulanges, and his clique, many of whom have their eyes too on Les Aigues and are furthermore annoyed by the social aloofness of the Montcornets and their friends.

The local magistrates and deputies are in sympathy with the schemers, and Montcornet's legal proceedings prove ineffectual. But behind them all is the ex-monk Rigou, 'l'usurier des campagnes', a worthy parallel to all the other bloodsuckers of the 'Comédie Humaine'. His appearance inspires Balzac to take an interesting glance backwards over his collective work:

Vous vous rappelez peut-être certains maîtres en avarice déjà peints dans quelques Scènes antérieures? D'abord, l'avare de province, le père Grandet de Saumur, avare comme le tigre est cruel; puis Gobseck, l'escompteur, le jésuite de l'or, n'en savourant que la puissance et dégustant les larmes du malheur, à savoir quel est leur cru; puis le baron de Nucingen, élevant les fraudes de l'argent à la hauteur de la politique. Enfin, vous avez sans doute souvenir de ce portrait de la parcimonie domestique, le vieil Hochon d'Issoudun, et de cet autre avare par esprit de famille, le petit la Baudraye de Sancerre. Eh bien, les sentiments humains, et surtout l'avarice, ont des nuances si diverses[2] dans les divers milieux de notre société, qu'il restait encore un avare sur la planche de l'amphithéâtre des études de mœurs. Il restait Rigou! l'avare égoïste, c'est-à-dire plein de tendresses pour ses jouissances, sec et froid pour autrui, enfin l'avare ecclésiastique, le moine

---

[1] See above, 205.
[2] Balzac's list of his own misers is far from complete.

demeuré moine pour exprimer le jus de citron appelé le bien-vivre, et
devenu séculier pour happer la monnaie publique.

Rigou is a former mayor of Blangy whom Montcornet has had
removed from his post. A libertine as well as an extortioner, he
holds the local peasants in the hollow of his hand by virtue of the
loans he has made them. Over against this combination Balzac sets
only a few benevolent personages—the charitable countess with
the amused and amiable Blondet, the devoted but unheeded Abbé
Brossette, later to become the ghostly counsellor of the Duchesse
de Grandlieu,[1] Michaud, and the sturdy old peasant Niseron, a
stoical republican whose wisdom and moderation fail to restrain
the rebels of the Grand I Vert. Michaud is shot dead in the forest.
Montcornet's life too is threatened. He gives up the struggle and
sells the property. Rigou buys it up cheaply and shares the best
part of it with his middle-class accomplices. The rest is split into
small lots and sold to the peasants. The 'bande noire' of speculators who batten upon the great estates has triumphed.

'La vie campagnarde et paysanne', Balzac had written in 1832,[2]
'attend un historien'. Not until Zola's *La Terre* (1887) was such
another unflattering picture of French peasant life to be painted.
Hatred, cunning and lustful promiscuity are the chief qualities
of the Tonsard family. Kindred spirits are Bonnébault, Marie
Tonsard's lover; Godain, Catherine Tonsard's 'poursuivant . . .
avare sans or', of whom Balzac tells us that 'il ne suait jamais, il
résorbait sa substance'; Courtecuisse, a would-be climber who has
failed to 'passer bourgeois' in spite of sordid economy, but who
still has the saving grace of wishing to thwart Rigou's designs on
the virtue of his daughter; 'le père Fourchon', one-time schoolmaster, clarinet-player at village dances, toper, braggart, trick-
ster; and Mouche, his bastard grandson. Not least among the
effective scenes in the novel is the one in which this pair of
spongers hoax Émile Blondet by staging a mock otter-hunt on the
banks of the Avonne. There is light and shade, and plenty of
comic relief in Balzac's evocations. His pessimism, as nearly always
when he is in his most 'realist' mood, is tempered with humorous
observation of detail and nuance, although the undertone of

[1] In *Béatrix*. See above, 336.   [2] *Contes bruns*, 59.

grimness remains, as in the account of the assembly at the Grand I Vert, in that masterly chapter which he entitled 'Comme quoi le cabaret est le Parlement du peuple' because this tavern serves as a meeting-place for plots against Montcornet. Each individual has his distinct physiognomy, and all converse in a vigorous local patter. Grandmother Tonsard is one of Balzac's most colourful old hags, an incarnation of whining and querulous malevolence, whose avidity drives her to risk arrest and imprisonment in order to further Rigou's game of increasing Montcornet's unpopularity.

According to Champfleury, Balzac learnt a lot about the peasants while at Les Jardies, where he had to deal with a type sharpened by more immediate contact with Paris. According to Lovenjoul, he learnt yet more, while at Passy, from his landlord Grandmaison. It is still more likely that his observant eye gleaned information and understanding from wherever he travelled in the provinces. Michelet, that great historian and vehement democrat, was indignant at what he regarded as a travesty of the class which for him was the backbone of the French nation.[1] On the other hand, Montalembert is recorded as having vouched for the truth of Balzac's presentation. 'Je suis du Morvan, et je me disais: "il faut qu'il y soit venu".'[2] But Balzac was not too prejudiced to state the peasants' point of view.[3] In an important opening scene Fourchon is enabled by his modicum of education to put the case of the have-nots in his forceful patois before Montcornet and his guests. For Balzac himself it is simply a matter of individual and social determinism, the determinism of material facts. He had already said so in *La Rabouilleuse*:

N'en déplaise aux faiseurs d'idylles ou aux philanthropes, les gens de la campagne ont peu de notions sur certaines vertus; et, chez eux, les scrupules viennent d'une pensée intérieure, et non d'un sentiment du bien et du beau: élevés en vue de la pauvreté, du travail constant, de la misère, cette perspective leur fait considérer tout ce qui peut les tirer de la faim et du labeur éternel, comme permis, surtout quand la loi ne s'y oppose point. S'il y a des exceptions, elles sont rares. La vertu,

---

[1] *Le Peuple* (1846), Preface (*À M. Edgar Quinet*).

[2] *Journal des Goncourt*, I, 129.

[3] The Hungarian communist George Lukács (op. cit., 28) applauds Balzac's diagnosis while deploring his conclusions.

socialement parlant, est la compagne du bien-être, et commence à l'instruction.[1]

He says much the same in *Les Paysans*:

Il ne s'agit jamais pour eux de savoir si une action est légale ou immorale, mais si elle est profitable. La moralité, qu'il ne faut pas confondre avec la religion, commence à l'aisance.[2]

Yet *Les Paysans* is not merely a study of the economic factors which had caused the impoverishment of the French countryside. A feature more common in Balzac's Provincial Scenes is not absent—the satire of social pretentiousness. In the first chapter of Part II he gives a sardonic description of the salon of 'la belle Madame Soudry', a painted 'haquenée', once a lady's maid, now 'queen' of the top social coterie in the town of Soulanges where her husband is mayor. Here we are shown a grotesque collection of people. It includes the notary Lupin, the fatuous *arbiter elegantiarum* of that brilliant centre; Gourdon the local medical practitioner, amateur entomologist, conchologist, taxidermist; and his brother, the magistrates' clerk, author of heroi-comic poems, who is astonished one day to discover that Burgundy boasts *another* poet, one Lamartine, who 'met les nuages en vers':

'C'est un *embrouillamini* de tous les diables! Des lacs, des étoiles, des vagues! . . . Pas une seule image raisonnable, pas une intention didactique; il ignore les sources de la poésie. Il appelle le ciel par son nom, il dit la lune bonassement, au lieu de l'astre des nuits.[3] Voilà pourtant jusqu'où peut nous entraîner le désir d'être original!'

It includes also Sarcus the legal historian and political oracle; Guerbet the tax-gatherer and amateur fruit-grower; Vermut the chemist, a target for the witticisms of this cultured set; Taupin the comfort-loving and accommodating curé; and of course an appropriate assortment of wives. At a lower social level Balzac does here what he had done for the frequenters of Mme de Bargeton's salon at Angoulême and that of Dinah de La Baudraye at Sancerre. Nevertheless, before once again nourishing his sense of superiority as a Parisian with this banter, he has put his finger on what to him is the enervating principle in the government of

[1] Conard IX, 398.   [2] Conard XXIII, 56.
[3] This argues for no great attentiveness on Balzac's part when reading Lamartine, who was by no means averse from such periphrases.

France in a chapter entitled *De la Médiocratie*. In describing the 'invisible coalition' with which Montcornet has to contend, a close-knit texture of private interests, aspirations and jealousies, inter-family alliances and conspiracies, intrigues for legal and administrative posts, and political machinations, Balzac rails at this phenomenon which is a sort of nepotism—'le despotique cousinage bourgeois'. It paralyses the administrative machine and stultifies the rule of justice and integrity throughout the provinces of France. *Pierrette* had already provided a striking example of this hegemony of the mediocre.

Naturally he repeats his conviction that this state of things arises from the establishment of the representative system. He was never to tire of criticizing a regime in which, despite the restricted franchise, the counting of heads replaces the assessment of ability, which creates an electorate devoted to private and local interests and fills the Chamber of Deputies with time-servers. A writer in whom the creative instinct was less powerful, using the novel for the propagation of such ideas, would prove unconscionably dull. But Balzac is never dull, not so much because he holds his convictions so strongly as because they are founded in and fused with the luminous vision, which he communicates to his readers, of the people and groups of people who are living illustrations of the tendencies he discusses. *Les Paysans*, even though never completed by Balzac himself, is indeed a gripping novel. One is left wondering what rich development he would have given to the scenes of the second half to balance those of the first. The vexations which the composition of this work caused him, and the agony of neuralgia which beset him as he wrote the extant parts, made him regret that he had ever undertaken such a task.

From the ideas set forth in the chapter *De la Médiocratie* it is easy for us to pass on to *Le Député d'Arcis* as a satire whose main theme was to be the jobbery and knaveries emanating from the electioneering system of his day.

ii. *Le Député d'Arcis* (1847–55)

In these later years Balzac grows more and more conscious of the homogeneity of his work. By its setting and by the reappearance

of many families and characters, *Le Député d'Arcis* is closely connected with *Une ténébreuse Affaire*, and a background theme is
the long-standing enmity, now attenuated by common political
interests, between Laurence, Marquise de Cinq-Cygne, and
Malin de Gondreville. It has a link with *Pierrette, Les petits
Bourgeois* and *Le cousin Pons* through the person of Olivier Vinet,
son of the barrister of Provins.[1] At one time Balzac had thought of
it as a counterpart to *Un grand Homme de province à Paris*. Both
this work and *Le Député d'Arcis* are concerned with 'cette
hideuse bourgeoisie qui mène les affaires', but the latter was to
be more interesting than the former, 'car la cuisine de la Chambre
des Députés est moins connue que celle de la littérature; elle
touche à plus de sympathies. Faire le portrait du *bourgeois-homme-
politique*!'[2]

His correspondence from August 1842 to March 1843 is full of
references to this work, which he announced under several different titles. Then it had to give place to other commitments, and at
last, in April–May 1847, he published all he had written of it in
L'Union monarchique, under the title *L'Élection*. It remained for
Charles Rabou to write a continuation of it in *Le Constitutionnel*
in 1853, and to publish it in three parts and thirteen volumes in
1854–5.[3] The worthlessness of Rabou's continuation is now
generally recognized.

Balzac chose as a centre for his electioneering scenes a little
town of Champagne, the birthplace of Danton, Arcis-sur-Aube,
which in fact, as he pointed out, was not the centre of a consti-
tuency. He had visited it in the summer of 1842 in order to
gather local colour. He chose for the time of his action the eve of
the 1839 election, when the ministry of Molé, through whom
Louis-Philippe was reaching forward to the complete exercise of
personal power, was threatened by a coalition of opposition parties, and when discord between France and England over the
Eastern question was nearing its climax. At Arcis, according to
Balzac's fiction, the banker-politician Keller, supported by his
father-in-law Malin de Gondreville, has for twenty years been

[1] See above, 177 ff. and 372.   [2] E II, 93; 21 Dec. 1842.
[3] De Potter. Mme Houssiaux included Part I of the work in her edition of the
'Comédie Humaine' in 1865 (t. XII). The *Éd. Déf.* published Balzac's original
work and Rabou's continuation.

returned unopposed. In 1839 he wishes his son Charles to take his place as ministerial candidate. But a faction of liberals with a Bonapartist colouring, tired of belonging to what we may well call a 'rotten borough', plans to put forward an independent candidate, the barrister Simon Giguet, in order to restore free initiative to the electors. The novel as written by Balzac only goes far enough to show the notables of Arcis forming their groups and taking up their positions. For this purpose Balzac gives a satirical account of a preliminary meeting organized by Mme Marion, Giguet's aunt, a defaulter from the Gondreville faction. This meeting is 'la réunion préparatoire de la réunion préparatoire', as one of the persons present ironically defines it.

A wily notary, Achille Pigoult, acting for the Gondreville faction, succeeds in weakening the claims of the dull and pompous Giguet. But the death of Charles Keller changes the situation. Another stake in the game, besides the criss-cross of factional motives, is the hand in marriage of the richly dowered Cécile, acknowledged by the mayor of Arcis, Philéas Beauvisage,[1] as his daughter, though her real father is the Vicomte de Chargebœuf. The novel breaks off just as a mysterious stranger, none other than Maxime de Trailles, turns up at Arcis with a mandate from the minister, Rastignac. He is to manage the elections in favour of a ministerial candidate, and his arrival puts the local inn and indeed the whole town into a flutter of conjecture amusingly described.

This last-minute reappearance of one of Balzac's most resilient high-society adventurers arouses a piquant interest and the regret that the novel was to peter out in its initial stages. Like Bianchon and de Marsay, de Trailles is one of those characters in the 'Comédie Humaine' who give the impression that one knows them familiarly, although they have never figured as chief characters in a novel. Here he was evidently destined to do so. A conversation in the Marquise d'Espard's salon, which results in the hatching of the political plot centred in Arcis, enables Balzac to gather threads together and give something like a coherent picture of de Trailles' personality and career. We know him so far as the parasite of *Gobseck* and *Le père Goriot*, who has wrecked the

[1] See above, 387.

happiness of the Restaud family but is a poor match for the formidable Gobseck. We have seen him, in *Un Homme d'affaires*, out-witted over a debt he is reluctant to pay, but losing none of his aplomb and *savoir vivre*. In the preface to *Pierrette* Balzac had facetiously apologized for creating such an unprincipled person and promised to marry him off and make a respectable man of him—respectable that is according to the moral standards of the times. The last part of *Béatrix* had again predicted this transformation. And now, in *Le Député d'Arcis*, we are vouchsafed a complete view of his career from the time when he was Napoleon's page-boy until the moment when, after the untimely death of his protector de Marsay, who had used him as a pliable instrument for unavowable political missions, he has reached such a low level of fortune that du Tillet wonders why he does not blow his brains out.

This still athletic dandy of forty-eight, with his dyed hair and his glazed gambler's stare, in whose physiognomy the ravages of vice contend with the determination to preserve the advantages of apparent youth, seems to excite more admiration than reprobation in Balzac. But whether we can share it or not, Maxime de Trailles stands as a good illustration of Balzac's ingenuity in maintaining the illusion of continuous reality by this to and fro movement of his characters. Putting aside Rabou's spurious continuation of the novel, we may conjecture that, armed with ministerial protection and the support of such varied persons as the Princesse de Cadignan, the Marquise de Cinq-Cygne and Malin de Gondreville, he was intended eventually to succeed in promoting his candidate and also—the concluding part of *Béatrix* foreshadows this[1]—in winning Cécile Beauvisage and her fortune as a prelude to rehabilitation and a diplomatic career.

Balzac proposed to make a four-volume novel of *Le Député d'Arcis* and to put a hundred characters into the action. He confessed in 1843 that he found the task long and difficult. 'Ce n'est pas une bagatelle que de faire un livre intéressant avec les élections.' But the fragment has brilliant features, and is interesting to compare with Stendhal's account of managed elections in the posthumously published *Lucien Leuwen* of 1834–5. One of

[1] See above, 335.

these features is the scene of the unofficial election meeting, in which Balzac parodies the pompous absurdities of political speechmaking, and lets off another squib against 'Progress' as a meaningless slogan.

. . . Se dire un homme de progrès, c'était se proclamer philosophe en toute chose et puritain en politique. On se déclarait ainsi pour les chemins de fer, les mackintosh, les pénitenciers, le pavage en bois, l'indépendance des nègres, les caisses d'épargne, les souliers sans couture, l'éclairage du gaz, les trottoirs en asphalte, le vote universel, la réduction de la Liste Civile. Enfin, c'était se prononcer contre le colosse du Nord, la perfide Albion, contre toutes les entreprises bonnes ou mauvaises du gouvernement. Comme on le voit, le mot *progrès* peut aussi bien signifier: Non! que Oui! . . .

With Mme Marion's salon as the social hub of the Arcis universe, *Le Député d'Arcis* promised some lively sketches and some more amusing scenes. One figure, that of the manufacturer of bonnets and stockings, Philéas Beauvisage, roped in initially as a supporter of Giguet, is especially interesting. This perfect type of provincial bourgeois, this model of inanity, with his fixed smile and strings of clichés punctuated by imbecile cackles, this man who was completely devoid of ideas outside his business was destined in due course, if we are to judge by references in *La cousine Bette*,[1] to occupy the Parliamentary seat of Arcis, for we find him at Paris in 1841 in the capacity of deputy. So that out of the humbug and intrigue, the pretence and altruistic speeches of electoral proceedings, a nonentity, a ministerial 'yes-man' was to emerge triumphant. One of the original titles of the work, *Un Ambitieux malgré lui*, seems to bear out this conjecture.[2]

Beauvisage is also useful for the glance we get through him at one aspect of the textile industry, as it was in the France of Balzac's day. Beauvisage had made his fortune by cornering supplies of cotton and the bonnets made from them during the *débacle* of 1814. The Industrial Revolution was yet to get under

[1] Conard XVII, 350.
[2] Rabou gives Cécile Beauvisage to Maxime de Trailles in 1841, but the Parliamentary seat to a newly invented person, Sallenauve. Then in 1841 he makes Sallenauve resign, and Philéas Beauvisage is elected in his place. Finally Giguet is elected in 1845.

way in France, and it did so very slowly. Troyes and the neighbouring countryside was the centre of the bonnet-making industry. Workmen plied their looms at home, and the so-called
'fabricants' furnished the material, collected the finished products
and served as middlemen by selling them to the wholesalers and
retailers. *Le Député d'Arcis* shows that in 1839 this was still the
case, and Beauvisage was a large-scale 'fabricant'. It is not surprising that, at so early a date, Balzac did not foresee to what
extent the invention of power-looms was to make the domestic
system obsolete. In fact his concern is with the increase of cost
involved in the operations of the middleman. He scolds the
philanthropists for not turning their attention to such matters,
and for preferring to obtain cheap glory as champions of negro
emancipation and prison reform. It was for Zola to reveal the
ravages brought about by the development of the heavy industries
in France.

iii. *L'Envers de l'histoire contemporaine* (1842–8)

This work as known today consists of two parts: *Madame de La
Chanterie* and *L'Initié*. The first part was produced piecemeal between 1842 and 1844.[1] The second part, much of which Balzac
conceived and wrote at Wierzchownia in 1847, did not appear
until the late summer of 1848.[2] The complete work was not put
together until 1855.[3] The fact that it was one of those novels for
which Balzac vainly hoped to win the Prix Montyon helps to
explain why he took pains to finish it while leaving such works as
Les petits Bourgeois, *Le Député d'Arcis* and *Les Paysans* incom-
plete.

Balzac had some justification for this hope. As an antidote to
ideological 'beneficence' and 'philanthropy' which he so often

[1] *Les Méchancetés d'un saint* (twelve chapters, in *Le Musée des familles*, Sept.
1842); *Madame de La Chanterie* (thirteen initial chapters of the later work, ibid.,
Sept. 1843); *Madame de La Chanterie*, 'suite et fin', ibid., Oct.–Nov. 1844. The
whole of the first 'episode' was co-ordinated and published in the 'Comédie
Humaine' (*S. vie politique*, t. XII) with its final title, in 1846. The same year
Roux and Cassenet published it as *La Femme de soixante ans* (3 vols.).
[2] In *Le Spectateur républicain*, Aug.–Sept. 1848.
[3] In t. XVIII of Mme Houssiaux' supplementary publication. See above,
269, n. i.

castigated and which, according to him, was divided 'en plusieurs branches exploitées par des filous de probité comme autant de commerces',[1] *L'Envers de l'histoire contemporaine* offers the organized application of Christian charity to the problems of the needy and the sick, whether respectable or reprobate. This final 'Scene of Political Life'[2] is to some extent a sequel to *Les Chouans*. Balzac was hoping to write one novel, *Les Vendéens*, as a prelude to the latter, and another, entitled *Mademoiselle du Vissard*, as a sequel to it.[3] In *L'Envers*, a certain number of characters, connected with *Les Chouans*, *Mademoiselle du Vissard* and *Une ténébreuse Affaire*, having passed through tribulation in Revolutionary and Imperial times, have come to realize that self-abnegation is the only valid rule of life, and have banded together to form a religious welfare association whose aims and ideals are the very opposite of the other secret societies imagined by Balzac, the 'Thirteen' and the 'Chevaliers de la Désœuvrance'. They call themselves 'Les Frères de la Consolation'.

One of them is Nicolas de Montauran, younger brother of Alphonse de Montauran, 'le Gars'. Their founder and leader is an exceptionally saintly woman, Mme de La Chanterie, whose life has been marked with tragic suffering. She had seen her daughter Henriette, married in 1807 to the infamous Baron Bryond des Tours-Minières, later known as Contenson,[4] become the mistress and accomplice of Rifoël, Chevalier du Vissard—a Royalist *condottiere* whom Balzac substituted for the historical Cottereau in the 1845 edition of *Les Chouans*. At one moment Balzac evidently thought of identifying her with the 'Mme du Gua-Saint-Cyr' of *Les Chouans*, but was thwarted by chronological difficulties.[5] Henriette and Du Vissard had been brought to trial and guillotined in 1809 for participation in a Royalist highway robbery,[6] and Mme de La Chanterie, though probably innocent, had been

[1] Among these 'filous' he no doubt counted Edme Champion, 'l'homme au petit manteau bleu', who distributed alms, food and clothing. See Bertault (2), 282 and n. 1.
[2] The Catalogue of 1845 (see below, 421–2) shows that Balzac's later intention was to put it among the 'Scenes of Parisian Life'.
[3] See the fragments edited in Castex (2).
[4] See above, 360.
[5] Conard XXII (*Les Chouans*), 160 and note p. 410.
[6] Founded on fact. See Lotte (4), 666, n. 62.

implicated, and was incarcerated until the fall of Napoleon. The case against her, Henriette and Du Vissard, had been prepared and mercilessly pursued by a Napoleonic magistrate renowned for his severity, the Baron de Bourlac.

Such are the preliminaries to the story, whose awkwardness of construction bears witness to its spasmodic composition. The story itself amounts to this: a young Parisian named Godefroid, weak in character, disillusioned and aimless in life, comes into contact with Mme de La Chanterie and her associates, finds increasing comfort and fulfilment in their way of life, and is eventually admitted to the Order after discharging a certain charitable task assigned to him. It is that of bringing succour to an old man, 'Monsieur Bernard', who is living in destitution with his daughter and grandson. The daughter is afflicted with a strange and distressing neurosis diagnosed as *plica polonica*, on the nature of which Dr Fernand Lotte has given some information.[1] Godefroid secures the intervention of the only doctor who can cure the disease, a Polish Jew named Halpersohn, an interesting addition to the medical confraternity of the 'Comédie Humaine'. To complicate all this, 'Monsieur Bernard' is threatened with distraint through the rapacity of a bookseller-discounter, Barbet, whom we have met in *Un grand Homme de province à Paris*, and who is publishing a legal treatise which Bernard has written. The latter's grandson steals money in order to extricate him. Mme de La Chanterie, knowing that Bernard is none other than the Baron de Bourlac, responsible for her daughter's execution and her own twenty-year sentence, uses the funds of the Brotherhood to save the situation. On learning this Bourlac throws himself at her feet in contrition and gratitude. He is pardoned.

After digesting *Le Curé de village* and certain parts of *La cousine Bette*, the reader of *L'Envers* is not likely to feel surprised at Balzac's new incursion into the realm of piety and disciplined other-worldliness. What value has it? One critic has written in especially disparaging terms of Balzac's religion:

... il n'a pas compris ce qui fait l'essentiel du christianisme ... je reste convaincu que lui, qui était affamé de gloire et d'amour humain, n'a pas personnellement prié ... il reste donc, malgré son désir de

[1] Lotte (1). See also Korwin-Piotrowska, 444 ff.

trouver une explication unique du monde créé, inhabile à sentir Dieu et à nous le rendre présent. De même qu'il n'était pas naturellement poète, il n'était pas naturellement mystique . . . il manque une dimension, la dimension chrétienne, à l'humanité qu'il a peinte.[1]

This is a bold affirmation for one man to make about another. It is true that Balzac's lip-service does not always carry conviction. What he says about the edifying influence of the *Imitatio Christi*, the Bible of 'les Frères de la Consolation', may be a tribute to Mme Hanska, who prized the work. Yet we cannot pass over the testimony, founded on deep study and prompted by gentle and reflective charity, which the Abbé Bertault has given in favour of a genuine religious sense to be discovered in Balzac, a real belief in Divine providence, and sincere movements of prayer, supplication and resignation.[2] He writes with respect for Balzac's understanding of the selfless charity of the five members of the Brotherhood. He also points out that in this work Balzac was 'plus historien que romancier', for in describing the activities of the Brotherhood he was summing up those of various real societies, notably the Confrérie de Saint-Vincent-de-Paul, founded in 1834, and the Société d'Économie charitable, founded in 1844.[3] In *L'Envers de l'histoire contemporaine* Balzac not only writes about religious devotion: he enters into the spirit of it. That of Mme de La Chanterie, Frère Nicolas, Frère Joseph, and 'Monsieur Alain' has the ring of truth, even though Balzac does not refrain, in one brief passage, from bringing in the apprentice-angels of Swedenborg[4] in order to explain the tender sublimity of the 'mother' of the Association. We are familiar with his assertion 'J'écris à la lueur de deux Vérités éternelles: la Religion, la Monarchie.' We are familiar too with his pessimism about a humanity whose evil tendencies can only be corrected by the discipline of strong government and the restraints, the menaces even, of organized Catholicism.[5] But in *L'Envers* a new flavour of thought on Society and the State is to be detected. Through the mouth of 'Monsieur Alain' Balzac utters sentiments which reflect

[1] Houdin, 234–8. Mr Aldous Huxley, op. cit., 320–30, expresses a similar view more trenchantly and more flippantly.
[2] Bertault (2), 226–7.   [3] Ibid., 284–8.   [4] Conard XX, 343.
[5] See the *Catéchisme social*, one of his last fragments, published in 1923 by M. Guyon, reprinted in Conard, *O.D.* III, 690–709.

adversely upon, without condemning outright, the conduct of the State towards its recalcitrant members.

'La Société seule a sur ses membres le droit de répression; car celui de punition, je le lui conteste: réprimer lui suffit, et comporte d'ailleurs assez de cruautés.'[1]

'Monsieur Nicolas' carries the thought further and says, about the famous Lacenaire case of 1836,

'. . . il n'y a pas d'atroces coquins, il y a des natures malades à mettre à Charenton; mais, en dehors de ces rares exceptions médicales, nous ne voyons que des gens sans religion ou des gens qui raisonnent mal, et la mission de l'homme charitable est de redresser les âmes, de remettre dans le bon chemin les égarés. . . . Les gens de qui vous parlez, entre nos mains, seraient devenus des hommes très-distingués,[2] ils sont d'une immense énergie; mais, dès qu'ils ont commis un assassinat, il n'est plus possible de s'en occuper, la justice humaine se les approprie.'[3]

Since his plea for the hangman and the assassin in *Les Mémoires de Sanson*,[4] Balzac had not often shown himself disposed to weep over the lot of criminals. *La Comédie du diable*, of November 1830, contained a passing gibe on philanthropists like Saint-Denis, who protested against capital punishment. In 1838 Balzac had suggested, perhaps jestingly, that candidates for the scaffold should not be executed, but handed over for scientific experiment.[5] If in 1839 he had attributed the multiplication of murders to the existence of the death penalty, he still referred to it as 'le grand soutien des sociétés'.[6] In 1840 he had approved of the English way of founding penal settlements for criminals and converting them into colonists.[7] In the dedication of *Les Paysans* in 1844, he had deprecated literary sentimentalism about the matter: 'On a fait de la poésie avec des criminels, on s'est apitoyé sur les bourreaux, on a presque déifié le prolétaire!'[8] But in *L'Envers* his ideas on the subject have something of the Ballanche

---

[1] Conard XX, 280.   [2] Balzac surely has Vautrin in mind.
[3] Conard XX, 295-6.   [4] See above, 36, n. i.
[5] *Traité des excitants modernes*, Conard, *O.D.* III, 182.
[6] *Le Curé de village*, Conard XXV, 52 and 55.
[7] *Fragments*, Conard, *O.D.* III, 361.
[8] The substance of this occurred in the opening chapter of the 1838 version.

touch,[1] with this difference that whereas Ballanche proposed a kind of politico-theocratic organization for the regeneration of criminals, founded on the law of 'expiation',[2] Balzac seems to intend no more than the handing over of such a task to the enterprise of pious people. The activities of these, embodying the principal of impartial succour to all who need it, constitutes what Balzac means by the 'reverse side of contemporary history'. We may reasonably conclude from this that, at the same time as he was seeking to expose, in *Le Député d'Arcis*, the hollowness of political principles and the selfishness behind political activity, in despair perhaps over the light which might be cast by one of his 'Vérités éternelles', Monarchy, he was pinning his faith more and more on the other verity, Religion, as a torch to illumine the human race.

---

[1] Ballanche, op. cit. [2] See Hunt (2), 92–3.

XIX

OTHER WORKS AND PROJECTS

i. *Petites Misères de la vie conjugale* (1830–46)

BALZAC WAS NEVER EXPLICIT about the function the 'Études analytiques' were to perform in his great scheme. We may remember that in October 1834 he had referred to the search for 'principles'—opposed to 'effects' in the 'Études de Mœurs' and to 'causes' in the 'Études philosophiques'—as being their ultimate purpose.[1] The analogy he had drawn from the theatre—'Les *mœurs* sont le spectacle, les *causes* sont les *coulisses et les machines*. Les *principes*, c'est l'*auteur*'—sheds no light on the nature of these principles. Félix Davin, in *L'Introduction aux 'Études philosophiques'*,[2] had been no more specific, although he had referred to the 'Études analytiques' as being 'l'examen *railleur* [my italics] des principes sociaux'. The *Avant-Propos* had merely mentioned *La Physiologie du mariage* as a sample. In the meantime, from 1839 to 1846, Balzac had been working spasmodically on his second and last completed 'Étude analytique'—*Petites Misères de la vie conjugale*.

Although two sketches, destined later to form chapters, had been printed as early as November 1830 in *La Caricature*, the foundations of the work were not really laid until the period September 1839–June 1840, when about one-half of Part I of the definitive work and some chapters of Part II were given to *La Caricature provisoire*.[3] Part I was virtually finished, though the chapters were to be rearranged and some of their titles altered, in *Philosophie de la vie conjugale: Chaussée d'Antin*,[4] published in

---

[1] See above, 126.   [2] Lovenjoul (1), 206.
[3] A non-political revival of the former periodical.
[4] The Chaussée d'Antin was the business and banking centre in Paris. The indication is therefore that Balzac was confining his attention to the class occupied with such activities.

August 1844.[1] Nearly all of the remaining material, that is to say most of the definitive Part II, appeared in *La Presse* in the last month of 1845. In the meantime Chlendowski was publishing the reconstituted work—Part I towards the end of 1845 and, in 1846, Part II, which of course included the contributions to *La Presse*. Although several editions, partial or complete, were produced in 1846, the work was not incorporated in the 'Comédie Humaine' until 1855.[2]

A remark made near the end of *Petites Misères*—'cette œuvre . . . est à la PHYSIOLOGIE DU MARIAGE ce que l'Histoire est à la Philosophie, ce qu'est le Fait à la Théorie'—squares ill with the idea that the 'Études analytiques' were to be concerned with principles. But it takes the work back into the right context, and shows that we are indeed dealing with the author, not only of *La Physiologie du mariage*, but also of the *Contes drolatiques*, where serious thought is often disguised in banter, light wit and humour, and jovial libertinism. There is much wisdom in this more Rabelaisian Balzac, who crops up quite frequently throughout the 'Comédie Humaine', and who is freed in those less responsible writings from the sentimentality, the heightened sense of drama and the pressing didacticism which are so frequently found in the novels.

With a wealth of scenes, anecdotes, 'axioms' and sardonic apophthegms, Balzac here evokes the 'minor vexations' with which the wedded life of Adolphe and Caroline de Chodoreille is beset. First there are those which puncture the dignity and self-esteem of the husband: all those pinpricks of feminine petulance, vanity, illogicality, possessiveness and jealousy that pierce the chinks in his armour of self-complacency. The second part constitutes 'le côté femelle du livre', and sets in sharp relief all the manifestations of obtuse self-centredness, unconscious cruelty and episodic disloyalty which can by degrees bring a wife to the point of condoning her husband's infidelities—clandestine meetings passed off as business appointments[3]—in return for a similar toler-

---

[1] In vol. I of a miscellany by various authors: *Le Diable à Paris* (1844–6). On the question of the exact date of this publication, see Lovenjoul (1), 214, and Conard XXXIII, 210, n. 3.

[2] See above, 269, n. i.

[3] 'L'affaire Chaumontel' serves as Adolphe's normal alibi.

ance on his part. Our bachelor author, now well on in his forties and still straining every nerve to achieve the matrimonial status at which he so freely mocks, is even more diabolically perspicacious than the bachelor of thirty had been about the intricacies of married life. His experience has increased. Some of it is direct, for he lived with Mme de Brugnol on a quasi-matrimonial footing for some years. But it is mostly indirect. One can imagine with what curiosity he scrutinized his fellow-creatures in the street, the drawing-room, the homes of friends and relations, and even in public vehicles. The picture he gives in *Petites Misères* of Adolphe de Chodoreille gleaning information in a 'coucou' reminds us of what he had told us in *Facino Cane* about his own faculty for observation:[1]

'Rien ne m'amuse plus que de soutirer à chacun, à l'aide de ce foret nommé l'interrogation, et de recevoir au moyen d'un air attentif et jubilant la somme d'instruction, d'anecdotes, de savoir, dont tout le monde désire se débarrasser; et chacun a la sienne, le paysan comme le banquier, le caporal comme le maréchal de France.

'J'ai remarqué combien ces tonneaux pleins d'esprit sont disposés à se vider quand ils sont charriés par des diligences ou des coucous, par tous les véhicules que traînent les chevaux, car personne ne cause en chemin de fer.'[2]

In spite of the frivolous tone of the whole, it is an eternal tragedy which Balzac unfolds, one of progressive disillusionment and estrangement in the hearts of a married couple, no less pathetic because its dénouement, the establishment of a *modus vivendi*, is described with a sort of cynical approbation. In thus reverting to a form of literary exercise calculated, on the face of it, to give most diversion to a male reader, Balzac shows himself as ready as ever to break a lance in favour of the sex with which he has been so popular. We close the book with the impression that the vexations a wife has to endure strike deeper than those she inflicts on her partner.

La femme vit par le sentiment, là où l'homme vit par l'action. Or, le sentiment peut à tout moment faire d'une petite misère soit un grand

[1] See above, 13, and *Biography*, 7–8.
[2] Conard XXXIII, 153. The passage is also reminiscent of the 'voyage en coucou' in *Un Début dans la vie*.

malheur, soit une vie brisée, soit une véritable infortune. . . .[1] Dans un mari, il n'y a qu'un homme; dans une femme mariée il y a un homme, un père, une mère et une femme. Une femme mariée a de la sensibilité pour quatre.[2]

So, while the husband's 'petites misères' are invariably a matter for mockery, those of the wife sometimes evoke sympathy. Nothing serves better to illustrate this fact than those chapters in Part II[3] which tell how a mortified Caroline, once a simpleton, now grown wise through suffering, uses an innocent, orthodox but effective stratagem to punish Adolphe for the hypocritical excuse—'mais c'est purement moral'—which he offers for a passing infatuation. These two chapters belong to December 1839. In the second part of the previous chapter,[4] first published near the end of January 1840, Balzac dwells on the self-denial and self-abasement a wife may have to accept in order not to handicap her husband in his career. It is in this connection that Balzac evidently remembers the case of Lucien de Rubempré coming up to Paris to make a name for himself. Adolphe de Chodoreille who, in Part I, and later again in Part II, appears to be some sort of businessman, who moreover has been introduced to us as being, like his wife, a Parisian born and bred, is temporarily metamorphosed into a struggling writer, an immigrant from the provinces. In the first part of this same chapter, added in 1844, he is even written down as a literary failure; and Balzac is inspired to repeat his oft-expressed conviction that hard work and seclusion are the only means of bringing budding talent to fruition.

This digression from the main theme, and this inconsistency about Adolphe's profession, may serve as a warning to those who, like Dr Lotte in his *Dictionnaire biographique*, are inclined to treat *Petites Misères* as a novel and admit those who appear in it to the fellowship of Balzacian characters. Granted that a few people within the Chodoreilles' social orbit—the Fischtaminel couple for example, the much-married 'dévote' Mme Deschars, and perhaps also the Foullepointe couple and the 'cousin Ferdinand' who becomes Caroline's accepted lover under the terms of

[1] Conard XXXIII, 147.   [2] Ibid., 175.
[3] *Souffrances ingénues* and *L'Amadis-Omnibus* (xviii, xxiv).
[4] *Les Ambitions trompées.*

the final *modus vivendi*—almost acquire individual personality.[1]
Granted also that the mention here and there of such persons as
Horace Bianchon, Léon de Lora, Mme Schontz and du Tillet
suggest that Balzac might eventually have drawn the figures of
Petites Misères into his confraternity. He might have equated
'Cousin Ferdinand' with the Ferdinand de Bourgarel, politician,
art critic and *viveur* who, it is hinted, paid court to Caroline in her
early married life.[2] But it is clear that the Chodoreilles and their
acquaintances scarcely get beyond the stage of serving as coat-
hangers. Not only does Adolphe change from a businessman to a
man of letters and back again. As the director of a periodical he
appears to be split into two individuals at that point of this desultory narrative where, disparaging a *nouvelle* which he does not
know has been written by his own wife, he refers to the editor of
the journal in which it has been printed as 'M. Chodoreille'. In
Partie Remise (chapter xxviii) Caroline surprisingly figures as a
'dévote'; and the last of Adolphe's infidelities,[3] from which Dr
Lotte has extracted material for his 'life' of Adolphe, is patently
hypothetical.

None the less we must recognize *Petites Misères* as a storehouse
of 'scenes' and embryonic *nouvelles* possessing the real Balzacian
stamp. Among them we may quote *Les Taquinages* (v), the
account of a family outing in a barouche, during which Adolphe
has to face a cross-fire of reproaches from his wife, mother-in-law
and child; *L'Amadis-Omnibus* (xxiv), which shows Caroline exploiting the fatuity of an elderly beau, the Vicomte de Lustrac,
in order to bring her husband to heel; and *Partie Remise* (xxviii),
which draws pathos as well as humour from the picture of a pious
but love-starved wife awaiting her husband's return after a long
separation.

Petites Misères is also a 'keepsake' of incisive home-truths and
bons mots:

Rien ne vous inquiète comme d'être protégé par votre belle-mère.
Elle est hypocrite, elle est enchantée de vous voir aux prises avec sa

---

[1] The coquettish Mme de Fischtaminel had obtained a passing mention in
La Physiologie du mariage. An authoress named Mme Fischtaminel (of Lausanne)
is also referred to in *Monographie de la presse parisienne* (1842–3).
[2] Conard XXXIII, 124.   [3] Ibid., 182–3.

fille; elle jette, tout doucement et avec des précautions infinies, de l'huile sur le feu.[1]

. . . Tout ménage a sa cour de cassation qui ne s'occupe jamais du fond et ne juge que la forme.[2]

. . . Quand on donne à une femme des raisons au lieu de lui donner ce qu'elle veut, peu d'hommes ont osé descendre au fond de ce petit gouffre appelé le cœur, pour y mesurer la force de la tempête qui s'y fait subitement.[3]

. . . 'Elle me dit quelquefois [says Adolphe, boasting of the late-found harmony which reigns in his household]: "Je suis grognon, laisse-moi, va t'en." L'orage tombe sur mon cousin' [Ferdinand, the 'minotaure'].[4]

Balzac has the knack of completing droll descriptions with an un-expected simile. Caroline, having retired to bed in dudgeon after a disappointing ball,

se range dans son coin de la façon la plus déplaisante et la plus hostile; elle est enveloppée dans sa chemise, dans sa camisole, dans son bonnet de nuit, comme un ballot d'horlogerie qui part pour les Grandes-Indes.[5]

A blasé husband takes his wife to town:

Vous regardez, à droite et à gauche, les curiosités sur les boulevards, en gardant votre femme d'un bras lâche et distrait, comme si vous étiez le remorqueur d'un gros bateau normand.[6]

His manipulation of antitheses can be very effective, as in the following instance, where the second term is sufficiently delayed, yet so similar to the first in its verbal components, that the opposition seems to be strengthened by the very means which might have been expected to attenuate it:

Pendant leur jeunesse, les femmes veulent être traitées en divinités, elles adorent l'idéal: elles ne supportent pas l'idée d'être ce que la nature veut qu'elles soient.

Two short paragraphs follow, and then:

Dans leur dernière jeunesse, les femmes veulent être traitées en mortelles, elles aiment le positif: elles ne supportent pas l'idée de ne plus être ce que la nature a voulu qu'elles fussent.[7]

---

[1] Conard XXXIII, 27. Balzac proposed in 1845 to write a novel *Gendres et Belles-Mères* to be added to the *S. vie privée.*   [2] Ibid., 40.   [3] Ibid., 187.
[4] Ibid., 204. For 'minotaure' see above, 21.   [5] Ibid., 34.   [6] Ibid., 48.
[7] Ibid., 148–9.

The concluding dialogue in *Petites Misères* gives a cachet of dry wit and irony to the whole. It is a semi-dramatic fantasia in which the various protagonists make their last bow and pay their several tributes to the ideal arrangement—the *ménage à quatre*—into which the once incompatible partnership of Adolphe and Caroline has resolved itself.

ii. The *Catalogue* of 1845

Balzac had more 'Analytical Studies' in view, just as he also intended to swell out his other categories. In 1845, though the first edition of the 'Comédie Humaine' was still far from complete, he drew up a Catalogue[1] of actual and projected works in twenty-six volumes. To the ninety-seven novels, short stories and other 'studies' already produced, or which were destined to be produced by 1848, were added the titles of fifty-one new ones,[2] some of which had been conceived or sketched out, but most of which were never even to take provisional shape. Besides these, he had among his papers about fifty plans or rough drafts.[3]

Sooner or later, no doubt, someone will write a thesis on Balzac's programme of future work. For us it must suffice to note various interesting features in the Catalogue. The Scenes of Private Life were to include novels about school and convent education. The career of an actress was to furnish another Scene of Provincial Life. The hospital, the theatre, the law-courts were to receive attention in new Parisian Scenes; so also were the rivalries between scientists. To the Scenes of Military Life, for which he had never found time to make the necessary researches, were to be added twenty-three novels. The Philosophical Studies contain several interesting new titles, as well as *Les Martyrs ignorés*,

---

[1] Given in Lovenjoul (1), 217–20, in Conard I and the Pléiade edition, and in Lotte (4), xxvii–xxix. It was slightly modified in the prospectus for a new edition which Balzac drew up in 1846.

[2] All these figures are approximate. They are computed from Lovenjoul's *Catalogue*; Lotte numbers them differently. The computation depends on various factors—are we to count as separate items the novels in the different cycles (*Illusions perdues*, *Splendeurs et misères*, *Sous Vienne*, etc.) or to treat each one as one novel? Also Balzac counts in *Les Employés* twice, and forgets other works.

[3] See Bardèche (3), Introduction.

fragment du Phédon d'aujourd'hui, which had begun as *Ecce Homo* in the *Chronique de Paris* (9 June 1836), had appeared in the 'Études philosophiques' of 1837, but had been omitted from the Furne 'Comédie Humaine'. It is tantalizing to wonder what he might have made of one of his proposed new philosophical studies, *Le Philanthrope*: would his hero have been a compound of Benjamin Appert, Montyon and Edme Champion? As for the proposed new 'Analytical Studies'—*Anatomie des Corps enseignants, Pathologie de la vie sociale*,[1] *Monographie de la vertu*,[2] *Dialogue philosophique et politique sur les perfections du dix-neuvième siècle*—there is a strong presumption that in many of these, as in the extant 'Analytical Studies', Balzac would have persevered in what Montesquieu considered to be the true tradition of the French mind:

Qu'on donne un esprit de pédanterie à une nation naturellement gaie, l'État n'y gagnera rien, ni pour le dedans, ni pour le dehors. Laissez-lui faire les choses frivoles sérieusement, et gaiement les choses sérieuses.[3]

At any rate the guiding principle in the new 'Analytical Studies' would have been the same as in the others: *faire . . . gaiement les choses sérieuses*.

iii. Theatrical works: *Vautrin* and *Les Ressources de Quinola*

'Je suis loin de vouloir décourager Monsieur votre fils, mais je pense qu'il pourrait mieux employer son temps qu'à composer des tragédies ou des comédies.'

Since Andrieux, the Collège de France professor, had written these lines in 1820 to Mme Balzac,[4] her son had certainly devoted his time to better purposes. But he never gave up his ambition

[1] See Guyon (1), 432. The idea for this work was adumbrated in *Traité de la vie élégante* (1830), and M. Guyon makes much of the elements to be found dispersed in various novels of the 'Comédie Humaine'.

[2] Lovenjoul (1), 184–5, gives two epigraphs for *L'Élixir de longue vie*, published in the *Revue de Paris*, 24 Oct. 1830, which are alleged to be taken from '*Monographie de la vertu*, ouvrage inédit de l'auteur'. Apparently Balzac negotiated for the sale of this non-existent book with two different editors round about 1831.   [3] *Esprit des Lois*, XIX, v.   [4] See *Biography*, 7.

for the theatre. The two volumes of M. Milatchitch[1] afford ample proof of this. It is not too much to say that, in 1848, he was perceptibly turning away from the novel in favour of the theatre, though mainly for mercenary reasons. Needless to say, neither his finished plays nor his many scenarios and dramatic fragments, interesting as they are, have any place in the 'Comédie Humaine'. Nor for that matter have the *Contes drolatiques*, though as good tales they lie so close to it that it would have been absurd to ignore them. Similarly, although it is unnecessary to tell the story of Balzac's efforts to win fame in the theatre,[2] the finished plays themselves suggest some relevant points of comparison and contrast with the novels of the 'Comédie Humaine', and therefore merit consideration.

Balzac rarely tried his hand at verse drama after his disappointment over *Cromwell*. He never again attempted to write pure tragedy after the classical model. Nor was he minded to vie with Victor Hugo, whose plays he scorned, or to further the cause of Romantic drama in general. He had many plans for pure comedies. Molière and Beaumarchais were beacon lights at which he would fain have lit his own torch. At the same time, since the business of writing plays was unfortunately so linked up with the need to make money, he was drawn to that lighter, more ephemeral kind of comedy which appealed to his contemporaries as it does to all generations of playgoers. He was enticed by the success of the Eugène Scribes of his age, by the vogue which the actor Frédérick Lemaître gave from 1823 to 1834 to the burlesqued melodrama *L'Auberge des Adrets* and its hilarious sequel *Robert Macaire*; he was no less fertile in imagining plots for the exploitation of that figure of caricature, Joseph Prudhomme, whom Henry Monnier had bequeathed to the world.

But between comedy and pure tragedy lay an indeterminate realm which had been revealed by eighteenth-century writers— that of 'tragédie bourgeoise', 'tragédie domestique', 'drame bourgeois', etc. It was in part from the 'drame bourgeois' that the melodrama of the Revolution and Empire had sprung. Moreover,

---

[1] Milatchitch's second volume (400 pages) contains a multitude of plans and sketches from *Cromwell* onwards.

[2] For summary information, see *Biography*, 102–5, 119–22, 156–7, 183.

thanks to the social turmoil which the Revolution aroused, thanks also to the rise of socialism, there was a tendency from 1820 to 1850 to reach forward to a kind of social drama inspired by modern subjects; and this in spite of the fact that the Romantic dramatists, in the main, thought of themselves as filling the void left by Corneille, Racine and Voltaire and replacing classical by a sort of historical tragedy. The elder Dumas, fond as he was of historical subjects, catered for this more modern vogue in *Anthony*, *Teresa* and *Angèle*. Vigny's *Chatterton* too, though a play about eighteenth-century England, is clearly a modern and social drama. We should expect Balzac, as the social and moral historian of his times, to follow the same trend in his dramatic works as in his novels, to evoke aspects of social and family life, and to air the problems arising therefrom.

This is in fact what he does, except in his first two performed plays, *Vautrin*, which is simply a melodrama, and *Les Ressources de Quinola*, which is a historical comedy. But he oscillates between the various forms. The earliest written of his six acted plays, *L'École des Ménages*, is styled a 'tragédie bourgeoise'. *Paméla Giraud*, though its nature is not specified in the subtitle, is in essence a 'drame social'. *La Marâtre* is called a 'drame intime'; it is in fact a very serious play about family relationships. *Le Faiseur*, or *Mercadet*, is rightly styled a comedy. In fact, Balzac seems to have been pulled simultaneously in three different directions: towards the ever-popular melodrama, towards a sentimental and moralizing drama in keeping with certain aspects of the 'Comédie Humaine', and towards a fairly astringent and perspicacious sort of comedy of manners which accords with other aspects of the 'Comédie Humaine' but which also makes of him a continuator of the *Turcaret* tradition and enables him to point the way to such satirists of manners as the younger Dumas (*La Question d'argent*, 1857), Émile Augier (*Les Effrontés*, 1861), Henry Becque (*Les Corbeaux*, 1882) and Octave Mirbeau (*Les Affaires sont les affaires*, 1902).

The first finished play, *Vautrin*, was a failure, not only because of Frédérick Lemaître's tactlessness in guying Louis-Philippe,[1]

[1] See *Biography*, 103–5. Or was the scandalizing toupee which he disclosed in Act IV merely a property taken from *Robert Macaire*?

but because of its intrinsic absurdity. Presumably Balzac wrote it to make capital out of his striking invention, the master criminal. But Vautrin in the 'Comédie Humaine' has some philosophical and symbolic justification as a rebel against society. Here he has no such significance. Though still a social outcast, he falls back into the role of the righter of wrongs, the mysterious *justicier* who had for so long been a stock figure in the novels of terror. But he keeps his weakness for attractive young men, and his task in the play is to see that Raoul de Frescas, deprived of his heritage by the suspicions of a jealous father, shall recover it, satisfy the longings of a mother whose instinct tells her that he is her son, and marry the girl he loves. And so our diabolic gangster, peerless in the arts of machination and disguise, is also presented to us in the part of a kindly nanny who has brought up the hero from boyhood, educated him in the narrow way of moral rectitude and gentlemanly deportment, and who finally hands him over to his mother with the gesture of one who has discharged a sacred trust. Other characters—Vautrin's ineffectual foil 'le Chevalier de Saint-Charles', the exemplary hero and heroine, the yearning mother, the stern father and the odious half-brother—are in keeping with the spirit of the play. Balzac himself vetoed an attempt made in 1848 to revive it.

Les Ressources de Quinola aroused almost as much turmoil among the audience of the Odéon Theatre in 1842 as *Hernani* had done at the Théâtre-Français in 1830. It ran for nineteen performances, and, when revived in 1863, for forty-three. It is a romantic comedy built upon the freer Spanish or English models; there are five well-filled acts preceded by a vivacious prologue. For most of its comic effect it depends on the attempt to endow a new stage serving-man with the mental and verbal agility which belong to Beaumarchais' Figaro. But the adventurer Quinola is concerned with a more serious problem than that of furthering a nobleman's amorous or thwarting his libidinous designs. He is at once the factotum and protector of Alfonso Fontanarès, whom Balzac credits with having invented, in the latter half of the sixteenth century, a system of steam-propulsion for ships, and who obtains the consent of Philip II to adapt it to a warship at Barcelona. We are thus brought back to a favourite theme of Balzac:

'les souffrances de l'inventeur'. Like all creative spirits, Fontanarès has to fight obscurantism, suspicion, derision, envy, and prosecution for debts. He thus carries much of Balzac's own bitter experience—lightened, like that of Balzac, by love and the hope of marriage, but also darkened by the intrigues of a passionate courtesan, Faustine Brancadori, who wants Fontanarès for herself and impedes him in the building of his machine until she has driven her rival, the faithful Maria Lothundiaz, out of his life. Against her stratagems those of Quinola, bold and varied as they are, are of no avail. In the end, thanks to the hostility of the local authorities, Fontanarès is even forced to cede the glory of his invention to a pseudo-scientist. He takes his revenge by sinking the warship and destroying the invention.

In spite of its anachronisms, the play is an interesting one to read. It has many good scenes, some stirring situations, and some liveliness of dialogue. The effort to make a Figaro of Quinola is too plainly visible; none the less his vivacity might have saved the play. The dead weight is in Fontanarès the *beau ténébreux*, his martyred Marie, and the too black-and-white courtesan, now diabolically ruthless, now—once she has gained her ends—passionately submissive. There is colour and vigour, but this compound of farce and melodrama is too strained; and through it all goes the refrain of Balzac's railings against his century. 'O monde des intérêts, de la ruse, de la politique et des perfidies, à nous deux maintenant!' exclaims Fontanarès-Rastignac as he shakes the dust of Spain off his feet and sets out for France, taking with him his invention, the loyal Quinola, and the now servile mistress whose machinations have turned his heart to bronze.

iv. Theatrical works: from *L'École des Ménages* to *Le Faiseur*

M. Milatchitch discerns tragic grandeur, and something of the 'âpre génie et l'observateur pénétrant de la "Comédie Humaine"' in *L'École des Ménages*. Its composition is anterior to both *Vautrin* and *Quinola*, but as a 'tragédie bourgeoise' it heralds the later plays. It had been long in coming to fruition, and though it obtained a trial reading at the Renaissance Theatre in February

1839 and was much admired at readings in two fashionable salons of the time, it was not put on any stage until 1910—at the Odéon, where it lasted for seven performances.

M. Milatchitch's enthusiasm for the play is not easily shared. If in the early nineteen-hundreds it was hailed as an early example of 'naturalism' in the theatre, this was because of the potentialities of the subject rather than the mastery with which it is treated. Its theme is the threatened break-up of a family through the overwhelming passion of an elderly husband and father, Gérard, a large shopkeeper, who has fallen in love with a girl half his age, his chief saleswoman, Adrienne Guérin. Balzac no doubt wished to make of Gérard a figure as intense as Goriot, Claës or Hulot, without throwing him into so extravagant a predicament as Nucingen the lover of Esther van Gobseck. After a lifetime given to money-making comes the poignant awareness of approaching old age and then the sudden vision of youth and beauty—not, as in Nucingen's case, in a ravishing harlot, but in a young woman of candour, integrity and devotion.

'. . . toutes les délices de la vie, toutes les fleurs de l'amour, elle a tout offert à mes yeux altérés, elle a rafraîchi mon âme qui se desséchait, la vie s'est réveillée, j'ai ressenti cette soif du bonheur qui nous poursuit tous! Dans la jeunesse nous aimons avec notre force qui va diminuant; mais, à mon âge, on aime avec la faiblesse qui va croissant; aussi la vie me paraît-elle impossible sans elle.'

These are familiar data, and so is the 'axiom' about youth and age which Balzac loved to repeat, sometimes in humorous, sometimes in serious vein.[1] Gérard is born of this formula, and the drama which his case provides is that of an honourable and scrupulous man torn between concern for his wife and two daughters and exasperation at the hostility they show to the interloper. But living characters are not made out of formulas, and his reactions are too much those of a puppet pulled by different strings. The position of the women is curious. Balzac is fair to both sides. Adrienne is no intriguer, although Gérard's passion and her own efficiency have made her the virtual ruler of the household. Her love for her employer is pure, and she tries to

[1] See above, 104 and n. 3.

keep the peace between him and his family. Mme Gérard is as reasonable as a wife in her position could be expected to be. The elder daughter, Caroline, is helpless and pliable. The younger one, Anna, is resourceful and implacable: another Rosalie de Watteville, but one whose demonic activity, which brings the struggle to a tragic issue, is prompted by loyalty to her mother.

Comic relief is furnished by two persons: the vacillating cashier Roblot, who admires Adrienne but loves his account-books still more, and the pusillanimous druggist, Mme Gérard's brother, whom Anna vainly tries to stiffen in his support of her plans. Then, as the final crisis approaches, Balzac again serves up the strong meat of melodrama—the threatened suicide of Caroline to avoid an odious marriage with Adrienne's none the less admirable brother, the attempted murder of Adrienne by the determined Anna, and Gérard's desperation which culminates in an access of emotion that drives him mad. Adrienne too goes out of her mind, and the last act shows the deranged lovers, now repentantly tended by the Gérard womenfolk, cherishing the memory of the passion that had united them, but each unable to recognize the other.

'Elle!' [says the distracted Gérard to the examining judge brought in to verify the fact of lunacy] 'c'est une pauvre fille. . . . Son amant est mort.'—'Lui?' [says Adrienne] 'Un vieux fou, un homme de soixante ans qui se teint les cheveux, qui s'adonise, qui fait le jeune, qui met des bottes vernies, un ci-devant jeune homme!'

Each is doomed to await for ever the return of a non-existent lover.

This ought to be a powerful dénouement. Balzac had obtained the material for it from an anecdote of real life, told him by Metternich in 1835.[1] The difficulty lay in grafting it into a play whose subject, grave as it is, is scarcely strong enough to bear it. In the 'Comédie Humaine', as *Adieu* sufficiently proves,[2] Balzac could have made the overthrow of a violently passionate man's reason entirely convincing. Here the development of the action and the texture of the dialogue are unequal to the task of preparation which the detailed narration of antecedents and events could carry out in a novel. But what can be said for

[1] Bouteron (2), 35–6.　　　　　　　　　　　[2] See above, 32.

L'École des Ménages is that Balzac has a feeling for tremendous scenes, and that, if he has failed in his presentation of characters like Gérard, and perhaps Adrienne too, Anna is a lively, vehement specimen of adolescent femininity.

Paméla Giraud, which M. Milatchitch aptly classifies as a 'mélodrame vertueux', achieved twenty-one performances at the Théâtre de la Gaieté in 1843, and thirty-five at a posthumous revival in 1859. Its structure and the progress of the action are better than in the previous plays, perhaps because two experienced comedy writers, Bayard and Jaime, pruned it down.[1] It had stuff in it to please the socialists, and indeed a journalist of *La Démocratie pacifique* pronounced it to be 'une critique sanglante contre les mœurs de notre société, où l'intérêt étouffe tous les sentiments du cœur'. The theme of the play is precisely that: the selfishness of a prosperous middle-class family contrasted with the generosity of a poor flower-girl who sacrifices her reputation to save their son from arrest and probable execution as a Bonapartist conspirator. As soon as the danger is over, the Rousseaus and their snobbish circle contemptuously suppose that money will settle their debt to Paméla. They are thwarted by the intervention of Dupré, a high-minded barrister who has some affinity with Derville of the 'Comédie Humaine'. Paméla marries her Jules. Such is Balzac's version of 'Virtue Rewarded', in which characterization, emotion and pathos scarcely transcend the conventional. No doubt he was trying to cater for the taste of the theatre-going masses.

But he moved on to better things. His 'drame intime', *La Marâtre*, was his first real success on the stage, and justifies the opinion that, had he lived longer, it might have been to future plays what his first successful story, *Les Chouans*, was to the rest of his novels. It might have had a long run at the Théâtre Historique in 1848 but for the disorganization of theatre life caused by the February Revolution. It won even Jules Janin's approval, and had a resounding success when the Vaudeville Theatre revived it in 1859.

---

[1] Milatchitch (1), 157–61, examines this question, and has compared the original manuscript with the printed version of 1843, which the modern editions of Balzac's work reproduce.

According to Hostein, the Director of the Théâtre Historique, Balzac got the idea of it from a casual observation of the virulent hatred, hidden behind a mask of tenderness, that existed between a stepmother and stepdaughter of his acquaintance.[1] *La Marâtre* proceeds, then, from the study of an observed situation and is based on an observed psychological fact. This gives it a force and originality only diminished by the difficulty of devising a fiction to incorporate it.

It was perhaps a foregone conclusion that Balzac would hit upon the notion of giving the greatest possible intensity to such an antagonism by making stepmother and stepdaughter rivals in love: a promisingly sensational theme which has often been treated since, particularly in French drama. He was also at pains to devise so ingenious a situation that the hatred between the two women should be fed still more by the difficulties and dangers that threatened each of them. The essential data may be regarded as almost banal: a woman who has taken an elderly husband in the hope of early widowhood, so that she may bring wealth to the man she loves, whom she has actually succeeded in introducing into her husband's household. Here then are the three points of the triangle: the Général de Grandchamp, his wife Gertrude, and Ferdinand de Mercantel. To this is added the necessary complication of Pauline, Grandchamp's daughter by a previous marriage, falling in love with Ferdinand, and he with her. Balzac gives the decisive touch of complexity to the imbroglio by setting his action in the Restoration period, in order to make a powerful psychological factor of the still prevalent fanaticism for Napoleon. The General sees red even at the thought of those Napoleonic officers who deserted the Emperor in 1814. Ferdinand de Mercantel is the son of one of them, and bears an assumed name to keep the General off the scent. In the case of both women therefore, rivalry is still further exasperated by the necessity for concealment: the passionate and possessive Gertrude has to hide her guilt, and Pauline, though she is as headstrong as her father, has to keep her love secret in case the General discovers Ferdinand's real identity and is thereby incensed to the point of challenging and killing him.

[1] See Milatchitch (1), 184–5.

On this foundation Balzac builds his study of a conflict whose deadly nature he was eminently capable of bringing out in its every phase, a tooth-and-nail struggle in which no quarter is given on either side. Gertrude and Pauline hold the stage:

Pauline
Nous nous faisons, vous le savez, une guerre de sauvages?

Gertrude
Dites de femmes, c'est plus terrible! Les sauvages ne font souffrir que le corps; tandis que nous, c'est au cœur, à l'amour-propre, à l'orgueil, à l'âme que nous adressons nos flèches, nous les enfonçons en plein bonheur.

Ferdinand, around whom the contest rages, is a supernumerary. The General, for all his testy authoritarianism, is a blind and bewildered old man. An official suitor of Pauline, Godard, has some individuality as a would-be gentleman, and is used now and then to give the action a jog. Napoléon, the General's eleven-year-old son (or is he the son of Ferdinand and Gertrude?),[1] is used for the same purpose. But everything pales in comparison with the women's battle, fought out with buttoned foils when others are present, with bared steel when they are alone; a ruthless affair, whose moves and counter-moves consist of threats, ruses, blackmail and even physical violence. It culminates in the suicide of Pauline and Ferdinand, the reduction of the General (still unaware of his wife's guilt) to numb despair, and Gertrude's last-minute acceptance of survival in order to look after her husband in his uncomprehending grief. The fact that this 'demon' of a woman is capable of an unselfish impulse when she sees her step-daughter and her former paramour dying or dead serves as a measure for gauging the intensity of the passion which has possessed her hitherto.

Balzac has treated his subject with more discretion than his successors. We are left to surmise the nature of Ferdinand's relations with Gertrude during the three years he has spent at Louviers, to guess at what moment he severed them, and to wonder why it needed a nocturnal interview between Ferdinand

---

[1] This seems to be suggested in Act I, Scene viii.

and Pauline to make Gertrude realize that Ferdinand was slipping from her grasp. It seems that the virtuous Pauline is not aware of the physical implication of her lover's liaison with Gertrude. Few post-Balzacian heroines in her predicament would have doubts on that score; but in fact it appears that Balzac intended us to credit her with the chaste ingenuousness of an early nineteenth-century heroine.

This is a pity, for it weakens his plot. Had he been able to endow Pauline with the 'toughness' of the modern young woman, she would have been more of a match for Gertrude, and the conclusion might have been less pathetic, but more stark. Pauline's capitulation to Gertrude, and her choice of suicide as the only issue left to her if she is to escape marriage with Godard, depend too completely on the thought of her father's ferocity if Gertrude reveals Ferdinand's identity to him. The poignancy of her dilemma is thus tied up again with the convention of the too passive *ingénue*. As Mme de Sévigné said (with less pertinence) of Racine's *Bajazet*, 'on n'entre point dans les raisons de cette grande tuerie'. But there is Racinian quality, as well as this allegedly Racinian defect, in *La Marâtre*.

Balzac's last play, *Mercadet ou Le Faiseur*, is of a very different kind. It is more in tune with that view of life which made him choose, as the collective title of his novel-cycle, 'la Comédie' rather than 'la Tragédie Humaine'. It comes from a long-standing desire to pillory the financial and commercial dishonesty of his age in a striking and yet amusing fashion; and to reach a wide public in doing so. He had the first idea of it in 1839, worked on it in 1840, and completed the primitive version of it in 1844. In the summer of 1848 it only just missed being adopted for production by the Théâtre-Français. In 1851 Mme de Balzac agreed to the play being revised and reduced from five to three acts by the playwright Adolphe d'Ennery, and it was given seventy-three performances at the Gymnase Theatre. It was adapted for the English stage in the same year by George Henry Lewis[1] as *The Game of Speculation* and had a successful run in London with Charles Mathews in the main part. M. Milatchitch[2] compares the

---

[1] Under the pseudonym of 'Slingsby Lawrence' (published by T. H. Lacey, London, 1852).   [2] (1), 253–67.

original version with the d'Ennery revision,[1] and it is clear that although d'Ennery gave it the pruning which a play of Balzac always needed, and tightened up the action, he also spoilt some of Balzac's best ideas and either misunderstood or violated some of his intentions. *Mercadet* has had many revivals. The last one was in 1957 at the Théâtre National Populaire.

In the 'Comédie Humaine' the type of *faiseur* or *homme d'affaires*, the banker, broker or speculator of various grades is generally an objectionable figure, a Nucingen, a du Tillet or a Claparon. As company-promoter or share-pusher he embodies that urge to swift enrichment which was robbing the merchant or manufacturer of his traditional virtues, and *Le Faiseur* does not fail to emphasize this truth:

'En spéculant, monsieur,' [says the heroically honest Mme Mercadet to her dangerously resourceful husband, who is the *faiseur* of the title] 'il y a mille manières de faire fortune, mais je n'en connais qu'une seule de bonne, que la brave bourgeoisie n'aurait jamais dû quitter: c'est d'amasser l'argent par le travail et par la loyauté, non par des ruses. . . .'

Yet Mercadet is far from being an odious figure. Balzac himself was prone to the temptation against which he warns his contemporaries. He was fertile in speculative schemes, sometimes brilliant, sometimes absurd, and perhaps would have tried more of them out in earnest had he possessed the time and the means. He has put this side of himself into Mercadet. Reduced to financial straits because his partner Godeau has absconded with 150,000 francs of their common capital, spurred on by his versatility, and enjoying Stock Exchange operations as an exciting game, prolific in the invention of specious enterprises, Mercadet uses his insight into the greed and gullibility of his fellow-speculators to gain time and stave off distraint or liquidation. Out of this arises the pleasant comicality of Greek meeting Greek, of tricksters vying with tricksters. Mercadet is the most keen-witted of them all.

The originality of *Le Faiseur* lies in the ingenuity with which Balzac keeps his hero constantly on the brink of flagrant roguery, and yet sees to it that this man whom his wife believes to be by

---

[1] See Conard XXXV.

nature honest, loyal and courageous is preserved from a definite fall, not only by the embarrassing situations into which his own nimbleness plunges him, not only by the probity of his wife and daughter and the latter's lover, but also by his own goodness of heart. These impediments to irretrievable dishonesty provide the sentimental interest of the play, which asserts itself as soon as Balzac has sufficiently demonstrated Mercadet's adroitness in duping or cajoling his creditors. It is a trite one, but treated with some novelty: shall his daughter Julie, a plain but spirited girl, marry her unmercenary admirer, Adolphe Minard—by an excellent touch of realism Balzac shows his disinterestedness wavering for a time under the influence of Mercadet's worldly reasoning— or serve her father's schemes by marrying a supposedly rich, elegant and aristocratic suitor, Michonnin de La Brive? The question scarcely needs answering, since here, as in *Paméla Giraud*, Balzac was in a mood to give true values the victory over false ones. The scenes in Act III, which bring Mercadet and La Brive together and show them coming to the realization that they are each of them frauds, are no less entertaining because they are reminiscent of similar scenes in *Robert Macaire*. Discomfiture gives place to mutual admiration, and soon they are in concert for a final fraud. From this the women and Minard pull back Mercadet before he has gone too far; the return of Godeau makes a happy solution possible, and Mercadet, converted but not deflated, decides to try his luck in agriculture instead of bucket-shop ventures.

Undoubtedly *Mercadet* is Balzac's best play because, in spite of technical defects, it is a happy combination of satire and good humour. Like all the others, it suffers from his determination to get in too much, and his customary sallies against the moral and social evils of his time, though here more epigrammatic and concise, sometimes obtrude and give artificiality to the dialogue. Yet these are only relative flaws, and the invention of a 'coup de théâtre' to wind up his action—the arrival of a fortune from India 'pour la millième fois'—may be a stock device, but it keeps him in famous company. What is surprising is that this comedy, which so clearly points forward to the nineteenth-century *Turcarets* staged by such dramatists as Augier, the younger Dumas and

Henry Becque, is devoid of the hardness and bitterness to be found in them. The reason may be that these authors took their inspiration from Balzac's 'realist' novels rather than from *Mercadet*. The greatest of these subsequent plays is *Les Corbeaux*, and Becque's sharks, Teissier and Bourdon, like Dumas' Jean Giraud and Augier's Vernouillet, are blood-brothers of the du Tillets of the 'Comédie Humaine', and not of Mercadet. So too was the original Turcaret of Lesage. It is not unpleasing that Balzac, in his last dramatic experiment, should have lifted himself on to the kindlier and more serene plane on which a Molière dwells.

What inference may be drawn about the possibilities of a triumphant exploitation, had Balzac lived on, of the drama of passion exemplified in *La Marâtre*, or the jovial comedy of manners exemplified in *Mercadet*? That he would have made further progress is extremely likely. But it is doubtful if he would have reached the summit of attainment. In order to achieve the dramatic power which was his objective in the 'Comédie Humaine' he needed the support of background description and preparatory narrative which the permissible prolixity of the novel could give him, but which is out of place on the stage. Such at any rate was the opinion of Louis Jouvet:

Par une singulière contradiction, c'est le roman qui, dans ses dialogues et la description constante de sa mise en scène, offre au public une action représentée, tandis que la pièce de théâtre n'aide en aucune manière la représentation que veut s'en faire le lecteur.[1]

This of course is the judgment of a reader, not of a spectator, but of one who was also an experienced actor and producer.

[1] Jouvet, 179.

XX

RETROSPECT

i. The Challenge of the 'Comédie Humaine'

THIS SURVEY of Balzac's writings has involved consideration, at relevant moments, of many general questions about his outlook, intentions and methods. A final question presents itself. What is the worth of this monumental creation? Many and diverse have been the answers given over the space of more than a century. They cover a wide range of attitudes, from ecstatic eulogy to systematic denigration. Many of them are extremely subtle and illuminating. If this book has fulfilled its purpose, it will have laid before the reader the sort of information upon which, once he has verified and enriched it by personal exploration, he may found his own judgments. But he has the right to expect a summary assessment in these concluding pages.

Balzac's ambition was a vast one, and in its totality beyond the compass of any single person, however great his energy, however wide the span of his interests, however steady and penetrating the glance into reality made possible by a rare combination of acutely developed faculties—observation, intuitive sympathy and imaginative vision; and, we may add, however enormous the conceit, the swagger, as Henry James puts it,[1] which induced Balzac to believe himself capable of carrying such a task through to completion. In making himself the 'secretary' of a society deemed to be dictating its own history,[2] it is astonishing that he should have succeeded in doing so much, that the fictitious world he created should stand so four-square and be so convincing a

---

[1] James (3), 41. 'One would really scarce have liked to see such a job as "La Comédie Humaine" tackled without swagger. To think of the thing really as practicable *was* swagger, and of the very highest order.'

[2] See above, 277.

replica of the real world. Only a great inventive genius could have gone so deep and reached out so far.

Of course there are gaps in his total picture, as he himself was ruefully aware. Of course the picture he presents, objective as he intended it to be, is that of a reality viewed through his own experience, arranged to his own perspective, enhanced with the tones and colours, the effects of light and shade, which only his eye was capable of perceiving. This was inevitable. Other minds occupied with the same task at the same period, viewing material and spiritual reality from a different vantage-point, would have seen other aspects, complementary to or corrective of those which stand out through the powerful lens of the Balzacian vision. Of course his picture is also strongly particularized by idiosyncrasies of conception, composition and style. Balzac plans and executes in an idiom which may serve to separate him from some kinds of readers. The medium he uses owes its success or failure to the fact that it is his own personal adaptation and exploitation of the language of his time, somewhat rhetorical, sometimes swollen, too poetic and sentimental for our taste, and for that reason not perfectly apt for the kind of objective notation for which Balzac often requires it. That is probably why Dr F. R. Leavis, for instance, finds fault with Balzac's language for its 'excited emphasis, top-level assertion and explicit insistence'.[1] It can indeed give this impression at times. But at its best the medium Balzac uses is resourceful, exuberant, picturesque, capable of great orchestral variations. It is a gigantic language in the hands of literary giants, and Balzac was one of them. Much has been said for and against his style. He himself was aware of its shortcomings and worked hard to improve it, though without conspicuous success. Yet he made language and style adequate to his purpose: evocative, forceful, explicative, portentous, sentimental, jovial, humorous by turns. In the words of Mr Raymond Mortimer:

A more disciplined and limpid style would probably fail to carry so irresistible a sense of life. Balzac impresses us like a force of nature, a summit or a Niagara. . . . I do not believe that Balzac in his most hard-pressed moments ever wrote a sentence that he did not himself find interesting, and his style, however reproachable, is the result of this

[1] Op. cit., 29.

impetus. Foaming, sparkling, hasty, scummy and opaque, it is a boulder-encumbered, whirlpool-forming torrent into which you hesitate to plunge; but once you are in you are swept irresistibly along.[1]

What of the gaps in his picture of the half-century—Empire, Restoration and July Monarchy? Considered as social history, it is remarkably dynamic. He shows France on the move, though he believed her to be moving in the wrong direction. He testifies to the weakening of monarchy, the defeat of the aristocracy, the advance of individualism, the adaptation and misuse of Parliamentary institutions, the reign of greed, the upward surge of an over-acquisitive commonalty, the progressive 'embourgeoisement' of French society. Omissions fade into insignificance in comparison with the area covered. Paris and the provinces; town and countryside; cross-sections of life in nearly thirty provincial towns; the physiognomy of many regions and departments evoked.[2] Half a dozen Balzacs, working in collaboration, might have surveyed the whole of France. One Balzac, working alone, had to be content to show what he regarded as most typical. But his boldest claim was to be the historian of social classes.

What of the aristocracy, Parisian, provincial and rural? A number of critics—not contemporaries like Sainte-Beuve, who might have been expected to score this point against him had he thought it valid, and not specialists in 'high life' like Proust[3]— have sneered at the 'novelette' element in his depiction of aristocratic society. It is true that at times he writes of it with the naïve snobbery of one flattered at the thought of hobnobbing with it. But the range of his inspection is astounding. He deserves a passing tribute for the skill with which he has drawn into his orbit such historical figures as Napoleon, Louis XVIII, Talleyrand and Fouché. But, in the sphere of pure invention, how many grades and types he has conjured up and classified in their characteristic attitudes and physiognomy! elder statesmen like the Dukes of Lenoncourt, Grandlieu and Chaulieu, the Comte de Fontaine and the Comte de Sérisy; austere representatives of the 'noblesse de

[1] Op. cit., *Introduction to Balzac*. Philarète Chasles wrote an admirable page on Balzac's style in 1858. See A. Levin, 144.
[2] See the *Liste topographique des endroits* in t. I (xxvii–xxviii) of the Pléiade edition.   [3] See *Biography*, 44 and n. 2.

robe' like the Granville father and son, Octave de Bauvan and the Baron de Clagny; survivals from the past, sometimes heroic, like the Marquis d'Espard and Laurence de Cinq-Cygne, sometimes amusing but still admirable in their rigidity, like the Baron du Guénic and the Marquis d'Esgrignon, sometimes comic in their effort to maintain the *panache* of former times, like the Chevalier de Valois; careerists and intriguers from lower strata like des Lupeaulx and scions of impoverished houses like Eugène de Rastignac; military and administrative *anoblis* who have come to the surface through war and turmoil, like Montcornet, the Hulots and Malin de Gondreville.

And if we confine our attention even to the top grade we get the same impression of variety. Balzac's noble families have each their distinct characteristics—the Grandlieus, the Chaulieus, the Vandenesses, the Maufrigneuses. Viewed as individuals, it is the younger people who stand out more sharply, and not always by their good qualities: the cold and libertine Charles de Vandenesse, his smug but mellowing brother Félix, the vain and weak Victurnien d'Esgrignon, the stupid Paul de Manerville, the brilliant and cynical Henri de Marsay, the opportunist Eugène de Rastignac; and those insolent but elegant cads Maxime de Trailles and La Palférine. Except for the rakes and the *arrivistes*, the men are somewhat colourless. Balzac's aristocratic women, of whatever generation, are more individual and more vivid, probably because Balzac, so keen was his scrutiny of the 'weaker sex', did not allow the fact that they were daughters of the nobility to blind him to the fact that they were also daughters of Eve. They form a fascinating collection, as mothers, wives, hostesses, schemers, idealists, coquettes, passionate victims of love or victimizers of lovers according to their temperaments. It is no small thing to have made a gallery of such figures as Mme Firmiani, the Marquise d'Espard, the Vicomtesse de Beauséant, the Duchesse de Langeais, Diane de Maufrigneuse, Béatrix de Rochefide, Louise de Chaulieu; or to have interspersed among them such provincial respresentatives as the Baronne du Guénic, Armande d'Esgrignon and Mlle de Pen-Hoël; or to have added to that aristocratic genius, Mlle des Touches, such aspirants to social and literary glory as Mme de Bargeton and Dinah de La Baudraye.

Nor are his well-born young ladies insipid—for example Émilie de Fontaine, Sabine de Grandlieu, Rosalie de Watteville, Modeste Mignon. Strange to say, it is when he is dealing with his own class that he sometimes fumbles with his *ingénues*, witness Victorine Taillefer and perhaps Césarine Birotteau. In spite of occasional *gaffes* like the 'Hein? fit la vicomtesse' of *Le père Goriot*, his accomplishment in this domain is worthy of admiration, even if it is the affectionately humorous admiration of Henry James:

Balzac carried the uppermost class of his comedy, from the princes, dukes, and unspeakable duchesses down to his poor *barons de province*, about in his pocket as he might have carried a tolerably befingered pack of cards, to deal them about with a flourish of the highest authority whenever there was a chance of a game. He knew them up and down and in and out, their arms, infallibly supplied,[1] their ramifications and other enthralling attributes.[2]

The population of the 'Comédie Humaine' has been roughly computed as amounting to 2,472 named and 566 unnamed persons.[3] The greater number of recurrent characters are those of the upper and middle classes who wind in and out of the scenes of private and Parisian life. Their continual reappearance might be expected to give the impression that Balzac's world is a disappointingly small one; but this is not the case. The marvel is that these characters do turn out to be so variedly representative and that duplication is so rare. As we move downwards from the social apex through the marginal nobility, and through the almost serried ranks of social climbers of whatever provenance, we get the impression, not of monotony, but of kaleidoscopic differentiation. This impression of inexhaustible fecundity is increased as we run through the numerous strata of middle-class society, as we envisage the great vocational groups clustered round the outstanding individuals: a rich assortment of clergymen ranging from that inexorable intriguer the Abbé Troubert to the saintly Abbés

---

[1] These arms and quarterings, by which Balzac laid great store, were regularly supplied by his one-time secretary, Count Ferdinand de Gramont, who thus became the Herald's College of the 'Comédie Humaine'. The Fonds Lovenjoul at Chantilly has some interesting collections of his blazons: A 247 and A 248.

[2] James (3), 44–5. [3] Lotte (4) and supplementary vol. of *Anonymes*.

Bonnet and Loraux; the Phellions, Thuilliers and Collevilles of the Civil Service class centred round Xavier Rabourdin; the various grades of legal men, judges like Popinot and Camusot de Marville, solicitors like Derville and Desroches, Paris notaries like Roguin, Crottat and the younger Cardot, provincial ones like Mathias and Chesnel, barristers like Bordin, Massol and Fraisier; financiers with the Midas touch, bankers and 'hommes d'affaires' like the Mongenods, the Kellers, Nucingen, Du Tillet, with their satellites and cat's-paws the 'escompteurs' and usurers, from Gobseck and Gigonnet to Claparon and Cérizet; the mercantile or shopkeeping groups like the elder Camusots and Cardots, the Guillaume and Lebas families, the Matifats, the Ragons and the Pilleraults, César Birotteau and his successors, and even the picturesque, hard-bitten greengrocers and fish-wives like Mme Madou and Mme Cardinal; the doctors like Desplein, Bianchon, Martener, Poulain; the artists of varied talent and integrity, painters like Bridau and Grassou, architects and sculptors like Grindot, Stidmann and Steinbock, caricaturists like Bixiou; and the innumerable types of men of letters, similarly diverse, like d'Arthez, Rubempré, Nathan, Du Bruel; and, lastly, closely associated with many of these, the newspaper-founders, journalists and critics like Finot, Blondet, Vignon who, with their train of loose-living artistes around them, help to form that miscellaneous 'Bohemia' to which Balzac devotes many brilliant pages. The variety of vocational and social groups would have been richer still if Balzac had not worn himself out in accomplishing what he did.

He was not, either by his affinities or his artistic instinct, drawn to the description of the urban working-classes, although many examples can be quoted to show that he lacked neither the knowledge nor insight necessary for a vivid and faithful evocation of them had he felt inclined to do so.[1] His incursions into the realm of industry are infrequent, but not negligible—the cosmetic industry in *César Birotteau*, the printing-house and the paperfactory in *Illusions perdues*, the bonnet and stocking industry in *Le Député d'Arcis*. He was vitally interested in the peasant-class, but perhaps his view of it is too coloured by his political and

[1] See above, 141, 384 and 395.

economic prejudices. The study of an older, semi-patriarchal peasantry in *Le Médecin de campagne*,[1] which tallies remarkably with that of Rétif de la Bretonne in *La Vie de mon père* (1778), is a less usual feature, but there is the suggestion of a similar atmosphere in the description of the mass said in the church at Montégnac, in *Le Curé de village*. To his depiction of present types in general Balzac brings his habitual keenness of observation and feeling for nuance, though his more attractive peasants are apt to be romanticized, like La Fosseuse or Farrabesche, or a little pallid, like the Tascheron family redeemed and civilized by Catholic piety. In *Les Paysans*, for the ideological reasons we have mentioned, the country population, although individually solid, real, full-blooded and diverse, is as a whole too 'red in tooth and claw'. Curiously enough, one thinks of certain characters from other stories, two of them provincial studies, as his greatest peasant creations: Grandet, Séchard senior, Sauviat. Wrongly perhaps, because Sauviat is a town-dweller, a scrap-iron merchant; Séchard has spent most of his life as a printer before he becomes a besotted vine-grower; Grandet is a rich proprietor and mayor of Saumur. Yet they have in them the sturdiness, the tight-fistedness, the earthy realism we traditionally assign to the peasant. But Grandet in particular, as well as being one of the great energumens of the 'Comédie Humaine', is more important as one of the dynamic rather than the static type since, unlike the peasants rooted in the soil, he represents that upward surge, that social fermentation of the period which Balzac illustrates in so many *milieux* and walks of life.

ii. Balzac and Reality

So much for the social historian—and many trained historians have testified to the unique value of the 'Comédie Humaine' as a historical document. But this of itself would not make a great novelist of Balzac. Many readers indeed may excusably confess to some impatience, not only at the sight of Balzac pursuing his sociological role, but also at the pains he forces them to take in

---

[1] Chap. ii, the funeral wake in the mountains.

absorbing his long pages of background description and argument.[1] What of his conception of human nature in general, and his psychological acumen in particular? In judging of this we have to keep in mind a number of features which are bound to affect our appreciation and assessment of his work.

One is a corollary of the sociological preoccupation just referred to: the continual awareness of an interrelationship between character and environment which puts such a special stamp on his novels—the emergence of his men and women from their surroundings and habitat, from the rural community, village, town or town quarter to which they belong. Without this awareness he could scarcely have arrived at the principle which binds his novels together—the classification into Scenes, private, provincial, Parisian, etc. But its importance can be exaggerated. It is not clear that, in the 'Comédie Humaine', the environment inevitably produces the character. It can be and has been argued that the character finds or produces a physical or spiritual environment which is appropriate to him; or that Balzac was not so much illustrating the operation of a law as yielding to an æsthetic instinct which urged him to conceive and create harmony between character and surroundings. But there is a more general determinism in the 'Comédie Humaine' which makes the majority of his characters more or less responsive, as Balzac himself was responsive, to two universally operative driving-forces of the age. The first is the individualist impulsion, summed up for its social effect in Balzac's own phrase *Ôte-toi de là que je m'y mette*, and for its economic effect in Guizot's *Enrichissez-vous!* The second is the habit of seeing life, especially on its sentimental and passionate side, in glaring colours, the urge to heighten its contrasts of light and shade, a sort of melodramatic *bovarysme*. The two things may appear incompatible, yet they exist together and blend with one another. To the first we must presently return more specifically. But together they go to form that strange mixture of 'Realism' and 'Romanticism' which is a feature of the age as it is of the 'Comédie Humaine'. While it is true that the fixing

---

[1] Mr O'Connor (65) asserts that Balzac's 'local colour rarely fails in interest; it frequently fails in beauty because he has not managed to assimilate it to the art of writing'. In my view it often fails quite simply because Balzac's vision of it is too minute and detailed: he describes exhaustively instead of evoking.

of such labels as 'Realist' and 'Romantic' to a man or his work is an unprofitable and often a meaningless amusement, there is aptness in the observation a literary historian has made about both Victor Hugo and Balzac as beacon-lights of the century: 's'il [Hugo] est "réaliste", c'est à la manière de Balzac, pour accréditer une histoire éminemment romantique'.[1] What does this mean for present-day readers of Balzac? It means that, even while they are looking in him for something other than the social history of an age which in some respects has become foreign to them, they must still be ready to accept in him what does belong more particularly to his time.

Another salient feature, one which, though connected with the ideology of the early nineteenth century, is also conspicuously Balzacian and must be considered, not so much in its historical context, as for whatever intrinsic value it may possess, is his theory of the concentration and expenditure of vital energy—a 'delusion' according to Mr Raymond Mortimer and many other critics—the theory of the fixed idea which is behind his conception of the *homme à passions*. In the words of Vautrin, certain people

. . . chaussent une idée et n'en démordent pas. Ils n'ont soif que d'une certaine eau prise à une certaine fontaine, et souvent croupie; pour en boire, ils vendraient leurs femmes, leurs enfants; ils vendraient leur âme au diable. Pour les uns, cette fontaine est le jeu, la Bourse, une collection de tableaux ou d'insectes, la musique; pour d'autres, c'est une femme qui sait bien leur cuisiner des friandises.[2]

We have no need to attach names to the incarnations of obsessions thus defined by Vautrin. Balzac's interest in them is perhaps largely due to his acceptance of the Mesmeric theory, or rather his incorporation of it into a philosophic doctrine which he drew in almost equal proportions from what he knew about the physical sciences and what he had learnt about illuminism. But it corresponds also, by his own assertion, with what he had actually observed in people around him. This man of phenomenal vitality must have observed it in himself as well, for the determination to 'carry an entire society' in his head is surely one of the most

[1] Barrère (5), 183.   [2] *Le père Goriot*, Conard VI, 268.

tyrannical *idées fixes* that any man ever cherished or so extensively applied. Subsidiary to this purpose, but of a like intensity, was his pursuit of Mme Hanska from 1843, so complicated with dreams of making a fortune by speculation and traffic in antiques that the impassioned tones of his *Lettres à l'Étrangère* are vividly reminiscent of the ravings of Claës in *La Recherche de l'absolu*. Can one dare, in the face of such evidence, to assert that such obsession is psychologically inadmissible; or even that it is rare? The usual complaint of hostile critics is that it is foisted upon them as something they must accept without the stages in its progress being meticulously explored;[1] or that it is exaggerated beyond the limits of verisimilitude, so that Goriot, for instance, becomes not a man with an obsession but an obsession personified. This very important element in Balzac's view of human personality certainly takes many of his creations beyond the realm of normal humanity; but, thanks to the intensity of his conception, they are in fact his strongest creations. They are pitiful or hateful, admirable or contemptible; but they are fascinating and compelling. Perhaps that is because in some way they respond to a craving for the absolute that is in us. We love to analyse and isolate, and so we are not alienated, but rather captivated, when we see some character of fiction—Dickens had a like propensity—attaining or reaching towards that absolute homogeneity which we know real persons never attain. Dickens' own father, for example, was never wholly or simply a Wilkins Micawber. Grandet no doubt had his models, and the search for them by Balzacian enthusiasts may in part have been inspired by the subconscious desire to prove his existence possible; but such prototypes could not have been all of one piece as Grandet is. However this may be, there will always be, among readers of Balzac, those who turn to him because of the fascination of his 'monsters'. To reject Balzac because of this feature is to refuse one of the most intense experiences he has to offer.

A third feature is the preoccupation with money, not solely as the root of all evil, but as the mainspring of activity, as one of those powerful motive forces of which we have already spoken. No one before Balzac had paid such minute attention to money or

[1] E.g., Turnell, 221.

445

been at such pains to tell us how much each character has, how he got it, why he wants more, and how he sets about getting it. In the 'Comédie Humaine', hard cash is the symbol of reality breaking into and transforming romantic fiction. Money is the 'Open sesame' to passionate adventure, the avenue to success, luxury, power and all the many forms of self-fulfilment which the many kinds of men and women desire. Pick up almost any novel of Balzac, except of course those in which he is dealing with people born with silver spoons in their mouths, and you will find that behind the particular heroes and villains looms a universal hero or villain, the 'pièce de cent sous'. No doubt Balzac, who was himself so harried financially, exaggerated the omnipotence of money even in the increasingly acquisitive society of his own times. And yet, though greed is so often a ruling passion in the 'Comédie Humaine', it is often outrivalled by other motives. By bad ones—a Baron Hulot will lay waste his family's resources and swindle his country for the sake of a harlot—and also by good ones: a man's concern for his integrity or for his peace of mind, a woman's love for her husband or children, nay even a prostitute's devotion to her lover. Balzac's loftiest, and often his humblest, characters, are in no sense the slaves of lucre. He knew very well that there are people like this, and it was not merely in order to point a moral or preach a cause that he offered us characters like César Birotteau, the Séchard couple, Judge Popinot, Benassis, the Abbé Bonnet, Mme de La Chanterie, etc. But he found it difficult not to make money troubles or financial intrigues a touchstone, the occasion through which the spiritual worth or worthlessness of human beings, and also their weakness or strength as players in the game of life, are tested and manifested. And such a touchstone it normally is, together with the other material factors in life which affect our physical well-being and help to make up the texture of our lives: food, clothing, physical attractiveness or repulsiveness, our occupations and our pleasures. Selfish materialism is rampant in the 'Comédie Humaine'. Is it less rampant, because as a rule less dramatically evident, in real life either of the nineteenth or the twentieth century?

But there is a fourth element in Balzac's own make-up which contributes potently to his general psychology, one which is peculiarly French perhaps, or at any rate peculiarly Romantic: the conception of love as the most exalted and most ecstatic experience in life. It haunted him from beginning to end. It helped to determine the trend of his own life and to inspire him for the creation of such women as Marie de Verneuil, Mme de Beauséant, Mme de Mortsauf and Louise de Chaulieu. It is not merely because of their position or status that passion, and not money, is the ruling principle in the novels in which they appear. A noteworthy fact about Balzac's treatment of love is that, although in many males—from Raphaël de Valentin onwards—it begins as a selfish calculation of interest before it develops into a dominating passion, more often, in the female, whatever be the individual temperament or the walk of life, it is all that matters: the world can be well lost for love. Is it not because, all the time, the artist —'Il n'y a que les artistes qui soient dignes des femmes, parce qu'ils sont un peu femmes'[1]—was looking for the same thing as they: the perfect and permanent union which in the usual course of things, as his novels show, is unattainable? This quest, and the attribution of it to some of the characters on whom he lavished most attention, accounts for what we may well find to be an exaggeration of the importance and imperiousness of love between the sexes, a too great idealization of its quality, and an excess of rhetorical sentimentality—witness his lovers' letters, and his own letters—in his way of expressing the emotion it arouses in its votaries. This attitude amounts to a religion; so much so that it frequently blends with and is expressed in terms of the only religion to which, for the greater part of his inner life, Balzac whole-heartedly and even naïvely adhered—the illuminism of Swedenborg and kindred spirits. Yet we have seen that the love at whose shrine Balzac mostly worships is extra-conjugal love, or love which can hope for no consummation in marriage. It is in fact an all-absorbing passion more liable to destroy than to make marriages. There is here an apparent inconsistency in Balzac's outlook. In a large part of his work he assumes the role of a matrimonial counsellor, and generally he rules out passionate attraction as a condition for happy mating. At bottom he no doubt regards a great passion as an experience which only a privileged

[1] E I, 126.

few can enjoy—or suffer—as he himself did in the court he paid to Mme Hanska.

That is why love is the be-all and end-all in only a minority of his novels and *nouvelles*. *La Bourse, Madame Firmiani, La Femme abandonnée, Le Lys dans la vallée, Béatrix* and *Albert Savarus* are exceptions. When his young men fall in love or set out to conquer a woman, their motives are usually mixed. And generally love has to take its place, often a subordinate one, in the rough-and-tumble of ambitions and calculations. All the four elements we have considered join together and go to make the Balzacian presentation of human character, thought and action a confusing and sometimes, perhaps, a disconcerting one. But it is one of real complexity and not a mere synthesis of disparate elements. When the balance seems to be too much upset in favour of one or other of the elements, we may be inclined to reject, or only grudgingly to accept, such and such a character— Mme de Mortsauf and Vautrin, to take two opposite extremes. Yet the fact remains that the 'Comédie Humaine' introduces us to a crowd of men and woman, primary and subordinate, rich and poor, elegant and threadbare, wise and foolish, cunning and obtuse, grotesque and commonplace, tragic and silly, worthy and ridiculous, who have been discussed, admired, condemned, whose biographies have been scrupulously compiled by such enthusiasts as Cerfberr, Christophe and Lotte, and who, in short, even if they never could have lived within the strict bounds of real human experience, have the stuff of life in them and still have to be reckoned with as embodiments of what men and women think and feel about men and women. A large number of them have become immortal because they possess a superabundant vitality which real life rarely if ever affords. It is not given to many writers to create characters who live on outside the pages within which they were originally confined, whom we should not be surprised to meet in the home or the street, whose sayings we quote, at whom we laugh or shudder as if they really formed part of our daily experience.

iii. Judgment of Life

Increasing attention has been given, during the last thirty years or so, to the metaphysic substratum of the 'Comédie Humaine'; so much so that a commanding position has been allotted to such works as *La Peau de Chagrin*, *Les Proscrits*, *Louis Lambert*, *Séraphita* and kindred writings. Balzac's metaphysic may in many respects seem amateurish, but it was a part of the dynamic urge within him. It proceeded from his desire, evident even in his earliest literary efforts, to understand the universe in its totality before he undertook the task of reproducing it in fiction. Without so avid a lust for all-embracing knowledge it may be doubted whether the 'Comédie Humaine' would have been conceived. From it also proceeds his judgment of life as a whole and the deeper morality perceptible in his work once one has allowed for the inconsistencies that spring from the ebullience of his temperament and the voracity of his appetite for all kinds of experience, physical and spiritual. Thanks no doubt to this ebullience, his morality is by no means translucid or homogeneous. He is by turns or simultaneously a materialist and an idealist, a cynic and a sentimentalist, a pessimist and an optimist, an anticlerical and a pietist. He can be apostolically edifying and sardonically ribald, as we have seen when passing from *L'Envers de l'histoire contemporaine* to the virtually contemporaneous *Petites Misères de la vie conjugale*. He is rarely indecently suggestive or baldly outspoken when dealing with sex. If it would be going too far to call him chaste, he shows a certain discretion and even, except possibly in *Les Contes drolatiques* and *La Fille aux yeux d'or*, what the French call *pudeur*. The taste of his age demanded such reticence. His real indiscretions are on the emotional or the didactic side. There is an element of ingenuousness, of childishness even, in his temperament, just as there is in his view of life and the world, for all the sharpness of his inspection of them and his relentless exposure of the calculating egoism concealed behind fair-seeming. This ingenuousness is most likely to show itself at certain moments: when he is too jubilant about his knowledge of 'high life'; when he displays conscious wit instead of letting his pen be guided by the irony and humour which never fail him as

2G

a detached observer and recorder; when he buttonholes his readers and proceeds to enlighten them, whether relatively to his theme or not, about the mysteries of art, the arcana of science, the truth about politics or the real nature of religion.

In the long run such foibles amuse and endear. At worst they are the price one pays for great instruction and entertainment; at best they help to build up the total conception of a remarkable and many-sided personality. But they can arouse irritation. They have prompted some English critics to accuse him of immaturity of outlook. Yet to challenge the cogency of his judgment of life and society on these grounds is to remain on the surface of the 'Comédie Humaine'. There may indeed be more solid grounds for such a challenge. Even with the unhappy experience of the twentieth century to draw on, we may feel that the more forbidding Balzac whom we find confronting us when we strike deep into his work is too much of a Jeremiah. Despite his natural exuberance and his enormous zest for living, his presentation of human life, and of ourselves through his *milieux* and characters, is unflattering and even humiliating. Claude-Edmonde Magny has summed up as follows the impression Balzac makes on her:

. . . ce qui donne à l'œuvre de Balzac sa richesse et son épaisseur, c'est le contraste perpétuel entre les opinions avouées, légitimisme, cléricalisme, et le profond pessimisme, à la fois psychologique, social et politique, qui se manifeste dans la trame de ses romans et n'épargne ni la noblesse, ni la monarchie, ni les institutions, ni les hommes.[1]

This is true, and it is what constitutes the genuine 'naturalism' of Balzac. However much he may indulge, in his more exalted moods, in poetic flights about human life and sentiment, he is, once he starts thinking, an anti-Rousseauist. He is starkly conscious of original sin. And if he rubs in the legitimism and clericalism, it is because he is genuinely persuaded that they are the only possible antidotes, even though he shows them only too often to be mere palliatives. These remedies are no doubt questionable, and the combination of them is unthinkable today. Balzac's Catholicism is too emotional and too much mixed up with the Romanticism which, had he confined himself to thinking and

[1] Op. cit., 31.

refused himself 'les délices du sentiment', he should have forsworn. But his diagnosis commands attention. Perhaps a disconcerting fact is that it often seems too impartial. Like Bianchon, he is intensely interested in the diseases he discovers. He finds his reprobates much more exciting than his righteous persons. He may occasionally wag the finger of reproof, but it would not be too much to say that he loves his mean and bad characters. Creative paternity in him is so strong, and the sympathy it engenders so keen, that he seems to participate, even to revel in the desires, motives and machinations of his knaves.

But what a catastrophe it would have been, in a writer with such a taste for moralizing, to have lacked this gift for participation! Thanks to it every one of Balzac's characters is in a real sense Balzac himself. That is why they are so superbly, so galvanically alive.

iv. Permanence

The 'Comédie Humaine' is not historical in a narrow sense, that is to say merely a resuscitation of fifty years of the nineteenth century. It is true that the numerous types that flit through its pages are unmistakably clothed in the garb of their time. The society Balzac perpetuated in print seems vastly different from our own. Darwinism, psycho-analysis, the revolution in the means of communication, entertainment and propaganda, the advent of the atomic age, the shifting of political and social axes, the weakening of Western Europe, the uncertainty and anxiety through which humanity is passing, all these things may seem to give a flavour of obsolescence to the nineteenth-century vision of life. But to delve into the past is only another way of looking at ourselves. Whatever revolutions come about, the human beings of one generation are fundamentally identifiable with those of another. Their motives and conduct are the eternal stuff of the novel. At a time when only vague premonitions about coming upheavals were possible, Henry James said of Balzac: 'What he did above all was to read the universe, as hard and as loud as he could, *into* the France of his time.'[1] More recently, in the full

---

[1] James (3), 26.

flood of the twentieth-century maëlstrom, stress has been laid, notably by M. Bardèche,[1] though with some exaggeration, on the pertinence and the prophetic value of Balzac's diagnosis of modern ills. It is commonly recognized that Balzac foresaw the trend of things and presented problems which society and the individual still have to face.

His treatment of the novel is all-embracing. He lacked the perfectionism of a Flaubert—the deliberate, obstinate attention given to language, style and structure as the sole possible avenue to a consummate artistry envisaged as the end of creative endeavour. But he had his own art of composition. He has in general a way of building up his subject, of arriving at the heart of his theme, of assembling and releasing the moral and material forces operating in human lives, which imparts unequalled vigour and conviction to his tales. He has pre-eminently the talent for surprise, that surprise which results from a slow and sometimes laborious preparation of an action culminating in a precipitous surge of events,[2] narrated as a rule though a dialogue which is superlatively dramatic. He was right in characterizing his stories as 'scenes' and the whole body of his work as a 'comédie'. With him the novel becomes an original kind of drama, but a drama enriched with all the contributory facts and factors which it is not possible to represent on the stage. And if it is a comedy rather than a tragedy, in spite of his acute awareness of the tragedy, both splendid and sordid, that haunts human effort and human ambition, it is because he is also constantly aware of all that is deflatingly comic in human experience. He is a humorist as well as a dramatist. In his laughter are the echoes of Rabelais, Molière, Sterne and Beaumarchais.[3]

Drama presupposes psychology. Though Balzac lacks the subtlety of a Stendhal or a Proust, the habit of viewing continuously from inside which also distinguishes a Henry James or a Joyce; though he seems to go from the exterior to the interior, to present human reality as objectively observed rather than intuitively

[1] Bardèche (4). See also Estrada.

[2] 'Singulière *pression* du sujet', says Gide, writing of 'cette espèce de génie qu'il a pour faire un nœud subit de tous ses fils' (*Journal* I, 198).

[3] See on this point the sensitive and perceptive chapter on Balzac in Professor G. Turquet-Milnes, op. cit.

sensed; although (or because?) his conception of character is concrete and classical and his instinct for what he calls 'typisation' exceptionally strong, he has pierced through to the core of human nature and shown it as it is: potentially good, potentially bad, rarely neutral, often mediocre, capable of great extremes, but always human and therefore never entirely alienated from human sympathy. And if the note of determinism is conspicuous in the working-out of his characters, they do often take control—he himself testified to this during the composition of *La cousine Bette*—and exhibit in themselves that element of the incalculable and the unforeseen which baffles deterministic explanation and gives them the depth and mystery inherent in the human person. We should however take note that for Gide,[1] this does not happen often enough in the 'Comédie Humaine'.

He enriched the domain of fiction with very many new themes and subjects and many new ways of treating them. Although his technique is broadly consistent, he gives glimpses of other methods—the 'flashback', as in *La Duchesse de Langeais*, the 'Hall of Mirrors', as in *La grande Bretèche*, and even the 'stream of consciousness', as in the contrast he draws, in *Le Curé de Tours*, between the spoken and the unspoken dialogue between Mme de Listomère and the Abbé Troubert.[2] Although as a rule omnipresent in his ordering of events and, in his manner of presentation, omniscient as a creator of character and a witness of life, he can withdraw himself and, as in *Le Succube*,[3] leave us to guess at the facts. That he is a pioneer in the realm of the police and detective novel confers on him no obvious claim to greatness; but it illustrates his variety and versatility. Is he the inventor of the 'roman-fleuve'? Those of Zola, Romain Rolland, Jules Romain, Georges Duhamel, Roger Martin du Gard, Galsworthy and the rest are more evidently a development of the novel-sequence. Nothing comes more naturally to a novelist with a lot to say than the idea of widening his conspectus and illustrating the continuity of existence by adding sequel to sequel. The conception behind the

---

[1] *Journal* II, 1218.

[2] I borrow these examples from the succinct and perspicacious assessment of Balzac's achievement by Mr. H. O. Stutchbury (Stutchbury (2)).

[3] *Contes drolatiques.* See above, 105–6.

'Comédie Humaine' is much more involute and complex; but it no doubt served as an example—and especially to Marcel Proust.

To gauge Balzac's influence and to assess his contribution to the development of the novel as an art-form is beyond the scope and intention of this book as it is beyond the capacity of its author.[1] The novel has always been and will be a chameleon among the literary forms. It lives by innovation and experiment. From time to time it strikes out along new paths, as it has done in our century, becoming an accommodating vehicle for the expression of anything a man has to say of social, religious or metaphysical import, or lending itself to the cult of subjectivity and the exploration of 'interior vision'. In the long run, new techniques invented or new fashions exploited, that for instance of the blurring or elimination of plot and character, are little more than ripples on the surface of a genre which, basically, is 'a story, perhaps borrowed from reality, but reality transformed and reimagined, endowed with form, made fictitious';[2] a fiction held together by what has been aptly described as 'the imaginative logic of the great and effusive liars'.[3] But where exactly does Balzac come in behind all this? One could draw up a list of great or reputable novelists who, at some time or other, and in one way or another, have taken stock of Balzac, have been inspired or repelled by him, or both inspired and repelled, like Flaubert. What proof would that afford of Balzac's intrinsic worth? There have been many outstanding novelists since his day, of all the major nationalities. Some of them can be measured against Balzac or differentiated from Balzac by virtue of the territory they explore and their manner of exploring it, the penetration or the comprehensiveness of their vision, the cogency of their appeal, the quality of genius that lies in them. But it is not necessarily what they have in common that gives them whatever stature they have achieved. Tolstoy, Turgenev, Dostoievsky, Henry James, Proust, Thomas Mann, D. H. Lawrence, James Joyce—it seems ungracious not to lengthen the list still further—are marked with a certain stamp of uniqueness. Balzac's uniqueness is of a higher

[1] M. Weidlé has made an interesting assessment of Balzac's 'place dans l'histoire des lettres'.

[2] Peyre, 10.   [3] Pritchett (2).

order than that of most if not all of them. Out of the ten greatest novelists whom Mr. Somerset Maugham recently selected for study, he would unhesitatingly ascribe genius to Balzac alone, because of his 'instinctive and extraordinary capacity for imaginative creation'. It is worth noting that experienced novelists, among whom must be counted such illustrious ones as Henry James and Proust, have often been less reserved than the critics in the homage they have paid to Balzac. Henry James, in the article from which I have already quoted,[1] after affirming his belief that 'Balzac stands signally apart', that he is 'the first and foremost member of his craft', puts him in immortal company:

The authors and the books that have, as we say, done something for us, become part of the answer to our curiosity when our curiosity had the freshness of youth, these particular agents exist for us, with the lapse of time, as the substance itself of knowledge: they have been intellectually so swallowed, digested and assimilated that we take their general use and suggestion for granted, cease to be aware of them because they have passed out of sight. But they have passed out of sight simply by having passed into our lives. . . . We have largely been living on our benefactor.

Significant also is the fact that a history of Balzacian criticism would show how frequently the name of Balzac has been coupled with that of Shakespeare. Cool judgment might object that only at supreme moments could Balzac rise to such Olympian heights. But, like Shakespeare, Dante, Molière and Cervantes, he offers a wealth and breadth of experience, a knowledge of human nature on which each successive generation can draw according to its tastes and needs. His work forms part of that immense literary treasure which the novel-form has accumulated during the centuries.

And finally this 'spirited, effusive, good-humoured egotist, half innocent, bursting with invention and fizzing with sardonic irony',[2] makes his own personal claim to our attention. In the last resort perhaps the most interesting, the most original, the most enigmatic character of the 'Comédie Humaine' is the creator of that 'Cyclopean city'. As Proust has maintained, it is not only his unimpeachable qualities that attract:

[1] James (3), 24. [2] Pritchett (2).

... les autres romanciers, on les aime en se soumettant à eux, on reçoit d'un Tolstoï la vérité comme de quelqu'un de plus grand et de plus fort que soi. Balzac, on sait toutes ses vulgarités, elles nous ont souvent rebuté au début; puis on a commencé à l'aimer, alors on sourit à toutes ces naïvetés qui sont si bien lui-même; on l'aime, avec un tout petit peu d'ironie qui se mêle à la tendresse; on connaît ses travers, ses petitesses, et on les aime parce qu'elles le caractérisent fortement.[1]

This attachment is one of the most important ingredients which go to the making of a 'Balzacian', that member of a special but widespread confraternity whose moral physiognomy the Abbé Bertault has discerningly sketched.[2] To be a true 'Balzacian' is to become passionately and indefatigably interested in Balzac's life, person and writings: the writings as elucidated through the person, the person as sensed in the writings.[3] In some cases the cult is carried to the point of idolatry. Few Englishmen will go as far as that. But to embark on the reading of his works, to set out in a modest way, and, little by little, to find oneself venturing farther and farther into the seas he charted until one begins to perceive more reasons for going on than for stopping or turning back, can become a most exciting and fascinating experience.

But where should a reader start, and what order should he follow? The order in which Balzac himself arranged the novels? He never really settled it finally. The order in time of his fictitious scenes and events? This is what that veteran Balzacian, Mr. W. H. Royce, advises,[4] and the 'Formes et Reflets' edition arranges the novels in accordance with this principle. The order in which he conceived or wrote the works? There is much to be said for this, as the present work has tried to show. The order devised by M. Bardèche, based on the formulation, illustration and application of Balzac's central philosophy, the destructive power of thought?[5] Usually readers have to content themselves with the edition which comes to hand, or upon available translations. It does not matter much. The essential is to make a start, and to let personal caprice and mounting curiosity dictate the course of further exploration.

[1] Proust (3), 216.   [2] Bertault (8), 155–68: 'Sur le mot "Balzacien".'
[3] See Gaëtan Picon for an interesting, though too ingenious and over-systematic attempt to show Balzac as revealed in his writings.
[4] Royce (2).   [5] André Martel edition.

APPENDIX I

SCHEME OF THE 'COMÉDIE HUMAINE'

The Conard arrangement is given here. It follows Balzac's own revised classification of the original 'Comédie Humaine' (1842–8), based on the Catalogue of 1845 [c], with subsequent modifications—the 1846 Prospectus for a projected new edition by Furne and Balzac's corrections on his own copy of the original edition [FC = 'Furne corrigé']. The distribution of stories in the 'Édition Définitive' (Calmann-Lévy, 1869–76) is faithful neither to Balzac's original nor to his final intentions.

TITLES AND SUCCESSIVE CLASSIFICATIONS[1]	CONARD VOLS.
Avant-Propos	I
ÉTUDES DE MŒURS	
SCÈNES DE LA VIE PRIVÉE	
La Maison du chat qui pelote	
Le Bal de Sceaux	
Mémoires de deux jeunes mariées	
La Bourse (priv. 1832; par. 1835; priv. 1842)	
Modeste Mignon	II
Un Début dans la vie	
Albert Savarus	III

[1] Notes on classification are only given against stories whose classification was altered. The first category indicated is that in which a story that was subsequently shifted was inserted when it was first classified; it may or may not have already been previously published. Entries dated between 1842 and 1848 inclusive indicate the original 'Comédie Humaine' edition. 'phil.' may refer, according to the date given, either to *Romans et contes philosophiques* (1831), or to *Nouveaux contes philosophiques* (1832), or to Werdet's 'Études philosophiques' (1835–7), or to the 'Études philosophiques' (1846) in the original edition of the 'Comédie Humaine'.

La Vendetta
Une double Famille (priv. 1830; par. 1835; priv. 1842)
La Paix du ménage
Madame Firmiani (phil. 1832; par. 1835; priv. 1842)
Étude de femme (phil. 1831; par. 1835; priv. 1842)

La fausse Maîtresse   IV
Une Fille d'Ève
Le Message (priv. 1832; prov. 1833; priv. 1842)
La Grenadière (prov. 1833; priv. 1842)
La Femme abandonnée (prov. 1833; priv. 1842)
Honorine

Béatrix   V
Gobseck (priv. 1830; par. 1835; priv. 1842)

La Femme de trente ans   VI
Le père Goriot (par. 1842; priv. c)

Le colonel Chabert (par. 1835; priv. c)   VII
La Messe de l'athée (phil. 1837; par. 1844; priv. c)
L'Interdiction (phil. 1836; par. 1839[1]; priv. c)
Le Contrat de mariage
Autre Étude de femme

SCÈNES DE LA VIE DE PROVINCE

Ursule Mirouët   VIII
Eugénie Grandet
Les Célibataires

  Pierrette   IX
  Le Curé de Tours (priv. 1832; prov. 1833)
  La Rabouilleuse
Les Parisiens en province

  L'illustre Gaudissart   X
  La Muse du département
Les Rivalités
  La vieille Fille
Les Provinciaux à Paris

  Le Cabinet des antiques   XI
Illusions perdues
  I. Les deux Poètes

[1] Charpentier edition.

458

APPENDIX I

APPENDIX I

APPENDIX I

APPENDIX II

PRINCIPAL EDITIONS AND ENGLISH TRANSLATIONS

THE COMPLETE WORKS

For the original edition (1842–8) and the Houssiaux 'tomes complémentaires' (1855) see above 268–9 and 269 n. 1.

Calmann-Lévy, 24 vols., 1869–76. 'Édition Définitive.'

Conard, 40 vols., 1912–40, ed. M. Bouteron and H. Longnon, illustr. Ch. Huard. See Appendix I.

'Pléiade', 11 vols. up to date, 1935–58, ed. M. Bouteron. Vol. x includes some *inédits*. Vol. xi includes *Les Contes drolatiques*, the Prefaces, other *inédits*, Notices sur les œuvres (R. Pierrot) and Index des personnages (F. Lotte).

André Martel, 30 vols. & Postface, 1946–51, ed. M. Bardèche. Limited edition, arranged according to the development and expansion of Balzac's ruling ideas, with illustrations, in colour, by modern artists.

'Formes et Reflets' (Club français du livre). 16 vols., 1951–3, ed. A. Béguin, J. A. Ducourneau, Henri Evans. Limited edition, arranged according to the chronological order of events in the stories, with illustrations from the original editions.

'Club de l'honnete homme' (Société des Études balzaciennes), 1955–, 4 vols. to date, ed. M. Bardèche and others, with illustrations by artists contemporary with Balzac, selected for general value.

OTHER EDITIONS

'Les Classiques du monde' (Publ. Fernand Hazan, ed. A. Prioult), 1947 sqq. 25 vols. proposed, but publication suspended.

Classiques Garnier. Some 19 vols. They were formerly edited by M. Allem. The latest vols. have been taken over by other scholars. See Bibliography under the names Adam, Allem, Castex, Guyon, Regard.

LETTERS

Corresp., 1819–50, vol. xxiv of *Éd. Déf.*, Calmann-Lévy, 1876. An unreliable collection.

Lettres à l'Étrangère, 4 vols., Calmann-Lévy, 1899–1950 (vols. i and ii ed. Spoelberch de Lovenjoul, vols. iii and iv ed. M. Bouteron). Vol. v in preparation (ed. R. Pierrot). Letters of the period 3 Feb.– 29 June 1848 (except for the period 18–30 Mar.) have been published as follows in *La Revue de Paris*: Nov. 1949, Aug. 1950, Aug. 1952 (ed. M. Bouteron); Sept. and Oct. 1954, Nov. 1956, Aug. 1957 (ed. R. Pierrot).

Lettres à sa famille, Albin Michel, 1950, ed. W. S. Hastings.

Corresp. avec Zulma Carraud, Gallimard, 1951, ed. M. Bouteron.

Corresp., vol. xvi, 'Formes et Reflets' edition (ed. J. A. Ducourneau).

Corresp. générale (excluding letters to L'Etrangère). To be published by Garnier in 4 vols. from 1959; ed. R. Pierrot.

Hanotaux, Gabriel and Vicaire, Georges, *La Jeunesse de Balzac*, Ferroud edition of 1921. Gives some corresp. between Balzac and Mme de Berny.

Hastings, W. S. *Balzac and Souverain. An unpublished Corresp.*, New York, 1927.

Les Cahiers balzaciens, ed. M. Bouteron, Cité des livres (Nos. 1–4), Lapina (Nos. 5–8).

No. 1 (1923), *Corresp. inédite . . . avec le lieut.-col. L. N. Périolas.*
No. 3 (1924), No. 5 (1927), *Lettres de Femmes.*
No. 6 (1928), *Corresp. inédite avec la duchesse de Castries.*
No. 8 (1928), *Corresp. inédite avec le Dr Nacquart.*

ENGLISH TRANSLATIONS

i. *Collected Editions*

Dent edition, 1895–8, 40 vols. General Preface by G. Saintsbury. Omits *La Physiologie du mariage, Sarrasine, La Fille aux yeux d'or, Une Passion dans le désert, Petites Misères de la vie conjugale.*

Caxton edition, 1895–1900, 53 vols., including Cerfberr and Christophe's *Repertory of the Characters.*

Lotus Library (from 1887). About 5 vols.

Everyman Library, 14 vols., of which only five are in print; see below.

ii. *Separate Novels recently in print*

At the Sign of the Cat and Racket, Everyman 1908 and 1944 (trans. Clara Bell). Includes *Le Bal de Sceaux, La Bourse, La Vendetta, Madame Firmiani.*

A Bachelor's Establishment [*La Rabouilleuse*], G. Weidenfeld & Nicholson, 1951 (trans. Eithne Wilkins).

Béatrix, Elek Books, 1957 (trans. Rosamund and Simon Harcourt-Smith).

César Birotteau, Elek Books, 1957 (trans. Frances Frenaye).

Conjugal Life, Neville Spearman, 1957. Pt. I, *Pinpricks of Married Life* (trans. Geoffrey Tickell). Pt. II, *The Physiology of Marriage* (selections, ed. Derek Stanford).

Cousin Bette, Hamish Hamilton, The Novel Library, 1948 (trans. Kathleen Raine). Out of print, but may be reprinted.

Cousin Pons, ibid., 1950 (trans. Norman Cameron). Out of print, but may be reprinted.

Droll Stories (selections), Bourbon, 1948 (trans. Lignolles).

—, Elek Books, 1958 (trans. Alec Brown).

Droll Stories, John Camden Hotten. Illustrations by Gustave Doré. Out of print, but listed as being a memorable edition.

The Duchesse de Langeais, reprinted from Everyman in *Great French Romances*, Pilot Press, 1946 (trans. Ellen Marriage, Introd. R. Aldington).

—, Euphorion Books, 1950 (trans. D. Mitford). Text not complete.

Eugénie Grandet, Everyman, 1907 and 1956 (trans. Ellen Marriage; new introd. by M. Marcel Girard).

—, Penguin Classics, 1955 (trans. M. A. Crawford).

The Fatal Skin [*La Peau de chagrin*], Hamish Hamilton, The Novel Library, 1950 (trans. Cedar Paul). Out of print, but may be reprinted.

The Wild Ass's Skin, Everyman, 1954 (trans. Ellen Marriage; new introd. by M. Marcel Girard).

The Girl with the Golden Eyes, Peacock Press (privately printed), Chicago, 1928 (trans. Ernest Dowson; illustrations by Donald Denton).

The Gondreville Mystery [*Une ténébreuse Affaire*], Elek Books, 1958 (trans. Gerard Hopkins).

The Lily in the Valley, ibid., 1957 (trans. Lucienne Hill).

Lost Illusions, John Lehmann, 1951 (trans. Kathleen Raine).

Old Goriot, Everyman, 1907 (trans. Ellen Marriage).

—, Penguin Classics, 1951 (trans. M. A. Crawford).

The Physiology of Marriage. Privately printed 1904.

—, Casanova Society, 1925 (trans. F. J. Macnamara).
[See also above, *Conjugal Life.*]

Ursula Mirouët, Everyman, 1915 (trans. Clara Bell).

The Vicar of Tours, Euphorion Books, 1950 (trans. D. Mitford). Includes also *Pierre Grassou.*

GENERAL BIBLIOGRAPHY

This Bibliography does not claim to be exhaustive and does not normally include biographical material. For a full list of works before 1929 see Royce (1). The place of publication is only given for works published elsewhere than at Paris.

Abraham, Pierre, (1). *Balzac, Recherches sur la création intellectuelle.* Rieder, 1929.

—, (2). *Créatures chez B.* Gallimard, 1931.

Adam, Antoine, (1). *Illusions perdues.* Garnier, 1956. Introd., Notes and Selected Variants.

—, (2). *Splendeurs et misères des courtisanes.* Garnier, 1958 Introd., Notes and Selected Variants.

Alain. *Avec B.* Gallimard, 1937.

Allem, Maurice, *Balzac.* Encyclopédie par l'image. Hachette, 1950. Also Introductions, Notes and Selected Variants in the Garnier edn.

—, (1). *La Peau de chagrin,* 1933.

—, (2). *La cousine Bette,* 1937.

—, (3). *Eugénie Grandet,* 1950.

—, (4). *Le père Goriot,* 1950.

—, (5). *La Rabouilleuse,* 1950.

—, (6). *La Femme de trente ans,* 1952.

—, (7). *Ursule Mirouët,* 1952.

—, (8). *Le Curé de Tours, Pierrette,* 1953.

—, (9). *César Birotteau,* 1954.

—, (10). *Le colonel Chabert, Honorine, L'Interdiction,* 1955.

—, (11). *Le cousin Pons,* 1956.

Altzyler, Hélène, *La Genèse et le plan des caractères dans l'œuvre de B.* F. Alcan, 1928.

Arrault, Albert, (1). *La Touraine de B.* (Preface by Horace Hennion.) Arrault et Cie, Tours, 1943.

—, (2). *Histoire de Jane la pâle* (edn.), ibid., 1947.

Arrigon, L. J. (1). *Les Débuts littéraires de H. de B.* Perrin et Cie, 1924.

—, (2). *Les Années romantiques de B.* Ibid., 1927.

—, (3). *B. et la 'Contessa'.* Edn. des Portiques, 1932.

Atkinson, Geoffroy, *Les Idées de B. d'après la 'C.H.'* 5 vols. Droz, Geneva, and Giard, Lille, 1949–50.

Aubrée, Étienne, *B. à Fougères.* Libr. Académique Perrin, 1939.

Baldensperger, Fernand. (1) 'Une Suggestion anglaise pour le titre de la "C.H." de B.', *RLC*, Oct.–Dec. 1921.

—, (2). *Orientations étrangères chez H. de B.* Champion, 1921.

Ballanche, P. S. *La Ville des expiations* (1820–36). Edited by A. Rastoul. Bibliothèque Romantique, 1926.

B. et la Touraine. Rapports lus au Congrès d'Histoire littéraire. Imprimerie Gibert-Clarey, Tours, 1950.

Bardèche, M. (1). *B. romancier.* Plon, 1940, reduced and revised 1943.

—, (2). *La Physiologie du mariage pré-originale.* Droz, 1940.

—, (3). *La Femme auteur et autres fragments inédits* (edn. and Introd.). Grasset, 1950.

—, (4). *Une interprétation de B.*, supplementary vol., André Martel edn. of B.'s works.

Barrère, J. B. (1). 'B. créateur. Introduction au problème du réalisme imaginaire', in *B. et la Touraine*, q.v.

—, (2). 'Hugo jaugé par B.', *MF*, 1 Jan. 1950.

—, (3). Victor Hugo, l'homme et l'œuvre. Boivin, 1952.

Barrière, Marcel, *L'Œuvre de B. Étude litteraire et philosophique de la 'C.H.'* Calmann-Lévy, 1890.

—, Pierre, (1). *H. de B. Les romans de jeunesse.* Hachette, 1928.

—, (2) *H. de B. et la tradition littéraire classique.* Ibid., 1928.

Bartlett. See Maxam and Bartlett.

Barzun, J. *Berlioz and the Romantic Century.* 2 vols. Gollancz, London, 1945–50.

Beckett, W. *Liszt.* Dent and Sons, London, 1956.

Béguin, Albert, (1). *B. visionnaire.* Skira, Geneva, 1946.

—, (2). 'Formes et Reflets' edn. of B.'s works. Co-editor.

Bellessort, André, *B. et son œuvre.* Libr. Académique Perrin, 1924.

Bérard, Suzanne, 'A propos des "Chouans"', *RHLF*, Oct.–Dec. 1956.

Bertault, Abbé Philippe, (1). *B. et la musique religieuse*. J. Naert, 1929.

—, (2). *B. et la religion*. Boivin, 1939.

—, (3). *Traité de la prière (texte inédit)*. Ibid., 1942.

—, (4). *B. L'homme et l'œuvre*. Ibid., 1946.

—, (5). 'Le Cycle tourangeau de la "C.H."', *Au Jardin de la France*, Spring No., 1949.

—, (6). 'B. précurseur du Catholicisme social', *Matines*, Aug. 1950.

—, (7). 'Introduction au "Prêtre catholique"', *Études balzaciennes*, 3–4, June–Dec. 1952.

—, (8). *Introduction à B*. Odilis, 1953.

Bertaut, Jules, '*Le père Goriot*' *de B*. Malfère, Amiens, 1928.

Beuchat, Ch. *De Restif à Flaubert*. La Bourdonnais, 1939.

Billy, André, (1). *Vie de B*., revised edn., Flammarion, 1944.

—, (2). *Sainte-Beuve. Sa vie et son temps*, t. i. Ibid., 1952.

Biré, Edmond, *H. de B*. Champion, 1897.

Blanchard, Camille, 'B. en Dauphiné et "Le Médecin de campagne"', *RHLF*, Oct.–Dec. 1955.

—, Marc, (1). *La Campagne et ses habitants dans l'œuvre de H. de B*. Champion, 1931.

—, (2). *Témoignages et jugements sur B*. Ibid., 1931.

Bonnier de la Chapelle. See Parménie and Bonnier de la Chapelle.

Borel, J. 'Un Modèle d'Horace Bianchon', *RSH*, Oct.–Dec. 1955.

Bourget, Paul, (1). *Études et portraits III* ('B. nouvelliste'). Plon Nourrit, 1906.

——, (2). *Nouvelles pages de critique et de doctrine*. Ibid., 1922, vol. i.

Bouteron, Marcel, (1). *Les Cahiers balzaciens*. 8 numbers, 1923–8. For Nos. 1, 3, 5, 6, 8 see Appendix II (*Letters*). The other Nos. contain hitherto unpublished writings of B., i.e. No. 1, *Les Fantaisies de la Gina*, 1923; No. 4, *Les cent Contes drolatiques. Quatriesme Dizain*, 1925; No. 7, *Lettres sur Kiew*, 1927.

—, (2). *Une Année de la vie de B. 1835*. Monaco, 1925.

—, (3). 'En marge du père Goriot: B., Vidocq et Sanson', *La Revue*, 1 Jan. 1948.

—, (4). 'Anthologie de la vie provinciale d'après la "C.H."', *RSH*, Jan.–June 1950.

—, (5). 'L'Inscription de "La Peau de chagrin" et l'orientaliste Joseph de Hammer', *RHLF*, Apr.–June 1950.

—, (6). 'Avant-Propos', in F. Lotte, *Dictionnaire biographique*, 1952.

—, (7). *Louis Lambert*, t. i. Edn. by M. Bouteron and J. Pommier. José Corti, 1952.

—, (8). *Études balzaciennes*. Jouve, 1954.

Bouvier, René, *B. homme d'affaires*. Champion, 1930.

—, and Maynial, Éd. (1). *Les Comptes dramatiques de B.* F. Sorlot, 1938.

—, —, (2). *De quoi vivait B.?* Edn. des Deux Rives, 1949.

Bowen, R. P. *The Dramatic Construction of B.'s Novels*. University of Oregon, 1940.

Bridgers, F. A. 'Faire concurrence à l'État civil', *RHLF*, Apr.–June 1950.

Brunetière, F. *Honoré de B.* Nelson, 1913.

Brunot, F. *Histoire de la langue française des origines à nos jours*, t. xii (Ch. Bruneau). Armand Colin, 1948.

Burton, J. M. *H. de B. and his Figures of Speech*. Princeton, New Jersey, 1921.

Canfield, A. 'Les Personnages reparaissants dans la "C.H."', *RHLF*, Jan.–Mar. and Apr.–June 1934 [t. 41].

Castex, P. G. (1). *Falthurne, manuscrit de l'abbé Savonati* (edn.), José Corti, 1950.

—, (2). *Mademoiselle du Vissard* (edn.). Ibid., 1950.

—, (3). *Le Conte fantastique de Nodier à Maupassant*. Ibid., 1951.

—, (4). *Histoire des Treize*. Garnier edn. Introd., Notes and Selected Variants, 1956.

—, (5). *La vieille Fille*. Garnier edn. Introd., Notes and Selected Variants, 1957.

Cazenove, Marcel, *Le Drame de B.* Delmas, 1950.

Cerfberr, Anatole and Christophe, Jules, *Répertoire de la C.H.* Calmann-Lévy, 1887.

Cesari, P. *Les Passions dans l'œuvre de B.* Presses Modernes, 1939.

Chaillet, J. 'Le Cycle de Touraine'. 'Formes et Reflets' edn. of B.'s works, t. vi, Preface.

Chamberlin, Wells, 'The Zweig Manuscript Proof of "Une ténébreuse Affaire"'. Appendix to Dargan and Weinberg, q.v.

Chancerel, André, 'Quelle année vit naître le titre de "La C.H."?', *RHLF*, Oct.–Dec. 1952.

Christophe. See Cerfberr and Christophe.

Conner, Wayne, 'La Composition de "La Fille aux yeux d'or" ', *RHLF*, Oct.–Dec. 1956.

Courrier balzacien, Le. Ten numbers Jan. 1949–Dec. 1950. Continued as *Les Études balzaciennes*: Four numbers Mar. 1951–June–Dec. 1952. Edited by J. A. Ducourneau and Léon Gédéon, then by the former alone.

Crain, W. L. (1). See Dargan, Crain and others.

—, (2). 'An Introduction to a critical edition of "Le Secret des Ruggieri" ', in Dargan and Weinberg, q.v.

Crépet, J. *H. de B. Pensées, sujets, fragmens.* Blaizot, 1910.

Curtius, E. R. *Balzac* (1923). Trans. H. Jourdan [in French]. Grasset, 1933.

Dagneaud, R. *Les Éléments populaires dans le lexique de la Comédie Humaine d'H. de B.* Ménez et Cie, Quimper, 1954.

Dargan, E. Preston, *Honoré de B. A Force of Nature.* Chicago, 1932.

—, Crain, W. L. and others, *Studies in B.'s Realism.* University of Chicago Press, 1933.

—, — and Weinberg, Bernard, *The Evolution of B.'s 'C.H.'* Ibid., 1942.

Dedinsky, Brucia, *The Development of the Scheme of the 'C.H.' Distribution of the Stories.* See preceding item. Also printed separately, University of Chicago Libraries.

Descaves, Lucien, *Le Président Balzac.* R. Laffont, 1951.

Ducourneau, J. A. See *Courrier balzacien, Le,* and above, Appendix II, 'Formes et Reflets' edn. of B.'s works, t. xvi.

Easton, M. F. 'The Origins and Early History of the Artist as a Bohemian.' Unpublished thesis of the University of Leeds, 1954.

Eigeldinger, Marc, *La Philosophie de l'art chez B.* P. Cailler, Geneva, 1957.

Émery, Léon, *Balzac.* Éditions Balzac, 1943.

Estrada, E. Martinez, 'Philosophie et métaphysique de B.', in *Hommage à B.* Unesco, Mercure de France, 1950.

Études balzaciennes. See *Courrier balzacien, Le.*

Europe. Nos. 55–6. July–Aug. 1950 [Marxist interpretations of Balzac].

Evans, Henri, (1). 'La Pathologie de Louis Lambert: B. aliéniste', *RHLF*, Apr.–June 1950.

—, (2). *'Louis Lambert' et la philosophie de B.* José Corti, 1951.

—, (3). 'Formes et Reflets' edn. of B.'s works, Annotations.

Faguet, Émile, *Balzac*. Hachette, Grands Écrivains Français, 1913.

Failletaz, Emm. *B. et le monde des affaires*. Payot, 1932.

Fargeaud, Madeleine, 'Autour de B. et de Marceline Desbordes-Valmore', *RSH*, Apr.–June 1956.

Fernandez, Ramon, *Balzac*. Stock, 1943.

Flat, Paul, *Essais sur B.* and *Seconds Essais sur B.* Plon Nourrit, 1893–4.

Forest, H. U. *L'Esthétique de B.* Presses Universitaires, 1950.

Fouquerre, André, *H. de B. à Angoulême*. Soc. Gen. d'Imprimerie et d'Édition Levé, 1913.

Gancier, Pierre, 'Le Peuple dans la "C.H." ', *Rev. de l'Université Laval*, Quebec, Feb. 1955.

Gautier, Théophile, 'Honoré de B.' in *Portraits contemporains*, Charpentier, 1874. Reprinted in *Souvenirs romantiques*, Garnier, 1929.

Gide, André, *Journal*. I (1899–1939); II (1939–49). Pléiade edn., 1948 and 1956.

Gillot, Hubert, (1). *Le Médecin de campagne*. G. Courville, 1938.

—, (2). *Modeste Mignon*. Les Belles Lettres, 1945.

Giraud, Raymond, *The Unheroic Hero in the Novels of Stendhal, Balzac and Flaubert*. Rutgers Univ. Press, New Brunswick, New Jersey, 1957.

Godin, Henri, 'Variations littéraires sur le thème de la Confession', *FS*, July 1951.

Goncourt, Edm. and Jules de. *Journal*, t. i. Flammarion and Fasquelle, 1887–1892.

Goulard, R. 'B. et les "Mémoires de Sanson" ', *MF*, 1 Nov. 1950.

Gould, Ch. 'The Present State of B. Studies', *FS*, Oct. 1958.

Gourmont, Rémy de, *Promenades littéraires*, 5e Série. Mercure de France, 1913.

Gozlan, Léon, (1). *B. en pantoufles*. 3rd edn., Michel Lévy frères, 1865.

—, (2). *B. chez lui*. Lévy, 1862. Both works are included in edn. of *B. en pantoufles* by L. Jaffard, Delmas, 1949.

Guignard, Romain, 'La "Rabouilleuse" de B.' Lecture given at Frapesle, 30 May 1949. Gaignault et fils, Issoudun, 1949.

Guyon, Bernard, (1). *La Pensée politique et sociale de B.* Armand Colin, 1947.

—, (2). 'B. et le mystère de la création littéraire', *RHLF*, Apr.–June 1950.

—, (3). *La Création littéraire chez B.* Armand Colin, 1951.

—, (4). *Une ténébreuse Affaire.* Garnier edn., Introd., Notes and Selected Variants [forthcoming].

Haas, J. *H. de Balzacs 'Scènes de la vie privée' von 1830.* Halle, 1912.

Hanotaux, Gabriel and Vicaire, Georges, *La Jeunesse de B.* Ferroud, 1921.

Hastings, W. S. (1). *B. and Souverain. An unpublished Correspondence.* New York, 1927.

—, (2). See Appendix II (*Letters*): *Lettres à sa famille.*

Hennion. See Arrault (1).

Hirschfell, G. *B. und Delacroix. Streiflichter auf den Roman 'La Fille aux yeux d'or'.* Alsatia, Haut-Rhin, 1946.

Hofmannsthal, Hugo von, 'L'Univers de la "C.H." ', *Études balzaciennes*, No. I, Mar.–June 1951 (trans. A. Béguin).

Hourdin, G. *B., romancier des passions.* Éd. Les Temps Présents, 1950.

Hunt, H. J. (1). *Le Socialisme et le romantisme.* Clarendon Press, Oxford, 1935.

—, (2). *The Epic in Nineteenth-century France.* Blackwell, Oxford, 1941.

—, (3). 'The "Human Comedy": first English reactions', in *The French Mind.* Studies in honour of Gustave Rudler. Clarendon Press, Oxford, 1952.

—, (4). 'B. and the English Tongue', Modern Language Review, Oct. 1954.

—, (5). *Honoré de B., a Biography.* Athlone Press, London, 1957.

—, (6). 'Balzac's Pressmen', *FS*, July 1957.

—, (7). ' "Portraits" in the *Comédie Humaine*', *Romanic Review*, Columbia University Press, Apr. 1958.

—, (8). 'B. and Lady Ellenborough', *FS*, July 1958.

Huxley, Aldous, *Music at Night and Other Essays.* Chatto and Windus, London, 1949.

Hytier, J. 'Un Chef-d'œuvre improvisé: "La cousine Bette" ', *Romanic Review*, Apr. 1949.

Jackson, O. E. 'Summaries of Variants in "Les Secrets de la princesse de Cadignan" ', in Dargan and Weinberg, q.v.

Jaffard, L. (1). *Journaux à la mer. Textes inédits 1830–9* (Introd., Notes and Comments). Édns. du Conquistador, 1949.

—, (2). See under Gozlan.

James, Henry, (1). *French Poets and Novelists*. Macmillan, London and New York, 1878.

—, (2). *The Question of our Speech* and *The Lesson of B*. Houghton, Mifflin and Co., Boston and New York, 1905.

—, (3). *Notes on Novelists* (Dent, London, 1914) as reproduced in *The Art of Fiction and Other Essays*. Oxford University Press, 1948 (pp. 24–47: 'Honoré de B.').

Jarblum, I. *B. et la femme étrangère*. Boccard, 1930.

Jouvet, L. *Témoignages sur le théâtre*. Flammarion, 1952.

Korwin-Piotrowska, Sophie de, (1). *B. et le monde slave*. Champion, 1933.

—, (2). *B. en Pologne*. Ibid., 1933.

Lalande, R., 'Les États successifs d'une nouvelle de B.: "Gobseck" ', *RHLF*, July–Dec. 1939 and Jan.–Mar. 1947.

Lambinet. See Léger (2).

Lanson, Gustave, *Histoire de la littérature française*. 18ᵉ edn., Hachette, 1924 (pp. 1000–5).

Leathers, V. L. *L'Espagne et les Espagnols dans l'œuvre de H. de B.* Librairie Ancienne H. Champion, 1931.

Leavis, F. R. *The Great Tradition*. Chatto and Windus, London, 1948.

Le Breton, André, *B. L'homme et l'œuvre*. Armand Colin, 1905.

Lecuyer, M. *B. et Rabelais*. Les Belles Lettres, 1956.

Lefèvre, André, 'Dans l'ascendance de Benassis', *Le Courrier balzacien*, Oct. 1950.

Léger, Ch. (1). *A la recherche de B*. Le Goupy, 1927.

—, (2). *B. mis à nu* [attributed to Lambinet]. Edn. with Preface and Notes. C. Gaillandre, 1928.

Levin, A. *The Legacy of Philarète Chasles*, vol. i. University of North Carolina Press, 1957 [especially pp. 127–84, where some of Chasles' writings on B. are reprinted].

—, Harry, 'B. et Proust', in *Hommage à B*. Unesco, Mercure de France, 1950.

473

Le Yaouanc, Moïse, (1). 'Notes balzaciennes', *RHLF*, Oct.–Dec. 1953.

—, (2). 'Notes sur le titre de "La C.H." ', ibid., Oct.–Dec. 1956.

—, (3). 'Autour de "Louis Lambert" ', ibid., Oct.–Dec. 1956.

Livre du Centenaire. Compendium of studies on B. Flammarion, 1952.

Lotte, Dr Fernand, (1). 'L'Histoire de Wanda de Mergi', *Le Courrier balzacien*, No. 6, Dec. 1949.

—, (2). 'La Chronologie de "La Femme de trente ans" ', ibid., No. 10, Dec. 1950.

—, (3). 'Chronologie de "La C.H." ' in 'Formes et Reflets' edn. of B.'s works, t. xvi.

—, (4). *Dictionnaire biographique des personnages fictifs de la 'C.H.'* José Corti, 1952. With supplementary vol. (*Anonymes*). Ibid., 1956.

—, (5). 'Autour du "Médecin de campagne" ', *Rev. des deux Mondes*, 1 Apr. 1956.

Lovenjoul, Comte Spoelberch de, (1). *Histoire des œuvres de H. de B.* Calmann-Lévy, 1886 (2nd edn.).

—, (2). *Études balzaciennes. Un Roman d'amour.* Ibid., 1896.

—, (3). *Autour de H. de B.* Ibid., 1897.

—, (4). *La Genèse d'un roman de B.: 'Les Paysans'.* Ollendorff, 1901.

—, (5). *Une Page perdue de B.* Ibid., 1903.

—, (6). 'Les "Études philosophiques" de H. de B.', *RHLF*, 1907, xiv, 393–441.

Lukács, G. *Studies in European Realism.* Hillway Publishing Co., London, 1950.

Magny, Claude-Edmonde, *Les Sandales d'Empédocle.* La Baconnière, Neuchâtel, 1945.

Maigron, L. (1). *Le Roman historique à l'époque romantique.* Champion, 1898.

—, (2). *Le Romantisme et les mœurs.* Ibid., 1910.

—, (3). *Le Romantisme et la mode.* Ibid., 1911.

Malo, Henri, (1). *Une Muse et sa mère. Delphine Gay de Girardin.* Émile Paul frères, 1924.

—, (2). *La Gloire du Vicomte de Launay. Delphine Gay de Girardin.* Ibid., 1925.

—, (3). *Les Années de Bohème de la duchesse d'Abrantès.* Ibid., 1927.

Marash, J. G. *Henry Monnier.* Harrap, London, 1951.

Marceau, Félicien, *B. et son monde*. Gallimard, 1955.

Marhofer, Esther, ' "Le Curé de Tours". A Study in Topography'. See Dargan, Crain and others.

Marix, Thérèse, 'Franz Liszt et H. de B.', *Rev. des Études hongroises*, Jan.–June, 1934.

Martineau, René, 'B. influencé par Stendhal', *Le Divan*, Oct.–Dec. 1945, No. 256.

Massant, Raymond, (1). 'B. disciple de Rabelais et maître du conte drolatique', in *B. et la Touraine*, q.v.

—, (2). Preface to *Contes drolatiques* in 'Formes et Reflets' edn. of B.'s works, t. xiii.

—, (3). 'A propos des Contes drolatiques: réalités et fictions dans *La belle Impéria*', *RHS*, Jan.–June 1950.

—, (4). 'B. historien pittoresque de la France', *RHS*, Apr.–Sept. 1951.

Matoré. See Robert and Matoré.

Maugham, W. Somerset, *Ten Novels and their Authors*. Heinemann, London, 1954.

Mauriac, Claude. *Aimer Balzac*. La Table Ronde, 1945.

Maurice-Amour, Lila, (1). 'La musique que B. aimait', in *B. et la Touraine*, q.v.

—, (2). 'B. et la musique', *MF*, 1 Jan. 1950.

Maury, Lucien, *Opinions sociales et politiques de B. Textes choisis et préfaces*. Stock, 1941.

Maxam, Mary H. and Bartlett, F. R. 'Summaries of Variants in "Le Cabinet des antiques" ', in Dargan and Weinberg, q.v.

Mayer, Gilbert, (1). *La Qualification affective dans les romans de H. de B.* Droz, 1940.

—, (2). *La duchesse de Langeais* and *Un Début dans la vie*. Introd., Notes and Variants, edn. Nizet, 1949.

Maynial. See Bouvier and Maynial.

Melcher, Edith, *The Life and Times of Henry Monnier*. Harvard Univ. Press, Cambridge, Mass., 1950.

Merlant, Joachim, (1). *Honoré de B. Morceaux choisis*. Didier et Privat, La Littérature Française Illustrée, 1912.

—, (2). 'Le manuscrit de "Béatrix" de B.', *RHLF*, July–Sept. 1913.

—, (3). 'B. en guerre contre les journalistes', *Rev. de Paris*, 1 Aug. 1914 and 1 Jan. 1915.

Métadier, P. B. *Saché dans la vie et l'œuvre de B.* Gibert-Clarey, Tours, 1950.

Michelet, Jules, *Le Peuple* (1846). Soc. des Textes Fr. Modernes. Marcel Didier, 1946.

Milatchitch, D. Z. (1). *Le Théâtre de H. de B.* Hachette, 1930.

—, (2). *Le Théâtre inédit de H. de B.* Ibid., 1930.

Monod, Marie O. *Daniel Stern, comtesse d'Agoult.* Plon, 1937.

—, S. 'La Fortune de B. en Angleterre', *RLC*, Apr.–June 1950.

Montalée, Rémy, *En lisant B.* Figuière, 1925.

Moore, George, (1). *Avowals.* Ebury edn., Heinemann, London, 1936.

—, (2) *Confessions of a Young Man.* Ibid., 1937.

—, (3). *Conversations in Ebury Street.* Ibid., 1939.

Moore, W. G. (1). 'The B. Centenary', *FS*, Oct. 1951.

—, (2). 'Vers une édition critique de "César Birotteau" ', *RHLF*, Oct.–Dec. 1956.

Mortimer, Raymond, *Channel Packet* ('Introduction to B.'). Hogarth Press, London, 1942.

Nadau, Maurice, 'B. et la Presse', *MF*, 1 Jan. 1950.

Nicolson, Harold, *Sainte-Beuve.* Constable, London, 1957.

Nouvelles Littéraires, Les. 'Hommage à B.': No. of 19th May 1949 consecrated to B.

O'Connor, Frank, *The Mirror in the Roadway.* Hamish Hamilton, London, 1957.

Parménie, A. and Bonnier de la Chapelle, C. *Histoire d'un éditeur et de ses auteurs, P. J. Hetzel (Stahl).* Albin Michel, 1953.

Partridge, Eric, *The French Romantics' Knowledge of English Literature (1830–48).* Champion, 1924.

Pearson, Geoffrey, 'B. critique des mœurs administratives sous la Restauration et la Monarchie de Juillet'. Unpublished thesis of the University of Birmingham, 1957.

Perre, P. van der, *Les Préfaçons belges. Bibliographie des véritables originales de H. de B. publiées en Belgique.* Gallimard, 1940.

Peyre, Henri, *The Contemporary French Novel.* Oxford Univ. Press, 1955.

Peytel, Adrien, *B. juriste romantique.* Poinsot, 1950.

Pichois, Claude, 'Les vrais "Mémoires" de Philarète Chasles', *RSH*, Jan.–Mar. 1956.

Picon, Gaëtan, *B. par lui-même*. Éditions du Seuil, 1956.

Pierrot, Roger, (1). 'Hetzel et l'Avant-Propos de "la C.H." ', *RHLF*, July–Sept. 1955.

—, (2). 'B. et Hugo d'après leur correspondance', ibid., Oct.–Dec. 1955. See also above, Appendix II, Pléiade edn., *Lettres à L'Étrangère*, and *Correspondance générale*.

Pommier, Jean, (1). *L'Église* (edn.). Droz, 1947.

—, (2). 'Les Préfaces de B.', *RSH*, Jan.–June 1950.

—, (3). 'Naissance d'un héros: Rastignac', *RHLF*, Apr.–June 1950.

—, (4). 'Querelle de naturalistes (Notes balzaciennes)', *RHS*, Apr.–Sept. 1951.

—, (5). *Louis Lambert*, t. i, ed. M. Bouteron and J. Pommier. José Corti, 1954.

—, (6). 'B. et Musset', *RHLF*, Oct.–Dec. 1956.

—, (7). 'Le petit Vicomte [de Lovenjoul]', *Nouvelles littéraires*, 24 Oct. 1957.

—, (8). *L'Invention et l'écriture dans 'La Torpille' d'H. de B.* Droz (Geneva) and Minard (Paris), 1957.

Ponceau, Amédée, *Paysages et destins balzaciens*. Edn. du Myrte, 1950.

Pontavice de Heussey, R. du, *B. en Bretagne*, Caillière, Rennes, 1885.

Poulet, G. *Études sur le temps humain*, t. ii (*La Distance intérieure*). Plon, 1952 (t. i published by the Edinburgh Univ. Press, 1949).

Pourtalès, Guy de, *La Vie de Franz Liszt*. Gallimard, 1927.

Pradalié, G. *B. historien*. Presses Universitaires, 1955.

Praz, Mario, *The Romantic Agony*, trans. Angus Davidson. Oxford Univ. Press, 1951.

Preston, Ethel, *Recherches sur la technique de B.* Presses Françaises, 1926.

Prévost, J. C. *Le Dandysme en France (1817–39)*. Droz (Geneva) and Minard (Paris), 1957.

Prioult, Albert, (1). *B. avant la 'C.H.'* G. Courville, 1936.

—, (2). *Sténie ou Les Erreurs philosophiques* (edn.). Ibid., 1936.

—, (3). Introductions to 'Les Classiques du monde' edn. of B.'s works. See above, Appendix II.

Pritchett, V. S. (1). *The Living Novel*. Chatto and Windus, London, 1946.

—, (2). 'B. and the Human Appetite for Life', *The Listener*, 26 May 1949, London.

Proust, Marcel, (1). *Pastiches et mélanges*. Nouvelle Revue Française, Gallimard, 1919.

—, (2). *A la Recherche du temps perdu: Sodome et Gomorrhe*. Ibid., 1924.

—, (3). *Contre Sainte-Beuve* (preface by Bernard de Fallois). Gallimard, 1954. Chs. xi and xii.

Reboul, Jeanne, 'B. et la "Vestignonomie" ', *RHLF*, Apr.–June 1950.

—, Pierre, 'Les Anglais de B.', *RSH*, Jan.–June 1950.

Regard, Maurice, (1). 'B. est-il l'auteur de "Gambara"?', *RHLF*, Oct.–Dec. 1955.

—, (2). 'B. et Charles Didier', *RSH*, July–Sept. 1955.

—, (3). *L'Adversaire des romantiques, Gustave Planche*. 2 vols. Nouvelles Éditions Latines, 1955.

—, (4). *Les Chouans*. Garnier edn. Introd., Notes and Variants, 1957.

—, (5). *L'Envers de l'histoire contemporaine*. Garnier edn. Introd., Notes and Selected Variants, 1959.

Revue d'histoire littéraire de la France. Nos. entirely or chiefly consecrated to Balzac: Apr.–June and July–Sept. 1950, Oct.–Dec. 1956.

—, *de littérature comparée*. 'B. dans le monde': No. consecrated to Balzac, Apr.–June 1950.

—, *des sciences humaines*. No. consecrated to Balzac, Jan.–June 1950.

Richer, M. F. 'Autour de la pièce "Vautrin" ', *MF*, 1 Nov. 1950.

Robert, Guy and Matoré, G. *Un Début dans la vie*. Edn. Droz (Geneva) and Minard (Paris), 1950. Introd., Notes and Variants.

Rogers, Samuel, *B. and the Novel*. University of Wisconsin Press, 1953.

Roux, Fernand, *B. jurisconsulte et criminaliste*. Dujarrie et Cie, 1906.

Royce, Wm. Hobart, (1). *A Balzac Bibliography*. University of Chicago Press, 1929. Now being brought up to date by a committee of Syracuse University.

—, (2). *B. as he should be read*. Auguste Giraldi, New York, 1946; reproduced in *Adam*, London, June 1949.

Sacy, S. de, (1). 'B. et le mythe de l'aventurier', *MF*, 1 Jan. 1950.

—, (2). 'Ursule Mirouët', *Le Courrier balzacien*, No. 7, Oct. 1950.

—, (3), 'B. et Geoffroy Saint-Hilaire. Problèmes de classification', *MF*, 1 Nov. 1950.

Sainte-Beuve, Ch. A. de, *Causeries du lundi*. Garnier, 1851–62, vols. ii and iii.

Saint-Germès, Madeleine, *B. considéré comme historien du Droit*. Nizet et Bastard, 1936.

Saint-Girons, Pierre, 'Les barons Hulot et le comte d'Aure', *Études balzaciennes*, No. 2, Sept.–Dec. 1951.

Saintsbury, G. (1). Introductions to Dent edn. of B.'s works, London, 1895–9.

—, (2). *A History of the French Novel*, vol. ii. Macmillan and Co., London, 1919.

Sand, George, (1). *Histoire de ma vie*. Calmann-Lévy, 4 vols. 1854–5.

—, (2). *Autour de la table*. Dentu, 1862.

Savant, Jean, (1). *Les vrais Mémoires de Vidocq*. Corréa, 1950.

—, (2). 'Formes et Reflets' edn. of B.'s works, t. xiii, Introd.

Savey-Casard, P. *Le Crime et la peine dans l'œuvre de Victor Hugo*. Presses Universitaires, 1956.

Ségu, Frédéric, *Un Maître de B. inconnu, H. de Latouche*. Études Romantiques. Les Belles-Lettres, 1928.

Seillière, Ernest, *B. et la morale romantique*. Félix Alcan, 1922.

Serval, Maurice, (1). ' "La Rabouilleuse" de B. Les sites et les gens; les personnages; B. à Issoudun', *MF*, 1 Apr. 1911.

—, (2). *Autour d'un roman de B.: "Les Chouans"*. L. Conard, 1921.

—, (3). 'Autour d'un roman de B.: "Une ténébreuse Affaire" ', *RHLF*, Oct.–Dec. 1922.

—, (4). 'Autour d'un roman de B.: "Le Lys dans la vallée" ', ibid., July–Sept. and Oct.–Dec. 1926.

—, (5). 'Les Sources d'un roman de B.: "La Recherche de l'absolu" ', *Rev. Bleue*, 18 May and ff. 1929.

—, (6). 'Autour de B.: "César Birotteau" ', *RHLF*, Apr.–June and July–Sept. 1930.

Smith, S. R. B. *B. et l'Angleterre*. Printed by Williams, Lea and Co., London, 1953.

Stevenson, N. W. *Paris dans la "C.H."* G. Courville, 1938.

Strozier, R. M. 'Genesis and Structure of B.'s "Splendeurs et misères des courtisanes" '. Unpublished thesis, University of Chicago, 1945.

Stutchbury, H. O. (1). 'English Writers on B.', *Adam*, June 1949.

—, (2). 'The Balzac Centenary', *Contemporary Review*, Sept. 1950.

Surville, Laure, 'Notice biographique' (1858), Éd. Déf. of B.'s works, t. xxiv.

Swinburne, Algernon Charles, (1). *William Blake. A Critical Essay.* J. C. Hotten, London, 1868.

—, (2). *A Study of Shakespeare.* Chatto and Windus, London, 1880.

Taine, Hippolyte, 'Balzac', in *Nouveaux Essais de critique et d'histoire* [1858]. Hachette, 1909.

Taylor, A. Carey, *Non-French Admirers and Imitators of B.* J. W. Ruddock and Sons, London, 1950.

Thibaudet, Albert, *Histoire de la Littérature française de 1789 à nos jours.* Stock, 1936 (pp. 219–38).

Thouvenin, G. (1) 'La Genèse d'un roman de B.: "La Recherche de l'absolu" ', *RHLF*, Oct.–Dec. 1911.

—, (2). 'La Composition de "La duchesse de Langeais" ', ibid., Oct.–Dec. 1947.

Turnell, Martin, *The Novel in France.* Hamish Hamilton, London, 1950.

Turquet-Milnes, Gladys, *From Pascal to Proust.* Jonathan Cape, London, 1926.

Vernière, P. 'B. et la genèse de Vautrin', *RHLF*, Jan.–Mar. 1948.

Viatte, Auguste, (1). *Les Sources occultes du romantisme*, 2 vols. Champion, 1928.

—, (2). *Victor Hugo et les illuminés de son temps.* L'Arbre, Montreal, 1942.

Vicaire. See Hanotaux and Vicaire.

Vier, Jacques, (1). *Marie d'Agoult, son mari, ses amis.* Éd. du Cèdre, 1950.

—, (2). *La Comtesse d'Agoult et son temps*, vol. i, Armand Colin, 1955.

—, (3). 'Comment B. composait un roman: l'affaire *Béatrix*', *L'École*, 5 Feb. 1955.

Vouga, Daniel, *B. malgré lui.* José Corti, 1958.

Weidlé, Wladimir, 'La Place de B. dans l'histoire des lettres', in *Hommage à B.* Unesco, Mercure de France, 1950.

Weinberg. See Dargan and Weinberg.

Wenger, Jared, *The Province and the Provinces in the Work of H. de B.* G. Banta Publishing Co., Princeton, New Jersey, 1937.

Werdet, Edm. (1). *Portrait intime de B.* Dentu, 1859.

—, (2). *Souvenirs de la vie littéraire.* Ibid., 1879.

Wilde, Oscar, (1). 'B. in England', in *A Critic in Pall Mall*. Methuen, London, undated.

—, (2). 'The Decay of Lying', in *Intentions*. Osgood, McIlvaine and Co., London, 1891.

Wurmser, André, 'La Comédie inhumaine', *Europe*, July–Aug. 1950.

Zweig, Stefan, *Balzac*, trans. Wm. and Dorothy Rose. Cassell and Co., London, 1948.

SUPPLEMENTARY BIBLIOGRAPHY

1959–1964

(I am grateful to the Abbé Philippe Bertault and Dr Charles Gould for help with this revision.)

COLLECTIONS AND EDITIONS

Œuvres Complètes (Club de l'honnête homme). Consists of 28 vols. up to date (1956–63).

Les Œuvres de Balzac (notices et notes de Roland Cholet). Lausanne. Editions 'Rencontre', 1958–62, 30 vols. Tt. i–xxiv (Edn classée suivant l'ordre de publication des romans et nouvelles). Tt. xxv–xxx: *Contes drolatiques*, *Théâtre* and *Romans de jeunesse*.

Romans de jeunesse. Le Cabinet Romantique. Les Bibliophiles de l'Originale, 1961–3. Pieree Barbéris. Text, xv vols. Vol. xvi: *Aux Sources de Balzac. Histoire des Romans de jeunesse* (not sold separately).

Contes choisis (A. W. Raitt). O.U.P. 1964.

Correspondance. t. I (1809–June 1932); t. II (June 1832–5); t. III (1836–9). Garnier (R. Pierrot). In progress.

Eugénie Grandet. Les Petits Classiques Français, Presses Universitaires, 1959 (R. Pierrot).

Illusions perdues, le manuscrit de la Collection Spoelberch de Lovenjoul. A. Colin, 1959 (S.-J. Bérard).

Le Chef d'œuvre inconnu (Un Catéchisme esthétique). Didier, 1961 (P. Laubriet).

Le Colonel Chabert. Edn critique. Marcel Didier, 1961 (Pierre Citron).

Le Curé de village, première édition conforme à la publication des feuilletons de 1839. Texte établi par M. Henriquez. José Corti, 1961.

GENERAL BIBLIOGRAPHY

The following works (unrecorded in the original edition of this book) have appeared since 1959 in the new series of Classiques Garnier:

Béatrix, 1962 (M. Regard); *César Birotteau*, 1963 (P. Laubriet); *La Maison du Chat-qui-pelote, Le Bal de Sceaux, La Vendetta*, 1963 (P.-G. Castex); *Le Cabinet des Antiques*, 1958 (P.-G. Castex); *Le Père Goriot*, 1960 (P.-G. Castex); *Les Paysans*, 1964 (J.-H. Donnard); *Les Petits Bourgeois*, 1960 (R. Picard).

PUBLISHED WORKS

Album Balzac (J.-A. Ducourneau). Pléiade, Gallimard, 1962.

Armorial de 'la Comédie humaine' (F. Lotte). Garnier, 1963.

Bertault, Abbé Philippe, *Balzac*. This is Bertault (4)—see p. 468— 'revu et augmenté'. Hatier, 1962. Also translated into English: *B. and the Human Comedy* (Richard Monges). New York University Press, 1963.

Bérard, S.-J. *La Genèse d'un roman de Balzac, 'Illusions perdues'* (1837). 2 vols. A. Colin, 1961.

Borel, Jacques (1). *Personnages et destins balzaciens*. José Corti, 1959.

—, (2). *Le 'Lys dans la vallée' et les sources profondes de la création balzacienne*. José Corti, 1961.

Bory, J.-L. *Eugène Sue. Le Roi du roman populaire*. Hachette, 1962.

Canfield, A. G. See General Bibliography, p. 469. Revised edition by E. B. Ham. University of North Carolina Press, 1961.

Castex., P.-G. *Nouvelles et contes de Balzac*. 2 vols. Centre de documentation universitaire, 1961–2.

Citron, P. *La Poésie de Paris dans la littérature française de Rousseau à Baudelaire*. 2 vols. Éditions de Minuit, 1961.

Delattre, Geneviève, *Les Opinions littéraires de Balzac*. Presses Universitaires, 1961.

Descaves, P. *Balzac dramatiste*. La Table ronde, 1960.

Donnard, Jean-Hervé, *Balzac. Les réalités économiques et sociales dans 'la Comédie humaine'*. A. Colin, 1961.

George, Albert J. *Books by Balzac. A Checklist of books by Honoré de Balzac*, compiled from the papers of W. H. Royce. Syracuse University Press, 1960.

GENERAL BIBLIOGRAPHY

Gould, Charles, art. 'Balzac', in *Encyclopaedia Britannica*, 1961, vol. iii.

Laubriet, Pierre, *L'Intelligence de l'art chez Balzac.* Didier, 1961.

Levin, H. *The Gates of Horn. A Study of Five French Realists.* O.U.P., New York, 1963 [Balzac: chapter IV].

Le Yaouanc, Moïse, *Nosographie de l'humanité balzacienne*, Librairie Maloine, 1959.

Lukács, G. *The Historical Novel.* Translation from the German by Hannah and Stanley Mitchell. Merlin Press, London, 1962.

Oliver, E. J. *Balzac the European.* Sheed and Ward, London, 1959.

Perrod, P.-A. *En Marge de 'la Comédie humaine'.* Henneuse, Lyon, 1962.

Royce, W. G. *A Balzac Bibliography.* Revised edition. University of Syracuse, U.S.A. (in preparation).

Teuler, Gabriel, *Du Côté de Balzac.* Nouvelles editions Debresse, 1959.

Wurmser, André, *La Comédie inhumaine.* Gallimard, 1964.

PERIODICALS AND ARTICLES

Bulletins 'Balzac à Saché' (Société Honoré de Balzac de Touraine, edited by Paul Métadier, Conservateur du Château de Saché), i–ix, 1951–64.

Cahiers de l'Association internationale des études françaises, No. 15, March 1962. Articles by J. Pommier, Wayne Conner, K. E. Sjörden, Fr. Bar, S.-J. Bérard, J.-H. Donnard, M. Le Yaouanc, A. Lorant, Ch. Gould, G. Delattre.

Castex, P.-G. 'Aux sources d'Eugénie Grandet', *RHLF* janv.-mars, 1964.

Cesare, Raffaele de (1). 'Un Mese della vita di Balzac (gennaio 1836)', *Contributi del Seminario di Filologia moderna*, Serie francese, i, 1959.

—, (2). 'Balzac nel febbraio 1836', *Saggi e ricerche di letteratura francese*, i. Feltrinelli, Milan, 1960.

—, (3). 'Balzac nel marzo 1836', *Contributi del Seminario di Filologia moderna*, Serie francese, ii, 1961.

—, (4). 'Balzac nell'aprile 1836', *Saggi e ricerche di letteratura francese.* Feltrinelli, Milan, 1963.

483

Chamberlin, W. P. 'Une Ténébreuse affaire, roman policier', *Annales publiées par la Faculté des Lettres de Toulouse*, Littérature VI, 1958.

Citron, Pierre, 'Du nouveau sur le titre de *la Comédie humaine*', *RHLF*, janv.-mars, 1959.

Courrier balzacien, Le. Continued as *Les Études balzaciennes*, 1951–1952, 1958-March 1960; as *L'Année balzacienne* from 1960.

Dédéyan, Ch. 'Le fanatisme romantique de Balzac', *Revue des lettres modernes*, v, 1958.

Ducourneau, J.-A. and Pierrot, R. 'Calendrier de la vie de Balzac', in *Études balzaciennes*, 1951–1960, and *L'Année balzacienne*, 1960–64. In progress.

Gould, Charles, 'Monsieur de Balzac. Le dandysme de B. et son influence sur sa création littéraire' *Cahiers de l'Association internationale des études françaises*, No. 15.

Guyon, Bernard, 'Balzac "invente" les Scènes de la Vie de province', *MF*, July 1958.

Pugh, A. R. (1). 'Recurring characters in *Le Père Goriot*', *Modern Language Review*, Oct. 1962.

—, (2). 'Personnages reparaissants avant *Le Père Goriot*'. In *L'Année balzacienne*, 1964.

Taylor, A. Carey, 'Balzac et Thackeray', *Revue de littérature comparée*, July Sept. 1960.

Tolley, B. R. (1). 'Balzac the Printer', *French Studies*, July 1959.

—, (2). 'Three articles wrongly attributed to Balzac', *Modern Language Review*, Jan. 1960.

—, (3). 'Balzac et "La Caricature"', *RHLF*, janv.-mars, 1961.

—, (4). 'The Cénacle of Balzac's *Illusions perdues*'. *French Studies*, Oct. 1961.

—, (5). 'Balzac and the *Feuilleton des journaux politiques*', *Modern Language Review*, Oct. 1962.

—, (6). 'Les "Œuvres Diverses" de Balzac (1824–1831)', in *Année balzacienne*, 1963.

Wais, Kurt, 'Le Roman d'Artiste: E. T. A. Hoffmann et Balzac'. In *La Littérature narrative d'imagination*, Colloque de Strasbourg, 1959. Presses Universitaires, 1961.

INDEX

Names of 'Comédie Humaine' characters are marked with an obelus (†); those of characters from Balzac's plays are marked with a double obelus (‡). For general topics (aspects of Balzac's work) see under Balzac, Honoré de, and 'Comédie Humaine'.

INDEX

Balzac, Honoré de—cont.

vital energy and monomania, 40–4, 56–7, 64–8, 70–1, 79–80, 86–8, 98, 134, 199 and n. 3, 278, 304, 338–9, 380–2, 390–2, 444–5

determinism in its relation to the question of Balzac's 'realism': (a) as universal law, 54–5, 67, 272–3, 274–6, 390, 402; (b) as against 'a priori' conception, 55, 272–4, 443; (c) as against coincidence and chance, 161, 357; (d) as against autonomous development of character, 55–6, 169 n. 1, 350, 453

'physiognomy', etc., 3, 8, 54–5, 65, 119 and n. 1, 139, 172, 253–5, 259–60, 273, 295, 302 and n. 3, 331–2, 353 and n. 1

transformism, 55, 273, 275–6

intervention of imagination and fantasy, 10, 37, 39, 78, 85, 121–2, 136, 137, 143, 285–6

impact of the age on Balzac's conception of reality, language and style, 63, 78, 109, 323, 324, 367–8, 432, 437–8, 443–448

validity of his philosophy, 53–4, 449, 451–2

5. *Religion*

early scepticism, 4

Swedenborgism, 48–53, 57–8, 295, 412, 447

'angelism' and 'angelic' characters, 51, 52, 58, 67, 147, 231, 297, 385–6, 412

attitude to clergy, 26–7, 33–4, 105, 162–3, 190, 199, 336

view of Protestantism, 18, 148–149, 152–3, 278

defence of Catholicism, 38, 72–3, 153–4, 248, 250–1, 277–8, 284, 286, 291, 385–6, 412–14, 450–1

charity v. philanthropy, 129, 141, 366, 385, 402, 409–14, 422

underlying pessimism, 29, 34, 45, 83, 92–3, 180–2, 342, 390 395–6, 450

quality of Balzac's religious feeling, 114, 230 and n. 1, 251–2, 411–14, 450–1

6. *Social Outlook. Economics*

money, 'le seul dieu moderne', 9, 23, 27, 28, 36–7, 38, 45, 65, 66, 67, 75, 80, 83, 118, 128, 136, 178, 194, 197–8, 353, 378, 389–90, 445–6

legal and illegal acquisition, 9, 77, 92–3, 135–6, 138–9, 193, 201–2, 214, 326

usurers and misers, 27, 38, 57, 64–6, 98, 171, 198, 212, 246, 352, 373, 400–1

industry, commerce and speculation, 28, 135, 171, 172, 174 n. 1, 177–8, 191, 192–4, 201, 353, 370, 432–4, 441

publicity and advertisement, 64, 194–5, 214

financial intrigues in the stories, 186, 192–4, 201–2, 341, 353, 359, 370, 372, 381, 400–1

fiscal economy, 184–5

rural economy, 72–5, 248–50, 398–9, 401

domestic industry and middlemen, 408–9

socialism, attitude towards, 15–16, 64, 384

7. *Social Outlook. Justice, etc.*

civil procedure in bankruptcy and debt collection, 198, 352

justice and expediency, 139, 165, 167, 180–2, 263, 361, 369

criminal types and associations, 6, 77–9, 91–3, 360, 362, 425

penal system and its consequences, 35, 36 n. 1, 365–6, 413–14

police system and its agents, 16–17, 257, 263, 360–1, 368–369

8. *Social Outlook. Politics*

early political tendencies, 4, 16, 20, 71

programme of 1832–3, 71–2, 80, 243–4

INDEX

INDEX

INDEX

Davin, Félix, 11 n. 2, 43, 126 n. 1, 127–9, 130, 132, 133, 134, 135, 168, 199, 244, 245, 256, 269, 270, 274, 280, 415

Début dans la vie, Un, 288, 289, 316–20, 332, 361, 419 n. 2

Defoe, Daniel, 4

Delacroix, Eugène, 37, 85, 211 n. 1, 339 and n. 3

Deleuze, J. P. F., 3

Delloye and Lecou, 132, 156 n. 1, 267

Démocratie pacifique, La, 429

Député d'Arcis, Le, 176 n. 6, 187, 243, 258, 290, 312, 335, 397, 398, 404–9, 414, 441

Dernière Fée, La, 6, 10

Dernière Incarnation de Vautrin, La, Part IV of *Splendeurs et misères des courtisanes*, q.v.

†Derville, Maître, 27, 34, 98, 139, 320, 429, 441

Desbordes-Valmore, Marceline, 380 n. 1

†Deschars, Mme, 418

†Descoings, Mme, 338–9

†Desmarets, Jules, 78–9

†Desmarets, Mme Jules, 57, 78–9, 195

†Desplein, 137–8, 180, 441

†Desroches (senior), 342

†Desroches, Maître, 139 n. 1, 318, 320, 341, 370, 441

†Desroys, 188

Deux Ambitieux, Les, see *Député d'Arcis, Le*

Deux Amis, Les, 168, 387

Deux Amoureux, Les, see *Modeste Mignon*

Deux Frères, Les, see *Rabouilleuse, La*

Deux Musiciens, Les, early title of *Cousin Pons, Le*, q.v.

Deux Poètes, Les (*Illusions perdues*, Part I), 133, 167–75, 210, 274 n. 1, 347

Diable à Paris, Le, 369 n. 2, 416 n. 1

Dialogue philosophique et politique sur les perfections du dix-neuvième siècle, 422

†Diard, Pierre-Fr., 76–7

†Diard, Mme, 76–7

Dickens, Ch., 172, 181–2, 196, 294, 331–2, 445

Diderot, Denis, 4, 22, 145, 206, 240

Didier, 173

Dinah Piedefer, see *Muse du département, La*

†Doguereau, 210, 211

Dom Gigadas, 5 n. 1

†Dominis, Abbé de, 114

†Doni, Massimilia, 143–6

†Don Juan, 37

Doré, Gustave, 106

Dorval, Marie, 84

Dosne, Mme, 218

Dostoievsky, 454

Double Famille, Une, 26–7, 86, 133, 222, 247, 258, 390 n. 1

Drame au bord de la mer, Un, 133, 135, 141, 224, 384

Drame dans les prisons, Un, earlier title of *Dernière Incarnation de Vautrin*, q.v.

Dubochet, 268

Ducange, V., 5

Duchesse de Langeais, La, 46, 72, 76, 78–83, 145, 162, 167, 234, 453

Duckett, Wm, 193, 223

Ducray-Duminil, 5

†Dudley, Lord, 84, 113

†Dudley, Lady Arabella, 113, 114–16, 223

Duhamel, Georges, 453

Dumas, Alexandre (*père*), 137, 213 n. 2, 375, 397, 424

Dumas, Alexandre (*fils*), 337, 424, 434–5

†Dumay, 326, 331

Dumont, 352 n. 2

‡Dupré, Maître, 429

Dupuytren, G., 137, 138 n. 1

Duranty, 285

Duras, Duchesse de, 173

Durham, Lord, 365 n. 2

Dutacq, Armand, 106

†Dutheil, Abbé, 247, 251

†Dutocq, 185, 187, 188, 372

Ecce Homo, see *Martyrs ignorés, Les*

Échantillon de causeries françaises, see *Conversation entre onze heures et minuit*

INDEX

INDEX

†Ferraud, Comtesse, 33–4

Fétis, J. Fr., 145

Fielding, H., 4

Figaro, Le, 183, 213 n. 2, 228 n. 1

Fille aux yeux d'or, La, 76, 79, 83–6, 97, 117, 121, 122, 131, 268, 368, 449

Fille d'Ève, Une, 94 n. 2, 96, 117, 142 n. 2, 145, 205, 206, 208, 209, 220–4, 235, 239, 270, 272, 276, 283, 334, 388

†Finot, Andoche, 95, 194, 203–4, 205, 211–15, 213 n. 2, 217–18, 221, 255, 320, 340, 360 n. 1, 441

†Firmiani, Mme, 38, 140, 186, 439

†Fischer, Élisabeth ('la cousine Bette'), 158, 312, 376–8, 380–1

‡Fischtaminel, Mme de, 418, 419 and n. 1

Fitz-James, Duc de, 71, 217 n.1

Flaubert, Gustave, 44, 53, 120, 190, 196, 197, 232, 247, 251–2, 282, 332, 379, 452, 454

Fleur-des-Pois, La, original title of *Contrat de mariage, Le*, q.v.

Fleur-des-Pois, La, (fragment of *Vieille Fille, La*), 155 n. 1

†Fleury, 187

†Florentine, *see* Cabirolle, Florentine

†Florine, *see* Grignoult, Sophie

†Fœdora, Comtesse, 40, 44, 45, 46, 56, 80, 126, 231, 279

†Fontaine, Comte de, 438

†Fontaine, Mlle Émilie de, 186, 195, 223 and n. 1, 440

†Fontaine, Mme, 295, 371, 392, 394, 396

‡Fontanarès, Alfonso, 425–6

†Fortzheim, Comte de, *see* Hulot, Maréchal

†Fosseuse, La, 75, 442

Fouché, J., 16, 17, 255–6, 257, 260, 360, 438

†Foullepointe, Mme, 418

†Fourchon ('le père'), 401, 402

'Fragments inédits', 384, 413 and n. 7

†Fraisier, Maître, 389–90, 393, 396, 441

Français peints par eux-mêmes, Les, 314 n. 1, 348 n. 2

†Franchessini, Col., 365

†Francine, 17

Frapesle (residence of the Carrauds near Issoudun, from 1834), 168, 343

†Frenhofer, 37, 142, 143

†'Frères de la Consolation, Les', 410–411

‡Frescas, Raoul de, 365, 425

Furne, Ch. (co-publisher with Dubochet, Paulin and Hetzel of 'La Comédie Humaine', first edn), 156 n 4, 174 n. 1, 268–9, 287 n. 1, 313 n. 1, 314 nn. 2 and 3, 391 n. 1, 422; *see also* Hetzel, P. J.

†Gaillard, Théodore, 213, 217, 371

†Galathionne, Prince, 236 n. 2

Galériens, Les, ou Les Amours forcés, *see Béatrix*

†Galope-Chopine, 19, 20

†Galope-Chopine, Mme, 20

Gall, F. J., 3, 54, 158, 279

Galsworthy, J., 453

†Gamard, Mlle, 34, 158, 279

Gambara, 142–3, 156

†Gambara (the character), 142–3, 144, 145

†Gambara, Mme, 144

Gars, Le, see *Chouans, Les*

Gars, Le (Avertissement), 13–14, 15, 47

†Gasselin, 233

†Gaston, Louis, 63

†Gaston, Marie, 63, 304

†Gaston, Mme Marie, *see* Chaulieu, Louise de

†Gaubertin, Fr., 400

†Gaudin, Pauline, 40, 41, 44, 46

†Gaudissart, Félix, 64, 194, 203, 204, 344, 388, 394

Gaudissart II, 290, 369–70

†Gaudissart II (the character), 370

†Gaudron, Abbé, 190, 199

Gautier, Théophile, 45, 147, 211 n. 2, 213 n. 2, 221, 227 n. 3, 228 n. 1, 292, 324, 333, 362–3

Gavault, S. P. B., 352 n. 4

Gazette étrangère de Saint-Pétersbourg, La, 98 n. 1

†Gazonal, S. P. B., 371

INDEX

INDEX

†Mignon de la Bastie, Mlle Modeste, 323 n. 2, 325–31, 386, 440

Milton, 4

†Minard, A. F. Jr., 187, 372

†Minard, Julien, 372

‡Minard, Adolphe, 434

†Minoret, Dr Denis, 293–6

†Minoret-Levrault, Fr., 282 n. 1, 292–6

†Minoret-Levrault, Mme Fr., 293, 295, 296

†Minoret-Levrault, Désiré, 292, 295, 296

Mirabeau, 23

†Mirah, Josépha, 378, 382–3, 385–6, 394

Mirbeau, Octave, 424

†Mirouët, Ursule, 293–7

Miroir, Le, 213 n. 2

†Mistigris, *see* Lora, Léon de

Mode, La, 24, 27, 32, 38 n. 3, 60 n. 1, 100, 189 n. 2, 244

Modeste, early title of *Petits Bourgeois, Les*, q.v.

Modeste Mignon, 145, 290, 320 322 n. 2, 325–33, 376 n. 1

Molé, Comte L. M., 405

Molière, 4, 65, 191, 196, 281, 313, 373–4, 423, 435, 452, 455

†Molineux, J. B., 194

Monet, Claude, 37

†Mongenod et Cie (bankers), 373 and n. 1, 441

Moniteur de l'Armée, Le, 397

Monnier, Henry, 25, 159, 188–90, 195, 423

Monographie de la press parisienne, 208 n. 1, 219

Monographie de la vertu, 60, 422 and n. 2

Montalembert, M. R. de, 60 n. 2, 402

†Montauran, Marquis Alphonse de, 16–21, 410

†Montauran, Marquis Nicolas de, 410, 412, 413

†Montcornet, Maréchal Comte de, 205, 398–402, 404, 439

†Montcornet, Comtesse de, 205, 217, 222, 400, 401

†Montéjanos, Baron Henri Montès de, 378–9

Montesquieu, 4, 422

Montivers, Abbé, 90 n. 1

†Montriveau, Général Marquis Armand de, 78–82, 97, 110, 121 n. 1, 170, 236 n. 2, 315

†Montsaurin, Mlle de, 391 n. 1

Montyon (Prix), 73, 291, 409, 422

Moore, George, 399

Moore, Thomas, 4

†Moreau ('de l'Oise'), 316–20

Moret, 391

Morillon, Victor, 13–14, 47

Mortimer, Raymond, 437, 444

†Mortsauf, Comte de, 57, 110–16

†Mortsauf, Comtesse de, 110–16, 119 n. 1, 222, 279, 281, 447, 448

†Mortsauf, Jacques de, 111

†Mortsauf, Mlle Madeleine de, 111, 113–14, 115

†Mouche, 401

Murger, Henri, 220–1, 242

Muse du département, La, 131, 169 n. 1, 205, 239 n. 3, 280 n. 1, 288, 289, 315, 344, 345–52, 370 n. 4

Musée des familles, Le, 409 n. 1

Musset, A. de, 25, 227, 349 n. 1

†Nanon, 65, 67

Napoleon I, 4, 19, 27, 30, 35, 72–3, 74, 160, 196, 240, 243–4, 256, 257, 258, 259–62, 277 n. 3, 314, 340, 344, 353 n. 1, 355, 358, 407, 411, 430, 438

†Nathan, Raoul, 208, 212, 213 n. 2, 215, 216, 217, 220–3, 227, 239, 320, 337, 350 n. 1, 351, 360 n. 1, 441

Nerval, Gérard de, 221

Ne touchez pas la Hache, first title of *Duchesse de Langeais, La*, q.v.

†Niseron, J. Fr., 401

Nodier, Charles, 3, 37, 213 n. 2, 339 n. 2

Noël du Fail, 99

†Noswell, Mrs, 370

†Nourrisson, Mme, 371 and n. 1, 379 and n. 1

Nouveaux Contes philosophiques, 38

†Nucingen, Frédéric, Baron de, 86, 89, 97, 136, 192–3, 198, 200–3, 206, 222, 359–60, 361, 364, 373, 400, 427, 433, 441

INDEX

INDEX

INDEX

INDEX

INDEX